The World Today Series®
Stryker-Post Publications, Harpers Ferry, WV • USA

East & Southeast Asia

Steven A. Leibo

2010

43rd edition
Next Edition: August 2011

Steven A. Leibo Ph.D.

A former Fulbright Scholar, Leibo is a Professor of International History and Politics at the Sage Colleges in Albany and Troy, New York, and a lecturer in Asian history at the State University of New York (SUNY) in Albany. Dr. Leibo was educated at the University of California at Santa Barbara and Washington State University. He is the author/editor of many scholarly books and articles, including *Transferring Technology to China: Prosper Giquel and the Self-strengthening Movement, Journal of the Chinese Civil War, 1864, International Conflict in the 20th Century* and the historical novel *Tienkuo: The Heavenly Kingdom*, which was written to introduce readers to 19th century China.

Leibo is also a filmmaker. His latest work is the historical documentary *From Albany to Saigon: Vietnam & the Capital Region*. Widely experienced with the electronic media, he has served as an international political analyst for television and, since 1997, as a commentator for WAMC Northeast Public Radio. Within the Internet, Professor Leibo is also known as the co-founder and long time editor (1994–2004) of H-ASIA, a global forum for Asian studies professionals. In 1994, he founded and served as the first director of the Sage Colleges' Shanghai Institute of Foreign Trade exchange program. The author travels extensively throughout Asia and has often led study tours through Vietnam and Cambodia. A popular public speaker, Dr. Leibo, regularly gives talks in both the United States and China on topics from Globalization to Global Warming. He blogs at "Leibo's World Watch."

First appearing as a book entitled
The Far East and Southwest Pacific 1968,
revised annually and published in succeeding years by

Stryker–Post Publications
P.O. Drawer 1200
Harpers Ferry, WV 25425
Telephones: 1–800–995–1400 (U.S.A. and Canada)
 Other: 1–304–535–2593
 Fax: 1–304–535–6513
www.strykerpost.com
VISA–MASTERCARD–AMERICAN EXPRESS

Photographs used to illustrate *The World Today Series* come from many sources, a great number from friends who travel worldwide. If you have taken any that you believe would enhance the visual impact and attractiveness of our books, do let us hear from you.

International Standard Book Number: 978-1-935264-11-8

International Standard Serial Number: 1043-2140

Library of Congress Catalog Number: 67-11540

Cover design by nvision graphic design

Cartographer: William L. Nelson

Typography by Barton Matheson Willse & Worthington
Baltimore, MD 21244

Printed in the United States of America
By United Book Press, Inc.
Baltimore, MD 21207

The World Today Series has thousands of subscribers across the U.S. and Canada. A sample list of users who annually rely on this most up-to-date material includes:

Public library systems
Universities and colleges
High schools
Federal and state agencies
All branches of the armed forces & war colleges
National Geographic Society
National Democratic Institute
Agricultural Education Foundation
ExxonMobil Corporation
Chevron Corporation
CNN

CONTENTS

Fast food lunch in Bandung, Indonesia

Photo by Steven Leibo

Downtown Jakarta

ACKNOWLEDGMENTS

Many people made the author's task much easier as he attempted to both update the book and to revise it in the twelve years since the task was undertaken. Most of those who helped can be named, but some, for reasons readers can guess, cannot. The author would like to thank those who have helped make the volume much better than it might otherwise have been. They are Mary Shinners, Kelly Ryan, Marilyn Levine, Robert Swartout, Stephen L. Schechter, John Tribble, A. Tom Grunfeld, Robert Drake, Pam Katz, Robert Cribb, Malcolm Russell, Susanna Fessler, Ekaterina Matusevich, Salley Zgolinski, Paul H. Kratoska, Andor Skotnes, Morris Rossabi, Amanda Attendorn-Nedelsky, Bradley Martin, Batbold Bayaraa, Gloria A. McLaughlin, Ed Tick, Sara Colaneri, Dawn A. Walker, John Y.C. Chu of the Taipei Economic & Cultural Office in New York City and the former American Vice President Al Gore, whose effort to educate the world about the threat of global warming has enriched several sections of this text.

At a more fundamental level, a large number of organizations, funding groups and individuals played a major part in helping the author prepare to undertake this yearly task, and they too need to be acknowledged. Most importantly, the Fulbright-Hays Program, the Semerad and Sherman David Spector Funds of the Sage Colleges, The Climate Project and the National Endowment for the Humanities contributed enormously. Additionally I would like to thank many organizations from CNN to the American Central Intelligence Agency for their excellent websites that help many authors and students keep up with the latest information available for each country.

Among my former teachers I would especially like to thank Irving Roth, Joachim Remak, Howard Payne, Thomas L. Kennedy, Immanuel Chung-Yueh Hsu, and Matthew Lamberti. Without their early training and support this work would never have appeared.

My wife, Sara Zaidspiner-Leibo, has also been deeply involved in the book's production. Her help is always of enormous consequence and is much appreciated. Special thanks must also go to the late Philip Stryker for asking me to take on this exciting project in the first place. Lastly, the author would also like enthusiastically to request that future readers, teachers and students alike, contact him with suggestions on how the book can better serve their needs.

Steven A. Leibo leibos@sage.edu
Albany, New York, June 2010

Voting in Mongolia

Photo by Bob Beatty

UNIFORMS . . . lifesize clay warriors, 4000 strong, somberly guard Chinese emperor Qin Shihuang Di's tomb near Xian, while Japanese baseball ("Yah-kyu") players thrill their fans in Tokyo.

East and Southeast Asia Today

In a great many ways 2009 might one day be seen as a more significant Chinese "coming out era" than many had hoped the 2008 Olympics would turn out to be. Certainly, the Olympic effort offered China, as it did Tokyo in 1964 and South Korea in 1988, the opportunity to show the world just how far their economic development had come. In China's case, of course, it was to highlight how much they had accomplished since its leadership made the historic decision to tap into global market forces while energizing its economic development with a significant dose of free enterprise. But, even as their Olympic effort was especially successful, just how much China had changed did not become really obvious until the following year when its economy, like much of the world's, started sliding into one of the worse economic downturns of the last hundred years. Indeed many influential observers both within China and beyond wondered aloud how well China would handle the emerging stresses.

Indeed its own leaders had often spoken of their absolute dependence on a spirited economy to maintain stability. However, while the early signs were as depressing within the PRC as elsewhere, the leadership had other ideas. In fact, this time the most influential thinker was neither socialism's Karl Marx nor capitalism's Adam Smith, but England's John Maynard Keynes. He had argued early in the previous century that only governments had the necessary resources to pull economies back from the brink of economic collapse. With that warning in mind, China began a massive stimulus plan that was even larger than America's efforts. The spending was especially well planned as Beijing poured money into all sorts of new infrastructure efforts from high speed trains to a wide range of green energy projects. All were designed not only to spur recovery but to push the country into becoming a manufacturing center for these new green energy technologies likely to dominate the 21st century.

The overall result of that massive commitment has created a very new dynamic in the international community. Having spent the decades since 1978 working to transform itself into a successful modern nation, China was finally fully emerging as the world's newest superpower. Chinese banks, for example, have become the world's largest, and that was only one of the most dramatic of developments.

In short, one could easily say that China had "arrived," or for those with longer historical perspectives "returned" to its previous position of prominence in world affairs. The signs of that "arrival" were increasingly obvious over the last year as individual Chinese to government ministries seemed to take on a new confidence in their role in the world. Even as China's overseas activities from South America to Africa, from UN security missions in Haiti to its concerns about its own offshore claims, all seemed to carry fresh energy. How Beijing's new role will grow over the decades and how its neighbors in the region will respond to the newly assertive and confident China are likely to be topics very regularly covered in the coming years' annual editions of *East and Southeast Asia*.

Clearly every day brings news of developments important for an understanding of the entire region. With that in mind, for almost four decades the annual publication of *East and Southeast Asia* has allowed readers to keep abreast of developments. With the arrival of the Internet and its plethora of online newspapers, materials never before available have become so at the click of a computer mouse. Thus, at least in theory, it is extraordinarily easy to "keep up." Unfortunately, the availability of materials on the day-to-day developments of, for example, Indonesian politics is still meaningless without the broader context necessary to understand those events. Thus, the goal of *East and Southeast Asia 2010* remains that of offering enough of the political, social, environmental and economic background needed actually to understand those current events. As a final note—all listed GDP-per capita figures refer to "purchasing power parity."

Vietnam's Halong Bay

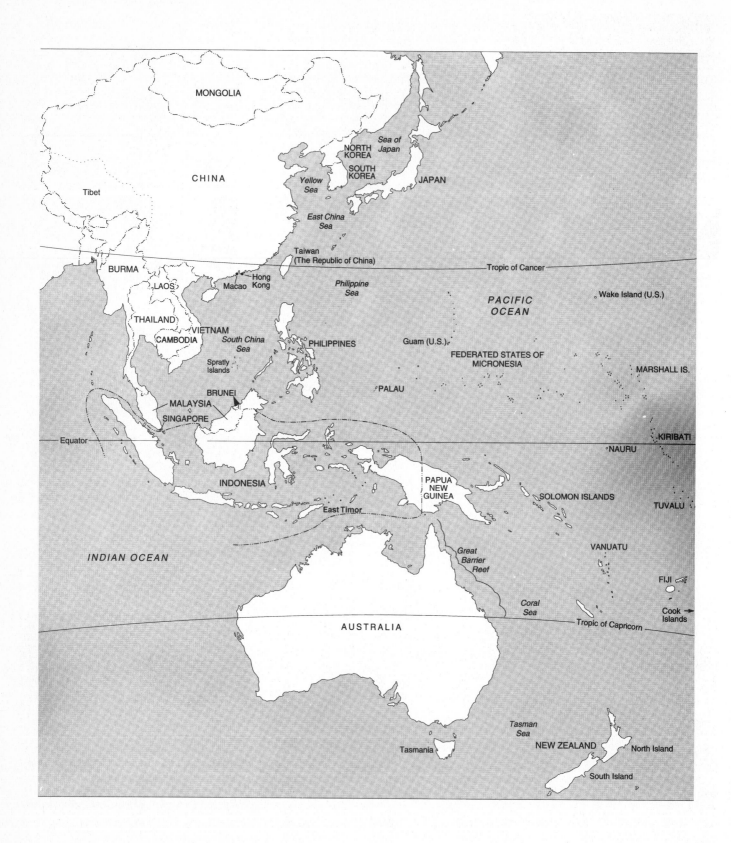

A Diversity of People

The region discussed in this volume covers an enormous range of different ethnic and linguistic groups—from the Mongoloid communities of East Asia and the Caucasian immigrant communities of Australia and New Zealand to the heavily pigmented peoples of Micronesia who most closely resemble the aborigines of Australia. With the exception of a few countries like North Korea, almost every nation in the area includes many different ethnic and linguistic groups. While East Asians, Chinese, Japanese and Korean are largely made up of people from the "Mongoloid" racial community they are sharply divided by their linguistic heritage.

Chinese, for example, is part of a Sino-Tibetan language group that looks somewhat similar in its written appearance, but is totally different from the languages spoken in Japan and Korea. Southeast Asia is even more diverse and has at times been called an "anthropologist's delight" in recognition of the extraordinary diversity of ethnic communities found there. Although most nations in Southeast Asia have a "dominant majority" ethnic community, almost all of them include both indigenous minority communities like the Montagnards of Vietnam and more recent ethnic communities, often made up of Chinese and South Asians, who immigrated to places other than their region of origin during the colonial era. The island communities of the Western Pacific themselves include a wide variety of peoples most notably divided into three groups, Polynesian, Melanesian and Micronesian. More than a thousand different languages are spoken among them.

Although not often discussed in the West, many of these countries from East Asia to the Western Pacific have experienced considerable tensions between the majority and minority communities. In some parts of the region, people of Indian origin are regularly treated as second-class citizens, and the Chinese in places like Indonesia have had similar treatment. In Burma, now known as Myanmar, the efforts by the Burman majority to dominate the political life of the nation have led to decades of tensions and struggle with non-Burman peoples.

1

Historical Background

Lhasa, Tibet

Photo by Steven Leibo

Religious Beliefs

Confucianism

The original Confucianism of early Chinese civilization was more a social philosophy than a religion—perhaps more like the Hellenic thoughts of Aristotle and Plato than the divine musings of the Hebrews across the Mediterranean. In fact, Confucius himself was not particularly interested in issues of the supernatural. For Confucius and his followers, what mattered was the world of human, and how they could best govern themselves.

Originating from a feudal elite society of blood nobility, Confucius nevertheless developed a new theory of nobility based on merit, rather than birth. How was that merit defined? By a single-minded commitment to nurturing the truly "noble heart."

Traditional Confucianism's core emphasis was on the family and hierarchy. This was reinforced by the belief that true stability was attained when everyone within a society understood the appropriate relations among people. How was that stability to be maintained? By an extraordinary emphasis on the ability of education to elevate the soul of humanity.

Later Confucian thinkers, especially people like Mencius, further emphasized the necessity of the development of "virtue" specifically through the study of various writings from antiquity known eventually as the Five Classics. Over time, mastery of the material came to be the key to a successful career through the developing Chinese Civil Service Examinations that dominated the selection of elites during the last 1,000 years of traditional China's existence. As time went on, however, Confucianism was challenged by other more spiritual philosophical and religious traditions—like Daoism and Buddhism—and began to assimilate aspects of their more metaphysical orientation. Thus was born the Neo-Confucianism of later traditional history.

Although it has been generations since millions of Chinese males spent their lives preparing to pass the Confucian civil service exams, Confucian influence as a social philosophy remains tremendously strong in China. In fact, Confucianism, both as a religious and intellectual tradition and as an ongoing theory of social behavior, continues to be very influential. From China to Korea, from Taiwan to Japan, Confucianism remains influential not only among the millions of ethnic Chinese who live in the People's Republic, Singapore and Taiwan, but also among those millions of others who live as Chinese minorities from the Philippines to

Malaysia and Indonesia. Moreover, it remains important among many other societies whose people if not ethnically Chinese were nevertheless fundamentally influenced by Confucianism, even as they developed their own unique cultures. These include not only the Vietnamese and Koreans but also other more distant neighbors, like the Japanese, who did not share a common border with China.

Obvious examples of Confucian influence are easy to note. Despite the assaults on Confucianism under Mao Zedong, the Confucian priority given to education and the family remain strong in East Asia. Moreover, the strong sense of the group over the needs of the individual, while perhaps diminishing somewhat at the beginning of the 21st century, still figures prominently as a clear contrast to the Western preoccupation with the individual. Interestingly, Confucianism has been undergoing something of a more official revival in China in recent years.

Buddhism

Buddhism remains one of the strongest religious traditions throughout East and Southeast Asia. From Thailand to Vietnam, from Myanmar to China, Buddhism is present if not in the lives of everyone in the region, then as part of their cultural and architectural heritage. Even within the People's Republic, which saw so much energy directed against traditions like Buddhism in the 1960s, a revival has been going on. Emerging about the same time that Confucius lived, Buddhism was founded in Nepal by Gautama. (See Russell, The Middle East and South Asia). It eventually became an extraordinarily influential tradition through much of Eastern Asia.

Given the vast differences between the traditions of South Asia and East Asia, it often required considerable modification of the originally rather pessimistic Buddhist message to assimilate into the generally optimistic Chinese environment. It actually was, in some ways, a protest against the teachings of Brahmanism, or Hinduism, which was then dominant in India. The Buddha, as Gautama is called, preached the message that beings moved through a series of lives in this world which was largely an experience of pain and suffering. Within Buddhism there is a deep belief that fate can be influenced by human efforts through the force of "Karma." A good person moves upward through successive existence to an ultimate reward. The greatest

reward possible, according to this belief, was the attainment of Nirvana, a philosophically complicated concept that essentially postulated that a person who had attained "Nirvana" reached a state of individual nonexistence, that is often compared to the snuffing out of a flame which as a "practical" matter ended the process of constantly being reborn into a series of burdensome lives.

These teachings, which urged withdrawal from the world for meditation, created monastic communities in the ensuing centuries. The stress on personal and universal religious experience made this much more of a missionary religion than Hinduism and was thus more similar to Islam and Christianity in its core belief in the universality of its message.

The form in which Buddhism migrated to Southeast Asia is known as Hinayana ("the Lesser Vehicle"), or more recently, Theravada ("the Way of the Teachers") or simply, the Southern School of Buddhism. This school, which is closest to original Buddhism in its early years, had its major home on the island of Sri Lanka (Ceylon) which converted to Buddhism in the 3rd century B.C.

Theravada countries in Southeast Asia—Vietnam, Laos, Cambodia, Thailand and Burma—all have large communities of monks devoted to the daily practice of Buddhism. In recent times, these communities have been influential and increasingly active in national and political affairs. Although the Theravada Buddhists share the same central beliefs, there is no overarching system of central authority comparable to Vatican Catholicism that attempts to regulate the entire community. Almost every country has its own individual Buddhist sects.

Buddhism also spread north and northeast from India in the first centuries of the Christian era in the form known as Mahayana ("Greater Vehicle"), which entered Tibet, China, Korea and Japan. This form of the religion places less emphasis on good works and monastic withdrawal for contemplation, and greater weight on elaborate scriptures and faith. The canon (authorized texts) was printed in China in the 10th and 11th centuries, using some 130,000 wooden blocks on which characters had been carved. It was widely followed in central Asia until almost eliminated by the growing influence of Islam.

Inside the Liu Rong Buddhist temple (479 A.D.) in Guangzhou, China   Photo by Miller B. Spangler

Historical Background

Mahayana Buddhism became widespread in China in the first centuries of the modern era, during a period of considerable social disruption associated with the collapse of the Han (206–222 BC). It continued to grow in influence until it reached its height under the Tang Dynasty (618–907). Thereafter, its official influence began to wane although it continued to be profoundly influential in the lives of ordinary Chinese.

A form of Buddhism developed in Tibet known as Tantrism, which was heavily influenced by a type of Hinduism that engaged in demon worship and varieties of magical practices. It still exists today, particularly in eastern Tibet, but has been largely replaced by another form known as Lamaism, or "The Yellow Sect" to distinguish it from Tantrism. This is a combination of a purer form of Buddhism similar to Mahayana with an elaborate monastic organization common to Theravada, but even more highly formalized. Lamaism, of which the Dalai Lama is the leading figure, spread to Inner and Outer Mongolia in the sixteenth century. (See Tibet section for more details.)

The teachings of Buddhism have changed over the centuries and have been modified by many varied external influences. It does not contain a formal universal hierarchy, as does Catholicism. It is in general more administratively decentralized in the fashion of traditions such as Protestantism, Judaism, Hinduism and Islam.

Naturalism

Long before the formal development of the major schools of Chinese thought, Confucianism, Taoism and Buddhism, the Chinese had already developed an elaborate intellectual system. It covered ideas of governance (see Mandate of Heaven in the China section) to metaphysical ideas associated with the stability of the entire cosmic order—from the universe to each person's physical body. Chief among those ideas were the concepts of yin, and yang, and qi.

Yin and yang are often difficult for Westerners to understand because they superficially resemble aspects of the Western idea of duality, of the idea of "good" and "evil." The resemblance, though, is purely superficial. In the West, this ancient idea, originally derived from the Persian religion of Zoroastrianism, involves a duality of forces in the universe, one evil, one good, that struggle over the fate of the universe and humanity.

Yin and yang are quite different. This Eastern version of duality is one of complementary opposites that need each other. Some things are associated with yin more than yang, but both are always pres-

Panda Research Center, Chengdu   Photo by Steven Leibo

ent and vital for cosmic and personal stability. This distinction may appear minor but it has had a significant impact on how the two civilizations have viewed the world around them. An understanding of yin and yang are critical to an understanding of things Chinese, from philosophy to medicine. In the same vein, qi is another important aspect of this naturalist worldview.

According to Chinese tradition, every living thing possesses a sort of "vital element" that, in the case of humans, is drawn both from our parents and our environment. This qi, which is said to flow through the body, is considered to be absolutely vital to good health. It is the flow of qi that Chinese traditional physicians still attempt to manipulate with techniques like acupuncture and acupressure to heal patients. Thus, an understanding of issues like naturalism, yin and yang and qi remain even today a vital part of the tools necessary to understand the enormous civilization that has so influenced most of the rest of East Asia.

Daoism (Taoism)

Daoism (Taoism) is in many ways a complementary parallel to China's long Confucian tradition. Daoism, which was formalized at about the same time as Confucianism, is often portrayed as a clear contrast to Confucianism's obsession with how human beings in society should behave. Daoism is less social in its orienta-

tion and more interested in the individual's relationship with the natural and metaphysical world. A flavor of this tone is captured in the famous Daoist dictum for government that what was really important was keeping people's heads empty and their stomachs full. Overall Daoism is more personal and self-consciously contemplative than the social activism of Confucian practice. Daoism varies enormously from an association with a popular religion of magic and spirits to a very philosophical discussion of the relationship of beings to the universe. On a practical level, the early Daoism's interest in the search for elixirs of life brought to Chinese civilization an acute interest in nature, which continues to have a strong influence on contemporary Chinese food and medicine.

Christianity

Although Christian missionaries have been active in Asia for centuries few people in the region have been influenced by any of its various sects. In China, for example, Christianity was often seen simply as an element of Western imperialism and rejected out of hand. Today, although Christianity is a vigorous tradition within the People's Republic, the actual numbers, given China's enormous size, are relatively insignificant. On the other hand, some of the countries covered by this text have been tremendously influenced by Christianity. The Philippines and Vietnam both

4

developed large Catholic communities during the colonial eras. The Philippines today is almost exclusively Christian with the exception of the southernmost island of Mindanao where Islam remains dominant.

Among the East Asian nations, Korea is the most influenced by Christianity due to a curious irony of history. During the nineteenth century Christian missionaries in Korea often sided with the Koreans against the colonizing Japanese, thus linking Christianity to the emerging Korean nationalism. In today's Korea Christianity is a very influential tradition with millions of followers.

The Pacific Islands people are largely committed to the various Christian traditions. Christians are found widely throughout the region among those whose families were originally converted by the earliest Protestant and Catholic missionaries and, more recently, to new denominations ranging from Jehovah's Witnesses in Tahiti-Polynesia, Fiji and New Caledonia and the Solomon Islands, to Mormons in Tonga and Western Samoa. The Anglo communities of New Zealand and Australia, made up as they are largely by immigrants from England, are, of course, largely Christian as well.

Shinto

Shinto emerged in the earliest period of Japanese history, and originally was an animistic religion that gave human form to the various gods that rule the forces of nature. Although indigenous to the Japa-nese home islands, this religious tradition is in many ways similar to the animistic beliefs found among Southeast Asian and African groups. As in many traditional Native American beliefs, it embraces the sense that a "divinity" of sorts exists among many natural objects in nature from beautiful trees to waterfalls. Shinto, a tradition that refers to the "Way of the Kami," puts emphasis on what might be called entities of "awe," the Kami that include myriad objects from ancestors to legendary heroic figures and natural phenomena. Especially important within the tradition is the belief that the Sun Goddess, Amaterasu, sent her descendants to Earth to create the Japanese home islands. It was the association of the Yamato clan line with that tradition that became the basis of its claim to imperial power.

Unlike religions such as Buddhism and Christianity that developed very elaborate traditions of religious ritual and sacred texts, Shinto tended to be very much more loosely organized and was overshadowed in Japan by the arrival of Buddhism in the sixth century. As Mahayana Buddhism entered the islands, the two beliefs tended to influence each other. Thus, it was possible to profess the ideologies of both without feeling inconsistent.

Buddhism in Japan eventually split into numerous sects, and for several centuries Shinto beliefs were somewhat dormant, although not forgotten. In the late nineteenth and early twentieth century, the Shinto heritage became the state religion; it was reemphasized that the emperor was a descendant of the Sun Goddess and possessed her divine powers. Although the imperial house had long been respected in Japan, the late nineteenth century development of a cult-like imagery around it was not a product of Japanese tradition, but rather part of the modernizing effort. It was believed by nineteenth century thinkers that Japan needed a "unifying element" to fully join the nation. Enhancing the symbolism of the emperor was thought the most appropriate way to do so. Thus, the imperial house was far more celebrated in the late nineteenth and early 20th century than it had been for centuries. In many ways it is helpful to think of this revival of Shinto as "State Shinto" in contrast to the more decentralized tradition of Japan's earlier history.

This revival corresponded with a rise of militarism in Japan, culminating with World War II. After defeat by the allies, Japan renounced the idea of the "divinity" of the Emperor. Shinto lost its official status. Ironically the supposed "imperial divinity" which Westerners found offensive about the Japanese system was only remarkable when viewed from the outside by Westerners bred in the traditions of monotheism. In Japan the spiritual aspects of the emperor had operated in a very different context for the Japanese.

Islam

Although most Americans tend to associate Islam with the Arab communities of the Middle East, the reality is that the larg-

Photo by Steven Leibo

5

Historical Background

est communities of Muslims in the world are found in Asia and among a very wide variety of ethnic groups. Especially large communities of Muslims are found in South Asia (see Russell, The Middle East and South Asia), but they are also a very important religious community in East and Southeast Asia as well. From western China to the southern Philippines, from Malaysia to Indonesia (the largest Muslim nation in the world) Islam is very important to this region.

Islam, which emerged in the 7th century, is part of the enormously rich Middle Eastern monotheistic religious tradition that had earlier seen the development of Judaism and Christianity. Muhammad, a poor merchant from the Arabian Peninsula, developed the religion after experiencing what he called a revelation from the angel Gabriel regarding the Unity of God. As a tradition, Islam is a militantly monotheistic creed that requires giving charity to the poor and a life of regular daily prayer as well as, if at all possible, a pilgrimage to the holy places at Mecca in today's Saudi Arabia.

Although Islam is a growing movement within the United States, few Americans know much about it and would probably be surprised at how much of its theology is shared with both Christianity and Judaism. The tradition includes the idea of a heaven and resurrection and a system of predestination. Seeing itself as a clear continuation of the line of revelation that had begun with the Patriarch Abraham, Muhammad revealed himself to be the "final prophet" in a long tradition that extended back through both the Old and New Testaments. Basically, Muhammad taught that the Judeo-Christian biblical texts are not complete. Thus, the Islamic movement embraced a new document, one, said to have been dictated by God. That text is known as the Qur'an (Koran). This new sacred document, which makes regular reference to biblical personalities and events, is distinctly influenced by the Judeo-Christian traditions which had preceded it.

Sometimes stories are derived from the bible texts and modified with startling results. For example, the story of the fall from Eden is also found in the Qur'an, yet in the Islamic version, the female, Eve, is not blamed for the transgression against God, a very thought-provoking modification, especially for those who think Islam can be easily categorized on issues of gender. The text of the Qur'an itself includes 114 chapters that Muslims believe confirms and clarifies the revelation received earlier by the Christians and Jews.

Like many religions, Islam spread through a complicated series of developments that ranged from militant conquest to merchant activities and mystical religious missionaries. Today it is found widely in parts of Southeast Asia and western China.

The resurgence of militant Islam in the Middle East and northern Africa has had its effect in such Southeast Asian countries as Indonesia and Malaysia. Here, it has taken the form of increased wearing of the traditional dress, stricter dietary rules, and the establishment of Muslim banking operations. Though Islam is more strictly adhered to in Malaysia, religious resurgence in that country or in any other part of Southeast Asia does not usually approach the fervor which is found today in the Middle East. Until recently few of the Muslim states in the region—Brunei, Indonesia, Malaysia or the Philippines (the latter has only a small Muslim minority) had seen the extensive level of Islamic militancy experienced elsewhere. Nevertheless, such tendencies have grown considerably in recent years and have become a significant factor in public affairs from Thailand to Indonesia.

Women in Traditional Asia

Although until recently women have lived in few societies that have afforded them even a semblance of equality with men, the women of Asia have often been particularly challenged by the limitations of their own unequal status. Nevertheless, our region is large and it is difficult to make generalizations. In some traditional societies and especially hierarchical societies like those dominated by Confucianism, which has had such an important influence throughout much of the region, women are regarded as decidedly inferior to men. As elsewhere, they were commonly less valued both as infants and as adults. Female babies were less likely to be nurtured when young and more frequently experienced infanticide than males. They were raised to serve as a wife for a male chosen by others (if they were lucky). Too often, in times of financial distress, daughters found themselves

Woman with bound feet

sold into virtual sexual slavery by their parents.

The specific nature of their unequal status has varied widely from region to region and from period to period. In China, for example, it appears that women were more influential early on and that their status deteriorated around the 8th century A.D. By about the 11th the horrendously painful practice of foot binding, that is, of forcing the female child's foot into an artificially tiny shape, had emerged, a practice that would cause immense suffering among Chinese women until the 20th century. Elsewhere though, the status and circumstances were quite different. In early Japan, women appear to have been much more important than their latter status suggests and imperial women of the court, individuals like Lady Murasaki, are credited with creating the modern form of the novel, most notably in works like the Tale of Genji written around 1000 A.D.

In Southeast Asia, peasant women remained much more important than their peers in either East Asia or South Asia and played an important role in the local economies. In places like Vietnam, whose elite was especially influenced by Confucianism, the peasant women's lives remained much less constricted than the elite women of the Confucian aristocracy. And among the latter, women played a more significant and respected role than they did in Vietnam's giant neighbor to the north.

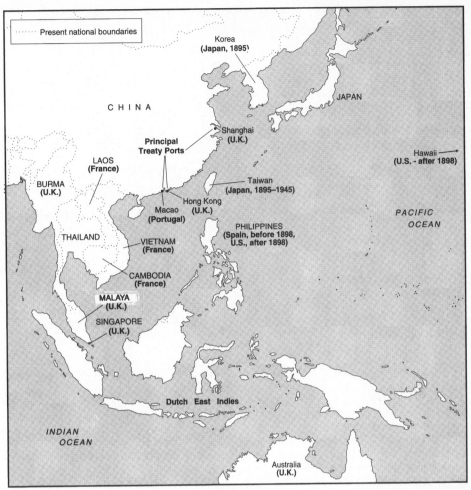

Colonial Era

The Impact of the West

One of the most dramatic aspects of modern world history was the enormous movement of colonialism and imperialism that saw the various Western nations spread their influence and direct administrative control over a large percentage of the globe. From a period running from approximately 1500 through the early 20th century, the various Western powers, and eventually Japan, gained control over much of the world. Only a few nations remained outside of their control. In Africa the ages-old empire of Abyssinia, today's Ethiopia, managed to resist an Italian effort at conquest in 1896 and in Southeast Asia the kingdom of Siam, today's Thailand, survived albeit hemmed in by English and French colonies on either side.

It was that world of colonial and imperial control that brought the globe into the 20th century, and much of the 1900s, dealt with the reversal of that process as individual national communities eventually found their way to national freedom from colonial administrations. East and Southeast Asia were not exempt from this global phenomenon and in fact, they were part of the region whose products had originally attracted the 15th century Europeans at the dawn of the modern colonial age.

The countries of early modern Western Europe, especially Spain, Portugal and the Netherlands, tried to reach East Asia and the Western Pacific in order to acquire the profits from the extraordinarily lucrative spice trade, to gain converts to Christianity and to acquire new territories for their respective governments. Especially significant in those early years were the Iberians, adventurers from Spain and Portugal, who had also led the efforts in the Western Hemisphere.

Ferdinand Magellan, a Portuguese in the service of Spain, was the first to lead Europeans to the region. He was killed in the Philippines in 1521. Half a century later Spain, operating from its bases in the New World, began to colonize the Philippines, which it eventually held for three centuries. In the 16th century, Portuguese explorers, traders, and missionaries spread similarly from the Indian Ocean to Southeast Asia and the coast of southern China. They were not strong enough however to make much of an impact on the region, and most of their holdings soon fell to the Dutch.

The Dutch East India Company was the strongest European influence in East Asia and the Western Pacific in the 17th century. Its main theater of operations was the Dutch (or Netherlands) East Indies (now Indonesia), the richest in the region in the resources then in most demand in Europe (spices, coffee, etc.). Although the Dutch government eventually took direct control of the East Indies from the Dutch East India Company in the early 19th century, its rule was distinctly paternalistic and did little to develop the islands from either an economic or a political point of view.

The British impact on the region was less than they had in the Indian Ocean and South Asia, where they built up their enormous empire in India, but it was still significant. In Southeast Asia, the British colonial presence began first in Burma. For the British, expanding control was usually a response to growing commercial interests. In Burma, territorial disputes and issues of sovereignty arose in the late eighteenth century. Anglo-Burmese relations deteriorated until 1823, when British forces captured Rangoon. By the end of the 1860s, the British had integrated all of

Historical Background

A Chinese Opium "den" in 1898

the Burmese provinces into British Burma and into the Indian empire.

By 1826, they had established what was known as the Straits Settlements along the coast of Malaya (today, Malaysia). These settlements consisted of the island of Penang, just off Malaya's north coast, Malacca, formerly a Dutch possession on the central coast, and Singapore at the southern tip of the Malay Peninsula. Over the next fifty years their control extended over all of Malaya. They obtained vast quantities of tin from the interior and commerce from the Straits Settlements. An Anglo-Dutch Treaty of 1824 recognized British dominance along the Malay coast and also acknowledged Dutch interests to the south. This resulted in the effective splitting up of the old Malay world. The Dutch eventually established their control over all of Sumatra and Java, and became the colonial masters of the future Indonesia. The British controlled Malaya and Singapore until their independence.

In the 19th century the British East India Company had also become a major commercial force along the South China coast, its main interest being Chinese tea, silk and porcelain. Merchants brought opium, usually bought from the Company in India, to the South China coast and sold it in defiance of an official ban. Machine-made British textiles eventually became a major Chinese import in the 19th century, especially after the British East India Company lost its legal monopoly of its share of the China trade early in the century.

The British government used armed force at intervals to compel China to lower its barriers to expanded foreign trade (in-cluding opium imports) and residence (including missionary activity). These pressures eventually culminated in the famous "Opium Wars" of the early nineteenth century and resulted in a series of unequal treaties with the Chinese that saw Westerners establish themselves along the China coast in a series of "treaty ports" which were outside of formal Chinese control.

Although the United States had been late to enter the competition for empire in the Pacific, it eventually became very involved there. By the mid-nineteenth century, the United States had established itself on the American West Coast and had begun the effort to extend its influence into the Pacific. The Hawaiian Islands came under American control in 1898.

Meanwhile, by the late nineteenth century, a number of educated Filipinos were moved by modern nationalist ideals to declare independence from Spain and cooperate briefly with the United States in expelling the Spanish during the Spanish American War of 1898. Unfortunately for them, after the defeat of Spain, the United States proceeded to take over the Philippines for itself. After crushing a spirited Filipino resistance, the U.S. set up a reasonably efficient colonial regime and did a good deal to prepare the Filipinos for self-government, but like the other colonial powers in the region it did not qualitatively develop the economy, which remained essentially an extractive (mining) and plantation one.

Earlier, the U.S. had, beginning in the mid-19th century, spearheaded the western entry into Japan. In contrast to many other communities in what became the colonial world, the Japanese, were much better able to control the process, and Japan never became a colony of the West. In effect, in attempting to avoid the fate of so many other Asian peoples, Japan decided to dramatically transform its society. Thus, it borrowed from the West (mostly technology and organization) and combined it with the essentials of its own culture. In the process, Japan became a military and imperial power strong enough to defeat China (in 1894) and Russia (in 1905) and itself emerge as a major colonial power with control over the Chinese island of Taiwan and the Korean peninsula.

Certainly not content to be left behind their colonial rivals, Paris was involved in Southeast Asian colonialism. The Treaty of Saigon of 1862 established the French colony of Cochin China in southern Vietnam. The conflict leading to this treaty was in response to several decades of tension as a result of inroads into Vietnamese society by French Catholicism. The French seemed to be as much interested in the spread of their religion as the potential for economic gain. Especially important, in the minds of the French, was the necessity of keeping up with their English rivals. French control of Cambodia and Laos followed and, with Vietnam, became French Indochina. The Laotians and Cambodians were more favorably disposed toward the French, having been under the authority of both Siam and Vietnam previously. For Vietnam, the period of French domination was culturally much more difficult.

Remarkably, even though it was sandwiched between the British colonies of Burma and Malaya and the French in Indochina, Siam (now Thailand) was able to survive under its own monarchy without being colonized by any European power. This was partly because the British and French were more interested in penetrating Southwest China from their bases in Southeast Asia than in colonizing Siam and because they both saw the benefit of Siam as a buffer between their respective territories. Siam also benefited from a highly talented monarchy that earlier saw the need to learn about western institutions and governing methods. When the British did come, the Siamese showed considerable diplomatic skill in meeting the challenge.

An important product of western colonial rule in Southeast Asia was the influx (from about 1850 to 1920) of large numbers of Chinese immigrants, driven by poverty and chaos at home and drawn by the economic opportunities created by colonialism. These "overseas" Chinese have tended to be resented by the indigenous peoples and have never been allowed a share of real political power (except in Singapore, where they are the majority), but their economic activity and influence have been very great.

Major political and military trends of the twentieth century, culminating in Japan's launching of World War II in the Pacific (see Japan), were to sweep away Western colonial rule in Southeast Asia, and make its restoration after the war a practical impossibility. As we shall see, during the post war era, colony after colony emerged from Western control although some anti-colonial struggles, like that of Vietnam, were to become particularly bloody as anti-colonialist momentum became entwined with the struggles of the Cold War.

The islands of the Western Pacific were no exception to this process. Even as they were among the first communities absorbed into the Western colonial empires, many of them have only recently gained their autonomy. A few, like New Caledonia, still remain as colonies.

Nationalism, Communism and Revolution

One of the most predictable results of Western colonialism was the emergence of an organized resistance to that control. Not surprisingly the effort to reject imperialism eventually became a fundamental part of the struggle for Asia's modern identity. But initially Western political control over colonial Asia seemed unshakable, and there was thus little basis for the emergence of such nationalism. When Japan defeated Russia in 1905, however, the myth that the Western powers were invincible was shattered.

Japan also showed by its example that it was possible, however difficult, for an Asian country to modernize itself along

the lines of Western nations. During the brief period that it controlled substantial portions of Southeast Asia, Japan weakened the prestige of the colonial powers to the point where it would be all the more difficult for them to reestablish themselves in the region after the war.

Next to the influence of the West itself and that of Japan's successes, the third great external influence on the emergence of modern Asian nationalism was the example of Soviet Russia. Before 1917 Marxism had almost no following in the area, but many Asian leaders became impressed with the seemingly rapid success of Lenin's Bolsheviks in seizing power within Russia in 1917. Of even greater importance was the loudly declared determination to modernize Russia along socialist lines, and to help the people of the non-Western world to throw off alien influence. The communism of Marx, prescribed for industrial nations of Europe and America, was billed as the medicine that would allegedly cure the ills of the poor, non-Western countries of Asia.

Lenin attracted great attention with his theory that the main obstacle to progress in the non-Western world was Western "imperialism"; he urged that local nationalists, supported by Soviet Russia, could make progress toward expelling this imperialism. This would be, according to Lenin a preparation for the day when "proletarian" parties, in other words, communist parties, could emerge and seize power. The combination of the concept of imperialism, the exploitation of existing nationalism and the triumph in Russia of a communist party had an enormous influence in Asia as well as elsewhere in the world. These ideas became part of the mental equipment of many, although by no means all, Asian nationalists, whether

or not they consider themselves communists. Stated otherwise, many Asian nationalists adopted some communist ideas and techniques without becoming communists—or for a time found it politically useful to act as though they had.

The result was often a complex alignment of nationalist and communist elements, in which it is often difficult to see where the nationalistic spirit ends and the communist aims begin. Ho Chi Minh was a member of the Communist International and the founder of the Vietnamese Communist Party but he was also a committed Vietnamese nationalist. Unlike the situation in Eastern Europe where communists and nationalists were often bitter enemies for most of the 20th century, the dynamics of anti-colonial struggles in much of the world often saw the two groups not only closely aligned but united in the personalities of many of the anti-colonial leaders. Unfortunately this reality was often misunderstood by Western leaders and analysts, who were often far better trained in the politics of Europe than Asia.

Anti-colonial movements began to assume importance in the colonies of Asia about 1920. The spread of Western education and political ideas, the limited measure of self-government granted by the colonial powers, the influence of Woodrow Wilson's doctrine of self-determination—the idea that every people has the right to choose the form of government under which it will live—and the Bolshevik Revolution in Russia, all played parts in the spread of nationalism.

The Chinese communities living in Asian countries other than their homeland (the "overseas Chinese") were stimulated to nationalist activity by the revolutionary forces then at work within China, but usually preferred a continuation of Western political rule to the possibly oppressive rule of the native majorities where they lived. Non-Chinese nationalists usually resented the Chinese for their hard-earned wealth and economic influence, to the same degree that they also opposed the political control of the Western powers. As a result, their agitation was usually directed against both groups of outsiders.

Prior to World War II, there were no nationalist movements in Southeast Asia able to challenge the well-armed colonial governments. Nationalists were unable to gather sufficient support for the independence cause until the outbreak of the war changed the dynamics of the entire region. As will be seen in the individual national state sections, the combination of the Japanese temporary occupation of the region and the weakening of the colonial powers made a complete reestablishment of the former Western colonial world in East and Southeast Asia simply impossible. Cer-

Historical Background

tainly in some areas, like Indonesia and Vietnam, the colonial powers attempted to reestablish their power but each in turn was eventually stymied in the face of the worldwide anti-colonial momentum. The age of formal colonies had passed. Only the rise of the Cold War in the late 1940s made this trend somewhat less certain as many nationalist and economic struggles became entwined with the politics of Soviet/American rivalries.

Communist challenges arose in the Philippines, in the form of the Huk rebellion in the early 1950s; in Malaya, under the "emergency" declared from 1948 to 1960; and in Indochina and Indonesia. Burma, Thailand and even Singapore also experienced communist activities. In Indonesia, the movement was strongest in Central Java. The Indonesian Communist Party met its bloody demise in 1965 when it was destroyed by the Indonesian military under Suharto whose regime continued to maintain stability under an authoritarian government until 1998.

Presently, Vietnam is the only surviving nominally communist regime in Southeast Asia, and that will be increasingly debatable as reforms move ahead. Laos no longer qualifies as a genuine Marxist state. In Laos, as in other nations of the region, the military has emerged particularly important.

Nevertheless, communism was often an essential ingredient in the emerging nationalism of the region. In some cases, it forced colonial and then newly independent governments to address social problems that they might have otherwise ignored. In contrast to Eastern Europe, communism still remains a vital if evolving force. The tensions of the old Cold War have dimmed in East Asia much more slowly than they have in Europe.

Women in Modern East and Southeast Asia

Along with many women of the Western World, the women of the East, Southeast Asia and the Western Pacific have often made enormous strides during the 20th century. Although the dominant figure as the century began was a woman, the famous Cixi, the dowager empress, most women in China labored under both the physical pain of foot binding and the limitations of their educational and career possibilities. Yet within the first quarter century not only was foot binding outlawed and eventually suppressed, but those years saw women in large numbers begin to gain higher education and to take part in political activism as shown in their role in the famous May Fourth Movement.

When the communists came to power in 1949 one of their first moves was to legislate improvements in the lives of women that, if not creating a society of equality, have much improved the lives of millions of Chinese women.

In Japan, the century began with a few women striving to establish their own political and literary activities and more often ending up in trouble with the conservative governments of the time. Nevertheless, Japanese women gained the vote as a result of the changes brought about during the American Occupation of Japan and the end of the century even saw a woman emerge for a time as the head of one of the major Japanese parties, the Japanese Socialist Party.

Throughout the world the development of better contraceptive devices and the growing perception that women need to be educated in order to contribute to the economic lives of their families has also spurred improvements in many areas of East and Southeast Asia. Not surprisingly the women of the more urban classes have gained the most from these changes while poorer women are less likely either to have the finances, access or education necessary to take advantage of the new technologies available for family planning. In some areas, like the Philippines, where the Catholic Church is influential, there is considerable opposition to birth control.

Politically the single most important element to affect the lives of women of the region was probably the emergence of nationalism as a driving force. In many regions, especially in places like Vietnam, women played important roles in the anti-colonial struggles of the postwar era. Moreover, in recent years, women activists have been especially involved in encouraging democratic growth in the region. Corazon Aquino emerged triumphant in the struggle that saw the end of the Marcos dictatorship in the Philippines and elsewhere in the region, most notably in Burma, where Aung San Suu Kyi has led the democratic opposition. During 1996 Megawati Sukarnoputri the daughter of the late Indonesian ruler Sukarno, attempted (unsuccessfully) to challenge the continuing dictatorship of Suharto. By mid-1999 she had become vice president and eventually emerged as Indonesia's first female president. Meanwhile, the Philippines have had their second female president, Gloria Macapagal Arroyo, while in both Taiwan and South Korea women have held national office as the vice president and premier respectively.

Despite these changes, real improvements in the lives of women have never been even or routine across the region. In some areas like China where recent economic liberalization has at times given more discretionary power to families and individual factory managers, we have seen the emergence of more traditional values regarding the worth of daughters than was experienced under the height of socialist control. These new freedoms have sometimes actually worked against women's rights. Elsewhere a religious backlash against Western secularism has also challenged those gains.

From Post-Colonialism to Globalization

As the new states of East and Southeast Asia began to emerge after the demise of colonialism, hopes were high, especially in the West that economically vibrant western style capitalist democracies would emerge. In fact, many new states began their existence as free countries using models borrowed from the Western liberal democracies that had originally colonized them.

Today Singapore and Malaysia—the latter to a diminishing extent—survive as single-party-dominated systems while Thailand, after years of military domination, appeared for a time to be evolving toward a much more open democracy. Recently that evolution seemed to backslide toward the sort of one-party "guided democracy," common elsewhere, at least until the Thai military once again intervened. It remains unclear how real a blow to Thailand's democratic momentum recent events will be since the supposedly pro-military military coup was itself rejected in the most recent elections. On the other hand, the Philippines, and even more recently Indonesia, have recently returned to the democratic fold after decades under dictatorship.

In what became known as the East Asian Newly Industrialized Countries (NICs), like Taiwan and South Korea, extended periods of strongman government lasted until the late 1980s. Although the American occupation authorities re-established its 1920s-era parliamentary system, Japan was until quite recently largely governed by the combination of a single party (The Liberal Democratic Party) and an especially powerful bureaucracy.

Economically, after the Second World War, the hope was to see the region smoothly recover from the devastation of the war. Sadly, that was not the case. Their economies were weakened by the anti-communist struggles of the era, wars in Korea and Vietnam, and related struggles like those in the southern Philippines. The region's natural economic structure was also undermined by the turmoil that engulfed China during the first decades after the People's Republic emerged in 1949.

Of course, the communist states initially embraced a system of single party domination over their countries' economic and political life. Nevertheless, by the late-1970s in China and the mid-1980s in Vietnam, political decisions were made that led their peoples farther and farther from the communist command economies that had once dominated their lives.

In fact, by the late-20th century, China in particular had largely traded the central planning of communist economic systems for a vibrant and more mixed economy that included very significant levels of private capitalist activity. However, the rejection of communist economics was not paralleled by an equally impressive move toward more open political systems. Nevertheless, as people found themselves less economically dependent on the state, their lives were often increasingly freer.

If the immediate postwar years were not very successful in establishing more democratic governments and economically open capitalist systems, the region's more recent record is much more promising. As we enter more deeply into the 21st century, East and Southeast Asia, so recently an area in constant turmoil, has emerged as an extremely dynamic part of the world. The Industrial Revolution that transformed Western Europe a century ago and has now dramatically hit East and Southeast Asia has not only radically changed the economic life of its citizens but raised their educational and political aspirations.

Most important has been the role East and Southeast Asia have played in the phenomenon of globalization that was so obviously transforming the planet by the early 21st century. In fact, it has probably impacted Asia more than almost anywhere else—in both positive ways and negative ways.

"Globalization" is the term that refers to the increasing integration of the world, particularly economically. It has been a phenomenon particularly nurtured by the combination of lowered legal barriers to international trade, the acceleration of international communication through such vehicles as the internet, and dramatically faster and lowered cost for international transport of manufactured goods.

The combination of the above made it possible for many of the region's less developed countries to transform themselves economically by placing their primary emphasis on exports while attracting foreign investors who, in the 1990s, poured huge amounts of money into the region in search of lower production costs and higher financial returns. At least initially, East and Southeast Asia's movement into the global marketplace seemed mostly without great costs.

In the ensuing years national and personal incomes often rose substantially while their cities began increasingly to resemble the ultra modern skylines of many long developed nations. If Japan had initially led the way during the 1960s and 1970s, by late century nations from Thailand to South Korea and Indonesia where experiencing similarly impressive growth rates and the emergence of new and urbanized middle classes. Unfortunately, the price of such growth became more obvious when the combination of over-heated construction markets and poorly timed liberalization of their economic markets (encouraged by the International Monetary Fund) caused many to fall into a deep economic slump as the Asia's economic crash set in during late-1997.

For a time East and Southeast Asia's recession seemed to destroy the momentum of decades of growth. For many it would take years to recover. Nevertheless, by 2007 most of the region from Malaysia to South Korea was back on track. For the largest economy of the area, China, the decision to reject communism for a major role in the newly globalized world economy was transforming the nation faster than any other in world history. More importantly, that decision helped China develop the necessary economic resources to confront successfully the challenges of the latest economic downturn that hit in late 2008.

Arriving from Hong Kong by train, these high rise buildings are the first evidence of new development seen by visitors at Shenzhen's commercial center, Luohu.

Courtesy: Caltex Petroleum Corporation

11

Historical Background

Not surprisingly, given all the economic changes, authoritarian regimes have been more and more challenged in their efforts to dominate national political life. From South Korea to Taiwan and Indonesia new leadership has been elected democratically with the support of more politically involved middle classes, the very middle classes required and nurtured by economic changes. Even the seemingly all-powerful Communist Party of China has seen its authority challenged in ways unimaginable only a few years ago.

How these economic and political changes will ultimately transform the entire region is only just beginning to become clear. What is certain is that the entire region will play a much more significant role in the global arena in the 21st century than it did during the 20th.

The Price: East and Southeast Asia's Environmental Challenge

The largest environmental issue that faces humanity today is the phenomenon known as "global warming." Asia might seem, at first glance, less responsible for this problem. In fact, it has been the United States that has made the largest contribution to the production of the "green house gases" that are threatening our world. It alone is responsible for around 30 % of the total, while all of Asia, including not only East and Southeast Asia but India, produce approximately 16%.

Readers may have heard recently that China has passed the United States as the major emitter of green house gasses, such as CO_2. However, the problem is the cumulative amount. The United States has been a large industrialized society for generations while China has only recently started down that road. Thus while Asian emissions are important, the primary responsibility for the developing "climate crisis" still lies at the feet of the Western industrialized societies. Due to its more recent industrialization, much of Asia bears less responsibility for what is occurring.

But carrying such a conclusion to far would be wrong. In fact, if humanity is to avoid some of the worst predictions scientists are warning us of—from rising sea levels that could swamp regions from the Mekong Delta to Shanghai, to other areas from North Central China and central India to Africa destroyed by drought—some of the most important decisions will have to be made by Asian leaders.

The reason is obvious to those who have studied, lived or traveled in Eastern Asia. Because of the very economic success that has raised hundreds of millions of Asians from poverty and has seen millions of them advance from foot power to bicycles and then motorcycles and increasingly these days into automobiles, decisions about how much of Asia will develop have been turned into critical questions for all of humanity. In short, if Asians follow the same industrial development and transport choices that western nations, particularly the United States, have pursued over the last several generations, the world will confront challenges unlike anything that has ever faced us.

Moreover, Asians are particularly at risk because the glaciers on the Tibetan plateau have been particularly impacted by global warming. That region holds more than a hundred times more drinking water than the Alps and produces water for the forty percent of humanity that draws its water out of rivers from the Ganges and the Mekong to the Yangtze and the Yellow.

Looking at only one country, China can reveal something of the challenge. It has been predicted that the number of vehicles on China's roads could increase by fifteen times over the next 30 years, perhaps tripling the amount of carbon dioxide pollution emitted into the air. Certainly anyone who has seen the rows of shiny new car dealership in some of the most obscure Chinese towns would have little reason to challenge predictions of this sort.

For those closer to the sea, from Japan to Southeast Asia, the most immediate threat is that increasing ocean temperatures are making the famous storms of Asia, the typhoons, known as hurricanes in the Atlantic, regularly more powerful than in the past. The smaller communities of the South Pacific are even more immediately threatened as rising sea levels and more powerful storm surges threaten their very existence.

On the more positive side, our region has also been particularly involved in helping to organize a world-wide attempt to confront the climate crisis. In fact, from the famous Kyoto Treaties of the late 1990s—which began the first serious efforts to create a consensus for action—to the 2007 international meeting at Bali, Indonesia, held to move the effort even further forward, East and Southeast Asians have been at the forefront of the global response to man-made climate change. If China received significant criticism in late 2009 for its unwillingness to accept outside monitoring of its energy efficiency efforts, it was nevertheless true as well that the nation had fundamentally committed itself to working toward a clean energy future within its own borders. That matters given that China today accounts for approximately 20% of the world's carbon emissions.

Great Buddha at Kamakura, Japan, 1252

Internet Café in Chengdu China   Photo by Steven Leibo

The People's Republic of China

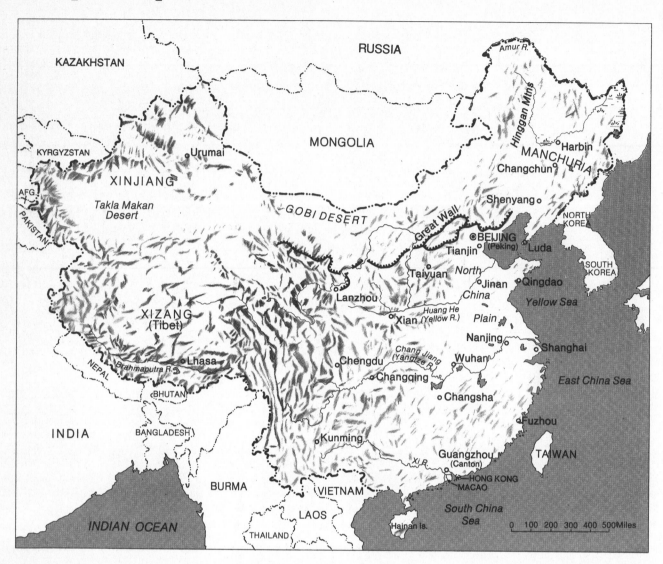

7 Area: Approximately 3.7 million square miles, including Inner Mongolia and Tibet. (As large as the 50 United States plus another Alaska).

Population: 1,321,851,888 (July 2007 estimate)

Capital City: Beijing, Pop. 14,930,000 (2004 estimate)

Climate: Dry, cold with bitter winters in the mountainous West and North, temperate in the East, subtropical with rainy monsoons in the South.

Neighboring Countries: Russia (Northeast, sharing a tiny border on the Northwest); Mongolia (North); Kazakhstan, Kyrgyzstan (Northwest); Afghanistan, Pakistan (East); India, Nepal, Bhutan (Southwest); Burma, Laos, Vietnam (South); Korea (Northeast) and Taiwan (not considered a separate country by the PRC)

Official Language: Mandarin Chinese, the dialect of the Chinese language spoken in Central and Northern China.

Other Principal Tongues: South and West Chinese dialects, including Cantonese, Hakka, Fukienese and Wu, the Tibetan language. Tribesmen of remote Xinjiang, Inner Mongolia and Manchuria have their own languages and dialects.

Ethnic Background: Chinese, or *Han* (about 91.9%). Relatively small minorities of Mongol, Turkic, Tibetan, Thai and Korean ethnicity

Principal Religions: Confucianism, Taoism, Buddhism, Islam and Christianity.

Main Exports: machinery, plastics, optical and medical equipment, iron and steel, toys, footwear, textiles, agricultural products, oil, minerals

Main Imports: machinery and equipment, oil and mineral fuels, plastics, optical and medical equipment, organic chemicals, iron and steel

Currency: Renminbi (people's currency) expressed in units called Yuan.

Former Colonial Status: Some regions were colonized by various Western powers.

National Day: October 1, anniversary of the founding of the People's Republic in 1949.

Chief of State: Hu Jintao, President (since March 2003).

Head of Government: Wen Jiabao, Premier (since March 2003).

General Secretary, Communist Party: Hu Jintao.

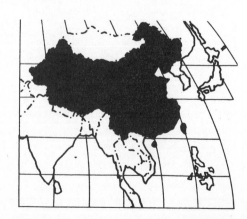

14

China

National Flag: Red, with one large and four small five-pointed stars at upper left.

Per Capita GDP Income: U.S. $5,300 (2007 estimate-purchasing power parity)

(Note: At the beginning of 1979, the People's Republic of China officially adopted an already-existing system known as Pinyin for writing out Chinese names and terms in the Western alphabet. That system is now increasingly used in both the West and even on Taiwan. Thus the capital of China, once known commonly as "Peking" is now more often rendered "Beijing." The Pinyin system is used in the following text except where possible confusion might occur with terms already quite familiar, thus "Daoism," will also be followed by the less correct but more familiar "Taoism.")

Occupying a land area larger than that of the 50 United States, China stretches for a distance of 3,400 miles from its Northeastern region adjacent to remote Russian Siberia to the mountainous regions of Tibet bordering on Nepal and India. As for temperature, altitude and roughness of terrain, fertility of the soil, and rainfall, there are two distinct regions. The invisible line that divides the two starts in the distant north at the Amur River and runs southward through the crest of the Great Khingnan Mountains. It follows the contours of the Huang He, or Yellow River, turning northwest and then west to accommodate that part of the river that arches toward Mongolia. Turning again southward, it searches out the upper part of the river, passing through the region around Lanzhou and Chengdu and finally becomes obscure in the hilly southern area of Kunming near the Vietnamese border.

A mother and child framed in a decorative wall-window in Hangzhou
Courtesy: Jon Markham Morrow

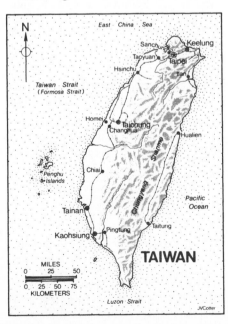

In the West, on the left-hand side of the rough demarcation line, the land is a combination of closely crowded mountains with rough surfaces possessing little greenery even in the warmer regions of the lower altitudes. The towering peaks are occasionally interrupted by expanses of flat territory that is also desolate and dry, being surrounded by a natural barrier that withstands the invasion of rain clouds. The mountains in the North on the edge of the "line" give way to the Gobi Desert, filled with shifting earth, harsh rock formations and severe extremes in temperature, all of which combine to exclude more than occasional visits of man and beast. The mountains envelop this desert which extends from Manchuria into southern Mongolia.

These areas of outer China are largely unmapped by Western standards. The thinly scattered people of Tibet, Xinjiang and Manchuria have traditionally relied on herds of animals as their principal resource, although great treasures of mineral wealth may lie buried below the surface of the earth. A short growing season provides the small amount of greenery available. The air is dry in both summer and winter, blowing out of Asiatic Russia (Siberia). The great distance the wind has traveled prior to its arrival in China has taken almost all moisture from the air. The lack of significant bodies of water in the endless expanses also makes the dry winds cold—bitterly so, almost beyond belief, in the winter.

In the spring enough warmth arrives to melt the snow in the lower altitudes of the mountains. This is sufficient to support limited agriculture at the lower edges of the mountains bordering the Gobi Desert of western Manchuria and Mongolia in the area between the mountains and the Takla Makan Desert in Xinjiang and the valleys of Tibet, but only during the brief summer season.

To the south and east of the "line" the land changes into temperate farmland; it is relatively flat and somewhat drier in parts of northern China, notably in the North China Plain. The hillier and more mountainous areas found in southern China have more moisture and warmer temperatures, producing thick growths of forest on the land not under cultivation.

The three main rivers, the Huang He (Yellow), the Yangzi and the Xijiang (West River) have their origins deep within the remote territory west of the mountains, but flow through the more level eastern regions in a sluggish manner. Refreshed by the cool water of melting snow, they are quickly swollen in the spring by rains brought by the southeastern monsoon, and overflow their banks, spreading rich silt over the surrounding land. Rivers overflowing their banks continue to be a major problem. They also are a traditional source of communication and transportation in the region, but this is being replaced by railroads.

The lower valley of the Huang He is temperate and is the area in which the major aspects of Chinese civilization were born. The river itself is unpredictable. It left its old course south of the Shandong peninsula in which it had flowed for more

China

than 800 years, and assumed its present course north of the peninsula in 1853, a shift of more than 500 miles. The immense quantities of silt it carries in its waters gave it the name "Yellow River" and also have built up a riverbed so much so over the years that is higher than the surrounding land. When it enters flood stage, the results have been catastrophic.

The growing season increases in the central and eastern region of China that is drained by the Yangzi River; it becomes almost continuous throughout the year in the southeastern area through which the Xijiang (Sikiang) River flows. If the rainfall in these regions were uniform from year to year, both would produce great quantities of food to feed the huge number of Chinese. The variations in rain, however, cause periodic loss of crops by either drought or flood. During a prolonged drought, even the violent summer rains are not of much help, since they run quickly into the rivers and flow into the sea rather than watering the land, which then dries out, unless there is further, preferably steady, rainfall.

The island of Taiwan has an elongated oval shape and its entire length is dominated by a chain of mountains rising with regularity to heights of 6,000 to 11,000 feet.

These peaks lie close to the eastern side of the island and drop steeply at the coastline into the warm waters of the Pacific. The western slopes descend gently to a fertile plain that occupies almost one-half of the island's surface. The climate varies from tropical to temperate, depending upon altitude. As is true on the Chinese mainland 100 miles across the Taiwan Strait, the summer winds bring abundant rain, which supports intense agriculture. The smaller rivers do not cause the catastrophic floods of the three mighty rivers of continental China, so that bountiful harvests of a variety of produce, principally rice, are regularly gathered.

History

The Formative Era

China is the world's oldest continuous civilization in the sense that contemporary Chinese civilization recognizably resembles its earliest origins. Today's Arabic and Islamic Egypt, for example, is far more different from the civilization of the Pharaohs than China is from its early years. Still China is actually of much more recent vintage than the major early civilizations of Southwest Asia and North Africa.

Archeological evidence from north China, where its drier climate better preserves artifacts, reveals Neolithic communities based in several parts of the region dating from around 5000 B.C. These communities cultivated dogs and pigs and, even at that early date, silk worms.

By the period 1800–1000 B.C., the Chinese had begun to develop into a highly stylized, complex pattern. Advanced and very artistic techniques of casting bronze developed. The system of *ideographic* writing was refined and became the method of communicating and recording of ideas. But it did not and it does not now have an alphabet; it consists of a collection of thousands of symbols, each of which represents a word. Somewhat similar to Egyptian hieroglyphics, these characters have evolved far beyond their original graphic origins. Today, merely looking at a character provides few clues to its meaning. For many hundreds of years this system of writing was known only to scribes and intellectuals and has only recently become more widely known among the general population.

Nevertheless, using this tremendously demanding writing system, the Chinese developed quite early a society more dependant on a wide dispersal of learning than almost any other major civilization. The 20th century saw many modifications to both the format and structure of the characters to make them more accessible to the average person.

The Early Dynasties

From around 1800 B.C. the Chinese were ruled by kings of the Shang, an apparently feudal and aristocratic dynasty. The Shang rulers were replaced by the Zhou (Chou) dynasty, which formally governed from about 1100 to 800 B.C., after which their power rapidly diminished until it was destroyed centuries later. Although the details of the fall of the Shang need hardly concern us here, what is astonishing is that from that collapse emerged one of the most significant Chinese contributions to political philosophy ever devised, The concept of the "Mandate of Heaven."

In originally justifying their conquest of the Shang, the Zhou leaders explained that the Shang, due to their degeneracy, had forfeited the "Mandate." According to their reasoning, which would dominate Chinese political thought down through the ages, "Heaven" was not viewed as a spiritual place of post-life salvation. It was a conscious entity that insisted that governments on earth must rule for the benefit of the masses. And leaders maintained

Shanghai's skyline

. . . to the parched wastes of the Gobi Desert

the right to do so only as long as they continued to behave well toward the people. In a world where too often political power has derived more from the sword or inheritance, this provisional nature of power has been an important idea first developed in ancient China and eventually complementary to many modern democratic theories of government. Some early Chinese thinkers even went so far as to claim that the "Mandate" actually justified the right of the masses to revolt!

The real power of the Zhou dynasty lasted only a few centuries before North China then disintegrated into a number of feudal states led by "princes" who occupied their time and that of their subjects in a variety of wars against each other. The use of iron tools in agriculture during this period produced a high yield from the earth, which, together with irrigation and (after 1,000 A.D.) the widespread cultivation of rice permitted a correspondingly high rate of population growth. As the people pressed outward, they came into greater conflict with non-Chinese people who inhabited central China around the Yangzi River. The stronger rulers subdued the weaker and smaller states, and the number of feudal princedoms became less, gradually falling under the control of two major states: Qin, which ultimately triumphed in the 3rd century B.C., was in the west central and northwestern part of China and Chu in the central Yangzi valley. Graphically, this period is known as the "Warring States Period."

The Hundred Schools

Though China was divided during the later Zhou period, this diversity of political power proved to be a major benefit for its cultural development. In fact, one of the most interesting features of Chinese civilization is that, given its usual tendency toward centralization and successive government enthusiasm for promoting an orthodoxy of thought, it is most often during periods of relative weakness that Chinese intellectual life most dramatically has flourished.

Several points in modern history, the 1920s and most recently in the era before the clashes at Tiananmen Square in 1989, serve as good examples. The later Zhou was just such an era, a time when in the 5th and 4th centuries B.C. China enjoyed an intellectual blossoming comparable to that of Greece during the same period. Literature and the arts flourished, and the desire for knowledge and social order led to the creation and formalization of the two intellectual systems which originated in China: Confucianism and Taoism, the latter a mystical and contemplative system of belief and magical imagery (see Historical Background).

Confucianism, in contrast, is largely a system of social philosophy, and became a very influential source of satisfaction for the learned Chinese as well as providing a sense of imperial legitimacy and the security arising out of its emphasis on hierarchy and deference to authority, a feature many in East Asia today claim still plays an important role in their recent economic successes.

The First Empires

By 221 B.C. the Qin ruler, who led a highly organized and militarily strong state, conquered his rivals and established control over all of north and central China as well as part of the southern region. For China this was one of the darkest periods in its history. The Qin dynasty unified the empire in more ways than military conquest; the Great Wall of China was constructed laboriously over a period of years to ward off the periodic raids by the nomadic central Asians from the North. Roads and other public works were built and the system of writing and weights were standardized. Obsessed with the needs of state power, the Qin leadership ignored the precepts of Confucianism, even killed many of its adherents, rejecting totally the idea that the state existed to serve the masses. Not surprisingly the rule of the Qin was extremely oppressive and produced much discontent among the Chinese people. It was soon overthrown by a new dynasty that took the name Han.

These new rulers, successfully avoiding the arrogance which had brought down the Qin, eventually governed for almost 400 years (2nd century B.C.–2nd century A.D.) before and after the beginning of the Western Christian era. The people of China today are sometimes referred to as Han to differentiate them from the minorities that live in the outer part of what is modern China. In spite of a brief collapse at the halfway point of its reign, the Han Dynasty succeeded in making China into an empire of power, wealth and cultural brilliance comparable to the other great civilization of the same period, the Roman Empire.

Technologically, it was in fact far more advanced than its Roman counterpart on the other side of Eurasia. Its boundaries were pushed well into central Asia, where local leaders were awed by the brilliance of Chinese advances in learning and military prowess. Even if not directly supervised by the Chinese, rulers of the outlying states of Asia were often willing to acknowledge themselves tributary and vassal states of the mighty empire.

When the Han dynasty collapsed, the following four centuries were marked by frequent nomadic invasions from the North which resulted in a series of states in northern China ruled by non-Chinese. A few Chinese, or Han states, did survive in the South, however, under a series of weak dynasties. During this time of uncertainty, Mahayana Buddhism, sometimes referred to as northern Buddhism (see Historical Background), spread quickly following its arrival from northern India by way of Central Asia at the beginning of the Christian era.

China

The Middle Dynasties

China was reunited by the Sui and Tang dynasties after 581 A.D., and under an energetic succession of emperors it once more extended the area of its power far into Central Asia. For the first time in world history, a written examination was developed for civil servants, appointment of whom was based more and more on ability rather than family ties. Ironically, aspects of this movement away from aristocracy and toward a more individually based system of merit had begun earlier under the generally hated Qin dynasty.

Although the officials of the Tang Dynasty were largely Confucian in outlook, it was in this period that Buddhism reached the height of its influence in Chinese civilization. Nevertheless, that influence was not long lasting and the later Tang era saw many cruel persecutions of Buddhists. Though losing its hold on official Chinese thought to Confucian scholars and Daoists (Taoists), this South Asian belief system would nevertheless remain influential on the popular level into the modern period.

There was a short period of disunity following the decline and fall of the Tang dynasty in the 10th century A.D. The brilliant cultural advances of the ensuing three-century period centered chiefly on painting and the discipline of philosophy. Under the influence of Buddhist theology, official Confucianism was modified by about 1200 into Neo-Confucianism which concerned itself more with abstract philosophy than had the original form of this belief.

The country was ruled by emperors of the Song (Sung) dynasty, and was continually threatened by a succession of powerful non-Chinese states that emerged along the northern border. The end of this era came with defeat by the most powerful northern force, the Mongols, who were able to succeed in their conquest only after a long and bitter campaign. The Song had withstood the Mongols longer than any of the other civilizations of the world into which the conquerors intruded, but ultimately became a part of a vast empire stretching from the Pacific to what is now the Middle East.

The Mongols finally unified all China in 1279 and ruled for a century, taking the name Yuan dynasty. Already disliked by the Chinese in a number of ways, the Mongols had but slight respect for Confucianism and the civil service examinations. These factors led to even greater opposition by the Chinese, particularly the upper classes. The rulers were religiously tolerant and permitted small communities of Franciscan missionaries to introduce Christianity into several parts of coastal China.

The Mongols were expelled from China in 1368 in a great upheaval with strong anti-foreign tendencies. This new, ethnically Chinese dynasty that came to power, the Ming (1368–1644), at first ruled firmly and energetically and created a powerful empire.

Following the momentum of the outward-looking Yuan Dynasty, the Ming Emperor even sent out huge overseas flotillas toward the west to explore and demonstrate the might of the Chinese Empire. Starting in 1405 the Ming Emperor Yong Le sent out an extraordinary series of naval expeditions which over the years eventually traveled throughout Southeast Asia and parts of India and ranged as far away as Aden in Arabia and Mogadishu in East Africa. The final expedition in 1431 even sent some ships as far as Jedda on the Red Sea. The efforts, whose motives are not exactly clear, certainly had its impact. The Chinese flotilla intervened in a number of local disputes and worked to further the prestige of the Chinese emperors.

However, they lacked the ongoing significance of the voyages Westerners mounted in the opposite direction several generations later in the 15th century. By the time the Europeans attempted similar voyages, memory of the early Chinese flotillas had been all but forgotten.

Within China, a period of decline began about 1500. Japanese pirates began to increase their activities along the coast. Internal weakness became an increasing problem which was transformed into an even greater liability by the rise in power of the Manchu rulers to the north. In 1644, a combination of domestic rebellion and Manchu might was sufficient to overthrow the Ming dynasty; within a few decades, the Manchus had subdued all of China.

The Manchus

The new rulers took the name Qing (Ch'ing) dynasty, but are more commonly referred to in the West as the Manchus. Although Chinese culture was by this time static to a degree that made basic changes difficult, under them the country was once again united and became rapidly powerful. In an effort to consolidate their positions, they ruled through existing Chinese institutions, including the very formal civil service examination system with its Confucian orientation. For this reason, and others, they were accepted rapidly by their Chinese subjects.

Interestingly, they devised a system whereby major offices and responsibilities were shared by matched sets of Manchu and Chinese officials. After an initial period of wise and successful rule, the Manchus indulged themselves in a period of energetic, but arbitrary and costly, warfare in the late 18th century that undermined the dynasty and coupled with internal

The 1,400 mile long Great Wall of China

Courtesy: Bruce Terry Howe

corruption and a number of internal revolts combined to make China less able to deal with the challenges the nineteenth century would bring.

The Western Arrival

Although Westerners from the Roman era on had periodically visited China, the modern period of Sino-Western relations really begins in the 18th century when Europeans, principally British, started to seek Chinese silk and tea. Unfortunately for these early merchants they had, at first, little to offer, save silver bullion in exchange for the coveted Chinese goods. The Chinese seemed quite disinterested in Western products. In fact, the famous emperor Qian Long even explained to a Western visiting dignitary in 1793 that China had "all things" in abundance and was simply not interested in Western goods. Nevertheless, the trade did develop and at the insistence of the Beijing government it was confined to the southern port of Guangzhou known to foreigners as Canton.

For the English though, this "Canton System" although lucrative enough, did cause problems. They were interested in trading further north in China where there might be a better market for their goods and in having direct contact with Chinese officials when various problems, legal and commercial, arose.

None of these things was possible, given the prevailing Chinese disinterest in any Western style foreign relations or commercial exchanges beyond those considered important to maintaining the dignity and universal legitimacy of Chinese imperial claims. For the Chinese, foreign relations as understood in the West did not exist.

The Chinese emperor was considered the "son of heaven" and people interested in having relations with China were expected to take part in the Chinese "Tributary System," largely a symbolic system whereby other communities recognized the supreme symbolic authority of the Emperor. On a technical level, that required a physical prostration before the emperor known as the kowtow and an exchange of various presents. In fact, the presents the Chinese gave away were not uncommonly more valuable than those they received. For the Chinese emperors, it was the symbolism of the relationship that mattered, not the cash transaction. England, the country that some had disparaged as the nation of shopkeepers, had met an empire completely uninterested in commerce. It was a bad match.

But by the late eighteenth and early nineteenth century two developments occurred which led to dramatic changes in China's relations with the Western powers. The British discovered that opium, grown in their possessions in India, could be sold at a handsome profit in China. Over the next decades the amount of opium imported into China by the British grew enormously until by the first quarter of the 19th century the drug was devastating Chinese society, especially in the south.

After first undergoing an internal debate in the late 1830s about how best to deal with the crises, the imperial government decided to force the foreign traders to give up their trade. To that end, an imperial commissioner, Lin Zexu, was sent to Guangzhou in 1839 to attempt to suppress the trade. Although the imperial commissioner managed to confiscate the traders' opium stocks and destroy them, the British government, by then especially committed to the drug trade, declared war. Over the next generation and during two successive "Opium Wars" one of which culminated in the capture of Beijing itself in 1860, the British, and eventually their French allies, managed to impose a series of "unequal treaties" on the Chinese. Those treaties would dominate Sino-Western relations until the middle of the 20th century.

What had gone wrong for China? For most of world history Chinese technology had far outshone the skills of the Westerners, but by the 18th century, the industrial revolution, especially centered in England, gave the British enormous advantages over the once self-sufficient Chinese empire. That advantage would last for more than the next hundred years with profound implications for our own century.

The Diplomacy of Imperialism

Under the series of "unequal treaties" signed under pressure in the first half of the 19th century, China lost a large part of its sovereignty. The Westerners gained the right to dominate a series of ports, soon known as Treaty Ports along the coast. Hong Kong and Shanghai are the best known of them. The treaties also gave the foreigners immunity to Chinese law and control over China's tariffs. Additionally foreigners gained the legal right to preach Christianity in the interior of the country. Moreover, due to the concept of "most favored nation," the rights won by the English and French guns applied to all other foreigners in China including the Americans who had hardly taken part.

Cutting the Melon

The culmination of this era of imperialist greed occurred just as the 19th century was coming to a close. Known as the "Cutting of the Melon," one European power after another began demanding further spheres of influence in China. The British demanded an expansion of their influence in the region west of Shanghai and north of Hong Kong while the French pushed into southern China from their base in Vietnam. To the north the Russians and Germans made their demands while the Japanese insisted on gaining further rights in the Chinese coastal areas opposite Taiwan. In each of these, a particular Western power (with the exception of the United States) was granted sweeping and exclusive economic rights in its area, coupled with a great degree of political influence.

Russian domination was established in Manchuria, but the fertile southern portion of that region went to the Japanese in 1905 after their victory in the Russo-Japanese War. The Germans established themselves in the province of Shandong (Shantung); the British became the major power in the Yangzi valley region; the Japanese controlled Fujian (Fukien) Province and the French asserted their dominance over Southwest China.

The Chinese Exam System

The Chinese examination system, which existed in various forms until the early 20th century, was truly remarkable for a traditional society. Rather than relying on birthright to choose the bulk of their elites, as was so common among the Europeans and even their East Asian neighbors, the Japanese, the Chinese eventually developed a massive system of offering Confucian-based exams to thousands upon thousands of males annually. Those who advanced beyond the first demanding tests went on to even more rigorous exams at the provincial and eventually imperial level. Although few became great government officials, the system created an enormous pool of educated people who served the needs of society as local leaders and, for the lucky few, officially within the imperial bureaucracy.

Not surprisingly those who came from educated and reasonably well-off households had a major advantage in the competition. Nevertheless, the record of graduates shows that it was a true system of social mobility that allowed many people year after year to rise beyond their families' earlier accomplishments.

China

Marble sculpture of a Ming soldier at the Imperial Tombs

Interestingly for students of modern Chinese history, the new demands were often made in the form of forced 99-year leases. Although most of these arrangements were long ago terminated, the lease on the New Territories of Hong Kong ran its full course.

That imperialistic high point known as the "Melon Cutting" did not stop at the century's end. Outside what had been China, places like Korea and Okinawa, which had paid tribute to the Manchu emperors, also became colonies or spheres of influence of Britain, France, Russia and Japan. Russian influence became paramount in Outer Mongolia, and penetrated into Xinjiang (Sinkiang) in the 1930s. The British became a powerful influence in Tibet.

These losses of territory and authority were dramatic demonstrations of China's basic weakness by the standards of the 20th century Western powers and were an insult to the sense of national pride of the Chinese. The economy of the coastal regions, traditionally more wealthy than the interior areas, was almost totally dominated by foreign trade and investment.

Although many among the Chinese tended toward an inwardness that made

effective response to these pressures difficult, there were other more far sighted individuals within the Chinese leadership. They foresaw crises developing and began as early as the 1860s to adapt to the various Western military techniques needed to maintain the country's sovereignty in that imperialistic age. Led by perceptive individuals at both the imperial and military level, most notably the Manchu Prince Gong, a period known as "Self Strengthening" was begun. He was aided at the provincial level by leaders like Li Hongzhang and Zuo Zongtang. Under this program, during an energetic era dating from the late 1860s through the 1890s, several military arsenals and dockyards were founded and scores of students sent abroad—to America and Europe—to learn Western military and engineering techniques. Sadly, though considerable effort was put out and significant gains made, they were overall too little to stem the flow of China's diminishing strength nor to equal similar but more energetic efforts like those of their neighbors, the Japanese, which were simply far more successful.

As seen below, in the first test of their respective efforts at mastering Western military techniques during the Sino-Japanese war of 1894, the Chinese accomplishments proved sorely lacking and the country experienced yet another massive humiliation. The significance of these humiliations and the various unequal treaties cannot be underestimated. It is important to understand that even today many of China's oldest citizens grew up when these special Western and Japanese privileges were still in effect.

The Heavenly Kingdom of Great Peace

Although the long term implications of the Western pressures on China were enormous, the larger issue at the time for the Chinese themselves was the outbreak in 1851 of an enormous rebellion which eventually devastated much of the country over the next fifteen years. The origins of the Taiping Heavenly Kingdom, as the rebels called themselves, lay in the startling increases in population which had added enormous pressures on the land. Moreover, the Opium Wars themselves had disrupted economic life in southern China. It was in that disrupted environment that one of the more curious dramas of world history arose.

The story began in the early nineteenth century when a frustrated Confucian scholar, who had for years been unable to pass the demanding Confucian civil service exams, decided that he was the younger brother of Jesus Christ. He developed a new "trinity" that included

"God, the Father", "God, the Son" and in this new theology, himself, the "little brother."

For fifteen years, dating from the original revolt in 1851, China was divided between two governments, the ethnically Manchu, but Confucian-oriented Qing Dynasty, and the unique Chinese Taiping Rebels with their semi-Chinese semi-Christian orientation. Following ideas found both in the Old Testament and drawn from mythic memories of early China, the Taipings established a theocracy with a communal economic structure. Life was organized, especially at their capital at Nanjing, around a religious military structure which at least on the surface seemed quite puritanical. Women, in sharp contrast to traditional Confucian practice, were far freer. Foot binding was not practiced and the women also took part in battle. But the assault on traditional practice had been too great and by 1864 the Heavenly Kingdom of Great Peace collapsed under pressures from Qing Militia leaders aroused by the struggle to preserve Confucianism (and assisted by Western military soldiers and advisors).

Following the death of the Emperor in 1861, his widow, referred to as the Empress Dowager Cixi, became co-regent during the reign of her son and wielded considerable influence. When he died in 1874 the throne then passed to Cixi's own young nephew and her power continued as before. Probably the most powerful woman in world history, Cixi dominated China, the largest population under a single government in the world, from the early 1860s through 1908. Her influence cannot be underestimated. Ruthless, able and extremely conservative, she embodied the traditions cherished by the Manchu court officials who clung to the security of the past. Nevertheless, under her reign, the first efforts to deal with the Western challenge in the form of the various industrial efforts known as "self-strengthening projects," were begun.

Cixi's power was so great that when she felt threatened by the Emperor Guang Xu's dramatic effort during the summer of 1898 to drastically reorganize the Chinese government and educational system, the better to make it able to withstand imperialistic pressures, she had him arrested. But if the Empress Dowager Cixi had intensely disliked the Emperor's response to the weakening of China, that did not mean that she failed to recognize the peril the dynasty faced. It is probably with that reason in mind that she soon pinned her hopes on yet another approach to the question of saving China. And in that case, one that arose from the popular masses' anger with the disruptions in

Traditional *Junk* on the China Sea

the overthrow of the Manchus and to the modernization of China along semi-Western lines. Although he was eventually able to attract a relatively large following, Sun was not very effective in organizing his followers. Nevertheless due to the drama of Sun having been unsuccessfully kidnapped by Chinese agents in London in 1896, he became very well known in the West and eventually personified, in the minds of many Westerners, the goal of a Chinese republican revolution.

When the Empress Dowager died in 1908, the Manchu court installed the two-year-old Pu-Yi as child emperor. He reigned through regents appointed by the court until 1912. Later he was to serve as the "Emperor" of Manchukuo (Manchuria) when the Japanese attempted in the 1930s to colonize northern China.

The Revolution of 1911

In the fall of 1911, the ability of the Court to maintain the two-hundred and fifty year old Qing dynasty finally failed. A rebellion broke out in the city of Wuhan which, given prevailing frustrations with the Manchu leadership, spread rapidly across the country. One after another, various provinces declared themselves for the revolution. Sun Yat-sen, although at the time visiting the United States, emerged by December as the provisional president of a new Chinese republic. It appeared at first that China was about to take its place among the democracies of the modern world. But that was not to be. If the forces of the old regime had been unable to maintain themselves, portions of their strength remained potent enough to direct the course of events over the next several years.

To avoid a civil war, Sun turned over power to Yuan Shikai, a former Qing general who still held considerable loyalty among many government soldiers. There was actually little choice. A civil war between the new revolutionary forces and those of Yuan Shikai would have only weakened China further. The compromise seemed necessary to save what had been already won. But sadly, Yuan was more interested in establishing a new dynasty than serving as a true democratic president, and within a few years China literally collapsed from the stress.

By 1916 China had disintegrated into a score of petty states run by individual military governors, usually referred to as "warlords." They had little governing ability and their rule was almost uniformly oppressive. The legal government of China in Beijing continued to be recognized diplomatically by the foreign powers. In reality, this "government" was an ever-shifting combination of one or more

their lives said to be caused by the foreigners. The results came to be known as the Boxer Rebellion.

At the popular level, there were many anti-foreign and anti-Christian outbreaks of violence in the years following 1870. Both sentiments joined to provide discontent resulting in the famous 1900 Boxer Rebellion a dramatic effort by thousands of Chinese to literally drive the Westerners out of China. In fact, the "Boxers" as the foreigners called them because of their ritualized style of physical and mental exercise, were encouraged by influential members of the Manchu court. For months, especially in north China, the Boxers terrorized Westerners and their Chinese converts.

Eventually, a joint military expedition sent by the Western powers crushed the Boxers. American and other foreign troops stormed Beijing in August 1900. Less than fifty years after the 1860 capture of Beijing by the Westerners, it was again under their control.

The Empress Dowager, who had fled the city as a young woman in 1860 was understandably shaken by the defeat and granted her reluctant assent to certain innovations in the imperial government. But it was too late. She died in 1908. The Manchu Qing dynasty had only a few more years to survive.

Trying to Save China

In the years after the 1839–42 Opium War several important officials and thinkers had come forward with theories and projects for reforming the Chinese empire. Some among them, as influential provincial leaders, put into place the various projects of the "Self-Strengthening Movement." More radical reformers later in the century played an important role in the Emperor's dramatic and failed reform effort of 1898, the so called "100 Day Reform." Nevertheless, as China moved into the 20th century its problems worsened and the ability of the imperial Manchu government to respond to the crises became less and less significant. These early reformers were not unified and their disunity prevented them from achieving any real influence on the Manchu court until it was too late.

As the situation deteriorated, the influences of these reformers became increasingly irrelevant, and leadership passed to those calling for more radical actions. It was in that context that a new generation of leaders arose, men not interested in reforming the Manchu Qing Empire but in replacing it with a republic more along the lines of Western models.

The most important of these radicals was Sun Yat-sen, who dedicated himself to

China

warlords, sometimes under the influence of foreign nations. Communications were extremely poor and there was a thin scattering of modern arms in the outlying regions, making it almost impossible to achieve any genuine national unity.

Sun Yat-sen, the "Father of the Revolution," embittered by his experiences in these developments, established himself in the south and tried in various ways, without success, to overthrow the shadow government at Beijing and to reunite the country. During those years he devoted himself to the building up of the Guomindang (Kuomintang)—"National People's Party," or "GMD." But far to the north, an intellectual energy and nationalist momentum was growing that would go far beyond even Dr. Sun's revolutionary plans.

The May Fourth Movement

The May Fourth Movement of the years 1915 to 1921 was a multi-dimensional era which embraced few central themes save a general disregard for China's traditional Confucian culture. On an individual level many of those involved loudly advocated a reorientation of cultural values. The young were told to become more independent, less tied to the more tradition-bound older generation. Confucianism, it was said, simply did not allow China the vitality necessary to withstand the aggressive modern world.

In addition to the trend toward economic modernization in the cities and coastal regions and cultural speculation during the 1920s, there was a marked growth of nationalism among the Chinese, who sought an end to foreign influence in their country. The "central" government was in the hands of a group under Japanese influence who cooperated with the latter's efforts to have their control over the Chinese province of Shantung formalized by the treaties that ended World War One. An outburst of patriotism, led by students, which became known as the May Fourth Movement, prevented the actual signing of the treaty and sparked an era of intense popular political activity.

On the national level the people of China, particularly the youth, desired the end of imperialism and internal disunity and came to believe that these goals could only be achieved through a major political and social revolution. Some chose the Guomindang, while a smaller number joined the infant communist movement.

Communism

The Chinese Communist Party (CCP) was founded in 1921 mostly by young Chinese intellectuals. The movement quickly came under the control of the Third International, more familiarly known as the Comintern of Russia under its energetic revolutionary leader, Lenin. The picture became even more complicated when the Comintern decided to enter into an alliance with Sun Yat-sen's Guomindang and ordered the local Chinese communists to do the same. This unstable union was produced by a common, overwhelming desire to expel Western and Japanese influence from China and to eliminate the power of the warlords.

To accomplish these aims, the Comintern reorganized and greatly strengthened the Guomindang through money and military aid, but it also hoped that communists could gradually acquire control over it by infiltrating top positions, and by putting pressure on the party through communist-dominated labor and peasant unions. Although there was considerable uncertainty about the collaboration of the Guomindang's nationalists and the communists, what mattered above all was that their cooperation help unify the country once more. In 1926 that great effort, known as the "Northern Expedition," began. For the next several years, sometimes by fighting, sometimes by negotiation, the nationalists marched north enthusiastically attempting to build a new, stronger and now unified China. The march was to prove ultimately successful, although tensions inherent in the nationalist/communist alliance eventually broke out.

While Sun Yat-sen had been alive, the effort to both unify China and to maintain the coalition of nationalists and communists continued fairly well. But after his death in 1925 he was eventually succeeded by General Chiang Kai-shek, who had become increasingly alarmed at the threat of Soviet domination of China and the more immediate threat of potential communist revolution.

Chiang determined to head off these threats by military force and in 1927 sent his forces into the newly liberated Shang-

Kunming Shopkeeper 1945

Courtesy of Gregg Millett

hai to slaughter his communist allies. The alliance between the Chinese nationalists and the communists was thus broken. For the moment the nationalists—the Guomindang forces, under Chiang—seemed triumphant.

Chiang captured Beijing in 1928, and proclaimed the renewed Republic of China with its new capital at Nanjing, a city which has often served as an alternative capital in Chinese history. Actually the GMD controlled only the eastern provinces of China and was faced with tremendous problems: a large army that had to be fed and clothed, floods, famine, and political apathy. After a generation of struggle the Guomindang had finally come fully to power. But its ability to attempt a rebirth of China was soon to be severely curtailed when, in 1931, the Japanese began their effort to dominate the country.

The Japanese Invasion

Japanese efforts to establish an East Asian empire began in the late nineteenth century. By the early 1920s, their influence had grown considerably. Korea and Taiwan were already colonies and Japanese influence in Manchuria was considerable. China's weakness during the era of the "Warlords," 1916–1928, had given them even greater leeway to assert themselves. Moreover, the worldwide depression, which struck at the end of the 1920s, convinced many Japanese nationalists that Japan's future lay in furthering their hold on northern China. That commitment led to the Japanese Manchurian army's (see Japan) decision to provoke an incident which would allow them to take over Manchuria.

The Japanese seized it in 1931–32; the territory was renamed Manchukuo and the former Manchu emperor of the Chinese Empire, the youthful Henry Pu-Yi, took the throne as "Emperor of Manchukuo." This interesting character had been tutored in the Western classics by an Englishman after the ouster of the Manchus, who suggested that he take an Anglo name. Having been enthroned as emperor and deposed while still a child, the possibility of once again becoming an emperor must have been exhilarating for the young man. Nevertheless, during his years as emperor over Manchuria, he would prove as powerless under the Japanese control as he had been as a child under the direction of the adults around him in the Chinese imperial court. His story is a fascinating one, and it eventually became well known to millions of filmgoers through the movie "The Last Emperor."

To Chiang Kai-shek, the Japanese assault, while dangerous, was still not his most immediate concern. The Generalissimo was

大清國當今慈禧端佑康頤昭豫莊誠壽恭欽獻崇熙聖母皇太后

The Empress Dowager Cixi

China

more concerned about what he saw as a disease of the "heart," the Chinese communists, who, while weakened by his assault in 1927, had remained a potent force. While Chiang had managed to weaken the city-based Shanghai communists, many others, most notably Mao Zedong in southeastern China, had managed to establish communist strongholds far beyond GMD control.

Chiang Kai-shek then made the poorest of choices. He decided to concentrate his energies on dealing with the Chinese communists rather than the Japanese invaders. That decision would eventually put into question whether the GMD really had any right to call itself the "Nationalists." His primary opponent, Mao Zedong, himself both a nationalist and committed communist, was often alienated from the leadership of the Chinese communist party; it often saw him as less orthodox in his ideological outlook. But these differences were hardly significant to the Guomindang which set out in the early 1930s to destroy the Chinese communist base known as the Jiangxi Soviet.

After long and difficult campaigns—the communist resistance was initially very effective—the communists were forced by overwhelming Guomindang military pressures to evacuate their base areas in Central and South China. Eventually, after a long dramatic trek of thousands of miles and extraordinary hardships later known as the "Long March," the temporarily defeated Chinese communists took refuge in the remote and desolate regions of Northwest China. During the march, after a crucial meeting at Zhunyi, Mao Zedong at last emerged as the leader of the Chinese communists, a position he would not relinquish until his death in 1976. While Chiang Kai-shek may have felt some satisfaction with the weakening of the communists, he had more pressing pressures to the north.

World War II

By late 1936 in the midst of yet another effort to completely destroy the Chinese communists, Chiang was kidnapped by his own troops who were angry about his preoccupation with the communists in the midst of the imminent Japanese threat. After a dramatic episode that came close to bringing China to civil war, the Guomindang and Chinese communists made yet another alliance. From Mao's perspective and that of many patriotic Chinese, it was absurd for Chinese to fight in the interior while Japan pressed forward in the northeastern part of the country. Moreover, Russia's Stalin had been urging the communists to enter into another alliance with the Guomindang in order to resist the invaders. Mao probably saw an opportunity

General Chiang Kai-shek

not only to resist the Japanese, but to ultimately overthrow the Nationalists after they had been weakened by the enemy.

The new alliance came none too soon, for Japanese forces invaded eastern China in 1937 and started an assault of extraordinary brutality that at times foreshadowed later Nazi acts in Eastern Europe. The Japanese conquered the prosperous coastal regions of China, depriving the Guomindang of its major economic and political bases. Driven into the hills and mountains of southwest China, it became even more conservative and subject to corruption than before. Under Japanese control, cities like Nanjing, the Nationalist's capital, experienced a horror of mass murder and rape that went on for weeks. To the north, Japanese doctors would

eventually establish a medical experimentation center that carried out live vivisections on hapless Chinese captives. Though less well known than the Nazi brutalities, they left a legacy of bitterness between China and Japan that still exists.

The expansion of the communists from that time forth was actually at the expense not only of the Japanese but also of the Guomindang. Inflation and weakness also sapped the strength of the Nationalists, enabling the Japanese to inflict further heavy defeats on it as late as 1944. Nevertheless, the Japanese were unable to prevent the communists, more skilled in the art of guerrilla warfare than the Nationalists, from infiltrating and setting up base areas within territory that was supposed to be Japanese. Partly in retaliation for this resistance, the Japanese committed more atrocities against the Chinese people in the occupied areas, driving many into sympathy with the communists and thus assisting them to seize political control on an anti-Japanese, more than an anti-Guomindang, platform.

The Struggle for Power: Nationalists and Communists

Increasing numbers of Japanese soldiers were withdrawn from China starting in 1943 because of the defeats that were being suffered in the Pacific war. This permitted the communists to expand rapidly, so that by the end of the war they controlled nineteen base areas, in various parts of China, principally in the North and Northwest.

The elimination of Japanese troops from China at the end of the war brought a frantic flurry of political and military ac-

Dr. Sun Yat-sen addresses a crowd before departing with his troops on the campaign against Beijing

24

Japanese troops in China, 1937

and equipment. After igniting a frequently violent purge against the rural landowning classes, small plots of farmland were distributed to the peasants and then as the years went on collectivized. The lives of women were improved with the passage in 1950 of a new marriage and divorce law that gave women more marital and property rights.

In short, China progressed from war-inflicted chaos toward a centralized, autocratic and rationally administered state. Traditional Chinese culture and society were forcibly changed in directions desired by the communists with widespread, fundamental and seemingly impossible effects. By 1956 the regime apparently felt confident enough to encourage the masses to voice their opinions on the many changes the CCP had brought about. "Let a hundred Flowers Bloom," Mao, the supreme leader, proclaimed although apparently what the CCP's leadership heard was not to their liking. By 1957 a cruel repression known as the "Anti-rightist Campaign" had commenced which was to destroy the careers of millions of Chinese intellectuals and others who had been naive enough actually to speak out.

In foreign relations, the Chinese regime initially established a close alliance with the Soviet Union, still led by the aging Stalin. Doing so was not without its difficulties. The Soviet dictator would clearly have preferred a Chinese leadership more servile to Moscow and had even made Mao wait three days in Moscow before receiving him in November of 1949. Nevertheless the tie was formalized into a thirty year treaty of friendship. China also entered into diplomatic relations with all communist countries and with a number of neutral and Western nations. The

tivity by both the Guomindang and the communists. In the immediate period after the war the U.S. was the major political power in the Pacific area and it attempted to bring about some sort of settlement between these two competing Chinese parties. The talks conducted under the encouragement of U.S. General George C. Marshall, special envoy of President Truman, completely broke down in 1946 because neither side had any real desire for an agreement. Each preferred a trial of armed strength. Neither political party had any interest in sharing China's future with the other.

Unfortunately for the Guomindang, the Nationalists, nominally more powerful, were plagued by their inability to deal with China's most serious problems: inflation, corruption and loss of political unity. The military leadership also employed very poor tactics against the communists, especially in the battle over Manchuria, and soon found itself losing control over the mainland.

By the end of 1949 the Guomindang was driven to the island of Taiwan. The Chinese communists under Mao then controlled all of mainland China except for Tibet, which had been outside Beijing's control since the collapse of the Qing. They proclaimed the People's Republic of China and reestablished the Chinese capital at Beijing.

The next year the soldiers of the People's Liberation Army invaded Tibet. Although there was some initial resistance, the "roof of the world" was brought under Chinese control again; the Dalai Lama, spiritual leader of the Tibetans who also was vested with rather wide governing

powers, was soon made a figurehead. He eventually fled Tibet in 1959 after an unsuccessful uprising against the Chinese in the eastern part of the region.

The "People's Liberation Army" brought the new regime to power, and it remained important as a defense against possible enemies, both internal and external. The Chinese Communist Party, however, was the real instrument behind Mao and his regime; its members held and now hold all important public offices. It has proven to be the only political force since the Manchus that has demonstrated itself able to hold China together. For the first quarter century of the People's Republic's existence, Mao Zedong played an overpowering role. He made himself into a cult-like father figure whom all Chinese, especially the youth, were taught to worship to a degree that would have created envy in the hearts of previous emperors.

Building a New China

The team of Mao, the Chinese Communist Party (CCP) and the army, held together quite successfully through the late 1950s and achieved results which were quite impressive considering how devastated the country was after generations of invasion and civil war. The majority of the people regarded the regime as the only hope of escape from the long nightmare of civil and foreign war, chaos and abject poverty, and gave it overwhelming support. Initially following the Soviet model of development, China's new leaders restored the defunct economy and launched an impressive program of heavy industrialization with Russian technical assistance

Mao Zedong (Mao Tse-tung) in 1945

China

United States, which had become protector of the Nationalists on Taiwan, refused to recognize Mao's government. With only slight success, the Chinese communists initially tried to promote revolutions elsewhere in Asia. Eventually they retreated from this policy somewhat in order to be in a better position to cultivate the friendship of the neutral Asian nations.

The Korean War

Although the Chinese leadership may have wished to concentrate on solidifying their control over China in their first years of power, international developments became impossible to ignore. In June of 1950, the North Koreans, apparently with Soviet support, invaded South Korea with the goal of unifying the entire peninsula under their leadership.

Although the immediate Chinese reaction was somewhat restrained, the American decision to intervene through the United Nations aroused their ire. More to the point, after the American troops successfully drove the North Koreans back across the 38th Parallel demarcation line, they decided to invade North Korea with little thought to the consequences of moving toward the Chinese border. (See the Korea section.)

From the Chinese perspective, the American troops (the apparent allies of their enemies the Chinese Nationalists) were pushing toward their borders and ignoring Beijing's warning that they would intervene if the Americans continued north. Unfortunately, the American forces did continue north and the Chinese, urged on and with the support of the Soviets, committed massive numbers of "volunteers" to stop the Americans and to the aid the besieged North Korean communist government. Whatever possibilities might have existed for a successful relationship between Washington and Beijing was destroyed in the explosion that followed and killed so many Americans, Chinese, and Koreans over the next few years. By July of 1953 an armistice was signed dividing the peninsula between the North Koreans and their communist allies in the north and the South Koreans and their American allies to the south. U.S. forces have remained in South Korea ever since.

The "Great Leap Forward"

By the mid-1950s, the Chinese leadership had at last successfully stabilized the economy and begun the long effort to recover from so many decades of war and civil war. The Soviet model of a command economy with its five year planning models was being used and significant progress was made.

Silk tapestry B. R. Graham

But Mao wanted more; he wanted China to literally leap forward toward a more industrialized and socialized future, not at some distant point in the future but immediately with one giant effort of the Chinese people united in the endeavor. By 1958, new and far more ambitious plans were announced for the country. Mao declared that China should catch up with industrialized England within fifteen years.

The "Great Leap Forward" as it was known was to have two fundamental aspects; one industrial, one social. Toward the first, enormous industrial goals were announced. Each work unit was, among other things, expected to create "backyard furnaces" to boost iron production. Every industry was expected to dramatically increase its output of goods using an emphasis less on industrial know-how than the cumulative willpower of the energized population.

Taking a Break Photo by Steven Leibo

On the "communitarian/socialist" side Mao's planners herded people into what would become known as "People's Communes," which would dominate almost every aspect of their lives from child care to the use of their labor. Moving far past the Soviet model of state farms and limited private plots, the peasants were now told to live in completely egalitarian communities where there was literally no room for individual family initiative (or privacy). Even such mundane activities as growing a pig and raising it for market were branded "capitalist" and made impossible to carry out.

Most of these programs were terrible failures. Industrial production collapsed. The famous "backyard furnaces" often produced completely useless materials. The harvest revenues plummeted horrendously. Amidst the propagandistic circus of claims and boasts, a very real food disaster developed which turned into an enormous famine. Millions of people died in the following years due to this manmade disaster.

Late in the decade, policy differences and political tensions began to appear between the aging Mao and some of his colleagues who were more pragmatic than he and obviously worried about the suffering brought on by the failures of the Great Leap Forward. Few though were willing to challenge the Great Leader openly. Moreover, problems with their enormous socialist neighbor were as well beginning to develop.

Relations with the Soviets

By the late 1950s, relations with the Soviet Union, the principal source of economic and military aid, were becoming severely strained. The Soviet leader Khrushchev cut off all aid in 1960. Actually a clash between Mao and Nikita Khrushchev was probably inevitable—the former regarded the younger Khrushchev as an upstart and at the same time Khrushchev, blessed with an over abundance of ego, considered Mao a fanatic and an adventurer. China's enthusiasm for considering itself, rather than Moscow, the leader of their world revolutionary movements hardly endeared it to the Soviet Union either.

Soon growing Chinese political pressures on the Soviet Union, calculated to prove the correctness of Mao's brand of communism and the error of the Soviet "deviation," produced serious and fundamental tensions not only between the Soviets and the Chinese, but within the entire communist world. Over these years relations with the Soviets, never close, would continue to deteriorate until by 1956 they seemed in competition for leadership of the communist world.

In the summer of 1958, Mao engaged in another unsuccessful gesture—the shelling of the islands of Quemoy and Matsu, controlled by the Nationalists, close to mainland China in the Taiwan straits. Whatever his original intentions had been, nothing more than an artillery and air-power duel occurred, notwithstanding the alarm of other nations because of the possibility of a Chinese-U.S. confrontation. The Soviet Union's unwillingness to be supportive during the crises and later when tensions developed with India further alienated Beijing's leadership from Moscow.

The Soviet Union was accused of being as great if not greater political enemy than the United States. The task of struggling against the supposed imperialistic designs of the U.S. was in effect assigned to other revolutionary movements in Asia, Africa and Latin America.

The revolutionary zeal of the Chinese, and their tendency to urge radical and nationalistic movements to greater tasks than were possible, with endless quantities of advice and of Mao's "thoughts," coupled with quantities of arms, did not produce the desired results. A number of moderate nationalist and socialist leaders of Asia and Africa became rapidly aware of the not yet serious threat, and took steps to expel Chinese agents. There were especially serious setbacks in Indonesia and in sub-Sahara Africa, which had seemed promising to the Chinese in the years 1963–1965. After the fall in 1964 of Khrushchev, who had handled the revolutionary impatience of the Chinese rather clumsily, his more practical successors offered China a limited agreement, which was spurned by Mao. With this refusal, Mao worsened his relations with some of his critics at home and abroad who wanted a less antagonistic attitude toward Russia.

By the early 1960s, tensions within China's leadership had become more obvious. Mao had withstood the direct criticism of former allies like Peng Dehuai regarding the disasters caused by the Great Leap Forward. But by the early 1960s his influence over events within China was being lost to the more pragmatic bureaucratic leadership of the Chinese Communist Party, most notably individuals like Liu Shaoqi and Deng Xiaoping. For the aging leader Mao Zedong, this development was completely unacceptable.

The Great Proletarian Cultural Revolution

By the last half of 1965, Mao became convinced that the time had come to silence his critics within the party. Thus began another mass campaign: the "Great Proletarian Cultural Revolution." His first obstacle, the reluctant municipal boss of Beijing, Peng Zhen, was soon overthrown by a combination of political pressures and military threats. Mao then proceeded to call on the revolutionary young people, organized into "Red Guards" to root out his enemies. Moreover, in his struggle with the leadership of the Chinese Communist Party, Mao also had the support of Lin Biao, the commander of the People's Liberation Army. The youthful Red Guards attacked and terrorized Mao's real and imagined opponents in the universities, in the party structure and anywhere else they were thought to be found.

The victims ranged from party officials to teachers and other professionals in almost all fields from medicine to religion. Almost anyone the young enthusiasts could accuse of being insufficiently Maoist was in danger. The students created their own kangaroo courts to punish their victims and broke into homes looking for anything considered counter-revolutionary. Those found with materials ranging from books by Confucius to Western writings, even possession of materials written by the now purged former leadership of the Communist Party, could cause an individual serious problems.

Throughout the country, former officials and others who had held authority previously were beaten and humiliated as they were marched through the streets wearing banners proclaiming their supposed guilt. The lives of countless millions were affected by the malicious chaos of the era.

The struggle was as much an assault on the full heritage of Chinese tradition as it was against Mao's enemies. Throughout the country the "Red Guards," aroused as they were against almost any object connected to China's imperial past, destroyed or defaced materials of enormous beauty. Practitioners of traditional arts,

from Buddhist monks to magicians and fortune tellers, were hounded from their professions.

Eventually even central power began to break down in many parts of the country as Mao's "Cultural Revolution" went far beyond what even he had envisioned. By early 1967, it was necessary for Mao to urge the army to intervene in order to prevent chaos and yet to keep the Cultural Revolution moving. The army quickly discovered that these two tasks were inconsistent and increasingly began to emphasize the restoration of order in place of the disorder created by the unruly Red Guards. In 1967, Mao was brought, willingly or unwillingly, to endorse a turn towards a more conservative line. After that time, the impact of the Cultural Revolution on everyday life lessened. During 1968 the army acquired more and more local power, and with Beijing's consent, it forcibly suppressed the Red Guard movement. The young Red Guards were banished to the countryside to "educate" themselves among the peasants.

How much they actually "learned" is less certain. What is clear is that a huge percentage of the young people of that era lost their opportunity for higher education and a better life. Many of their older contemporaries whom they had been persecuting were able to resume their former lives once calm was restored. That was less true for many of these youth, who were in many ways the real victims of the Cultural Revolution. Not only were they as individuals to lose, but China itself ultimately lost out on the professional skills they would have potentially made available to build a new, more modern China.

Kaifeng Shoe Repair
Photo by Steven Leibo

China

The Vietnam Wars

While China itself was going through the chaos of the Cultural Revolution, just to the south one of the longest struggles of the twentieth century, the Vietnam War, was entering an especially critical stage (see the Vietnam section). For China, despite the eons of tension and ambivalence that separated the Chinese and Vietnamese, there was no question but that Beijing would support North Vietnam in its struggles against the Americans during the Vietnam War (approximately 1965–1975 for the American stage). But here, unlike in Korea, China did not play a major role.

China did though send some arms and personnel to North Vietnam cooperated for a time in transshipping Soviet weapons by rail. Additionally, Beijing sent railway engineering units to help keep the main Vietnamese railway lines open in spite of American bombardment. After the American withdrawal in 1973, China stepped up its flow of arms to Hanoi and in this way contributed significantly to the rapid fall of South Vietnam in the spring of 1975.

By that time, however, Hanoi had already begun to show signs of abandoning its neutrality in the Sino-Soviet disputes. It was "tilting" toward Moscow. By 1977 Vietnam was involved in a border war with Cambodia, where the pro-Chinese rather than the pro-Vietnamese wing of the Khmer Rouge (the Cambodian communist movement) had come to power in 1975. When China began in 1978 to put pressure on Vietnam in support of Cambodia, Hanoi expelled several hundred thousand "boat people," many of them of Chinese ancestry, and moved still closer to Moscow. At the end of 1978, Vietnam invaded Cambodia and installed a puppet government in Phnom Penh. Accordingly, China then experienced its own Vietnam War for a time by invading Vietnam briefly in February–March 1979 with the announced purpose of teaching Hanoi a lesson.

The lesson did not take. Vietnamese forces did far better than expected against those of their giant neighbor, and relations were tense for decades. Not surprisingly, despite the alliances of the war, the animosity that had existed between China and Vietnam for centuries was revived.

Tensions have continued for years in the vicinity of their common border, as well as in the South China Sea, where a naval rivalry took place. Nevertheless, the collapse of the Soviet Union eventually led to a slight warming of relations between China and Vietnam.

A Fundamental Shift

The military clash along the Sino-Soviet border in early 1969, which turned out

Mao Zedong in 1966 AP/World Wide Photos

badly for the Chinese, eventually led to some astonishing shifts in East Asian politics. Given the reality that China was finding itself "squeezed" between two different antagonists, the jealous Soviets to the north, and the Americans struggling against communism in Vietnam, many in China felt it was time to rethink China's international position. A moderate coalition, led by Premier Zhou Enlai and some of the military, tried to restore a greater degree of domestic stability and more workable foreign relations.

Zhou felt it advisable, after several months of Soviet threats, to enter into negotiations on border problems and related matters, and to downgrade disputes concerning communist theory. Nevertheless, by the end of 1970, it appeared that the negotiations had resulted in a deadlock.

Internal politics also played a role in bringing about the new international alignment when Lin Biao, the long-time leader of the contentious PLA, who had supported improved Sino-Soviet relations, conspired against Mao. He was eventually killed in a 1971 abortive plan to flee the country. The way was clear to open relations with the United States, a relationship many in the Chinese leadership hoped would serve as a balance to the potential threats posed by the Soviet Union.

To the surprise of the Americans, China extended in 1971 an invitation to an American ping pong team to visit. This was quickly followed by a visit by Dr. Henry Kissinger in July 1971 and later by President Nixon in 1972. For the Americans, of course, better relations with Beijing offered the possibility of finding a new tool to end their frustrating involvement in Vietnam. Beijing's help did eventually prove significant in developing the treaties that allowed for the United States to withdraw, even though that aid hardly

affected the ultimate outcome of the Vietnam War itself.

Nevertheless, American ties to China continued to improve, and by 1978 President Carter of the United States formalized diplomatic relations with Beijing. At the same time, the United States terminated its formal diplomatic relations and defense treaty with the Republic of China on Taiwan. Other important ties, however, remained intact and the U.S. continued to sell arms to Taiwan and to offer considerable "moral support." Once Beijing and Washington began to improve their relations Taiwan's international position began to deteriorate. In a humiliating move, Nationalist China was expelled from the United Nations and the People's Republic of China became the official representative of China at that organization.

The Emergence of Deng Xiaoping

In the mid-1970s an upsurge of political ferment reflected radical dissatisfaction, especially from the individuals eventually known as the "Gang of Four" which included Madame Mao, Jiang Qing, as its most prominent representative. They were clearly dissatisfied with Premier Zhou Enlai's more moderate policies, desiring another dose of Mao's sloganeering agitation. In spite of this, Zhou, a highly skilled and educated person, though suffering from cancer, remained in power until his death, counterbalancing the influence of the waning Mao, who though physically frail was still perceived as supporting, or at least protecting, the more radical Maoists.

Zhou Enlai was still effectively in charge, though in a hospital, possibly hoping that an early demise on his own part would not give the radicals an opening to resume their initiatives. Whatever his goals, Zhou died in January 1976, more than ten months before Mao Zedong passed away. The timing appeared to allow Madame Mao and her radical allies their opportunity to come to full power at last.

The death of Zhou Enlai deprived the world of one of its most astute statesmen and placed the future of the moderates in Beijing in jeopardy for a time. Vice Premier Deng Xiaoping, Zhou's main assistant since 1973, had badly antagonized the Maoist radicals and did not remain in office long; he was forced out by April, presumably with Mao's approval. The new premier announced at that time, however, was not formally a radical, but a compromise choice, Hua Guofeng, whose record suggested a closer affinity with the moderates than the radicals.

A major earthquake in July 1976 tightened the political ties between Hua and the army, which handled most of the relief work. Given the trauma and demands

China

Shanghai Bund   Photo by Steven Leibo

required to recover, it was apparent that China needed a breathing spell away from the political bickering of the communist era.

Frail, senile and moribund, Mao died in September 1976. His death removed the main shield of the leading radicals, including his widow, Jiang Qing. They were purged by Hua a month later. The so-called "Gang of Four" soon came to be seen as central symbols of the suffering experienced by so many during the previous decade's Cultural Revolution. After their purge, propaganda against them continued unabated.

Deng Xiaoping, the leader of the more pragmatic communist officials was "rehabilitated" and soon became the most powerful man in the country. His general approach could not be more in contrast to Mao Zedong, his long-time leader. Mao had been committed to an ideological approach to governing that often excluded basic realities, thus making possible movements like the "Great Leap Forward." In dramatic contrast, Deng was more concerned about emphasizing a pragmatic approach to issues, preferably devoid of ideology. And it was with that approach that he set about, in what in hindsight turned out to be an incredibly successful effort, to build a new China.

Opening to the World

Under Deng Xiaoping's leadership China underwent an extraordinary series of changes almost unprecedented in Chinese history. Famous for his comment that "it did not matter if a cat were black or white,

as long as it caught mice," Deng, while committed to the political power of the Chinese Communist Party was first and foremost a pragmatist. Early on he forced the retirement of Premier Hua Guofeng. Ultimately he was replaced by Hu Yaobang. Deng then successfully went forward with the trial of the "Gang of Four," thus neutralizing radical opposition, some of which was within the army, making it easier to move against the ideas and policies they and Mao had represented.

The purge of radicals continued in both the party and the bureaucracy during the early 1980s. In 1985, 64 members of the Central Committee "resigned" under pressure from Deng. Zhao Ziyang was named General Secretary of the party in 1987, replacing Hu Yaobang. Eventually, he in turn, after the crises of Tiananmen Square, was replaced by the Jiang Zemin, in 1989.

Deng was also the driving force behind significant agricultural reforms during the 1980s, which led to partial decollectivization. In 1984, control over industry was eased, giving local managers more authority. Prices were set at the local instead of the national level (at least in theory), and food and housing subsidies were reduced for urban dwellers. In 1985, the economy grew by 15%. That astounding leap in GNP would begin a pattern of growth that continued for decades.

Unfortunately, inflation and corruption also exploded. Attempts by more conservative forces to rein in the freer economic environment were not as successful as they would have liked. Deng also took a more "open" approach toward the outside

world. Relations with the U.S. improved after the issue of American arms sales to Taiwan was aired in 1982. From Deng's perspective, that was particularly important given his assumption that China could not accomplish its modernizing goals without good relations with the United States. A cautious move to improve relations with the Soviet Union was also undertaken, but in the aftermath of the Soviet invasion of Afghanistan that became more difficult.

1989—Tiananmen Square

The death of Hu Yaobang, once considered the likely successor to Deng, in April 1989, ignited demonstrations by students who had long idolized him as a true reformer. By early May they had turned out by the hundreds of thousands in the larger cities, particularly Beijing, waving banners with statements unheard of in China: "Down with Corruption! . . . Long Live Democracy! . . . . Press Freedom!" . . . "Down With Rule By Men, Long Live The Rule Of Law!" A level of student and public activism emerged that had not been seen since the most dramatic days of the 1919 May Fourth Movement seventy years before.

Tiananmen Square was literally taken over by a huge encampment of protesting students some of whom gained even more support by going on a hunger strike to demonstrate their commitment. Not only students but workers in cities throughout China became involved and their demands ranged from moderate calls for further democratization in China to protests against political and economic corruption. A shaken Communist Party leader, Zhao Ziyang, mingled with the student demonstrators and made some vague concessions, but was swept aside by Deng Xiaoping and the more conservative Premier Li Peng.

There were clearly conflicting opinions among the leadership on just how to deal with the protesters. Moreover, the leadership itself appeared divided on larger issues of policy regarding the economy. Should it continue its rapid growth or reign in the increasingly open economy toward a more party-dominated one? Who would win in the leadership struggle thus had clear ramifications for China's entire economic future as well. But the more immediate crisis was in the streets and for the moment, the hardliners both political and economic were in the ascendance. For weeks, during a period of leadership indecision complicated by the visit of the Soviet leader Mikhail Gorbachev, the crisis grew and the humiliation of the government leaders along with it.

Suddenly on June 4th tens of thousands of well-armed troops smashed their way

China

through Beijing to the heart of the city, Tiananmen Square. The tanks crushed many in their path; estimates of those killed and wounded were in the thousands. There were reports of soldiers firing indiscriminately into the crowds, invading hospitals to yank out life-support systems of the wounded, attacking doctors and engaging in other violent acts. The hardliners had won, at least for the time being.

The massacre in Beijing was followed by a massive nationwide campaign of political repression involving many arrests. This evoked outrage abroad and some limited, largely temporary, sanctions on the part of China's major trading partners, which had little effect on the hardliners dominant in Beijing. Clearly China's Communist leaders had weathered the storm, but the events of June 1989 would continue to haunt them for decades to come. The CCP had come very close to losing control of the country. The fall of eastern European communism over the next few years only reinforced that sense of vulnerability.

Parallel with this political crackdown, Deng Xiaoping's economic reform program went into reverse. In fact, some have surmised that the economic conservatives among the leadership had used the confrontation for their own ends, to return to a more Soviet style command economy at almost the same time that the Soviet Union was unraveling. Central control over the economy was strengthened, prices were more closely controlled and there was even talk of the "voluntary" re-collectivization of agriculture.

Whatever senior leader Deng's commitment to stopping the political challenge and chaos of the streets in 1989 had been, he himself clearly remained convinced that China needed more, not fewer, economic freedoms. But for a time after the clashes on Tiananmen Square, Deng's pro-economic reformers were clearly in the minority among China's leading decision makers.

President Nixon contemplates the Great Wall, 1972

AP/World Wide Photos

Eventually, though, by 1992, Deng Xiaoping and his supporters once again prevailed over the economic conservatives to reinvigorate the reforms. The private sector received encouragement, and in 1993 the free market concept was legitimized in the constitution. The "open" policy toward the outside world remained in effect, and foreign investment continued to flow in from the United States as well as from other sources.

Although opposition continued to be sternly repressed, China in the early 1990s experienced one change with important political possibilities. The provinces were gaining in autonomy and authority at the expense of the center. This was especially true of the comparatively prosperous and dynamic provinces along the coast.

The Death of Deng Xiaoping

After years of waiting, the world heard of the news of Deng Xiaoping's death in February 1997. While he had not been influential in decision-making for years, many had waited for word of his death with trepidation. After all, more than once before, the death of a senior leader had set off dramatic developments in the People's Republic. In 1976, both the early death of Zhou Enlai in January and Mao's death in October had set off dramatic changes in the leadership of the country. Indeed, it was only with Mao's death that the forces were released that brought Deng Xiaoping to supreme power. And more recently the death of the former party Chairman Hu Yaobang, had set off the chain of events that eventually brought on the Tiananmen Crisis of June 1989. But in the first weeks after Deng's death it appeared that nothing of the sort was likely to occur this time around.

Chief among the differences was the very success Deng had brought about. When Deng first emerged in real power in the late 1970s he led a weak China with a military that would soon embarrass itself in the expedition against Vietnam, one that hardly made a dent on the international, political or economic scene. A generation later the China of Deng has been drastically transformed.

In 1978 when Deng's authority began to be significant, Chinese exports to the world were U.S. $9.8 billion by 1995 they were U.S. $149 billion! Steel production had tripled and urban Chinese lived increasingly in cities that often resembled huge construction sites that were the product of a building boom. More than a decade of double-digit growth rates had transformed China. Even the World Bank estimated that the number of people living in poverty had been cut by two thirds.

Thus by the time Deng died, an enormous percentage of Chinese felt invested in the new changes. While there were clear differences between some of the top leaders, the sort of issues that had divided the leadership in 1976 and for a time in 1989 seemed much milder. With even the conservative military making billions from their role in the surging economy there was clearly no turning back from the world that Deng had built. China would be an involved player in the world community. Only the details needed to be worked out. The dramatic and sometimes deadly struggle between the Maoists and the Pragmatists that had characterized aspects of the earlier Mao years seemed to have passed. There was far more general agreement on the new China that Deng had set in motion.

By Deng's death, Jiang Zemin was already well positioned to establish himself as the new dominant figure. His prominent role during the July 1997 Hong Kong transition and later his leadership at that fall's 15th congress of the Chinese Communist Party only confirmed his power through late 2002 when another smooth transition of power occurred.

New Generations Emerge

In the fall of 2002 the long awaited 16th National Party Congress took place and a new generation of leaders finally emerged from the shadows. Most importantly, Hu Jintao, 59, the vice president and previous party boss of Tibet was chosen to head the 65 million member Chinese Communist Party while a host of older leaders, men long known to the outside world from Zhu Rongji, the long-time premier, to Li Peng who became infamous during the Tiananmen Crisis of 1989 retired. Even as President Jiang was leaving office his influence remained obvious not only in the make up of the new politburo which was still packed with his supporters but the apparently forced retirement as well of Li Ruihuan, one of Jiang's principal rivals.

Still, China's new leader, Hu Jintao, has steadily expanded his influence since coming to power in 2002. In fact, by the fall of 2004 former President Jiang formally surrendered his last official position of significance, as leader of the party's military commission. Hu Jintao added this to his other titles as president and head of the party.

Both leaders Jiang and his successor Hu Jintao have clearly been committed to continuing the general lines of reform begun by Deng Xiaoping, but they have faced a China much different from that Deng had led. China has become far more integrated into the world system, its military and economy are far stronger and the challenges its leaders face quite are different from those Deng had dealt with.

Deng Xiaoping

The NPC or National People's Congress is no longer the rubber stamp it had once been. Over the years it has become more and more effective in occasionally challenging the Communist Party and in pushing for an enhancement of the rule of law. In 1995, it successfully opposed changes in the education system and banking reform sponsored by party leaders. The body has also become the locus for increasingly popular expressions of opposition to government policies. Congress members are free to introduce their own legislative bills and members have even been willing to publicly oppose the government on matters as sensitive as politburo nominations. Public polling in recent years has shown that more and more citizens view the NPC as an important institution to which they can address their complaints.

This is certainly a new development in a society so long exclusively dominated by the Chinese Communist Party and its powerful leaders. Of particular recent interest were both the decision taken by the 10th People's Congress in 2007 to allow foreign journalists easy access to the event and the more general focus at the gathering on the sort of issues—health care, corruption and the environment—that in more open democracies are usually considered "populist" policies.

At the local level it is now more possible for non-party members to hold important positions of influence, something that would have been practically impossible in the past. Even more interesting has been the decision to allow local elections. Still, the Chinese Communist Party has made it clear that it intends to remain in ultimate control. It has worked vigorously to reinvigorate and train its more than 14 million members with precisely that goal in mind. Nevertheless, it has also been willing to allow extraordinary new freedoms in the social and economic arenas and on the local level even greater political freedoms.

But retaining control does not preclude seeking competence over ideological purity or party cronyism. It looks like China plans to return to some of the roots of its own civilization for help in recruiting qualified personnel. Since 1994, China has moved to return to the time honored system of examinations to recruit candidates for government jobs. The government has continued to battle economic corruption, especially that associated with the families of the senior leaders that have been fundamentally weakening the Communist party's ability to lead. In recent years the government has charged and convicted of corruption people holding positions of great political and economic responsibility.

Quite clearly China's new leadership generation has enormous challenges ahead given the reports of wide-spread alienation among so many Chinese and the severe social dislocations that people have experienced as China moves even more deeply into the world economy. They find themselves out of work. In fact, recent polls have suggested that the majority of Chinese not only wants more social programs made available by the government but a greater role in choosing their own leaders. Clearly the days when the Chinese Communist Party could simply call the shots and expect the population to follow through on whatever demands it made are rapidly fading away.

Looking Forward: Thematic Issues for the 21st century

As we move into the twenty-first century, the People's Republic is not simply going to proceed on the path Deng laid out a generation ago. Deng Xiaoping was trying to "jump start" an economy that had been artificially wounded by impractical economic leadership. His goal was to reinvigorate that economy through internal reforms and an external opening to the world. But those initial goals were accomplished and his heirs, especially Jiang Zemin, and Hu Jintao are committed to refining the economic and social message that dominated Deng's years. Given the current weakness of communism as an important unifying message, Jiang embarked upon several efforts to revitalize the party's rule starting with a call for a new "spiritual civilization" that combined elements of economic growth with both communitarian and nationalist elements.

More specifically, Jiang moved to revitalize the Chinese Communist Party by successfully opening up party membership to practicing capitalists. In short, China's leading party may still formally call itself "communist," but it has evolved far beyond the purely working class ori-

May 21, 1989: *A People's Liberation Army* convoy is engulfed by demonstrators in Tiananmen Square, Beijing.　AP Wide World Photo

China

entation of early communist theorists. But opening the doors of the party to members who are clearly not "communists" in any real sense of the word is hardly the same thing as opening up the political system. In short, is there any chance of a parallel opening toward democracy on the national level? At this point it seems not at all probable. Nevertheless, as discussed in the human rights section below, real changes are occurring at the grass-roots level.

Overall, day-to-day developments will have to be understood in the context of an evolving China that is quite unevenly moving toward a more open future. For example, throughout the last few years the government continued to give mixed signals on its attitude toward reform. On the one hand, a new more open attitude evolved for a time that allowed for the publication and discussion of quite radical political ideas. Moreover the government has allowed village level elections and expanded those elections to the regions in China's far west. China's current leader, President Hu, has at times spoken very positively of expanding what he has called democratic participation and democratic scrutiny of government activities. But that has not always been the case in reality.

Those who have challenged the ultimate authority of the Chinese Communist Party—however subtly—have over the years felt its wrath. This was well demonstrated by the harsh sentences handed down in late 1998 to several dissidents for attempting to organize a new party called the China Democracy Party.

Even more dramatically, the government moved in 1999 against those who had involved themselves in spiritual activities that seemed beyond official control. Most prominent was the official banning and at times brutal persecution of members of the Falun Gong, a quasi-religious movement that practices physical and meditative activities and had become enormously popular. In fact, the movement was so popular that the authorities, nervous that a mass movement able to attract such support and mindful of how dangerous such movements had been in earlier eras, set out to suppress Falun Gong. In the years since, thousands of Falun Gong followers have been arrested. Many of its leaders were given long prison sentences for having played a role, not in an organization that had formally challenged the authority of the state, but apparently for having taken part in a movement that might potentially do so.

More recently, partly as an off-shoot of China's growing economic transformation and the stresses that is putting on rural communities, China has been experiencing a regular series of violent local protests. Tens of thousands of these have been suppressed by local authorities. The incident that received the most publicity was a confrontation in a village near Guangzhou in late-2004. Over twenty people were killed by police officials attempting to quell demonstrations against land seizures.

Despite such incidents, there is still, in the long run, reason to hope for the appearance of a more open China. After all, an increasingly educated and sophisticated society has emerged. More institutions of civil society are emerging, and it is more respectful of the rule of law and tolerant of a more divergent leadership.

Of more immediate interest is the fact that, unlike Deng Xiaoping or Jiang Zemin, whose emphasis was largely on economic growth, China's leadership team, President Hu Jintao and Premier Wen Jiabao, seem much more concerned about dealing with the more negative consequences of China's spectacular recent growth, from environmental degradation to social inequality. This focus, as mentioned above, was particularly evident during the Fifth Plenary Session of the People's Congress in 2007.

As a practical matter, though, it has not been domestic democratic activists or even religious or spiritual movements like the Falun Gong that have really challenged the party lately. Rather, it was the drastic economic downturn that began in the United States in late 2008 that started to undermine the economic strength that has long been one of the most important features of the CCP's retention of power in China. All of this is probably one of the primary reasons the government moved quickly in the aftermath of the crisis of 2008 to implement a massive stimulus program to jump-start the economy.

Sources of Domestic Unrest

Other important issues to monitor are developments in Western China and especially in Xinjiang, where outbreaks against Chinese rule have resulted in riots followed by harsh retribution by officials. Ironically, the September 11, 2001, terrorist attack in the United States turned out to be somewhat advantageous for Beijing. It allowed it to align its on-going effort against the Muslim separatists of Xinjiang with the larger American-led war on terrorism. In fact, the PRC's leadership even claimed, probably with some justification, that the infamous al Qaeda had trained large numbers of Uighur militants. That is not surprising given the complications of life for the region's non-Han largely Muslim community.

For the most part, Beijing remains very suspicious of the influence Islam could potentially have on the region's inhabitants, and it closely controls it. Neither students nor government workers are allowed to fast during Ramadan, and taking part in non-officially sanctioned religious activities can put a person's career prospects in jeopardy. The effort is quite invasive ranging from limiting how long sermons can be to outlawing private teaching of either Arabic or the *Quran*. Long-standing tensions erupted dramatically in July 2010 after an incident in a factory in Uumqi, Xinjiang's capital. Sadly, the incident resulted in vicious ethnic fighting and the deaths of almost 200 people while about 2,000 were injured. Eventually the government executed many of those it thought primarily responsible for the violent disturbances.

Yet another area of concern is the potential for significant labor unrest as tensions mount over the growth in unemployment

Deng Xiaoping with the Reagans, Beijing 1984

associated with reforms of the government-owned enterprises and over the more recent global economic downturn. Understandably, the millions of workers being laid off by the state-owned enterprises are adding to the potential for social unrest. Further tensions have arisen from the fact that Chinese society has become far more fragmented than it once was. In today's China, some people are moving smoothly into the new world of global consumerism. Other areas, largely in the rural countryside, continue to stagnate. Some Chinese depart for uncertain lives in the cities and become part of the "floating population" of underemployed. More positively, the situation improved somewhat when governments in places like Shanghai agreed to allow the children of migrant workers into local schools. At the same time, the central government has made it more attractive through a series of reforms, such as introducing health insurance and tax relief for the rural population, to entice them to remain at home rather than flooding into the cities, which until recently teamed with jobs.

Economy: Moving Away from Communism

As the Chinese moved into the new millennium there was plenty of reason to feel both confidence and some concern. On one hand, the economies of many of her neighbors had been terribly hurt by the economic meltdown of the late 1990s and were only just beginning to recover. This was a meltdown that China itself had managed largely to avoid. In fact, despite her neighbors' problems the PRC maintained a very positive growth rate throughout the period. She had also had major advantages over her neighbors during the crisis that had settled into the region in 1997. For example, her currency was not traded on the world market, and the government boasted enormous economic reserves—said at the time to be around $150 billion—that most governments in Southeast Asia, often fighting to defend their currencies, could not even dream of. But the next global economic spiral downward turned out to be much more serious.

For Beijing, moving decisively was of fundamental importance. After all, the economy which had boasted double digit growth rates in the previous decade had slowed to 9.7% in 1996 and dipped to an official 7.8% in 1998. And much of that growth was simply a result of government infrastructure spending. The numbers continued to dip for a time, but by 2000 they had started climbing again. GDP for 2002 came in at 8%, that for 2003 at 9.1%. By 2007 the figure had grown to over 11%. But that growth streak drew to an abrupt

President Hu Jintao

halt in late 2008 as the newest world economic crisis set in.

Unlike in 1997, China was far more impacted, especially as exports to the United States slowed dramatically. In fact, as the crisis set in, it began to look like China's growth rates were likely to dip to under 8%. However, while China did take a dramatic economic hit in the 2008 global economic downturn, decisive leadership by the central government was able to avert much of the damage. They did so by instituting a massive economic stimulus plan of over $586 billion coupled with directions to the nation's bankers to loosen credit restrictions to spur growth. The effort worked and China ended 2009 with a growth rate again over 8%. Still, there are plenty of reasons for long-term economic concern.

The entire economy continues as it has for years to be handicapped by the inefficient state-owned enterprises (SOEs). China has hundreds of thousands of SOEs, many of which operate at a financial loss. The total cost of propping them up over the years has been enormous. Chinese leaders have long been aware of the problem, but doing something about it has been quite another matter. After all, Beijing's leadership has understood that hundreds of millions of workers are still employed in the state sector. Fearing social unrest, the government until recently was very hesitant to begin the reorganization, especially given the subsequent growth in unemployment that reforming that sector would require.

With Deng's departure and Jiang Zemin's solidification of power, the leadership was finally ready to bite the bullet and begin in earnest the transformation of the state enterprises. At the 1997 fall party Congress, Jiang announced that a major effort would commence—despite the perhaps necessary massive layoffs—to reform that lagging part of the economy. The program called for a range of actions from complete shutdowns to mergers and reorganizations to deal with the problem. Recognizing by the spring of 1998 the dangers of further economic dislocation given the regional economic slowdown and the anticipated problems associated with reforming the state enterprises, Beijing decided to move even more dramatically. It committed itself to further reforms and a massive economic stimulus effort, especially aimed at the agricultural and the housing sector, to spur the economy.

However, China's leadership has been interested in far more than merely reforming the state enterprises. More recent years

Young workers exercising in the Shanghai Petro-Chemical Works

China

have seen a very committed effort to move dramatically away from the entire system of a communist-based command economy. Building on the momentum begun during Deng Xiaoping's tenure in office, the last decades have seen an incredible array of changes that in their totality fundamentally represent an almost complete repudiation of communism as China's governing economic principle.

Thus during the late spring of 1999 the Chinese Parliament finally decided officially to recognize capitalism as an important part of China's new socialist market economy. A few months later Beijing announced that henceforth private enterprises would be placed on an "equal footing with state-owned enterprises." Capitalists have officially been invited to join the Communist Party, and China's national legislature moved to amend the constitution to protect private property. By 2004, while the state-owned enterprises were still undergoing massive changes, more than three million private companies had emerged that were themselves employing close to 50 million workers. Perhaps most interesting was the decision to strengthen the laws on private property. This was another clear sign of Beijing's fundamental rejection of formal communism as a guiding economic principle. Of special interest in this regard was the adoption of the new Property Law in 2007, which finally passed after years of controversy. It dealt with issues ranging from transferring property to ownership. While not overturning the core socialist assumption that the state owned all land, it did provide important new safeguards for individual citizens and businesses. That momentum continued into 2008 as moves were underway to give rural Chinese the right to buy and sell long-term land rights.

China's entrance into the World Trade Organization has also forced many new challenges on the once relatively isolated Chinese environment. The gradual opening of markets forces enormous changes. They range from continuing efforts to transform the Chinese legal system so that they conform to international norms to putting even more pressure on her still important state enterprises to become more financially efficient.

Another important milestone was a new economic survey conducted by the government during 2005 that has indicated that China's economy had not been properly measured. Apparently the economy was thought to be 17% larger than previously believed, a figure that made China's economy the world's sixth-largest in 2004.

Aside from the years of obvious growth, other signs indicate the changing international economic environment. That the

People's Republic of China emerged a few years ago as an even bigger market for Volkswagens than the United States is a fact that highlights the growing interest by Chinese consumers in purchasing their own automobiles. This is a development that was unimaginable only a few years ago. China's trading patterns are also evolving. In recent years Southeast Asia has become a particularly important market for Chinese goods and might one day soon even pass the United States as a market.

Of particular interest for outside commercial interests is the reality that after generations of frustrated foreign entrepreneurs who mistakenly embraced the famous image of China as a vast untapped market, the situation is finally starting to change for the better. For more than a hundred years the idea of the endless "China Market" was one that had seduced foreign businessmen. They embraced the dream of seeing hundreds of millions of Chinese becoming a vast heretofore-untapped market for foreign sales. Alas, for most of China's recent history, that rarely turned out to be true. But soon after the dawn of the new century, a majority of American firms reported that their Chinese efforts have finally become profitable. Even the Chinese government has gotten involved in China's new consumer market. Concerned that the nation is too dependent on foreign export markets, Beijing has been encouraging the growth of

its own consumer markets to insulate the nation's economy from the sort of economic shocks that were arriving by early 2009.

Looking Closer:
The Human Rights Question

Certainly one of the most difficult issues in the Sino-American relationship is caused by tensions over human rights. Here, as with questions over Tibet, emotions sometimes get in the way of thoughtful analysis of the situation. From the U.S. side, many Americans have been appalled by various reports about the far fewer personal, religious and political freedoms the Chinese enjoy compared to citizens of most Western countries. Of course, images remain powerfully charged by memories of Chinese tanks sent to drive peacefully demonstrating students from Tiananmen Square in 1989, the violent suppression of the 2008 uprising in the Tibetan-populated areas of southwestern China, or the somewhat similar developments in the Muslim areas of the far west.

The many reports Americans hear of forced abortions in the People's Republic, imprisoned democratic activists and the persecution of some religious figures are true enough. But these reports alone often fail to project an accurate image of developments in the People's Republic where the general trend is usually toward a far more open society than Chinese have ex-

Chengdu's Famous Panda Park

Photo by Steven Leibo

perienced in their entire history. Today's China, despite the very real issues Western human rights activists decry is a far freer place than is generally understood. Millions of people have much more control over their daily lives, worship openly with little interference from the state have the power to sue the government and even to take part in political elections at the local level.

That momentum toward an even greater level of individual freedom largely continued into the opening years of the new century as today's Chinese citizens no longer need, as they once did, permission from their work units either to marry or to apply for a passport. For those citizens who find themselves on the wrong side of the law, more legal aid resources have been established by the government. Unlike in the past, criminal lawyers are now officially allowed to represent their clients, rather than the state. People have successfully sued the government for false arrest and detention. Nevertheless, the People's Republic remains a country of swift justice. Every year thousands of convicted criminals are immediately executed after their sentences are handed down.

However, the evolution toward a more open society has not always continued smoothly. Over the last year the government has seemed less and less tolerant of dissent and in the opinion of some observers has backtracked significantly. Still, if a generation ago the Chinese leadership insisted on controlling practically every aspect of people's lives, the formula today seems a far narrower one. The government allows people far more social, religious, political and intellectual rights as long as they do not challenge the unity of China or the power of the Chinese Communist Party. Thus, for example, religion—Catholicism and even Tibetan Buddhism—has been allowed to flourish as long as its followers do not tie themselves to the leadership of outside figures, such as the Dalai Lama or the Pope. Space has even opened up somewhat for more toleration of gays and lesbians

Nevertheless, it is still dangerous to question the national leadership itself. That last point was graphically demonstrated in the fall of 1998 when several democratic activists were given long prison terms for attempting to form a new political party, the Chinese Democracy Party, to challenge the Communist Party. Similar developments have continued to happen on a regular basis in the decade since.

Clearly, despite the much greater freedoms available to the Chinese people, the government and party are determined to maintain for itself the right to decide how far and when those freedoms might expand. It is clear as well that Beijing's leaders have been quite willing to withdraw some of those liberties when they felt compelled to do so.

An issue that rose to particular prominence over the last decade was Beijing's harsh reaction toward religious movements that were perceived to be beyond state control. From the Falun Gong meditative exercise group to Tibetan Buddhists and Catholics who continue to associate with the Vatican, China's leaders have shown little hesitancy in suppressing any religious movement they considered capable or even potentially capable of challenging their authority. More recently, spiritual communities that have operated outside of the structure of the official religious establishment have seen large numbers of their church buildings demolished.

One of the most obvious signs of China's internalization of the phenomenon of globalization as it relates to human rights was the proclamation on December 10, 2008—the sixtieth anniversary of the universal declaration of human rights—of a new Chinese call for a fundamental transformation of Chinese political life. The document was signed by hundreds of people, many of them in positions of relatively significant importance, calling for an end to China's system of one-party rule and its replacement by a more fundamentally democratic system built on the usual checks and balances common to true democracies. To no one's great surprise, the proclamation's signers soon found themselves harassed and often imprisoned by the regime. A year later, in 2010, the well known writer Liu Xiaobo, who had organized the Charter 08 Manifesto, was sentenced to an eleven-year prison term. Perhaps more ominous has been the regime's growing intolerance of those lawyers willing to defend individuals who have crossed swords with the government.

In short, the Chinese still have far fewer freedoms than Westerners, but far more than many Westerners believe they do. Very real changes, for example, have come in their rights to choose their own employment and where they wish to live. They are even occasionally successful suing the government and winning in court. In fact, the state is simply less involved in the lives of average Chinese. The real challenge for those outside critics of the PRC will be to respond to the situation in China as it actually exists rather than to the often sensationalist reports in the foreign media.

Foreign Relations of the People's Republic

The People's Republic has begun to play a much more significant and cooperative international role than it did in the early years of its existence. Beijing successfully served as the site for the 1995 UN-sponsored Fourth World Conference on Women. More recently of course it hosted the highly successful Olympics of 2008.

It is also true, however, that China has entered a more assertive period in its foreign relations. Its economic progress has created conditions where the country's leaders feel it appropriate and necessary for China to assume a higher profile inter-

Morning exercises in Shanghai   Photo by Steven Leibo

China

Carved Buddha in Tibet

Photo by Steven Leibo

nationally. In effect, after more than a century of weakness, Beijing seems ready to resume its former place of significance in the world. Moreover, as mentioned previously, with the weakening of communism, nationalism remains the best means of unifying the Chinese people. The central government needs it to survive. The most recent example was seen during 2008 when, as much of the world condemned Chinese practices in Tibet, a significant part of the domestic Chinese population strongly supported the government's policies there.

Thus events over the last decade have shown that China's leaders are at times quite willing to play the nationalist "card" to ensure their continuing legitimacy in the eyes of the Chinese public. Nowhere have these nationalist tensions been as obvious as between the increasingly self-confident People's Republic of China and its long-time nemesis, Japan.

The recent attempts by Japanese extremists to assert their control over the islands known in Chinese as the Diaoyus were a good example of the complexities of nationalism in this new era. Chinese of all stripes, from Hong Kong to Taiwan and the People's Republic, were united in anger against these Japanese efforts. Even more recently Japan's efforts to gain a permanent seat in the United Nations Security Council have also aroused considerable public anger.

But the tension cannot be exclusively associated with Beijing's desire to justify its leadership in the vacuum left by the weakening of communism. The sentiments are quite genuine among the Chinese population. In part they are caused by the postwar unwillingness of Japan, as the Germans have in Europe, to confront fully the reality of the horrors Tokyo inflicted on so many peoples of the region during the Second World War. The issue was particularly obvious during the spring of 2005 when thousands of Chinese demonstrated against the Japanese government's continuing effort to downplay the violence of its World War II assault on China as portrayed in its school textbooks. Significantly though, some of that tension had dissipated by 2008.

Relations with North Korea's remain very important to Beijing. In fact, Beijing's new international role has been especially obvious when one looks at her growing involvement in the issue of North Korea's on-going and controversial efforts to develop not only a nuclear weapon's program but the complementary missile systems necessary to deliver such weapons. Over the last few years not only have Beijing leaders made it quite clear that they oppose their old ally's efforts to develop such weapons but have become the host and sponsor of a new set of multi-lateral talks between the regional powers and the

United States on the problem. Perhaps most significant of all, Beijing, rather than Washington D.C., has in many ways emerged as the most important player in the effort to confront North Korea's nuclear ambitions.

Beijing's growing efforts to resolve the standoff over North Korea's weapon's programs have not been the only area where it has become more involved in the rest of the region. For example, the economic crisis that enveloped much of the region in 1997 also gave the People's Republic an opportunity to expand her influence. In contrast to tensions over competing island claims, the 1997 economic crisis allowed Beijing to show its support for the region both by offering financial help and by making pledges not to undermine the region's recovery by devaluing her own currency. But it has not lessened her interest in maintaining her claims to those potentially lucrative offshore waters.

Even more significant was the decision by ASEAN to work toward a new Asian free trade zone that would include both China and her neighbors. This would perhaps eventually include over 1.7 billion people. The fact that China ended one millennium and entered another with growth rates that were still reasonably impressive has also helped expand her influence. That influence continued even as the economic crisis of 2008 unfolded. Somewhat

Lake Side in Kaifeng   Photo by Steven Leibo

nese goods become especially common in the central markets of those nations, but Beijing has offered significant levels of support to help the region build up its infrastructure.

Particularly interesting has been China's growing economic and diplomatic relationships with the countries of Latin America and Africa. President Hu has visited both continents and was well received. While Beijing's ties to South America are currently dwarfed by the relationship the region has with its northern neighbor, the United States, they are likely to grow significantly over the next several decades. In the case of Africa, both China and the United States have been showing renewed interest because of the available oil resources. For its part, China has promised enormous loans to various African nations as well as a program of debt cancelation. Both efforts complement the large sums China is investing in the continent.

Sino-American Relations

A significant part of China's foreign policy in recent years has centered on resolving issues with the United States. Unfortunately, relations continue to be very complicated, at times quite tense. Those tensions were particularly exacerbated in 2005 by one of China's leading energy firm's offer to purchase the relatively unknown American oil company, Unocal. This company has been especially involved in efforts to develop central Asian oil fields. Although the company itself was a minor player, and American companies, particularly banks, have of late been buying into the Chinese banking industry, the Unocal offer set off a dramatic set of concerns in Washington that ultimately resulted in the cancellation of the offer and a new round of anti-Chinese American rhetoric in the United States.

None of the charges were particularly new, but they did represent a growing American anxiety about China's emerging world influence and economic power. Overall, though, they differed little from the earlier moments of tension that have been so common a feature of the complicated relationship that exists between the two world giants.

During the early Clinton administration, the United States government's policy was geared toward exacting human rights concessions from China before economic relations could progress. This included holding up most favored nations (MFN) status for China. In May 1994, however, the policy was modified. Despite his early campaign statements, President Clinton changed his approach to one of "comprehensive engagement," assuming the same approach to China as the ad-

protected by its huge internal financial reserves, Beijing began to speak more assertively about a new economic order that might better include less global dependence on the American dollar as the major economic tool of global commerce.

On a different front, relations with India became much more complicated over the last few years as India's new government not only officially announced its new status as a nuclear power by setting off a series of underground nuclear tests but did so while citing tensions with China as one of the reasons to do so. Not surprisingly that outraged Beijing and played a role in its willingness to work with Washington to try to avoid a nuclear arms race in South Asia. Nevertheless, by the spring of 2003 relations between Beijing and New Delhi were improving and eventually culminated with the visit by India's Prime Minister Vajpayee. Still Sino-Indian relations have remained quite volatile and clearly lack the on-going cordial relations Beijing has long maintained with India's arch rival Pakistan.

Within the United Nations China has also played an increasingly important role. In 1999 China opposed NATO'S violent intervention in Kosovo. On the other hand Beijing has not always been absolutely against intervention in the internal affairs of other nations. When the United Nations decided in mid-1999, with the permission of Indonesia, to send a force to East Timor, China cooperated

by sending a team of Chinese policemen to help. That continuing commitment to the work of the United Nations has continued. By 2004 Beijing had even dispatched a contingent of Chinese security people to help out in Haiti, China's first contribution to such a force in the Western Hemisphere.

China has also been involved in the controversy that arose in recent years over the question of whether Saddam Hussein's Iraq was sufficiently complying with its international obligations, which emerged after the first Gulf War, to end the most dangerous of their weapons programs. Within that context the PRC often worked closely with other Security Council members like France and Russia in attempts to resolve peacefully the successive series of crises that have arisen from time to time. When, the United States chose to overthrow Saddam Hussein's government in Iraq, China, along with many nations from France to Russia, made it clear that it would have preferred a less violent and diplomatic resolution to the crisis than what eventually transpired. Eventually, though, Beijing has become a major investor in the new Iraq, something the United States with its major interest in Iraqi stability can hardly object to.

One of the newer dimensions of China's international role has been a newly developed relationship with the nations of Central Asia that emerged out of the collapse of the Soviet Union. Not only have Chi-

China

Soccer game—China vs. Japan
Courtesy of Pam Katz

ministration of George H.W. Bush. The change was not surprising. Clinton had come to understand that the People's Republic was simply too large and too important economically and diplomatically to ignore. Far too many economic and geopolitical issues required Beijing's cooperation. China was critical for dealing with issues ranging from North Korea's nuclear aspirations to progress on nuclear non-proliferation to working within the United Nation's Security Council where China holds a permanent veto. But that change hardly resolved all the problems.

The 1994 decision again to allow high-tech exports to China had by 1999 become very controversial. At that time charges surfaced that sophisticated missile technology had "accidentally" been transferred to the PRC by American companies as well as claims that the Chinese had gained valuable nuclear technology by spying. These charges, which put the Clinton administration on the defensive, eventually forced a cut-back in nuclear cooperation.

Moreover, the American-led military campaign in Yugoslavia also added to the tensions when the People's Republic sided with those nations which found the NATO bombing campaign unacceptable. Concerns over the NATO campaign in Yugoslavia and most probably the accumulated tensions that had developed over the years were dramatically revealed when in May 1999 the United States accidentally bombed the Chinese embassy in Belgrade, Serbia. The resulting explosion of Chinese

anger clearly highlighted how potentially divisive the relationship can become.

Ironically, given the fact that former President Clinton had largely adopted the China policy of his predecessor, George Herbert Walker Bush, his own successor, George W. Bush, began his administration with a China policy considerably more critical than either of his two predecessors. In fact, from the new American president's plans to build a missile defense system (which the Chinese feared would negate their own limited nuclear missile program) to the mid-air crash in early 2001 between an American surveillance plane and a Chinese jet, a host of tensions emerged.

Thus, it is not surprising that the Chinese side too has plenty of its own criticism of America. Especially important was the sense by many in China that the Americans were frequently unwilling to treat them with the respect and equality their size and accomplishments have earned them. The Chinese were also particularly aware that many American groups, from environmentalists and human rights activists to religious fundamentalists and many politicians, had "adopted" China as their "favorite whipping boy." America's continuing support of the Tibetan exile community and Taiwan remain long-term irritants given the Chinese perspective that the U.S. has too often intervened in what are seen as domestic issues.

Fortunately after the drama of September 11, 2001, as Americans began to focus

on the war on terrorism and the ways China might help in that struggle, the more immediate tensions between the two nations started to wane and a level of cooperation not seen for years began to prevail. It was unfortunately that smoother relationship that again began to unravel later in the decade as more Americans once again started vocalizing their anxiety about the eventual impact on the United States of China's extraordinary recent growth.

Today, many Americans openly talk of the People's Republic with considerable antagonism and argue that China's growth fundamentally threatens the United States. Of course, many in China are themselves very critical of the United States' decision to invade Iraq and its attempt to remake that country by force. Interestingly, that tension was momentarily revealed when, on the eve of the hard-fought American presidential election of 2004, Chinese Vice Premier Qian Qichen came out with a broadside criticizing President Bush and severely questioning his international leadership.

More recently issues, from the recall of Chinese products to Tibet, from Darfur to environmental concerns, have added fuel to the frequently open tensions between the two nations. On an even more fundamental level, there is a very good chance that Sino-American relations will become dominated in the near future by tensions stemming from their respective need to find new sources of oil. One should not forget the simple reality that irresponsible financial policies in the United States have left it increasingly dependent on Beijing's good will to maintain the flow of Chinese money invested in American treasury bills. They are, of course, needed to keep America's precarious financial house in relative health.

Increasingly there are very few areas where Chinese and American relations do not come into contact. One of the best examples is China's willingness to invest in both Iraq and Afghanistan, two areas whose economic health is vital to America's long term-goals. Not surprisingly, another area is energy use. This is a reality that President Obama has clearly taken to heart in his calls for a much more cooperative relationship between the U.S. and China in dealing with the emerging 21st century energy issues.

Interestingly the American administration has considered the evolving global realities. During President Obama's first official visit to China in late 2009, he was much more conciliatory toward China's leadership than visiting presidents have usually been. Eschewing the long-term American enthusiasm for confrontations over human rights and trade imbalances for a more positive and respectful tone, Obama was willing to recognize Beijing's significant accomplishments. Still he has forged ahead in areas that the PRC's leadership still finds especially irritating: the official reception of Tibet's long-exiled Dalai Lama and support for Taiwan

As always, there were many persons willing to oversimplify issues and fatalistically to predict a new cold war. The reality, though, was more complicated. As former Secretary of State Henry Kissinger counseled in the days after Deng Xiaoping died, the United States needs to differentiate between what in Beijing's activities represents the natural behavior of a newly powerful great nation and what might more specifically be a threat to the United States. Clearly they are not necessarily the same thing. But a more sophisticated view is required than many are willing to adopt to understand the difference.

But tensions over energy, competition for fossil fuels and their impact on the larger global climate system are relatively new issues. Over the decades another issue tended to dominate U.S. China relations. The fate of a relatively small island, once known as Formosa, has long remained at the core of American Chinese relations.

The U.S./PRC/Taiwan Triangle

From Beijing's perspective, Taiwan remains the single most important issue in Sino-American relations. That is not surprising. The PRC's leaders and much of the Chinese population continue to see the island as a fundamental part of the Chinese homeland and remain deeply committed to seeing Taiwan become part of the People's Republic one day. Perhaps of even more immediate concern is the general impression among China's leadership that an official loss of the island might ultimately signal its own downfall. After all, communism no longer commands much allegiance in the People's Republic, and the party has had to define itself in much more nationalist terms. This new legitimacy requires the CCP to do everything it can to keep the hope alive of Taiwan eventually reuniting with the mainland.

Thus it is from that on-going aspiration that Beijing constantly works to negate Taiwan's efforts to join the international community officially. In fact, Beijing has long applied pressure to any country that cooperated with Taiwan's efforts to integrate itself more formally into the world community. In that context, relations with the United States have been particularly problematic due to Beijing's constantly frustrated hope that the United States would lessen its long-term support of Taiwan. From Beijing's perspective the hope

is that the island's leaders might be more willing to resolve their differences with the mainland if America were not so openly supportive.

During 1996, U.S.-China relations were especially tense as Taiwan's first presidential election campaign was going on. In fact, concerned that voters would support a pro-independence party, Chinese naval forces initiated very provocative military maneuvers off the coast of the Republic, actually firing live shells vaguely in the direction of Taiwan's leading port. As the election decision drew near, Beijing kept up the threatening stance, clearly hoping to weaken the popularity of those who

were calling for Taiwan's independence from the mainland.

For its part, Washington responded by sending two carriers into the waters off Taiwan. When the election finally took place, the result was an impressive victory for then Taiwan's President Lee, who had maneuvered his campaign brilliantly between those on the island who emphasized independence and those who wanted reunification with the mainland. China had not succeeded with its scare tactics. Sadly, tensions over this issue are easily aroused. During 1999 Taiwan President Lee started another firestorm of new tensions by announcing that henceforth

In 1996, China became the largest steel producer in the world.

China

discussions between Taiwan and the People's Republic should be carried out as equal "state-to-state" relations. But that was nothing compared to the reaction when, in the 2000 elections, the Democratic Progressive candidate, Chen Shuibian, long an advocate of formal Taiwanese independence from China, was quite unexpectedly elected the new president.

It is true that Beijing's reaction to Chen's election was reasonably restrained. Nevertheless, Taiwan's slow yet obviously committed efforts to keep distancing itself from the mainland continued to be a constant irritation. Sometimes the efforts were quite subtle, as when Taipei decided to print the word "Taiwan" on its citizens' passport—a move that was done. It was said simply to make things easier during international travel.

Sometimes the efforts have been much less subtle: during the run up to the 2004 presidential elections on Taiwan, President Chen's government backed plans for a referendum on the question of Beijing's military threat toward the island. In that particular case the administration of George W. Bush, putting aside its usually strong commitment to Taiwan, publicly aligned itself against Taipei and argued against holding the referendum, a move that gained Beijing's public gratitude.

It is important, though, not to overemphasize the tensions that are often at the heart of the Taiwan-People's Republic relationship. Over the years, the two have become closer and closer in economic ar-

eas, and the days when it was impossible to travel or communicate directly from Taiwan to the mainland are long over. In fact, in 2007 an extraordinarily new development occurred. After years of discussion, both governments officially agreed to begin direct flights. Finally, at very long last, travelers were not required to go first to some alternate destination such as Hong Kong before moving on to their final Taiwan destination. The first official and regularly scheduled direct flights began in the summer of 2008.

But far and away the most important development in Taiwanese-Chinese relations has been the Nationalists' return to power through the Presidency of Taiwan. Taiwan's new president, Ma Ying-jeou, specifically ran on a platform of lessening tensions with Beijing with the hope of using those improved relations to help Taiwan's weakening economy. Since coming to office, Ma has carried out that pledge despite criticism from some quarters in Taiwan. On its part, Beijing has also become somewhat more flexible and more willing to work with Taiwan, especially as the island nation began to use more commonly the term Chinese Taipei, a term the PRC finds more acceptable. Still, that improving relationship did not prevent Beijing's irritation when the United States agreed in the fall of 2008 to sell the island billions of dollars more in defense equipment. Overall, Americans need to understand that when dealing with Beijing on issues related to Taiwan, the fate of the lat-

ter is viewed through mainland Chinese lenses as primarily a domestic issue and more specifically one tied to the long-term viability of China's Communist Party.

U.S.-China Economic Relations

The Sino-American economic relationship has taken on a new and potentially burdensome dimension in recent years. Although arguments about differing methods of registering trade persist, it is clear that frustrations associated with the trade imbalance between the United States and China have come to resemble the sort of economic tensions that once dominated the American-Japanese relationship. That trade imbalance is enormous; according to one estimate, it is currently somewhat over $226 billion annually. It is also true that the numbers can vary considerably, depending on who is consulted and how the figures are calculated. The Chinese estimates of the imbalances are generally lower than those the U.S. claims. Of course, it is usually forgotten that most of the so-called Chinese "sales" are not really Chinese goods per se. They are outside goods produced by Western—often American—companies that arrange for the manufacture within China of goods they plan to sell in the United States. Perhaps most revealing is the example of the very familiar American product, the Barbie doll. Such a doll might sell for $20 in an American store, but the Chinese themselves only pocket around 35 cents from its production. Even more importantly, much of the imbalance really reflects the centralization of Asian manufacturing in China from other Asian countries, something very few commentators have apparently noticed.

Regardless of the different interpretations and explanations, the Clinton administration, the second Bush and the Obama administration have been committed to basing these newly established economic ties on a more equal footing than had evolved over the years with Japan. Unfortunately, the success of the agreements too often relied on success in other areas of the complex relationship. Progress in other areas, such as weapons sales and nuclear technology, seemed likely to impact positively on the trade imbalance if politics did not intervene.

One of the most important economic issues in Sino-American relations over the years was the question of whether the United States would support China's entry into the World Trade Organization (WTO). The principal problem was whether China would be admitted as a developing nation or as an already developed one. The definitional issue was important in that each carried with it different requirements concerning a country's

Downtown Chengdu

economic obligations to the rest of the world. The Chinese wanted to be admitted as a developing nation. The West insisted it adhere to the standards set for the developed world. Obviously, given its enormous size and diversity, China represents aspects of both. After years of negotiations, real progress was made in 1999 when the U.S. and China finally signed and ratified an agreement on China's bid to enter the WTO. The deal itself obliged China to cut tariffs an average of 23% and offer greater access for U.S. firms.

By 2001 China finally did enter the WTO. It was accomplished with the support of the United States although that hardly made their economic relations any less complicated. By 2005, an entirely new dimension had been added to their relationship as American coat hanger manufacturers began using China's new status as a WTO member to attack their Chinese competitors. China fought back with a combination of American law firms and their own anti-dumping legal charges. Concerns about trade could often go far beyond that of coat hangers. Chinese purchases of Boeing airplanes have been among the most important products the Americans have been able to sell to the Chinese.

But Boeing's future in China is not certain. During 2005, Chinese officials signed a very lucrative deal with Boeing's principal competitor, the European firm Airbus, for the eventual purchase and cooperative assembly of 150 planes. There were, no doubt, many reasons for the Chinese decision. Boeing's chances were not helped by the discovery that a new Boeing aircraft that had been ordered by the Chinese leadership was "somehow" built with dozens of spying devices included.

Moreover, in 2005 the most dramatic issue was the American decision to put limits on the growth of Chinese textile exports to the United States. In response, hoping to avoid an escalation of tensions, China raised its own export tariffs, while slightly revaluing its currency around 2.5%. This was, in some measure, a response to its critics. Still, as mentioned above, the majority of American companies are now reporting that their Chinese-based operations have become profitable.

Although rarely discussed publicly, one aspect of enormous significance to the Sino-American economic relationship is that the United States has been running extraordinarily large budget deficits that have been kept largely manageable only because the PRC, with its growing economy, has been making huge purchases of dollar-based goods, including American treasury notes. In fact, the amounts are so large that they have helped keep Ameri-

can interest rates low and the American economy vital. However, China's willingness to continue to "subsidize" the American economy with its purchase of treasury notes has started to come into question. By early 2009, even as the United States was going deeper and deeper into debt to jump-start its dramatically weakening economy, China itself was not only starting to spend billions of dollars on its own infrastructure-building stimulus programs. It was also reportedly more wary of becoming even more deeply linked to America's financial problems than it already was. Dramatically, the governor of the People's Bank of China even suggested during 2010 that the world consider ending its reliance on the dollar as the most important international currency.

Perhaps most important is the reality that as the global economic recession of 2008–09 emerged, it was increasingly obvious that the United States and China were linked at the hip economically. The deep linkages between the two societies had created a situation that made the economic health of each nation of vital interest to the other. This was becoming more apparent with each passing day and one made especially graphic by the fact that America has over the years become the world's biggest debtor nation while China has emerged as the world's creditor nation. China itself had replaced Japan as the nation to which America owes the most.

While not yet as significant an issue as it is likely to become in future years, China's increasing need for more imported oil to fuel its growing economy is certainly going to add to the tensions with

the United States, which itself continues to demand more and more of the world's limited oil resources for its own needs. Sadly, some have already predicted a future "resource war" between Washington and Beijing. On a more positive note, the American administration under Barack Obama has offered to work with Beijing more creatively and cooperatively with regard to energy. This would not only reduce the likelihood of a clash over diminishing energy based on fossil fuels, but it would affect their mutual impact on the global climate as well.

Defense Issues for the People's Republic

The military has been enjoying the fruits of economic expansion and has been very involved in commercial ventures. In fact, at one point it was estimated that about one fifth of all domestically produced consumer goods in China was produced in factories owned by the military. All this certainly helped the military's bottom line, but in the view of some analysts it also threatened to undermine the effectiveness of China's army. Not surprisingly the lure of huge amounts of money was also causing a flurry of stories about officers taking advantage of their positions to earn illegal funds.

Regardless of whether the entrepreneurial army was hurting its military orientation, its activities were getting in the way of the leadership's desire to remove the government from the economy. Thus as part of Beijing's effort to lessen the importance of the state-owned enterprises

Chengdu

Photo by Steven Leibo

China

Catholic Church in Shanghai   Photo by Steven Leibo

it also recently ordered the military to withdraw from business. Officially at least, the military did so in 1999 although the People's Liberation Army was allowed to keep control of those industries that directly served its needs. Still, because of this new wealth, China has purchased billions in military hardware from Russia.

Given how close the CCP came to losing control of China in 1989, it is not at all surprising that the party leadership has in recent decades been particularly generous with the military. After all, without the military's support in 1989, China's CCP might have lost everything, and a similar circumstance could easily emerge in the future.

Predictably China's military growth—which rises about ten percent a year—has begun to worry her neighbors. They are concerned about the possibility of military expansionism. This has been most prominent with regard to Beijing's willingness to assert itself in disputes regarding many islands in the region. It has become public enough for very high officials, upwards to the Japanese Foreign Ministry, to have commented about them publicly. These disputes have ranged from the Diaoyu islands in the East China Sea to the Spratley islands. Happily, some of the tensions that at times were quite high only a few

years ago have calmed considerably over the last decade or so. However, they have not gone away.

One issue that has already raised international concern is the growth of China's naval forces. That is probably not surprising given the fact that it is now importing close to fifty percent of its petroleum needs through relatively narrow and vulnerable water lanes in Southeast Asia. Nevertheless, China's decision to give itself more power to protect those vital shipping lanes has raised international "interest" in some quarters.

For the Chinese this associated problem has become known as the "Malacca Challenge." On the one hand, they understandably want to develop a naval presence in that particularly narrow strait through which so much of their energy needs to pass. On the other hand, their efforts to protect their energy security through a more significant naval capacity has aroused those in Washington who see such efforts as a threatening challenge to American naval predominance. This provokes the sort of potential insecurity Chinese has been hoping to avoid.

On the other hand, decisions on the other side of the world have also had an important impact on Chinese defense plans. Most significantly, the decision by former President George W. Bush to de-

velop an anti-ballistic missile system was seen by Beijing as a direct threat to its own limited ICBM program.

Clearly the growing Chinese economy is giving the People's Republic the ability to strengthen its forces although for the immediate future their effectiveness remains limited. But China does have ambitious goals. Most obviously, it has again moved to downsize the military. During 2003 it began efforts to demobilize another 200,000 troops while making it clear that its goal is to have a smaller but more technologically sophisticated force ready to serve the nation's military needs. As the 20th century passed into history, the commander of China's air force announced major plans to build a stronger air force with greater capabilities beyond China proper. Still, while some might be concerned about the increasing sophistication of the Chinese military, defense spending by the People's Republic is still only around ten percent of the figure spent by the American military.

Perhaps an even more significant sign of China's arrival as a major player on the international scene was its late-2008 decision to commit its navy to a long-term effort to help suppress the Somali pirates that have plagued international shipping in the Gulf of Aden. This was the first such long-distance effort since 1949 for China's navy. But that was not the only new development. During 2008 the Chinese navy has become less willing to tolerate American surveillance ships in nearby waters. Those changing attitudes were particularly obvious a few years ago when Chinese naval vessels approached and apparently harassed an American ship operating about 75 miles off the coast of China's Hainan Island.

China's Space Program

Particularly fascinating has been China's decision to enter that rare club of nations that have been able to put manned spaceships into orbit. That goal was ultimately realized in the fall of 2003 when Beijing successfully sent its first astronaut into an orbital flight that lasted twenty-one hours. Once that was accomplished, China set out to prepare for its first lunar launch, a goal that was realized in the fall of 2007 as the People's Republic's first unmanned lunar rocket settled into orbit around the moon. By September 2008 China accomplished yet another milestone by successfully carrying out its first 13-minute space walk.

All the talk of moon missions has had a very significant impact on a more widespread interest in returning to the moon. Washington's attention has been aroused while Japan, China's arch rival, has also placed a moon orbiter in place. Even India is planning its own efforts.

It was not merely talk of going to the moon that raised alarms in Western capitals, but China's successful shooting down of a satellite in early 2007. This was a feat that demonstrated its growing ability to undermine any American defense of Taiwan. It was not simply the fact that China demonstrated it could carry out such an impressive accomplishment that raised concerns. After all, the U.S. had demonstrated such capacity decades before. But China's move into space obviously had strategic military implications.

China and the World of Globalization

If making the transformation from a communist command economy to a more capitalist market economy was the biggest economic challenge the People's Republic faced in the last decades of the 20th century, the opening years of the 21st century have been dominated by her entrance into the new globalized world economy. In doing so China has done particularly well. The combination of a very industrious work force, particularly low wages and a government deeply interested in economic matters has increasingly made China the official workshop for much of the world. In fact, by 2004 China had overtaken Japan to become the third-largest exporter of goods, in her case goods valued then at over $600 billion.

In keeping with the general evolution of industrial globalization, that is from outsourcing manufacturing to that of service activities, China's Dailin region has become filled with "call centers" where Japanese-speaking Chinese handle technical service calls for Japanese customers. In fact, China has become so involved in the manufacture of goods by outside companies that the term "China Price" has come to refer to the power of China to offer the best possible manufacturing base for corporations all around the world. It is the price other nations and industries have to compete with to be competitive.

The downside, of course, was that China, in its role as the world's workshop, had become so deeply tied to the global economy that its own long-term economic growth was deeply threatened by the slowdown in the purchase of its exported consumer goods. This was especially obvious by early 2009. Nevertheless, the decades of strong growth had given the nation's leaders the hundreds of billions of dollars necessary to stimulate the economy with thousands of basic infrastructure projects China needed anyway. Of course, they had also created the enormous numbers of new jobs required to

survive the loss of so many international export markets.

Culture and Society in China

The twentieth century has seen extraordinary changes in culture and society in China. Ironically, Chinese communities in Hong Kong, the PRC and Taiwan spent much of the 20th century moving farther apart while more recently their societies have started to appear more similar again. Keeping up with these changes is breathtaking for the outside observer; actually living them would be astounding.

In 1900, most Chinese were rural peasants living very simple lives as farmers. The fundamental and lasting institutions of family life and farming completely dominated Chinese culture for thousands of years. This was certainly true throughout most of Asia, but these two foundations were developed to a higher level within China. Agriculture combined the careful cultivation of cereal grains, skillful efforts to control water by the construction of levees and irrigation ditches, and the return of all available fertilizer, including human waste, to the soil. This permitted high nutritional content of the harvests, which in turn permitted a rapid rate of population growth. The family was the

basic social unit—above it stood the village, governed usually by the heads of the leading families.

Society was dominated by an intellectual elite known as the scholar gentry who were very influential on the local level and supplied most of the personnel for the imperial bureaucracy that ran the empire. The traditional upper class culture was also based on the family and on the group of related families that together formed a clan. Ancestor worship, involving sacrifices to dead forebears, who were not considered to be actually divine, had begun among the upper classes and spread to the lower classes. The wealthy avoided manual labor and regarded literacy and education—especially in the Confucian tradition—ownership of land and public service, as the highest social goals and symbols of status. This upper crust, dominating education, government service and land ownership, was not so exclusive that the lower classes were entirely excluded from it. Unlike India, China never had a caste system as part of its culture, but in reality, it was highly unusual for a person of peasant origin to acquire enough education, wealth or influence to move to the top of the social scale.

In spite of tendencies toward conservatism and anti-foreignism, traditional

Billboard encouraging family planning

Photo by Miller B. Spangler

China

Chinese culture was the richest, and certainly the longest lived and most continuous of the great civilizations, ancient and modern. It was relatively free from the religious bigotry and intolerance that was evident in much of Western history. In contrast to the principles of decaying despotism of France under the Bourbon kings, China's traditional philosophy and culture greatly impressed well-educated Jesuit missionaries who came to China in the 17th century.

Sadly, the decline of the traditional Chinese political system in the late 19th and early 20th centuries brought a loss of confidence in many aspects of traditional Chinese cultural values. Education was increasingly altered to conform to Western ideals; literature began to be written in the vernacular, or conversational language, rather than in the old, more difficult and formal literary language.

By early years of the 20th century new groups of elites and workers became significant. On the elite level, new types of soldiers, business people, and intellectuals emerged as well as the formation of a new industrial working class that lived in the Western ports. China was starting its extraordinary century-long transformation.

During the 1920s, the new ideas and values including Marxism were gaining ground among intellectuals. At the level of the uneducated, the solidarity of the family was greatly weakened by the beginnings of economic progress toward industrialization, which created jobs for women, drawing them away from their families to the factories in the cities. The Japanese invasion in 1937 and the ensuing chaos uprooted millions of people and heavily contributed to the further breakdown of the traditional social and cultural order.

In the first generation after the Second World War, society in the several parts of China began to diverge. Both Taiwan and Hong Kong were aligned with the Western capitalist economies and each saw tremendous economic changes in their respective communities over the years. Economic growth was significant and people's lives were dramatically altered by the changing circumstances.

Within the People's Republic in contrast, while economic growth remained the principal goal, Mao Zedong's ideologically driven approach as demonstrated in the Great Leap Forward and the Cultural Revolution, failed to economically raise people's living standards; indeed at times the situation simply deteriorated dramatically. Even a casual visitor to the area in the late 1970s and early 1980s could see great differences in the life style of these different parts of the Chinese community.

But again, the revolutionary cycle has changed and since the late 1970s under the direction of Deng Xiaoping, the People's Republic has itself chosen to enter and compete in the world market. It has done so with enormous success. Real gains have been made in people's economic possibilities. Individual citizens can now purchase their own apartments. In Shanghai, which has been allowed to experiment with private housing more than ninety percent of the homes are privately owned but of course such changes are also required an on going effort to make the laws of the People's Republic more compatible with such private ownership.

These dramatic changes go far beyond property issues. Professionals like lawyers are now free to privately organize themselves to develop clients. Chinese citizens can now travel abroad far more often then they ever did before. And the luxury practically unimaginable only a few years ago, that of owning a private automobile has become very real for a growing number of Chinese. Although the West hears much about the harsh repression of individual dissidents who have chosen to challenge the state, the reality of a more general improvement in human rights is also true.

Urban life has become increasingly the norm in China as well. Today China has over 174 cities with more than a million people, and forty percent of the population lives in those cities. By 2020, the expectation is that 55 percent to 60 percent of the population will have become city dwellers.

Other changes are underway as well with one of the most controversial aspects of modern Chinese social legislation. For a generation the leadership has been encouraging the famous "one child policy." Designed to allow the PRC to get its long-term growth under control the program was a complicated combination of propaganda, financial incentives and disincentives and social pressure brought against families wishing to have more than one child. Although the program often had a significant impact on urban Chinese, it has been more difficult to implement in the countryside.

As is well known, the policy brought China under considerable outside criticism for the excesses of the program which critics charged included forced abortions. In recent years the policies have evolved to allow more flexibility within the program, and only recently a new law went into effect that has altered the rules to give it a more voluntary dimension.

But there are as well deeply gloomy aspects of contemporary Chinese life, such as the enormous growth in numbers of people with AIDS, often contracted by efforts of the poor to sell their blood using unsanitary conditions. The government has finally admitted that the number of AIDS victims has grown to more than a million and has committed itself to attempting to produce locally its own drugs to deal with the crisis. During the spring of 2003 China's health establishment was universally embarrassed by how poorly its health authorities dealt with the chal-

Mall Shopping in Shanghai

lenge of SARS, the virulent pneumonia-like disease that emerged in Southern China during late 2002 and began spreading around the planet. Given that embarrassment, it is not surprising that Beijing has taken a much more visible role in trying to organize a world-wide effort to deal with the potential challenges of Avian Flu.

One of the most interesting ironies of recent Chinese social development is the changing circumstances associated with her evolving demographic dilemma. While a generation ago China's primary challenge was limiting its population growth so they could maintain their population at a reasonable living standard and even advance. The first years of the 21st century have begun to illuminate a new and very different challenge. After decades of lowering their fertility rates and increasingly people's lives with better health care China's population is now becoming, like much of the developed world, increasingly older. The result is that just as in the United States, China will in coming decades see far fewer workers attempting to support a much larger number of aging citizens. Unfortunately, unlike most other developing countries that have arrived at this new demographic challenge, China's overall wealth will not be nearly as great as the new challenge sets in.

Nevertheless, the Chinese people certainly have plenty of reason to be pleased. For the older generation today's commonly improved life styles are truly remarkable. For the generation that remembers decades of war and economic turmoil it must be truly astonishing to see how much Chinese living standards have improved in recent decades. Three hundred million people, a figure somewhat larger than the entire United States has been pulled from poverty while the average income has quadrupled over the last generation. This is something to be very proud of. However, the price has not been insignificant. It managed initially to avoid a too great and potentially divisive gap between rich and poor within China during the mid-20th century.

But by the early 21st century the chasm between China's wealthier citizens, people often living in luxurious Western-style "gated communities," and the millions of still deeply poor Chinese has grown enormously. Today, the richest 10 percent hold 45 percent of the country's wealth, and the gap in average income between urban dwellers and those who live in the countryside is enormous.

The impact globalization initially had on raising living standards does not seem to have had as much of an impact in recent years as it once did. Today the national poverty rate appears frozen at eleven per-

cent and is not improving. On the more positive side, it has become clear that China's leadership is determined to rectify the situation before the problem gets completely out of control. One measure that has been adopted is to abolish school fees for the 150 million pupils who live in the country's poorer provinces. The PRC is also moving to establish a medical insurance program for those who live in the countryside and offer farmers more control over land rights. But much more will have to be done before the growing tension in the countryside starts to subside.

One of the most interesting developments over the last year has been the efforts of the government to back off somewhat on the long established One-Child policy, which had so effectively limited the growth of the population during the last decades of the 20th century. However, today's China has different problems. The number of working adults is soon expected to decline as the population of aging citizens grows. This would create a very problematic demographic imbalance between retired and working adults. For example, in 1975 China had 7.7 working adults available to support each citizen over 60. By the middle of the 21st century,

that number has been projected to drop to only 1.6. In short, while still largely a developing country, China is experiencing the same sort of demographic problems that more economically mature societies from Japan to America have long faced.

Chinese Women

Chinese women were among the biggest winners of the 20th century. Beginning the century with almost neither rights nor education, they were more often than not controlled partly through the painful process of foot binding. Yet by the early years of the century, women's education, even at the college level was much more common and foot binding, long outlawed, was less and less practiced. The Communist Revolution of 1949 moved as well to improve their status and the next year laws were passed giving them more rights. At the height of Mao Zedong's influence, the circumstance of women and men did not widely vary. Neither gender had much personal freedom.

On the other hand, it was difficult for those who controlled the factories to dismiss anyone, so at least more economic security was possible. The more recent eco-

Mahjong Players in Kaifeng

Photo by Steven Leibo

China

nomic changes though have again altered the circumstances of many women and given the progress made in earlier years of the century have at times seemed to have slowed the momentum toward improving women's rights. For example, given the decision-making powers to hire and fire, many employers have made it clear they prefer males as workers to avoid the expenses associated with maternity leave. Industries that have been associated with female labor have been especially hit by cutbacks. This was despite the fact that women, in the rural areas, generally get only around 77% of men's wages for the same work. Moreover, in the rural areas, given the incentives for families to take responsibility for growing more on the land and the common migration of men toward city work, agriculture itself is increasingly becoming a female activity.

Thus, since more than 80% of Chinese women still live in rural areas, traditional attitudes toward women still strongly affect their lives. Most importantly, it is the still common practice of women to leave their native villages and move to the village of their new husbands, thus making their own social position less secure than that of their spouses. Sadly, rising school fees are making it more and more difficult for families to afford to send their daughters (and sons) to school. Another issue, of course, is the simple reality that the schools are often too far away to make it convenient to send one's daughters. These pressures often mean keeping the girls out of school.

Among the urban and more educated classes, women have made important strides, but they are limited. They consti-

tute around 14% of the communist party's membership, but their representation goes drastically down as one looks at the higher ranks of party administration. Although traditional values often prevail with regard to women's roles, the new openness has allowed Chinese women far more outlets to reflect on their circumstances. The new social and political openings have allowed for an enormous expansion of media outlets from radio talk shows to magazines that often frankly discuss women's concerns. If issues like sex, domestic violence and individual self-fulfillment were hardly discussed at all a generation ago, today they are often a common part of the public culture.

Moreover, as has happened in other parts of Asia, fetuses, once determined to be female by modern technologies like ultrasound, are more likely to be aborted. And when such drastic choices are not taken it is also common for rural families to simply not register their newly born daughters, a decision that can have drastic effects on the young women later when their lack of legal existence will hurt their chances for education and health benefits. Here again, China is following the path common elsewhere in Asia, where the number of boys sharply exceeds the number of girls. For China, official reports suggest there are 100 women for every 119 males.

Clearly these "missing" Chinese females may merely be unreported, but it is clear as well that in China, as with many other Asian countries, the traditional preference for boys still determines the numbers of female fetuses that will be carried to term and eventually raised. Given the

extraordinary imbalance between males and females that is developing in parts of the country the nation's leaders are finally coming to the realization that they have to act decisively to deal with the problem. The rules against using modern technology to make gender based abortion decisions have been significantly strengthened. President Hu Jintao has officially spoken of the need to deal with the problem while a commission has been appointed to investigate the growing crisis, that some have predicted will leave China within only a few decades with tens of millions of males unable to find potential wives.

The long-established "one-child policy" has, of course, been very controversial both inside and outside China. Yet until recently, no one would argue against the importance of China maintaining a stable rather than constantly rising population. But the burden of adhering to the population control measures affected women more often than men. They are, of course, the principal targets for efforts to monitor fertility and are most responsible for pressuring people to adhere as well.

On an international level, the "face" of China has become far more feminine recently. Vice Premier Wu Yi became very well known in her role as the leader of the delegation Beijing sent to Washington during the summer of 2007 to help reconcile tensions within the Sino-American relationship. She was recently named the third most powerful woman in the world by the influential Forbes Magazine.

In short, Chinese women have experienced extraordinary changes during the 20th century although those changes have been most obvious in more urban areas and especially in large coastal cities like Shanghai and, of course, on Taiwan and in Hong Kong. However much these women's lives have been enriched by the changes, most Chinese women remain in the huge Chinese interior, much less affected by the changes brought on by modernity.

The Internet

Like so much of the rest of the world Chinese society ended the 20th century grappling with the meaning of the emergence of the personal computer and the networking of much of the globe through the Internet. Even in the People's Republic, which initially lagged behind in computer use, sales are booming as parents buy PCs hoping to give their children an edge in the future job market. The government itself has committed the country to a major Internet presence as it moves into the new millennium. The Internet, which included no more than 100,000 people in

Shanghai's High Speed Mag Lev Train

Photo by Steven Leibo

46

1996, was said to have reached over 253 million users by 2008. While it is more and more common for Chinese citizens to have Internet access from their homes today, the country also has almost two million internet cafes. In fact, the Chinese are apparently now the most prolific users of the internet globally. The leadership has joined in. In 2008 both premier Wen Jiabao and President Hu Jintao signed up for their own Chinese language Facebook pages.

The government, while well aware of the importance of the Internet to its goal of building a modern economically sophisticated nation, is also aware of how easily the Internet can bring in unwanted outside influences and undermine the communist party's power. For example, when mainland Chinese students used the Internet to create their own organizations dedicated to protesting Japanese occupation of controversial islands, the leadership became uncomfortable and closed down the student networks. 1998 saw the first arrest of a Chinese businessman specifically for the crime of distributing Chinese e-mail addresses to overseas organizations.

Citing the growing number of sites devoted to vices from gambling to pornography, the government recently ordered 18,000 Internet cafes to close down temporarily, accusing them of having allowed children to play adult-only games. This is an issue about which many Americans are themselves concerned. The effort to keep the internet under control continues. The authorities have decreed that anyone who writes a web blog or keeps a personal webpage must register with the government. They also employ thousands of people to browse the web and block "questionable" material. Still their effectiveness has frequently been shown to be relatively limited, given the availability of various software resources that allow for accessing supposedly "forbidden sites."

Clearly the Chinese government is concerned about both the positive and negative aspects of the Internet. It is worried about its potential to cause internal disruptions. But it is equally concerned about of losing out on the new globalized world economy that is emerging partly through the Internet. The Internet represents both a tool to integrate China further into the world economy and a threat of further Westernization of the sort the government found so threatening in 1989. Do not expect China's "Internet dilemma" to be resolved any time soon. Those concerns were most obvious over the last year as Beijing and the Internet giant Google sparred over charges that the latter's sites had been hacked by authorities in search of political dissidents. This threw into question Google's continuing presence in the ever growing Chinese internet market. Eventually the clash saw Google relocating its operations to Hong Kong. American Secretary of State Hillary Clinton weighed in with criticisms of China's Internet practices that were, to say the least, not particularly well received by Chinese authorities.

Shanghai's Stock Exchange building

China

The Price: China's
Environmental Crisis

Just as China's traditional leaders were often judged by their ability to maintain adequate levees against the all-too-frequent floods caused by the Yellow River, today's leaders are likely to be judged by their ability to regulate and preserve the environment for the nation's future generations. Unfortunately if such a judgment does come about, her leaders are likely to have a lot to explain. China's extraordinary commitment to modernization has often come at the price of destroying the environment and putting the people's health seriously at risk.

In recent years, not only has China had to deal regularly with flooding caused by deforestation. Many in the world were horrified in late-2005 by images of the Songhua River in China's far north saturated with carcinogenic chemicals floating by Harbin, a city of 3.8 million people, that suddenly found itself without water for days. Even more disturbing were early reports, uncovered by "muckraking" local Chinese journalists, that the government had initially tried to cover up the spill. This was an error similar to the SARS cover up a few years earlier.

The chemical spill into the Songhua was obviously an accident. But an even more environmentally catastrophic development has been China's abundant use of coal, the world's highest, to fuel most of her industrial growth. The resulting pollution has strongly hurt the quality of air in large parts of China and damaged the health of countless people.

More quietly and far from the headlines has been the growing desertification of much of the country literally from north-central China to Inner Mongolia and Gansu Province. Desert landscapes, which once competed with rivers and lush grasslands for space in these regions, are now growing enormously. Today the residents' lives are dominated by the drying out of the land and the ever present threat of huge dust clouds that can easily kill those caught within their grasp.

Even the Yellow River has been impacted. Where once it readily inundated north-central China, today a combination of factors, from poorly planned economic development to overgrazing and the slowly rising temperatures, has created a situation that has seen extended periods when the Yellow River has not even made it to the open sea. In fact, in 2003 the river reached such a low level that 12% of the entire country was short of water while one-third of the fish that once lived within its waters are said to have become extinct.

It is also worth noting that given the common international condemnation of China's environmental problems, estimates are that between 20% and 25% of the pollution the Chinese emits is released while making goods for foreign countries. In a sense, those foreign consumers are enjoying the fruits of Chinese manufacturing while exporting their own pollution back to China.

While recent changes in attitude and new long-term goals offer some reason for optimism, it is also true that historically many environmental organizations around the world have morphed into successful political movements. This is something the Communist party is determined to avoid. Thus it is reasonable to assume that China's ability to deal successfully with its many environmental challenges may be severely hampered by the national leadership's concern about the emergence of movements that might effectively check its authority.

Looking more broadly, the issue is hardly a mere Chinese domestic issue. We must not forget the very real challenge of climate instability caused by global warming. If continued unchecked, it could see significant parts of the world and much of China's recent accomplishments destroyed by rising waters near great cities like Shanghai. More immediate is the significant damage being caused by more violent storms in some areas and drought, an increasingly common reality, in others.

It is, of course, important to add that China's contributions to the global CO_2 emissions that are largely causing the problem are becoming more significant each year. China is said to have caught up with the United States as an "annual" emitter of CO_2 gasses although its cumulative contribution of these—that last a hundred years plus in the atmosphere— will continue to be far less than the United States. Ominously China still continues vigorously to build more and more coal plants to meet it exploding need for energy.

China's reputation took a significant hit during late 2009 when it was widely seen as having played a significant role in the Copenhagen climate talks' having accomplished so little. Apparently, Chinese officials were particularly unhappy with demands for formal monitoring of their emissions being included in any potential international treaty to succeed the earlier Kyoto Accords. They were more interested in offering improvements in energy efficiency as measured against GNP than more absolute reductions. By the time the conference ended, China had taken part in talks with some of the major players in international climate negotiations. These nations from the United States to India forged what became known as the Copenhagen Accord, which many hoped would move the process along toward more formal agreements.

But if China was less than cooperative in forging a new international consensus its leaders were making extraordinarily significant decisions about the nation's future energy use by using their significant influence to nurture the nation's green industries and to position the economy to be a major player in the sale of new non carbon based technologies.

China's Energy Challenge

Like the rest of the world, the People's Republic faces critical energy choices over the next several years. China is growing very fast, and the growth of its energy needs is one of the most important features of our modern world. Overall, the story of China's energy use is a mixed one.

The best way to understand the patterns of recent Chinese energy usage is to recognize a series of distinct periods. From 1949 to 1980, it followed the Soviet model, that basically meant state-subsidized energy prices and no concern about the environment. In the early 1980s, China began an aggressive effort to manage energy much more efficiently and did so even as it had also begun going down its now famous path of explosive economic growth. The PRC did so quite successfully. Even as the nation's GDP doubled over the decade of the 1990s, its energy use only went up by a fourth.

Unfortunately, in the years after the new century began, the commitment to energy efficiency seemed for a time to collapse even as its energy needs continued to grow. More recently China has begun again a major commitment to improve its energy efficiency. The newest five-year plan specifically calls for the nation's energy consumption per unit of GDP to drop by 20% below 2005 levels by 2010.

That, of course, is in the context of a growing Chinese GDP. This still means a greater and greater demand for energy. For example, the Chinese have already begun to import additional coal to meet their demands and are investing billions in an Iranian oil field while becoming an even bigger importer of Saudi Arabian oil than the United States. In 2009, they triumphantly opened up a big new oil pipeline from central Asia to add to its available supplies. In late 2009 a new pipe line to transport natural gas from Turkmenistan to China was opened with great fanfare. More positively, it also announced plans to close some older less efficient industrial plants, many of which emit particularly large amounts of pollutants.

There is significant evidence that China is beginning to confront the challenge of converting its energy base more seriously.

Travel on the Yangtze River

In contrast to earlier years, China's current leaders do understand the problems. The nation has already committed itself to expanding significantly the number of nuclear reactors with plans that vastly exceed the goals established within any other nation.

Efforts are also underway to introduce alternative energy methods, to design "greener" communities and to push up mileage standards on vehicles. That last issue is particularly important since China passed the United States in 2009 as the largest global market for automobiles. They are also embracing vehicle energy standards that American car dealers have long rejected and are only now adopting under pressure from the Obama administration. More significantly China has announced that it wants to move dramatically into the development and eventual production of completely electric cars. Impressively the Chinese spent approximately $12 billion in 2007 to develop various forms of green energy. By 2009, they were investing more in clean energy than even the Obama administration. Under the pressure of the world economic downturn of 2008, Beijing like so many other nations

began to "prime" their economy with billions of dollars in stimulus money. A particularly large percentage of this was specifically directed toward building the nation's green energy infrastructure. For example, while its growing deserts are a major threat to society, they are also important areas for solar production. The government has already committed $200 billion to developing it.

Concerned about the nation's energy security, many Chinese businesses have made significant progress in developing sophisticated technologies to convert coal to a liquid form usable for transport. The question remains in what final form such efforts will emerge. Limited technology does exist to carry out coal liquefaction in a fashion that removes atmospheric pollutants from sulfur to CO_2. Nevertheless, it is significantly more expensive than making the conversion from coal to liquid without such environmental concerns.

The final decisions on China's efforts to meet both her security and environmental needs have not yet been made. Still there are reasons for some optimism. In fact, the Chinese government recently issued an official report outlining China's failure to

protect its environment properly during its generation-long effort to modernize the country.

As in the United States, a growing awareness of the importance of introducing alternative energy sources into the mainstream of China's energy grid is growing dramatically. Moreover, China's industrial establishment has taken up the challenge with a clear commitment. Although its production has still largely been for the foreign market, China has already become by far the largest producer of photo-voltaic cells.

Energy production is yet another area of important future cooperation between the United States and China. While some worry about a future geopolitical energy competition between the United States and China over fossil fuels found in nations like Venezuela, Sudan and Iran, a much more positive outcome may well emerge as the world's two greatest energy importers begin to cooperate on green energy production. Signs of that more positive future are emerging. Already there exists the new private-industry based Joint US-China Cooperation on Clean Energy initiative created with exactly that pur-

China

pose in mind. The Obama administration has signaled an interest in establishing an even more formal energy cooperation model. If the world is to avoid the dangers of resource wars based on fossil fuels and the worse effects of global warming, such cooperation is absolutely vital.

China at the Copenhagen Climate Talks

In December 2009, the Chinese premier Wen Jiabao arrived in Copenhagen as part of the more than hundred world leaders to take part in the effort to advance humanity's effort to confront a warming climate. That challenge, of course, has been caused by the burning of fossil fuels that have dramatically increased the ability of greenhouse gases to maintain the earth's long-term temperature balance. The result as increasingly understood around the planet is a dramatic altering of the global climate. However, this time China's circumstances were quite different from previous meetings.

When the first efforts began to confront the climate crisis in the mid 1990s China was still only just emerging from its long period of economic stagnation. As an official "developing" country, it was not obligated to carry out the carbon emissions cuts of the long-developed powers. Moreover, that did make sense. After all, the Western countries, themselves long industrialized, had emitted the vast amount of the long-lasting green house gases like CO_2 that were causing the problem.

Nevertheless, by 2009, the situation was entirely different. China itself was now extraordinarily more industrialized than it had been only a generation before. Moreover, it had become the leading emitter of such green house gases. It had become obvious that developing countries, of which China was the most important member, had to be brought under the carbon reduction regime if the world were to have any chance of staving off the worst aspects of dramatic climate change.

From the perspective of many developing countries, though, that reality seemed quite unfair. After all, their populations per capita used infinitely less energy than citizens of the developed countries and were themselves in the process of bringing their citizens' lifestyles up to western standards.

Nevertheless, over the last few years the government has recognized that, justice aside, China itself is deeply vulnerable to the threat of climate change. It began to speak, if not of exact carbon reductions, of efforts to make their economy more energy efficient by dramatically lowering the amount of energy they used relative to GDP growth. In short, it had to make the economy much more energy efficient,

but not to offer exact reductions. It was a compromise that complemented their status as a still developing country. But it was not well received in many quarters, especially Washington. Of course, Washington's approval of China's policy is an absolute prerequisite for meaningful American carbon reduction targets.

At the Copenhagen Conference itself, China was widely criticized in some quarters for resisting calls for international monitoring of their emissions and for demanding that the developed world contribute more to the developing nations' efforts to reduce their carbon emissions. Eventually, the conference ended without the world reaching a consensus on legally binding international carbon emission caps. While many blamed China for contributing to that failure, it was true as well that the American president arrived at the conference unable to commit his own country to the level of international cooperation necessary to confront the challenge of climate change. Eventually the United States and China, as well as an increasingly growing number of other nations, signed the much weaker "Copenhagen Accord." The simple reality, though, is that until both the United States and China become more willing to confront the challenge, little is likely to be accomplished in this critical area.

China's Olympic Challenge

Given how much controversy surrounded China's decade-long effort to bring the Olympics to Beijing, it should not be a surprise that in the final year-long run up to the games, one issue after another rose to complicate Chinese efforts to present an unsullied event to the world. It began with a series of product recalls, from children's toys to pharmaceuticals and cosmetics. The government initially reacted defensively. But it later proactively promised better supervision of those export industries after China's international position had taken a major hit.

Even before that crisis simmered down, China's international human-rights record, both international and domestic, began to arouse concern. With reference to the former, China's long-time energy-driven ties to the government of the Sudan came under increasing international concern due to the general sense that Beijing could do more to pressure the Sudanese government to end the genocidal murders reported in the western province of Darfur. Domestically, China's found itself internationally embarrassed as the first large-scale demonstrations against Chinese rule in decades broke out in Tibet.

Most upsetting to the Chinese leadership were probably the fairly widespread

calls for a boycott of the Olympics. This was the sort of international condemnation that had so effectively ruined Moscow's Olympic effort in 1980. But by the time the games began in August 2008 the world seemed willing to give the Chinese a chance to live up to their promise of a very successful and well organized Olympic celebration. For the most part they did. The opening ceremonies were as impressive as anything ever seen at an Olympic venue, and for the most part, the games went off very successfully. In a great many ways, the 2008 Olympics had accomplished with an extraordinary level of success the same symbolism that Tokyo's 1964 and South Korea's 1988 Olympics had. In a sense, China's successful Olympic effort showed that it was back as a major player on the international scene. However, the truth of that assertion ironically would not become fully obvious until later that fall as the world's economies fell into an economic crash much more serious that seen for decades.

The Future: The People's Republic

For much of human history China was at the forefront of the human experience in both the arts and sciences. Indeed, in the early 19th century China's economy has been estimated to have equaled a third of the world manufacturing output. But that extraordinary series of accomplishments ground to a halt in the mid 19th century as the West, newly invigorated by the Enlightenment and the Industrial Revolution, surged ahead. For almost two hundred years, dramatic internal problems and external pressures ranging from Western imperialists to Japanese invaders kept China from regaining its traditional place at the forefront of the human drama.

However, things have now changed. The generation-long surge of economic building set off by Deng Xiaoping has helped China pull itself out of the two-century-long doldrums in which it had fallen. In fact, even as the world entered into what seemed likely to be an extended economic downturn during the late fall of 2008, China appeared better prepared than many to weather the challenge by virtue of its long built-up economic reserves and prompt action in stimulating its economy domestically. Be early 2010 that expectation had become the reality as China's economy, temporarily stalled by the recession, came roaring back. It was stirred by the massive government stimulus package that not only put people back to work but saw enormous investment in that nation's infrastructure. These were precisely the sort of investment the still developing nation would have needed in the coming decades whether the recession had occurred or not.

As a matter of fact, in many ways the downturn that hit the global economy might well be seen one day as the true "coming out" party for the People's Republic in a way that even the spectacularly successful 2008 Olympics did not quite live up to. After all, China entered the global downturn still seen as a thriving export nation so dependent on selling its goods abroad, especially to the consumer crazed Americans, that it was surely going to be among the victims of the global recession. Nevertheless, as the global economy spiraled down, China's leaders not only ambitiously launched a massively ambitious stimulus plan to enhance the nation's infrastructure. They did so in a fashion likely to make its transition into the 21st century more successful. Moving from huge and ambitious expansions of the nation's high-speed rail systems to a green energy package significantly larger than what Americans were spending under their own stimulus efforts, China began moving beyond the recession much faster than many initially imagined. Even more importantly, they began efforts to make sure their own peoples' purchasing behavior would in the future be strong enough to lessen the dependence on international exports.

However, the fact remains that over the last two years some of the most significant developments in China included the regime's growing intolerance of dissent and the fact that it had to commit hundreds of billions of dollars to revive the economy after the disaster of 2008. The stimulus may have worked, but it was still based on government spending, not on a healthy world economy ready and eager to buy Chinese goods. Eventually the stimulus will end. If the government continues to show the level of intolerance it has in recent years, pressures may soon build up that could once again bring into question the legitimacy of the CCP to rule. For the moment, though, that challenge, apparently almost always in the background of the leadership's thoughts, was averted. For the moment at least, Beijing has plenty of reasons to be pleased and to be relieved by its growing influence in the world.

By 2010 it was more and more obvious that Deng Xiaoping's long-term goal of bringing China back from the "dead," caused by generations of imperialism, Japan militancy and the excesses of Mao's administration, were largely becoming issues of an increasingly forgotten past. Of more immediate concern for much of the world is the impact of a newly powerful and consumption oriented China.

For example, many have warned about the dangers of China's industrialization for the world's environment. The nation's recent emergence as the country that spews the most green house gases in the world is only the most obvious example of the global impact on international prices of China's growing need for oil and other commodities. These are hardly pessimistic long-term concerns. By 2008, many of those fears were proving prescient as China's new appetites for food and energy were playing a significant role in the price rises that were becoming ever more common globally. At least they were so until the international recession that began in the late fall of 2008 temporarily halted that momentum.

The only thing that is certain is that one of the world's great peoples has found its way into the modern industrialized world as a more confident major player. Enormous adjustments will have to be made, not only for the Chinese people, but for their leaders as well. China is not only entering the modern world, but it is also transforming itself as it goes. The leadership is committed to making that leap toward the future while maintaining itself in power. The dissident movement fights for and undergoes a political transformation as well. The democracy movement may not attract large numbers of followers. But movements based on spirituality, from the Falun Gong to Catholicism, have attracted large numbers of new followers whose strength has clearly made the country's leadership feel threatened. Within the country a new middle class—estimated at almost twenty percent—is emerging that is eventually likely to make its voice heard at the highest levels. That is something that was less true only a few years ago.

Perhaps of even greater importance is the growing economic gap between those Chinese who have gained the most from China's entrance into the more capitalistic globalized economy and the hundreds of millions of Chinese who have been left behind. Today's leaders are finding themselves increasingly having to confront the social problems caused by that growing gap, even as local uprisings, usually directed against land confiscations or industrial pollution, are becoming more and more common.

Nevertheless, today's Chinese leaders have every reason to feel satisfied. They handled the last two year's economic challenges with a very professional and long-term plan not only to stimulate the economy, but to do so in a fashion that emphasized those energy-efficient policies and technologies likely to serve it very well in the new century. Not that many democracies could claim the same success.

Spring 2008's earthquake

China-Hong Kong

HONG KONG
Special Administrative Region of the PRC
since July 1997

Hong Kong Harbor

Photo by Steven Leibo

Area: 398 square miles.
Population: 6,977,700 – 2008 estimate
GDP per capita: $42,700 (2009 est. purchasing power parity)

The former British Crown Colony of Hong Kong consists of four distinct areas. The first is the island of Victoria (better known as Hong Kong Island) immediately off the coast. The second part is the small area known as Kowloon, at the tip of the peninsula jutting from the Chinese mainland toward Victoria. Between Victoria and Kowloon lies one of the world's busiest and most beautiful harbors in the world though the air pollution in recent years has diminished the number of days when its beauty can be easily appreciated.

The third part is composed of the "New Territories," which extend northward from Kowloon to the Chinese border. Kowloon is connected by rail to the Chinese cities of Shenzhen and Guangzhou and during 2009 one of the big issues of the day was whether Hong Kong would take part in creating an ultra high speed railroad from the former colony northward.

In recent years the largest of the islands, Lantau has become much more developed. The relatively new and ultra modern international airport is located on the island as well as a Hong Kong's own Disney Land that has been success-

ful enough to be planning an expansion of the property.

Most of the area of Hong Kong consists of hills and low mountains, but there are enough level lands in the New Territories for large quantities of food to be harvested. It is actually dependent for much of its food and water on the mainland of China. The population is almost totally Chinese, many of them having arrived since 1949 in order to find greater safety, freedom and economic opportunity than was allowed on the mainland of China. The climate is subtropical and experiences monsoon rains in the summer, but is relatively cool in the winter.

Realizing the potential value as a naval base, although not seeing at first the commercial possibilities of Hong Kong, the British annexed it from the Manchus in 1842, after the first Opium War. Under an effective British administration, and sharing in the increase of British trade with and investments in China during the nineteenth and early twentieth centuries, Hong Kong experienced rapid growth as a port. Kowloon was annexed in 1860, after Anglo-French forces again attacked China. The New Territories were added in 1898 in order to provide agricultural land and living space for the growing population but were held on a 99-year lease. It was the impending end

of that lease that brought about the eventual return of Hong Kong to Chinese sovereignty in 1997.

Toward Unification with the Mainland

Much of Hong Kong's recent economic success is directly tied to the changing policies of the People's Republic of China. The ideologically driven PRC of Mao Zedong hardly needed Hong Kong's economic strengths, but Deng Xiaoping's arrival to power in the late 1970s brought change. Deng was determined to open China up to the world and to begin that effort in the southernmost parts of China. Under the circumstances, the British colony, with its abundant knowledge of both China and the Western world was in a perfect position to contribute to and take advantage of Beijing's changing economic policies.

Just north of the Hong Kong border, Beijing established special economic zones that, coupled with Hong Kong's strengths, eventually became the earliest engines of China's resurgence. During those years Hong Kong's economy, which had earlier been less tied to the People's Republic, actually began its first steps, at that point economic, in its reintegration with the mainland. Thus, China's economic accomplishments became Hong Kong's as well, and the momentum toward 1997's reunification with China had already begun.

Ironically, given some of the tensions that arose in the years before the 1997 hand-over of Hong Kong to the PRC, it was the British who had pushed for treaties to resolve the impending end of the 99-year leases of 1898. In Beijing's perspective, none of the nineteenth-century treaties imposed on China by the imperialistic West had any validity, so there was no reason to consider 1997 any different.

However, the British wanted the fate of their colony, the last Asian remnant of their once enormous Asian colonial system, resolved, and insisted on negotiations. During those years the two powers worked well together and the Sino-British Joint Declaration on Hong Kong was signed in 1984. The United Kingdom even agreed to coordinate its changes in Hong Kong with the People's Republic.

Within the agreements, Britain unilaterally gave up the right to change the Hong Kong political system. For more than a hundred years that had meant being ruled undemocratically by British governors sent from London. For its part, Beijing

Hong Kong Disney Entrance   Photo by Steven Leibo

seemed an especially appropriate choice. His personal background had well prepared him to deal with challenges ahead. A Shanghai-born Chinese who spoke the same dialect as many of China's leaders, Tung lived for a decade in the United States and has many ties there. He has been involved with the United States Chamber of Commerce, the Hoover Institution and the Council of Foreign Relations.

He was even said to count former President Herbert Walker Bush among his personal friends. Moreover he had already served as an advisor in the British administration of Hong Kong. That China's leader Jiang Zemin favored him was also known previous to the election and no doubt helped his candidacy considerably.

A Not So Smooth Transition

Throughout early 1997 tensions ran high regarding the upcoming transition. Following through on its long-standing rejection of those political changes Britain had made since the hand-over agreement, Beijing repealed many of the new laws—some made within hours of the changeover.

During the transition there had also been considerable talk about the undemocratic aspects of Tung's election though with little appreciation that he was actually the most democratically elected leader in Hong Kong's history and the first Chinese. If anything, the tensions during the hand over underscored how little the two groups had come to understand each other despite more than a century of interaction.

The last minute British efforts toward democratization clearly complemented Western political and social values though

promised to leave the existing economic and social systems essentially unchanged for at least fifty years after 1997 and to permit a degree of self-government.

In the years immediately preceding the hand-over, there was considerable concern among Hong Kong's residents about whether Beijing could be trusted to honor the promises it had made. For that reason, many people, especially white collar and professional workers, emigrated in considerable numbers. They numbered over 500,000 alone in the decade before the hand-over.

Unfortunately, during the last years before 1997 both Beijing and London showed an increasing willingness to violate the spirit of the 1984 treaty. Britain on its part, long happy with governing Hong Kong under its own benign colonial dictatorship, moved aggressively, especially under its last colonial governor, to transform Hong Kong into an increasingly democratic political entity, something Beijing had hardly agreed to. Even a bill of rights was introduced by 1991.

With the appointment of former Conservative Party MP, Chris Patten, to the post of Governor of Hong Kong in 1992, the British had apparently decided to take a stronger hand in determining the future of the colony's government prior to their withdrawal. Even before Governor Patten's appointment, the British had taken steps to strengthen the democratic process in Hong Kong. In September 1991, elections were held for 18 of the 61 seats on the Legislative Council (Legco). Sixteen of those seats were won by pro-democratic candidates. That election gave a considerable boost to the pro-democracy movement although it did not make the Chinese on the mainland happy. Two years, later, in 1995, the first truly free election took place.

Predictably, those last minute British changes aroused the anger of the Chinese government. The basic disagreement between the British and the Chinese had to do with the type of government Hong Kong would have. Beijing had in mind an executive-dominated government for Hong Kong, where the legislature plays the role of an adviser. The British in contrast were moving to establish a strong, elected legislative assembly and more freedoms than they themselves had ever tolerated.

In December of 1996 Tung Chee-hwa, a shipping company magnate, was elected by the 400 member selection committee to be the first chief executive for Hong Kong after the transition. Almost 6000 people had applied for membership in the committee and a final 400 eventually selected Tung. To many persons, Tung Chee-hwa

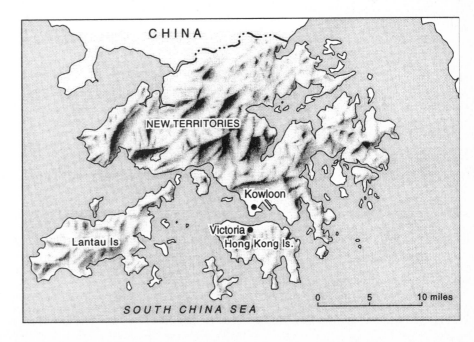

China-Hong Kong

Former Chief Executive Tung Chee-hwa

one might ask sarcastically why Britain had waited so long to introduce them. What they did not complement was efforts to make a smooth transition from Hong Kong's earlier status as a colony to its future as part of the People's Republic, which despite Western preferences, continues to be controlled by an authoritarian single-party government.

Hong Kong and China: The First Years

In the months leading up to the handover, commentators varied widely on what would occur next. Some predicted that China would dramatically transform the colony for the worst, stifling its freedoms and dynamic economy. Others insisted with equally great conviction that little would actually change within the former colony and that the doomsayers were raising unnecessary panic. They were both wrong. The first year after the transition turned out to be quite traumatic though for reasons few had predicted.

The principal menace arrived not from Beijing, but from the failing economies of her East and Southeast Asian neighbors. As well known financial institutions faltered and the Hong Kong markets plummeted, Hong Kongers found their life styles and hopes under siege. Throughout 1998 and early 1999 economic news continued to be very discouraging. Hong Kong, following the lead of its Southeast Asian neighbors moved into the worst recession since the early 1970s. Unemployment was up to a fifteen-year height and tourism, an important source of revenue down.

Responding to the crisis the government not only expended considerable resources to defend the Hong Kong dollar but announced several economic stimulus packages. Ironically, considering all the Western rhetoric about how Hong Kong

might be threatened by its reintegration into the People's Republic, Beijing now turned out to be a source of strength. Not only did the PRC's leaders work to defend Hong Kong's economy, they went as far as to threaten international currency speculators against efforts to weaken her currency and even began encouraging more mainland tourism there.

But what of all those fears of Beijing's new power over Hong Kong? The PLA soldiers who had marched into the territories with such fanfare in July 1997 withdrew from public eye. Perhaps most controversial were the new pressures upon the educational system regarding the expansion of education in Chinese. From the fall of 1998 the expectation was that Chinese, both the local Cantonese dialect and Mandarin, would become the principal language of instruction. Given the importance of English for international business, this demand was heavily criticized in some quarters.

Also of particularly significance was the furor raised in early 1999 over a ruling by the Hong Kong Court of Final Appeal that children born of Hong Kong residents had the right to reside in the former colony. Clearly a blessing for many Hong Kong parents of mainland children but one that raised considerable controversy over the local court's right to decide such important immigration issues and fears about a too large influx of new residents to Hong Kong especially as it was struggling with a financial turndown.

When, somewhat later, the Chinese National People's Congress, following a request by Tung Chee-hwa, chose to modify the Hong Kong court's decision, concerns were also raised about Beijing's growing power over Hong Kong. Eventually, by the spring of 2002 the news was filled with stories of the adult children of Hong Kong residents being forced to return to the PRC because they lacked the necessary papers to remain in Hong Kong.

Politically the long anticipated May 1998 elections brought the return to power of many of the former colony's most outspoken democrats. Martin Lee's Democratic Party did especially well in the elections, both in competition for those openly allocated seats and for those reserved for the professional classes.

Overall, it is clear that a majority of the Hong Kong population would like to see a more democratic environment. In both the elections of 2000 and 2004, local democrats won clear majorities. Still, in the election that took place during the fall of 2004, supporters of Beijing won 34 of the 60 possible seats. However, this was not an unexpected outcome given that the majority of members are not chosen in open elections. The election results hardly

Hong Kong Chief Executive Donald Tsang Yam-kuen

changed public attitudes. In the late fall of 2005 Hong Kong's streets were again full of demonstrators demanding direct elections for the former colony's leaders. But that enthusiasm failed to achieve much beyond its early starts. As we will see below, more recent elections have not seen a significant growth in voting support for the more democratic parties either.

Hong Kong between Two Worlds

In fact, Hong Kong's government has revealed no great commitment to expanding its resident's democratic rights. For example, in late 1999, when new councils were formed at the local levels they were even less democratic than their predecessors. Clearly, Hong Kong's new government, despite the gains made by some democratic activists, remained similar to the relatively open but also authoritarian regimes of countries like Singapore. In fact, when Anson Chan, who had long led Hong Kong's civil service, recently resigned she publicly decried the weakening of Hong Kong's publicly minded professional civil service.

As for the first Chief Executive, Tung Chee-hwa's his popularity dropped dramatically not only among the local population but among many of the former colony's most influential figures. For a time Tung managed to retain the all-important support of Beijing and was able to win his position anew when his first term expired in March of 2002. Despite his lessening public popularity the situation was different administratively. Early on Tung saw his powers enhanced by the introduction of a new ministerial system consisting of a fourteen-person cabinet of policy officials whom Tung personally selected.

Beijing's unwillingness to consider expanding Hong Kong's very limited experiments with democracy was reinforced in the spring of 2004 when the National People's Congress ruled that only China's central government had the right to modify the former British Colony's political structure. But while some decried the decision it was also clear that Hong Kong's people still retained enough power to limit the authority of their own government if they exerted themselves enough.

That "people power" was especially evident during the summer of 2003 when tremendous numbers of Hong Kong residents took to the streets to protest a proposed anti-subversion bill law that would have given the Hong Kong's leaders the right to ban certain groups and allow the police to carry out searches without warrants. Eventually, under pressure from the population, Tung Chee-hwa agreed to modify the measure and remove its most onerous provisions. Nevertheless, the crisis had contributed to the weakening of Tung's support.

By the winter of 2005 Tung had become increasingly unpopular and eventually resigned his office a full two years before this term was set to expire. Meanwhile Beijing, once again asserting its authority, announced to considerable controversy that Tung Chee-hwa's successor as Chief Executive, Donald Tsang Yam-kuen, would only be allowed to serve out the final two years of Tung's term in office rather than the full five-year term of a new chief executive.

For many in Hong Kong, Beijing's decision was another example of China's willingness to interpret at its convenience Hong Kong's constitution. Public polls have also reinforced the impression that China is losing much of its popularity among Hong Kong's population. Over the last year the numbers claiming to be dissatisfied with Beijing has grown considerably.

As for Donald Tsang himself, he eventually won election in his own right in a contest against pro-democracy leader Alan Leong. Chinese Prime Minister Wen Jiabao then officially recognized the result by awarding Mr. Tsang the "instrument of appointment" at a ceremony that took place at the famous Chinese leadership compound of Zhongnanhai. Mr. Tsang's new term began on July 1, 2007, exactly a decade after Hong Kong officially returned to China.

Within a few months Mr. Tsang found himself facing a particularly impressive critic. Anson Chan, Hong Kong's long serving head of its civil service under both British and Chinese rule, won election to the legislative council of Hong Kong in December 2007. Ms. Chan, a formidable politician and bureaucrat, had emerged in the period after Hong Kong's formal return to China as both a member of Tung Chee-hwa's government and one of its best-known critics. Later, after she left her position as the head of the civil service, Chan became for a time a leading advocate of constitutional and more specifically democratic reform in the former colony. This stance allowed her to consolidate opposition forces behind her electoral victory.

But Chan did not prove to be a long-term political foe. During the summer of 2008 she announced that she would not stand for reelection in the upcoming elections. When those elections did occur, many expected the democratic movement to weaken significantly, given Beijing's heightened status after its successful Olympics and growing public concerns that centered more on economic issues than democratic aspirations. In the end, though, the democratic movement representation, while weakened somewhat by the loss of two seats in Hong Kong's legislature, still retained enough to remain major players in Hong Kong's political life.

The Environment

The environment is becoming more and more of a problem. The air pollution that has been growing over China's cities is severely affecting the living conditions in Hong Kong. Most recently, it was announced that during 2009 the air quality at street level in parts of Hong Kong was at life-threatening levels one in eight days of the year. While air quality at the higher levels was somewhat better, the murky haze that floats above Hong Kong has gotten so bad in recent years that it is not only threatening human health, but depressingly the views within Hong Kong's harbors, which were once among the most beautiful in the world.

But all of this is hardly China's fault. Indeed authorities claimed that the worst increases were the result not of regional pollution coming in from the People's Republic, but locally produced pollutants stemming from Hong Kong's own fossil fuel energy uses. Local medical experts report that the increasingly foul air contributes to as many as 2000 deaths a year. The employees of the many international companies that have bases in Hong Kong are becoming more and more vocal about the problem. However, there is little evidence that the situation is having an immediate economic impact on the former colony.

The Future

Particularly important for Hong Kong's future has been the obvious commitment Beijing's leaders continue to feel toward the former British colony. After all, one might have imagined a greater emphasis on Shanghai as the latter continued to grow. Nevertheless, it has remained obvious that despite the PRC's devotion to Shanghai, Hong Kong's vitality continues to be a very important priority. But still, one might assume that over the years, as the People's Republic of China enters the world economy even more directly through its membership in the World Trade Organization, the importance of Hong Kong as an economic intermediary between China and the world might well diminish.

Hong Kong

China-Hong Kong

For the immediate future, though, there seems little reason to be concerned. Indeed, the new high-speed trains that were beginning to emerge within the People's Republic are now expected to have an impact on Hong Kong's future as well. In fact, by 2015, Hong Kong will be linked to Guangzhou by one of those 300-kilometer-per-hour trains. The proposed plan encountered considerable resistance especially among those New Territory residents who would be most directly impacted by the train. On the other hand, the proposal was backed by Hong Kong's merchant community, which expected it significantly to raise the number of mainland tourist arrivals in the territory. In January 2010, the plan passed the territory's legislative council by a vote of 31 to 21. It is clearly another example of how, in so many ways, China itself was being knitted back together by the new railroad planned to link Hong Kong more closely to the Chinese mainland and by those that were being build within the People's Republic itself.

On the other hand, the hopes of some that Hong Kong might over time become more democratic have clearly been dashed.

Moreover, Beijing's willingness to exert its will when it chooses has been demonstrated more and more frequently. Donald Tsang, the SAR's leader, has promised to move Hong Kong even further toward full democracy by the end of his term in 2012. Realistically there are plenty of reasons to be cynical. After all, the chances that Hong Kong will be allowed to move toward democracy faster than the People's Republic itself seem quite unlikely. The fact that China has in the last few years become relatively less tolerant of dissent makes any further opening within Hong Kong even less likely than it was once thought to be.

Economically, as the world's most recent economic slowdown commenced, Hong Kong found the mainstays of its economy, finance, property and trade all weakening dramatically, even as the first months of 2009 saw its exports drop by almost 25%. Hong Kong's position appeared particularly vulnerable, given that its economy was especially tied to the export market, a sector that has been particularly hard hit by the 2009 recession. Recognizing that reality, its leadership announced its own extensive stimulus plans to provide jobs for the recently unemployed within Hong Kong and those who were expected to return home as other economies from the Gulf States to Macau weakened.

But 2010 saw quite a different situation emerging. Beijing's leadership committed itself to an enormous stimulus program. Not surprisingly it spilled over into Hong Kong as the numbers of Chinese who could visit and spend money dramatically rebounded even as the housing market surged again. By mid 2010, the first reports were that a healthy 8.2% growth rate had returned.

One interesting economic development of the last year that might offer a hint to Hong Kong's future was the decision by the American Internet giant Google to relocate its offices to Hong Kong. Apparently the decision was related both to China's increasing efforts to control its population's too open-ended access to the global media and to concerns about mainland-based hacking into Google's proprietary software. Whatever the motives, the fact that a global corporation was moving to Hong Kong rather than the reverse might offer an interesting hint of the future if the climate for foreign businesses in China itself deteriorates further.

Inside Hong Kong's famed Star Ferry

Photo by Steven Leibo

Macau Special Administrative Region of the People's Republic of China

MACAU
Portuguese Dependency until 1999

Senato Square, Macau

Area: 6 square miles
Population: 567,957 (July 2010 est.)
Per Capita GDP: $33,000 (2009) purchasing power parity
Chief Executive: Fernando Chui Sai-on since December 2009

Until its late 1999 return to the mainland, Macau was Portugal's only remaining overseas territory. Macau is divided about equally into Macau proper, which has a common land frontier with the Chinese mainland, and two nearby islands. The terrain is mostly flat. The offshore waters are muddy with silt carried by the Pearl River. The climate is subtropical with a summer monsoon and a relatively cool winter. Except for a small community of Portuguese (officials, soldiers, police, missionaries, businessmen, etc.) and other Europeans, the population is overwhelmingly Chinese.

Portugal acquired Macau in the mid-16th century for use as a base from which to trade with nearby Canton by an agreement with the Ming dynasty of China. It prospered in the 18th century, but during the 19th it was rapidly overshadowed by

Hong Kong. From its earlier days of prominence, Macau has retained some beautiful old buildings and something of a Mediterranean flavor. It has a reputation, partly justified, as a center of opium and gold smuggling and assorted vice. Gambling is unquestionably the major feature of the economy, and auto racing and bullfighting have been introduced as well.

The new government of Portugal after 1974 wanted to return Macau to China, but Beijing would not accept it because of the disturbing effect such a transfer might have had on Hong Kong. Portugal did agree to allow more internal autonomy to its former colony in 1976 and granted it increased powers in 1990. After the Sino-British agreement was reached on Hong Kong in 1984, negotiations began between Lisbon and Beijing for the reversion of Macau to Chinese control. It was agreed in April 1987 that reversion would take place in December 1999, along lines similar to those already worked out for Hong Kong. Certain concessions were granted to Macau's leaders. For example, it was later agreed that capital punishment, com-

mon in the People's Republic, would not be employed in Macau.

In the months leading up to the handover two issues dominated the life of the colony. First the on-going gang violence and the question of who would lead the colony after its return to mainland control. As in Hong Kong, a special committee of 100 notables was formed to plan for Macau's future leadership. Edmund Ho, the 44-year-old son of a well known diplomat and banker, was selected. More recently Fernando Chui Sai-on, who had served as the secretary for social and cultural affairs in Ho's administration, declared his own candidacy for chief executive in June of 2009. The following July he was "elected" by 282 of the potential 300 votes possible in the election committee. There were no "no" votes.

In sharp contrast to Hong Kong's reversion to China, Macau's was a much smoother transition with a considerably more cooperative attitude on both sides. Nevertheless, there were some features of the transition that were harder on Macau than Hong Kong. For example, unlike

China-Macau

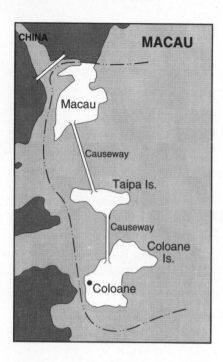

marily concerned with either business issues or ties to Beijing. The pro-democracy candidates did manage however to capture 21% of the vote and doubled their representation from one to two members.

But the fact remains that within Macau there has been no more of a renaissance of democracy than there has in Hong Kong. The largely anti-democratic tone was particularly obvious in the transition from the leadership of Edmund Ho to Fernando Chui Sai-on. It saw no real competitive contest for leadership and only a few blank ballots and absenteeism offered in opposition to Chui's election.

It is also true that the less populated Macau has had fewer problems than Hong Kong in reintegrating into the People's Republic. That does not mean that real problems have not emerged from time to time to complicate matters. Most recently there have been tensions over the former colony's system for legal education. Ironically students whose training has focused on the legal system of the mainland have fared far less well than those who have specialized in the more Portuguese-based system long in effect. Clearly those with a better knowledge of mainland law will most probably have an advantage in the future. But for the moment their options apparently remain limited compared to those who were trained in the more traditional legal system. This problem has emerged even as the lack of lawyers has become a significant problem given the growth of the casino industry.

Overall, Macau entered the millennium with a positive outlook. The economy has done relatively well in recent years although it too was hit hard by the world economic recession that began in the fall of 2008.

There has also been considerable progress in improving transport links between Macau and the outside world with particular progress made in linking Macau to Taiwan. Tourism is also looking up, and efforts to have Macau listed as one of the United Nation's "World Heritage" sites are in progress.

Former Macau Chief Executive Edmund Ho Hau-Wah

In another sign of Macau's evolution, the decision by the government to open up the former colony's gambling industry to international investment has attracted investors who are hoping to transform the once sleepy Macau into a Las Vegas-like gambling and resort destination capable of attracting a much larger number of visitors than ever before. While hoping the new investments will add to government revenues, Beijing is also aware of the potential problems and has already forbidden its own officials from gambling in Macau. Beijing's concern about its own officials' potential corruption was not the only impact of Macau's greater involvement in the globalized world economy. But there have been downsides as well to Macau's decision to become more involved in the world economy. Just as some American casinos had invested in Macau when they had been financially stronger, by 2009 there was talk of those same American businesses selling off Macau-based properties to make up for their own recent losses.

Gambling was not the only development that brought Macau into the international spotlight over the few years. As one of the principal means of putting pressure on the North Koreans regarding their nuclear programs, the American administration used its influence to freeze Pyongyang's financial assets in a local Macau bank.

There is also some sign that Macau's growth as the new "Las Vegas" of Asia is putting some strains on its relationship with Hong Kong. Some within the former English colony are clearly concerned that Macau might soon become a serious rival for foreign tourist dollars. For its part, Macau has taken to refusing entry to Hong Kong residents it finds unacceptable. Those recently rejected include a number of relatively influential Hong Kong political activists.

Hong Kong that had already put into place a largely home-grown bureaucracy, the departure of the Portuguese left Macau without as many trained administrators in place. To deal with the problem, the government arranged to have some of its civil servants trained in Singapore.

One important controversy was the mainland's decision during the fall of 1998 to station troops in Macau after the handover. It was a decision that clearly contradicted previous understandings, but one that was probably a logical outcome of Beijing's concern about criminal violence. For a time just before the turnover, gang warfare became a particularly violent part of the life of the colony. Once the turnover occurred, Beijing carried out a crackdown that drastically reduced the violence.

Politically the former colony has evolved in a fashion somewhat similar to its neighbor Hong Kong. The fall 2001 direct elections, which provided some of the representatives to the 27-seat assembly, resulted in a body filled largely by candidates pri-

Constructing Macau's new MGM Grand   Photo by Steven Leibo

Tibet

Globalization Meets Lhasa's Potala Palace

Area: 1,200,000 square miles, most above 14,000 feet

Population: 2,620,000. Officially 95% Tibetan (probably misleading because official Chinese sources only list Han Chinese with official permission to live in Tibet). Other ethnic groups are Han, Hue, Melba, Luoba, Naxi and Nu.

Status: September 1, 1965, declared Tibet Autonomous Region (TAR).

Note: The term Tibet and Tibetans can have many meanings. On one hand, it usually refers to what the Chinese now call the Tibetan Autonomous Region (TAR), roughly the area the modern Dalai Lamas governed. It is that region on which this "looking closer" section of our text focuses. But the term can have broader meanings. Of the 4.6 million ethnic Tibetans reported in a 1990 census, only 46% lived in the TAR while 54% lived in Western Chinese provinces from Qinghai and Gansu to Sichuan and Yunnan. This latter area might best be thought of an ethnographic extension of the Tibetan community. Of course, one cannot forget the influential Tibetan community that followed the 14th Dalai Lama into exile in the years after 1959 and established itself in nations from Nepal to India.

Introduction

Whether one arrives by bus, airplane or perhaps the world's first pressurized railroad train that began operating in July 2006, it soon becomes obvious that Tibet is something truly astonishing. Situated at an average height of 4,000 meters, most of the country is over 14,000 feet high. Tibet is found on what is known as the Qinghai-Tibet plateau, to which many have long referred as the "roof of the world." It is surrounded by four different mountain ranges: the Qilian Mountains, the Mt Kunlun-Bayan Har Mountains, the Mt Karokoram-Tanggula Mountains and, of course, the internationally famous Himalayas. The Tibet Autonomous Region itself is located on approximately half of this enormous region.

Sadly, for those interested in understanding the Tibetan situation, discussion of the issue is often marred by the emotionalism that both Tibet's supporters and the representatives of the People's Republic tend to carry into each discussion. The result is that all too often it is difficult to find an objective account of Tibetan-Chinese relations.

On the Tibetan side, charges from violations of human rights to genocide are often bantered about. The Chinese usually vehemently defend their control of Tibet and speak with pride of their liberation of the Tibetan people from the previously existing system of serfdom and peasant exploitation under which many had previously suffered. Putting the relationship in the context of larger global trends, it is of-

ten apparent that China's relationship with Tibet is similar to that found during the colonial era. That is, China frequently exhibits a recognizable "colonial" attitude of superiority toward the Tibetans. Tibetans for their part deeply resent that obviously unequal relationship.

More fundamentally, Beijing has usually viewed supporters of the exiled Dalai Lama as enemies seeking to dismember the Chinese homeland. When that support has come from official U.S. sources, such as the American Congress or even more dramatically from U.S. presidents, Beijing has felt particularly threatened. As a practical matter, pre-modern Tibet's cultural and ethnic identity long existed outside the direct control of China's many imperial governments. In fact, until recently Tibet's population did not include Han Chinese. Nevertheless, Tibet has long been under either direct or indirect Chinese influence. As so often is the case, zealots from both sides of the argument cite the historical record to justify their claims. It is to that early Tibetan history that we turn first.

Tibet's 7th Century Unification

Tibet has had a long and impressive national existence separate from that of China. This distinguishes it from other communities designated by Chinese authorities as separate "autonomous" or

China-Tibet

His Holiness The Dalai Lama of Tibet

"administrative" areas, locations from Macau to Hong Kong and or even the physically independent Republic of China on Taiwan, all which are products of recent historical developments.

The emergence of a unified Tibet occurred during the late 7th century as regional tribes were brought together under the leadership of Songsten Gampo who is today considered the first ruler of Tibet. Ironically, given later developments, Tibet's leader chose to solidify his relationship with his powerful Chinese neighbors by a marriage with a princess from the Tang dynasty. What is particularly interesting about the marriage is that while Buddhism was to that point relatively unknown in Tibet, it is thought that under the influence of the newly arrived bride, Wen Cheng, Buddhism began to grow in influence. During those years Buddhist missionaries from India, China and Nepal were apparently welcomed in Tibet, and it was scholarly Indian Buddhists who over time would have the most influence on the evolution of Tibetan Buddhism. Eventually Tibetan Buddhism would become far more important than the indigenous Bon tradition, and by the eighth century it was declared the official state religion. The transition did not come without considerable internal strife between the adherents of the two religious traditions.

During those early years of a unified Tibet, the nation was a major player in central Asian politics and drew cultural inspiration from both of its huge neighbors, China and India. Such basics as the use of butter, tea, cheese and knowledge of astrology came from China. Policies on monasteries and their financial arrangements were adopted from India. Also because of Indian influence, the Tibetans began using a written alphabetic writing system quite different from the ideographs that might have been borrowed from China, as so many other Eastern Asians eventually did. Today's Tibetan alphabet was adapted from an Indian script studied by one of Songsten Gampo's ministers. Meanwhile ties with China remained very strong. More than a hundred and fifty missions were undertaken between the two capitals, and many treaties were signed. But that relationship eventually ground to a halt by the early tenth century as both kingdoms, Tibetan and Chinese, collapsed.

Relationship with the Mongols

In contrast to the complicated relationship between China and Tibet in the late 7th through 9th centuries, by the time the Mongols rose as a power the two often competing nations had not been in contact for generations. But the emergence of the Mongol empire was to change all that dramatically.

By the 13th century Mongol tribes under Genghis Khan had burst out of central Asia, intending to conquer all whom they encountered. Arriving in Tibet by 1207, they forced the Tibetans to submit without a fight. The latter agreed to accept Mongolian suzerainty over Tibet and to pay tribute to the great khan in order to avoid a bloody invasion. But the decision only put off the violence to a later era when, after Tibet had stopped sending the required tribute, the forces of the new Khan Ogedai advanced toward Lhasa looting monasteries and killing all who opposed his forces.

In the aftermath, not only did Tibet make a full submission to the Mongols, but the Mongolian leaders decided to adopt the Tibetan religious traditions. Eventually a fortuitous tradeoff emerged: Mongolia would help Tibet in secular matters while the Tibetans served as Mongolia's spiritual guide. Thus began that complicated relationship that eventually saw Tibet's leaders serve as Mongolia's religious teachers, carrying out religious obligations, doing divination and other rituals deemed necessary for the good health of the Mongolian leadership. Within Tibet itself the Mongols chose to grant the Buddhist religious leaders from the Sakya monastery secular authority, thus creating the tradition of theocratic rule that would become the norm for most of Tibet's history until modern times.

By the time Kublai Khan arrived on the scene, Tibet was administered by a Tibetan leader who had once served as tutor to the great khan and was able to gain recognition from the Mongol ruler of his superior status as a religious leader. The best example of the relationship is the term Dalai Lama itself. The title is an obvious reflection of the relationship combining as it does the Mongolian word for "ocean," *dalai*, with the Tibetan word *"lama"* for spiritual teacher.

By the 14th century Sakya rule over Tibet ended, while the Mongols, during the same period, lost their control over China. During the following years, an era that paralleled the famous Ming dynasty, the Chinese had no administrative influence over Tibet. Ignoring that reality, Ming emperors continued to confer titles upon the Tibetans as if they still did.

The Emergence of Modern Tibet

It was not until the rise of the Geluk Sect (system of Virtue) that Tibet's modern history really began. That reforming tradition began with the career of the scholar, Tsongkapa, whose travels in the late 14th century convinced him of a profound moral decline. Eventually, he began to preach a revived Buddhism that emphasized strict monastic celibacy and academic study as the truth path to enlightenment. By 1409 Tsongkapa founded his own monastery: the famous Ganden Monastery just outside of Lhasa. It was the sect's choice of the Yellow Hat to distinguish themselves from the older "red hats" that was to give Tsongkapa's followers their best known name, the Yellow Hat Sect. Within only a few years two more monasteries, the Drepung and Sera, were constructed. These were religious settlements that housed over 15,000 monks on the eve of the 20th-century Chinese occupation. Even today, though they operate with significantly reduced numbers living in buildings that were only recently rebuilt, the monasteries continue to house hundreds of members.

Predictably, the rise of the Yellow Hat Sect aroused considerable tension with the older monastic Tibetan sects. During the following centuries, significant strife developed between the differing religious communities. By the early 17th century tensions had become so great that Karma Kagyu sect Tibetan king ordered the Geluk monasteries occupied. Moreover, the search for the newest reincarnation of the fourth Dalai Lama was forbidden. Eventually, with the help of the Mongols, who were still influential despite their withdrawal from China, the Yellow Hat Sect reasserted itself.

Early Modern Tibet and the Outside World

In 1644 China's new leaders, the Manchus, established themselves in power. Unlike their Ming predecessors, the Manchu Qing dynasty was to be quite involved in Tibetan developments. It was in this period that the first Chinese imperial

Lhasa Pilgrim
Photo by Steven Leibo

magistrate was stationed in Tibet while Qing forces regularly intervened within Tibet during periods of internal strife. They also dispatched an army to defend Tibet when Hindu Gurkhas threatened the nation from their base in Nepal. The Manchus were not the only regional power interested in Tibet.

From the perspective of the India-based British, Tibet was for centuries seen as a potentially significant route to Western China and an important buffer between themselves and growing Russian strength in Central Asia. During the late 18th century British diplomats and missionaries were able to enter Tibet relatively easily, a situation that the Manchus stopped by the end of the century. The Qing did so in part because, as so often before and after, China's leaders saw Tibet as deeply within their sphere of influence. They were understandably concerned about the presence of the English, who were by then becoming more and more powerful in India.

But Qing efforts to exclude them hardly diminished British interest. From the British perspective, a foothold in Tibet would make the growth of Russian influence in Central Asia easier to contain. Thus, by the early 20th century, British forces under Colonel Francis Younghusband invaded Tibet and easily destroyed the weak Tibetan forces sent against the invaders. By the summer of 1904, Lhasa was occupied by the foreign troops while the thirteenth Dalai Lama fled to Mongolia. While insisting that Tibet was part of China, the Qing government was powerless to oppose the British advance toward Lhasa. Once there Younghusband forced a treaty upon the Tibetans that in effect

made Tibet a protectorate of the British Empire. This was something the colonel's superiors in London had hardly authorized. Once word of the settlement arrived in England, the decision was made to repudiate significant parts of the agreement. Britain even officially agreed that Tibet was part of China, regardless of what the Tibetans themselves might think.

In the aftermath of the reasonably successful resolution of the crisis created by the Younghusband expedition, Beijing, in a burst of renewed confidence, sent troops to forcibly reenter Tibet. Following their arrival, the Qing forces worked to administer Tibet directly in a fashion that Chinese governments had not done for centuries. This time it was China, not Britain that was imposing its will on Tibet. Ironically, given earlier events, the Dalai Lama then fled to British India for support.

That renewed Chinese claim to Tibet in the early 20th century could not be maintained. In the aftermath of the Chinese Revolution of 1912, the Tibetans expelled the Chinese forces. The new Chinese Republic, the successor to the Manchus, was not in a position to challenge Tibet's assertion of independence. For the next several decades, two different Dalai Lamas successively governed Tibet as an independent, if not internationally recognized, sovereign country.

Tibet's Era of Independence 1912 to 1951

Unfortunately for Tibet's long-term future, during the several decades of Tibet's *de facto* independence the government failed to establish for itself either an internationally recognized legitimacy or the military power necessary to resist China if Beijing ever again chose to reassert its authority. Most importantly, the government was unable to move forward with a military modernization program that was opposed by Tibetan conservatives. Even more enervating was an explosion of internal violence that broke out between forces based at the famous Sera monastery and those in Lhasa. Nevertheless, Tibet did manage to defend itself successfully from occasional Chinese encroachments through the early 1930s.

Overall, those years represented an era when Tibet remained especially isolated from the outside world. But it has ironically become particularly well known today because of the writings of visitors like Heinrich Harrer and famous films from *Seven Years in Tibet*—made from Harrer's memoirs—to the movie *Kundun*. Both are set during this period of Tibetan independence.

After World War II ended, the situation in central Asia became considerably more complicated. The Chinese Communists

were moving closer and closer to a defeat of their long-time enemies, the nationalists, while below Tibet's southern border the long-influential British were preparing to leave India. With that decision, a significant part of their long-term interest in Tibet's fate began to fade.

Accordingly, Tibet's leadership began making efforts to develop relations with the outside world including a successful invitation to the internationally famous broadcaster and explorer, Lowell Thomas, to visit and report on Tibet. As a practical matter, given the sorry state of Tibetan military preparations, hoping the support of the larger international community might protect them from China was probably their only option. Moreover, Lhasa's leaders, in what would eventually seem a vain effort to maintain their authority in the waning days of the Chinese Civil War, expelled all those Chinese associated with the Nationalist government of Chiang Kai-shek. Ironically, the gesture provoked one of the few moments of agreement between the increasingly ascendant Chinese Communists and the nationalists. Both Chinese political parties, true to their mutual assumption that Tibet was part of China, denounced the decision.

The Chinese Return to Tibet: The Early Years

One of the primary goals of contemporary Chinese civilization has been to piece back together various regions perceived to be "Chinese" that were lost during the years of China's greatest weakness in the era from the Opium Wars through the Second World War. During the late 20th century, that goal meant the successful efforts to reabsorb Hong Kong and Macau not forgetting, of course, the long-term desire to bring Taiwan back into the fold.

The Chinese have seen Tibet no differently. For most Chinese it remains a fundamental part of China. That perception helps explain why China, in October 1950, only a year after the People's Republic had come into power and while the Korean War was getting more and more bloody, the forces of the PRC entered Tibet. The Chinese military was easily able to overcome the poorly equipped Tibetan forces and once again, as so often in the past, to reoccupy Tibet, destroying the independence it had enjoyed for the decades since the Chinese Revolution of 1912.

As for the Dalai Lama, he temporarily left Lhasa with an apparent intention of going into exile. Eventually, though, the young leader chose to return to his capital while his representatives soon found themselves in Beijing forced to agree to Chinese military and administrative authority over Tibet. Known as the Seventeen Point

China-Tibet

Agreement, the document called for the establishment of Chinese civil and military facilities at Lhasa while promising Tibetan domestic political autonomy and recognition of its religious heritage. Most important to later developments was the first point, which stated that the Tibetans were officially recognizing Chinese sovereignty over their land. This was something they had never done before. For its part, China promised to recognize Tibet's traditional political and economic system as headed by the Dalai Lama.

As for the outside world, while nations from Britain to the United States understood that Tibet had quite obviously been independent during the decades before China's return, neither Western power had ever recognized Tibet's official independence nor would they now come to its aid. Behind the scenes, though, the United States would eventually become increasingly involved because of the growing tensions of the Cold War.

Still, in the early years of China's reoccupation, Beijing's control over Tibet was relatively light. Reportedly this was the case because Mao Zedong understood that Tibet's situation was different from other regions in China and that caution would have to be exercised. For example, during those early years, no Tibetan aristocratic or monastic property was confiscated, and the local landlords, long dominant over Tibet's deeply feudal and theocratic system, maintained their judicial authority. The long-term goal of transforming Tibet and integrating it into the People's Republic did not, of course, change. However, Mao was willing to approach the challenge with a relatively moderate initial hand.

That early caution did not last long. Nevertheless, during the early years there was general agreement among both Tibet's secular and religious leaders that they could successfully co-exist with the new leaders of the People's Republic. As for the Dalai Lama, he was apparently confident enough with developments that he had a new and quite impressive mansion built for himself within the famed summer palace retreat of Lhasa's leaders. This was an impressive building that included the first Western style toilet in the entire country.

Tibet and the International Cold War

The roots of the later estrangement between Tibet and the Chinese were embedded in both the Cold War then engulfing the world and the more immediate circumstances of the ethnically Tibetan people who lived in those regions that lay beyond the area the Dalai Lama's government had previously controlled. Unlike within "political Tibet," Beijing had no reluctance whatsoever to intervene in those places. Thus, the revolutionary social transformation of the mid-1950s that was then raging in much of China affected as well on Tibetans in Sichuan province. It eventually provoked a rebellion that quickly spilled over into Tibet proper.

By 1957 the United States was no longer dealing with the challenge of the Korean War, which had until 1953 seen America and China fighting a vicious conventional war on the Korean peninsula. It began to intervene more enthusiastically on behalf of those Tibetans willing to confront Beijing's power. Working with the Dalai Lama's brother, half a dozen Tibetans were trained on the American island of Saipan by members of the American Central Intelligence Agency. Other training facilities were established in the mountainous areas of Colorado. Meanwhile several dozen supply drops were made, and much more elaborate training facilities were set up in Nepal.

From the Chinese perspective, the fact that the United States, its long-time Cold War foe, had become involved was particularly alarming. It most certainly contributed to the much more violent crackdown Beijing imposed on Tibet in 1959, a crackdown that saw the 14th Dalai Lama flee to India. Eventually, within India, a relatively large Tibetan exile community developed. For a time their host, the new Indian democracy, itself having border tensions with China, would lend its support to the Tibetans. After the Sino-Indian clash of 1962, the Indian government began working closely with the Americans and Tibetans in these training efforts.

But American covert support for the Tibetan independence effort only lasted through the late 1960s. As for the Dalai Lama, he himself received generous American government funding at least through the early 1970s. Not surprisingly, U.S. support for the Tibetan independence movement dwindled as U.S.-China relations improved. Meanwhile, as it slowly improved its own relationship with Beijing, New Delhi also withdrew formal military sup-

---

"Tibetan Buddhism"

By Jeannine Chandler

Tibetan Buddhism (also called Vajrayana or Tantric Buddhism) claims roughly 20 million practitioners around the world. Although most are found in the Himalayan region (Tibet, Nepal, Bhutan, Sikkim, Ladakh), Mongolia, Manchuria, China and Russia, in the last half century converts have appeared in the West as well. In contrast to Mahayana or Theravada Buddhism, Tibetan Buddhism combines esoteric practices with the rigorous study of texts in order to hasten one's journey towards enlightenment. Tibetan Buddhists use meditation, deity visualizations, ritual prostrations and the chanting of mantras to achieve this end. However, the defining characteristic of Tibetan Buddhism is its emphasis on guru (lama) devotion, as knowledge of and initiation into these practices is reliant upon one's relationship with a guru and his lineage.

In the eighth century, Indian master Padmasambhava brought the Tantric Buddhist teaching to Tibet and initiated Buddhism's integration with Tibet's indigenous religious tradition of Bön. Following a period of Buddhism's persecution and subsequent revival in Tibet, in the eleventh century the adept Atisha introduced reforms to Buddhism in Tibet, intent on correcting what was perceived by many to be an overemphasis on tantric practices to the detriment of moral discipline. He also is known for reviving the monastic tradition in Tibet (for which it is now famous) as well as stimulating the creation of the New Translation schools in Tibet: Sakya, Kagyu, and Geluk. With the Old Translation School (Nyingma), these traditions remain today the four schools of Tibetan Buddhism.

The development of Tibetan Buddhism was influenced for centuries by secular political struggles as well as competition between (and within) religious schools, often with Mongol involvement. After centuries of sectarian conflict, the Geluk tradition eventually became the dominant school, headed by the Dalai Lama, a reincarnation of the bodhisattva of compassion, who came to be revered as the spiritual and temporal leader of the Tibetans.

Within the past twenty years, the Fourteenth Dalai Lama has become the international embodiment of Tibet and the face of Tibetan Buddhism (and often of Buddhism in general). A winner of the Nobel Peace Prize (1989) and the United States' Congressional Gold Medal (October 2007), the Dalai Lama has campaigned for Tibetan independence, human rights, religious tolerance and world peace. With his image behind the religion, Tibetan Buddhism has become globalized, with on-line sanghas and booming sales of Buddhist merchandise.

Monks debating at the Sera Monastery in Tibet

Photo by Steven Leibo

port even as it continued to host the large Tibetan community within its borders. If Britain's colonization of India earlier in the century had helped Tibet in its efforts to stave off China's demands, the fact that New Delhi chose not to assume Britain's role in Central Asia in the years after independence probably sealed Tibet's fate. Eventually, India's leaders would officially announce that also New Delhi considered Tibet officially part of China.

Tibet Under Chinese Rule: The Situation Becomes Complicated

If the early years of China's occupation of Tibet had been relatively successful, the situation changed dramatically in the late 1950s. Responding to what it saw as more foreign encroachment, the Chinese government dropped is previous reticence as it put down the rebellion. Even more tragically for Tibet's fate, China would soon enter the era of the Cultural Revolution, which by the mid-1960s saw enormous numbers of young Chinese attacking and destroying the symbols of China's cultural heritage. While it took place all over China, that assault was particularly destructive within Tibet. In those years, huge numbers of its cultural monuments were destroyed. Its monks were driven from the monasteries, and most of these facilities were devastated. Of course, feeding the assault was the fact that many of the monasteries had taken part in the earlier 1959 revolt. Moreover, their very existence as largely feudal theocratic organizations fundamentally clashed with the emerging Chinese communist sensibilities.

By late 1966, as the Cultural Revolution grew to a crescendo of chaotic political ac-

tivism and violence across the rest of China, large numbers of Red Guards, despite the orders of leaders like Zhou Enlai, began to arrive in Tibet. They were ready to take on what was for them the quintessential feudal society they had long hated. Significantly, it was not just Han Chinese youth who became involved. Large numbers of Tibetans themselves, caught up in the enthusiasm of the moment, took part in the assault. People were even attacked in the streets for wearing traditional Tibetan clothing.

All across the country monasteries were attacked and destroyed while pitched battles took place between Tibetan monks and the assaulting Chinese and their Tibetan allies. All was done in the name of reforming the Tibetan consciousness from the traditional mindset to one more closely adhering to the new socialist "man" the leaders of the Chinese revolution had long striven to create. They believed this would require the complete suppression of Tibet's religious heritage in the name of building the new socialist society. In the aftermath of the wholesale assault on Tibetan identity, the once proud Tibetan society and religious establishment suffered an assault from which they would barely be able to survive.

Contemporary Tibet

In the years after Deng Xiaoping came to power, much was done to rebuild Tibet's monasteries and reestablish its religious and cultural traditions. Today families again dedicate their children's lives to serve in the monasteries, and the Tibetan language is widely taught in primary schools throughout the country. Without

fluency in Chinese though, the number of professional career possibilities available to ethnic Tibetans is very limited.

For a time, under the relatively liberal communist leaders who dominated in the 1980s, efforts were made to find a compromise between Beijing's identification of Tibet as a part of China and the supporters of the Dalai Lama. Nevertheless, little was accomplished.

The horrors of the Cultural Revolution have passed, but the fate of Tibet still remains deeply in question. Though various Chinese governments have tried from time to time to find common ground with the Dalai Lama and his supporters, Beijing is absolutely unwilling even to consider Tibet's demands that have ranged from independence to complete autonomy. Thus while Tibetan cultural and religious life has been allowed to reemerge, any activities that have appeared to support the Dalai Lama and the independence movement have been ruthlessly suppressed.

The commitment to maintaining Tibet within the Chinese orbit was particularly evident in 1989 when Beijing violently suppressed an uprising. More recently, in March 2008, another series of demonstrations led to violence not only in Lhasa, but in the neighboring province of Gansu. This is an area of Tibetan presence, as explained above, that is beyond the frontiers of Tibet proper. The more recent tensions, which may have claimed more than one hundred lives, were relatively predictable given Beijing's on-going tight control over Tibet. Of course, many of Tibet's worldwide supporters used Beijing's expanding international profile during the run-up to the Olympics to highlight the plight of Tibet. This most certainly added fuel to the fire of discontent. That discontent continues today. Over the last year, Beijing has sent significant numbers of soldiers not only to Tibet, but into the larger ethnographically Tibetan regions. This has created a sort of unofficial martial law environment while smaller incidents from public demonstrations to bombings have continued.

As for the Chinese reaction, Beijing has behaved defensively over the last few years. It recently issued a series of reports outlining how much their control has improved the lives of the Tibetans. According to the documents, the sixty years since China assumed control have distinctively improved Tibetan infant mortality rates, lengthened life spans and raised their incomes significantly. Unfortunately, from the Chinese perspective, while their impact on Tibet over the years probably has brought improvements, such developments have historically not lessened the sorts of tensions aroused by "foreign" oc-

China-Tibet

cupations, as the Tibetans most certainly see the Chinese. Still the Chinese keep the focus on the positive improvements they believe they have brought to the Tibetans. They have even gone so far as to set March 28, the anniversary of the 1959 uprising, as a day officially to commemorate the liberation of Tibet's serfs.

Meanwhile, to facilitate the region's fuller incorporation into the People's Republic, Beijing has moved vigorously to extend and enhance its land-based communication routes to Tibet. In 2006 the world's only atmospherically sealed train began its first run from Beijing to Lhasa traveling the enormous distance and scaling the extraordinary peaks, at one point at a height of 16,640 feet. The new train is expected to play a significant role in dramatically transforming Tibet, which was once one of the most isolated countries in the world. Meanwhile, the Chinese authorities have announced plans for an expansion of Tibet's airport facilities to link it more effectively with the rest of China.

Things have obviously not always gone smoothly for Beijing. China's efforts to weaken the influence of the Dalai Lama suffered an enormous setback in 1999 when the 17th Karmapa, the third-most important leader in Tibetan Buddhism, fled Tibet complaining that the Chinese authorities had denied him the ability continue his studies. The Karmapa Lama was hardly the only Tibetan to flee. Since 1990, thousands of Tibetans have arrived in Nepal as refugees. Moreover, in recent years the largely passive resistance of the Tibetans has moved to a new level with the emergence of terrorism being carried out in the name of Tibetan independence. Predictably, Beijing has struck back harshly, and in early 2003, it executed a former monk, the first Tibetan executed for such activities in a very long time. How many others might have died as a result of the more recent disturbances of 2008 may never be known. What we do know is that nineteen people, mostly Han Chinese, died in Lhasa, but the rioting went far beyond the capital.

Meanwhile, the last few decades have also seen an enormous increase in Western interest in Tibet. Films from *Seven Years in Tibet* to *Kundun* and the well-publicized interest of various celebrities from Richard Gere to Harrison Ford have brought Tibet's problems to the American public. In addition, the 14th Dalai Lama's many international travels brought the concerns of that troubled nation to the world community as never before. More recently, in 2009, the American House of Representatives overwhelming passed a resolution calling for Beijing to treat Tibet more humanly.

Sadly, while the Dalai Lama has been extraordinarily successful in building sup-

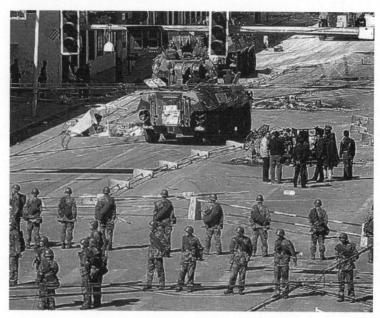

Chinese reestablish order in Lhasa, 2008

port in the Western world, Beijing appears to have lost interest in seeking a compromise. It is perhaps merely waiting for his death in exile to help resolve the problem.

As a practical matter, Tibet's internationally respected but exiled leader would probably be better off cultivating more friends in Beijing than in Washington D.C. Only in Beijing could a path be found that would likely offer a compromise that would see Tibetan culture thrive in the 21st century.

Of course, that assumes that Beijing remains interested, as it once was, in finding such a compromise. Chinese economic policy in recent years has encouraged large numbers of Chinese to move to Tibet. While it is true that only a small percentage have official permission to live there, the number of "illegal" migrants has grown enormously. This has swamped the region's original inhabitants while developing those Tibetan community leaders, both secular and religious, who have shown themselves more cooperative and supportive of Beijing.

Most significantly, the politics of Sino-Tibetan relations has of late begun to focus not only on the 14th Dalai Lama, but on the question of who will succeed him after he leaves the scene. During the summer of 2007 Chinese authorities issued a new regulation outlawing anyone from recognizing a child as the official reincarnation of the Dalai Lama. This is an effort obviously designed to allow the PRC—at least within its border—the power to control the naming of the next Tibetan leader. Meanwhile, taking a page from his more western allies and despite the obvious contradictions with Tibetan tradition, the

Dalai Lama has begun to talk of having the next Tibetan leader chosen by more democratic means. How all this might turn out is anyone's guess, but the odds are that Beijing, with both territorial control and Tibetan tradition on its side, is likely to win this battle.

Meanwhile the fires of nationalism can burn both ways. It is true that Tibetan nationalists can cause Beijing significant problems. However, ethnic Han nationalist sentiment that Tibet is indeed part of China and a sense that the Tibetans have not been sufficiently grateful for the People's Republic's development efforts often pushes the P.R.C. leadership's popularity higher when they energetically reject Tibetan calls for greater autonomy or, in some cases, independence.

Nevertheless, not all Han have supported their administration's policies on Tibet. In June 2010 approximately 200 Chinese legal professionals published a report condemning the government's disruption of Tibetan economic, religious and cultural life and blaming those policies for the deadly riots of 2008.

For its part, the Beijing government continues to believe that their on-going effort to improve the Tibetan region's economic prospects will eventually gain them more support among the indigenous Tibetans. It is a policy frequently followed in the past by other governments in similar situations. Frankly it has not had much success elsewhere.

What would most likely impress the Tibetans themselves is a major government effort to ensure that their population is not totally swamped by Chinese immigrants. However, that seems less likely to occur.

Taiwan: Republic of China

Taipei 101, among the world's highest buildings

Photo by Steven Leibo

Area: 13,885 square miles

Population: 23,024,956 (July 2010 est.)

Climate: Subtropical and humid in the lowlands, with an eleven-month growing season; in the higher elevations of the central mountains the temperatures are cooler.

Neighboring Countries: The Republic of China has been on the island of Taiwan, located 100 miles from the southeast China mainland, since 1949. It is about 300 miles north of the Philippine island of Luzon.

Official Language: Chinese ("Mandarin" also known as Guoyu or Putonghua)

Other languages: Taiwanese (Min), Chinese Hakka dialects. Indigenous tribal communities speak a number of Austronesian languages.

Ethnic Background: Chinese, also known as Han. The highlands are occupied by relatively small groups of Austronesian ancestry who resemble other indigenous people found in parts of Southeast Asia. They make up around 2% of the population

Principal Religions: Confucianism, Taoism, and Buddhism. These three, which migrated with the earliest Chinese from the mainland, are generally intermixed. The indigenous communities practice various forms of Christianity.

Main Exports: (to the U.S., Japan, Hong Kong & China) Textiles, clothing, plas-

tics, metals, electronic equipment, processed foods.

Main Imports: (from U.S., Japan, Kuwait) Industrial equipment, automobiles, oil, minerals, precision instruments

Currency: New Taiwan dollar

Former Colonial Status: Taiwan was a Japanese colony from 1895 to 1945.

National Day: October 10, anniversary of the Chinese Revolution of 1911.

Chief of State: Ma Ying-jeou (since May 20th 2008)

National Flag: A red field with a blue rectangle in the upper left containing a 12-pointed white star.

Per Capita GDP Income: $29,800 (2009 est.) purchasing power parity

Note: Unlike the Hanyu Pinyin Romanized transliteration of the mainland, Taiwan has long used the older Wade-Giles and postal system spellings. For consistency this chapter will follow the style used on the island except for well-known mainland terms. It should be noted that Taiwan's new President Ma has indicated that he wants to have the island adopt the Hanyu pinyin system used on the mainland.

History

Although the bulk of the population of Taiwan is and has been for centuries ethnic Han Chinese initially from the continent, the island's evolution through time has been significantly different from that experienced on the mainland. Archeological evidence suggests that people have lived in Taiwan for at least 15,000 years, and, in fact, it was not until the 17th century that the arrival of large numbers of ethnically Han people from the mainland began significantly to impact the island's demographic balance.

Before that the island's predominant population, like other relatively nearby Pacific communities, consisted of a wide variety of Austronesian peoples whose descendents today constitute about two percent of the population. But even after the island became predominantly Chinese in ethnicity, it long remained outside the direct control of China's many imperial and more recently republican governments. This is a historical evolution quite different from the mainland. That very different historical experience constitutes one more element in the perspectives that have separated Taiwanese from their mainland cousins.

Taiwan's Pre-Modern Historical Experience

Taiwan's formal encounter with Western colonialism began at the end of the 16th century when a group of Portuguese

Taiwan

was shipwrecked on the shores of what they would come to call "Ilha Formasa," Portuguese for "Beautiful Island." But it was the Dutch who would be the first Westerners to establish a lasting presence on the island, an effort that began in 1624 and that eventually saw them drive their primary European competitors, the Spanish, from Taiwan by the early 1640s.

During the years of Dutch domination a significant transformation of the island's demography began as they encouraged mainland Chinese to resettle on the island as sugarcane and rice production workers. The newly arriving Han Chinese added to the number of ethnic Chinese already on Taiwan. Those newcomers were soon joined by other mainlanders who arrived after fleeing from the chaos associated with the collapse of the Ming Dynasty and the subsequent arrival to power in 1644 of the Manchu Qing Dynasty.

If the Dutch encouragement of Han migration to the island had a significant impact on the ethnic balance of Taiwan, it was the arrival of the anti-Manchu, Cheng

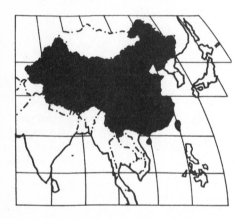

Cheng-gong, better known as Koxinga, who even more profoundly moved the island into a Chinese political and cultural environment. A Ming family loyalist, Koxinga's forces were among those who resisted the Manchu conquest of the mainland by establishing themselves on Taiwan and creating the first formal Chinese administration the island had ever experienced. Koxinga's forces drove the Dutch from the island and were themselves able to resist the Qing forces for a generation. Eventually, though, by 1683 the effort failed and Taiwan was absorbed into the expanding Qing Dynasty.

Over the subsequent decades Taiwan was considered part of Fujian Province. Meanwhile the population continued to grow significantly. By the mid-19th century it was estimated to have reached two and a half million people while once again Western interest in the island was aroused. As a result of the 1858 Treaty of Tianjin, two of the island's ports were designated treaty ports, adding to those that had already been established on the mainland from Hong Kong to Shanghai. But it would not be the imperialist Western powers that would ultimately make the biggest impact on Taiwan during the era. Rather it would be imperial Japan, which by mid-century was already beginning the steps that would see it emerge as a major colonial power by late century.

Taiwan and the
Emerging Japanese Empire

Almost as soon as Japan's own modernization effort began in the aftermath of the Meiji Restoration, Tokyo started showing interest in the island. That was most dramatically demonstrated in 1874 when Japanese soldiers arrived in Taiwan claiming that the island's indigenous inhabitants had attacked fisherman from the nearby Ryukyu island chain, which Japan also claimed. From Beijing's perspective, the temporary Japanese expedition was of real concern. A Chinese force was then dispatched to the island to help settle the conflict. Subsequently Beijing upgraded the island's status to that of an independent province. But its growing concern about the island's status did not stop the Qing Empire from eventually losing control of the island completely.

In 1895 as a consequence of the Sino-Japanese War of the previous year, Taiwan was absorbed by the emerging Japanese empire. The initial occupation was quite traumatic. Some locals vigorously resisted the Japanese even as they vented their anger against local Qing officials, who, it was felt, had abandoned them. To some extent that was true. Officially Beijing chose to accept the loss of Taiwan though

President Ma Ying-jeou

some of its local forces attempted to carry out their own resistance under the banner of a newly proclaimed "Taiwan Republic." That effort failed after only a few months. But if both the official and unofficial Qing defense of island was short lived, locals, both Chinese and the indigenous Austronesian community, continued their resistance for years. The violence was at times so intense that at one point over six thousand Taiwanese were massacred by the Japanese. Despite that opposition, the Japanese managed to repress the resistance and establish themselves on the island. The occupation would last until the middle of the next century.

Like Korea, whose absorption into the growing Japanese empire took place during the same era, the people of Taiwan were pressured over time to become assimilated into Japanese culture. Initially there had been some ambivalence among the Japanese about making such an effort, literally to turn the native Taiwanese into second-class "Japanized" citizens of the new Japanese empire. But by the middle of the 20th century the effort was well underway.

Japanese was designated the language of instruction, and the new generation became increasingly literate in the language of their conquerors. Many locals even studied in Japan. Economically, the Japanese worked to enhance the island's infrastructure and to use it as an area for agricultural production, particularly rice and sugar for the Japanese home market.

Nevertheless, given how traumatic the next decades were to be on the mainland—the several civil wars and brutal Japanese invasion—Taiwan's people were to be spared much of that horror. Ironically Taiwan ended the period in significantly better economic and social circumstances that their ethnic cousins on the

the nationalists, who frequently saw them as potential agents of Japan. While the island's citizens had already come a long way in developing a new identity that was neither Chinese nor Japanese, it was one that would eventually give the name "Taiwanese" new meaning.

If the nationalist's initial welcome had been enthusiastic, some of their earlier decisions were less appreciated. The island was placed almost exclusively under the direction of mainlanders cutting off the upper administrators from a more sophisticated knowledge of the sentiments of the locals. Particularly important among those perspectives lost would be the experience the Taiwanese had previously gained in working with and pushing for greater rights under Japanese colonial control.

But it was not merely prejudice that kept the mainlanders from understanding the locals. After half a century of Japanese control, significant numbers could not even communicate with the new arrivals. Japanese had become commonly spoken, and Mandarin, the newly designated "national language" of the government, was very different from the southern Chinese dialects better known in Taiwan. Given official insistence that those who worked for the new government understand the national language, many Taiwanese lost their jobs and were not even deemed eligible for official employment.

Unfortunately for the newly arriving nationalists, they were soon seen by many locals as simply another colonial force and one that governed less well and with more corruption than the departed Japanese. The charges were, of course, quite understandable. The nationalists, long infamous for the level of corruption among their ranks, were also increasingly distracted by the struggle on the mainland. Under the circumstances, there emerged among local Taiwanese the goal of winning greater local governing autonomy. This was a movement that was for the most part continuing the momentum already begun under the Japanese.

Ironically, given how passionately the nationalists had resisted communism, their own ideas about the role of government in the economy clashed deeply with the Taiwanese, who often resented the nationalists' intrusions into the local private economy. Squabbles over the fate of abandoned Japanese holdings only added to the tensions.

An Open Conflict Erupts

The developing tensions exploded in February 1947 when the nationalist administration was temporarily swept aside by a local revolt initially sparked by

A Paiwan man from Austronesian Community

Photo by Steven Leibo

mainland. Especially helpful were the implantation of new health regulations that allowed for dramatic improvements in the rates of disease, from cholera to small pox. At least that was true until the era of the Pacific War when Tokyo used the island as a staging area for its thrust toward Southeast Asia. During those years many Taiwanese served in the Japanese military, and the islands themselves were bombed by allied forces.

Taiwan's Reunification with China 1945 to 1949

After Japan's Second World War defeat at the hands of the Allies, the nationalist government, which had emerged while Taiwan's people were still living under Japanese rule, arrived to take control of China's long-lost possession. It was just as abrupt a change in administration as the previous one had been in the 1890s. Suddenly Taiwan was Chinese again. As time would reveal, both China and Taiwan had changed dramatically during their years of separation.

Initially, though, while there was some ambivalence, certainly most Taiwanese had accepted Japanese control, and many served in their war effort. The arriving Nationalists were greeted enthusiastically. Beneath the surface, though, the seeds of future tension already existed. During the war itself, many Taiwanese on the mainland had experienced discrimination by

Taiwan

economic tensions complemented by reformist demands for greater autonomy. General Chiang Kai-shek's forces, already hard-pressed on the mainland would have none of it. Nationalist soldiers arriving from the mainland massacred thousands of local Taiwanese-estimates suggest some eight thousand people died—and quickly crushed the revolt. Of course, this created a legacy of bitterness that would continue for decades. It is not surprising that the nationalist forces were hardly in a mood for careful negotiation and fence building. Their soldiers on the mainland were trapped in a life or death struggle with the communists. Taiwan was seen as the location of what might become their last stand. They were right. By 1949 Chiang Kai-shek's nationalists had been decisively defeated on the mainland, and the last remnants of their forces retreated to the island.

From Chiang Kai-shek's perspective, the situation could have been worse. His forces had, after all, reestablished themselves on a productive and relatively well developed island—at least compared to the mainland. It was an island whose infrastructure had been carefully nurtured by the now departed Japanese. Certainly, there was much wartime damage to be repaired, but compared to the problems on the mainland they were manageable.

For the locals themselves, though, many would soon evolve from seeing themselves as liberated by the land of their ancestors to simply living under a new foreign occupation. Most significantly, the mainlanders had shown with what brutal force they were willing to suppress Taiwanese demands for autonomy.

Internationally, of course, the pretence was maintained that the Nationalists, as the Republic of China, still represented the mainland of China in the United Nations. This was a facade that their continuing friendship with the powerful Americans facilitated for another generation.

Taiwan and the Cold War

The outbreak of the Korean War in June of 1950 proved a disaster for the people of Korea and for the many Americans who were soon caught up in the struggle. But for Taiwan's nationalists, the war brought real advantages. If the United States had earlier been reluctant to become involved in the on-going competition between the Nationalists and the Communists, its support for Taiwan now became much more open. By 1954 a defense treaty was signed with the United States, and the island's fate clearly became linked to America's Cold War struggle with the communists. No longer would the Americans see Beijing's desire to retake Taiwan as merely a potential last act in the Chinese Civil War.

Taiwan's eventual fate had now become an issue of international Cold War tensions. This was particularly so during the American presidential election of 1960 when the defense of Taiwan's few remaining near mainland islands curiously emerged as a fundamental part of the debates between the then presidential contenders Richard Nixon and John F. Kennedy. But America's solidarity with Taiwan would experience a diplomatic revolution by the early 1970s.

Taiwan's Fate and Sino-American Relations

By the late 1960s Taiwan's fate was again buffeted by forces beyond the island, as so often before. The United States, its long time ally, was trapped in the Vietnam War, and the new Nixon administration was committed to using the growing rift between Moscow and Beijing to pressure North Vietnam to make the concessions the US required to withdraw from Vietnam. But gaining Beijing's cooperation required a significantly improved relationship with mainland China, which Richard Nixon's administration set out to accomplish. The price, of course, was Taiwan.

Over the next several years, the ROC would not only lose its seat at the United Nations and be replaced by the mainland Chinese. By the late 1970s it would see the official withdrawal of formal ties with the United States. None of that meant that America had completely abandoned Taiwan. Actually the ties on a less official status have continued to this day. Nevertheless, the battle over Taiwan's international legitimacy had formally sparked a struggle that saw Taiwan increasingly isolated, at least formally, from much of the international community.

Recent Political Developments on Taiwan

Politics in the Republic of China constitutes one of the most encouraging cases of how democratization can take place over time alongside a modern, rapidly developing economy. Even critics of the Guomindang, the Nationalist Party that completely dominated the political system from the break with the mainland in 1949 until recently, would acknowledge that substantial progress has been made.

But those more democratic changes did not occur for decades after the Guomingtang's abrupt withdrawal from the mainland. In fact, for the first several decades, the island's inhabitants, both the newly arrived mainlanders and the locals lived under a dictatorship dominated by Chiang Kai-shek himself and then his son Chiang Ching-kuo. That dictatorship could at times be quite harsh. During the era of martial

Former President Chen Shui-bian

law, formally begun in 1949, the government imposed censorship over the media, refused to allow competing political parties and suppressed any political activities it found suspicious.

But Chiang Ching-kuo's policies were not limited to suppressing all potential opposition. He also took care to encourage as many Taiwanese as possible, at least those who were thought loyal to the Nationalist party, to become part of the GMD's ruling elite. Thus it was through a combination of repression and co-option that the nationalists worked to retain their authority over the island.

Over the years, though, their harsh control would diminish significantly. Especially important in that evolution was the lifting of martial law in 1987 in the last years of Chiang Ching-kuo's administration. But even in the years before the ending of martial law, more informal political opposition groups were beginning to emerge. Most significant was the more tolerant legal environment that allowed the formation in 1986 of the Democratic Progressive Party. It would eventually become the Nationalist Party's biggest rival. As so often has been the case, developments on Taiwan have been deeply linked to both international events and, more specifically, to its critical relationship to the Chinese mainland.

Taiwan's Democratic Emergence

In late 1989, the world was riveted by the image of peoples throughout the world of Eastern European communism casting off their anti-democratic leaders while some even within the Soviet Union were starting down the road of more open elections. Given that international environment, it is not surprising that Taiwanese political activists began to agitate aggressively for more democratic reforms. By the spring of 1990, the pressure became such that critical decisions were made to

Wind Power Facility at Taiwan's Changhua Coast Industrial Park

move toward a more open system. Particularly important was the support of Lee Teng-hui, a native Taiwanese, who succeeded Chiang Ching-kuo as president and who would eventually become the first democratically elected president.

Naturally it should not be forgotten that all this was going on in the aftermath of Beijing's violent suppression of the Tiananmen Square demonstrators of June 1989. Surely, it was argued that having Taiwan move toward a more open democracy, just as Beijing's international prestige was at its nadir, would be advantageous to the island nation. Of particular interest was that Taiwan saw its own version of the confrontation between students and the government, which had riveted the world the previous year.

In March 1990, just as the first anniversary of the Beijing confrontation was approaching, Taiwan students began their own demonstrations and hunger strikes demanding more political opening. But this time both the Taiwan government and the students themselves had the benefit of hindsight. They carefully avoided the mistakes made the year before. The students' demands were more reasonable that those made in Beijing, and the GMD government approached the challenge from a more flexible position. Indeed many of the

demands for a more open political system complemented the goals of then President Lee. Finally the confrontation ended in a reasonably amicable fashion, and Taiwan moved further along a path toward democratization.

The upshot of the changes was the end of the Guomindang's decades-long domination of Taiwan's political scene. By the mid-1990s, most of the holdovers from the National Assembly—originally elected on the mainland in 1948—had retired. Discussion of politically sensitive issues, such as whether Taiwan should be independent of the People's Republic, was at last permitted.

More significantly, the Democratic Progressive Party had grown more influential, and relatively clean elections became more and more a common part of the political landscape. Eventually the Guomindang even lost its hold over the presidential office. But those changes occurred slowly and revolved around issues ranging from which party should lead the country to its relationship with the mainland.

Not surprisingly much of the contention among the competing parties has centered on the independence versus unification issue. The New Party that emerged for a time was more representative of the old line GMD, Nationalist Party, in its claim

that it had the right to rule over all of China. However, the Nationalists, under the direction of former President Lee, took a more centrist approach. Meanwhile, the DPP was openly supportive of an independent Taiwan.

Further evolution of the political system also came about when steps were taken to strengthen the position of the president. New constitutional amendments provided for the direct election of the president. They also granted the president the authority to appoint and dismiss high-ranking government officials without the consent of the prime minister.

Taiwan held its first ever direct presidential election in March 1996. Lee Teng-hui, the long time incumbent, was elected with 54% of the vote. The voters rallied around their president, who had skillfully raised Taiwan's diplomatic profile by meeting with several ASEAN heads of state, and who had visited the United States. Peng Ming-min, the Democratic Progressive Party candidate that year, came in second. Peng himself was known as an open supporter of Taiwan's independence, a stance of which leaders on the mainland have long been very wary.

During the election Beijing, no doubt concerned about the rising popularity of efforts to disassociate Taiwan further from the mainland, made a crude effort to intimidate voters by staging provocative military maneuvers in the weeks leading up to the election. While Beijing's exact motives are not completely clear, the result of its threats was to complement President Lee's efforts to fix his candidacy in the middle of the Taiwan political spectrum. Thus he became the election's big winner while the votes of both those openly advocating formal independence and those encouraging closer ties to the mainland went down.

Even as Taiwan's evolution toward a more democratic system has progressed smoothly in recent years, the ever-present issue of relations with the mainland has continued to complicate matters considerably. In fact, there has at times been a growing popular support for the Democratic Progressive Party's calls for more formal and official independence from the mainland. For a time that momentum seemed to be waning when in late 1998, Chen Shui-bian, the DPP mayor, was defeated by Ma Ying-jeou, a member of Taiwan's Nationalist Party.

All that occurred before the presidential election of March 2000. To the frustration of outgoing President Lee Teng-hui and his Nationalist Party, hopes of a smooth transition from President Lee to another Nationalist Party president were dashed when former Provincial Governor James Soong declared for the presidency. His

Taiwan

Commuting in Taipei   Photo by Steven Leibo

challenge was particularly galling to some Nationalist Party members because he had once served as their own party's secretary-general before falling out with his former colleagues. By early spring 2000 the race had become a three-man struggle between Soong, the pro-independence candidate, Chen Shui-bian of the DPP and President Lee's hand-picked successor, Vice President Lien Chan.

When the results of the 2000 presidential election were finally announced, they proved to be far more of a watershed than almost any analyst had predicted. Chen Shui-bian, the former mayor of Taipei and leader of the pro-independence forces, had won election to the presidency. The split within the ranks of the ruling nationalists had made Chen's victory possible. More important than the details of the win was the reality that after half a century of rule by the Nationalists, who had moved their government to the island after their defeat on the mainland, the Guomindang no longer held the presidency of the Republic of China. This was an astounding step forward in Taiwan's path toward building a more modern democratic society. While some were celebrating this demonstration of the growing vitality of Taiwanese democracy, many were concerned about how Beijing would respond to the arrival to power of the Democratic Progressive Party, which had been so much blunter in its calls for a formal declaration of official independence from China than had the Nationalists.

As a practical matter, Chen appeared to have won far more of the votes of those who were angry about corruption in Taiwan than any specific support for a confrontation with China. Needless to say, Beijing was very unhappy with the results.

Nevertheless, initially cautious statements by Chen and soothing diplomacy by the United States kept the "fallout" to a minimum. To the surprise of many, the arrival to the presidency of a representative of the independence-minded Democratic Progressive Party was at first received with far more toleration by Beijing than many would have predicted.

However, surviving Beijing's initial reaction was hardly the new President Chen Shui-bian's only problem. He himself had won a three-way race to become president, but the GMD still controlled the country's legislature. By the end of the following year, Taiwan's political system continued its dramatic evolution. His party, the DPP, won the parliamentary elections thereby becoming the largest party in the country. Meanwhile the old

GMD Nationalist party saw its influence, which had been paramount in Taiwan so long, shrink further.

By spring 2004, Taiwanese political life was dominated by yet another presidential campaign that saw the incumbent, Chen Shui-bian, running once again against the GMD's chairman, Lien Chan. The campaign was a heated one. As so often before, it was dominated by questions surrounding Taiwan's relations with the People's Republic and the concern among some of the president's opponents that his ongoing effort to move Taiwan farther from Beijing might one day provoke the mainland to attack.

As the election neared, popular interest was so high that thousands of voters headed back from the mainland to cast their votes. More than the choice of parties and presidents faced Taiwan's voters as they anticipated the spring 2004 electoral choice.

On the ballot were two very significant measures: first, Taiwanese voters were asked to offer an opinion on whether Taiwan should strengthen its anti-ballistic missile defenses if the People's Republic did not withdraw the hundreds of missiles it had aimed toward the island. The second ballot initiative dealt with the question of whether Taipei should reopen peace talks with the PRC. Beijing itself made it very clear that it considered both ballot initiatives provocative. In the end neither initiative gained enough votes to validate them, but by then the election had become even more complicated and impassioned.

On the final day of campaigning both President Chen and Vice President Annette Lu were shot by a gunman who fired at their motorcade in the southern city of Tainan. Although both leaders experienced only minor injuries, the next day's

The new high speed train   Photo by Steven Leibo

election results, which saw Chen and his Democratic Progressives very narrowly defeat the GMD leader by a mere 30,000 voters, set off a dramatic campaign of demonstrations and protests by Lien Chan's supporters.

Over the following weeks Taiwan's politics were convulsed by tensions as Lian Chan's supporters denounced the election results and demanded that army personnel who had been unable to vote at the last minute due to the assassination attempt be allowed another opportunity to do so. Eventually, though, the nationalists withdrew their demand, and it became obvious that President Chen would indeed have another term. But even as Chen claimed he was theoretically open to the idea of a recount, he also proclaimed that his reelection victory had vindicated his efforts to move Taiwan even farther toward full legal independence, a move Beijing vehemently opposed.

Moreover newly elected President Chen proposed creating a new constitution that would replace the one that has governed the island since the 1940s. More specifically, Chen wanted to create a constitution that more closely reflects the reality of Taiwan's separate existence from the mainland. When the vote was finally held to elect representatives to the ad hoc assembly needed to ratify the proposed constitutional changes, Chen's supporters once again out polled those of the Nationalists. But that hardly solved the ongoing internal debate over Taiwan's relationship with the mainland.

During the same period the leader of the Nationalists made a dramatic and historic visit to Beijing. This officially ended six decades of animosity between the Chinese Communist Party and Taiwan's former ruling party, the Nationalists. In the course of the trip the two leaders agreed to cooperate in opposing efforts to declare Taiwan independent. In the same period members of Taiwan's other opposition parties made their own trips to Beijing and announced that they too agreed that Taiwan was part of China.

For its part, Beijing, which was encouraged by the activities of Taiwan's opposition party, went so far as to offer the Nationalists previously unreported credit for their role in resisting Japanese aggression during the Second World War and offered Taiwanese students the same tuition rates as mainlanders in the People's Republic's universities. Unfortunately for Taiwan's then current government, tensions between it and the Nationalists continued unabated. President Chen himself seemed caught between the proverbial rock and a hard place. His hard-core supporters wanted him to keep pressing his campaign to disengage Taiwan from the mainland

while the population at large apparently preferred a more conciliatory approach.

Moreover, charges of corruption continued to hound President Chen's administration. His son-in-law was indicted during 2006 for insider financial trading while his wife faced charges of having mishandled diplomatic funds. The charges did not remain exclusively focused on the president's close associates. He himself was charged with misusing state funds and ended up handing over some of his presidential powers to the premier while he just barely survived a parliamentary recall vote during the summer of 2006.

During his last years in office President Chen's problems became even more dramatic. The parliamentary elections of early 2008 saw his nationalist opponents win a strong majority of seats in the parliament. The vote was a clear repudiation not only of the corruption that has plagued his government, but of his frequently provocative policy toward the mainland, which Taiwan's former leaders, the Nationalists, so obviously rejected during their well publicized visits to the mainland.

As for the spring presidential elections, the only thing that appeared clear even before the election took place on March 22 was that the era of President Chen's more confrontational approach with Beijing was likely to be coming to an end. His own DPP nominated Frank Hsieh, the former prime minister, who had already made known his desire to lower the level of tension with Beijing. At the same time, Ma Ying-jeou, the Guomingtang's presidential candidate, had long made it clear that his party rejected the politics of confrontation. In fact, the Guomingtang Nationalists promised that if their candidate was elected, they would terminate Taiwan's provocative official independence drive and move vigorously to improve relations with Beijing.

Once Taiwan's population made its choice, the earlier January 2008 defeat of the DPP parliamentary candidates by the newly revived Guomingtang was reconfirmed by the election of the latter's presidential candidate, Ma Ying-jeou, who won by an overwhelming 60% margin. The decision, which some had thought in jeopardy due to Beijing's then ongoing harsh crackdown on dissidents in Tibet, apparently did not turn Taiwan's voters away from Ma's calls for improved relations with the mainland.

As of summer 2009, it is far too early to predict reliably how ultimately successful the GMD will be, given their return to power after so many years. But it does seem possible to begin a preliminary evaluation of former President Chen's term in office as the country's first DPP president. While his power remained limited and much of the nation's bureaucracy was still in the hands of GMD supporters, President Chen clearly pushed Taiwan closer to a two-party democratic system. No longer were those who supported the party's more pro-Taiwan independence stance beyond the mainstream.

In fact, despite the DPP's loss of power, one thing remained clear. Even in the face of the DPP's defeat, Taiwan has continued down the path of creating a more stable two-party system than had existed in the early years of the country. Still, the fact that the former president eventually ended up in jail on charges of corruption is not likely

Presidential Palace

to enhance his historical reputation nor help the DPP's future electoral prospects

Interestingly, by the time President Chen left office, the island's citizens had come to think of themselves more commonly as Taiwanese rather than Chinese. This is a transition likely to have profound implications in the future if it continues. It is worth mentioning, however, that Taiwan's new president seems to have significantly less interest in promoting an especially unique "Taiwan" identity among the island's people.

It would be a mistake, though, to assume that only the question of relations between Taiwan and the mainland separate the two competing parties. Ethnic differences often split them as well. While the Guomindang has evolved into a more Taiwan-based, rather than mainland-oriented political party its roots tend to be stronger among those of the distinctive Hakka background. The DPP usually gains wider support among those groups that distantly hail from China's Fujian Province. But it is also true, as is often the case, that one's political preferences can be tied to location. Regardless of ethnic background, people who live in southern Taiwan have tended to be more supportive of the DPP than the GMD, which counts on strong support from the economically better off northern part of the island.

Taiwan's Foreign Relations

The long-time goal of Taiwan's foreign policy has been to gain international recognition. This has been seen as essential to the island's survival as an independent state, and this goal became even more important under the DPP party. Because of its huge investments on the mainland, the majority of Taiwan's overseas investments are located there. It is growing progressively closer to the People's Republic of China. Thus her leaders know that they need a counter-balancing political legitimacy capable of preventing the country from being swallowed up. There is also a growing sense that the question of Taiwan's separate status needs to be resolved as soon as possible, given the PRC's extraordinary growth in economic power and influence. Otherwise it would become impossible as time goes on. But while both parties have generally agreed with the above, there have, of course, been many tactical differences that separated the different political parties—GMD and DPP—that have dominated Taiwan's political life in recent years.

There is no question that Taiwan is an independent entity in economic terms. But the issue of its official political standing has not yet been settled. Nevertheless, with its impressive economic power Tai-

At the National Health Service

Photo by Steven Leibo

wan has long been viewed as an independent actor by much of the global community. However, things are much more complicated politically. Over the years Taiwan's efforts to gain further international recognition have regularly met with Beijing's active opposition.

Beijing's influence has continued to ensure that Taiwan's president is not able to take part in the annual meetings of the Asia-Pacific Economic Cooperation (APEC) forum. Nor has Taiwan been able to make any real progress in regaining admission to the United Nations. Among the significant disappointments was South Africa's decision to withdraw its recognition and open relations with Beijing. Taiwan also lost official recognition from nations from Tonga and the Central African Republic to Guinea Bissau and Macedonia. By 2005 there was even talk that the Vatican itself might soon abandon ties to Taiwan in order to improve relations with the much larger People's Republic.

The new Guomindang government has indicated that it plans to put less emphasis on the political struggle over diplomatic recognition. This is one more step in its efforts to lower the level of tension with Beijing. Nevertheless, Taiwan—as the Republic of China is now increasingly calling itself—did manage to enter the World Trade Organization (WTO) as a "separate customs territory." After years of frustration in its efforts to gain admission to the World Health Association as an "observer," Taiwan finally accomplished that goal. This was part of the generally improving relationship with Beijing that had been developing in recent years and was particularly enhanced after the GMD returned to power in 2009. Not being part of the WHO had had at times put Taiwan at a significant disadvantage in dealing with quickly developing health threats. Taiwan's unusual political status can also be a very significant problem for its international business community. It can be very frustrating for Taiwan's businessmen to have to obtain individual visas for coun-

tries they would like to visit when their competitors from nations like Japan and Singapore enjoy much greater ease of international travel.

Over the years, Taiwan has at times used every advantage it has at its disposal to try to assert its independent existence. For example, the Asian economic crisis that began in 1997 opened up new opportunities for the island to expand its influence throughout Southeast Asia. Taking advantage of its relatively stronger economic position, Taiwan's government and business community were quick to act as their neighbors' economies went into tailspins. Acting under a program called "Go South," its economic leaders looked for ways to expand Taiwan's economic and diplomatic influence in the area. The goal was to strengthen ties to the larger region as an important economic counter-balance to her growing links with China. Helped by very healthy financial reserves, the government itself made it clear it was willing to help her neighbors through the crisis. After all, it was a rare opportunity to expand Taiwan's international position even as Beijing, as usual, sought to lessen it.

On the diplomatic level former President Lee was especially active working to distance the island further from China diplomatically. In fact, he spent a lot of effort publicly emphasizing Taiwan's independence in tones that often antagonized Beijing. Lee's campaign even included a warm reception for the visiting Dalai Lama, Tibet's exiled leader.

Interestingly, that visit had a significant impact that had perhaps not been anticipated. After the visit Beijing added a new demand to those it expected of the Tibetan leader. If he wished to work with Beijing, he was to officially announce that Taiwan was part of China.

Former President Lee also infuriated Beijing before he left office by announcing that henceforth relations between the island and the mainland should be carried out in the manner of "state-to-state" rela-

Direct flights to China begun 2008

tions. Although it was not quite a declaration of independence, the pronouncement set off another firestorm of denunciations from Beijing, which was as determined as ever eventually to integrate the island into the People's Republic.

Of course, once the DPP party won the presidency under Chen Shui-bian, its new government continued, however cautiously, to carry out an agenda designed further to distance Taiwan from the mainland. That commitment and the dangers of such a stance were particularly obvious during the summer of 2002 when President Chen both suggested and backtracked on the idea of a referendum on independence in the same week. Despite the setback, he continued to make publicly clear his opinion that Taiwan was already an "independent state." He even went so far as officially to dismantle a government committee responsible for overseeing an eventual reunification with China. These were potentially provocative policy decisions that the newly returned nationalists have vowed to end.

As we have seen, once back in power the Nationalists have moved quickly to improve relations with Beijing. They made it officially clear that they would back off from the long-time obsession with expanding Taiwan's diplomatic ties. For its part, Beijing has been somewhat more flexible, as in its decision not to stand in the way of Taiwan's entrance into the World Health Organization. Not surprisingly, though, it was not as Taiwan or even as the Republic of China that Taipei gained admission, but rather as the more neutral "Chinese Taipei."

Of interest to Tibet's supporters is the question of the island's relationship with the Dalai Lama. For a time it seemed that the door had been closed to another visit by Tibet's exiled leader. But in the aftermath of the devastating earthquake of August 2009, he was allowed to visit to help comfort the survivors.

Taiwan's current government appears no longer to be interested in going out of its way to irritate Beijing. It was also quite unwilling to receive the Uighur human rights activist Rebiya Kadeer, who had also requested a visa to visit.

Taiwan and America

Relations with the United States have remained strong over the last few decades despite occasional irritation in Taiwan, for example, over President Clinton's comments during his official 1998 visit to the People's Republic of China. He unambiguously stated that the United States did not support moves toward official independence for Taiwan. Obviously aware of how easily the United States could be dragged into a crisis between Taiwan and the People's Republic, the American president wanted to eliminate any uncertainty that might make confrontations more probable in the future. But that hardly calmed Beijing, which was also hearing a contrasting and decidedly more pro-Taiwan tone from members of the United States Congress. Many had been working to strengthen American-Taiwanese military ties.

With the arrival to the White House of George W. Bush, many on Taiwan had reason to feel pleased. This was especially true because the new American president, far more than many of his predecessors, had made his support of Taiwan more public. The US even suggested a willingness to take part in Taiwanese war "games," something that had not occurred in a generation. Moreover, for the first time in years Taiwan's defense minister had an unofficial meeting with the American Deputy Secretary of Defense. The fact that Washington was willing to make such gesture was yet another sign of its increased commitment to Taiwan regardless of what Beijing thought.

Nevertheless, the new and apparently more pro-Taiwan government of George

W. Bush, like its predecessor in the White House, has been just as concerned that Taiwan might drag the United States into an unnecessary confrontation with the People's Republic. That was especially obvious during the spring of 2004. When Taiwan's voters cast their presidential ballots, they found themselves also voting on a referendum sponsored by President Chen that queried them on whether they felt threatened by the mainland's military posture toward the island. Predictably, Beijing was less than pleased with the ballot initiative.

More surprisingly, President George W. Bush, usually a strong supporter of Taiwan, also cautioned Taipei on the inadvisability of holding such a vote. This was a bit of advice Taiwan's president chose to ignore. Certainly the negative attitude of both Washington and Beijing regarding Taiwan's apparent gestures toward an official declaration of independence is important.

It is also true that the majority of Taiwan's citizens have made it clear that they too want a relaxation of tensions between the island and the mainland. Former Premier Frank Hsieh clearly had that in mind when he spoke of finding a less confrontational "middle way" between the various extremes found within Taiwan on the question of the Republic of China's relationship with the mainland. Interestingly when Hsieh resigned in early 2006, one of his last public statements reiterated his belief that as long as Taiwan benefited, the island itself should continue to find ways to work cooperatively with Beijing. This is a position the departing premier made clear was not universally supported by his former government colleagues.

It was hardly surprising that Mr. Hsieh was willing to suggest that there was dissension within the government's ranks. Emotions regarding Taiwan's relationship with the mainland run deep and lie just beneath the surface. In fact, they can appear quite suddenly depending on events, such as the temporarily explosive environment that emerged after Beijing's national assembly proclaimed that the mainland retained the right to use force to reunite Taiwan with the mainland. On that occasion over 500,000 people in Taiwan went into the streets to protest. But developments on the island are only one element of the complicated relationship. The evolution of the mainland has also affected matters as well.

The rejection of the Maoist economic ideology under Deng Xiaoping has ironically had a deep impact on relations with Taiwan. Mao had been somewhat casual about Taiwan's fate in the years before he came to power. But his regime was quite nationalist in its orientation and saw the

Taiwan

loss of Taiwan in the same context as China's earlier loss of territories, such as Tibet to Hong Kong. Still, Mao's primary emphasis was on the series of famous ideologically driven public campaigns, such as the Great Leap Forward and the Cultural Revolution.

Once Deng Xiaoping came to power and ended China's obsession with communist purity, the core legitimacy of the Communist Party became an issue. To fill that void, mainland governments have over the years focused on nationalism and the party's credentials as the defender of the nation. In that context the question of Taiwan's fate has grown to the point where today's leadership no longer controls the issue, which the population has taken up as its own. Thus the CCP leadership has little choice but to take the hardest line possible on issues related to Taiwan's continuing ties to the mainland. Most important is Beijing's need to have Taiwan accept the idea that there can be only one China. The fundamental reality, though, is that regardless of who is in power in Beijing, the communist party would find a declaration of independence on Taipei's part to be a threat to the CCP's legitimacy. It would almost certainly feel compelled to act militarily against the island.

On the other hand, not coming to Taiwan's defense would be a geo-political disaster for the United States. In short, Beijing and Washington have often found themselves trapped in a potentially explosive situation largely out of their control. Over the last year or so, though, the situation has again evolved. On the one hand, the United States has continued to sell Taiwan billions of dollars worth of new weapons that Beijing deeply resents. On the other hand, with the arrival of the less confrontational Nationalists to the Taiwan's leadership, Washington's own concerns about being dragged into an unnecessary conflict have lessened. It is also true, though, that China's growing naval strength also makes the likelihood of a successful American intervention on Taiwan's behalf more problematic militarily.

More significantly both governments are beginning to recognize that the United States is likely to be less influential in the future while China is becoming more and more important and economically powerful. That evolving reality and the fact that Taiwan's nationalists have returned to power make the present a particularly good time to resolve their differences.

Taiwan's Economy

As was common among several of its Southeast Asian neighbors, Taiwan's decision to turn itself into a relatively inexpensive exporter of products for the richer

National Palace Museum

countries of the developed world was a key to its economic takeoff in the 1960s. Of course, doing so required not only taking advantage of its relatively low wage level, but also encouraging the improvement of the educational system. However, that decision to tie the nation's future to the international economy and especially in those years to the American economy did not come without significant challenges.

As for much of the world, the oil shocks of the mid 1970s forced Taiwan officials to begin to move the island's economy away from a more resource- and material-intensive economy to one more focused on high technology. In short, the decision was made to focus on the talents of Taiwan's human capital by nurturing a less resource-intensive, more scientific and technological base for the economy. In that spirit, and somewhat based on California's Silicon Valley, the nation established its own technology incubation system, based at what would become Hsinchu Science Park. Today Taiwan's premier "science park" has become a centerpiece of government and private sector cooperation. It has played a major role in facilitating Taiwan's more recent economic development and its transition away from the older resource hungry and environmentally damaging industries.

Although Taiwan's economic record had been somewhat spotty in recent years, the economic turmoil of 1997–1998 saw the island relatively unaffected by the economic crisis that hit its neighbors so hard. In general, trends continued as before. In 1997, the economy repeated the performance of previous years with growth at about

6.7%. The year 1998 ended with a healthy growth rate of around 8%. This was a figure many of its neighbors facing negative growth rates surely envied.

Nevertheless, Taiwan has not been immune to the region's problems. It too has experienced weaknesses in its banking sector and a growing unemployment rate. Though Taiwan weathered the initial years of the Asian economic crisis, it entered the new millennium with a more negative economic environment.

Its economy declined dramatically in 2001 and only recovered slightly the following year. Not surprisingly, the slowing economy on Taiwan proper has proven to be an incentive for the island's business community to search for more opportunities within the People's Republic.

It also played a role in seeing Taiwan's Standard and Poor economic rating go down somewhat the end of 2002. By mid-2004, though, the economy appeared to be recovering. While lower than some had expected, Taiwan's growth rate for 2004 came in at a healthy 4.9%, a figure certainly helped by Taiwan's expanding ties to the still fast-growing People's Republic. Although the figure for 2005 was a somewhat more disappointing 4%, 2007 came in at a healthier 5.7%. However, that was before the explosion of oil prices began to unhinge the international economy in the first months of 2008.

By late 2008, Taiwan, along with much of the world, was deeply impacted by the economic downturn that saw the island's export economy contract by just under 5%. Given that its economy is increasingly linked to the mainland's, which was

Historic Newspaper Edition 2008

one of the first countries to start emerging from the dramatic downturn, it is altogether logical that the current Nationalist government would use the last year to further strengthen the economic links across the Taiwan Straits. Of course, that was in large measure only continuing policies that had been growing for years.

In recent years, plans were formalized to allow direct shipping between Taiwan's largest port at Kaohsiung to Xiamen and Fuzhou. The initial arrangement was only for the ships of foreign nationals, and no direct cargo shipments was allowed from the mainland to Taiwan. But even those rules have loosened.

Most recently direct links have been allowed between China's Fujian Province and some of Taiwan's offshore island holdings. Influential businesses have been encouraging such direct trade. Acer, the well-known Taiwan-based computer maker, even opened a production facility in Guangdong province. During early 2002, plans were underway to allow Taiwan banks to start operations on the mainland. By 2005 such banking investment had become a reality.

By 2003 regular chartered flights became available to link Taiwan to Shanghai. Although the planes were still expected to touch down in Hong Kong or Macau before flying on to the People's Republic, passengers no longer had to go through the inconvenience of switching planes before going on to their final desti-

nation. Making connections even easier, direct flights between Taiwan and the mainland were temporarily allowed during the Chinese New Year holidays. Passengers, business travelers and tourists alike did not even have to land in Hong Kong during the holiday period. Although only temporarily allowed, such flights clearly reflected the government's awareness that the majority of Taiwan's population wanted to be able to travel easily to the mainland.

Overall, significant progress was made under President Chen to make it easier for the residents of both communities, Taiwanese and Chinese, to visit and work with each other. Thousands of Taiwanese have worked in the People's Republic, and mainland tourists have regularly visited the island. One long-lasting impediment, though, was the absence of regular direct flights and ocean-going ferries between Taiwan and the coast.

By mid-2008, after the Nationalists reestablished themselves in power, even those last impediments rapidly fell away. In July, it became much easier to take a ferry from the mainland to China's Fujian province. Regular direct flights that were not required to touch down initially in Hong Kong began.

The following year saw even more economic links forged under Taiwan's nationalist government. Almost two hundred sectors of the island's economy were opened up to direct mainland investments, and PRC groups gained the right

to purchase real estate. In Addition, the government moved vigorously to reduce tariff barriers between the communities. To no one's surprise, the DPP legislators were very unhappy with these efforts and vowed to oppose them.

Over time, the increasing ease of transportation and investment between these two long-estranged communities is likely to transform both peoples fundamentally. If in the recent past the lives of those who lived on Taiwan and the mainland often differed dramatically from each other, the current century is likely to see a major reduction of those differences. If China somehow becomes more democratic as well, the merging of cultures could become even more dramatic.

Society and Culture

Taiwan's primary ethnic roots have long resided both in the Chinese mainland cultures that came to dominate the population over the centuries and in the indigenous Austronesian communities. The Taiwanese sense of identity remains an evolving concept. While a generation ago most Taiwanese, obviously of Han ethnic background, considered themselves "Chinese," today they are much more likely to identify themselves as "Taiwanese." In doing so they are reflecting a growing sense that the people of Taiwan represent a more diverse community with differing ethnic and historical experiences than those on the mainland.

Certainly the emergence of a Taiwan-based consciousness was one of the most significant developments of the DPP's years in office. Just how real that shift in self identity is, though, has been questioned. Some have suggested that it is less a substantive change in long-term self identification than a short-term reaction to the tensions with Beijing, a sentiment likely to diminish as relations improve.

The differences that separate those of Han ethnicity themselves are less rooted in recent political developments. Although intermarriage is more and more common, the non-indigenous population is made up of people from different communities within China. The most significant distinctions are between those whose families migrated generations ago from China's Guangdong province, often known as the Hakka, and those whose lineage initially began in China's Fujian province. The somewhat more diverse groups that arrived along with the fleeing Guomindang after the Chinese Civil War should not be forgotten. It is also true that many of the island's Han inhabitants trace part of their roots to the intermarriage of their ancestors with the indigenous communities that once dominated the islands.

Taiwan

Taiwan's Indigenous Austronesian Communities

The vast majority of the Taiwanese are ethnically Han Chinese. However, approximately 2% of them make up a community of indigenous Austronesian peoples more similar to those found in Southeast Asia. Their origins seem to lie not only to the far south, but among the non-Han peoples who previously inhabited the southern coast of China. Not a homogeneous group, the community is made up of some fourteen officially recognized and quite distinctively different groups that have over the years often found themselves pushed into the mountains, particularly along the east coast of the island.

Often in conflict with the Han peoples arriving from the mainland, the diverse Austronesian communities were not completely subdued until the Japanese did so after they acquired the island at the end of the nineteenth century. Once that was accomplished, the Japanese initially set up a reservation system that isolated the various indigenous peoples from the majority Han community. Over time, though, the Japanese began to exploit indigenous land and encouraged them to assimilate into Japanese culture. Long isolated and often discriminated against by the dominant majority population, these communities have in recent years begun to assert themselves and even became active in the various groupings of indigenous Pacific peoples. Delegations have even traveled to Canada to confer with native peoples there about asserting their economic rights.

Taiwan's New National Health Service

One of the most obvious signs of Taiwan's maturity as a society has been the successful implementation of a national health care system that covers all residents. Begun in 1995, Taiwan's Nationalist government, with some nudging from the emerging DPP movement, concluded that Taiwan's recent economic success had reached the point when a medical system that would cover the entire population had become feasible. There was reason to do so. As was the case in the United States, a significant part of the population, something over forty percent, had no medical insurance and were therefore eligible only for as much health care as they could afford.

More surprising was the fact that compared to the effort undertaken at approximately the same time in the United States, there was very little opposition. Unlike within the U.S. there has been a general consensus in Taiwan that health care is a human right with which the government

Delta Electronics builds first green rated building in Taiwan

should concern itself. Those that disagreed did not have the political clout to stop the effort. There are, of course, some who are dissatisfied. But the vast majority of the population is quite pleased with the system, which is both quite affordable and universal. Of particular interest was the fact that the government of Taiwan, as a sign of its continuing friendship, sent an expert on the Taiwan medical system to the United States as a resource just as the American government was itself—during the spring of 2009—taking up the challenge to provide its own population with such universal care.

Taiwan and the Climate Crisis

Although Taiwan's contribution to global warming is relatively small, it is still a highly industrialized nation. It was recently ranked as the 23rd largest producer of CO_2, the best known of the green house gasses that humanity keeps pumping into the atmosphere. Taiwan is particularly vulnerable to the effects of global warming because scientists believe it leads to the intensification of tropical storms, the kind that already cause considerable damage in Taiwan from time to time.

Many of its important urban centers are also located along the ocean's edge where water levels are steadily rising. A mere one meter rise in sea levels could, for example, see the ocean claim 272 square kilometers of land. Additionally, because Taiwan is located close to the equator, it is vulnerable to the arrival of new diseases as global warming permits these medical challenges to move further north into regions they had not previously inhabited.

That problem has, in fact, already developed. Dengue fever, which plagues people in much of Southeast Asia, has begun to arrive in southern Taiwan much earlier each season. It remains longer and is expanding further to the north in its area of contagion.

On a more positive note, Taiwan's leaders have recently begun to address efforts not only to research the island's green house gas emissions, but to work to reduce them. Legislation has been created to establish a national goal to keep emission levels from climbing above those of 2005. This is an important but not very ambitious goal. Thus far this has been a voluntary effort among the nation's top two hundred energy producers. The year 2007 was designated Taiwan's inaugural year of carbon reductions, and authorities began a publicity campaign to teach the public how to reduce their own carbon energy impact. For professional men this has involved the encouragement to dress down, ending the use of heavier suit coats that require more summertime air conditioning.

The nation has also moved to use more green energy. Major efforts are underway to encourage people to use mass transit, and Taiwan has become the third-ranking nation in the use of solar water heater installation density. Wind energy is also being installed, though largely as a way to augment, not replace, energy produced by fossil fuel.

One especially impressive example is the southern city of Tainan under the direction of its long serving mayor, Hsu Tain-tsair. He has been particularly aware of the threat of climate change and has worked not only to expand the city's green spaces, but to develop its mass transit facilities. Given that parts of Tainan are very close to sea level, that attitude is especially important.

The challenges of a changing global climate were especially apparent to islanders in August 2009 when the devastating Typhoon Morakot struck the southern part of the island killing over 600 people. The vast majority were from the island's indigenous community. While no single weather event can be directly attributed to man-made climate change, the devastation caused by Morakot was exactly of the sort one would expect from the more powerful storms scientists have attributed to a warming international climate.

The Future: Taiwan

As so often in the past, Taiwan's people have reason to be both concerned and satisfied. On the one hand, its budding dem-

ocratic tradition survived the crisis of the 2004 election. Leadership of Taiwan was smoothly handed back to the Nationalists when they won the most recent presidential election. For those who measure a democracy's viability by the real possibility of those in power giving it up to those who win at the ballot box, it was yet another marker in Taiwan's democratic evolution.

On the other hand, former President Chen's efforts further to legitimize Taiwan's independence from the mainland had the potential of provoking Beijing into an aggressive policy that could, at the very least, have undermined Taiwan's economy and conceivably prompted a military response. Complicating matters enormously is, of course, the fact that Taiwan's relationship with the mainland is so deeply linked to the more immediate political competition between the island's two main contending parties. For the moment, though, tensions have calmed significantly. With the Nationalists' return to

power and President Ma Ying-jeou's commitment to creating a more positive relationship with the mainland, the years of dramatic flag waving on the part of Beijing and Taipei are probably over for now.

Perhaps the most important point is that both sides understand that a new era is emerging. Considering that the Nationalists are back in power, Beijing believes that now is the time to create a more successful relationship, Moreover, many people on Taiwan understand that creating a more positive relationship with Beijing is really their only choice, given China's growing influence and their deeply shared cultural values. That choice also allows Taiwan to gain the most from the mainland's economic accomplishments. Nevertheless, it will not be easy. The combination of Beijing's growing international confidence and more repressive internal administration will most likely make attaining that "balance" an especially challenging effort over the coming years.

Japan

Area: 142,726 sq. mi (370,370 sq. km.)
Population: 126,804,433 (July 2010 est.)
Capital City: Tokyo 12,527,115 million (2003 estimate)
Climate: Sub-tropically warm in the extreme south, becoming temperate in the north. The high elevations have much lower temperatures than the coastal areas. There is a rainy monsoon from June to October.
Neighboring Countries: The islands of Japan are closest to Russia (north); Korea (west); and mainland China (southwest).
Official Language: Japanese
Ethnic Background: Overwhelmingly Japanese—99.4%—and some Koreans. There is a very small community of Ainu on Hokkaido Island who are physically significantly different from the Japanese, possibly descended from the earliest inhabitants of the islands.
Principal Religions: Shinto, the earliest religious tradition, and Buddhism. The latter is especially widespread and split into many old and new sects; Christianity (less than 1%).
Main Export (to U.S., nations of Southeast Asia and Western Europe): Products of heavy industry, including ships and autos, products of lighter industry, including consumer electronics, cameras, and a wide range of other items, i.e., textiles, iron, steel, fish.
Main Imports (from nations of the Middle East and Southeast Asia): Oil, raw industrial materials, foodstuffs, textiles
Currency: Yen
National Day: December 23 (birthday of the Emperor)
Special Holiday: Sept. 15, "Respect for the Aged Day"
Chief of State: Emperor Akihito
Head of Government: Prime Minister Naoto Kan (since June 2010)
National Flag: White, with a red disk representing the rising sun in the center.
Per Capita GDP Income $32,600 (2009 est.)

The island nation of Japan consists of four larger bodies of land, Hokkaido, Honshu, Shikoku and Kyushu and the smaller Ryukyu Islands south of Kyushu. The southern half of Sakhalin and the Kurile Islands to the north, which Japan possessed at the height of its World War II power, were lost to the Soviet Union at the close of the conflict.

Geographically, Japan is part of an immense hump on the earth's surface which extends from Siberia on the Asian continent through Korea and Japan southward, rising above water again in the areas of Taiwan and the Philippines and extending further south toward the eastern portions of Indonesia and Australia. As is true in other portions of the ridge, Japan is geologically unstable and subject to frequent and sometimes violent earthquakes. Thermal pressures from deep in the earth escape periodically through the many volcanoes that are interspersed among the mountains. Mt. Fuji, its lofty crater surrounded by a mantle of snow, is visible from the streets of Tokyo on a clear day—one of the most beautiful sights in Asia. It has not been active since 1719. All of the mountainous areas, volcanic and non-volcanic, are scenic—the taller peaks on Honshu have justly earned the name "Japanese Alps."

The mountains leave little level space; only about 15% of the total land area is level, and much of the only large plain is occupied by the huge and busy capital of Tokyo. As a result, farms are located in the hilly areas of the islands and are made level by the labors of the farmers, who have constructed elaborate terraces in order to win more land for their intense cultivation. Japanese farming is actually better called gardening, since the small units of land, an average of 2.5 to 5 acres per farm, are tilled with such energy that none of the soil or available growing season is wasted. This tremendous agricultural effort produces almost enough to feed the people, most of which live in densely packed urban areas.

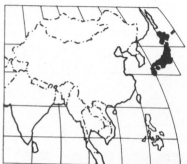

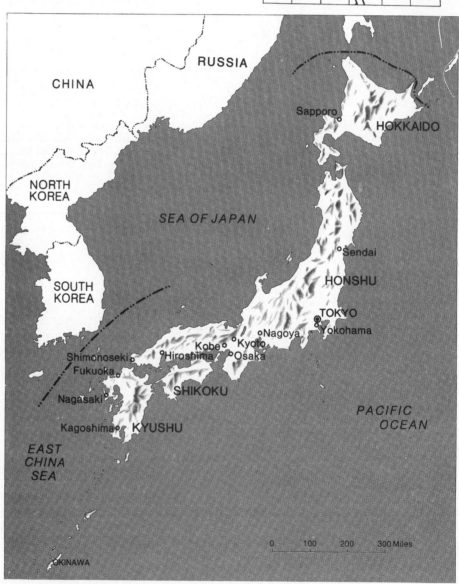

"Bullet" train streaking commuters home against the majestic background of Mt. Fuji

The climate of the islands is totally dominated by the seasonal winds, or monsoons. Cold winds blowing from the Asian continent invade the land beginning in September each year. All of Hokkaido and some of Honshu lie buried in snow from December to March. In the spring, the winds shift, blowing from the warm equatorial South Pacific; the growing season of Honshu and Hokkaido then commences.

The subtropical island of Kyushu remains warm all year around, permitting two or three harvests of paddy rice each year. Only one crop of dry, or field rice, grows in the much shorter summer of Hokkaido. In the last half of August and in September, the southern monsoon brings typhoons (hurricanes), laden with rainfall and often destruction from the Pacific to the shores of Japan.

Rainfall and weather are also affected by the oceanic water currents that envelope the islands. The warm southern Kuro shio dominates the summer months; the arctic Oya Shio descends as far south as Tokyo in the winter. Both currents bring a huge number of fish to the offshore areas on the Pacific side, and an even larger number to the Sea of Japan. Depending almost wholly for animal protein upon this bounty from the sea, the Japanese raise only an insignificant number of livestock on the islands.

History

The earliest known inhabitants of the Japanese islands were probably the Ainu,

a people who are physically very different from the Japanese. For much of Japan's history the Ainu people were driven steadily northward by settlers arriving from mainland Asia. The Ainu exist today in small reservations on the island of Hokkaido where in recent years they have tried to revive their ancient culture.

The men have much more body and facial hair than the Japanese. Archeological evidence reveals the existence of a Neolithic culture in Japan from about 10,000

B.C. known as Joman, from the rope-patterned ceramics they produced. This community was apparently displaced around 300 B.C. with the arrival of other people from mainland Asia who introduced a rice-growing culture known as Yayoi.

The people who eventually formed the community we know as "Japanese" had come primarily from the mainland of northeast Asia, by way of Korea, and are of the same linguistic ancestry as the Koreans. They were mainly of Mongolian

An Ainu elder   Courtesy: Jon Markham Morrow

79

Japan

stock whose ancestors had lived a nomadic existence on the continent of Central and Northeast Asia. This ethnic group became the predominant one, but there were also other elements from the South China coast and the Southwest Pacific.

All of these elements gradually blended into a people possessing very similar physical characteristics, considering the large size of the present population. In the first centuries A.D., the Japanese lived mainly around the Inland Sea, a body of water almost completely enclosed by three of the four large islands. They were organized into many warring clans and had no writing system with which to express their language, which is derived from dialects originally spoken in what is now Manchuria, Mongolia and Siberian Russia.

Japanese tradition tells of the creation of the islands by the sun goddess whose descendants founded the Yamato clan that eventually emerged as the Japanese imperial family. Actually, there is considerable evidence to suggest that the real origins of the imperial elite are to be found, not in Japan itself, but in Korea. Some authors, going beyond the more vague references to "continental influences" have argued succinctly that the original Japanese ruling family was founded by the early southern Korean kingdom of Paekche. Whatever the specific ties to Korea, it is certain that the evolution of Japan was fundamentally altered by its leadership's decision to immerse itself in the culture of the continent in the 6th century.

Encounter with China

The Japanese were greatly impressed by the tales told of Tang (618–907 A.D.) and China's power, wealth, prestige and culture. They quickly set about importing many aspects of Chinese civilization. Buddhism was at its height and it was through that medium that a range of cultural, linguistic and political elements of Chinese civilization entered Japan. On a political level, the Yamato clan was interested in borrowing the Chinese imperial system since it offered the possibility of greatly enhancing their power far above the influence the clan had long held.

In an attempt to imitate the Tang dynasty, the Japanese imperial court built a capital at Nara, near the Inland Sea on the island of Honshu. They also worked to establish a centralized governing system along Chinese imperial models. For a time the influence of China was enormous. The Chinese language was adopted as the official writing system and played a role similar to that of Latin in the medieval west. Kyoto emerged as the new imperial capital in the late 8th century and became the home of a brilliant culture. Histories

were produced to "prove" the divinity and supremacy of the Yamato imperial clan. The 7th century B.C. was selected as the time that the sun goddess was said to have given the blessing of creation to Japan, and established the reign of her descendants on the islands.

Within court life at Kyoto, the arts flourished, especially a particularly distinctive literature that many believe to have been the world's first formal novels. The physical form of the novels, produced by women of the imperial court, was influential as well. Interestingly, although literary production was considered a fundamental talent for both men and women of the court, the men largely wrote in the adopted language of Chinese. Women, who in contrast, wrote using a system of modified characters known as *kana* to represent the sounds of Japanese, went on to write these profoundly influential works.

The best known of them, the *Tale of Genji*, a 1,000 page story about the romances of Prince Genji of the imperial court, is a sophisticated novel which deals with an extraordinary range of human emotions and sentiment. It is a far more

personal and introspective work than the romances that had preceded it either in Japan or elsewhere. Written by Murasaki Shikibu during the early 11th century, it became the model of refined behavior for educated Japanese, a literary influence that could only be compared to that of Shakespeare in the West.

As time passed and Imperial Tang China itself faded, the more direct links to China were severed. After the 10th century no more formal missions were sent to the Chinese court. By then the Japanese aristocracy was ready to build their own syntheses from both earlier Japanese traditions and the more recent borrowing from the court. If, however, many aspects of the period of tutelage continued to influence Japan over the centuries, the Yamato imperial family's attempts to establish themselves as Chinese-style emperors failed.

The creation of a true central government was not possible because many clans, particularly those in central and northern Japan, were strong and independent and were preoccupied with battling the Ainu people and each other. These clans did not attempt to overthrow the imperial court, however. They contented themselves with largely ignoring it. Moreover many had ties to powerful court factions that gave them additional autonomy.

Although the more martial, semi-independent clans outside the capital admired and imitated the cultural achievements of imperial Kyoto, they were primarily interested in the military power. The Taira, one of the two most powerful military clans, defeated the other, the Minamoto, in 1160 and then temporarily seized control of Kyoto. Shortly afterward, the Taira were in turn defeated by the Minamoto, whose leader Yoritomo was appointed as the first *shogun*, or generalissimo, of Japan by the emperor. Thus was founded the Kamakura *shogunate*, which remained in power for 150 years and an entirely new system of ruling.

The Shoguns

With the emergence of the Minamoto family and the Kamakura *shogunate* they founded, Japan moved into a new phase of its development, one that would last in various forms until the 19th century. Although it varied over the centuries, it usually operated as a generally feudal society dominated by successive shogunal families best thought of as military dictators. For the next seven hundred years real power usually existed in a somewhat precarious balance between regional lords and various shogunal families that emerged from time to time.

The imperial court remained largely irrelevant to the real issues of power. In fact, not until the nineteenth century, and then more in symbol than reality would power appear to gravitate once again around the emperor. For the feudal era even that appearance of power was gone.

Japan's "medieval" era has often been compared to feudal system in Western Europe, and indeed there were many similarities. Although Japan's feudal experience developed later than that in Europe it too was characterized by the dominating presence of an aristocratic military elite loyal to various regional lords or *daimyo* as they were known in Japan. In both regions, feudalism reflected the decentralized nature of power and a system that was built upon the labors of peasant farmers. Nevertheless, there were clear differences as well.

The ties between the military elite, *samurai*, and the *daimyo* tended to be more personal and based on kinship than that of the more contractual-minded Europeans who developed elaborate contracts to cement feudal relationships. Western Europe never developed the institution of the *shogunate* that eventually became a sort of "halfway stage" between feudal society and the centralized governments of a modern country.

The Kamakura *shogunate* was soon faced with the external threat of the powerful empire established by the Mongol emperor Kublai Khan in China in the 13th century. Two attempted Mongol invasions were defeated by a combination of Japanese military resistance and timely, violent typhoons. Interestingly, the Japanese perception that they had been saved by the intervention of divine winds, i.e. *Kamikaze*, was an inspiration under far different circumstances many centuries later as young Japanese suicide bombers attempted once again to save their country from invasion

during the last days of the Second World War.

The 14th century fall of the Kamakura *shogunate* led to other weaker powers moving into the breach to establish their own dominance for a time. More importantly, the powerful regional lords known as *daimyo* came to dominate the life of the islands. These feudal lords were supported by highly trained and loyal *samurai*, that is by the soldiers, men who followed a warrior's creed of honor and loyalty known as *Bushido*. It was the bloody struggles among these regional leaders that made the late 16th century an exceptionally violent time in Japanese history.

The Tokugawa System: 1603–1868

Japan disintegrated into a state of feudal warfare in the 16th century resembling that of the Wars of the Roses in England. Commercial interests continued, however, to promote trade and build roads. Warfare was gradually brought under control in the later part of the century by two persons—Oda Nobunaga and his brilliant general, Toyotomi Hideyoshi, who succeeded Nobunaga as dictator when his overlord was killed by a dissident general. After two unsuccessful attempts to invade China (see Korea section), Hideyoshi was assassinated. Though things were a bit unsettled for a time, Japan was about to enter into one of its most stable eras, the *shogunate* of the Tokugawa.

In 1603 Tokugawa Ieyasu, a feudal lord from the region where modern Tokyo is located, emerged triumphant. He established a new *shogunate* which lasted until the nineteenth century. The Tokugawa developed a complicated system that can be described as a sort of "centralized feudalism." On one hand the Tokugawa retained very considerable power, yet the regional lords, the *daimyo*, controlled their own domains. To retain power, the Tokugawa insisted that the lords maintain a residence and the permanent presence of themselves or family members at Edo. In short, the Tokugawa maintained control through a formal hostage system.

For generations thereafter, anyone on Japan's main thoroughfare was treated to the spectacle of aristocratic lords and their *samurai* entourages regularly traveling through the countryside to and from Edo. There is a curious irony to this system, sometimes known as the "alternative attendance" system. The Tokugawa *Shogunate* was powerful enough to impose it on the many feudal lords of Japan, yet weak enough to need such a system to maintain control. The system, designed to freeze the political and social structure of Japan under the Tokugawa, had the unexpected effect of vastly improving the resources of

the despised merchant class that served this enormous and peripatetic nobility.

The Arrival of the West

It was in the 16th century that the western ships, Spanish and Portuguese, began to arrive in Japanese waters and the various Catholic missionaries, from the aristocratic Jesuits to the more populist Franciscans, began to build commercial and religious ties to the islands. The Jesuits converted a large number of people, particularly on the island of Kyushu and its largest city, Nagasaki. Their position was enhanced by the conversion of a leading feudal lord of the island, which led many vassals and followers into the arms of the Church. Firearms and other Western methods of violence were introduced and eagerly adopted by the Japanese.

Spanish Franciscans, who arrived in 1593, began a period of even greater efforts toward conversion of the Japanese and also complicated the situation by periodic bickering with the Jesuits. Though the missionaries were often initially well received, such a positive reception did not last long. It was especially undermined by a growing Japanese awareness of the role they had played in supporting Western conquests in other regions of East Asia.

Hideyoshi, who was in domination by the 1580s, became convinced that Christianity was nothing but a veil concealing a future European invasion and embarked on a course of persecution directed to-

Japan

ward the Western priests and their converts. Somewhat later, concerned that the Westerners could threaten their own power, the Tokugawa authorities moved not only to persecute Christians but to close the entire country to the outside. For the next two hundred years the only Westerners allowed into the country were those on a yearly Dutch ship permitted to trade at Nagasaki.

Ironically, Japan under the Tokugawa chose to isolate itself just as the West was beginning to dramatically emerge. During this period of isolation, the clans, each ruled by a powerful *daimyo*, built ornate castles around which towns arose. Agriculture prospered, though sporadically interrupted by revolts of the peasants, who lived in abject poverty. Trade flourished and the population increased. A merchant class emerged which quickly acquired a great deal of influence over the *daimyo* and the martial *samurai* by making loans to them. There was much intellectual activity, which was conservative, to the extent that it advocated that the imperial clan, which had survived over the centuries, be restored to full power and to replace the "usurping" *shogunate*.

Over the next centuries sporadic attempts by the Western powers to "open" Japan to foreign trade were largely unsuccessful. This lasted until the mid nineteenth century when the Russians, British and Americans developed more serious plans to penetrate the islands.

For the United States, which was to take the lead in Japan's departure from isolation, the effort was a logical extension of its generation-long thrust toward the Pacific and beyond. In 1846 San Francisco had been taken and an eye clearly directed to the possibilities of commerce beyond. Though Japan was of less interest than the riches of China, it was seen as a stepping-stone to the Asian continent. Ironically, if the Americans who wanted to open the islands knew very little about Japan, many in Japan were quite knowledgeable about the outside world—they had had access to Western materials smuggled into Japan during the periodic visits of the Dutch ships at Nagasaki.

The Opening of Japan

The uncertainty among the Japanese when Commodore Perry of the United States sailed his fleet into Tokyo Bay in 1853–1854 is understandable. They had a good understanding of the military power the Westerners had demonstrated against China in the Opium War a decade earlier and knew they did not have the weapons to match the West. On the other hand, the policy of exclusion, now more than two centuries old, had become the accepted

Commodore Perry's fleet in Tokyo Bay

custom. No mere request by the arriving American flotilla could easily change that. The situation was even more complicated by the continuing antagonism of the southwestern domains of Satsuma and Choshu and the growing imperial sentiment which itself undermined the authority of the Tokugawa *Shogunate*.

The *shogun's* government uncertain how to respond to Commodore Perry's demands, took the unprecedented step of asking the several hundred *daimyo* for their advice. Even though the answers received were not unanimous, they did demonstrate a generally anti-foreign tone. Nevertheless, the *shogun's* government, facing the potential military power of the Americans, signed the foreign treaties anyway thus even further alienating them from many of the feudal lords over whom they had so long dominated. Commodore Perry was therefore able to get the treaty desired by the U.S. The other Western powers soon had their own agreements. All of these were patterned after the "unequal treaties" that were then being imposed on the waning Manchu dynasty of China.

The opponents of the Tokugawa, especially the powerful clans of the southwest, accused the government of weakness and continued an anti-foreign campaign under the slogan "Honor the Emperor—Expel the Barbarians." But their enthusiasm for driving the Westerners out proved militarily impossible. Western naval bom-

bardments at Kagoshima in 1863 and Shimonoseki in 1864 convinced them of the folly of their demands. Eventually they did an about-face, becoming eager advocates of learning as much as possible from the West in order to be better equipped to resist its influence and power.

The immediate problem though was frustration with the Western pressures. The *shogunal* court found itself caught between the Western demands and the aroused *samurai* class. After a series of confrontations, the two-hundred-fifty-year-old Tokugawa *shogunate* collapsed in the face of a coalition of forces which included the southern domains of Satsuma and Choshu in alliance with the Kyoto-based imperial court. Known perhaps inappropriately as the "*Meiji Restoration*" due to the reemergence of the imperial court as a player, this truly revolutionary development was to be the central turning point in modern Japanese history.

The Meiji Restoration

The *Meiji Restoration* was ostensibly the restoration of the Japanese emperor to power by the southern regions of the islands. What really occurred though was the arrival to power of an oligarchy of extraordinary young mid-level *samurai* mostly from the Southwest that was fundamentally committed to modernizing Japan in the face of the Western challenge. The leadership set up a strong central administration and governed in a style that nevertheless made some concessions to the concerns of those *samurai* elite left outside of the new constellation of power. Their fundamental goal was to build a "rich country and strong military" and to have Japan enter the Western family of nations as a full partner rather than, as was the case so often elsewhere, yet another victim of Western colonization.

Determined to make a dramatic break with the past, the new leaders issued a series of goals known as the "Charter Oath" which outlined their hope of reforming the social structure of Japan and to learn as much as possible from the outside world. The period of feudal isolation was clearly at an end. These new *Meiji* leaders wiped out the old clan system of authority and at the same time modernized land tenure. The landowning peasants were heavily taxed, however, yielding greater funds for modernization. Modern communications were established and new machinery was imported to manufacture textiles and other goods. An entirely new system of banking and other modern industrial techniques were imported, and many "foreign experts" were temporarily engaged to help in the transformation.

A modern education system, eventually geared to the production of literate and obedient subjects of the Emperor, was created. An effective army and navy and a modern legal system also emerged within a short time, eventually permitting the Japanese to renegotiate the "unequal treaties," but the leadership avoided foreign military adventures at first. On a political level, the *Meiji* oligarchies continued to dominate, though by the 1880s they found themselves pressed by a "popular rights" movement led by wealthier members of the peasant class and former members of the *samurai* elite. Eventually, after studying Western governmental systems, the leadership adopted a modified version of the imperial German parliamentary system.

A *Diet*, or parliament, was created under a constitution of 1889 that proclaimed the emperor as the supreme ruler. Nevertheless, behind the scenes the governing oligarchy continued to rule. The period of indiscriminately adopting foreign institutions and techniques diminished and practically ended by 1890. After that, although the interest in Western science and technology continued unabated, more emphasis was now placed on traditional Japanese institutions and customs. The emperor became the object of still greater glorification, even though he possessed little more than nominal power. This veneration interestingly was less a product of traditional Shinto imperial myths than Japan's search for modernity. The oligarchy that created the new governing system felt that the nation needed some sort of unifying principle to support its modernization and the ancient system of the imperial dynasty seemed to suit their purposes.

Economically, a small group of *zaibatsu* (large family-owned holding companies) arose that dominated the beginnings of industry in Japan in a manner reminiscent of Carnegie, Harriman and Morgan in the United States. But there was also abundant room for small business as well. This balance between central control and local initiative, coupled with the rapid urbanization of Japan, its fairly low rate of population growth and the fact that the people demanded little in personal comforts, permitted a rate of modernization unparalleled in history.

The late Emperor Hirohito at his coronation, 1926

By the end of the *Meiji* period (1868–1912), Japan had largely achieved its goal of modernization, a feat not duplicated by any other traditional nation in the world in such a brief period, or indeed anywhere on such a tremendous scale. Nevertheless, despite the changes in the material circumstances of Japan, many martial feudal values from the Tokugawa era would continue to be influential for generations.

The Rise of the Japanese Empire

The international arena that Japan had chosen to enter during the late nineteenth century was an aggressive one of imperialism. After centuries of colonization, the imperial urge had continued to grow at an even faster pace. Africa and Southeast Asia were then being carved up by the Europeans and the Americans were beginning to turn an eye toward the Hawaiian Islands and eventually the Philippines. In central Asia, the Russians and English were competing for influence and China, the giant of traditional East Asia, was struggling to maintain even a modicum of influence. Within Japan, many argued that they too had to take their place among the imperial powers and begin to assert themselves abroad.

For many, the first goal was obvious, the Korean peninsula. In fact, as early as the 1870s some in government had forcibly argued for a move against the then closed "hermit kingdom" of Korea. That early effort had not been carried out but by the 1890s the Japanese were aggressively competing with China for influence on the peninsula.

By 1894 a full-scale war had broken out. The Japanese army and navy seized control of Taiwan and conquered Korea, which was annexed in 1910. In its war with China, Japan fought alone, without the support of any of the major Western powers and somewhat predictably aroused the antagonism of the Russians who had their own interests in the area. Working with other European powers, Russia then forced the Japanese to give up at the bargaining table much of what they had won on the continent itself.

This lesson left a lasting impression on Japanese leaders. In their minds, the "Western imperialists" had their own set of rules; outsiders, like the Japanese, were not part of their "club" and were not permitted the same freedom of action as other world powers. Nevertheless, in 1903, the Japanese concluded an alliance with Britain that lasted until the 1920's. The ensuing period saw a tremendous growth in Japanese military and political power at the expense of its neighbors, in part a result of its strengthened position as a member of a Western alliance.

The Japanese, of course, were not alone in conquering territory from the Chinese. By the turn of the century the dramatic episode known as the "Cutting of the Melon," had begun which saw the Western powers grabbing even more power for themselves throughout China. The Russians' actions particularly aroused Japanese anger. The two were competing for influence in northeast Asia. The Russians had, for example, established a "sphere of influence" in Manchuria dating from 1898. By 1904 the Japanese felt ready to challenge them and launched a victorious land and sea campaign (the Russo-Japanese War) thereby establishing themselves as the leading power in East Asia—in fact, one of the world's major powers.

A decade later, Japan did not waste the opportunity offered by the vulnerability

Japan

of Germany during World War I. It quickly declared war and seized the German holdings in China's Shandong Province, as well as several small island groups in the Pacific. At the same time, it shipped considerable quantities of munitions to the Allied Powers, including Russia, its former enemy. A few years later after the Bolshevik Revolution of 1917, Japan sent a large military force to occupy eastern Siberia to see if the region could be added to the growing Japanese empire. By 1922, internal and external pressures eventually forced them though to withdraw from Siberia and Shandong.

Taisho Democracy

The post-World War I period in Japan was one of transition. The original *Meiji* Constitution of 1889 had not worked quite as anticipated. The cooperation of the parliamentary parties had become more necessary than expected for the smooth operation of government and they had thus gained in power. Party leaders such as Hara Kei emerged as prime ministers, and Japan entered an era where more experimentation was carried out in democratic decision-making. The voting lists were also enlarged to include almost the entire adult male population. The political parties became more influential than ever before. By the 1920s two political parties had rotated in power and a system of formal parliamentary government seemed to be at hand.

The parliamentary leaders found much of the real power needed to run the country still denied them. The military and bureaucracy remained extraordinarily influential and the aging oligarchic leadership still powerful. On the more positive side, the parliamentary governments were more open to negotiation regarding issues of international concern such as the growing naval arms race of the period. In fact, much to the irritation of the Japanese right wing, Japan signed a treaty that theoretically limited the growth of its navy.

But the speed of modernization in Japan left unsolved some problems and created many others. The rural population remained isolated from urban progress, while continuing to pay for it by increased taxes, rents and difficult conditions in the countryside. All of this created considerable discontent.

Moreover, Japan had changed greatly since its days of isolation. The country's economy was far more integrated into the international order than ever before. Thus, the onset of the great depression hit the country very hard and the rural peasants especially so. The cause of the peasants was championed by ambitious army officers, who did so partly in sincerity but

Entrance of a Shinto temple at Nagasaki, c. 1880

also for political reasons. Those officers, who were often of rural origin themselves, found allies among civilian nationalists. They adopted the position that rural poverty had two basic causes: poor government by the political parties and economic practices by the large combines. They criticized the political parties, which were more influential during the 1920s than at any previous time. The *zaibatsu* also came under fire for their "materialist devotion."

The military and civilian nationalists also blamed injurious and "insulting" tariffs and discriminatory trade policies of

some foreign nations for the adverse conditions of the peasants. The answer to Japan's dilemma was, in their eyes, further expansion into the mainland which was seen as a "new frontier" one that be developed for Japan's benefit and receive its excess population.

This line of argument had a broad base of appeal, and the rightists strengthened their position by taking forceful action in the form of assassinations and coups. The more extreme of the right-wing groups never rose to power, but they were able to force the parliamentary parties from power.

Toward War with China

From the early 1930s, although the extremists failed to gain power, Japan was again controlled by conservative leaders often drawn from the military. Within China, Japan took advantage of the conflict between the nationalist forces of Chiang Kai-shek and the Chinese communists. Increasing pressures, both diplomatic and military, were brought to bear in order to give Japan great influence over China. The Japanese army seized Manchuria in 1931–1932, soon after the local authorities had threatened Japan's interests by accepting the authority of Chiang Kai-shek's government.

Renaming the area Manchukuo, the Japanese military established the youthful Henry Pu-Yi, the "last emperor" of the Manchu dynasty, as its puppet emperor. Frequent military clashes with China eventually led to an invasion of eastern China in 1937. During the invasion a multitude of atrocities were committed by the invading soldiers. The best known of these came to be called the "Rape of Nanjing" for the reign of mass murder and rape the Japanese soldiers inflicted on that city's helpless residents. With the start of the invasion, World War II had begun in Asia. Within two years it would be expanded by Hitler's invasion of Poland.

The merciless bombing of the mainland cities alienated the Chinese completely and enabled both Chiang and Mao to rally support for their separate struggles against the Japanese. Eventually an uneasy truce emerged between the two Chinese leaders because of the Japanese threat. The Japanese forces remained in occupation of the major cities of eastern China. The vicious Japanese assault led to increasing criticism and pressure from the outside world, including the United States. Unfortunately for the Chinese, only the Russians initially offered any significant official help.

Eventually, in an effort to limit the capability of the Japanese war machine, the U.S. gradually cut down shipments of oil and scrap steel. This reduced shipment of strategic materials caused the Japanese to look for sources elsewhere, particularly iron in the Philippines and oil in Indonesia. By the 1940s, the successful German victories provided an example of the rewards of aggression, and weakened those Western colonial powers the Japanese were soon also to challenge. Fortunately for the rest of the world, cooperation between Nazi Germany and Japan was always very unsteady even though they and Italy formed an alliance in 1940.

World War II in the Pacific

In late 1941, Japan decided to force the issue with the Americans. It demanded an

The newly installed *Orchid Emperor of Manchukuo* reviews Japanese troops at Dairen in 1934

unfreezing of its assets in the United States, a measure that had been undertaken in response to the July 1941 Japanese invasion of Indochina. However, Washington refused and continued to withhold oil and scrap steel shipments. Washington encouraged the Dutch in Indonesia also to withhold sales of oil unless the Japanese agreed to a political settlement. That would have involved an end to aggression and withdrawal from China. Since the Japanese had no interest in such a dramatic retreat and the Americans were unwilling to compromise with a nation many felt would not dare attack, the die was cast for an even greater extension of the developing world war.

Believing that the U.S. would oppose any Japanese seizure of the resources of Southeast Asia, the Japanese decided to destroy the U.S. Pacific Fleet stationed at Pearl Harbor in Hawaii. On December 7, 1941, Japanese airplanes without warning almost completely wiped out the U.S. battleship fleet stationed at Pearl Harbor. The imperial forces of Japan then quickly attacked the many Western colonies in Southeast Asia. Initially, their superior might in the Pacific was impressive enough to cause fear of an imminent naval attack on California. That threat never materialized. But it did arouse enough popular sentiment on the American west coast to inspire a round up of the region's Japanese-American population, regardless of their U.S. citizenship, and their relocation to prison camps over the next several months.

The Japanese army met its greatest resistance in the Philippines, where the people cooperated with the U.S. defense force led by General Douglas MacArthur. But ultimately the islands fell. Apart from unwise attempts to gain still further territories from Australia and India, the Japanese military settled down to occupy and exploit their newly won empire. The only

land resistance during this period was sporadic and weak, from Chiang Kai-shek's forces, which were contained in southwest China, and from Mao Zedong's troops in the northwest.

Although many Japanese were convinced that they were on a great mission to free Asia from Western colonialism, their brutality against the local peoples very quickly alienated these communities and created an anti-Japanese sentiment in parts of the region that continues to this day. In the later years of the war, active resistance to the Japanese occupation formed in most of the Southeast Asian nations they had conquered.

As the war economy of the United States came into full production, the Japanese suffered increasing defeats in naval and air battles with the U.S. Australia initially served as the main base for the Allied campaign; it and New Zealand also contributed fighting units to the war. Island after island fell to American Marines and Allied Army units. U.S. aircraft and warships, principally submarines, cut the Japanese islands off from Japanese Southeast Asian and the Southwestern Pacific conquests by sinking tremendous amounts of shipping and by defeating the Japanese navy.

By 1944 General Tojo, who had led Japan to war with the U.S., was deposed as premier and disappeared from the circle of military officers who were in control. Important persons in the imperial court and the government saw that the war was lost and believed that peace should be negotiated as soon as possible in order to save the Emperor and avoid a communist revolution. The military however insisted on continuing the losing battle; the Emperor might have overruled them but chose to remain silent fearing that a move on his part might create an even more destructive civil war. The stage was set for the Americans to force a surrender without invading the Japanese home islands.

Japan

The Atomic Bombs

On August 6, 1945, the sky above Hiroshima was lit by the fiery destructiveness of the first atomic bomb used in the history of the world. The Japanese were already hard pressed by the Allied troops, who were being reinforced by soldiers arriving from the now ended European theatre of war. Two days later, on August 8, the Soviet Union declared war on Japan. Moscow had agreed to do so the preceding February in exchange for postwar control of Outer Mongolia and territories like southern Sakhalin Island and the Kurile Islands. A second atomic bomb was dropped on Nagasaki on August 9. The next day the war and peace factions went to the emperor and submitted the choice of war or surrender.

The emperor, in an act of great moral courage, chose surrender. The final terms of capitulation were agreed to by August 14, 1945, and the formal agreement was signed aboard the *U.S.S. Missouri* in Tokyo Bay on September 2, 1945. The islands had been terribly battered and exhausted by the war. National morale was almost completely crushed; some army leaders and high government officials chose *seppuku*, a formal suicide that eliminated the necessity of facing their conquerors or the people they had led.

The American decision to use the atomic bombs has continued to arouse heated controversy more than a half century after their use. Some have argued that Japan was already defeated—that the bomb was used more to intimidate the Soviets than to end the Pacific War. Considerable documentation exists to suggest the usual combination of mixed motives on the part of the American leadership. Nevertheless, regardless of the decision-making process then going on in Japan, which American leaders were not privy to, many believed then and now, however correctly or not, that the use of the bombs would eliminate facing a bloody invasion of the Japanese home islands with an accompanying loss of lives which was incalculable. Whether the war could have been ended without resort to either atomic weapons or an invasion we will never know.

The Postwar Occupation

The American occupation of Japan after World War II was initially an ambitious attempt to remake Japan's political, economic, and educational institutions in a way that would prevent the future re-emergence of militarism. In reality, the occupation can be divided into two distinct periods, the period of the transformation of a defeated enemy and the period, after

Children visiting "Ground zero," Hiroshima

the commencement of the Cold War, of working to revive their former foe and transform it into a loyal ally in the struggle against communism. During that early phase, the Supreme Commander of Allied Powers (SCAP), MacArthur's headquarters, rewrote the Japanese constitution, began to break up the powerful *zaibatsu* business conglomerates, and completely revamped the Japanese educational system.

In many respects, some of the reforms forced on Japan in the war's aftermath were more liberal than many comparable U.S. policies. Most importantly, the circumstances of the rural Japanese were vastly improved as the occupation forces moved to lessen tenancy and help establish the peasantry as a land-owning class.

The right wing of both the military and civilian sectors, were purged with the goal of rebuilding Japanese governance on a new more peaceful basis. The prewar parliamentary system, which had been largely suppressed during the 1930s, was revived and this time its authority was more clearly established and codified. Unions were encouraged as never before as the America sought to rebuild Japan largely in its own image. Women were granted the vote during this restructuring as well.

As the Cold War developed by the late 1940s many American reforms were abruptly curtailed as the U.S. hastily sought to firmly anchor Japan as an anti-communist bastion in the Far East. Union activities, earlier encouraged, were now often suppressed in the name of the supreme struggle against communism.

The war in nearby Korea also had a profound impact on the course of the occupation. The socialists, who naturally supported some of the liberal reforms proposed by the Americans, were now eyed

with suspicion. Many were purged from government positions by SCAP authorities. Japanese moderates were genuinely frightened by prospects of political unrest and they feared a communist takeover right on their Korean doorstep. Discredited conservative politicians, removed from office due to their support of Japan's war effort, were rehabilitated as anti-communist allies.

The war had a number of other effects as well. While the Japanese adhered to the constitutional prohibition against maintaining armed forces, under U.S. pressure a national armed constabulary was formed. Heavily armed, these "police" effectively replaced U.S. occupation troops, freeing them for combat duty on the Korean peninsula. Japan's devastated industries were slowly revived by the Korean War boom, which allowed it to provide supplies and equipment for the U.S. war effort. Almost overnight, the nature of the U.S. occupation and U.S.-Japanese relations had changed dramatically.

In 1951 a peace treaty was signed with the United States and some other Western and Asian nations, but the communist bloc refrained from concluding formal peace accords. Under the U.S. treaty, Japan regained its independence, but lost all of its empire outside the home islands. Further reparations were left to be deter-

Japan's Foreign Minister Shigimitsu signs the documents of surrender aboard the *U.S.S. Missouri*, while General MacArthur broadcasts the ceremonies

Their Imperial Majesties the Emperor Akihito with Empress Michiko

mined between Japan and each individual country concerned. A security treaty was signed with the U.S. under which America was to maintain military bases in Japan and to administer Okinawa in the Ryukyu Islands, where the U.S. had established its largest military base in the western Pacific. Okinawa was eventually returned to Japanese jurisdiction in 1972.

The Structure of Postwar Politics

The constitution introduced under the occupation in 1947 established a constitutional monarchy and a parliamentary system based largely on Japan's government as it had operated in the 1920s with modifications borrowed from Britain. It also provided (in the famous Article Nine) that Japan forever relinquished the right to make war and or to even maintain armed forces. This article though, which on the surface would appear to ban even self-defense, has significantly loosened over the years. In the early 1950s, Japan created an armed constabulary that, after being armed with heavy weapons, aircraft, and tanks, eventually expanded into today's sophisticated Japanese Self Defense Force.

Over the years Japan's commitment to the U.S. alliance and its growing global importance has seen the responsibilities of the self-defense forces expand to include responsibility for protecting vital shipping lanes to a 1,000-mile radius from the Japanese islands. Today Japan's navy (Maritime Self Defense Forces) is one of the largest in Asia.

The new constitution also failed to mention, and in that way repudiated, any divine attributes or political power on the part of the emperor. In spite of this, or perhaps because of it, Emperor Hirohito remained a respected symbol of the nation for the rest of his life. In 1986 he celebrated

his 85th birthday and also the sixtieth anniversary of his accession to the throne.

After one of the longest reigns in history, Emperor Hirohito died on January 7, 1989. He was succeeded by his son Crown Prince Akihito, who upon assuming the throne took the title *Heisei* or Achieving Peace.

The transition evoked a great deal of soul searching in Japan about their responsibility for World War II in the Pacific and more specifically about Hirohito's own role in the origins of that bloody struggle. Some historians, such as the scholar Herbert Bix have suggested that Hirohito was considerably more involved in Japan's prewar imperialistic decision making that many had previously thought. Information that became available after his death does suggest that the Emperor had feared that an intervention on his part against the most extreme militarists within Japan might have provoked a civil war.

Ironically the parliamentary parties that had represented the moderate left wing of Japanese politics in the prewar era became in the post war years, after the militant ultra-nationalists were purged, to represent a conservative front of big-business, pro-American politicians. Merging in 1955 into the *Liberal Democratic Party*, the domination of the *LDP* was so great that the opposition parties had no opportunity to come to power for years.

In fact over the next several decades, real politics within Japan played out within the *LDP* where the party's many factional leaders competed for power within the party and thus over the Japanese government itself. They continued to dominate the political scene until the late 1980s when their power began to weaken. Still, though the *LDP's* influence was enormous in the decades after the war, even as its power was dramatically limited by the

extraordinary control of the entrenched Japanese bureaucracy.

Moreover, Japan, like so many other countries, has been dominated by "money politics." Politicians have very heavy expenses, since they are expected to offer presents to many of their constituents and to make outright gifts of money to their supporters. The funds for these transactions come mostly from business interests. For this reason, the political clout of the enormously wealthy business community has increased greatly over the years.

During the postwar era much of the wind was taken out of the opposition's sails by the remarkable growth of the Japanese economy which began in the 1960's and lasted until late in the century. Among the most significant foreign policy developments of those early years occurred under Prime Minister Eisaku Sato (1964–1972). In 1965 Sato announced his determination to regain jurisdiction over Okinawa. After prolonged negotiations with the U.S., the island as well as the rest of the Ryukyus, were returned to Japan in 1972. Sato also cooperated with the U.S. during the first years of the Vietnam War, a stance that helped Japanese firms make large profits by selling supplies and equipment to the U.S. for use in Vietnam as they had once supplied materials during the American struggle in Korean War.

But Japan's special relationship with the United States did not save it from the geopolitical dramas of the early 1970s. Long supporters of the pro-Taiwan stance of the United States, the Japanese were shocked when the White House, without any advance warning, set out to improve relations with the People's Republic of China. Although Prime Minister Sato hesitated, his successor moved quickly to establish relations with Beijing.

Kakuei Tanaka, a farmer's son and popular politician was elected president of the ruling *Liberal Democratic Party* in 1972, thus assuring him the prime minister ship. He then paid a successful visit to Beijing and established diplomatic relations with the People's Republic of China.

Meanwhile Japan's vulnerability due to its limited national resources was especially demonstrated in 1973 when a temporary Arab oil embargo against Japan was imposed during the Middle East War. The *LDP* government had of course long supported American policies in the Middle East and that policy had usually meant a generally pro-Israeli position. However, Japan was then importing 80% of its oil from the Middle East. The price of oil quadrupled. Recognizing the situation, the government made statements critical of Israel and began to woo the Arab states. Moreover, it set out, as the United States was doing as well, to create

Japan

a strategic oil reserve that, it was hoped, would make Japan less vulnerable in the future.

This crisis reduced Japan's economic growth and further weakened the Tanaka government. To recover, the ruling *LDP* spent large sums of money received from business contributions in an effort to influence elections for the upper house of the Diet, the House of Councilors. Despite that effort the party emerged with only half the seats they had previously held.

Over time the feeling grew that if the controversial Tanaka stayed in office until his term expired in 1975, he would bring disaster to his party. Meanwhile, the "Watergate Affair" in the United States and President Nixon's resignation in 1974 had heightened the Japanese public's interest in the behavior of its own leaders. The final blow fell that fall when a series of press articles exposed Tanaka's personal wealth and the questionable means by which it had been obtained.

Feeling that it might be facing its last chance to save itself from losing power, the Liberal Democratic Party dispensed with the usual jockeying for the premiership and chose the moderate Takeo Miki as its standard bearer. Nevertheless, in the years after the Tanaka scandal was exposed concern over corruption in Japanese politics and specifically within the LDP would continue to grow.

Worse news was to come. In early 1976 it was revealed that over the previous twenty years the Lockheed Aircraft Corporation had paid over twenty million dollars in bribes to various Japanese officials and politicians to promote the sales of military aircraft.

Over the next years the political domination of the LDP continued to flounder

Photo by Suzanne Marks

and a series of relatively nondescript leaders led the country until late 1982 when the energetic Yasuhiro Nakasone, emerged as Japan's new prime minister. Without opposition, Nakasone was later reelected to a second term as president of the party and prime minister.

While in power, Prime Minister Nakasone maintained a high profile abroad. He visited the United States and threw his considerable prestige and popularity behind an appeal to Japanese business and public to import and buy more foreign (especially American) goods, so as to reduce Japan's huge payments surplus. This appeal had little effect though and problems associated with Japan's balance of trade with the United States continued.

In the 1986 elections, helped by the premier's good image, the *LDP* made a significant comeback. Its main gains were in the cities and at the expense of the *Japan Socialist Party*. In an effort to make a fresh

start, the *JSP* then elected a woman, Takako Doi, as its chairwoman, an unprecedented step for a major Japanese political party.

Despite Nakasone's accomplishments his premiership did not always go smoothly. His efforts to reform the tax laws and to privatize institutions like the Japanese railroads aroused opposition. He also damaged his prestige with remarks he made in 1986 to the effect that Japan's relatively homogeneous population and at that point, stronger economy, gave it a marked advantage over the America's more multi-ethnic society.

Thus, in spite of the July 1986 electoral victory, Nakasone's political career was weakening and by 1987 he resigned in favor of Noboru Takeshita a low profile politician who had just taken over the leadership of former Premier Tanaka's sizable faction in the Diet. In the years that followed Japanese politics would be dominated by the efforts of the opponents of the LDP to end the party's long domination of Japan's political life.

Contemporary Government

Japan is a constitutional monarchy, with the constitution dating to May 3, 1947. Administratively, the country is divided into 47 prefectures. Twenty is the legal age for voters. The legal system is modeled after European civil law with some English and American influence. The Supreme Court has the power of judicial review over legislative acts.

The Emperor is the ceremonial head of state. The Prime Minister heads the government and has the power to appoint the cabinet. The legislature, or *Diet*, is bicameral, consisting of the upper House of Councilors and a lower House of Representatives. New electoral laws took effect on January 1, 1995. Under the new system, the lower house consists of 500

Houses and Rice Field

Japan

Former Emperor Hirohito addresses the opening of the Diet. Courtesy: Japanese Embassy

members. Of these, 300 are elected from single member districts. The remaining 200 are chosen through a system of proportional representation.

The *LDP* Falters

With the advent of the Takeshita government in 1987, Japanese politics became increasingly fragile. The years of domination and corruption charges had clearly taken their toll on the *LDP*. No longer were as the party the masters of Japanese politics, and an era of instability, of revolving door prime ministers and governments, began. In fact, there were eight prime ministers in the period from October 1987 to July 1998, with the longest term in office being just over two years! By the late 1990s though Japan's political situation seemed to again be stabilizing.

Leading the *LDP*'s comeback was Ryutaro Hashimoto, the reelected Prime Minister, who seemed posed to be a far more long-lasting leader than his weak predecessors. He first became prime minister in mid-January 1996. This was the fourth change in government since the July 1993 elections, and it had temporarily returned the *LDP* to control of the premiership. It then fell to Hashimoto to build on that temporary return to power.

Hashimoto was admired for his strong stand against former American Trade Representative Mickey Kantor in discussions over automobile imports and other issues. The Prime Minister also handled well the difficult negotiations over the American bases in Okinawa. In the end he built an agreement that seemed to satisfy at least some of the demands of each side.

Through mid-1997 Hashimoto, who was popular with the public, was well positioned to attempt major reforms of the economy. There were plenty of reasons to push for reform given Japan's poor economic performance during the 1990s.

For much of Japan's modern history, despite the domination of the *LDP*, the real governors of Japan were the prestigious bureaucrats that controlled the major government ministries. For a time it looked like the reign of the bureaucrats was at long last about to be challenged and significant reforms about to be implemented. In fact, a strong conviction has been growing that over-regulation has not only hurt the economy but made day to day life for Japanese citizens harder as they struggled with extraordinarily high prices on consumer goods.

Missteps weakened Hashimoto's efforts and slowed the progress of reform considerably. Especially embarrassing was his early decision to appoint a known bribe taker to a cabinet position responsible for rooting out corruption. Though the decision was reversed, the slide in Hashimoto's popular support had begun.

But the core of Hashimoto's problems was the reality that Japan's economy continued its slide from stagnation to genuine recession and by the elections of 1998 the voters were ready to make their dissatisfaction known. In an especially high voter turnout, the *LDP*'s vote totals went down as those of their opponents in the newly reorganized Democratic Party, the *LDP*'s largest rival, went up. Anti-*LDP* sentiment was so strong that even the votes of the Communist Party went up.

Hashimoto resigned the next day and after an internal struggle within the *LDP*, Keizo Obuchi, leader of the largest *LDP* faction, emerged as the party's new leader and Japan's Prime Minister. Seen as a relatively bland individual, Obuchi presented himself as a leader committed to regaining Japan's economic momentum. Obuchi attempted to strengthen his position by enlarging his government with new members that included important segments of the political opposition. But, Prime Minister Obuchi's personal luck ran out during the winter of 2000 when the newly installed prime minister suffered a massive stroke that eventually killed him.

His successor, Yoshiro Mori, though apparently physically healthier than Obuchi, was no luckier. Coming from one of the most unsophisticated wings of the *LDP*, Mori alienated many within Japan and abroad by espousing ideas more reminiscent of Japan's pre-war imperial past than that of a modern democratic society. And his nostalgic candor for Japan's imperial heritage hurt the *LDP* at the polls as well when, in the elections of June 2000, the opposition Democratic Party did particularly well capturing seats in Japan's lower legislative house.

Finally, amidst great public enthusiasm, Mori was replaced by the flamboyant Junichiro Koizumi, who became head of the LDP and thus Japan's new prime minister in the spring of 2001. Koizumi, who campaigned on a pledge to carry out needed reforms, was quite popular. He formed a coalition government that included not only his own LDP, but the New Komeito Party as well.

The new government's popularity did not last long. In the first year after he became prime minister, Koizumi and the co-

Prime Minister Naoto Kan

Japan

alition he directed saw its popularity drop by almost half in national public opinion polls. Koizumi's party, the LDP, lost some significant by-elections as well. Even more important, Koizumi then lost a major legislative battle to privatize Japan's massive postal-savings system. His loss was even more meaningful because the plan, part of his larger project for reforming Japan's economic system, was stymied not only by his political opponents, but by his supposed allies within the LDP. But those frustrations turned out to be temporary.

Responding to the setback, Prime Minister Koizumi called an unexpected election for September 2005. Using the rejection of his postal privatization plan as the center piece of his campaign to push reform even further, he impressively engineered a landslide victory that significantly renewed his reform agenda. It was a stunning reversal of fortunes not only for the prime minister, but for the LDP as well. The party won the highest percentage of votes since 1969. It was quite literally the biggest single election win ever. Clearly the nation at large was willing to support Koizumi's economic reforms, and the reformed postal legislation sailed through easily once the new government was formed. By September 2006, Koizumi was smoothly replaced by Shinzo Abe, who promised to continue Koizumi's economic reforms. But there were significant differences.

The new prime minister, who was well known due to his strong stand on North Korean developments, was particularly unwilling to support progress on resolving the nuclear issues until the remaining questions about earlier North Korean kidnappings of Japanese citizens had been resolved. Nor did Koizumi's legislative momentum, drawn from the September 2005 elections, flow smoothly into Abe's tenure in office. During the late summer of 2007 the LDP decisively lost control of the senate, the upper house of the legislature, to the emerging Democratic Party. Impressively for the Democratic Party, its accomplishment marked the first time the LDP had lost its majority in the upper house since the party was founded in 1955.

But losing the Upper House was not the only problem facing new Prime Minister Abe and the LDP he led. A series of financial scandals, the suicide of one of his cabinet ministers and a controversy surrounding Japan's commitment to maintaining its support of NATO activities in Afghanistan eventually drove Abe to announce his resignation in early 2007.

He was succeeded by Yasuo Fukuda, a professionally trained economist who had worked in the energy industry before becoming one of the longest-serving Japanese chief cabinet secretaries in the nation's history. But as it turned out, his reputation for retaining his previous political position did not carry through to his new position. Only a year after coming to power, Fukuda resigned citing his inability to make legislative progress, given the continuing divide within the national diet. It will be recalled that the LDP has only controlled the lower house while their political opponents, the Democratic Party, control the less influential upper house. Such divided government may be commonplace in the United States, but for Japan's long influential ruling party, the LDP and its then leader Fukuda, it was a new and quite unfamiliar situation. Fukuda was followed in office by his LDP colleague, Tara Aso. Aso had previously served as Japan's foreign minister and is the first Catholic ever to serve as the nation's leader.

Japan: Moving Toward a Two Party System?

The uniqueness of Aso's background was not what finally determined his election to the LDP leadership and the prime ministership. His colleagues were clearly hoping that he would be able successfully to bring them through the impending elections for the lower house of parliament from which Japanese governments are formed. The LDP needed to do more than command a majority within the lower legislative body. Without two-thirds control, passing legislative proposals is especially problematic. Thus, the importance of new

leadership was obvious. However, that all depended on the decision by Japan's population, which by the early summer of 2009 seemed only slightly to favor the LDP over their rivals. However, what mattered, of course, was the mood on election day itself, which officially had to be set sometime before early September 2009.

Though the LDP's leadership had occasionally faltered in the years of its most formal domination, from the mid-1950s through beginning of the 21st century its leadership has never been so fundamentally challenged as it has been over the last year. The fact that the LDP was in real danger of losing the election hardly came as a big surprise to its leadership. Prime Minister's Aso stalled until the very last moment before calling for elections in August of 2009. The delay hardly helped the LDP's prospects.

The campaign itself centered around fundamental issues like the relationship between the United States and Japan, with the Japanese Democratic Party challengers calling for a more equal relationship with the United States. Domestically the Democrats called for cutting what it called wasteful spending on LDP pet projects and a redirection of the funds towards increasing financial support for the nation's pension and child welfare programs.

When the results were reported, the LDP took a drubbing unlike anything they had previously experienced. They lost 177 seats

Tokyo's expressways curve and divide as they crisscross the city.

Courtesy: Japanese Embassy

Japan

The Democratic Party of Japan's Short Term Leader Yukio Hatoyama

in the Japanese House of Representatives while Yukio Hatoyma and the soon-to-be new prime minister's Democratic Party of Japan picked up an additional 195 seats and the right to form a new government. Certainly, the LDP had faltered in previous years. For example, it had temporarily lost power in 1993. However, that limited and temporary setback was nothing like the scale of its loss over the last year. Opponents of the conservative Liberal Democratic Party of Japan had waited for such a significant victory for a very long time.

The Democratic Party of Japan was formed in the late 1990s from a group of opposition parties that had never managed fundamentally to wrest power from the dominant LDP. But the elections of late August 2009 changed the situation dramatically. The new government that was formed by mid-September saw the DPJ holding the largest number of seats in both houses of the diet, the Japanese parliament. Meanwhile the new government pledged to look with a fresh perspective at an entire range of issues from relations with China and the United States to climate change.

As is so often the case, in the year since they arrived in power the Democratic Party has seen the initial enthusiasm that greeted their victory wane as controversies from their unsuccessful effort to renegotiate the Okinawa treaties with the United States to a noisy corruption scandal weakened them. By early summer 2010, the situation had become so critical that the newly empowered LDP Prime Minister Hatoyama was forced to resign his office in favor of Naoto Kan, his finance minister. The new prime minister immediately promised to reinvigorate the DPJ's ties to the public, which only recently had granted the party a mandate to govern, and to repair the nation's economy.

New Stresses

The last decade or so has or so has not always gone smoothly for Japan. The frequent political and economic uncertainty has been complemented by other even more disturbing events and trends. For example, the country experienced a "reality check" of sorts when its long assumption about being well prepared for earthquakes was severely challenged by the government's poor performance in responding to the Kobe Earthquake of January 1995. The quake measured 7.2 on the scale and the death toll eventually climbed over 5,000, with 26,000 injured and 300,000 left homeless. Offers for assistance poured into the country which in some cases the government was very slow in accepting. And that was not the only trauma of recent years.

In mid-1995 Japanese prosecutors secured the indictment of cult leader Shoko Ashara, for masterminding the poison gas attack that killed twelve people on the Tokyo subway earlier in the year. One observer referred to the matter as Japan's spring of terror. Aum Shinrikyo, the cult that had masterminded the gas attack, has now been shown to have had far more ambitious projects in mind. Investigations have revealed efforts to obtain samples of the deadly Ebola virus in Africa, the employment of nuclear engineers in Russia and an apparent effort to mine uranium in Australia. Eventually, Japanese courts handed out a death sentence to Ashara for his involvement in Aum Shinrikyo's terrorist assault on the Tokyo subway.

In fact, by late century the sense that Japan was somehow free from the social ills that beset much of the rest of the world was crumbling. During a 1996 holiday party in the Japanese embassy in Lima, Peruvian leftists broke in and took hundreds of guests hostage. That the rebels had singled out Japan, whose ties with Peru had grown since President Fujimori came to power in Peru, was something quite new for the Japanese.

By early 2004 it had become more common as Japanese T.V. audiences found themselves viewing images of their citizens held hostage in Iraq, one of which, a young tourist, was beheaded while several Japanese reporters were also killed. As had become more and more obvious, all of this seemed to suggest that Japan's role in the world was changing significantly.

For so many years such international incidents had been the problem of other nations, not Japan. Commenting on the full range of Japan's recent experiences, one writer even went so far as to write an article about Japan finally becoming an "ordinary" country. This was especially reinforced in the spring of 2008 when Japan experienced yet another mass horror as a deranged young man deliberately drove a truck into a crowd of people and then proceeded to kill even more with a knife. This massacre was worse than anything the normally so "safe" country had experienced in years.

Perhaps the most obvious example of Japan becoming an "ordinary" country has been the significant increase in the number of Japanese firms that have found themselves taken over by huge foreign multinationals. That more and more Japanese now find their employers to be foreigners is certainly something new for Japan but quite familiar elsewhere. A perhaps particularly graphic example of this evolution is the fact that just recently a Welsh-American was named to be the new head of Sony Electronics. Internationally Japan's image took a particularly strong hit during the last year as its long-heralded and extraordinarily successful Toyota car company found itself temporarily pilloried for delaying recalls of some of its most popular models that apparently required safety repairs.

Foreign and Defense Issues

For much of the post war era Japan was uninvolved in most international issues and largely followed America's lead. That stance has modified in recent years as its foreign policy and defense planning have become more robust largely as a response to a range of developments from the American war on terrorism, to the U.S. invasion of Iraq and more regionally the ongoing threat of North Korean efforts to develop nuclear weapons.

Then Prime Minister Koizumi made it clear that he wanted Japan not only to consider changes to its post World War Two pacifistic constitution, but to aggressively lobby for Japan to gain a permanent seat on the United Nation's Security Council. Unfortunately, that is likely to be more difficult than some might have imagined only a few years ago. China's government and especially many of its citizens have made it clear that they oppose Japan winning such a seat. Beijing's growing international influence ensures their opinion will be heard. Even the United States, which has been more supportive, has been unwilling to support Japan receiving official veto power along with the potential permanent seat.

Turning to Japan's all-important relationship with the United States, more often than not economic issues have been at the forefront of issues that separated the two powers. The trade imbalance between the two countries has long been an irritant in Japanese-American Relations. Over the years, Japan has consistently had a sizeable trade surplus with the United States.

Japan

In an earlier attempt to address this problem the U.S. Congress passed the Omnibus Trade and Competitiveness bill in 1988. The Special 301 section of that bill provided a powerful weapon in the form of heavy tariffs on U.S. imports from countries deemed to be engaging in unfair trading practices. The first Bush Administration also introduced the Structural Impediments Initiative (SII). SII talks were aimed at eliminating the fundamental economic differences between the two countries that some claimed resulted in large trade deficits. These areas included the high Japanese savings rate (an issue that is becoming less important as the Japanese population ages) and low level of support for public infrastructure, high land prices.

In a somewhat curious irony from the usual American association with free trade the Clinton Administration, which followed the first President Bush in office, opted for an aggressive "managed trade" approach that insisted on establishing set targets. In 1994 and early 1995, the major issue was access to the Japanese market for American autos and auto parts. When in May of that year the talks collapsed, the Clinton Administration responded with a plan to place a 100% tariff on the major Japanese luxury cars. Though the Japanese did not accept the U.S. concept of managed trade enough progress was eventually made to lower the level of rhetoric.

There have been some newer developments that are likely to improve trade relations. The long term weakening of the Japanese economy during the late 1990s added to the Japanese consumer's interest in less expensive goods and the drop in land prices combined to allow the introduction of more American style superstores and even for the planning of U.S. style malls. Changes in regulations regarding such investments have also facilitated this development.

As the new century began Japanese-American economic tensions were simply less likely to make the headlines. China had become the country with which America has its largest trade imbalance. Thus, "Japan bashing" seemed to give way to "China bashing" as the U.S. deficit with that country grew.

By 2004, the American media had switched somewhat from concerns about trade imbalances between the United States and its trading partners in East Asia to more immediate complaints about U.S. corporations that were increasingly "outsourcing" American jobs to factories in countries from India to the People's Republic. But if the once widely discussed Japanese-American Trade imbalance receded from public attention, other issues of concern continued to affect the Japanese American relationship.

Among the most important long-term issues was the controversy over the renewal of the American bases in Okinawa, which dated back to the era of the American occupation of the islands at the end of World War II. For years, resentments grew in Japan over the presence of the bases. Those sentiments are especially strong in Okinawa where the bulk of the American bases are located. Several factors have added to the tensions, some tied to a more general evolution of the international arena and others linked directly to events in Okinawa. The Cold War has been over for more than a decade and the Japanese public is no longer as supportive of the American presence as it once was.

Within Okinawa, American insensitivity and domination of some of the island's best lands added to the problem. The American establishment of an artillery range that once fired over a public road was only one of the most egregious examples. Accusations of rape against soldiers from the American bases by young Japanese women have occurred far too often and dramatically increase tensions on a regular base.

Former Governor Masahide Ota had been particularly anxious to expel the Americans from Okinawa, but the elections of November 1998 brought to power a more pragmatic conservative, Keiichi Inamine, a businessman who argued for a more gradual approach to the problem and one that recognized that the Americans did pump a considerable amount of money into the local economy.

While Americans were probably relieved that Governor Ota was removed from the scene, the issues that had concerned the former governor did not go

**Former Prime Minister
Junichiro Koizumi**

away. In fact, by the fall of 2002, when Keichi Inamine was reelected, he too was calling for a major withdrawal of American troops from Okinawa.

Finally, during late 2005 a treaty was negotiated that anticipated moving some Americans to Guam while relocating others to less populated parts of the islands. The cost of relocating the troops was expected to be born by both the United States and Tokyo with the latter expecting to spend over $15 billion in the effort.

Eventually a formal treaty was negotiated in 2006. However, once the LDP left office, the new JDP leadership sought to revise the new treaty again. For the JDP the issue is an especially sensitive one since it had campaigned on a platform of realigning the relationship between Japan and the United States to a more equal footing. Meeting the expectations of Okinawans, who are dissatisfied with the presence of American bases on their islands, has been a daunting one. As we have seen, the issue eventually undermined the government formed in September 2010.

Another important issue over the years has been the revision of the guidelines for the Japanese-American Security Pact, which dates from 1960. The 1999 revisions aroused considerable controversy within Japan and abroad. Though somewhat ambiguous, the guidelines suggested that Japan was willing to send military personnel abroad during times of crises. For example, elements of the Japanese military have played significant roles in South Asia alongside the United States

After the September 11, 2001, terrorist attack in the United States, Japan agreed to allow its military to serve in a non-combat role in the American led war in Afghanistan. Tokyo also sent a naval destroyer to the Indian Ocean to support the American activities in South Asia as well. More recently, the two countries concluded yet another agreement that called for a major reorganization of military cooperation between them. Officially, it was said that the new relationship would be a global rather than regional relationship. The new plan calls for the armies, air forces and navies of the two countries to work and train closely together.

Not surprisingly, the American decision in 2003 to overthrow the government of Saddam Hussein also complicated relations. A great many Japanese opposed their country becoming involved in Iraq even as they had already contributed to the struggle in Afghanistan. Nevertheless, Prime Minister Koizumi's government decided to send Japanese troops to Iraq to serve in non-combat roles. This was a decision that many of his parliamentary opponents did not support. Koizumi stood his ground, offering the United States all the support it could in Iraq. Eventually, only a few months before he left office, Koizumi brought the 600 Japanese troops home from Iraq even as they continued to offer logistical support. As for the Japanese activities in South Asia, their role in refueling ships in the Indian Ocean has continued to arouse tensions between the U.S. and Tokyo. It also emerged as yet another domestic political issue which the LDP and their critics argued over until Prime Minister Fukuda, in one of his few accomplishments in office, managed to get authorization for the renewal of the effort in mid-2008.

Relations between the United States and Japan have at times also been complicated by the question of North Korea's nuclear ambitions. In recent years, the most significant issue has been whether North Korea would continue on a path toward reconciliation with Japan and the larger world community, or, as often seemed to be the case, would decide to return to the policy of nuclear brinkmanship it usually embraced during the 1990s.

On August 31, 1998, North Korea fired what appeared to be a three-stage missile over Japanese territory. There was some uncertainty about whether they were a testing an offensive missile or merely trying to put a satellite in space. What was obvious was that North Korea had demonstrated an ability to hit urban Japan with missiles. Especially upsetting for the Japanese was that they needed to depend on the Americans for technical information on the launch. Most significant recently was North Korea's successful October 2006 detonation of a nuclear device. This followed the equally alarming demonstration of its growing missile prowess with a series of short- and long-range tests.

Under the circumstances, Tokyo's reaction was hardly surprising. Not only was there a step-up of efforts to work with the U.S. on building a joint missile-defense structure, but for the first time the possibility of Japan joining the ranks of those countries that possess such weapons became more and more openly discussed. This is a development that is in so many ways a real "sea change" in attitude by the only country that has ever experienced a nuclear attack on its shores.

All of this was quite ironic given that relations during much of decade seemed to be improving. North Korea, in an apparent effort at "clearing the air" regarding their past policies, had finally admitted that, yes, indeed, as long had been rumored, they had actually kidnapped Japanese nationals during the 1970s and 1980s to serve as language teachers and intelligence resources.

Even more surprising was Pyongyang's decision to allow the five survivors of the original thirteen kidnap victims to visit Japan. Predictably, the gesture backfired somewhat as tensions arose when the returning Japanese chose to remain in Japan and to demand that their North Korean children be given the right to join them. For a time the situation improved somewhat. During his visit to North Korea, then Prime Minister Koizumi even managed to convince its leader to allow five people, all children of the earlier kidnapped Japanese, to travel with him back to Japan. But while relations have improved, questions about the abductions have at times continued significantly to strain Japanese North Korean relations to the present. Those disagreements have at times also spilled over to Japanese-American relations as the two nations have sometimes promoted different policies *vis-à-vis* North Korea.

Japan's relationship with China has often been in the spotlight. In recent years Japanese ultra-nationalists have made efforts from time to time to stake claims to the Daiyous Islands, known to the Japanese as the Senkaku Islands. Predictably, Chinese from all walks of life, from Hong Kong to Taiwan and the People's Republic, have reacted angrily to such efforts. Of course, nationalism plays an important role in such tensions. But the issue is also a deeply economic one as well because the area around the islands, the East China Sea, includes energy resources both nations need.

The November 1998 visit of President Jiang of the People's Republic did not make much progress in improving relations either. Aware of the apology Japan had offered Korea a few months earlier China's leader made it clear he expected something similar regarding the brutal Japanese invasion of China earlier in the century. The Japanese government, apparently under pressure from its own conservatives, refused to offer a formal written apology. The educational establishment has also often played down the brutality of Japanese war-time behavior in China. The results have been quite predictable. Japan's efforts to become a permanent member of the United Nations Security Council have become considerably more difficult due to China's opposition.

But there are signs of an improving relationship. Most dramatically, in November 2007 the first Chinese warship since 1934 sailed into Tokyo harbor to begin a long delayed visit dedicated to improving relations between the two East Asian giants. Given how complicated relations can be between Tokyo and Beijing, it will not be a surprise to learn that the visit had taken seven years to schedule. Still it was an important development in an environment that has seen the Japanese become

more and more concerned about the growth of Chinese military power. More recently, Hu Jintao, China's current president, made his own state visit to Japan in May of 2008 as a follow-up to President Jiang's earlier visit of 1998.

Since Japan's new government, directed by the Japanese Democratic Party, took office, there has been a flurry of contacts between Tokyo and Beijing that has been so energetic that some have speculated that America, which has for so long enjoyed an especially close relationship with Japan, now has a real competitor in the People's Republic. Nevertheless, the initial JDP Prime Minister, Hashimoro, went out of his way to emphasize the importance of Japan's on-going alliance with the United States. Still, the situation is clearly evolving.

Another important symbolic development has been the decision of previous Japanese prime ministers to end official visits to Japan's memorial to their wartime dead. The Yasukuni Shrine has in the past so often aroused controversy with those who suffered during Japan's mid-twentieth century expansion into Asia.

Clearly Japan's defense and foreign policy have begun to evolve rapidly as the Japanese find themselves moving more deeply into the new century and farther away from the relatively pacifist stance they had taken during the first generations after World War II. These changes have been significant. Not only did Japan send its military to Iraq, but it has begun building its own spy satellite systems and has announced plans for an anti-missile defense system. The need for such systems has grown more and more obvious over the years as North Korea has continued its missile production programs that have caused considerable alarm within

Crown Prince Naruhito and Princess Masako visit a nursing home.

Japan

Japan itself. Recent warnings were given in 2008 as North Korea tested yet another missile in what it called an effort to launch a communications satellite. It tested yet another missile the following year.

Additionally, the country's recent participation in several UN-sponsored missions, from its activities in Central and South Asia mentioned above to sending forces to Rwanda to perform human relief operations, reveals an evolving and more military and international role than recent generations of Japanese have known. The arena of space is yet another area that sees Japan taking on a new role. Long a spectator watching American or Russian space efforts, the Japanese, like the Chinese before them, have started developing a significant space program.

CULTURE AND SOCIETY

Before the arrival of Chinese influence, Japanese culture was, compared to its giant neighbor, rather unsophisticated; it was centered on the Shinto belief in spirits existing everywhere in nature. With the adoption of so many aspects of Chinese civilization Shinto was somewhat overwhelmed by the growth of Buddhism. In the modern era though, Shinto, experienced a revival of sorts with the Meiji Government's decision to use it as a feature of its enhancement of the role of the emperor. After the Second World War, "State Shinto" as it is sometimes called, was again de-emphasized. Today both Shinto and Buddhism are somewhat eclectically interwoven in Japanese society which overall is quite secular. It is quite common for a Japanese to marry in a Shinto shrine and to venerate his ancestors at the Buddhist Temple. The Christmas season has become an important time for socializing. It is an event hardly tied to the religious context the holiday carries in the West.

Traditional Japanese society has experienced an extraordinary transformation over the years since the Meiji Restoration. Japan had begun the nineteenth century as a society that saw itself, largely divided hierarchically into classes of samurai, peasants, artisans and merchants with the samurai the uniquely dominant elite. By the late twentieth century Japan had become a much more homogeneous society more divided by intellectual and professional accomplishment than family background. Recent research has suggested that that too may be changing. Over the last few years a greater income disparity has emerged in Japan. In fact, according to researchers the gap between what the richest and poorest earn has grown by over 50% in recent years.

Since Japan was the first non-Western country to industrialize along Western models it faced earliest a dilemma that communities around the world continue to deal with—how to modernize one's society without simply becoming "Western." After considerable struggle they did manage to find a comfortable balance. Today, the older cultural patterns are not dead. In fact, they are often creatively blended with modernity.

The increasingly urban life of the Japanese is a distinctive one. The business sections of the city are usually constructed of reinforced concrete. Sadly, the simple, yet attractive wood and paper housing that so charmed earlier visitors to Japan, has given way in recent generations to long rows of concrete apartment blocks. The people who work in the city during the day commute to suburbs in the evening. Thus, the morning and evening commuting hours are as frantic as those in the cities of the United States. Very long commutes are the norm and the common pattern is one that Americans who commute by rail into cities like New York could easily identify with.

Happily for the Japanese their transport systems, particularly rail, are as modern as can be found in the world. The famous and efficient *bullet trains* run throughout the country. Television, radio and computer games are widely enjoyed and while not yet quite as enamored of the Internet as many Americans, its use is growing very rapidly.

All of the fine arts are widely found in the cities, particularly Tokyo. Traditional European and Western musical works and ballet are heavily attended, as are cultural expressions that are distinctly Japanese such as the Kabuki and Noh theater performances.

On another level, bluegrass and country-western music sung in Japanese has a large following. Today, McDonald's and

Former Prime Minister Tara Aso

Kentucky Fried Chicken are among the top restaurant chains in Japan. Underlying this shift to western food is a far more significant outcome. Rice consumption is dropped considerably in the last quarter century. Consumption of meat and dairy products is skyrocketing and Japanese young adults are growing taller and bigger. It is not just American fast food that has attracted many Japanese. A version of the popular American show "Sex and the City" has been created for the Japanese entertainment market.

As Japan entered the 21st century, the single most important aspect of Japanese society is the reality that it is aging rapidly. Today, more than 14% of the population is over 65. By 2020 more than a quarter will be. Most dramatically, it was announced just last year that for the first time since records were kept, Japan's population has officially begun to decline. This is a reality that forces the question of how more and more pensioners are going to be supported by fewer and fewer workers. Japan and many other developing countries are soon going to have to face this challenge. For example, Japan has always attributed part of its economic success to the high savings rates of its citizens. But the days of huge individual savings accounts that could be used to finance industry may soon be over as the rapidly aging Japanese begin to drain their accounts to support themselves in retirement. Some have suggested that the result could be as much as an 18% reduction in the Japanese standard of living in upcoming years. Within Japan, as in America, there is increasing concern about the long-term solvency of the nation's old age pensions due to these evolving demographic realities.

Perhaps even more of a challenge for the relatively isolated and homogeneous Japanese society is the diminishing number of workers available to run its economy. The most recent studies report that the percentage of Japanese under age fifteen is now at a record low and that the nation has the highest ratio of elderly to young in the world.

The upshot is that the aging of the population and the lowering of the birth rate have combined to create a decline in the number of potential employees so significant that economists have projected that Japan, a country long uncomfortable with outsiders, will either have to allow thousands of immigrants a year to enter the country or fundamentally alter their society by encouraging more older workers to delay retirement and significantly more women to enter the work force. Whether the Japanese would actually agree to such a change in their society though is quite another matter.

Former Prime Minister Shinzo Abe

The record thus far is not encouraging. Japan has long been one of the most homogenous societies in the world. In the past, groups, such as the often despised Burukum and Koreans, regularly faced discrimination from the larger majority society. In today's Japan, there are around 2 million foreigners among the 128 million population. The discrimination they often experience has been sufficiently obvious to attract the attention of United Nations observers who have studied the situation.

Despite Japan's obvious accomplishments in science and technology there are some unusual elements in its delivery of modern medicine. Until recently, Japan adhered to a more traditional definition of life that was defined by the presence of a beating heart regardless of the condition of the patient's brain. This definition has often made it difficult for Japanese medicine to offer its patients some procedures common in the rest of the industrialized world such as heart transplants. In contrast to the United States, procedures like abortion are not controversial in Japan while the use of the birth control pill has only just become legal for contraceptive purposes. It had previously been available for hormonal regulation.

Japanese Women

On paper Japanese women have rights that American women are still struggling for. More than a decade ago, a Japanese law similar to the American Equal Rights Amendment was passed. As in the United States, the issue of sexual harassment has become an important topic in contemporary Japan. Stirred on by a 1998 American court's expensive judgment against Mitsubishi Motor Manufacturing of America, Japanese political leaders strengthened their laws against sexual harassment and sex discrimination.

Despite these gains, Japanese women still earn only about 62% of what a man earns and hold far fewer seats in the lower house of representatives. Moreover, less than ten percent have managerial positions. There have of course been gains. A woman directed the Japanese Socialist Party early in the last decade, and more recently Fusae Ota, a career civil servant was named the first female governor of the Osaka Prefecture. Japan's former Prime Minister, Koizumi, has named an unprecedented number of women to his cabinet in the years since he came into office including having more than one woman serve in the important position of foreign minister. Moreover, during the last elections a significant number of women agreed to run on the LDP banner. A record number of them, 26, won.

Studies of Japanese women's lives suggest that they face many challenges when trying to establish themselves as professionals. The general tendency on the part of employers is to assume they will quit their job once they have children and of course society often does pressure them to do so. Thus, it is difficult for women to advance as easily as men. Later in life they are expected to spend more time with aged parents than their male counterparts. For those Japanese women who stay at home the demands of parenting are greater than for most Western women. Japanese men are not expected to take much responsibility in the home and even if they are so inclined, their work schedules rarely allow them enough time to actually do so.

As women age and find their children leaving the family home, many are now spending more time and money on themselves. In fact, older Japanese women, often traveling in groups of other women are becoming an important market for the international travel industry while an increasing number of Japanese women are choosing not to marry at all. Given Japan's declining work force, it also seems likely that more and more of them will remain in the work force longer in upcoming years.

Japan has also finally begun to make some progress in dealing with its responsibilities toward the World War II era "comfort women" it enslaved for sexual purposes during the war. Government-sponsored private charities are now funneling funds to its wartime victims though the government's unwillingness officially to confront its treatment of women during the war is still a subject of considerable anger in some parts of Asia. Unfortunately, coming to terms with this issue as well as with the larger one of

Former Prime Minister Yasuo Fukuda

Japan's overall behavior during World War II has still not been confronted as successfully as some might hope. It thus continues to complicate Japan's relationship with its neighbors.

EDUCATION IN JAPAN

In contrast to the more varied and decentralized educational system found in the United States, the Japanese system is much more centralized and thus easier to generalize about. At all levels the public schools, and to some extent also the private schools, are under the control of the Ministry of Education in Tokyo.

From kindergarten through high school, Japanese students and their parents are under tremendous competitive pressure, mainly because ultimate career success is assumed to require graduation from a prestigious university (ideally Tokyo University). Below the college level, students generally wear uniforms, and conformity is expected as to hairstyles, behavior and effort. Students who rebel, as some do, are usually severely dealt with and that in a system where corporal punishment administered by teachers is still common. The emphasis in education is on memorization. Individuality and creativity are discouraged, though less so than in the past.

Very competitive entrance examinations for schools are common, even below the college level. Parents and students spend an enormous amount of time and energy on special programs and "cram" schools to improve their chances of admission into the better schools. There are frequent reports of students committing suicide from the financial stresses on their families and the pressures imposed upon them.

Although hard to get into, Japanese colleges are not hard to stay in. The instruc-

Japan

tion generally adds little to what the student has already learned. There is slightly more scope for originality, but not much. The real accomplishment more often than not is admittance and graduation from a particularly prestigious college rather than the material learned. Professional training, except in law and medicine, tends to be learned on the job rather than in graduate schools as in America. By the "Nobel test," the Japanese system of higher education does not stand up well; relatively few of these prizes have been won by graduates. The growing awareness of the problem has been especially highlighted by reports of Japanese successes in science earned by those who have worked outside of the system in other countries.

One core challenge that is likely to have a very long-term impact on Japan's future is the reality that the educational choices its young adults are making are becoming increasingly similar to those made by students in the United States. Instead of choosing science and engineering, fields particularly important to a nation's long-term productivity, Japanese youth have been gravitating to fields from finance, medicine to the arts careers that are often perceived as more glamorous than jobs more immediately associated with manu-

facturing. The problem, of course, is that this evolution has created a major deficit in the number of engineers graduating from Japan's universities and has caused significant problems for its manufacturers.

ECONOMY

The experience of Japan in the half-century since World War II has been one of extraordinary sacrifice, impressive accomplishment and more recently often disappointment. World War II brought the virtual destruction of Japan's physical plant, but not of the human qualities that had built it. Among the most important of these were (and are) energy, persistence, a high level of education, impressive technical skills, a high rate of saving and a willingness (somewhat declining at present) to accept relatively modest living standards.

The American occupation helped the Japanese economy by not imposing war reparations or other excessive burdens on it. The Korean War gave it a major shot in the arm (as did the Vietnam War in the next decade), in the form of official U.S. "offshore procurement" of supplies. By that time, various American specialists were beginning to advise Japanese industry on how it could increase its productivity.

The Japanese government, after the end of the Occupation in 1952, systematically pursued an Asian capitalist style of "industrial policy" aimed at stimulating Japanese recovery on the basis of "export-led growth." Anti-trust policy in Japan is much less severe than in the U.S., and this made it possible for Japanese industry to "rationalize" itself to a high degree in the mid-1950s.

The government, through the Ministry of International Trade and Industry (MITI), was much more involved in economic planning than is common in the United States (at least at the federal level). More concern was put on retaining workers and markets than shareholder's profits. "Sunset industries," such as textiles, were de-emphasized while industries using "leading edge" technologies were promoted: steel, automobiles, electronics, etc. This "rationalization" process had a spectacularly beneficial effect on Japan's industrial production and its export position, beginning in the early 1960s. So too did such domestic factors as political stability, social cohesion and a low defense budget, held by treaty to a bit under 1% of the GNP until 1987. External factors, such as the relative openness of the vast U.S. market, also helped greatly. These elements were accompanied by relatively high tariffs the Japanese government imposed on imports, by a maze of import regulations that were actually barriers, by a generally stable international scene and by the conscious undervaluing (at least until 1971) of the yen, with its stimulating effect on Japanese exports.

But even from the Japanese point of view, there have been some real drawbacks to this process. The cost of living was kept unnecessarily high due to factors ranging from the undervaluing of the yen, the extensive system of middlemen in the distribution system, and barriers to imports, including agricultural products. The Japanese agricultural population is guaranteed high prices and protected from foreign competition for political reasons. Thus food is very expensive. The retail distribution system is very inefficient and costly. It is divided between chains of large, expensive department stores and a huge number of mom and pop corner stores. Housing, public utilities and the like have been the victims of cumulative under-investment. Thus the average Japanese lives under conditions considerably less pleasant than the overall wealth of the country would suggest.

In spite of these problems, Japan is an industrial giant, second only to the United States. It has proved better able than other industrial economies to cope with the rise in the cost of imported oil. Its large trading companies have proved

Morning traffic on Uchibori-dori Avenue

very effective in penetrating foreign markets, especially that of the U.S. They cope with import quotas, when imposed by foreign governments, through "up scaling" (keeping the number of exported units within the quotas, but improving their quality and increasing their price, while staying somewhat below the prices of competitive goods produced in the countries of destination).

Japan's regional economic role within Asia had also grown significantly over the past decades. In fact, Asia, rather than the United States, had become the principal area of Japanese trade before the drama of 1997s economic meltdown in much of the area. There were many reasons Japan had become so involved in the region.

Japanese corporations had turned to Southeast Asia to solve some of their own economic problems. Facing a tendency by Japanese workers to demand higher pay and shorter hours, Japanese industry moved much of its production overseas, especially to China and Southeast Asia. This Japanese investment, coupled with the opening of China under Deng Xiaoping, spurred impressive economic growth in much of Southeast Asia. Japan had also become a leading investor in Vietnam, a country that because of the long-lasting U.S. economic embargo was unable to obtain U.S. investment for years. In short, for much of Japan's post-war history, while the individual consumer was often hard pressed to make ends meet, the economy as a whole had done well.

But that situation changed significantly in the last decade of the 20th century. Bank failures became more common, and the entire Japanese banking industry was being dragged down by a bad loans. The stock market also has weakened, and the economy lost the momentum that had once

made it seem invincible. Moreover, the bubble burst on land prices and they too declined dramatically. Of course, the government tried to deal with the problem by employing a series of policies from direct "pump priming"—that is enhanced government spending—through more significant calls for major restructuring. In late 2002, for example, Tokyo approved a governmental spending package of more than twelve billion dollars to be spent on public works and various "safety net" programs to ease the hardship of these difficult economic times. Particularly important has been the effort on the part of the Japanese government to pressure the banks into dealing with the rising level of bad debts. This pressure was backed up by threats to nationalize the banking industry.

Another significant economic development within the Japanese economy in recent years has been the growth in foreign control of some of her most important industries. The American Ford Motor Company recently took over a controlling interest in Mazda, and Britain's Cable and Wireless bought Japan's International Digital Communications. The idea of foreign firms purchasing domestic companies was something quite familiar to citizens of many other countries. But for Japan it was something quite new. Clearly, the weak Japanese economy of the previous decade made these dramatic changes possible.

These changes have had positive aspects, if not for Japanese corporations then for the Japanese public. Consumers have long shouldered the burden of artificially high prices for most of the goods they consumed from rice to electronics. The Japanese model seemed to be one of excellent service coupled with high prices regardless of what people actually wanted. But

those days may be passing. The declining price of land coupled with changing consumer attitudes and regulatory changes made it possible for the larger American-style super store and malls to make significant inroads into Japan. These developments may not please the Japanese corporations or small businesses, but they will certainly have a positive impact on consumer satisfaction.

As the new century unfolded, the Japanese economy, after so many years of recession, finally started showing signs of a limited recovery. While part of the improvement was tied to the American economy, a more significant percentage is directly tied to Japan's growing exports to the increasingly large China market. In fact, "Greater China," that ethnic block that includes not only Hong Kong and Taiwan but the People's Republic, not long ago became the largest single market for Japanese goods. Even more recently China alone passed the United States as Japan's most important trading partner.

Perhaps the most dramatic example of Japan's economic recovery in the years before 2008 was the news that Toyota was on the brink of passing General Motors as the world's largest automaker. This is a reality made possible in no small part by the Toyota's willingness to embrace so much more enthusiastically the growing consumer demand for more environmentally green and economic hybrid cars.

But while embracing green energy hybrid cars was clearly an important strategic decision by the nation's automakers, it in itself was not enough to shield the nation's carmakers, or almost any other part of the economy for that matter, from the world-wide recession that set in and drained consumer demand for Japan's products from nations as diverse as China and the United States. For a nation that lacks the energy resources some other nations enjoy, the recession came as part of a double-edged economic body blow. Before the economic crash, Japan's energy bills for imported fossil fuels had gone up extraordinarily fast over the previous year. This was a burden that was only relieved as energy prices dropped in the wake of the even more dramatic crash in the demand for her products.

As in the United States and China, Tokyo immediately turned to the development of various government-sponsored stimulus programs that it hoped would keep the economy from doing a total tailspin and start moving the nation toward recovery. Eventually they implemented three different stimulus programs that totaled about $275 billion. The new Japanese Democratic government trimmed some of the spending after it came into power. Unfortunately, by late spring 2010

Japanese women enjoy brewery celebration

Japan

the Japanese economy had still not re-gained significant economic health. Rather it was still plagued by a deflationary process that also saw significant unemployment. In keeping with current international trends, the only really bright spot was that exports to China were up significantly, as growth there continued to recover nicely from the 2008 global economic collapse.

Energy and Environmental Challenges

As a nation Japan has few sources of energy on its soil and has had to import almost all of its needs from abroad, especially the Middle East. During the early 1970s oil embargo, that situation proved particularly shocking to Japan's elites. In the years since, Japan has become not only one of the most energy efficient nations on Earth, but it has built up an impressive strategic reserve to help cushion such oil shocks.

The Japanese government understands that meeting the current energy needs of the second largest economy in the world has become considerably more complicated in recent years. Historically Japan met the vast majority of its oil needs from the volatile Middle East region. More recently, its enormous neighbor, China, which had long been an oil exporter, has become a huge importer of foreign oil. In fact, China recently passed Japan to become the world's second-largest oil importer. Even more significant, the growing reality of needing to make a transition from fossil fuels to new "greener" energy sources absolutely demands a new direction for the nation's energy policies.

With that in mind, the Ministry of Economy and Trade recently issued a new National Energy Strategy that announced plans fundamentally to reduce the nation's dependence on world oil resources and to expand its commitment to nuclear energy. In the transportation area it is, for example, mandating that by 2010 all new cars be required to operate with fuel that includes ten percent ethanol, and it is instituting a national campaign to lessen dependence on air conditioning during summers. But despite those goals, the plan also called for a more powerful Japanese corporate effort to secure Japan's energy sources abroad. In perhaps a new sign of the future, Japan airlines carried out its first test of a new green energy fuel in January 2009.

Once the new government of the Japanese Democratic Party took office, Japan's environmental record received a major boost when the JDP's leadership promised—under the assumption that other governments would go along—a much more ambitious effort to cut the nation's green house gas emissions. However,

while that pledge impressed environmentalists, the Academy Award winning film, the *Cove*, which depicted a bloody Japanese dolphin hunt, had the opposite international impact.

THE FUTURE

The most important issue for the immediate future will be how well the Japanese face the many economic, social and international challenges that confront them. Internationally Japan is moving into uncharted waters. Despite some competition from South Korea, she has for decades been the preeminent economic power in East Asia. That situation, though, is changing very quickly as China's economy and increasingly its military power surge ahead. Especially obvious over the last year was precisely how much the situation had already changed. A significant part of the more positive aspects of Japan's economic well-being was directly linked to exports to China. Her new government was working to improve relations with Beijing while trying to refashion relations

with the United States into a more equal and nuanced relationship.

The reality of Beijing's enhanced influence is even more complicated by the fact that China's growth is occurring in an era when many in East Asia still harbor considerable resentment toward Japan due to its war-time behavior. Clearly one of the biggest challenges for Japan's leaders will be to accommodate comfortably their nation to China's renewed power and influence and to move more successfully past those lingering memories.

More immediately, the challenge will be to establish fully a genuinely two-party political system that could offer the sort of governmental and policy flexibility that the half century of LDP domination often lacked. There is certainly plenty to praise about those many decades of domination by the Liberal Democratic Party. Nevertheless, for Japan to implement more effectively a more responsive democratic system, it has long needed a genuine opposition capable of assuming power. In the relatively new Japanese Democratic Party, Japan finally has such an alternative.

Sketch of a street scene in Seoul about 1880

The Republic of Korea (South Korea)

Area: 38,452 sq. mi. (98,919 sq. km., somewhat larger than Indiana).

Population: 48,636,068 (July 2010 est.)

Capital City: Seoul, Pop. 10,500,000 (2005 estimated).

Climate: Temperate, with a short winter, hot and humid in the summer with a rainy monsoon from July to September.

Neighboring Countries: North Korea (North); Japan (East)

Official Language: Korean

Other Principal Tongues: Japanese also spoken by many older Koreans

Ethnic Background: Korean, related to Manchurian and Mongolian

Principal Religions: Buddhism, Confucianism, Christianity

Main Exports (to U.S. and Japan): Textiles and clothing, electrical machinery, footwear, steel, ships, fish, automobiles and electronics

Main Imports (from, Saudi Arabia, China, Japan and the U.S.): Machinery, oil, transport equipment, chemicals, grains, petrochemicals, electronics

Currency: Won

Former Colonial Status: Korea was a tributary state of the Chinese empires for certain periods until 1895; Japanese protectorate (1905–1910); Japanese Dependency (1910–1945); it was occupied by the U.S. from 1945 to 1948

National Day: August 15, 1945 (Republic Day)

Chief of State: President Lee Myung-bak (since 25 February 2008)

Prime Minister: Prime Minister CHUNG Un-chan (since 30 September 2009)

National Flag: White, with a center circle divided equally by an S-curve into blue and red portions; there is a varying combination of 3 solid and 3 broken lines in each corner.

Per Capita GDP Income: $28,000 (2009 est.) purchasing power parity.

The predominantly mountainous peninsula of Korea is actually an extension of the mountains of southern Manchuria, from which it is separated by the Yalu and Tumen Rivers. The spine of the mountains runs from northeast to southwest, but remains close to the eastern coastline area of Korea. Eastern Korea is thus rugged, containing many scenic mountain peaks. The famous Diamond Mountains (*Kimgan-san*) in North Korea are particularly spectacular, reaching their greatest height in the Changpai San at the northern border, where the peaks are snow-covered all year.

From these immense mountains, streams gather to form the Yalu River which empties into the Yellow Sea, and the Tumen River which flows into the Sea of Japan. The steep descent of these rivers provides one of the world's best sources of hydroelectric power, with a great potential that has only begun to be developed. The western coastal regions contain most of the peninsula's level plains, interspersed with frequent rivers. This is the agricultural belt where rice predominates, raised in wet

South Korea

Skyline of modern Seoul. The grounds of the Duksoo Palace, built in the 15th century and carefully preserved, are seen in the foreground, surrounded by the bustling city.

paddies in the South, where two crops are harvested each year, and grown in the North on dry plantations, where only one crop matures at the end of the summer.

Tidal variations along the west coast are extreme; there is sometimes a difference of 30 feet between low and high tide. The offshore islands, numbering about 3,500, are the remnants of the mountain chain, standing with their shoulders above water. The long coastline and the nearness to some of the richest fishing grounds in the world have made the people, especially in the South, skilled fishermen. This has led to frequent squabbles with individual Japanese and with Japanese governments because the people of the over-crowded neighboring islands desperately need the same protein which the Koreans harvest from the sea.

The cooler climate of North Korea resembles that of Manchuria. It is better endowed with minerals, hydroelectric facilities and capacity. The lower regions of the mountains support thick stands of timber. South Korea has a warmer climate, which supports a greater agricultural production. In December, the temperatures in Pusan may be mild at the same time that frigid blasts of below-zero arctic weather envelope the remote mountains of the North. The Siberian black bear and leopard mingle with fierce wild boars, Manchurian tigers and smaller Korean tigers in the thinly populated northern region. In the more southern part of the peninsula the warmth increases as the animal life be-

comes more nearly tropical, dominated by herons, gulls and other birds with colorful plumage.

History

Given their appearance and language, the Koreans seem to have similar origins to the Turkic-Manchurian-Mongol people who have inhabited northeastern Asia for thousands of years and migrated to the island of Japan as well as to the Korean peninsula. People have lived in Korea from long before 10,000 B.C. But the more specific origins of the Korean people lie with the arrival of two distinct groups to the peninsula: first a Neolithic culture of fishermen and shellfish gatherers who arrived around 3,000 B.C. and later, around the 7th century B.C., a community that lived as well by hunting. These early inhabitants of the peninsula were similar to other Altaic, Tungusic tribes that inhabited the regions now known as Manchuria and Siberia as is evidenced by comparing their various tools, from ceramics to daggers and mirrors. One particular type of knife associated with women was, in fact, common among peoples from East Asia to North American Indians and Eskimos.

Although the exact chronology is less than clear, it appears that the use of bronze metal technology came into existence somewhere between 1,000 B.C. to 800 B.C. Archeological evidence suggests the presence of many tribal communities of limited size, the most important of

which was eventually the state of Old Choson, which emerged around the 2nd century based in the northwestern part of the peninsula in the area around the present day North Korean capital of Pyongyang. Korean society then, as now, was intimately tied to developments within their enormous northern neighbor China and in the first centuries B.C. much of Korea came under Chinese control.

The Chinese Commanderies

By 108 B.C., the Choson capital had fallen to the Chinese armies and their leaders the emperors of the famous Han Dynasty which established several administrative divisions in the northern part of the peninsula. Especially important was the Chinese establishment of a base at Nangyang where an enormously sophisticated society, largely based on Chinese models, would emerge. New artistic and philosophical systems were introduced as well as the Chinese administrative styles. Significant numbers of Chinese colonists arrived as well, and Nangyang would remain important for the next several hundred years. Though the Koreans would strongly resist direct Chinese control and eventually regain their independence, the influence of Chinese cultural norms and the interest they would hold for Koreans would in many ways continue through the modern day. Like the Japanese, the Koreans would reject important aspects of Chinese civilization from the more merit-

The medieval dance-drama, *Tomi*.

based Confucian examination system to its historical disdain for the military. Both Korea and Japan, despite their twin enthusiasms for Chinese civilization, would retain their emphasis on a hereditary aristocracy and honored military elite.

The Three Kingdoms

By the first century B.C. three Korean kingdoms would establish themselves; Koguryo in the north, Silla on the southeast part of the peninsula and Paekche in the southwest. In each kingdom a powerful hereditary monarchy evolved that ruled with a centralized system of control. Each of these kingdoms was under strong Chinese cultural influence, including Mahayana (northern) Buddhism, Confucianism and the Chinese written language. Especially interesting is the fact that there is now considerable evidence to suggest that the original Yamato Japanese state that later developed on the nearby islands may have been an offshoot of the early Korean kingdom of Paekche.

During the 7th century, the Silla kingdom, initially working with the powerful Tang Dynasty of China, defeated each of its rivals and emerged in domination. Later in the century, Silla's leaders even managed to drive out the Chinese and establish themselves dominant over most of the peninsula.

Over the next years, as Silla's leaders established themselves, a more centralized Chinese style administrative trend was

adopted that even included an exam system similar to what the Chinese were employing. The Chinese language was used as the principal language of communication and even Tang clothing styles were adopted. It was during Silla's domination that the effort began to create a phonetic system for writing Korean which, by the 1400s would become today's modern alphabet-like system known as han'gul.

It was also during these years, inspired by the interest of Silla's leadership, that Buddhism became particularly important on the peninsula. A large number of Koreans studied in China itself and the Buddhist establishment grew enormously with the emergence of large numbers of monasteries.

Externally, Silla, although dominant on the peninsula, considered itself part of the Chinese world order. Practically, this meant sending tribute missions to the Tang capital and having their representatives perform the *kowtow* to the emperors, which meant to kneel and touch the forehead to the ground in deep respect. But if Silla managed to maintain Korea's independence from China it was less lucky with its own internal enemies, and by the early tenth century they had lost control of the peninsula to a new state that called itself Koryo, from which we derive the modern name for the country.

Korea's years of independence were brutally interrupted by the arrival of the Mongol armies who occupied the peninsula and used it as a launching pad for

their two attacks against Japan in the 13th century. At the beginning of the 13th century the Mongol attack forced the Koryo government to withdraw to an island north of modern day Inchon. Within a generation after more devastating attacks the Koryo leadership was forced to submit to Mongol demands that included taking part in what were fated to be the unsuccessful Mongol invasions of Japan. In two attacks late in the century, Mongol warriors, sailing in ships made by the accomplished Korean ship building industry, tried to expand their power to Japan. But as discussed in the Japan chapter, the attacks failed in the face of adverse weather conditions and Japanese resistance. For the Koreans, involvement in the campaigns was a disaster.

Even during the era of Mongol control Korean culture survived. Socially the aristocracy continued its influence and, now disdaining Buddhism, embraced a Chinese style neo-Confucianism, a particularly metaphysical form of the historical Chinese system of social relations.

Not surprisingly, the overthrow of the Mongol dynasty in China by the new Chinese Ming dynasty had ramifications within Korea that contained supporters of both ruling groups. For Korea itself, the ultimate outcome was the capture of the Koryo capital by General Yi Song-gye and the establishment of the longest lasting of Korean dynasties, which extended from 1392 to 1910 when it was abolished by the Japanese. Formally known as the Choson dynasty it is also known as the Yi dynasty after its founder. Its capital city, Hanyang, is today better known as Seoul.

Yi Korea (1392–1910)

Violent power struggles within the ruling family marked the first years of the dynasty. Still, overall the Yi showed great creativity, wisdom and artistry, advancing in the field of astronomy and perfecting han'gul, the alphabet-like system that by the 20th century would become the common instrument of writing Korean. Although governed by a local line of rulers, Korea remained a faithful tributary of the Chinese empire and one so devoted to Confucian civilization that it vehemently rejected the Buddhist orientation of previous generations. Eventually they were to embrace a neo-Confucian ideology so completely that most scholars believe them to have been far more Confucian than even the Chinese themselves. The government strengthened the Chinese style administrative structure and examination system even more thoroughly than previous Korean regimes though the Chinese emphasis on true social mobility never really took hold. For Koreans, the

South Korea

system of hereditary elites remained more attractive.

Despite their nobler births the Korean aristocracy in these years, like others in East and Southeast Asia, very consciously modeled themselves on China's scholar-gentry ruling class. Of course, as Japan would also do, they created their own distinctively Korean variation of the Chinese model. In Korea the elites were known as Yangban, a hereditary class whose members were most respected when they combined impressive ancestors, land and office holdings and, above all, devotion to scholarly accomplishments. This Korean version of elite society was to prove remarkably resilient and to survive well into the modern era. Given the introduction of Han'gul, the phonetic writing and the educational priorities of the Korean Confucian elite, it is not surprising that these years saw an enormous growth in the production of printing, the first large scale efforts anywhere in the world.

Socially, traditional Korea had differed dramatically from China in its earlier treatment of women. Korean women enjoyed a level of freedom that is said to have amazed visiting Chinese. They were able to inherit, and a new husband could marry into a woman's family and reside there among his in-laws in contrast to the usual Asian pattern of brides always being the ones to relocate.

As we have seen, during the 15th century Korea's new leaders embraced a neo-Confucianism that was more orthodox than even found in China itself. This closer embrace of Confucianism did not bode well for Korean women, whose status diminished over the centuries.

Technically, Korea was, throughout this era, more advanced than the West. From its accomplishments in printing to mathematics and instrumentation engineering, Korean society was very impressive on the eve of the Western arrival. But these accomplishments were dramatically interrupted when, once again, Korea's location between two powerful neighbors put its people at risk. Just as in the 13th century Mongol armies had used Korea to attack Japan, by the late 1500s Koreans once again found themselves condemned by their location. In 1592 the Japanese, led by Toyotomi Hideyoshi, invaded the peninsula with almost 160,000 soldiers in an ill-fated effort to conquer China.

The Koreans defended themselves with a remarkable flotilla of the world's first armor-plated warships, the famous "Turtle Ships" which effectively destroyed the Japanese fleets. Moreover, with the help of the Ming they were successful in defending the peninsula, but the damage was overwhelming. After a second assault in 1597 when, after Hideyoshi's death, the Japanese finally withdrew, both nations entered an era of increased isolation from their neighbors.

President Lee Myung-Bak

While life would soon calm in Japan, Koreans experienced more trauma. The recovery had hardly begun before Koreans faced yet another trial, the conquest of China by the Manchurians and their own inclusion in this new emerging Sino-Manchurian Empire. From the Korean perspective, the fall of the much-admired Chinese Ming Empire to the Manchurians was an astounding cultural disaster that left many of them believing that Korea alone remained the last bastion of Confucian civilization. It was a sentiment many Russians had felt a century before when the exalted Christian Byzantine Empire had fallen to the arriving Ottomans. In Eastern Europe many Russians had begun to think of themselves as the new or Third Rome after Constantinople fell. At the other end of the enormous Eurasian land mass, Koreans, observing the collapse of Ming China, often felt themselves to be playing a similar role as the last defenders of true Confucian civilization.

Over the next centuries, although Korean pride in its Confucian accomplishments soared, so too did intellectual and court factionalism that would eventually make the nation less prepared to deal with the challenges to come. On the international level Korea became intensely isolationist, as committed to its own inward looking perspective as its much disliked Japanese neighbors. But in contrast to Japan, Koreans did not have a group of scholars, the equivalent of the famous Japanese "Dutch Scholars" who could at least keep the nation somewhat aware of developments in the outer world. Thus when later forced open by the pressures of imperialism, Korea would have fewer resources to fall back upon than Japan.

Over the next centuries, Europeans who were occasionally shipwrecked on the rough coastline were held captive while Japanese and Chinese who happened upon Korean shores were expeditiously sent packing. It was a far cry from the Korea of earlier centuries which is said to have been much more open to the world. During these centuries that immediately preceded the arrival of the Westerners the Koreans were content with their many official expeditions to Beijing. Nevertheless even during those activities Korean concerns about the outside world remained profound. While they were able to roam freely within Beijing during their visits, the Chinese envoy's movements were severely restricted in Seoul.

The Dawn of Imperialist Pressures

By the middle of the nineteenth century, Western pressures in East Asia had become intense. The Europeans during the two Opium wars forced open China and the Americans had done the same thing in Japan. It was now Korea's turn to feel the pressures of imperialism, but in her case it would ultimately be Japanese greed that would determine its fate. But that thrust would be later. Early on it was the Westerners, specifically the French and Americans, who applied the first pressures. Within Korea, as we have seen, the Yi Dynasty like Japan a generation earlier was vehemently committed to maintaining its isolation and the first contacts suggested that goal might be possible.

In 1866, the Koreans successfully drove a French force away from an island near Inchon. A few years later a confrontation broke out between an American commercial vessel, the General Sherman, that ended with the death of all those on the American ship. But unfortunately, these early and successful efforts to resist outside pressures did not last. When, a few years, the Americans retaliated against Korea for firing on American ships, the assault resulted in the deaths of more than six hundred Korean soldiers.

In 1882 the United States became the first Western nation to open treaty relations with the Koreans. However, it was with Japan that Korea's external relations were to become particularly complicated and painful.

The Beginning of the Japanese Assault

Koreans had long looked with disdain at their island neighbor, Japan's, efforts to remake itself on a Western model in the decades after Perry's arrival. In fact, their attitude almost provoked an indignant Japanese attack early in the 1870s. For the moment the Japanese decided against an expedition but a generation later Japan's attitude would be quite different. Over the next years, at China's urging, the court signed a series of treaties with the various Western powers. From China's perspective, which saw Korea as part of its own world order, Korean treaties with the Western powers provided some protection from Japanese demands.

Inside Korea, nationalists and the more educated youth often looked to Japan as a source of inspiration and direction. On the other hand, the elderly conservatives remained attached to the traditional Confucian empire of the Manchus. When an internal power struggle broke out during the 1870s the Japanese decided to intervene and dispatched a flotilla to the peninsula. It was an act not so very different from the American effort in the 1850s. This time, though, it was the Japanese who were making the demands rather than being the victims. The resulting treaty opened several Korean ports to the Japanese and not surprisingly aroused the ire of Korean conservatives and their supporters in China.

In the following decade an intense rivalry between the Chinese and Japanese over their relative influence in Korea was carried out and was paralleled within Korea by different factions who preferred one or the other of their neighbors. Ironically, given later events, the more progressive among the Koreans favored the Japanese having been impressed with that nation's willingness to embrace Western technical skills. More than once tensions and violence between the two groups encouraged further meddling in Korean affairs by China and Japan.

Given the intense imperialistic tone of the age a clash was inevitable. The explosion came in 1894. Initially it was internal developments, not international events, which set the stage. Within Korea a new popular movement, the Tonghaks, somewhat like the Chinese Taipings, had arisen. It was a movement that emphasized both traditional values, including Korean spiritualism, elements similar to Catholicism and was inspired by a general egalitarianism.

The Tonghaks were also anti-Japanese as well as antagonistic to the Westerners. More immediately it was driven by the distress of many in the peasant class who were hard-pressed by the exploitative demands of the Korean ruling classes. The new Japanese economic demands also added to the peasantry's plight and by the early 1890s a full-scale revolt had broken out. By the time the movement turned into an uprising it had become a major agrarian revolution.

In the ensuing turmoil, the Korean King Kojong called for Chinese help. Meanwhile, the Japanese used the occasion to rush troops to the peninsula. With little resistance, the Japanese drove the Chinese forces out of Korea. It was the first stage of what would become Korea's nightmare experience as a Japanese colony.

But the Japanese were not yet able to establish their undisputed control over Korea. The nearby Russians, whose empire bordered on Korea, had also developed considerable interest in the peninsula. But within ten years the Japanese and Russians would also fight over the increasingly prostrate Korean peninsula. After more than a millennium of independence, Korea was once again caught by its own geography between more powerful forces.

Becoming a Japanese Colony

When the short Russo-Japanese War of 1904–1905 resulted in a Japanese victory and the establishment of a Japanese protectorate over Korea, Tokyo was ready to make its move. With no opposition, Japan simply annexed the peninsula in 1910; Korea became the largest dependency of the growing Japanese empire. It was, after all, the age of Imperialism and such exploitative moves were common during these years. In fact, the Japanese had only just finished watching the Americans subdue those Philippine forces who had attempted to resist the American occupation of their land. Sadly, the Japanese occupation was to prove considerably more brutal than what the Americans imposed in their colony.

Japanese rule was very harsh and devoted to creating investment opportunities for Japanese capital, raising rice to feed Japan and establishing military bases for further expansion on the Asian continent. Whether most Koreans agreed or not, the long-isolated peninsula was being transformed by the changes introduced by the Japanese.

On a purely technical level the Korea that eventually regained its freedom half a century later was the most developed of East and Southeast Asia's former colonies. But those industrial advantages hardly outweighed the humiliations of Japanese control.

Almost from the start a committed Korean resistance movement began which did everything in its power to resist Japanese control. They even managed to assassinate Ito Hirobumi, Japan's revered hero of the Meiji Restoration during his tenure as Japan's highest official in Korea. The Japanese were outraged and the peninsula's formal annexation occurred soon after.

The best-known resistance occurred in the spring of 1919 when, angered by open Japanese exploitation and inspired by newly learned democratic slogans used in World War I, hundreds of thousands of Koreans, many of whom had converted to Christianity, staged a massive, peaceful demonstration in favor of independence.

Outraged by the thousands of demonstrators who took part in declaring a Korean Declaration of Independence, Japanese officials brutally suppressed the peaceful demonstrations arresting and killing thousands. For Korea, those years were traumatic and resistance was common. Throughout the era, Koreans both within Korea and beyond its borders fought against Japan's control and hoped through efforts ranging from guerrilla warfare through international protests to force the Japanese out. But as with most other occupations it is true as well that many Koreans threw in their lot with the Japanese and attempted to advance by serving within the colonial administration.

The Gateway in the Ancient Walls of Seoul

South Korea

A game of *Go-ban*, or oriental chess. Korean Minister of War, Yun-Woong-Niel, is on left. (1900)

A young Korean and his wife in street dress, Seoul, 1902.

Relaxing their rule briefly during the 1920s because of adverse Korean and world popular opinion, the Japanese intensified their exploitation when they undertook the conquest of Manchuria and China in the 1930s. In an effort to avoid further unrest, they attempted to absorb the Koreans by forcing them to adopt Japanese names and to speak the language of their conquerors. This had no lasting effect and actually served to further embitter the Koreans against the Japanese.

As the Pacific War developed in the 1930s the Koreans naturally found themselves caught up again in Japanese ambitions first to conquer China and later the assault on Southeast Asia. What the Japanese colonial authorities wanted of their Korean subjects was their labor. Millions were sent to Japan to serve as forced laborers during the war.

But working in Japan's factories and mines was not the only thing the Japanese demanded of their Korean victims. Along with young women from other parts of Asia, thousands of Korean women were forced to serve as prostitutes for the Japanese army. Euphemistically referred to as "Comfort Women," somewhere between one hundred thousand and two hundred thousand Korean women were forced into sexual slavery during the Second World War.

It was also during these years that Korea's postwar leaders, men like the American-oriented Syngman Rhee and his later communist opponent Kim Il-sung, made their reputations as leading Korean nationalists. The groundwork was prepared for their later arrival to power in the months after World War II.

The Division of Korea

At the close of World War II, when Japan had all but surrendered to U.S. and British forces, the subject of the future of Korea was considered by the leaders of the "Big Three" at the Potsdam Conference in mid-1945. Russia's Stalin reaffirmed his promise that the U.S.S.R. would declare war on Japan, which it had refrained from doing prior to that time, and proposed that it would secure the Korean peninsula from the Japanese armies. It was ultimately decided that Soviet forces would occupy the northern part of Korea and accept the surrender of the Japanese troops in that region, and the U.S. forces would do the same in the southern portion.

The American expectation was that the whole peninsula would come under the supervision of the then infant UN. This decision, made halfway around the world from the helpless Koreans, was to be the basis of continued conflict and friction for years, and also was to cost the loss of thousands of lives. It also ultimately was to result in an economically harmful division of the peninsula.

Two days after the first atomic bomb had burst with a terrifying holocaust on the Japanese city of Hiroshima, the U.S.S.R. declared war on Japan. The Japanese accepted the Allied surrender terms on August 14, but during the few intervening days the Soviets had easily occupied North Korea. The boundary between U.S. and Soviet troops was fixed shortly afterward at the 38th parallel by two young colonels in the American army who were given about half an hour to pick a place on the peninsula to divide the two forces. It was a decision that Koreans themselves would think back on with bitterness from then until today.

In the North, the Russians promptly installed a satellite regime run by Korean communists under the control of the Soviet occupation forces. In the South, U.S. occupation forces, which operated a full military government from 1945 through 1948, followed a shifting policy primarily devoted to economic recovery and to the creation of a democratic government.

There were seemingly unending negotiations between the two powers in 1946–1947 on the formation of a provisional government for the entire peninsula. But events on the ground made most of these discussions irrelevant. The Soviets for their part had chosen to support Kim Il-sung, the well known anti-Japanese fighter, and the United States increasingly settled on supporting the aging Syngman Rhee who by then had lived in the United States for decades. In essence, the tensions associated with the Cold War of the late 1940s had already begun within Korea immediately after World War II.

The southern, American-oriented Republic of Korea was soon declared independent and was admitted to the UN. Elections, carried out under the occupation's mandate, confirmed Rhee as the new President and the American occupation officially ended. The Russians reacted by establishing the "Democratic People's Republic of Korea" in the North and withdrew their own occupation forces. Soviet control and support of local communists were sufficient to maintain North Korea within the Soviet bloc with little or no Russian military presence.

During the Cold War the two regimes were poles apart on what other nations they chose to associate with and on economic matters. But they did have an important concern in common. Each was led by committed nationalists who were determined to reunite their nations. Over the next two years activists in both parts of the peninsula hoped for some sort of clash that would ultimately reunite the peninsula under one or the other government's leadership.

The Korean War

America on the eve of the Korean War was very involved in developments in the Republic of South Korea. Not only was it contributing more than a hundred million dollars a year to the country but it was also influential in practically every aspect of the new state's existence from government through cultural and educational affairs. Clearly the United States wanted the South to be well able to withstand a potential attack from communist North Korea. On the other hand, many Americans were more immediately concerned about those South Koreans who were anxious to begin their own effort to unify the peninsula from the south.

President Rhee, the American sponsored president, was among those calling for an attack on the north. But despite Rhee's efforts to gain American support to unify the peninsula under his control, it was his northern rival Kim-Il-sung and the latter's Soviet allies that made the fateful decision to begin what would become a vicious civil war. In June of 1950, bolstered by a heavy dose of Soviet military aid, North Korean forces invaded South Korea. Their attack, well planned in advance, was very effective and they were barely prevented from overrunning all of South Korea.

Angered by the North's invasion, President Truman, despite earlier U.S. statements to the contrary, viewed the attack as an assault on America's national interests and ordered a military intervention on the side of the South Koreans. Choosing to work within the structures of the newly formed United Nations, President Truman arranged for the UN to condemn the aggressive acts of North Korea and to order military sanctions against the Soviet satellite. Ironically, the representative of the U.S.S.R., who could have employed its veto power, was not there to do so. The U.S.S.R. had been boycotting the council due to controversies surrounding the question of who should hold the China seat, the People's Republic of China or the recently defeated Nationalists on Taiwan.

The southern counter-attack, while nominally carried out by a UN force, was primarily an American military effort. General Douglas MacArthur commanded the UN forces. Demonstrating the same energy and self-will he had shown during most of World War II, MacArthur planned an aggressive campaign to drive the northern forces out of South Korea.

A combination of mass bombing of the North and a flank attack by an amphibious landing at Inchon, a coastal town near Seoul, succeeded in driving the North Koreans from the territory they had conquered. Then having successfully driven the northern troops from South Korea, MacArthur insisted, and found support among his superiors, for an attack on North Korea and yet another unification drive, this time from the south.

Even as the American forces were moving closer and closer to the Chinese borders, MacArthur, ignoring Beijing's warnings, was certain that the forces of the People's Republic would not intervene. Sure of his judgment, MacArthur ordered his forces toward the Yalu River, the border that divided Korea from China. MacArthur was wrong. China was not prepared to accept foreign and probably hostile troops directly on its borders. Moreover, both Moscow and Beijing wanted to save the communist regime in Korea.

Beijing's forces struck with great force, using the same successful tactics they had learned in their battles with the Japanese and Chinese Nationalists during the previous decade. The Chinese effort to drive the U.S. and UN forces out of North Korea succeeded, but they were ultimately unable to capitalize on their initial military successes and fully unite the peninsula. Nevertheless, they did temporarily manage to capture Seoul, the capital.

General MacArthur, realizing he had been put on the defensive, very publicly

U.S. Marines in Korea, November 1951

South Korea

advocated a wider war effort, including the bombing of Chinese Manchurian bases. Eventually the famous general's utterances caused a public break between himself and President Truman who had lost faith in his judgment. MacArthur was replaced, but the war itself waged on.

Chinese forces tried to retake Seoul in April and May 1951, but their supply lines had become too long to support the effort. Armistice negotiations began in July 1951, but since neither side had won a clear victory, the talks dragged on for two years, while fighting continued. Each side sought to obtain a defensible position, and gradually the lines of battle hardened with heavy fortifications that would have made a major breakthrough by either side almost impossible.

A crisis over the repatriation of prisoners also prolonged the conflict. The Chinese and North Koreans disliked and refused to recognize the proposition that their soldiers, many of whom were former Nationalist soldiers, might not want to return to their homelands. Nevertheless, an armistice was reached on July 27, 1953, a few months after the death of Stalin which had led to a reduction of Soviet support for the war.

American politics also contributed heavily to this armistice. The popular military hero of World War II, General Dwight Eisenhower, was chosen by the Republican Party to oppose President Truman's Democratic successor. Eisenhower's promise during the campaign to use his influence to end the Korean War greatly influenced the American public. Privately, President Eisenhower threatened to use nuclear weapons to settle the dispute. The threat worked.

The eventual armistice was a stalemate of military might, and the demarcation is along about the same line as it was prior to the conflict. The real result of the struggle was the loss of several hundred thousand lives and an almost utter devastation of both Koreas. The fighting may have ended, but the two parts of Korea then settled in for a generation-long struggle for domination of the peninsula. Over the years that new struggle would take many forms.

The Two Koreas in the Post War Era

Shortly after the armistice, the Soviet Union and China began providing substantial economic aid programs to North Korea. As a result, it acquired a broad industrial base and a per capita industrial production that rose to a level higher than that of China. Kim Il-sung, the political leader selected by the Soviets in 1945 to lead North Korea, soon acquired exclusive control over the local communist party at the expense of his rivals.

90 CHURCH STREET, ROOM 1303
NEW YORK 7, NEW YORK

7 November 1961

Dear Mr. Stryker:

Thank you so much for your cordial letter of November 4th. It was thoughtful of you to write me as you have and I appreciate it.

The Fuller's lived next door to the MacArthur's on Marshall Street in Milwaukee. My father made it his home on retirement from the Army and I visited him there many, many times. Secretary Stimson was a life long friend. I admired him greatly.

Had we gone on beyond the Yalu we would have destroyed Red China and it would no longer be a growing menace to the free world. We could have done so very easily and the whole outlook of mankind would be different today.

With best wishes,

Most sincerely,

DOUGLAS MacARTHUR.

Mr. Philip F. Stryker,
312 Marlborough Street,
Boston 16, Massachusetts.

MacArthur's blunt comment eight years after the Korean War

Eventually the Korean War and subsequent Russian-Chinese ideological disputes over what is "true communism" gave Kim a much wider degree of freedom of action within the communist sphere. For a few years after 1960 Kim tended to favor the Chinese. After 1964 he swung back toward the Russians, then again toward the Chinese for a time, and after 1983, toward Moscow until the Soviet Union collapsed.

In South Korea, despite massive American aid, the postwar economy floundered and the elderly President Rhee grew increasingly senile, autocratic, and unpopular. In 1960 he resigned and left the country after his government faced rebellious student demonstrations that the army made no effort to suppress. There followed a year of political ferment and regrouping under a weak government that ended in 1961 when the army seized control of South Korea.

South Korea Emerges Economically

After an initial period of direct military rule, General Park Chung-hee, the leader of the military junta that had seized power, nominally became a civilian and was elected president. He was reelected in 1967. In 1972, not satisfied with his authority as the elected president of South Korea, Park pushed through legislation that allowed him to become a dictator. With that development, the entire peninsula had fallen under the control of autocratic governments, the communists in the North and Park's supporters. Park justified his actions by citing the need to retain national unity in the south in the face of the northern threat. But if the political situation of the two Koreas was growing more similar, the beginning of their modern economic divergence was also gaining momentum.

South Korean children and video games.

The roots of South Korea's modern economic "miracle" are diverse, ranging from external to internal factors. What is clear is that the average per capita income in 1963 was around $100; by 2009 it was over $29,000. As the century reached its termination, some Korean laborers were earning salaries comparable to Americans in the Midwest. Obviously, such an economic transformation was caused by myriad developments, but for Korea, certain key factors can be noted. Especially important were ties with both the Americans and the Japanese.

Since the decision to intervene during the Korean War, the United States had been committed to a stable South Korea and had helped create the conditions there necessary to such stability. By the 1960s, the Korean willingness to align themselves with the internationally unpopular American effort in Vietnam was also very lucrative. In fact, some of the most important South Korean construction firms profited greatly from the projects they carried out in South Vietnam during the war. Their role, in some ways, resembled that of the Japanese during the American involvement in Korea during the earlier Korean War.

Though the memories of the Japanese occupation remained bitter, the reality was that the Koreans, and especially many in the elite, were well positioned to take advantage of the economic growth then going on in Japan. These Korean leaders, including General Park himself, were fluent in Japanese and quite willing to gain the advantages of close economic ties to Japan. That strategy worked quite well as Japan invested enormously in South Korea. For example, Mitsubishi owned about 10% of the South Korean company Hyundai and supplied many of the most important parts.

These advantages would not have been realized if the Park government had not chosen to move his committed and inexpensive labor force into the world export market, an economic decision already well trodden by Japan itself. President Park's economic policy and the advantages of the international environment, especially after the early 1960s, were major benefits. One has only to look at the Seoul's modern skyline to recognize the very real improvement in living standards and to appreciate how much was accomplished in those years. On the political level Park's leadership was much less successful.

President Park's increasing personal power aroused considerable opposition, especially from the intellectuals, students, and the powerful Christian churches. This opposition was cruelly suppressed on the grounds that it gave aid and comfort to North Korea at a time when American protection of South Korea was becoming increasingly unreliable. Kim Dae Jung, later president, though then an influential opposition leader who had received a large minority of the popular vote for the presidency in 1971, was kidnapped in Japan by the South Korean Central Intelligence Agency in 1973 and brought home. The next year President Park's wife was fatally shot in mid-1974 in what was officially described as an attempt on the life of the president himself. Since the assassin had some Japanese connections, the government launched a dispute with Japan. But there were reasons to believe that this quarrel, as well as tensions in North Korea-South Korea relations which existed in 1974, were at least partly inspired by the Park government's efforts to distract attention from its domestic difficulties.

Despite his easy victory in a rigged referendum held in February 1975, Park's heavy-handedness might have cost him crucial American support. For a time after Jimmy Carter became president, it even looked like the U.S. might withdraw its forces.

The fall of Indochina to communism in 1975 left South Korea the only non-communist nation on the East Asian mainland and intensified the sense of danger felt in the country. This was exploited by President Park to increase his rigid control through repressive measures.

Nevertheless, The ruling *Democratic Republican Party* came closer to defeat in a 1978 election when it won only 68 seats in the National Assembly to 61 for the opposition *New Democratic Party*. In reaction, President Park reorganized his cabinet and released a number of political prisoners, including the *New Democratic Party's* leader, Kim Dae Jung.

President Park's Death

President Park was assassinated by the head of the South Korean Central Intelligence Agency in October 1979. After an interlude of confusion, the army under General Chun Doo Hwan seized power in December 1979. In mid-1980 it proclaimed martial law and viciously crushed a revolt in the southwestern city of Kwangju. The Kwangju Massacre, as it was to become known, was one of the most violent incidents in recent South Korean history and has continued to affect the course of South Korean politics ever since. Chun then became acting president and began to install a new government. Martial law was finally lifted at the beginning of 1981.

Chun then launched a policy of "national reconciliation" under which thousands of people imprisoned or barred from public life were pardoned. Despite the repressive measures used by the government to control South Korea, the surging economic figures during the 1980s helped maintain a reasonable level of satisfaction among the population. Seoul's international prestige was helped as well when it was chosen to serve as the site of the 1988 Olympic Games.

In many ways the assassinated president's emphasis on economic growth allowed the Republic of South Korea to surpass its northern rival without a military confrontation. South Korea was increasingly able to demonstrate by virtue of its accomplishments that its own economic system was stronger.

South Korea

General Park Chung-hee

A Weakened Dictatorship

By the mid 1980s President Chun faced serious political problems. There were mounting student demonstrations against the government, and the leading opposition politician, Kim Dae Jung, had returned from exile in the U.S. Although Kim was placed under house arrest, a new political party with which he was affiliated, the *New Korea Democratic Party*, did unexpectedly well in National Assembly elections held shortly after his return, winning 50 out of 276 seats.

The events of February 1986 in the Philippines also had a considerable impact on South Korea, not only because Marcos, the dictator, lost power, but because the U.S. had withdrawn support from him in spite of its large strategic interest in the country. If the United States, reacting to popular Philippine democratic pressures, could turn its back on a long-time ally like Marcos, then it might just as easily do so in South Korea as well. The military generals who dominated South Korea thus decided it was time to move toward opening the system before they were forced to do so.

An intensified dialogue ensued between the government and the legal opposition centering on the *New Korea Democratic Party (NKDP)*. A deadlock soon developed, however. It related to the nature of a new constitution. The government and the ruling party, the *Democratic Justice Party (DJP)*, wanted a cabinet (parliamentary) system, with the real power vested in the premier who would presumably be a *DJP* member; the opposition insisted on a directly (rather than indirectly, as at that time) elected president as the effective head of the government. The opposition however was hampered by disunity within the leadership of the *NKDP*.

Other elements of the opposition, including Christian clergy, lay believers, and activist students, demonstrated from time to time against the government. The demonstrators, although fairly numerous, were generally outnumbered by the huge numbers of police that the government deployed to cope with them.

South Korea's huge ally, the U.S., clearly favored compromise between the government and the opposition, and a further democratization of the political system. The activist elements of the opposition tended to view the U.S. as the main supporter of the hated South Korean "establishment," which they regarded as a military and police dictatorship. Many also blamed the United States for the continuing division of their country caused by the tensions of the Cold War.

Toward A More Democratic Korea

In the summer of 1987, as Chun's *DJP* was preparing to hand over the reins of power to his designated successor, fellow former general and *DJP* politician Roh Tae Woo, a public outcry began. Recognizing he faced a potential disaster, Roh called for an end to press censorship and free elections. Roh was counting on a loyal (but minority) *DJP* rural political base and hoped he could count on a divided opposition to salvage victory. His assumption that he could still win the election given the splits in the opposition proved correct.

The first direct presidential elections in more than sixteen years were held in South Korea in December 1987. The candidate of the ruling *DJP* was Roh Tae Woo. The two top opposition leaders, Kim Young Sam and Kim Dae Jung, were unwilling to cooperate, and the result was predictable: the winner was Roh Tae Woo with 39.9% of the vote, while the two Kims split the majority opposition vote 27.5% and 26.5%.

Amid anti-government protests, Roh Tae Woo was sworn in as president in February 1988. For the moment Roh, the former general, had prevailed, but the momentum toward a much more open system had begun. Korea would never be the same.

In an election for the National Assembly held in April of 1988, the ruling *Democratic Justice Party* won only 125 of the 299 seats. Flexing its new power the opposition then held hearings on various abuses of power during the tenure of former President Chun Doo Hwan, and especially on the Kwangju Massacre of May 1980. Chun refused to testify, and President Roh refused to compel him to do so. Chun did make a public apology, turned over his assets to the state, and retired to the countryside. Dissatisfied, a number of opposition politicians and radicals continued to demand that he be put on trial. That demand, though, was to wait until more progress was made in the democratization of the country. Nevertheless, early in 1989, approximately fifty people, including two brothers of Chun, were arrested on charges of corrupt practices under his administration. President Roh had a better image than his predecessor, but the opposition in the National Assembly hoped to pass a vote of no confidence in his administration and compel his resignation.

The several years leading up to the 1993 presidential election was an important transitional period. Many did not trust the ruling party or President Roh Tae Woo. It was believed that he might seek extralegal means of holding onto power. The new constitution was untested and the opposition was, for the most part, weak. There was also concern that the United States might significantly downsize its commitment to the republic. In spite of these concerns, 1993 did mark the beginning of a new, more democratic era for the country.

An Emerging Democracy

The election of 1993 finally brought to power Kim Young-sam, a long time democratic reformer who along with Kim Dae-jung had been especially involved in trying to bring about democratic reform. His election represented the arrival to the presidency of the first civilian elected leader in a generation, though members of the former ruling elite were still very influential. Upon coming to power, the new president, who was initially quite popular, put forward very specific goals including the

General Chun Doo Hwan

108

achievement of civilian control over the military, a more caring government, and an anti-corruption program.

By 1994 President Kim had initiated reforms to improve the political process. In a bi-partisan move, the National Assembly passed bills dealing with campaign spending, election procedures and local government. Government subsidies for political parties and candidates were increased. The overall limit on campaign spending was lowered (how much a candidate could spend on his/her own campaign). The legislation did not place a limit on how much a *party* could spend on a candidate. Overall, these changes made it easier for the opposition to compete on even footing with the ruling party. The legislature was also given increased authority over the budget and actions of the *National Security Planning Agency (NSPA)*.

President Kim Young Sam also succeeded in obtaining the agreement of all top military officials not to interfere in the political process. Charges of corruption were brought against top military figures and several were relieved of their positions, including the army chief of staff. The new government also moved to dismantle the *National Security Planning Agency*. A further significant move involved the release of almost 40,000 criminals and political prisoners. Helmeted riot police withdrew from the streets and the number of student demonstrations decreased. Anticorruption measures were initiated against a number of high-ranking government officials. After some thirty years of military participation in the political process, it is remarkable that the new president had as much success as he did.

South Korea had changed a great deal since President Park had ruled with an iron hand. President Kim was even named the winner of the Martin Luther King Prize for his contribution to building democracy and human rights in South Korea.

To the astonishment of many who had watched the long-time domination of South Korea by the military, President Kim even put on trial his two predecessors, Chun and Roh, for their roles in both the coup that brought them to power and the subsequent 1980 Kwangju Massacre. The trials ultimately concluded with former President Chun sentenced to death and President Roh to life imprisonment (lessened on appeal to a life sentence and 17 years respectively.) If President Kim had thought the trials would work to his advantage, he guessed wrong. The investigations also uncovered the depth of corruption inherent in the South Korean political system that eventually spilled over on to Kim's own administration and even his son.

Economic Corruption Scandals

A flow of corruption revelations then swept over the political landscape in a tidal wave that has not ended. Former President Roh Tae-woo admitted receiving over $600 million in contributions from businesses during his term in office. Roh's admissions came after two of his associates, one of whom managed a secret fund, revealed its existence.

It then became apparent that in return for the huge payments, large corporations such as Hyundai, Samsung, Daewoo, and Lucky Goldstar received large government contracts. Another revelation was that Kim Dae-jung, an unsuccessful candidate for the presidency in 1992, had received over $2.5 million from Roh for his campaign.

The corruption charges though were not exclusively the problems of the former presidents Chun and Roh or even of President Kim's long time democratic rival Kim Dae-jung. Early 1997 saw charges of collusion between President Kim's closest advisors and even his son with the Hanbo Group industrial group. The president was struggling, as his last year in office began, to find a way out of the growing scandal with his own reputation intact.

But the corruption scandals that were rocking South Korea by mid 1997 were not the only thing that weakened President Kim's prestige. Well aware that South Korea's soaring economy of the 1980s had stalled, the president became convinced that new economic laws needed to be implemented to give South Korean businesses more flexibility over their work forces. That in itself might have been an understandable conclusion, but when President Kim's supporters called an early morning meeting of the Korean Parliament on December 26, 1996, and passed legislation allowing businesses to lay off workers or adjust their hours more easily, he aroused a huge civil disobedience movement.

For weeks, in late December and January of 1997–98, the world watched as South Korea's democratically elected president was challenged by thousands of workers for reducing their economic security and acting undemocratically. Eventually, President Kim, his earlier insistence on standing firm not withstanding, agreed to allow the parliament, including the opposition parties, the opportunity to review the legislation.

But the events of the fall of 1997 soon changed the international environment. As the economic collapse of Southeast Asia began to impact in South Korea, the economy, already faltering, went into a tailspin (see The Economy below). With the nation's confidence crashing, a long awaited presidential campaign began which would be among the most dramatic of Korea's long history.

Kim Dae Jung: Korean President

The election campaign opened up with President Kim Young Sam's popularity in tatters and his government unable to take decisive action to deal with the nation's growing economic crises. Given the new situation it now looked like Kim Daejung, the three time presidential candidate, frequent political prisoner and lifelong opponent of the military regime, might finally have a real chance of winning. Recognizing that this was his last chance at the presidency, the former political prisoner, so long labeled a leftist radi-

The Olympic Highway in Seoul along the Han River.

South Korea

cal by his opponents, moved decisively toward the political center and sought out allies on the middle and right of the South Korean political spectrum. Not giving up, South Korea's long time ruling party, the Grand National Party nominated Lee Hoi-chang as its standard bearer who not surprisingly worked to distance himself from the extremely unpopular Kim Young-sam.

A third candidate, Rhee In-je, angry that the ruling party had not nominated him, emerged to turn the struggle into another three-way race. But this time, unlike in his previous efforts, the momentum was behind Kim Dae-jung, the long time political dissident. When he won the December 1997 vote, it was as astounding a political transformation as when Lech Walesa had become president of Poland or Nelson Mandela of South Africa.

Having waited a lifetime to lead South Korea and then at 73 winning power as his country experienced its worst economic collapse in a generation, the new president had his work cut out for him. Much to the relief of many, he seemed ready to begin. Recognizing that he had been elected by less than a majority and knowing the importance of unifying the country, he named as his prime minister Kim Jong-pil, a long-time supporter of the former ruling party and a man who had even played a decisive role in bringing about the long years of military rule. If that move did not endear him to some of his long time supporters, the new president's decision to grant general amnesties not only to imprisoned political prisoners but to those who had been convicted of traffic violations certainly was popular.

Unfortunately, for the new president, the economic crisis of 1997 turned out to be far more difficult to manage. While Kim was able to replenish the country's foreign exchange reserves, which had been dangerously low in the months before he took office, real reform seemed far off. Initially successful in obtaining promises of cooperation from the labor unions, he soon found their leadership was quite unwilling to accept layoffs to strengthen the nation's businesses.

Thus, by summer of 1998 Korea was once again experiencing major labor unrest. Nor were the nation's economic leaders any more willing to cooperate with the government's plans for restructuring and thus despite considerable rhetoric on the new president's part little real economic reform has been accomplished.

One problem that also appeared to weaken the president's efforts was accusations that he was not only favoring his own political supporters but carrying out an anti-corruption drive against supporters of the previous regime. Not that his efforts were not warranted. One former director of the previous regime was even convicted of seeking to have the North Koreans take provocative acts that might have affected the results of the previous presidential election. Nevertheless, there were those who felt that the corruption drive was hurting the economic recovery effort. And those accusations of corruption were not merely the problem of members of previous regimes. Over the last few years some of President Kim Dae-jung's closest colleagues, friends and even his sons were accused of similar crimes and he found his party, the National Congress for New Politics, loosing ground politically. The situation became so bad that by Kim Dae-jung eventually felt it necessary to personally apologize for the scandals in his administration.

Reacting to the weakening of his power base, President Kim organized a new political grouping known as the Millennium Democratic Party that it was hoped, would do well in the spring 2000 elections. Unfortunately for Kim, when the elections actually occurred his new party came in a relatively distant second, 115 seats, to the 133 seats won by the former ruling party, the Grand National Party.

The Sunshine Policy Renewed?

Meanwhile, as the new American administration of George W. Bush established itself in power, President Kim Dae-jung found his "Sunshine Policy"—the

Former President Kim Young Sam

term used for his efforts to improve relations with North Korea (which eventually earned him the Nobel Peace Prize)—deeply undermined by Washington's newly renewed skepticism toward North Korea. In fact, the new American administration's stance not only undermined President Kim it eventually turned the next South Korean Presidential election into something of a referendum on Seoul's relationship with both North Korea and the United States.

That election occurred in November of 2002 when Roh Moo Hyun of President Kim's Millennium Democratic Party and Lee Hoi Chang of the Grand National Party battled to succeed President Kim who was not legally allowed to run for a second term. And, quite an election it was as twin dramas played out during the struggle. On one hand, relations with North Korea, that had seemed so full of promise only a few short years before, continued to spiral downward as Washington's relationship with Pyongyang deteriorated. Moreover, the deaths of two South Korean teenagers in a traffic accident with American soldiers (which subsequently saw the Americans acquitted of the charges by a U.S. military court) aroused considerable anti-American sentiment and a regular series of demonstrations against Washington's policies on the peninsula.

The Millennium Democratic Party's candidate, a labor lawyer, former political activist and supporter of President Kim, Roh Moo-hyun advocated a renewed effort to invigorate the Sunshine Policy and a less subservient and more equal relationship with the United States. His opponent Lee Hoi-chang stood for a policy much more in line with the Washington's and as

General Roh Tae Woo

South Korea's National Assembly in session. Housed in the nation's new building, legislators enjoy all modern technological innovations including electronic voting.
Courtesy: Embassy of Korea

an opponent of the outgoing president's efforts to improve relations with North Korea.

When the election of December 2002 finally took place, outgoing President Kim Dae-jung had considerable reason to be satisfied. The final vote had been very close, but Roh had won. His victory reinforced the impression that South Korea's population remained committed to the policy of reconciliation on the Korean peninsula regardless of what the United States might think.

The election that brought long time human rights activist Roh Moo-hyun to power by early 2003 may have resolved for the moment who would lead occupy South Korea's famous Blue House, but it hardly resolved the tensions that continued to exist within South Korean society and especially with the nation's conservatives that dominated the Grand National Party. While it is probably true that his decision to support the American effort in Iraq may have appeased some conservatives who felt Roh was likely to weaken South Korea's traditionally strong ties to the United States, which hardly satisfied his critics. And as so often before, the criticism of the new president was related less to relations with the United States or even with North Korea, but to financial and campaign scandals within South Korea itself. As a result, the Parliament dom-

inated as it was by the Grand National Party voted to impeach the new president who was temporarily removed from office amidst general public outrage that the parliament had misused its powers.

However, things did not quite work out as the leaders of the Grand National Party might have hoped. By April 2004, South Korea's political environment, already in turmoil, was again transformed by that month's parliamentary elections. The Grand National Party lost control of parliament, and the Liberal Uri party, which had been formed to support Roh Moo-hyun, enormously increased its representation and emerged as the dominant party. By the next month President Roh was back in office after the nation's constitutional court invalidated the impeachment efforts of the GNP and vindicated his leadership.

But political gains rarely last long in democratic politics. By early 2006 President Roh's influence seemed to be on the wane as his colleagues in the Uri Party began focusing on the upcoming parliamentary and presidential elections that, when they arrived in December 2007, saw the Grand National Party finally returned to executive power in the election of Lee Myung-bak, a former executive of the Hyundai corporation. Lee was elected on a platform that focused on the economy and the candidate's extensive business ex-

perience. However, once his election was secured, the next challenge was winning the upcoming parliamentary elections.

When those elections occurred, President Lee won the mandate he had hoped for. His revised conservative party, the Grand National Party, took 153 seats to the much lower 81-seat result for the United Democratic Party. It was a remarkable reversal of circumstances for South Korea's conservatives, who had not held such power in a decade.

Given that the transition from South Korea's left leaning politicians to the more

Former President Kim Dae Jung

South Korea

Former President Roh Moo-hyun

conservative Grand National Party was accomplished smoothly there is plenty to rejoice in how well the nation has made the transition to a more consistently democratic society. Nevertheless, the frequently "take no prisoners" nature of the system was unfortunately also demonstrated in the aftermath of the transition as well. In the early summer of 2009 South Korea's former president, Roh Moo-hyun, apparently depressed by the barrage of corruption charges leveled against him after he left office, committed suicide.

Economy

The late 1990s brought increasing levels of economic frustration to South Korea, but the drama that unfolded after the summer of 1997, when the Asian economic crisis began, was quite unprecedented. Still, it was hardly a surprise to close observers of the Korean economy. After spending a heady period as one of the exciting Asian "Tigers," South Korea, like Japan before, saw its economic vitality lessen as the 1990s unfolded. South Korean wage bills had been going up faster than their Asian competitors and the growth of productivity had not kept up either. They were losing markets to the newer emerging economies like that of the People's Republic and the smaller but until recently vibrant economies of Southeast Asia.

As we have seen, late in 1996, hoping to inject new life and flexibility into the system, then President Kim Young Sam, the first elected civilian president in a generation, reverted to a very undemocratic method of decision-making. In the early dawn hours after Christmas his party arranged for a secret parliamentary meeting where it used the absence of opposition delegates (who had not been informed of the meeting) to pass legislation that would have given Korean employers more leeway in firing workers.

The act, which on purely international economic grounds might have been defensible, only further undermined the reputation of the government while doing little to add strength to the economy. Unfortunately, these moves may have strengthened democracy in the long run but they did nothing to make South Korea more economically able to compete with the other Asian economies with lower wage demands.

By the fall of 1997, the economic crisis that had begun in Thailand, a relatively minor player in the international economic arena, had hit Korea, one of the largest economies in the world. With confidence much weakened in the currencies of the entire region the Korean currency, the *won*, went into a slide making it all the more difficult for Korean businesses to meet their international debt. All this came at the worst possible time as the country moved into a presidential election campaign.

Unable to meet its international loan obligations, South Korea was forced after so many years of economic growth to request an enormous aid package of around $60 billion in loans from the International Monetary Fund. Korea had as well to accept stringent IMF demands that it institute major changes in its economy. Many of those demands, which would see unemployment rise considerably within the country, were very difficult to accept but given the circumstances Seoul had little choice. For the first time in a generation the South Korean economy had begun to shrink, and unemployment for 1998 doubled to 7.4%. The year 1997 had seen the

economy grow by more than 5%, but 1998 registered a 5% contraction.

Fortunately, the President, Kim Dae-jung, after some initial hesitancy, heroically decided to accept the necessity of dramatic reform and took them on as his own. In sharp contrast to President Kim Young-sam's strong arm tactics of the previous winter, the new president used his long term ties to the labor movement to help gain their initial cooperation. Those efforts were not though as successful as the president might have hoped.

By century's end there were clear signs of recovery. In 2001 Korea's economy was no longer required to operate under the regulations imposed by the IMF during the Asian economic crisis. As the decade moved toward its second half, the South Korean economy had successfully overcome the crisis of 1997. Its economy was humming along at a respectable 4.6% growth rate for 2004. While it dipped to under 4% for 2005, by 2007 it was just under 5%. Then the most recent graphic economic downturn in 2008–2009 hit with a vengeance pushing the economy downward for a time. However, by the spring of 2010 the numbers were again looking reasonably positive.

Relations with North Korea

In the years since the collapse of the Soviet Union and the death of Kim Il-sung, the long time leader of North Korea, people in the South have been divided about how to deal with their northern neighbor. It is clear that the North Korean economy has been failing and the regime is losing

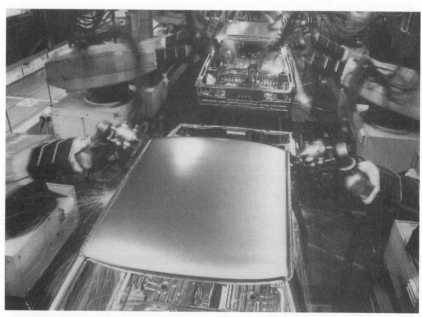

Assembly line at the Hyundai automotive company in Seoul—the *Excel*

its grip on the minds of its citizens. That the regime is likely to continue to weaken seems apparent, but how the South should react remains less clear.

Basically three different approaches seem to be in the forefront of public thought. First, the northern regime might collapse suddenly. Such an eventuality would please some of those in the South who have spent their lives struggling against the North. But such a collapse would leave to the Republic of Korea the burden of integrating the much less sophisticated infrastructure of the North into that of the South. The financial burdens would be enormous, as demonstrated in 1990 when West Germany had to do the same thing with East Germany. But South Korea does not have the same resources as Bonn did.

Others have hoped for a smoother transition, a so-called easy landing to North Korea's assumed collapse, emphasizing those programs that allow a smoother and less dramatic transition. Lastly, some people, aware of the enormous complexities of following either strategy, have understandably hoped for a simple stabilization of developments on the peninsula. But that is often difficult as incidents keep occurring that highlight both the tensions and the North's weakness.

Especially prominent among those incidents over the years was the landing and discovery of two different North Korean mini-submarines in South Korean waters. In the first incident, in September 1996, a mini-submarine accidentally beached in South Korea. Recognizing the dangers of their circumstances, the sailors on board appear to have killed themselves or to have been murdered while the soldiers among them set off into the interior of South Korea. Before the incident was over, 26 North Koreans and several people from the South were dead.

An even more dramatic incident occurred during the spring of 2010. Apparently, another North Korean submarine sunk a South Korean naval ship killing 46 sailors. Although as of the spring of 2010 the North was still denying the assault, a team of international investigators concluded that the fatal torpedo did come from the North Korean vessel. It was yet another in a long line of such provocative gestures.

Eventually the North apologized for the 1996 assault, but it will be some time before we know how the more recent assault will be handled. The North Korean regime makes decisions on a regular basis that suggest it is more interested in confrontation than dialogue. For example, during the summer of 1998 they test fired a missile that passed over Japan. That gesture came close to jeopardizing what limited trans-peninsula calm had been achieved,

and it inspired South Korean efforts to expand their own missile program. A similar series of reconciliatory and aggressive gestures have continued to today.

As discussed earlier, after Kim Dae-jung, the former democratic activist came to power, he established a more open policy dubbed the "Sunshine Policy" to improve relations with the North. Over the years considerable progress was made. For example, North Korea, in need of cash, has allowed South Korean tourists to make very controlled visits to its territory.

However, the most dramatic developments began when it was announced that Kim Jong-il of North Korea had agreed to meet with Kim Dae-jung in June of 2000, and meet they did. As people throughout the world watched, the two took part in the first summit ever between the leaders of that divided peninsula. Moreover, that dramatic meeting was followed by more reunions of individual family members many of whom had not seen each other since the Korean War began in 1950. For the first time in years not only did it appear that real progress was being made in North-South Korean relations but that for once events were being driven more by Koreans themselves than by outsiders like the Chinese and the Americans.

For President Kim Dae-jung himself, 2000 must have been especially gratifying when his "Sunshine Policy" received international accolades with his award of the Nobel Peace Prize for his efforts. But such accomplishments can be fleeting. By 2009 relations between North and South Korea had already turned sour again. North Korea continued with its efforts to develop nuclear weapons and the ability to deliver them with a complementary missile force while South Korea's conservatives returned to power. Making the situation even worse were the recent murder of a visiting South Korean tourist by a North Korean security guard who felt she had wandered off the tourist path and, as mentioned above, the torpedoing of a South Korean vessel by a North Korean submarine in the spring of 2010.

Over the long term, though, probably the most significant recent economic development has been the North's backtracking on the agreements associated with the joint ventures South Korea businesses have established in the North. Despite the fact that thousands of North Korean jobs are on the line, their government has begun to make life increasingly unpredictable for those involved in these once hopeful commercial ventures. This creates an uncertainty that is not likely to encourage growth in investment. It would seem that for the moment neither government, North or South, is particularly interested in improving relations.

Han Myung-sook, South Korea's first female prime minister

Foreign Relations

A large number of South Koreans have become strongly dissatisfied with the status of the relationship with the United States. The major issues are the American responsibility for the partition of Korea in 1945 (even given that the alternative was communist control over the entire peninsula), earlier American support for a series of authoritarian governments in South Korea, and the alleged lack of American enthusiasm for reunification of the country. Moreover, recent revelations about the murder of hundreds of South Korean civilian refugees by American soldiers during the chaotic early months of the Korean War as well as on-going tensions regarding the presence of thousands of American troops within Korea today have added to the tensions.

Over the last few years, the perception that the American government undermined the effort by South Koreans to improve relations with the North also emerged as a significant issue between the two nations. Certainly the most important element of the continuing tension between the United States and South Korea is the fact that, in large measure, the younger generation has become very skeptical of the Americans. In fact, until recently polls indicated that more South Koreans feared that the United State might start a war than North Korea, a perception that hardly helped American efforts to deal with the threat of North Korea's nuclear program. But such perceptions can be fleeting. By the summer of 2009 South Koreans were reportedly losing faith in the North's willingness to make the compromises necessary for a lasting peace.

How to deal with the reality of a weakening North Korea has added to the differences that divide these two long time allies. Chief among them is the ambiva-

South Korea

A railroad station plaza in downtown Pusan.   Courtesy: CALTEX Petroleum Corp.

lations in the future might not be as close as they were during previous decades. As was the case elsewhere in world, South Korea also had a great many skeptics about the US role in Iraq. Still it did commit itself to providing troops for the American effort there. Those troops have now left Iraq. It should also not be a surprise that relations have improved in the period since South Korea's conservatives returned to power.

On the American side, the war in Iraq has also affected very immediately relations with South Korea. In fact, by the summer of 2004 Washington had made known its decision to transfer some of those military units stationed in South Korea to the Iraqi theatre of operations. Plans were also announced to relocate many of the American troops to locations further to the south, away from the border and away from the more populated areas of South Korea.

Not surprisingly, though, American concerns about the growing nuclear capabilities of North Korea have continued to be a major complicating element in Seoul's relationship with the United States. The Bush administration was adamant about the importance of creating a coordinated regional approach to confront North Korea's nuclear weapons capabilities. It generally insisted that North Korea dismantle its programs before considering any offers of economic assistance to the beleaguered northern government. In contrast, South Korea's governments have tended—at least when the more leftist governments have been in power—to be much less demanding than the United States and much more interested in expanding regional and international cooperation. They have continued to carry out local initiatives from opening rail and bus lines between the divided nations to establishing more confidence-building measures than its huge American ally has usually been willing to contemplate.

Among the most important issues separating the two allies is the question of what to do with the partially constructed light water nuclear facilities that South Korea so heavily invested in as part of the mid 1990s agreement that saw North Korea freeze its plutonium programs for a time. Washington has since then apparently concluded that the program should be abandoned. In contrast, South Korea has been interested in salvaging something out of the project by perhaps finishing the energy producing facilities and then connecting them to the South Korean power grid with some sort of plan to supply part of the energy to North Korea.

More recently there has been some reason for optimism. After years of threats and very few accomplishments, the Amer-

lence among the South Koreans regarding the appropriate policy to take towards the North. For some Koreans this is believed to be the best time to push toward a complete collapse of the Northern regime regardless of the short-term difficulties involved in absorbing the communist government. Until recently though Washington with thousands of troops on the peninsula has at times seemed more interested in lowering the level of rhetoric and moving toward a smoother transition toward the future.

While the Clinton administration had been quite supportive of Kim's opening toward North Korea, things changed dramatically after the 2000 American elections. Almost as soon as the new American Republican administration organized in Washington, D.C., it pronounced itself far more skeptical about working with

North Korea. Given the enormously close political ties that exist between South Korea and the United States, this posture made Kim's policy of reconciliation far more difficult.

In the months that followed George W. Bush's arrival in power the momentum toward reconciliation all but vanished and a new climate of tension began to emerge on the peninsula. Nevertheless, as we have seen, when the South Korean presidential elections of 2002 turned into a virtual referendum on Seoul's relations with both the U.S. and North Korea, South Korean voters turned to Roh Moo-myun, the candidate who advocated continuing not only the "Sunshine Policy" and a somewhat more distant relationship with the United States.

There was thus reason to think that despite the long-term ties with the U.S., re-

ican administration of George W. Bush began to approach North Korea with more flexibility than it had previously shown. By the early winter of 2007 an agreement was concluded that officially saw North Korea promising to dismantle its primary nuclear facility at Yongbyon in exchange for a package of financial, security and energy incentives. By the next year that had been accomplished.

By the fall of 2008, for the first time in years, there was reason for real optimism. Not only had North Koreans allowed international inspectors to begin dismantling their nuclear facilities at Yongbyon, but a series of summit meetings, first between the two nation's presidents and then between their prime ministers, started opening the door for real progress. Plans were finalized to open cargo rail service between the two long estranged nations. There was even talk of creating a formal peace treaty to replace the armistice that had ended the Korean War a half of a century earlier.

With the arrival to power once again of South Korea's conservatives, some aspects of the reconciliation were modified. However, it seemed unlikely that the peninsula will return to the dark old days of complete estrangement. Or at least it did until the early summer of 2009 when North Korea once again began testing its nuclear and missile systems. It apparently set off yet another international incident with its sinking of the South Korean ship.

Overall, relations between Japan and South Korea have seemed on the mend recently as both countries worked to lessen the continuing tensions associated with the years of Japan's colonial control over Korea. Japan's government has finally issued an official apology for its earlier imperialistic policies toward Korea, and former South Korean President Kim has officially forgiven Tokyo. Going further than previous presidents, Kim even promised to ease the barriers against Japanese cultural imports into the republic though much of that was scuttled when yet another crisis developed over revisions in Japan's school books that failed to meet Korean demands for a more full accounting of Japan's behavior during the colonization of Korea. Eventually it was agreed that the three countries—China, South Korea and Japan—would work together to create a mutually agreed upon history of their often troubled relationship. More recently, as the most recent global economic meltdown unfolded, Japan and China both worked to help keep South Korea's financial house in order. This was a quite impressive example of regional cooperation. However, that has not and is not likely always to be the case in the future.

Another issue that has aroused significant tensions between South Korea and Japan has been competing claims to the islands known as Tokdo in Korean and Takeshima in Japanese. Although there are economic dimensions over fishing rights associated with the controversy, nationalist emotions have sometimes made the situation all the more complicated. A particularly dramatic example of the tension occurred during the summer of 2005 when Japanese and South Korean naval forces quite literally had a tug-of-war over a fishing ship the former wanted to impound. But more recently, yet another source of tension arouse as Japan, deeply involved in the on-going North Korean kidnapping scandal, refused to cooperate fully with efforts to reduce North Korea's nuclear capacities.

Relations with the People's Republic remain positive and are complemented by over a hundred billion dollars of yearly trade between the two countries. Still the South Koreans, like so many of their neighbors, have to deal with the complications associated with their ties to Tibet's exiled leader, the Dalai Lama. Some would like see him visit the country, a move strongly discouraged by Beijing. Moreover, controversies surrounding Tibet's status are not the only issues that have the potential to complicate relations. When it became known that Chinese imports of the Korean national dish, Kimchi, had been found polluted by parasitic eggs, emotions got quite heated.

Culture and Society

Korean culture, although distinct from that of Japan, resembles it in many respects. They have both also been exposed to Chinese influences over many centuries. Not surprisingly there are many cultural features that all three Confucian-influenced communities share in common. Nevertheless, Korea like Japan has also developed along its own unique cultural lines.

The ancient pre-Chinese aspects of Korean culture, such as shamanism—the belief in occult sorcerers and worship of demons—have a Northeast and Central Asian derivation. On this base the ingredients of Chinese culture, including Buddhism and Confucianism, were superimposed as a second layer. Since the 19th century there have been many conversions to Christianity. In fact, due to the support many foreign Christian missionaries gave to the Koreans during their years as a Japanese colony, the religion has an association with Korean nationalism not generally found elsewhere in East Asia. Today, the Christian community is a large and influential group that exerts a profound influence in the peninsula.

Health Care in Korea

The South Korean medical establishment has been deeply influenced by American medical practices. However, when it came to creating a health care delivery system that covered their entire population, the Japanese model was chosen as a more appropriate system. The struggle was hardly an easy one. Before the late 1970s, medical insurance in South Korea was a voluntary decision by individuals who could afford it. But in his last years in office before his murder, President Park's government began the process of putting into place a mandatory health care system that would cover everyone. It was quite a battle. In fact, it was to last a dozen years as previously uninsured groups were added to the program until, by the late 1980s, the entire population was eventu-

South Koreans protest policies toward North Korea

South Korea

ally covered. The funding has come from a combination of sources ranging from the individuals themselves to their employers and government subsidies to help pay the costs of the official medical societies that the government chose to administer the programs. The societies themselves were a conscious choice between the former voluntary private insurance programs and a full-blown government program that the administration wished to avoid.

Korean Women

Like most of Asia, Korea remains a strongly patriarchal society. Traditionally some women's roles as shaman-like priestesses in the traditional religion of the peninsula did give them levels of influence not always possible elsewhere. More recently, partly as a result of women's activism, laws have been passed improving their status within society. In 1991, the South Korean Family Law was amended to give women more property and divorce rights. Of college-educated Korean women less than 20% are employed and usually in non-professional positions. Viewing the situation from a more global perspective offers important insights. On issues of gender equality, South Korean women recently scored only 92nd on a scale of 110 countries while they hit the 95th spot in wage equality.

Still, South Korean women today have access to the same higher education that young men do although few hold positions of executive level responsibility in the country's businesses. The situation is improving, though. The number of women in more senior management positions has doubled over the last decade although in real terms the figures remain small.

Women have served in positions of influence in the government bureaucracy, and the legislative elections of 2004 turned out to be truly revolutionary in terms of women's political roles. More than 150 women sought seats in South Korea's 17th national assembly, and 39 of them took their places among their male counterparts. This was a significant increase over the sixteen women who had been part of the previous legislature. South Korea's women were also helped by a then new law that required political parties to nominate women for at least half of their proportional candidates. However, the victory went beyond that as ten of the female legislators were elected directly by the voters. It is important to note, though, that while it was the best showing for female candidates since the national assembly's founding in 1948, women still represent a mere 13% of the 2004 total. More significant was former President Roh's naming of Han Myung-sook as the nation's first female prime minister.

It is worth noting as well that prominent women are not confined to the supporters of former President Roh. Former President Park's daughter, Park Kun-hye, has emerged as the leader of the Grand National Party that once so dominated South Korean politics. She was one of the leading contenders in the presidential elections scheduled for the end of 2007. Eventually she failed to win her party's nomination for president, but it turned out her bid to become South Korea's first female president was not the only dramatic advance for the nation's women. In the spring of 2008, a 29 year old bioengineering student, Yi So-yeon, became the first South Korean to travel in space. In her case it was as part of the crew of a Russian space mission.

The Future: South Korea

South Korea faces many challenges in the decade ahead. While the political transition from South Korea's liberals to the more conservative followers of President Lee went very smoothly, South Korea's future still remains deeply challenged. The newly inflamed tensions with North Korea always have the potential to get out of hand. North Korea's recent pressures on those South Korean businesses that were willing to invest in the North only add to the economic challenges the nation faces. Beyond the financial concerns though is a growing skepticism among many in South Korea about their decade long effort to engage the North. Today more and more South Koreans feel they have very little to show for the effort. Despite years of improved relations, family visits, joint ventures and even the award of a Nobel Peace Prize for their gestures towards Pyongyang, the North often acts in a very aggressive fashion. The sinking of the South Korean ship in the spring of 2010, while very dramatic, was simply another example in a long line of North Korean provocations.

South Korea does have much to be proud of over the lasts few years. Not only was one of their career diplomats, Ban Ki-Moon, named secretary general of the United Nations, the first Asian in decades. Its economy for a time anyway broke the 300-billion-dollar mark in exports and achieved 11th place among the world's exporting nations. Moreover, while it was deeply impacted by 2008's major global economic downturn, the economy has recovered relatively well over the period since.

Environmentally, South Korea is also trying to make a difference. Recognizing the necessity of diversifying its energy resources and of dealing with the challenge of climate instability, it broke ground in early spring 2007 for what is expected to be the world's largest solar energy plant. Once operational, it will complement a large tidal power facility that is already under construction. The announced national goal is to raise South Korea's use of renewable energy from its current 2.28% use to 10% by 2020. A particularly important element of the nation's commitment to the challenge of climate change was its hosting during the early summer of 2009 of an international conference that dealt with the impact of global warming on some of the world's major cities.

South Korean War Memorial

Democratic People's Republic of Korea (North Korea)

North Korean leaders Kim Il Sung and Kim Jong-Il

Area: 46,814 sq. mi. (121,730 sq. km., somewhat smaller than Mississippi)

Population: 22,757,275 (July 2010 est.)

Capital City: Pyongyang (Pop. 2.5 million—2002 estimate)

Climate: Temperate, with a longer and much colder winter than in the South; summer wet season from July to September

Neighboring Countries: China (north); Russia (northeast); South Korea (south)

Official Language: Korean

Other Principal Tongues: Japanese, spoken by many older Koreans; Russian, spoken by many of educated North Koreans

Ethnic Background: Korean, similar to both Manchurian and Mongolian

Principal Religion: Buddhism, Confucianism. The government discourages religious activity

Main Exports (to South Korea, Russia, China, Japan): Minerals, meat products, fish, textiles

Main Imports (from China, Thailand, Russia, Japan): Petroleum, machinery, grains, coal

Currency: Won

Former Colonial Status: Korea was a tributary state of the Chinese empires for most of its history up to 1895; Japanese protectorate (1905–1910); Japanese Dependency (1910–1945); from 1945 to 1948 it was under Soviet occupation; after 1948 it developed an independent communist regime allied with both the Soviet Union and with China.

National Day: September 8, 1948.

Chief of State: Kim Jong-il, Head of State

National Flag: Two blue stripes on the top and bottom separated by two thin white stripes from a broad central field of red which contains at left center a white circle with a 5-pointed red star

Per Capita GDP Income: U.S. $1900 (2009 est. purchasing power parity)

Political System

The Democratic People's Republic of Korea (DPRK) is one of the world's few remaining hard-line communist states. The constitution was adopted in 1948 and was revised most recently in 1992. The legal system is built on communist legal theory and German civil law. The judiciary has no authority to review acts of the legislature. Suffrage is universal for everyone 17 years of age and older. The government has both a head of state and a Premier. The Supreme People's Assembly is the national legislature and has one house. Candidates for office are chosen by the Korean Workers' Party (DWP) and run unopposed though the assembly itself rarely meets. The National Defense Commission has emerged as the supreme decision-making body. For most of its history the state was dominated by one individual, Kim Il-sung.

117

North Korea

Politics and Government

The 1990s were a disaster for North Korea. The decade began with the collapse of its longtime supporter, the Soviet Union and even Beijing, its only other significant international friend, has been encouraging North Korea to dramatically transform its economy to survive. Despite North Korea's longtime reputation as the most isolated of national states, evidence of its dramatically faltering economy is everywhere. Recent years have seen disastrous floods that have devastated important farmlands, while the extremely proud regime has had to request enormous amounts of food aid from outside agencies. Visitors report as well that the country's electrical system is failing. Very credible reports of famine have been widely reported—some authorities have even suggested that as many as two million people or ten percent of the population have died. The regime's usual bluster aside, the defection of respected leaders and the departure of thousands of refugees to China in search of food all attest to the desperate situation Pyongyang finds itself in. Though foreign observers have reported that the food situation has improved somewhat in recent years, almost five hundred North Koreans managed to defect to the South during 2002 alone. In addition, large numbers of them live in China along the North Korean border while groups of North Korean defectors can also found living throughout many other areas of East Asia.

Life in North Korea

Through the middle of the last century, the lives of those who lived on the Korean peninsula were relatively similar whether they lived in the northern part of the country or the southern part. Both experienced the relative isolation of late Yi Korea and the traumas of both the Japanese occupation and the Korean War that ravaged the entire peninsula. From the mid 1950s though, their fate began to radically diverge. While South Korea moved unevenly toward becoming a major industrial power and by the mid 1990s a successful democracy, North Koreans lived their lives in a very different environment.

However, in those first decades after the end of the Korean War, that divergence was by no means self-evident. Initially North Korea was relatively better off both industrially and in terms of natural resources than South Korea was. By the mid 1970s, after America's embarrassing retreat from South Vietnam communism seemed to be on the accession.

Within North Korea, the government managed to meet the population's basic

North Korea's "Dear Leader" Kim Jong Il

material needs while building up an enormous military infrastructure dedicated to the unification, violently if necessary of the peninsula. That military infrastructure was complemented by an extraordinarily sophisticated leadership cult that was built around the accomplishments of Kim Il-Sung, the nation's longtime dictator.

That cult was rarely threatened, given the reality that for generations only a very few North Koreans had any opportunity whatsoever to learn what was going on outside the nation's borders. Only the elite could travel, and while the population had access to radios, their dials were permanently fixed to exclusively North Korean sources.

But North Korea's relative advantages over South Korea began to weaken over its southern rival by the 1980s as the North's economy began to falter and South Korea's economic take off began. By the 1990s, the situation had become dramatically different for by then, given the collapse of Eastern European communism the North found itself one of the last regimes still trying to maintain a Stalinist's style communist command economy. That effort along, with a series of natural disasters as well, decimated the economy of North Korea creating an environment of widespread hunger through much of the country by the last decade of the 20th century. In fact, the shortage of basic food stocks has even created a new generation of North Koreans who are known by some as the stunted generation that is a community of people that is significantly shorter and lighter than their South Korean neighbors. Deprivation led many of

them over the years to actually hope for war with the south as the only possible solution to the difficulties of their lives.

Still, things have changed somewhat in recent years both in terms of available food and knowledge about the outside world. And within the country life is becoming in some ways more sophisticated as cell phones, already very popular in other parts of East Asia, have become popular among the better off members of North Korean society as well. The government has not simply ignored its economic deterioration. Taking a page from the reforms in both the People's Republic and Vietnam even North Koreans have been allowed to set up semi-private markets where people can buy a wide variety of goods from shoes to hardware. A significant percentage of the nation's foreign policy in recent years has been directed toward finding ways to repair the nation's deeply weakened economic infrastructure.

For North Korean citizens the relative isolation of the population has diminished as more and more of them have heard stories of the growing wealth enjoyed by their neighbors from China and Russia to the prosperity of their archrivals in the South. Not surprisingly more and more North Koreans have begun to cross into China in search of food. There they live furtive lives trying to survive and to avoid Chinese authorities who often send them back to North Korea. However, the movement back and forth across the Chinese-North Korea border has in recent years played its own role in opening up life in North Korea to outsiders. It has now become more and more common for cell phones to be smuggled into North Korea. Today reports about life in the North relayed to the South by those very cell phones have, to Pyongyang's great dissatisfaction, been regularly posted on websites. While this new 21st century penetration into North Korea has become a useful tool for outsiders, those North Koreans who take part in the effort are putting themselves at great risk of being imprisoned in one of the North's infamous prison camps.

While life for the average North Korean has become more and more difficult in recent decades it is even far worse for those who have somehow roused the regime's anger. By 2004 outside experts estimated that the North Korean regime had developed its own Gulag Archipelago of prison camps that were said to include from 150,000 to 200,000 political prisoners. According to the respected British Broadcasting Company, North Korean prison authorities use the prisoners for medical experiments that rival those infamous efforts of Nazis or Japanese militarists of the Second World War.

A Communist Monarchy?
Kim Jong-il Emerges

In 1994, Kim Il Sung, the long time exalted leader, died just before he was to meet with South Korean President Kim Young Sam. After that, in a fashion more reminiscent of an imperial dynasty than a modern socialist state, his son Kim Jong-il who had been increasingly in charge for years assumed official power. For outsiders, the younger Kim's arrival to power had been of particular concern. He was not well known among North Korea watchers and rarely appeared in public. Moreover, he was thought to have been involved in some of the most egregious acts of North Korean terrorism. For most observers, though, the most immediate issue was whether Kim Jong-Il would be able fully to take control of the reins of power.

In the more than a decade since he assumed power, the answer to that question has become clearer. The younger Kim successfully solidified his authority and slowly assumed many of his father's official titles. More recently, Kim Jong-il was named the official head of state. Nevertheless, the question of just how powerful the current leader really is remains somewhat of a mystery. One thing is clear Kim Jong-il has given the nation's military significantly more power than it had held under his father.

For a time North Korea's new leader showed a side few had suspected. Until recently Kim Jong Il was devoting considerable time to improving relations with South Korea. He even toured Shanghai, the People's Republic of China's showcase of economic and industrial accomplishments. In addition, North Korea's leader, along with a large group of companions, traveled by train to confer with Russia's new leadership. Most interestingly, under Kim Jong Il, North Korea has made a significant effort to establish ties with the outside world. This is something in which North Korea, under the long years of his father Kim Il Sung's control, had been far less interested.

Clearly, these are very different activities from those that North Korean watchers had been used to observing. Some have even suggested that Kim was interested in emerging as North Korea's Gorbachev. But given what happened to the Soviet Union under Gorbachev's care, it seems safe to say that Kim Jong Il would probably prefer to be North Korea's Deng Xiaoping. Nevertheless, any real improvement is certainly dependent on North Korea being able to move out from under the obsolete economic and geopolitical environment under which it has operated for more than a half-century. Given the recent setbacks in its relationship with Washington and South Korea, this is perhaps even less likely than it was only a few years ago.

The most immediate political challenge, though, is of quite a different order. While Kim Il Sung was for years obviously grooming his son to assume the leadership, Kim Jong Il, who also has sons, has apparently not yet definitively designated his own successor. Some believe that he has chosen his third son, Kim Jong-Un, to succeed him.

Statue of Kim Il Sung and adoring children

Courtesy: Bradley Martin

That oversight, if that is indeed the case, became especially important over the last two years as Kim Jong Il disappeared from public life for a considerable period. Speculation was rampant that he had had some sort of health crisis, probably a stroke. When he did reemerge, the rumor seemed to be confirmed by how much his physical appearance had deteriorated over the preceding months. However, he did appear to recover relatively well over the following months. If indeed his son Kim Jong-Un is eventually to succeed him, the young man, now 27, will probably be aided by Kim Jong-Il's brother-in-law, Chang Song-Taek, whose influence has also been growing.

Economy

Obtaining authoritative data for the government of North Korea is a very difficult matter indeed. Massive floods and mismanagement of the economy have been responsible for disastrous economic results. The health care system has collapsed and the hospitals have none of the modern medicines necessary to keep the population healthy. Surgeons have been forced to operate without anesthetics.

South Korean watchers claim that the North's economy has shrunk by 3%–4% for each year of the 1990s. Only recently the government itself claimed the economy had shrunk by 50% during the late 1990s. More recent reports suggest that for 2007 the economy only shrunk by a bit more than one percent. Nevertheless, reliable figures are not available. The only thing that is certain is that the collapse of the socialist economies of the

North Korea

USSR and Eastern Europe hurt North Korea greatly.

The situation during the first decade of the 20th century appeared somewhat better than the previous decade. However, the continuing flow of refugees across the Chinese border clearly indicates that the plight of average North Koreans has not improved much. While the growth rate for 2009 was reported to be a reasonably respectable 3.7%, the situation for the nation's residents remains dire. In fact, what refugees from North Korea most commonly report are rising food prices and growing economic insecurity, especially for those North Koreans who live beyond the better-supplied capital city. More recently, the government's 2009 decision to devaluate North Korea's currency had a tremendously negative impact on the population, which saw the value of their savings collapse.

Perhaps most disconcerting for the northern government is the fact that modern technology, increasingly available even in the previously isolated North Korea is making it easier for its citizens to know what has been going on in South Korea and the People's Republic and compare their own lives to those lived by so many of their neighbors.

Recognizing their precarious economic situation, the government's struggle to find new funds has ranged widely from agreeing to allow international flights over North Korea in order to earn over flight fees from the airlines to the more controversial offer to accept some of Taiwan's nuclear waste. That deal which might have brought msillions of dollars into North Korea called for Pyongyang to accept and bury on its territory thousands of barrels of radioactive material from Taiwan. While not of potential use for military purposes, the agreement aroused considerable tension within South Korea that was especially unhappy with the decision to place the material in mine shafts near their common border. Recent reports suggest that the search for funds includes involvement in the international heroin trade and the counterfeiting of American currency. Though official South Korean sources now claim the latter activity has been terminated.

To an extent, North Korea has begun following the path long ago trodden by the People's Republic that of opening the country to global trade while liberalizing the economy. Following China's lead North Korea has finally established free trade zones at Rajin-Sunbong and at Sinuiju near the Chinese border. Like those established a generation ago by China near Hong Kong, the goal has been to attract foreign investment with promises of cheap labor and tax incentives. However, the new special economic zones have attracted little international interest. Even more recently, North Korea appears to have become ambivalent about their usefulness and is scaling back these tentative initiatives rather than expanding them.

Moreover, the government is making it difficult for outsiders to travel to the various commercial ventures South Koreans established there. By the spring of 2009, it began to demand a complete renegotiation of the contracts and pay scales.

For the average North Korean, the most obvious example of the government's belated efforts to move away—if only slightly—from a communist style command economy has been the right now granted to allow the sale of goods at free markets. However, opening up the system is hampered by the internal perception that the introduction of capitalist reforms had helped bring about the collapse of the Soviet Union. This is a road Pyongyang has no interest in following. Early 2001 saw North Korea's once reclusive leader Kim Jong-Il enthusiastically visiting Shanghai, a trip that was complemented by a much more extensive visit to Guangzhou in late 2005 and yet another similar trip during the last year. Clearly such travels by North Korea supreme leader suggest that he is considering reforms along the recent Chinese model. North Korea has even been making efforts to introduce a very limited internal version of the Internet into the country. Nevertheless, North Korean's own efforts to maintain its iron grip on the population make significant success in this area unlikely.

Moreover, the tensions between North Korea and South Korea have long made it much more difficult for southerners, the most logical investors, to play a part in northern economic development. Theoretically, though, the North is in a good position to arrest its drastic economic circumstances. After all, just to their south lies the Republic of Korea with which they share a common language and heritage. Economically the two are a fine match reminiscent of the relationship between China's Guangdong province and Hong Kong. The south has international economic sophistication but is burdened by wage bills that are moving ahead faster than both their competitors and their own productivity. In theory, an economic accord between Seoul and Pyongyang would help both, but examples of such successful cooperation are few. Daewoo, the huge South Korean industrial giant has set up a textile facility in North Korea. But tensions on the peninsula have made this possible avenue of potential growth considerably less than it might be. Still for a time, there were some hopeful signs. The two neighbors worked together to produce plans for another special industrial zone at Kaesong in North Korea. It was hoped that this facility would attract significant direct investment from South Korean firms. The decision in late 2007 to open up direct cargo rail service across the border also gave the project an additional boost. Sadly, most of that momentum has been lost as tensions have again risen between the two estranged communities.

North Korean Pageant

Photo by Bob Beatty

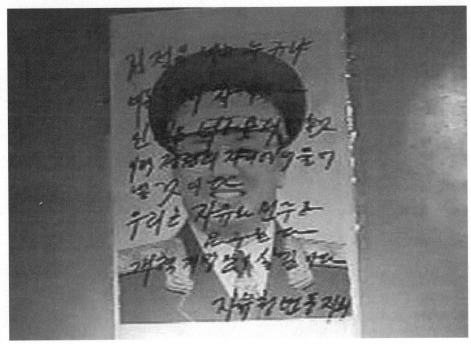

Defaced photo of Kim Jong-Il demanding his ouster

Foreign Relations: Survival North Korea Style

Although North Korea emerged after World War II as an independent state within the socialist world, it was long committed to maintaining something of a "distance" between itself and its largest allies the Soviet Union and the People's Republic. And that distance, nurtured by the regime's emphasis on *Juche* or self-reliance became particularly important after the outbreak in the late 1950s of the Sino-Soviet dispute that split the communist world.

Recognizing how much more complicated that rift made North Korea's international position Pyongyang's dictatorial leader Kim Il Sung worked to create something of a balancing act between relations with Moscow and the Soviet Union. Nevertheless, those ties were very important to the regime as it received from both communist superpowers regular shipments of subsidized foodstuffs that helped sustain its economy. But that support began to change in the late 1980s and early 1990s as both Moscow and Beijing worked to develop ties with North Korea's archrival the more economically dynamic South Korea. And more importantly by 1991 communism in the Soviet Union was failing even as Beijing continued to move dramatically away from the older Soviet style command economy that Pyongyang still embraced. Suddenly North Korea's isolated leaders found themselves adrift in an increasingly capitalist and globalized world system that appeared to threaten its very survival.

By the early 1990s North Korea's leadership recognized that their long term goal of growing powerful enough to unify the entire Korean peninsula under their control had now fallen to the wayside, and knowledgeable North Koreans found themselves increasingly concerned about the shear survival of their regime. With that in mind the Northern government began to tentatively reach out to the outside world. Kim Il Sung, for example, was engaged in organizing a meeting with his South Korean counterpart Kim Yong Sam the very day he died in 1994. His son and successor Kim Jong Il spent much of the 1990s attempting to move the country more into the international community they had previously largely shunned.

Thus by early 2001 Pyongyang had established diplomatic relations with nations throughout the world, literally from Great Britain and the Netherlands to Canada and Spain as well as the Philippines and Germany. Finally understanding the precarious position the collapse of the hard line communist world had caused them Pyongyang's leaders knew they needed to enter the larger international community to help ensure their survival as a nation. Those efforts also included working to improve relations in recent years with the leaders of post communist Russia as well.

Turning to China, relations with the People's Republic have also been quite strained at times. Beijing's decision to open up relations with South Korea was very disturbing to North Korea and probably of even more immediate concern was the PRC's decision to start demanding hard cash for the food stuffs they supplied the beleaguered state. Perhaps most significantly Beijing has used its influence to encourage North Korea to begin to implement economic reforms to open up the once closed system along the lines of those carried out by both China and Vietnam. It has also made significant efforts to show North Korea's leader, through a series of visits, the results of China's generation long economic drive. Moreover, China has become very involved in facilitating international discussions over North Korea's nuclear program.

Some progress has even been made with Japan. In an effort to improve relations with Tokyo, North Korea finally confirmed long-term Japanese suspicions that it had over the years kidnapped many Japanese citizens to serve as language teachers. Eventually a small group of surviving Japanese citizens, who had been kidnapped generations earlier, was allowed to return home to visit. Unfortunately, Pyongyang's decision hardly improved the "air" much as almost immediately more tensions emerged over the question of whether the "visiting" Japanese would return to their "adopted" homeland. It hardly helped when it was later discovered that some of the supposed "remains" of kidnapped Japanese turned out to be phony. By 2010 the many questions surrounding the kidnappings have still not been answered to Tokyo's satisfaction, and they continue to complicate relations.

While North Korea's gestures regarding the kidnapped Japanese were clearly tied with Pyongyang's desire to clear the air with Tokyo, their efforts to develop long-range missiles, especially of the sort they launched over Japan in 1998 have hardly helped matters. In addition, it's not just the developing missile technology that has caused international concerns. North Korea's hopes to move more deeply into the international community have also been enormously complicated by the regime's efforts to develop nuclear weapons that could be delivered with those increasingly sophisticated missiles North Korea has been developing.

The problem is that North Korea has long refused to play the "beggar" it has actually become in recent years. Instead, it continued to play the "nuclear card," i.e. threatening to continue development of nuclear weapons unless the world met its demands for outside assistance and new treaties to assure its safety.

North Korea's Nuclear Program

Pyongyang's nuclear activities date from the early 1980s when work first be-

North Korea

gan at Yongbyon a site around sixty miles from the North Korean capital. In those years, it is not surprising that the North Koreans were interested in nuclear weapons. After all, the United States, its arch-enemy, had hundreds of nukes in South Korea, and there was always the possibility that war could break out at any time. The United States, for its part, has long wanted to stop the North's nuclear programs. But little could be accomplished until America's own nuclear arsenal was removed from South Korea. The first Bush administration accomplished that goal.

Even as the American government was withdrawing its own enormous nuclear arsenal North Korea's leaders were coming to the realization that their nuclear program offered not only the possibility of deterring an attack, but could serve as well as a tool to gain economic and political concessions from the United States. Thus began the crisis of 1994 when Pyongyang publicly announced it was withdrawing from the Non-Proliferation Treaty, and apparently developing nuclear weapons at its nuclear energy plants at Yongbyon. It should be added that the situation with North Korea, as it is with countries like Iran, is complicated by the fact that international agreements do allow countries to develop nuclear capabilities if the facilities are dedicated to peaceful purposes such as electricity generation.

The crisis which brought Washington and North Korea to the very brink of war was eventually defused by the intervention of former President Jimmy Carter and the signing of what became known as the Agreed Framework. Under that agreement, North Korea promised to freeze their nuclear program in exchange for American promises of fuel deliveries to compensate for the loss of the electricity then being produced by the nuclear reactors. And an agreement that provided for the construction of two light-water reactors that unlike the older Soviet style reactors would not produce by-products that could be used in the manufacture of nuclear weapons-grade material.

The plan, loudly criticized in some conservative quarters in both South Korea and the United States, opened an era of relative calm that lasted for most of the following decade. Not surprisingly, there were many difficult issues involved in actually implementing the agreement. Still, ground was first finally broken in the summer of 1997 for the two new nuclear power plants that the international community had agreed to build in the north.

For a time things appeared to be going well. In fact, the last months of 2000 offered plenty of reason for optimism. Not only had the leaders of North and South Korea held a summit. The American Secretary of State Dr. Madeleine Albright

made a well-publicized trip to the Pyongyang. It even looked for a time as if President Clinton, building on all the earlier progress, might visit North Korea. Unfortunately that trip did not occur.

Once the administration under George W. Bush established itself, Washington became quite reluctant to continue the diplomatic momentum of the Clinton administration. As the American "War on Terrorism" unfolded, it became clear that Washington's new decision makers considered the North Korean regime, as the new president put it, part of an "Axis of Evil."

Relations were hardly improved when during the fall of 2002 the North Koreans were said to have admitted that they had, in a somewhat ambiguous violation of the previous agreements, carried out a clandestine uranium enrichment program. Whether such a program had ever been actually realized or more importantly whether it had been aimed toward civilian electrical production or the production of nuclear weapons (a much more technically demanding accomplishment) has never been made clear. Nevertheless, once the issue was raised the relative progress made since 1994 seemed to collapse.

During the winter of 2002–2003 tensions only rose higher as Washington and Pyongyang took part in a series of escalating steps that saw not only the end of fuel energy deliveries to North Korea by the Americans but North Korea's announcement that the agreements of 1994 were "dead." They also said they planned to restart their nuclear programs.

From the American perspective, the most important issue has been the growing North Korean nuclear program that has probably produced enough plutonium for between four and thirteen bombs. Adding to that concern has been Pyongyang's long-range missile program that may one day allow North Korea to threaten the American West Coast. Of more immediate concern has been America's fear that, given North Korea's economic situation, it could soon become a major exporter of weapons of mass destruction.

The most immediate impact of the increased role that China has been playing in the discussions was the agreement reached in September 2005 that saw North Korea promise to end its nuclear weapons programs in exchange for guarantees that the principal countries involved would promote international cooperation with the North on matters from energy to trade and investment. As part of that agreement, South Korea even offered to supply North Korea with electrical energy.

The agreement initially seemed to be a major breakthrough. However, over the next year it became clear that little had

"We will avenge anyone who hurts our self-respect wherever he may be."

Photo by Dave Pomeroy

122

been accomplished. In fact, North Korea's determination to move toward a nuclear-armed future continued unabated.

North Korea Crosses the Line

In the summer of 2006 North Korea began publicly testing its long-range missiles. While those tests were apparently less successful than Pyongyang might have hoped, they were more ominously followed up later that fall by its first apparently successful underground detonation. If this was not of a nuclear bomb, at least it was a nuclear device. A line had been crossed. On that day North Korea, one of the most brutal and closed society on the planet, entered the international nuclear club. This was a development that would immediately impact not only the Korean peninsula, but the international efforts to forestall the spread of nuclear weapons.

Still, for a time, during the winter of 2007 the momentum of negotiations appeared back on track. The American administration of George W. Bush, reeling from its defeat in the previous fall's congressional elections as well as set backs in Iraq and Afghanistan, appeared anxious to make progress on the de-nuclearization of the Korean Peninsula. Ironically, the soon to be ex-President Bush's new willingness not only to talk directly to the North Koreans, but to make concessions to the North's financial and security needs, was deeply reminiscent of the 1994 Agreed Framework developed by the Clinton administration more than a decade before.

Nevertheless, there were some differences. As in 1994, Washington promised to facilitate North Korea's access to fuel oil. Moreover, the Americans agreed to use their influence to release the monies the North had deposited in a Macau bank. Pyongyang, for its part, promised to dismantle its Yongbyon nuclear facility and to allow international inspectors to renew their monitoring of the North's nuclear activities.

Unlike 1994, the new agreement was much more incremental in its approach, promising the North specific gains for specific concessions over an extended time table. This time, the possibility of a continuation of the North's civilian nuclear energy programs was not on the table. Nevertheless, long interested in improving its relationship with Washington and anxious to regain access to its frozen financial resources, Pyongyang seemed initially enthusiastic to take part.

Amazingly, for long-time observers of the talks, real progress was accomplished by the fall of 2007 when international nuclear experts were allowed to begin the work of dismantling the Yongbyon facilities. While the agreements dealt only with North Korea's production efforts, rather than with the nuclear weapons they had already developed, the agreements were a major accomplishment. More ominously, by the time George W. Bush left office in 2009, North Korea seemed to have accomplished its long-term goal of developing a limited nuclear weapons capability and was working to improve significantly its ability to deliver such weapons on long-range missiles. Since 2008 not only has North Korea carried out more long- and short-range missile tests, but it has detonated yet another nuclear device.

The Future: North Korea

North Korea is clearly in trouble. The economy is a disaster and major supporters have been defecting. There have been reports from refugees in China that discipline has been breaking down among the ranks of the army. Moreover, protest leaflets have begun to appear within the cities. Even more significant has been the weakening of the wall of silence that has so long surrounded North Korea. Just recently a tape of secretly filmed public executions was smuggled out. One bold protestor even hung a defaced photo of Kim Jong-il under a bridge before fleeing the country. South Korean websites regularly report on life in North Korea based on reports phoned in from cell phones smuggled into the North.

Internationally, Pyongyang's complicated "relationship" with the United States has long isolated the regime further from the world economy. Pyongyang's one time hopes for an improved relationship with its neighbors was enhanced for a time by its willingness to cooperate on the nuclear issue. Most dramatically it recently even blew up a cooling tower located at the site of its best-known processing facility. For its part, the United States removed North Korea from its official list of states that sponsor terrorism.

But the American gesture hardly improved matters much. On a more immediate note, the tensions between Washington and Pyongyang were made worse during the spring of 2009 by North Korea's conviction of two American reporters arrested near the Chinese border. Eventually a stony faced Bill Clinton

ended up flying to North Korea to escort them home. It was the price the North's Kim, who claimed he wanted to meet the former president, had demanded for the release. But the tensely choreographed "private visit" by America's former president, albiet the husband of the current American secretary of state, accomplished little from a broader perspective.

The fact that North Korea has now increasingly demonstrated a growing nuclear capacity and an energetic missile program is not helping. After all, North Korea's neighbors, from Russia and China to South Korea and Japan, have consistently made it clear that they want the peninsula to be free of nuclear weapons and all vehemently condemned North Korea after the most recent nuclear and missile tests that took place in the early summer of 2009.

In terms of relations with United States, tensions were until recently moving in a very positive direction. Not only did the leaders of both nations exchange direct correspondence but the American navy actually came to the rescue of a North Korean ship attacked by pirates off the coast of Africa. The New York Philharmonic Orchestra even performed in Pyongyang in early 2008. For its part, the lame duck Bush administration seemed genuinely interested in making progress while President Barack Obama was elected on a platform that included a commitment to more flexible international diplomacy. But once in office Obama's explcit efforts to improve relations with the North Korea did not inspire a similar response from the North Koreans.

Unfortunately, North Korea's provocative missile and nuclear tests over the last several year have made it difficult to envision real progress in the short term. They make the resumption of significant tensions more likely. And while experts believe that it will be years before the North Koreans can successfully mount nuclear weapons on missiles, there remains considerable fear that North Korea may become even more involved in the dissemination of nuclear weapons technologies than it already is.

If there is any room for optimism, it is that North Korea's neighbors, from Russian and China to Japan and South Korea, have been much more unified in their condemnation of North Korea's provocative actions than was often the case in the past. That unified concern has resulted in somewhat stronger United Nation's Security Council resolutions against North Korea's increasingly provocative regime.

Mongolia

Contemporary Ulan Bator

Courtesy of Batbold Bayaraa

Area: 604,247 sq. mi. (1,564,619 sq. km., somewhat larger than Alaska)

Population: 3,086,918 (July 2010 estimated)

Capital City: Ulaanbaatar (Pop. 760,077, estimated)

Climate: Dry, with bitterly cold winters

Neighboring Countries: Russia (North; China (South, East, West)

Official Language: Mongolian

Other Principal Tongue: Turkic (mostly Kazakh) 5%, Russian

Ethnic Background: Mongol (about 97%); Kazakh (about 3%)

Principal Religion: The Lamaistic sect of Buddhism and a growing Christian presence

Main Exports: to China, U.S. UK, copper, textiles, beef, meat products, hides, wool, minerals, cashmere

Main Imports: from Russia, China, Japan, South Korea, U.S. cars, food products, chemical, sugar, tea, machinery, equipment, petroleum, electronics, building materials, clothing

Currency: Tugrik

Former Colonial Status: Tributary of the Manchu Dynasty of China from end of the 17th century until the Chinese Revolution of 1911; China recognized Mongolian independence in 1946, but withdrew recognition in 1952.

National Day: July 11th, in recognition of a communist/independence revolution in 1921

Chief of State: Elbegdorj Tsakhia President (since June of 2009)

Head of Government: Sukhbaatar Batbold Prime Minister (since 29 October 2009)

National Flag: Three vertical bands of red, blue and red. The band closest to the pole has a set of traditional symbols at the top in yellow.

Per Capita Annual GDP: $3,200 (2009 estimate.) purchasing power parity.

Mongolia is located in an area of extreme contrast in terms of geography. The arid rocks of the Gobi Desert in the southeast region of the country support almost no vegetation, and have a variation of temperature that splits the craggy rocks that interrupt the frequently monotonous landscape. Proceeding northward there is a gradual change, punctuated by the presence of mountains rising to heights of more than 13,000 feet. The desert gives way to mountainous forest areas whose own thick growth tapers off at the heights where perpetual snow dominates the landscape.

Water also becomes more abundant in the north, but the rivers are uncontrolled and rough, descending in cascades over rocky beds and resembling the swirling waters of the Pacific Northwest and Alaska. It is in this inhospitable part of the country that most of the people live. Their dwellings are constructed of felt that is made from wool and is stretched out over frames.

History

Prior to the 16th century, the people who inhabited Mongolia were famous as a world renowned warrior community that had periodically conquered vast areas as far away as Eastern Europe. This was principally due to the superior horsemanship and cavalry techniques of the Mongols, acquired as a necessity due to their traditionally nomadic lifestyle. This pastoral existence contributed to the superior stamina of their horsemen.

Several Mongolian leaders became well-known. The most famous was Chinggis (Genghis) Khan. He and his successors were able to lead his men in the conquest of vast areas of eastern and southern Asia as far as Baghdad, now the capital of Iraq. However, the Mongols were eventually "conquered" by the people they had subdued. Their empire broke up in the 16th century and the people were converted to Lamaist Buddhism, a pacifist religion, by contact with Tibet (see Tibet section). Economically the Mongolians were dominated by the Chinese, who possessed more sophisticated manufacturing skills. In more recent centuries the Mongolians have found themselves trapped between Russia and China, two large wealthy empires, both equipped with newly invented firearms and other instruments of modern technology that rendered the skills of horsemanship and prowess in cavalry warfare obsolete.

The Mongols were eventually reduced to the status of a tributary of the mighty Manchu Empire that came to power in 17th-century China. Later, in the 19th century, Russian interest in the area grew, and considerable economic and political power was gained in what was then called Outer Mongolia.

Over time the Chinese pressed northward settling Inner Mongolia to the edge of the Gobi Desert, and creating a threat to the people of Outer Mongolia. For this reason, when the Manchu Empire collapsed in 1912, the princes and lamas of Outer Mongolia refused to recognize the claim of the Republic of China to the lands within the region.

In order to gain support for their independence, they then appealed to the Russian tsar for protection. An agreement was reached in 1913 that stated that while China was to administer Inner Mongolia, and while Moscow "recognized" its legal "sovereignty" over Outer Mongolia, the "outer" region was to remain autonomous under local administration.

After the Russian Revolution of 1917, China attempted to seize control of Outer Mongolia. The attempt was initially successful, but in 1921 Outer Mongolia was invaded by a force of White Russian (anti-Bolshevik) troops from Russia. Eventually the Bolshevik forces wrested control from the White Russians and remained until 1925.

The Russians organized a communist government built around those Mongolians sympathetic to communism. Thus Mongolia became the first communist state in Asia. From the Soviet point of view, Mongolia served as a buffer against an increasingly powerful Japan, as well as separating it from any threat posed by China to the south.

In the succeeding decades, the communist regime brought the nomadic tribes and Lamaist monasteries under increas-

Former Prime Minister Sanjaa Bayar

ingly centralized control. Occasional resistance was easily crushed by Soviet troops armed with modern mechanized equipment. State services, previously unknown in the region, were provided, including badly needed livestock shelters to provide protection from the often bitter weather.

A defensive alliance signed in 1936 between the USSR and Mongolia allowed the former to drive a force of Japanese from eastern Mongolia in 1939. Military units from both nations worked together in 1945 to fight those Japanese troops still remaining in Inner Mongolia. At the same time, Stalin was able to obtain a Chinese promise to recognize Outer Mongolia's independence if a national vote showed that this was their desire. The proposed plebiscite was then held under carefully regulated conditions. The result, hardly a surprise resulted in a unanimous vote for independence from China.

Eventually, both the Nationalist and Communist leaders of China recognized Outer Mongolia's independence, and Beijing signed a boundary treaty in 1962.

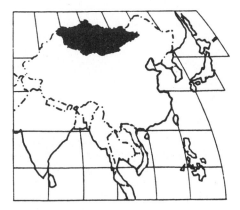

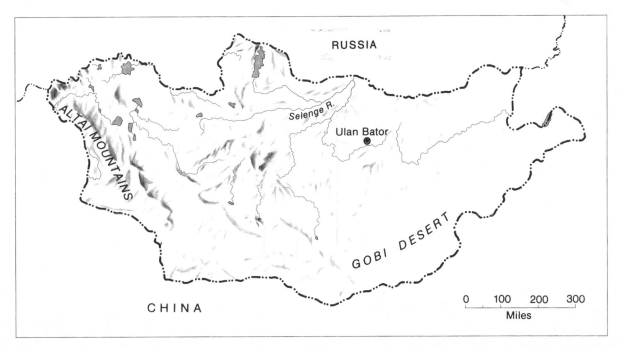

Mongolia

Former President Ochirbat's oath-taking ceremony   Courtesy: Government of Mongolia

China has over the years occasionally shown signs of wishing to increase its influence. These pressures caused Mongolia to cling to Russia for protection. The nation sided with the Soviet Union during the explosive Sino-Soviet dispute of the 1960s and 1970s. In return, Mongolia received substantial economic aid, which allowed the beginning of industrialization in the country. In 1981, as a gesture to Mongolian nationalism, a Mongol cosmonaut was even allowed to take part in a Soviet space flight.

Eventually, in 1986, the Soviet Union began to withdraw some of the military divisions it had long maintained in Mongolia. Diplomatic relations with the U.S. were established in late 1980s. By 1989 Mongolia opened its own embassy in Washington. Only recently the former American President George W. Bush made an official visit.

New Political and Economic Directions

Under the influence of developments in the Soviet Union, especially the ascendancy of Mikhail Gorbachev, the Mongolian leadership started down the path of political liberalization in 1985. By the end of 1989, the dramatic events in Eastern Europe had led to the emergence of several opposition movements in Mongolia, which called themselves the Mongolian Democratic Union (MDU), the Social Democratic Union (SDM), and the New Progressive Movement (NPM). They demanded an end to the Communist monopoly of power. Branches of these new movements were established in every province of Mongolia, and street demonstrations began while the

Communist government ordered troops to relocate near the capital. By March more than a dozen demonstrators had begun hunger strikes, and the nation's Communist leadership signaled its willingness to open negotiations.

The Mongolian communist leader Jambyn Batmunkh, formerly a professor at the State University, refused to authorize the use of troops. After negotiations the Communist Party Political Council resigned. The MDU tried to maximize its appeal to the voters by emphasizing nationalism, including praise for the medieval conqueror, Ghengis Khan, rather than communism. A few weeks later the entire Politburo of the ruling Mongolian People's Revolutionary Party resigned and was replaced by reformers; Batmunkh remained as chief of state for the time being. The ruling party formally gave up its monopoly of power. The new General Secretary, Gombojavyn Ochirbat, was a relatively unknown figure.

By July, although the communist ruling party won about two-thirds of the seats in an election for the Great People's Hural, the opposition parties achieved a recognized place in Mongolian politics. The beginnings of a new era of reform seemed imminent. After that changes came quickly. By 1992 a new constitution was in place that allowed for multi-party voting. Even the term People's Republic was dropped and the country was simply named "Mongolia."

Political ferment and liberalization continued after these dramatic events. Freedom of the press brought a mushrooming of newspapers and magazines. Freedom of religion led to a resurgence of Buddhism and even to some extent of Christianity.

The constitution provides for a popularly elected president and a Western-style parliamentary system of government, with a 76-seat unicameral legislative chamber, the State Great *Hural*. The president may introduce legislation before the *Hural*, and has a veto. The prime minister is the leader of the dominant party or parties in coalition, which control the *Hural*. A Constitutional Court has the authority to review the legality of laws.

The new constitution also allows for private property, but pastureland continues to be under public ownership. After the mid-1992 elections, the former Communist Party (MPRP) still controlled 71 of 76 seats in the Hural. But their domination was beginning to weaken.

In 1993, Mongolia held its first presidential election. Candidates for the post had to be over forty-five years of age and only political parties that held a seat in the parliament could select a standard bearer. The old-line Mongolian People's Revolutionary Party (MPRP) nominated L. Tudev, over the incumbent President Ochirbat. The opposition Mongolian Democratic Party (MDP) formed a coalition with the Mongolian Social Democratic Party (MSDP) and selected President Punsalmaagiin Ochirbat, who had been turned down by his own MPRP, to be their candidate.

In the election, Ochirbat was elected president with 58.7% of the vote. Perhaps as many as one-fourth of the MPRP supporters defected to support their old president. The newly reelected president promised to speed privatization but also to protect those who were hurt most by the process.

During 1994, the *MPRP* continued to rule under Prime Minister Puntsagiyn Jasray, but not without challenges. Street demonstrations broke out in April. The primary issue was apparently corruption in the *MPRP* that reached as high as the prime minister. Demands that the government resign were ignored. Perhaps as a way of making peace, the MPRP sat down with the opposition parties in the Great *Hural*, the Mongolian Democratic Party (MDP), and the Mongolian Social Democratic Party to create important reform-oriented legislation. One part of the agreement between the three parties was to require electoral reform to allow for a fairer representation among the parties in the Great *Hural*. The *MPRP* also agreed to the creation of an independent media, not under government control.

A Non-Communist Start

The weakening of communist control which had been going on since the early 1990s was finally fully realized during the 1996 elections when a coalition of democratic parties swept the communist Mongolian People's Revolutionary Party from power. The *MPRP*, which had been in power since 1921, saw its legislative control destroyed as its opponents won 48 of the 76 seats in the parliament! With that vote Mongolia took its place along side other former socialist states that have attempted to find a new future beyond their communist past.

The new prime minister was the 41-year-old M. Enkhsaikhan, leader of the Democratic Union Coalition. Moving beyond the economic liberalization that had already begun, the new prime minister promised to reform the economy to attract more foreign investment.

The prime minister certainly had his work cut out for him. Within months of his election in May 1997, Mongolian voters, who were frustrated by recent economic stresses, particularly the rapid pace of economic liberalization, elected Nat-

sagiyn Bagabandi, leader of the former dominant People's Revolutionary Party, as president.

During the spring of 1998, Prime Minister Enkhsaikhan resigned as the leader. Eventually, after more than six months of delay the popular mayor of Ulaanbaatar, Janlaviin Narantsatsralt, became the new prime minister only to fall from power a mere seven months later when he was replaced by Rinchinnyamyn Amarjargal. Clearly Mongolia's political elite were having problems. If maintaining a consensus about the office of prime minister was not serious enough, Mongolia was traumatized by the murder of Sanjaasurengiin Zorig, a long time democratic leader.

More important than finding a suitable individual to hold the position of prime minister has been the on-going competition between the market reformers and the former Communist Party members who make up the Mongolian People's

Revolutionary Party, the *MPRP*. Pushed from leadership by the results of the 1996 election, the former ruling party gained greatly from the reformist government's inability to cope with unemployment and inflation.

Thus, as we have seen, despite Mongolia's growing ties with the outside world and increased investment, the MRRP has made great strides in its effort to return to its former position of prominence. In 1997 its candidate for the presidency was elected. And in the elections of 2000, both at the national and local levels the candidates from the former ruling party won big at the polls. In fact, in the aftermath of the July 2000 elections for the national assembly they won 72 of 76 seats.

As a result of their defeat the Mongolia's democratic alliance reorganized itself creating a new party, the Democratic Party out of five former democratic groups. Nevertheless, the country's former ruling

Sukhbaatar Square in Ulan Bator

Courtesy of Batbold Bayaraa

Mongolia

**Former President
Nambaryn Enkhbayar**

party, the MPRP, had been returned to power. Its leader, President Natsagiin Bagabandi, was reelected in May 2001. Four years later, in May of 2005, another MPRP candidate, Nambaryn Enkhbayar, won his own presidential term. Overall the MPRP seemed to be making a significant effort at a comeback although its influence has certainly been limited at times. For a time it was forced to operate within a much larger grand coalition.

But the coalition hardly stabilized the political environment. By late 2005 the coalition collapsed when the MPRP left the government. In early 2006 a new government, dominated again by the former communist era ruling party, organized itself under its new prime minister, Meyagombo Enkhbold.

For many observers this seemed a clear rejection of Mongolia's efforts to turn away from communist past. All this, of course, was done legally as a result of political deal making. But that did not stop thousands of demonstrators, upset about the reemergence of the MPRP, from pouring into the streets of Ulaanbaatar to protest. Some observers have noted that the ideological lines between the two major parties are hardly as clearly drawn between communists and democratic capitalists as some have claimed. The latter, for example, had done particularly well in previous elections simply by promising to give each family government payments based on the number of children it had.

However, Mongolia's political environment remained in flux. In the summer of 2007 another crisis developed when charges of corruption were alleged against the chairperson of the legislative assembly. This resulted in the dismissal of the Grand Hural. Overall the prime minister's hold on power was clearly on the wane, and by the late fall 2007 his own party replaced him with Sanjaa Bayar the party secretary. The next elections, those for the

Grand Hural, were scheduled for June 2008.

When those elections finally took place, little was initially resolved. Indeed the early results were contested, and a riot broke out in the capital that resulted in the death of five people. Eventually, by the early fall, a new government was formed. Sanjaa of the MPRP retained his position as prime minister, and the new DP leader, Norovyn Altankhuyag, became the chief deputy prime minister. By the early summer of 2009 power relationships had begun to shift again as Mongolian Democratic Party's candidate, Elbegdorj Tsakhia won the presidency replacing MPRP's Nambaryn Enkhbayar.

Foreign Relations

The new Mongolia has been moving to improve its relationship with the outside world. Meetings have been held in recent years with important world leaders from Bill Clinton and François Mitterrand, to Boris Yeltsin, Vladimir Putin and George W. Bush.

Relations with Russia have been especially important though not always as smooth as one might want. Officials from both countries have met to discuss the terms under which Mongolia would repay its debt to Russia. The two parties disagree on the amount and the terms. One estimate puts the debt at about $15 billion. A second on-going problem, cross-border smuggling and rustling, is being addressed jointly. In late 2000 Russia's president Vladimir Putin visited and more recently Mongolia and Russia signed a security treaty that pledged each country never to align themselves with a third country against each other. The improving relationship with Moscow was particularly on display in the spring of 2008 as their military ties were resumed. Still relations have not always been smooth. More recently, the claims by Russian President Mevedev made during a visit in August that Mongolia had not yet fully satisfied its financial debt to the Russians were not particularly well received by his hosts.

Though decades of Soviet control played a role in turning Mongolia into a very secular society, a significant percentage of county's population still considers itself Buddhist. This was quite evident in 1995 when Tibet's exiled leader, the Dalai Lama, visited and attracted an enormous outpouring of interest. People from all over the country came to hear him speak. Clearly his presence signaled something of a rebirth of the country's religious heritage. During his initial ten day visit the "God King of Tibet" conducted a mass initiation to replenish the dwindling number of Buddhist monks. That very successful

visit was followed up during 2002 by a second two-day visit to Mongolia. Unfortunately, though Chinese authorities who have long accused the Dalai Lama of working to weaken China, showed their irritation with the visit by apparently stopping train traffic into Mongolia for two days.

The Dalai Lama's visit was probably not the only development in Mongolia that would have attracted Beijing's interest. In recent years Mongolia and the Republic of China on Taiwan established official commercial ties and exchanged representatives. Although the new ties did not constitute official diplomatic relations they were expected to increase tourism and the possibility of Mongolian laborers eventually being sent to Taiwan for work. There was even talk that Mongolia might one day serve as an important link in Taiwan's economic relations with Russia and Eastern Europe.

The Dalai Lama's visits and the new ties with Taiwan have not improved relations between Mongolia and the P.R.C. Relations have not weakened either. In fact, the two countries just signed a defense cooperation pact and Chinese officials have reiterated their respect for Mongolia's sovereignty and territorial integrity.

Looking beyond Northeast Asia, Mongolia has also been attempting to reach out internationally. A major foreign policy initiative of 1995 was launched when Natsagiyn Bagabandi, then chairman of the People's Great Hural (national assembly), publicly expressed Mongolia's desire to join the Asia-Pacific Economic forum. The country's leadership has felt that APEC membership was essential to open the door wider for foreign investment and economic cooperation.

In the spring of 1998 Mongolia was finally admitted to the ASEAN Regional Forum. By the next year, having paid its debts, Mongolia took up its seat in the United Nations' General Assembly. During 2002 United Nations Secretary General Kofi Annan visited Ulaanbaatar and officially thanked Mongolia for contributing two military observers to the United Nation's mission in the Congo.

Relations with Washington also continue to be strong. Mongolia was one of those few nations that agreed to contribute personnel to the United States' effort to transform Iraq. Somewhat later, a grateful Washington announced that Mongolia was among those "select" nations eligible to compete for Washington's new grant program, the "Millennium Challenge dollars." This was created to foster development among some of the planet's less developed countries. Even more dramatic for this land-locked nation, whose existence is so often overshadowed by that of its giant neighbors, a grateful George W. Bush arrived in 2005 to mark the first official visit by an American president.

Society and Culture

The traditional lifestyle of the Mongolians was that of a pastoral people largely living outside of cities. Even today, significant percentages of the population of Ulaanbaatar still live in traditional *gers*, the world famous Mongolian tent-like structure. Four times the size of California, Mongolia still has only a few hundred miles of roads (estimates range from 600 to 800 miles). Today, modernity is changing lifestyles quickly in Mongolia. On land once traversed by camels and horseback, Toyota Landcruisers and Russian motorcycles are a common sight.

Until the arrival of communism and its emphasis on atheism, the indigenous religious traditions of Mongolia were dominated by Tibetan Buddhist Lamaism and Shamanism with a small part of the population following Islam. Today's Mongolia is generally quite secular although there has been somewhat of a revival of Buddhism and a growing Christian community as well.

The traditional literature of the people is ancient. It first consisted mainly of oral epics passed down from generation to generation. In the 13th century the Mongols developed a system of alphabetical writing based on the Ugghur script that served to record the epics as well as being a tool for later literary efforts. Modern

Mongols were educated using Cyrillic letters. Knowledge of the traditional characters has largely been lost to the general public.

While the processes of industrialization and modernization intrude into the solitude of the people with increasing frequency, the Mongolians are still excellent horsemen, fond of festivals which stress the traditional skills of horsemanship, particularly racing, archery, wrestling and physical stamina. As the 20th century drew to a close, at least half the country still worked in the agricultural sectors of the economy even as many Mongolians are moving smoothly into the Internet world of the 21st century.

Today's Mongolia is undergoing the severe stresses common since the collapse of communism around the world. During this transition, as efforts have begun to build economic systems based on more open markets, the day-to-day lives of people have been shaken by the increase in unemployment. In the last several years, the number of people living below Mongolian poverty standards has risen sharply as have related problems such as alcoholism and spousal abuse. An estimated 36%, more than a third of the country, lives in poverty.

Women

Women have long been respected in traditional Mongolian society. The socialist state carried out proactive efforts to raise their status further. Today, the vast major-

Bush in Mongolia

Courtesy of the White House

ity of women are literate and they constitute significantly more than half of the graduates of higher education. Women play important roles in the professions and represent the majority of the physicians and academics and over forty percent of the agronomists, public servants, economists, and engineers.

Although recent years have seen a greater openness in the country's political system the end of the formally free health care system has especially hurt women, particularly pregnant and nursing women. Not surprisingly the maternal mortality rate has risen. Moreover, as with other collapsing socialist regimes, the withdrawal of government support for childcare facilities has inflicted additional burdens on women.

Economy

Agriculture and livestock production have been and remain the backbone of the Mongolian economy. Much of the country's industry, including wool production, clothing and leather goods is tied to this sector. The mining of gold, coal, copper, molybdenum, tin and tungsten also figure significantly in today's economy. In recent years the production of copper has also been especially important as world prices have grown higher. Today, copper plays a very significant part of Mongolia's economy and accounts for more than half of its annual exports. Mongolia's contribution to the world's copper supplies has become so significant that when the People's Republic temporarily suspended train traffic as a reaction to the Dalai Lama's visit, copper prices jumped.

The transition from communism has not been easy. The break-up of large collective farms has had a negative effect on livestock production. In 1995 livestock production (28.6 million animals) was only slightly larger than the previous record set in 1941. In 1998 it had gone up somewhat to 31.3 million. Despite the economic problems and political changes, efforts at privatization continued. Most re-

Campaigning in Mongolia

Photo by Bob Beatty

Mongolia

cently the decision was made to privatize housing without cost to the owners. The sale of small shops to private owners continues as well. By the end of 1996 there were over 30,000 private firms that employed hundreds of thousands of people. The private sector generates around 70% of Mongolia's GDP.

Because of the privatization movement, some one million Mongolians own stock. The initial director of the exchange, Naidansurengen Zolzhargal, an American trained Mongolian, was said to be working on a cellular phone system that would even allow herdsmen to trade directly with the exchange from horseback. Still, once the exchange actually opened, it did not prove particularly effective in the eyes of some observers.

There are more dramatic signs of the transformation of Mongolia's economy. The Mongolian Air lines purchased its first Boeing 737 aircraft and established its own Coca Cola bottling plant. Mongolia's interest in becoming more involved in today's dynamic and globalized economy has been particularly evident in the recent discussions concerning making English a second language for the nation's school children. The lack of trained English language teachers is likely to make that a major challenge for years to come.

After a number of sluggish years, the Mongolian economy has finally begun showing signs of life. Having registered growth rates of only around 1% in 2000–2001, its GDP jumped to 4% in 2002 and is officially said to have obtained a growth of 5.5% for 2005. Even more impressive were figures of around 9% that were recorded for 2007 and 2008. But of course, then came 2008's global downturn that lowered prices for the nation's mineral exports and pushed its growth figures into the negative numbers. Eventually Mongolia began to recover with help from the International Monetary Fund.

The economy also remains dependent on remittances sent home by Mongolians working abroad, as well as on assistance from international organizations and foreign countries. International donors, including the United States, the PRC, Japan and Russia, are deeply involved in Mongolia's economy. The same is true of organizations such as the World Bank, the International Monetary Fund and the European Union.

Private foreign investment has also increased in recent years as Mongolia has become more integrated into the world economy. Unfortunately, that has also apparently included Mongolia's new role as a place to "launder illegal monies." There

has been a growing concern among some outside investors about the government's support for such investments.

Of particular interest over the last few years was the arrival of large numbers of foreigners who wanted to mine for gold. They were hardly the only people mining for gold. An estimated 100,000 Mongolians have apparently abandoned their regular occupations to scour the countryside looking for gold. So intense has the activity been that it has been compared to California's mid-19th century Gold Rush. Mongolia's gold has not been the only natural resource to attract international interest. Mongolia has also just recently established a relationship with Russia to develop the nation's uranium mining and processing capacities.

Environmental Concerns

As a nation that remains particularly linked to its agricultural heritage, especially raising cattle, environmental issues are very important to Mongolians. Though long isolated from the outside world and land locked, the nation is not immune to the larger climate changes going on around the world. In fact, studies of Mongolian tree-ring patterns indicate that the area is hotter than it has been in a millennium. More immediately, like parts of nearby north-central China, Mongolia is experiencing significant levels of desertification and its former president was said to be especially concerned about Mongolia's environmental future.

The Future

In the last years Mongolia has made remarkable progress toward the goal of creating a politically and economically more open society. Its rulers have been especially successful in integrating the once isolated nation into the world community. The economy was experiencing positive growth rates before 2008's economic downturn took its toll and pushed the nation's 2009 GDP into negative numbers. Of interest for the future of Mongolia may well be the efforts to recreate the ancient "Silk Road" that made travel across Eurasia relatively easy during the Middle Ages. The plan, called the "Asian Highway Agreement," is intended to integrate an existing series of roads and canals into a modern transport system to link nations from Japan to Bulgaria.

As a relatively isolated and land-locked nation, Mongolia would likely benefit enormously from the effort. It is an idea that has been discussed for much of the last century. But only in recent years has there been a renewed growth in traffic between the Middle East and

Enthusiastic Mongolian Voter

Photo by Bob Beatty

Asia that is likely to have a significant benefit over the coming years for the people of Mongolia.

Still, the possibility of tension between Mongolia's new "friend," the United States, and Mongolia's neighbor, China, has the potential to make things very complicated. For a time the improved relationship between the United States and the People's Republic, partly the "fall out" from the terrorist attacks of 2001, made that challenge less of an issue for Mongolia. Nevertheless, by 2008 the growing tensions between the United States and China, despite the more general excitement over the Olympics, revived that particular Mongolian challenge.

Probably most important for Mongolia is to retain relatively good ties with all three major powers: the Russians and the Chinese (their immediate neighbors) as well as the United States. Mongolia's strong support of Beijing against those who challenged China's right to hold the Olympics and its sympathies when China experienced the horrendous earthquake in the spring of 2008 are both examples of that effort. The same applies to the new military and nuclear ties being developed with Russia.

The pastoral life of Mongolian sheepherders

131

Brunei Darussalam

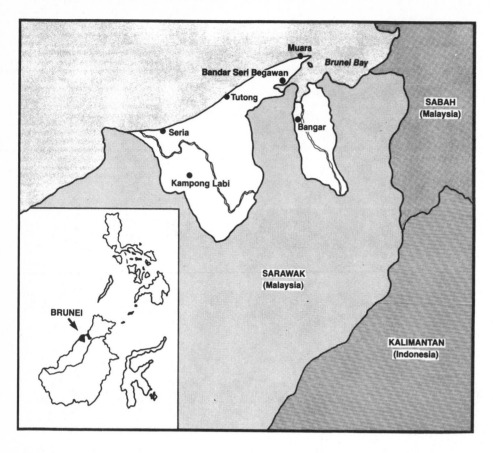

Area: 2,226 sq. mi. (5,765 sq. km., about the size of Delaware)

Population: 395,027 (July 2010 est.)

Capital City: Bandar Seri Begawan (named in honor of the present sultan's father, Pop. 46,000—estimates vary widely)

Climate: Tropical

Neighboring Countries: The East Malaysian states of Sarawak and Sabah enclose Brunei on the large island of Borneo, also known as Kalimantan, two thirds of which is Indonesian.

National Language: Malay. English is the second language

Other Principal Tongue: Chinese

Ethnic Background: Malay (67%), Chinese (15%), indigenous (6%)

Principal Religion: Muslim (60%, official State religion); Buddhist, Christian, traditional native beliefs

Main Exports: Crude petroleum, liquefied natural gas, and wearing apparel

Main Imports: Aircraft, electronics, other manufactured goods, and foodstuffs

Currency: Brunei dollar

Former Colonial Status: Previously independent, it was a British protectorate (1888–1983)

Independence Day: January 1, 1984

Chief of State: His Majesty the Sultan and Yang Di-Pertuan of Brunei Darussalam, Sultan Haji Hassanal Bolkiah Mu'izzaddin Waddaulah (b. 1946)

National Flag: A yellow field crossed diagonally by single white and black stripes upon which is centered a red crest

Annual Per GDP Capita Income: $50,100 (2009 est.) purchasing power parity

Brunei *Darussalam* (meaning "abode of peace") is one of the most unusual nations in the world. Having two distinct parts, with Malaysia's state of Sarawak plugging a 15-mile gap between the two, it is also one the wealthiest sovereign nations *per capita* on earth.

Much of inland Brunei is dense jungle scattered with remote villages and alive with brilliantly plumaged birds, but its gleaming capital city, Bandar Seri Begawan, on the Brunei River about nine miles from its mouth, is sleekly modern, and has several international-class hotels. The country's main port is bustling Muara.

Malays form the majority of the population, but there are also about thousands of non-ethnic Malays, most of them Chinese involved in trade and commerce. In 1961 Brunei passed a law allowing non-citizen Chinese to become Brunei citizens if they had resided in the country for 20 of the previous 25 years and could pass a Malay language test. There are also small groups of British, Dutch, Americans and Australians associated with the oil and gas industry. Education is free up to a doc-

torate if one's scholarship takes him that far. There are three streams in the educational program—Malay, English, and Arabic. Students may pursue advanced studies at schools at government expense.

Brunei has many splendid beaches, and hotels provide excellent service and delectable foods, often combinations of rice, meat and vegetables. The country's cattle are raised on a ranch in northern Australia, which is larger than Brunei itself. The cattle are flown into the country and slaughtered according to Muslim customs.

History

From the 14th to the 16th century, Brunei was the cornerstone of a powerful Muslim empire that encompassed most of northern Borneo and the Philippines. However, the advance of the Dutch and the British, internal corruption, and warfare took their toll as the 17th century dawned. Brunei's rule was confined to an area today formed by Sarawak and part of Sabah. Towards the middle of the century, in 1841, in a rather desperate move to secure military help against marauding South China Sea pirates, the sultan ceded to the English adventurer Sir James Brooke the entire region of Sarawak. Brooke styled himself *rajah* ("prince" or "king") of the area and was succeeded by his nephew and the latter's son until 1946.

By 1847 the British secured from the sultan the island of Labuan off the northwest coast of Borneo. They speculated that it could become an important naval base, but the plan was never realized. There were further concessions and treaties. In 1865 the United States government under President Abraham Lincoln's administration concluded a treaty with the sultan. The American Trading Company of Borneo was created and granted vast land holdings, but this venture was soon thought worthless and was abandoned. Sixteen years later the British set up the North Borneo Company, which acquired the assets of the U.S. firm and pushed further land concessions from the sultan who had little power to refuse the mighty British Empire. Brunei was thus reduced to its present size.

With a fragile economy and no way to defend itself against the many European powers that were continuing to colonize the entire area, Brunei chose British protection in 1888. In 1906 it permitted a British commissioner to take up residence in the country. The sultan was required to take his advice in all matters involving defense and foreign affairs, but not the Islamic faith and Malay customs.

During the next few years the country's economy began to grow, first with the cultivation of rubber. Then the eco-

Brunei

His Majesty The Sultan of Brunei, Hassanal Bolkiah Mu'izzaddin Waddaulah

entertainer, Michael Jackson performed for the guests.

Just recently, in a wedding some called the Asian "wedding event of the year" his son Crown Prince Haji Al-Muhtadee Billah was married in a very elaborate ceremony to Sarah Salleh, a young commoner whose mother is Swiss. But although the wedding was lavish enough it is also likely that it was all part of a process that might soon see the sultan, who has already led his nation for more than 36 years begin the process of turning power over to his son. But if the wedding was part of the process of succession it is clear as well that the sultan has even more wide ranging political changes in mind for his kingdom.

Politics and Government

According to its constitution Brunei is a "democratic Islamic Malay monarchy." However, it does not constitute a true democracy. The sultan and his family dominate the political life of the country. Although the constitution of 1959 did allow some sharing of political decision-making, the nation's legislative council was disbanded in 1962 after left-wing parties won a major victory at the polls, a victory which was complicated as well by an unsuccessful military coup. In the aftermath, the then

nomic picture drastically changed as vast oil reserves and natural gas were discovered in the 1920s in the western part of the nation, followed by offshore deposits in the 1960s. Brunei was on the road to enormous wealth.

When the Federation of Malaysia was established in 1963 to be composed of Malaya, Sabah, Sarawak and Singapore, the sultan of Brunei was urged to join. The then sultan rejected the plan, fearing for the erosion of his political position and determined that Brunei's oil and gas revenues would be reserved for the benefit of native Bruneians rather than becoming available to the proposed federation at large.

Brunei regained its independence after almost a century of colonialism on January 1, 1984. A member of the British Commonwealth, Brunei has since joined the UN and the Association of Southeast Asian Nations (ASEAN) among others. At the sultan's request, the Gurkha army units from Nepal stationed in Brunei while it was under British protection stayed on to aid the Royal Brunei Armed Forces. Decades later, they remain there with their own radio station, Gurkha Radio, available to fill their information needs.

The present sultan, Hassanal Bolkiah, heads the government, serving as prime minister, defense minister and more recently as finance minister. The other key government posts are held by members of his immediate family. Born in 1946, the sultan has more than one wife, as Muslim custom allows. A few years ago he divorced his second wife and more recently remarried a much younger Malaysian woman. This was a move that apparently irritated many of his female constituents. The sultan has three sons and six daughters. Educated in Brunei and Malaysia, he then enrolled as an officer cadet at the Royal Military Academy at Sandhurst, England.

He was crowned the 29th ruler of Brunei by his father in 1968 upon the latter's abdication. Easily one of the richest men in the world, the sultan controls the finances not only of his own family but that of the state itself. With such resources he can be quite lavish. For example, in 1996 to celebrate his fiftieth birthday, the sultan threw a party that cost over $25 million dollars and included Prince Charles, an old friend, as a guest. The American

Wedding of Crown Prince Haji Al-Muhtadee Billah

Brunei

The Sultan Omar Ali Saifuddin Mosque

sultan dissolved the legislature and suspended the constitution. By the mid-1990s though after a generation of absolute rule things appeared to be changing.

In February 1995, Haji Abdul Latif Chuchu, a political activist, was elected president of the Brunei Solidarity National Party, the country's only legal political party. Haji Latif and other party officials then called for democratic elections in a meeting with the sultan. That effort did not initially accomplish much. Haji Latif was banned from all political activity.

Things began to change again during the fall of 2004 when the sultan announced that he was creating a 21-member State Legislative Council with the stated goal of strengthening the monarchy and making the government more efficient. The move can hardly be considered a terribly dramatic step given the fact that the appointed members include the sultan and his brother as well as other family members and business elites. Still it was a gesture not to be discounted.

By the following year he introduced even more significant changes. New cabinet positions were added, and the State Legislative Council expanded in size while specific five-year terms were set for the individual members of the cabinet.

These changes were not insignificant. Brunei had not had an elected legislature since the early 1960s or even an appointed one since the mid 1980s. While the renewed State Legislative Council is hardly likely to call for dramatic changes in official policy, all this is said to be part of a process that will eventually lead to more open elections.

Despite the proposed changes, one thing remains absolutely clear. Sultan Hassanal Bolkiah, chief of government and head of state, still largely rules the country himself with the help of the Council of Cabinet Ministers, most of whom are family members. In fact, the government has said that although the State Legislative Council has now been revised to play a renewed role in the nation's governance, the sultan's goal is for it to improve the ties between the government and the people and to strengthen the monarchy rather than to make the state more democratic. A more obvious example was revealed over the last year when legal papers were released that showed that the new constitution has specifically claimed the sultan could do no wrong "in either his personal or any official capacity."

The sultan's desire to strengthen the monarchy was also evident in his efforts to start the formal introduction of the crown prince into the decision-making process. His son, Al Mutadee Billah, was appointed to the newly created position of senior minister.

He has also been emphasizing a more religious tone in some of his public talks, reminding his subjects of the importance of adhering to their Muslim duties. This approach has been a long-standing one. After his father's death in 1986, the present sultan devised an ideology designed to reinforce the monarchy. Known as *Malaya Islam Beraja* or *MIB* it is mainly an affirmation of Islam and the monarchy. The sultan's ideology, *MIB*, was brought into the secondary schools in 1992. More recently the constitutional amendments were introduced to make more explicit the sultan's right to make laws related to Islam itself.

But though there may still be little "public" politics within Brunei, there is certainly controversy within the ruling family that occasionally becomes more publicly known. A few years ago an open conflict broke out between the sultan and his brother, Prince Jefri Bolkiah, who was accused of financial mismanagement and removed as director of the Brunei Investment Agency (BIA). Surprisingly the break became very public, and Prince Jefri went into self-imposed exile for a time.

More recently, the tensions became so profound that for a while the public was witness to the spectacle of members of the royal family actually suing each other in court. This was a development that clearly added to growing public discontent. Finally the sultan stepped in to quell the lawsuits by settling the claims left by the collapse of Prince Bolkiah's business activities. Apparently family harmony has returned as Prince Jefri seems to be once again in the family's good graces. But the prince is not financially off the hook. The government is still trying to get him to surrender assets he owns around the world in compensation for his previous financial mismanagement. The saga continues. In 2008 Britain's High Court of London issued an arrest warrant for the prince. Again, he has been accused of financial misconduct. Apparently the Sultan's expectations for the next generation are more positive. He has named as his heir his twenty-four-year-old son, Prince Billah, a recent graduate of Oxford.

While Brunei may be an island of relative tranquility compared to many of its neighbors, it too has experienced a renewal of Islamic political activism. In the fall of 2003 it was reported that the government had detained a number of individuals because of efforts to revive the banned Al-Arqam movement, which had previously had many followers in Brunei and Malaysia.

Defense

While tiny in size, Brunei has a modern and capable defense force. Internal and external security is under the control of the Royal Brunei Armed Forces (RBAF), the Royal Brunei Police, the Gurkha Reserve Units, and the British Army Gurkha Battalion. Recent defense expenditures have been around 10% of the national budget. The RBAF has about 4,000 personnel and includes several hundred women who were recruited beginning in 1981.

The air force and navy are small but well equipped. Joint military exercises have been held with Malaysia, Thailand and Singapore. The latter trains its troops in Brunei's jungles. A Gurkha Reserve Unit is directly under the control of the sultan. The Royal Brunei Police Force is the fourth component of national defense.

Negotiations over a Memorandum of Understanding (MOU) with the United States on national defense matters were initiated in the early 1990s. The United States may be interested in using the country as a staging point for air surveillance in the region.

But as the world has learned in recent years, "defense" issues are not necessarily merely about the possible assault on one's nation by the forces of other countries. In July of 2003 ASEAN met in Brunei and agreed to work together to fight terrorists who have been active to various degrees in nations from Thailand and Malaysia to Indonesia and Singapore. Going beyond even that level of joint anti-terrorist activity, there is even talk of creating an ASEAN peace keeping force to deal with regional problems. More locally, the authorities in Brunei, following a similar effort in Malaysia, have begun efforts to eliminate illegal immigrants from Brunei and to make sure that their kingdom does not become a haven for terrorists.

Foreign Relations

Brunei foreign policy stresses the security of the nation. A true mini-state, the country must rely to a considerable extent on the goodwill of its neighbors. The fact that it is surrounded by its two Muslim brother states, Malaysia and Indonesia, is advantageous. Brunei joined the Association of Southeast Asian Nations (ASEAN) just after independence in 1984. Membership has helped the country establish close diplomatic and military ties with the other ASEAN states. Brunei also takes part in the ASEAN Regional Forum (ARF). The ARF is a consulting body that focuses on Asia-Pacific security matters. Last year Brunei became the chair of ASEAN and the host to their summit that took place in November 2001.

Brunei was the first Muslim state in the region to recognize Israel. Earlier on it had established ties with the Palestine Liberation Organization and opened an embassy in Iran. More recently Brunei has been strengthening its ties to other Muslim Middle Eastern states from Saudi Arabia to Morocco especially so with the hope of establishing Brunei as a safe haven for Muslims seeking to invest funds outside of the Western countries.

During the economic crisis of 1997 the sultan attempted to use his vast financial resources to shore up the collapse of his neighbors' currencies. Even his efforts failed to stem the tide of the currency debacle that hit the region. In years since the Asian economic crisis settled in, the sultan, despite weaknesses in his own economy caused by then falling oil prices, has vowed to take a more active role in helping the region progress. Not only has he been significantly involved in helping Malaysia and Indonesia recover financially, but he made his first official visits to his northern neighbors Burma, Laos and Vietnam. Going far beyond his region during 2002, he made an around-the-world trip that saw him meeting with leaders from George W. Bush in Washington to the leaders of Germany and Mexico.

The major recent complication in Brunei's foreign relations was a dispute over the rights to a huge oil field off the coast of Borneo that both Brunei and Malaysia claimed. Compounding the problem was the fact that both countries had contracted with different oil companies to survey the area in anticipation of drilling in the disputed area. Not surprisingly both Brunei's sultan and Malaysia's outgoing Prime Minister Mahathir became directly involved in the talks. Those talks were complicated still further by Malaysia's attempt to link the question of the off-shore oil resources to another sensitive regional issue, the question of Limbang, which Malaysia controls and which divides Brunei in two. Despite the tension, both nations have

Modern homes on stilts

Brunei

managed to keep the controversy from getting out of hand.

Culture and Society

The country is ruled by the royal family. The family line goes back some twenty-nine generations farther than any of the other twenty-eight monarchies in existence today. Brunei Malays are similar to the Malays of Malaysia and Indonesia. All are followers of Islam and speak the Malay language. They differ significantly from other ethnic groups in Brunei. Traditionally, Brunei Malays were fisherman, traders and craftsmen.

Today's generation is seeking more "modern" means of employment. About 10% of the Brunei Malays claim royal blood, having been descended from one of the sultans. Many of the Malays live in Kampong Ayer, the Malay community consisting of about thirty-five villages. Although under Muslim law a man is permitted to have up to four wives, this is actually rare in Brunei.

Contemporary life in Brunei for its citizens is one that many would envy. Perhaps to keep dissatisfaction with the sultan's political control to a minimum the state has used its oil resources to create a cradle-to-grave social security system. Almost every urban family owns at least one

car, often more, and there is no income tax. Both education and health care are free.

The Kedazans are the second most populous indigenous group. They are similar to Malays in their practice of religion, language and appearance. The greatest difference is that they have tended to be rice farmers. They do not have the same status in society as the Malays. Other smaller indigenous groups include the Bisayas, who follow indigenous religious traditions; the Penans, nomads of the jungle; the Muruts, who once populated the military for the sultan; and the Ibans, whose numbers are increasing compared to the other smaller groups and who are known for their past head hunting activities.

The Chinese are far more important than their numbers would suggest. They dominate the sultan's commercial sector. They also provide the managerial and technical talent for the country. The older generation follows Taoist-Buddhist traditions. Less than ten percent of the local Chinese have been granted citizenship. Still, their importance was recognized recently when the government's agreed to the founding of a Chinese language newspaper in the kingdom. Like Malaysia and Singapore, Brunei is a multiethnic society that can only survive with a good bit of tolerance and acceptance of diversity. But

maintaining tolerance is not the only thing that can offer challenges for Brunei. As the sultan has emphasized in his public talks, Brunei, like much of the world, is faced with the challenge of maintaining its cultural identity in the face of globalization.

Women

As is the case elsewhere, the experience of women in Brunei is a mixed one. While no women hold leading positions in the bureaucracy, large numbers hold positions at the lower levels. Today nearly two-thirds of the student body at the national university is female. They also serve in the military, though not in combat positions. However, since Brunei is officially a Muslim society, Islamic domestic law governs the life of women. Women have fewer rights in such important areas as divorce and inheritance, and, as is common in the region, they cannot pass on their citizenship to their children. Men also have considerable advantages over women in the government's civil service jobs.

Economy

Oil and gas provide Brunei with more than 90% of its export earnings. The nation is the third-largest oil producer in Southeast Asia after Indonesia and Malay-

Traditional houses in Brunei

sia. The Seria oil field was discovered in 1929, and by the 1950s it was producing 115,000 barrels a day. Offshore production began in 1964, and today there are hundreds of oil-rigs operated by Brunei Shell Petroleum Company, jointly owned by the government and Shell. Actual oil production is carefully watched since Brunei wants to conserve this source of income for the future. Almost half of its oil is exported to Japan, and the rest goes to other nations, including the United States. Brunei uses only about 3% of its production for domestic use.

Brunei is a major supplier of liquid natural gas, a venture owned by the government, the Royal Dutch Shell Group and Japan's Mitsubishi Corporation. Millions of tons are exported annually to Japan and Korea alone. During 2002, for example, Brunei sent over 200 cargos of natural gas to their East Asian neighbors earning an estimated two billion dollars. Overall, the petroleum sector—crude oil and natural gas—account for an enormous percentage, almost half of Brunei's gross domestic product (GDP).

The uncertainties surrounding the ongoing Middle East crisis and American Iraqi relations have made long-term economic planning for Brunei quite difficult. Certainly short-term hikes in the price of oil have been quite helpful for the kingdom. Still Brunei also needs its principal customers, such as Japan, to be economically healthy enough to pay those prices. On the other hand, a satisfactory resolution of the long-running Iraqi crisis could also see Iraq once again becoming a major oil exporter. This would lower the price of oil and hurt Brunei's government revenue.

As of the late spring 2007, though, the concern that oil prices might drop once Iraq stabilized seemed a long way off. China's growing demand for oil, natural disasters in the oil-producing regions of the United States, and instability in the Persian Gulf combined to keep oil prices high and Brunei's energy revenues flowing nicely. At least that was the case until the global slowdown of late 2008 dragged down the demand for world's oil with it and, of course, the revenues those who sold it earned. Eventually the impact of the declining demand for the nation's energy products saw Brunei's GDP drop by almost two percent in 2008 and only slightly improve during 2009, a year that came in at a somewhat less negative .4 growth rate.

The nation is also moving to play a bigger part in world petroleum production. The current plan is to go from a focus on selling crude oil to more emphasis on refinery activities and developing petrochemical industries within the kingdom. The fact that Malaysia and Brunei managed during 2009 to resolve a long-standing territorial dispute opens the way for more oil exploration in the waters shared by both Malaysia and Brunei.

Another source of revenue is foreign investment, which is now producing almost as much money as the petroleum sector. In 2002, for example, over a billion dollars U.S. was invested by outsiders in Brunei as opposed to only about half that amount the previous year. More recently the government has been in talks associated with expanding into cement production.

Overall, the government spent much of the last decade working on various plans to diversify the economy and more recently even moving toward privatizing some government agencies. One goal has been the plan to steer the economy away from dependence on oil and natural gas. They have reason to do so because current estimates are that the country's reserves will run out by 2025. For the moment, though, the efforts to diversify the economy have still often been tied to the energy industry.

However, this attempt to diversify the economy has been less than a smashing success although recent international events have complemented that goal somewhat. There is an interesting aspect of the kingdom's reaction to developments since the horrors of September 11, 2001, and the subsequent tensions between the United States and large parts of the Islamic world: Brunei decided to offer itself as an attractive banking alternative for those Muslims who are no longer comfortable having their investments in Western banks. That effort has seen a recent reorganization and merger of parts of the nation's banking industry and the emergence of the new Islamic Bank of Brunei Berhad.

Brunei is also developing plans to create a giant Mega port hub for handling the enormous container shipping that so dominates the region. Moreover, in yet another challenge to Singapore's accomplishments the government is also planning to push Brunei deeper into the internet revolution with the creation of a cyber park to encourage the nation's involvement in the emerging e-market developments.

Another factor that complicates Brunei's economy is that the government employs more than half of the labor force. A new joint-venture garment manufacturer was forced to import Philippine and Thai workers because locals were either too few in number or not willing to do such work. In reaction to such problems the government has frozen civil service pay in an attempt to make state employment less attractive. However, in a country where health care and education are free, and where subsidized loans are readily available, there is little pressure to change. There may be some ambivalence on the part of national leaders concerning economic change. An influx of foreigners and new ventures will surely disturb the comfortable and traditional environment of this Islamic mini-state. And such an influx is actually quite likely given that a new direct air link was recently established between the sultanate and Shanghai.

The Future

With a per capita purchasing power parity per capita of over $50,000, the country is doing far better than many of its neighbors. Although for a time there was some economic distress as unemployment grew significantly, things have improved considerably over the last few years. Income from oil fields has also gyrated dramatically.

Overall, the primary economic challenge still remains to diversify the economy enough to prepare it for the day when the oil lines do run dry, or realistically, when the world starts fundamentally to shift away from the fossil fuels on which Brunei depends for its livelihood. Given the generally growing global urgency about the importance of lessening our dependence on fossil fuels, as exemplified by the policies of the American Obama administration, that reality seems more likely today than it was only a few years ago. It is an example of the evolving global energy regime for which a nation like Brunei will have to carefully plan. However, the long-term impact of the planet's weaning itself from fossil fuels was not the only concern. Beside humanity's long-term use of fossil fuels that enhance greenhouse gasses, the kind of massive flooding that is so often associated with climate change hit Brunei in January 2009. It caused significant landslides and power outages in parts of Bandar Seri Begawan. It also devastated its neighbors in Manila.

The Kingdom of Cambodia

The temple of Angkor Wat built by Khmer warrior kings a thousand years ago

AP/World Wide Photos

Area: 68,898 sq. mi. (181,300 sq. km.; slightly larger than Missouri).

Population: 13,995,904 (July 2010, estimate)

Capital City: Phnom Penh (Pop. 862,000, estimate)

Climate: Tropically hot with a rainy monsoon season during the summer from May to October

Neighboring Countries: Thailand (North and West); Laos (Northeast); Vietnam (East)

Official Language: Khmer (Cambodian)

Other Principal Tongues: French, Chinese, Vietnamese

Ethnic Background: Cambodian (Khmer, about 90%) Vietnamese (semi-permanent or permanent, about 5%), Chinese (1%), other, (about 4%)

Principal Religion: Buddhism

Main Exports: to China, U.S. Germany, UK, Vietnam, Canada—Natural rubber, rice, pepper, timber, rice, fish, footwear, tobacco

Main Imports: from, Thailand, Singapore, Vietnam, Japan, Taiwan, and Australia—cars, pharmaceuticals, cigarettes, gold, construction materials, oil, machinery

Currency: Riel

Former Colonial Status: French protectorate (1863–1949); Associated State within the French Union (1949–1955)

Independence Date: November 9, 1953

Head of State: King Norodom Sihamoni (since 29 October 2004)

Head of Government: Hun Sen, Premier (since 1985)

National Flag: A plain red field upon which is centered in gold the ancient temple Angkor Wat

Per Capita Income: GDP per Capita $1,900 (2009 est purchasing power parity)

Cambodia has a rather short coastline that runs about one hundred and fifty miles along the warm waters of the Gulf of Thailand. The land stretches from this coast in a wide plain, which is traversed in the eastern part by the broad waters of the lower Mekong River. The western part of the plain is dominated by a large lake known as Tonle Sap, twenty miles wide and one hundred miles long. It is a body of fresh water that produces a heavy annual harvest of fish needed by those Cambodians, who do not eat meat because of Buddhist beliefs.

The borders with Laos and southern Vietnam run through thickly forested foothills that rise to highlands at the demarcation lines. The greater part of the northern border with Thailand consists of a steep series of cliffs; the part of Thailand closest to Cambodia is a plateau that is situated about 1,500 feet above the plain. The western border with Thailand and most of Cambodia's coastline is occupied by the Cardamom, Kirimom and Elephant Mountains, which rise to heights of 5,500 feet.

Much of the large central plain is regularly flooded by the mighty Mekong River in an uncontrolled fashion. There are no elaborate dikes to contain the waters such as are found along the Red River in northern Vietnam. The rains that begin in May are the first cause of flooding; melting

138

Cambodia

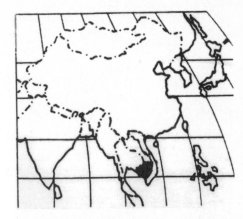

snows in Tibet and China in July add to the volume of water, which is also joined by monsoon waters from Thailand and Laos. By mid-September the floodwaters may cover as much as 8,000 square miles of land. These are not violent waters. Rather they deposit silt which enriches the land and they also bring huge quantities of fish to the Tonle Sap Lake, permitting annual harvests of up to 15 tons per square mile of water surface. The waters recede in October. The winter season begins in November, bringing slightly cooler and much drier weather except in the western and southern mountains, where there is sporadic rainfall.

History

The civilization of Cambodia first emerged as a product of indigenous communities of peoples and their interaction with peoples from South Asia. The Khmer people, from whom the modern Cambodians (Kampucheans) are descended, first organized themselves under a state usually known by its Chinese name of Funan, which emerged about 500 A.D. in southern Cambodia. This was apparently a result of trade with, and immigration from, India to Cambodia via the Kra Isthmus, which is now the southern part of Thailand. These early contacts were brought about by Southeast Asia's geographic location on the trade routes between South Asia and China. More significant for the development of society in Southeast Asia was that the region's powerful monsoon rain storms often forced the ships to spend long periods on the peninsula waiting for weather conditions to change. It was under these circumstances that the spread of Indian culture, including traditions like Hinduism and Buddhism, could spread widely.

Although Funan was not a centralized state as would later develop, it did have tributary relations with the Chinese to its north. But it would be Indian, not Chinese, society that would have the most profound influence on the region during these years. Just as Koreans would in these years model themselves after Chinese society, the Cambodian elites in the first centuries of the modern era strove to become more like their Western neighbors. They took Indian names and developed literary works in Indian languages. Hindu Gods, from Shiva to Vishnu, were worshiped, and local leaders strove to associate themselves with these powerful Indian images.

The Khmer Civilization of Angkor Wat

From the era around the early ninth century through much of the fifteenth century,

Cambodia was home to one of the world's most impressive civilizations. Located in Cambodia and parts of today's Thailand, this civilization, associated most with the extraordinary building structure at Angkor, has left us an enormous amount of information to try to understand it. Early leaders of this civilization were strongly influenced by Hinduism and identified themselves with the Hindu god Shiva. Because the temples were made of stone, many of which can be studied today, we tend to know more about elite religious society and less about the average "Cambodians" of the era. What we do know is that they were used by the monarchy to supply labor to the building projects of the empire. And their labor was impressive indeed. Angkor Watt, built in the twelfth century, remains the largest religious building in the world today.

The people were converted after 1000 A.D. to the older school of Buddhism now generally referred to as Theravada Buddhism. Mahayana, or Greater Vehicle Buddhism, was also influential but less so than the more austere Theravada (the way of the elders) Buddhism which prevailed over time. At its height in about 1200, the Khmer Empire controlled much of what is now Vietnam, Thailand, Laos and Burma. One of the main features of Angkor Civilization as we now understand it was a very attractive commitment to religious toleration.

In the later years of Angkor Civilization, the Cambodians were much influenced by the arrival of Muslim traders from India. They not only converted many Southeast Asians to Islam, but played a significant role in reorienting the inward-looking rice based economy of Angkor to one that was also interested in international trade.

In foreign affairs, the Angkor Civilization found itself by the twelve hundreds under pressure from the Thai forces as well as the Vietnamese, a community whose tensions with Cambodia lasted well into the modern era. Sadly, having flourished earlier, the Khmer Civilization of Angkor had collapsed by the 15th century and its people dispersed. The city itself lay forgotten until the 19th century when it was rediscovered.

For the next three and one-half centuries, Cambodia was sandwiched between the Annamese of Central Vietnam

139

Cambodia

Young King Sihanouk, 1946

and the Thais to the north and west. Sadly the once mighty Cambodian people were over the centuries to be almost continuously dominated by one or the other, or both.

The Arrival of the West

By the 1500s the Western missionaries had begun to arrive in Cambodia seeking converts to Christianity and influence for the Spanish Empire. They were not terribly successful and unlike their brethren in the Philippines, had little success in attracting converts. But while Western missionaries from the Iberian Peninsula were the first to appear in Cambodia, the Indochina's more fundamental encounter with colonialism would come from the forces of imperial France.

The beginning of formal French influence in Indochina was initially an offshoot of their activities in China during the Second Opium War. Once the Anglo-French forces had captured the city of Canton in southern China, French officials made the decision in 1859 to send a fleet to Vietnam to establish a presence there. From the French perspective, it was a way to successfully compete with their archrivals, the English, in the rush to establish themselves in East and Southeast Asia. French-specific interest in Cambodia was stimulated in the late 1850s by British advances in Burma. Both powers thought of Southeast Asia principally as a stepping stone to the supposedly vast treasures and markets of southwest China.

Although it established a protectorate over Cambodia in 1863, France did not de-

throne the reigning family; the area was increasingly drawn into the Indochinese colony created at the end of the century in an attempt to rival the much larger British Indian Empire. The French prevented the Thais from moving against Cambodia and protected it also from its other overlord, the Vietnamese, who had themselves become part of the French Indochinese Empire. Because this protection was welcomed by the Cambodians there did not develop the violently anti-French attitude that existed in neighboring Vietnam during the same era. Nevertheless, when the French in the early 1880s attempted to modify tax rates and introduce other administrative changes they provoked a revolt in 1885 that lasted for more than two years and required large numbers of French troops to suppress it.

During those early years of the French presence they ran Cambodia as a trusteeship and allowed the indigenous monarchy and its officials to largely administer the country. Nevertheless, the French held the ultimate strings of power and were usually instrumental in choosing who actually held the Cambodian throne during their years of colonial control. The hands-off policy was abandoned by the late nineteenth century as French officials began to interest themselves in internal developments and to more directly control it as a colony.

As in other parts of Southeast Asia, the existence of a stable colonial administration attracted a sizable number of Chinese immigrants, who quickly emerged in a virtually dominant position in profitable ventures as commercial middlemen. Many Vietnamese also immigrated to Cambodia during these years. Because they were more likely to speak French they were more able than the native Cambodians to advance themselves through links with the French.

Initial French enthusiasm for Cambodia lessened after it became clear that the colony itself lacked the rich mineral resources many had hoped for nor provided a convenient "back door" to the southern provinces of China. By the interwar period, the Cambodian economy, like many of its neighbors in Southeast Asia, was increasingly integrated into the world economy. For Cambodia this meant producing rice for the world markets and becoming, under the control of French companies, a major exporter of rubber.

The Second World War

Japan quickly overran Cambodia in 1941, and as a token of appreciation, two of the Cambodian border provinces were awarded to Thailand, by then an official ally of the Japanese. Although they were returned after World War II, the Cambo-

King Sihamoni

dians have a lingering suspicion that the Thais still covet them.

After the return of the French in 1946 politics in Cambodia were dominated by a popular yet unpredictable individual who initially ruled until 1970: Prince Norodom Sihanouk. He had been made king by the French in 1941, but became impatient with the conservative traditions of the monarchy and increasingly interested in the liberal political movements within the country. During the early 1950s he successfully convinced the French to grant full independence for Cambodia, an effort that gained him even more public appreciation. He abdicated the throne in 1955 in favor of his father so that he could organize his own political movement, *the People's Socialist Community* which he expected to have replace the existing political parties. Building on his widespread support among the population, Sihanouk dominated Cambodian political life for the next generation.

He skillfully used this popularity to cope with what he regarded as major domestic problems: the traditional aristocracy, the partly westernized intellectuals, the businessmen, the small communist movement and a segment of right-wing opponents who he believed were supported by Thailand. Initially, his efforts were almost uniformly successful. He continued to lead the *Sangkum*, or the *People's Socialist Community* that was the only significant political party. Sihanouk's sense of his own talents is difficult to exaggerate. During the same years he wrote and produced a number of feature films with himself as the leading man.

But for the popularity of Sihanouk at home, Cambodia would never have been able to deal with the external pressures with which it was faced. In order to keep open the largest number of possible alternatives, Sihanouk remained "neutral" in the international "Cold War" and aloof in the hot war in Asia. He engaged in active and skillful diplomacy that often puzzled the most astute foreign ministries.

The Vietnam War Era

To counterbalance the threat of North Vietnam, Sihanouk established close relations with the People's Republic of China, a nation that was not anxious to see Ho Chi Minh's Vietnam dominate Cambodia. Overall, Sihanouk hoped he could play off the powerful forces around his country to keep Cambodia safe and independent. But given the tensions of the Cold War era, Sihanouk's efforts to find a middle ground between the contending forces was complicated indeed and aroused the suspicions of the United States which saw him as an impediment to their own plans for the peninsula.

He was supportive of both sides in the Vietnamese struggle during the early 1960s. For example, he allowed the North Vietnamese to use Cambodian territory in their efforts to supply their troops in South Vietnam while keeping open his relations with the Americans.

For this reason, relations between Sihanouk and the U.S. were strained after the early 1960s. Complaints by the U.S. increased sharply in late 1967 as the fighting in South Vietnam became more intense. Clearly the United States wanted to pursue the Viet Cong into the eastern provinces of Cambodia. The whole situation was made even more complicated by Cambodia's claims to areas in South Vietnam, claims Sihanouk put forth at the bargaining table repeatedly when dealing with the U.S. Eventually Sihanouk did secretly agree to allow the Americans to bomb North Vietnamese supply lines in Cambodia.

The ever-changing diplomacy of Sihanouk worked to the extent that its Asian neighbors did not constitute a direct threat to the survival of Cambodia. Nevertheless, the unity of Cambodia and Sihanouk's direct control were weakening. There was a significant increase in communist-led revolts in the provinces bordering Thailand and Laos in the latter part of 1968, as well as the number of Viet Cong illegally present within Cambodia.

The displeasure of anti-communist Cambodians grew so great that in 1970, while Sihanouk was out of the country, major anti-Hanoi demonstrations broke out in Phnom Penh. General Lon Nol and Prince

Along the Tonle Sap, Cambodia's Great Lake

Sirik Matak, an older cousin of Sihanouk, proclaimed the ouster of Sihanouk and a new government under their leadership. The communist problem, however, was not the only issue—there had been disputes over Sihanouk's socialist economic policies that were thought to be hurting the economy as well.

Recognizing the more pro-American tone of the new Cambodian administration, the North Vietnamese and Cambodian communist forces, now supported by the ousted Sihanouk, promptly began to expand their military activities in various parts of the country. That same year, in April of 1970, twenty thousand American and South Vietnamese soldiers entered Cambodia to attack the communist bases along the border from which the communists had been conducting raids into South Vietnam. To their disappointment they found the bases had been abandoned weeks before. The Americans soon pulled out, but their bombers would return in coming years to carry out a massive campaign against leftist forces within Cambodia.

The country suffered severely as a result of this military campaign. Although Lon Nol was in poor health and under heavy military pressure from the communist forces he managed to remain in power until 1975. However, long before that Lon Nol had already dissolved the National Assembly and begun to rule by decree. He also proclaimed himself President. But none of these efforts helped. Public confidence in the government eroded badly. Meanwhile the expansion of the Vietnam War into Cambodia had fur-

ther outraged many Americans and by mid 1973 the bombing partly undertaken to support Lon Nol's pro-Western government was halted.

The Cambodian Genocide

Meanwhile the communist forces of Cambodia, dubbed the *Khmer Rouge* by Prince Sihanouk, who was quite publicly working with them, were growing stronger. Although fiercely nationalistic, they initially also had the support of the North Vietnamese. The *Khmer Rouge*'s most influential leader was Solath Sar, better known as Pol Pot, a Western-educated Cambodian whose family had earlier had significant ties to the Cambodian court.

Communist *Khmer Rouge* military efforts came close to isolating Phnom Penh by early 1975. Undermined by his own shortcomings, political bickering, and uncertainty about American support, Lon Nol's government evaporated. The rebels refused to negotiate, leaving it no alternative but to surrender amid ominous proclamations of a collection of "blood debts" from the leadership. The final collapse came in mid-April 1975, when Phnom Penh fell to the *Khmer Rouge*. It was to be the first step in the darkest chapter of Cambodian modern history.

The policies of the new *Khmer Rouge* regime, which was pro-Chinese and soon became anti-Vietnamese, reflected the ideological mentality of its leaders and personnel. Once in power the *Khmer Rouge* set out to brutally transform Cambodia, which they now renamed Kampuchea, into a classless agrarian society. It was to be an

Cambodia

Cambodian Prime Minister Hun Sen
AP/Wide World Photo

experiment in social engineering more radical than ever tried in modern human history. Going beyond the social reorganizations of Asian groups like the Chinese Taipings or what had gone on elsewhere in the communist world, the *Khmer Rouge* was determined to remold all Cambodians to fit their "idealistic" images. Those who were not perceived as "appropriate" for the new order were simply murdered. Over the next several years, civil society as Cambodia had known it simply disappeared. Money and wages were abolished, the cities largely emptied and all forms of religious life, freedom of the press and much of the middle class were simply eliminated from the life of the nation.

To build their new classless agrarian society the *Khmer Rouge* closed down institutions from hospitals to educational facilities and even monasteries. Private property, even down to the most personal hygiene supplies, was communalized while a policy of systematic mass murder was put into place. Over time what emerged was a genocide that rivaled the horrors experienced by Armenians and Jews earlier in the century or that experienced by others in Central Africa later on. As one writer has put it, Democratic Kampuchea was less a nation than a state prison camp.

The major cities, including Phnom Penh, were forcibly evacuated, allegedly on account of food shortages. There were executions of supporters of the former regime and widespread atrocities, mainly against persons of middle class background. Anything, even the wearing of glasses, could mark someone as too bourgeois and thus bring on a death sentence! Cambodians found themselves brutalized by one of the harshest governments of the 20th century. A veil of secrecy shrouded the once great nation. The formerly beautiful capital of Phnom Penh with 1.3 million people was left with 90,000. Boarded-over storefronts and virtually deserted streets told the story. The new regime wanted to stifle religion, wipe out any education system conflicting with the hopes of the "new order," and stamp out family ties.

Families were driven from the cities to labor from dawn to dusk in the fields. First priority was the destruction of the intelligentsia and middle class. Although estimates regarding the number of dead vary widely, the best scholarly estimates now put the number at between 1.5 and 1.7 million people dead from execution, starvation and overwork. Of the seven to eight million Cambodians before the genocide began, some have estimated that the death toll ranged from 15% to 40% of the entire population.

The regime's atheistic and racist mentality was particularly devastating for the nation's Buddhist community whose monks and properties were regularly singled out for destruction. Although much of the killings were of Cambodians by Cambodians, the nation's ethnic minorities were not spared; hardly surprising given the vehement racist/nationalist mentality the *Khmer Rouge* usually displayed. Previous to the *Khmer Rouge's* arrival to power the largest ethnic communities in Cambodia were the Muslim Chams, the Chinese and the Vietnamese. Together these minorities had traditionally made up about 15% of the nation's population but once in Cambodia the new leadership was determined to change the situation. The Vietnamese, who were particularly hated, were completely eliminated with many dead and others fleeing to Vietnam. Recent researchers have failed to find a single Vietnamese who survived the assault on their community in Cambodia. The Chinese, whose traditions as city dwellers made them particularly unpopular with the new rulers, saw more than half, about 200,000, of their numbers die during these years. The Muslim Chams faired no better. After first experiencing the *Khmer Rouge's* efforts to destroy their Islamic traditions, their people were systematically massacred after they attempted to resist.

Pol Pot's preferred method of execution even saved the cost of a bullet: a skull-penetrating blow to the rear of the head by a pickaxe used on a kneeling person. Massive piles of bones throughout the country attest to this grisly activity. Others simply starved to death.

Once Lon Nol's government was overthrown, the still popular Prince Sihanouk returned home. *Khmer Rouge* rule Cambodia was not run by Sihanouk, though, but by a shadowy leadership of the *Cambodian Communist Party* known as the *Angka* ("organization"), of which Pol Pot was Secretary General. An election held in 1976 filled 250 seats in the People's Representative Assembly. All of the 515 candidates were picked by the *Angka*. Sihanouk then resigned, together with the rest of the government. The former king was placed under house arrest. A government entirely of communists was announced, with Pol Pot in actual control.

Given the vehement nationalism of the new regime it is not surprising that it almost immediately provoked friction with its neighbors. The most serious case was

Mekong River tour boat

with Vietnam. On-going border warfare erupted between the two nations until late 1978 when a massive assault was launched on Cambodia by the Vietnamese.

Cambodia's Vietnamese Interlude

The new Cambodian regime had immediate friction with all of its neighbors, the most serious with Vietnam, which erupted into continuing border warfare from early on until late 1978 when Vietnam invaded. By early January 1979, Pol Pot had fled to western Cambodia, and a new pro-Vietnamese government known as the People's Republic of Kampuchea had been set up in Phnom Penh. Despite their defeat, Pol Pot's forces would then carry on a guerrilla war against the Phnom Penh government until the late 1990s.

Though Hanoi probably viewed its invasion as both a reaction to the *Khmer Rouge's* assaults and as an effort to free the Cambodians from Pol Pot's murderous regime, few in the international community viewed the invasion in that light. In general the world community viewed the invasion as an unprovoked Vietnamese aggression and responded negatively. Ironically, the world reaction produced some very strange informal alliances as both the United States and the People's Republic of China condemned the invasion, and to various degrees were supportive of the defeated *Khmer Rouge.*

The Chinese, long unhappy with Hanoi's ties to the USSR, staged a brief invasion across the Vietnamese border in early 1979 with the announced purpose of "teaching Vietnam a lesson." Unfortunately, for the PRC the only "lesson" learned was their own forces were ill prepared to deal with Hanoi's experienced troops. The attack had no impact on Vietnam's control of Cambodia.

For the next decade, regular fighting went on in western Cambodia between Vietnamese troops and Pol Pot's forces. Tension also arose between Vietnam and Thailand over the Cambodian refugees grouped near the border. A coalition under Sihanouk, including what was left of Pol Pot's regime, emerged in opposition to the Vietnamese-dominated government in Phnom Penh. This group retained Cambodia's seat in the U.N.

The Phnom Penh government, while hardly the genocidal regime of the *Khmer Rouge,* was itself repressive. Moreover because it was dominated by the Vietnamese it was understandably not very popular with the Cambodian population. For a time the government attempted to carry out socialist agricultural policies somewhat similar to those common during Pol Pot's years and within Vietnam itself, but these were eventually phased out. The

anti-religious policies of Pol Pot were also ended. Once again Buddhist activities were allowed. Monks could retake their traditional place in Cambodian life despite some restrictions. Though many Cambodians had been very relieved to have the Vietnamese drive out Pol Pot's murderous regime, the new Vietnamese-backed government was unpopular and thousands of Cambodians continued to flee the country.

It was during these years that Cambodia's later "strong man" Hun Sen emerged in importance. Originally, from a middle class family, Hun Sen had initially been part of the Cambodian Communist resistance to Sihanouk's government. He later joined the *Khmer Rouge* only to break with the regime in 1977. Hun Sen returned home as part of the Vietnamese invasion force. By 1985 he was prime minister.

Eventually, in May 1988, the Vietnamese Government announced that it would soon withdraw its troops from Cambodia. Hanoi

had done so by 1989. The reasons for this major policy shift included the dismal state of the Vietnamese economy, the small chances of attracting aid from abroad while the Cambodian occupation continued, and Soviet pressure, or at least persuasion. It is probably not a coincidence that only the month before Moscow had formally agreed to remove its troops from Afghanistan by February 15, 1989. Hanoi also wanted to improve its relations with the United States, something that its continuing hold over Cambodia made impossible.

The prospect of a Vietnamese withdrawal naturally accelerated the pace of political and diplomatic activity relating to Cambodia, both within and outside the country. Having lost its more immediate Vietnamese support, Hun Sen's government was faced with the necessity of building a strong popular base of its own within Cambodian society. It was thus during this era that he moved to reintroduce private

Monument filled with skulls at the infamous "Killing Fields"

Photo by Steven Leibo

143

Cambodia

Their Majesties the former King and Queen of Cambodia

property and expand further the role of Buddhism which had been allowed to revive in the years after Pol Pot's defeat.

The main problem that the Vietnamese evacuation created was the fear that it might lead to another seizure of power by the blood thirsty *Khmer Rouge*. Of course, the other contenders for power were Hun Sen's government in Phnom Penh, the Royalists around the former king, Prince Sihanouk, and a non-communist resistance group directed by the former Prime Minister Son Sann. The latter two in fact had received international recognition as a Cambodian government in exile but represented little of practical importance within the country.

The U.N. Sponsored Elections

As the 1990s unfolded a complicated series of international negotiations took place with the goal of establishing Cambodia on a healthier and more stable road to recovery. On October 23, 1991, the Paris International Conference on Cambodia adopted an agreement on a Comprehensive Political Settlement of the Cambodia Conflict, which created the United Nations Transitional Authority in Cambodia (UNTAC) with a force of 16,000 military and 6,000 civilians that began arriving in Cambodia in early 1992. UNTAC's function was to disarm the Cambodian warring factions and create a political climate where free elections could take place.

The long awaited free elections took place in 1993. But the victory of the royalist forces under Prince Ranariddh, the son of King Sihanouk, was overturned by Hun Sen, whose military forces remained stronger. Refusing to accept his party's political defeat at the polls, Hun Sen forced the creation of a very convoluted political system with two prime ministers.

Thus, from 1993 through 1997, Cambodia operated under the coalition government formed in the aftermath of the 1993 United Nations sponsored election. After more than a generation of civil war and totalitarian governments this was a remarkable improvement. Officially its government was a constitutional monarchy headed by Prince Norodom Sihanouk, who was once again officially sworn in as monarch in September of 1993.

Sihanouk's sons directed FUNCINPEC, the "royalist" party and Prince Norodom Ranariddh held the position of first Prime Minister. Hun Sen, the long-time leader of Cambodia, held the title of second prime minister although he actually held more power than his rival. The cabinet also featured dual ministers representing both parties.

The country operated as a parliamentary system though the judiciary was not as independent of the government as the constitution required. The unusual system of two prime ministers certainly helped get the government operating, but the more common pattern of having rotating prime ministers, as has occurred in Israel and Turkey, might have worked more efficiently.

From the start the two prime ministers were frequently estranged and actual

fighting often broke out between their supporters. Only the most optimistic believed the unstable coalition could survive. Norodom Sirivudh, half brother of King Norodom Sihanouk, was "encouraged" to go into exile for allegedly planning to kill co-prime minister Hun Sen. Many believed the Prince was framed in an attempt to silence his criticism of the government. The murder in 1996 of Hun Sen's brother-in-law was another example of the tension. Nevertheless, the coalition might have survived if the third factor in Cambodian politics, the blood thirsty *Khmer Rouge*, had not complicated the situation enormously.

The *Khmer Rouge* and what to do about it had, of course, long been the major issue that faced the government. Attempts to end the fighting took different forms over the years. The approach ranged from fighting to occasional efforts to reconcile with the *Khmer Rouge*, despite its bloody record of mass murder. Of those contending for power it was the royalists who were most willing to associate themselves with the *Khmer Rouge*. There was also a move to have Sihanouk form a provisional government of reconciliation that would have included the *Khmer Rouge*. Hun Sen's supporters opposed the plan, and Sihanouk withdrew his offer. Nevertheless, by the late 1990s the dynamics of Cambodian politics started changing dramatically.

The End of the Khmer Rouge

1996 saw major progress in the government's efforts to end the long-time insurrection of the *Khmer Rouge*. In August, Leng Sary, a senior leader of the *Khmer Rouge*, said to be second only to the infamous Pol Pot, broke ranks and offered to end his role in the insurrection. The offer, while greeted as an important step in the final reconciliation of the country, was complicated by the former *Khmer Rouge* officer's direct role (vehemently denied) in the genocide of the 1970s. After complicated negotiations, he was granted a royal pardon.

That Leng Sary's defection indicated a weakening *Khmer Rouge* was highlighted by the remaining leadership's willingness to allow a formal radio talk show discussion on maintaining *Khmer Rouge* solidarity. This was a remarkable step to take for a party with one of the most totalitarian records of the 20th century. These developments highlighted a blow to the *Khmer Rouge* as profound as their earlier loss of power after the Vietnamese invasion of 1979 and which later events showed they would not recover from.

By early 1999 the last of the major *Khmer Rouge* leaders had fallen into the hands of the government though it was unclear how many of the actual killers would ever come to trial before either a Cambodian tribunal or one organized by the international community. Over the years, though, there has been an almost constant effort to create a tribunal, rather like those that have dealt with crimes in the former Yugoslavia and the genocide in Rwanda, to confront the horrors of the Khmer Rouge years.

The world community had by 2006 finally agreed upon an institutional framework to accomplish such a goal. In January an international tribunal, which included both Cambodian and foreign nationals, was established just outside of Phnom Penh. The following summer prosecutors and judges were sworn in. In mid-summer of 2007 the new tribunal officially recommended that the Khmer Rouge leaders be tried for genocide and crimes against humanity. By the fall some of the most notorious of the surviving Khmer Rouge leaders had been arrested and began appearing before the newly established tribunal. By 2008 more formal trial procedures against some of the most infamous of the still surviving members of the Khmer Rouge had begun, including Kang Kek Leu, known as Duch, who had once directed the horrific Tuol Sleng detention camp.

Search for Political Stability

The unstable coalition government that had operated since the United Nations' sponsored elections collapsed during the summer of 1997. The actual break was caused not by tensions with Sam Rainsy's group but, as so often in the past, over relations with the then weakening *Khmer Rouge*. In early July, Hun Sen's forces carried out a coup against the supporters of his rival Prince Ranariddh. The second prime minister claimed that the Prince had finalized an alliance with elements of the *Khmer Rouge* and was planning to integrate them into his own forces. All this took place in the middle of a "circus" of international media attention as the *Khmer Rouge* itself seemed close to collapse and rumors abounded that the notorious Pol Pot might become available for trial at an international tribunal against genocide. What was actually going on behind the scenes was quite uncertain. What was clear was that after the dust settled Hun Sen's forces had driven the Royalists from the capital and Prince Ranariddh was in exile.

By mid July 1998 most of the major aid donor countries had temporally halted aid to Cambodia in protest against the coup and the country's hopes to join ASEAN were dashed as the leaders of the Associa-

tion of Southeast Asian Nations decided to postpone the planned admission of Cambodia. Apparently the proposed alliance between the Cambodian Royalists, assuming we accept Hun Sen's claims, caused major political waves within the *Khmer Rouge* as well. By the end of the month the movement's long-time leader, Pol Pot, had fallen from power, denounced by his former followers. Later that summer the world got its first glimpse in a generation of the fallen leader when Pol Pot was given a "show trial" by his former colleagues and sentenced to life imprisonment. Within months word came that the former ruthless dictator had died, *apparently* by his own hand.

In the months after the coup Hun Sen worked to establish his authority throughout the country while claiming he was ready to allow the continuation of parliamentary elections. He even retained the title of second prime minister while allowing a one time Royalist, Ung Huot, to replace Ranariddh as the first prime minister. As for King Sihanouk, the man who had spent his entire life trying to retain his influence within the Kingdom he had inherited, there was little room for hope. His comments seemed to suggest an ex-

hausted leader who had lost faith in the future.

Given the international community's negative reaction to Hun Sen's actions, Cambodia's strong man found himself still required to present to the world a Cambodia willing to continue the process of democratization. Well aware that the long-planned parliamentary elections of mid 1998 would not be accepted as valid unless Prince Ranariddh took part, the world was entertained in the months before the election with a show of the former first prime minister and his associates being tried for smuggling weapons and plotting a coup against Hun Sen. After being found guilty, the prince was sentenced to thirty-five years in jail and fined millions of dollars. Once that was done, the plan, arranged in advance, was carried out. The prince's father, King Sihanouk, granted him a full pardon that allowed the ousted first prime minister to compete in the elections of July 1998.

Cambodia's election of the summer of 1998 did not though improve conditions much. Once again, the players remained largely the same: the supporters of Hun Sen, the Royalists led by Prince Ranariddh and Sam Rainsy's followers. As expected

A young Buddhist monk

Cambodia

Victims of the Khmer Rouge

Photo by Steven Leibo

Hun Sen's backers dominated the country's media outlets making it hard for the opposition to get their electoral message out to the voters. Discouraging to supporters of the opposition was the decision by both Ranariddh and Rainsy to attack Hun Sen by stirring up anti-Vietnamese sentiment. Certainly, it was a tactic that could be effective against Cambodia's long time leaders who had initially been installed in power by Hanoi. Nevertheless, given Cambodia's recent history of ethnic-based genocide, few could find the decision an admirable one and it eventually caused several deaths among the local Vietnamese community.

Once the voting took place, a new controversy exploded over the counting of votes that eventually saw both opposition parties refusing to cooperate in the creation of a new government. Their cooperation was needed because Hun Sen's supporters had failed to gain enough seats in the national assembly to form a government on their own.

Officially the vote tally had given the government party, the CCP, 41.1% of the vote to 31.7% for the Royalists and 14.3% for Sam Rainsy's party. Whether the actual vote counting had been corrupt, the result was more months of political strife and public demonstrations before it was agreed that a new coalition government would be formed. Not surprisingly the compromise left Hun Sen as the main political leader and prime minister with Prince Ranariddh as the new president of the National Assembly.

Nevertheless, over the years, the most obvious development in Cambodia's political life has been the increase in long-time Prime Minister Hun Sen's power and influence. In recent local elections, his followers won the vast majority of votes. Although many have questioned the honesty of those polls Hun Sen's power has continued to increase.

The elections that took place during the summer of 2003 did not fundamentally alter the situation at all. As before, Hun Sen's CCP won 58 of the parliamentary seats while his rivals, the royalist party FUNCINPEC and the SRP of Sam Rainsy, got 26 and 24 respectively. On the positive side, a huge number of local and international observers testified that the election had been carried out in a reasonable fair manner.

At the time the Cambodian constitution required that a government could only be formed if a political party controlled a two-thirds majority, something Hun Sen followers lacked. Thus began, as it has so often before, months of political struggles over how the new government would be formed. FUNCINPEC and the SRP jointly insisted that they would not offer the required support unless a tripartite governing coalition was formed under someone other than Hun Sen.

The long-time prime minister absolutely refused to step down or allow more than a two-party coalition to form the new government. Eventually, FUNCINPEC broke with its ally the SRP and joined yet another coalition government. Fundamentally little had changed except that valuable time had been lost. The nation's entrance into the World Trade Organization had been delayed as were completion of plans for a joint Cambodian-United Nations tribunal to address the horrors of the Khmer Rouge era.

FUNCINPEC, the royalist party, was clearly losing its ability to be an effective national opposition. It had been additionally weakened by internal divisions that most recently saw Prince Ranariddh driven from the party's leadership. By early 2006 it was obvious that its members were reconciling themselves to a clearly secondary role and becoming less confrontational toward the government. They had good reason to do so. A new constitutional change reduced the number of parliamentarians whose support is needed to establish a government. The significance is that, in the future, the CCP will no longer need FUNCINPEC's support to form governments. The situation was further complicated in the late summer of 2007 when an entirely new opposition party, the Human Rights Party, was founded by a former political prisoner. However, that hardly affected real power in Cambodia. Indeed, during the summer 2008 election the CPP managed to win 73% of the seats in the national election.

As for Prime Minister Hun Sen himself, the only thing that is absolutely clear is that he has no plans to leave the prime ministership any time soon. There was even talk for a time that he was interested in founding a new Cambodian monarchy himself. Whether there is any truth to that rumor is unclear. But it may have played a role in Norodom Sihanouk's decision in the fall of 2004 that, after more than sixty years as the nation's on-again off-again monarch, he was simply too old and exhausted to carry on any longer.

The announcement set off a dramatic effort by the king's son and Hun Sen's rival Norodom Ranariddh to try to dissuade his father from abdicating. Nevertheless, the aging monarch was adamant and by mid October of 2004 his son Norodom Sihamoni, a former dance teacher and ambassador to UNESCO, was chosen to assume the throne. Unlike his half brother, Ranariddh, Sihamoni had never played a role in Cambodia's often troubled politics and vowed that he would continue that same approach once he assumed office.

Society and Culture

The art and culture of the Khmer Empire, based largely on its Indian, Hindu and Sri Lankan Buddhist origins, were an elaborate and highly developed combination to which distinctly local elements were added during the centuries that have passed. The surviving specimens of the Empire are mainly of stone and bronze that display highly stylistic and ornate techniques. The modern Cambodians are justifiably proud of their historical heritage. The Khmer (Cambodian) language was spoken prior to the arrival of Indian influence and is now written in a script derived from India. Sadly for Cambodia's cultural heritage an enormous percentage of the country's cultural leaders were murdered by the *Khmer Rouge*, a blow few nations could easily survive.

While it will take years for the nation's cultural heritage to recover, the damage goes far deeper. Cambodia remains a country where the ratio between men and women has been distorted by years of civil war and genocide. There are, for example, only 93 males for every 100 females in contemporary Cambodia. That is even more pronounced among the older generation where the loss of males to warfare and violence has been even more dramatic.

Perhaps worst of all, Cambodia may have survived the Khmer Rouge years and even seen its economy slowly improving, but infant mortality rates have actually climbed in recent years. According to the United Nations, the primary cause of this worsening of infant mortality has been the rising level of AIDS and a weakening public health service. No doubt recognizing the severe strains Cambodia's exceptionally high birthrate causes (the second highest in Southeast Asia), the government has introduced a program to encourage families to plan their childbearing decisions more carefully.

Life for minorities, especially the Vietnamese, remains especially difficult. Longtime antagonisms and current political tensions both play a role in keeping Cambodian hostilities toward Vietnam and their own Vietnamese residents strong. On the other hand, Cambodia's Chinese community has recovered from the blows it experienced during the Khmer Rouge era and has been growing rapidly in recent years.

There is also relatively good news for the Cham community, those Cambodian Muslims who found their ranks decimated during the Pol Pot years. Money has been flowing in from the Islamic world to help rebuild mosques and to found Islamic schools although there has been some concern that those schools may be fostering the sort of intolerance that has at times brought so much grief to people from the Middle East to South Asia. No doubt in response to those concerns, the United States itself has started to provide funding and training for Cambodian Muslims in the values of human rights and democracy.

Perhaps one of the most telling signs of Cambodia's return to normalcy has been the emergence of a problem with teenage drag racing. Where Khmer Rough thugs once murdered people in the nation's capital, today's population has become more concerned about dangers from wealthy teenagers racing through the streets disrupting traffic.

Women

Women make up the majority of the population and the largest percentage of the work force in most sectors, from agriculture to business, industry and service sectors. Because of the years of violence, women today head a quarter of the households in Cambodia. They do not, however, hold many significant positions of influence. Men continue to dominate decision-making.

Boat racing at the Water Festival in Phnom Penh.

Photo: Serge Corrieras

Cambodia

The country's new constitution explicitly contains language offering women equal rights, but in practice these are not normally carried out. According to a new report by the United Nations, the inequality between men and women has actually grown greater in recent years. Cultural traditions that emphasize male authority are still strong. Moreover, as is often the case, the return to a less authoritarian socialist economy, despite the many advantages, also frequently has the impact of reinforcing traditional attitudes that value females less than men. There are, however, many non-governmental organizations that are quite active and emphasize improving the lives of women. As in other Southeast Asian countries, stories of the trafficking in women are very frequently reported. The unfortunate young women and girls far too often end up as part of the region's well-known sex trade.

But new opportunities are also opening up as Cambodia enters more deeply into the globalized economy. Local workers, as part of a program to help Cambodia's least advantaged citizens have been trained to digitize Western literary classics by typing them into computers, activities that not only help them earn money but develop valuable computer skills.

Foreign Relations

Throughout its history, Cambodia has been in the unfortunate position of being caught between contending forces beyond its borders. In the pre-colonial era both the Thai and Vietnamese empires occupied parts of Cambodia. The country was also caught between the United States and the pro-communist Vietnamese during the Vietnam War. The North Vietnamese used overland routes through Cambodia to transport war materials. The U.S. bombed those same North Vietnamese supply lines through Cambodia thus disrupting life in many parts of the country.

Prince Sihanouk could neither prevent the North Vietnamese from using his territory, nor satisfy the United States that his policies were not pro-Hanoi. Later, during the Vietnamese occupation which was backed by the Soviet Union, Cambodia was again a pawn between the Vietnamese and their Soviet ally, on the one hand, and the Chinese, who backed the *Khmer Rouge,* on the other. Even today relations with Vietnam remain difficult as both nations continue to argue over where the border between the two states should be. Unfortunately, the last few years have also seen a growth in tensions with Thailand over their mutual borders.

The Thais have been angry about the establishment of casinos near their mutual border. Tensions reached a violent crescendo after a Thai actress was said to have claimed that the revered local heritage site, Angkor Wat, should belong to Thailand. In subsequent outbursts of Cambodian anger, Thai properties were attacked in the capital, and Bangkok had to evacuate its citizens quickly.

More recently things have gotten even more complicated. Both Cambodia and Thailand have long-standing claims to the ancient temple structure of Preah Vihear. Over the last year a dramatic confrontation developed over their competing claims. Making matters worse, the issue became even more complicated when the question of how supportive the Thai government was to Cambodia's plans to have the temple proclaimed a UNESCO world heritage site became yet another political "wedge" issue separating Thailand's "warring" political factions. Tensions have continued. Unfortunately the confrontation has taken on a very nationalist and populist tone within Cambodian society. This is likely to make concessions by the government even more difficult than it might otherwise have been.

Relations have also continued to be tense at times with Vietnam. Hanoi has, for example, continued to be suspicious about whether Cambodia has allowed access to its territory by groups the government considers anti-Vietnamese. On the other hand, the two governments have been cooperating on road building in the area near their shared borders.

The most important development for Cambodia in recent years has been the slow improvement in its relations with many of its Southeast Asian neighbors. In 1995, Cambodia secured "observer status"

Downtown Phnom Penh

within the Association of Southeast Asian Nations (ASEAN) and was then expected to become a full-fledged member. However, the 1997 coup delayed Cambodia's entrance until 1999, when it finally gained full membership.

Cambodia's positive relationship with China was graphically on display during 2009 when the government very publically deported more than a dozen Uighur men and boys. On the run from China's crackdown in its central Asian territories, they had been smuggled into the country by Christian missionaries. In fact, the government did more than merely deport the refugees, whom the Cambodians deemed illegal immigrants rather than potential asylum seekers. They had them placed on a special flight back to China provided by the Chinese authorities. Despite the accompanying protests from both the United States and the United Nations, the government's decision is probably understandable given that China has become the single largest investor in Cambodia's economic development.

For years, Cambodia's relationship with the larger international community beyond Asia has been complicated by differing attitudes towards the creation of tribunals to try the former members of the Khmer Rouge for their genocidal acts during the late 1970s. Until recently the Cambodian government resisted calls for international trials by claiming that such trials might destabilize the admittedly new and fragile peace that Cambodia has been enjoying. Nevertheless, efforts to reach an agreement regarding future criminal proceedings against the surviving leadership of the Khmer Rouge remain a major issue. By 2005 this culminated in an agreement to establish a special tribunal within the Cambodian judicial system. It would include international judges alongside local jurists to address this most horrid chapter in human and Cambodian history. As we have seen, by 2008 those trials had begun. By 2009, the infamous Kaing Guek Eav, better known as Duch, once the head of the horrific concentration camp S-21, had publically confessed in court. Final sentencing was scheduled for July 2010. There was also talk of putting other former members of the Khmer Rouge jointly on trail.

Economy

A major challenge for the new government is to establish a national economy. Two decades of conflict and revolution have destroyed much of the country's infrastructure. But finally significant progress is being made in replacing what was lost and damaged. The presence of UNTAC, the United Nations force, also caused distortions in the economy. The

Asian economic crisis of 1998 also affected Cambodia though it had, one might say, less far to fall given the long-term weakness of the economy compared to its neighbors.

As might be expected, the military commands about 20% of the entire budget though plans are now being made to scale back the military. Plans to demobilize the military have not gone as well as hoped and large numbers of former soldiers have not gotten the bonuses they were promised to help them rebuild their lives.

About half of the country's operating budget comes from foreign aid. The country has continued to receive substantial amounts of aid and loans from individual donor countries, the International Monetary Fund (IMF), World Bank, and the Asian Development Bank (ADB). For a time in recent years one bright spot for the Cambodian economy was the jump in foreign investment that included several major hotel chains. Unfortunately, the bloody struggle between the two prime ministers during 1997 temporarily set back much of this momentum.

By the new century Cambodia's tourist industry was again clearly on the mend. The number of new visitors grew rapidly, and foreign investment was again rising. Creating that sense of stability is particularly important given that outside aid remains so important to Cambodian success despite recent economic gains. International aid agencies have been hard pressed to provide larger and larger amounts of aid for new problems, such as the Asian tsunami victims. Given those new demands on the donor community, it has been particularly important for Cambodia to achieve economic success.

For Cambodians the end of the *Khmer Rouge* has allowed for Cambodia to start healing economically. Inflation has lessened and economic momentum has once again begun. It is true that Cambodia's growth rate in recent years has been relatively unimpressive—in the four to five percent range.

Still, unlike other parts of Southeast Asia, Cambodia is getting good marks from outsiders for attempting to reform its economy. In mid 2003 the Asian Development Bank announced a three-year loan program that would bring over $230 million into the country for development purposes. By mid-decade Cambodia's economy was doing well, largely due to the growth in the garment industry. But the growth rate in 2007 came in at over a ten percent. Predictably, 2008 saw the beginning of the slowdown, and 2009 ended up in the negative territory.

As is the case for so much of the world, the emerging economic giant China affects Cambodia as well. Cambodia entered the

World Trade Organization (WTO) in 2003. This was a change that offers many advantages. However, the nation has to compete even more for sales with the growing efficiency of Chinese factories. On the other hand, China's success has in part also been Cambodia's because the PRC has become a very major investor in Cambodia.

Perhaps somewhat macabre are the government's plans to capitalize on international interest in the Khmer Rouge years by creating a fancy "theme" park to receive visitors to various sites associated with the atrocities. The plans including the restoration of the buildings associated with the Khmer Rouge as well as the creation of a high-tech museum complex and tour guides apparently chosen from among former members of the Khmer Rouge. As of the spring of 2010, plans were even in place to turn Pol Pot's final stronghold and the site where he died into a tourist site to include a guidebook commissioned by the prime minister.

Regardless of how some might react to the plans, it also seems likely that many of the growing numbers of tourists who visit Cambodia each year will be attracted by the effort to capitalize financially on the horrors of the Khmer Rouge years and be willing to contribute to today's Cambodian economy in the process. More predictably, the growth of tourism around Angkor Wat, the nation's extraordinary medieval religious site, has grown enormously in recent years and is likely to continue to do so as more and more tourists grow comfortable visiting Cambodia.

Even more exciting in terms of revenue has been the growth of Cambodia's offshore oil industry. Current estimates suggest that in the next several years Cambodia could start seeing several hundreds of millions of dollars of income as a result of these resources. Obviously this is not great news for those hoping to wean the planet from its addiction to fossil fuels, but it is very good news for a nation sorely in need of new revenue streams.

But there are some real concerns. The growth of Cambodia's role in the world drug market is discouraging. Cambodia is rapidly earning a reputation as Asia's newest "narco-state." In 1996, Washington placed Cambodia on its "watch list" of trafficker states. As a demonstration of Cambodia's increasingly deep involvement in the globalized community its government found last year that it had to expel a large number of foreigners for using Cambodia as a base for internet financial scams. Moreover, major storms and flooding in recent years have also dramatically affected Cambodia at times, killing hundreds of people and hurting the economy. Only a year or so ago, some thirty million dollars worth of food was destroyed by

Cambodia

flooding, and a million people faced food shortages. Real growth is going to require a major effort to improve the roadways of Cambodia which remain in terrible shape with only 28% of them considered to be acceptable.

Cambodia's Environmental Challenge

Cambodia may be experiencing a level of stability the nation has not seen for decades, but that is not the case for much of its environment. It is currently thought that about half the nation is covered to some degree by natural forest cover, but that is changing rapidly as more and more forests are removed to make way for agriculture. Moreover, logging, both legal and illegal, is having an impact on marine and freshwater resources. Over fishing combined with greater use of dangerous pesticides are also negatively affecting the nation. As with many of its neighbors, Cambodia is particularly vulnerable to the threat of rising waters and more powerful storm systems associated with the phenomenon of global warming.

The Future

In a fashion so different from much of Cambodian history during the latter half of the twentieth century, the early years of the new century have been kind to Cambodia. Not only has the Khmer Rouge collapsed long ago, but a reasonable level of stability and cooperation has been reached. Unfortunately, that stability has emerged from the increasing strength of the ruling party, the CCP, which has largely eliminated the influence of the other smaller parties. In fact, international organizations have publically condemned the government's use of lawsuits to intimidate the opposition, which has little influence. In one especially notable case, Hun Sen sued the former minister of women's affairs after she demanded an apology from the prime minister after he made sexual comments about her in public. Not surprisingly, the court sided with the powerful prime minister and fined the former lawmaker thousands of dollars. By the early spring of 2010 the former minister, Mu Sochua, had unsuccessfully appealed to the nation's supreme court . She faced the decision either to pay the fine or go to jail. Clearly, the days when Cambodian politicians were able to challenge Hun Sen's power have long disappeared.

Until the most recent global economic slowdown, news on the economic front was mostly positive. Parts of the economy had been showing vitality, from the textile industry to the agricultural sector, while the tourist industry was growing nicely. Of course, hope for new oil revenues also brightened the economic future as well. This is an important development, given its ability to contribute to the country's overall wealth. Particularly impressive is that these accomplishments have not gone unnoticed. The International Monetary Fund recently decided to forgive Cambodia's $82-million-dollar debt in recognition of its accomplishments. Still, the .9% negative growth rate of 2009 is hardly encouraging. But given China's close economic ties and its own relatively successful rebound from the recent global recession, Cambodia's own economy is also likely to start growing again soon.

Of more immediate concern is the growing tension with Thailand over competing claims to the temple of Preah Vihear. The fact that the contemporary volatility of Thai domestic politics makes the situation on the shared borders more complicated is a cause for even more concern.

Statue at Angkor

150

Executive office building in Dili

Photo by Marc Cassidy

Area: 5,743 square miles
Population: 1,084,971 (July 2010 estimate)
Capital City: Dili (Pop. 150,000 estimate)
Climate: Tropical
Neighboring Countries: Australia and Indonesia
Official Languages: Portuguese, Tetum
Other Principal Tongues: Bahasa, English
Ethnic Background: Indonesian-Malay & Melanesian
Principal Religion: Catholicism
Main Exports: coffee, sandalwood, marble, natural gas and oil production is being developed
Main Imports: food, gasoline, kerosene, machinery
Currency: U.S. dollar
Former Colonial Status: previously controlled by Portugal & Indonesia
National Day: Independence celebrated May 20, 2002
President: Jose Ramos-Horta (since May 20, 2007)
Prime Minister: Kay Rala Xanana Gusmao (since August 8, 2007)
GNP Per Capita GDP: $2,400(2009 estimate, purchasing power parity)

Among the newest members of the community of nations, East Timor occupies only part of one island in the vast Indonesian archipelago. The other half of the island, "West Timor" remains part of Indonesia. To understand the origins of the region's newest independent nation requires a close look at the centuries of Portuguese and then Indonesian colonial control of East Timor.

HISTORY

East Timor, is approximately the size of the American state of Maryland. Historically it included about two-dozen different linguistic communities, most of which practiced an animistic religious tradition until quite recently.

The colonial history of East Timor began with the arrival of the Portuguese in the first years of the 16th century. Those early arrivals from Europe were initially interested in the sandalwood of the area and had little impact on the lives of the inhabitants who lived largely in small villages in the interior. By the late 16th century, Dominican friars from Portugal had begun to establish themselves as did people known as "Black Portuguese," a reference to the peoples of mixed Portuguese and local ancestry from the surrounding area. Long known for the sandalwood produced there the island found itself fought over by both the Portuguese and the Dutch during the era of colonial expansion. Eventually, but not until the early 20th century, the present boundaries were established between Dutch administered west Timor, part of the larger Dutch East Indies colony, and East Timor which was controlled by the Portuguese. As with the rest of the area, the British occupied the region during the Napoleonic wars. After the defeat of the French, the Portuguese reestablished their control.

Within East Timor, the Portuguese colonizers made little effort to develop their holdings. In fact, according to one, nineteenth century visitor no roads had been developed at all beyond the settlement of Dili itself. Lisbon put very little effort into East Timor until late in the nineteenth century when they feared losing it to the other, more aggressive, European powers.

As tensions built toward the Second World War, a group of Australians landed in East Timor and prepared to resist the advancing Japanese forces. Later, as with the rest of the enormous Indonesian archipelago, the advancing Japanese army occupied East Timor. Over the following years Western forces, frequently with the help of the East Timorese, worked to sabotage the Japanese holdings. After the war the Portuguese once again reestablished their control.

A generation later, in the mid 1970s, another even more dramatic trial began for the East Timorese when Portugal's authoritarian government fell from power, replaced by a more liberal government less committed to retaining the country's colonial holdings. The new government declared its intention to allow East Timorese to decide their own future in a referendum planned for the fall of 1976.

East Timor

Indonesia's Invasion and the Cold War

The promise of independence would sadly be forestalled for a quarter of a century as developments within East Timor and the larger international Cold War intervened to alter her fate. To understand the roots of the disaster that soon befell East Timor it is important to look at the colonial history of the larger Indonesian island chain that surrounds it.

In contrast to most of Indonesia, that had been administered by the Netherlands as the Dutch East Indies, for centuries, East Timor had been a Portuguese colony. In fact, like Portuguese Goa in India or Macao, it was one small reminder of the once energetic Portuguese role in colonization.

But just as India's government had moved into Goa in the early 1960s, and as China took back Macao in December 1999, Indonesia decided to absorb East Timor in 1975. Ironically, given more recent developments, Indonesian leaders had not been particularly interested in East Timor before the mid 1970s. It was often outsiders like the Australians who had at times encouraged them to integrate East Timor into Indonesia.

Other international forces and themes played out as well. The Cold War struggle between communism and democratic capitalism influenced events in East Timor also. During the mid 1970s communism was in ascendance in Southeast Asia. From Vietnam to Cambodia left wing political forces had advanced and as we have seen elsewhere in *East, and Southeast Asia*, communists came to power in both countries during the spring of 1975.

Within East Timor its own resistance group the *Fretilin*, the main independence group, was a nationalist party with a clearly leftist orientation. From the perspective of the very anti-Communist Indonesian military and the Western Democracies, the potential rise of the leftist East Timorese independence movement to power within a free East Timor was simply unacceptable. Thus, their support for Indonesia's occupation was quite predictable.

An Era of Mass Murder

When the Indonesia invasion began in December 7, 1975, the East Timorese were more prepared to resist Jakarta than one might have imagined. As a former colony of Portugal—a member of NATO—some East Timorese had had professional military training. The departing colonial power also left weapons behind that were later used effectively against the Indonesians.

But these advantages hardly made them a match for Indonesian forces. Unlike the East Timorese, Jakarta had the military support of the United States and thus the

Saluting the flag of the new nation of East Timor

ability to impose its will upon the resisting East Timorese. In the years after 1975, despite considerable efforts at infrastructure building and impressive educational gains made by the East Timorese under control from Jakarta, many East Timorese continued to work for independence. Meanwhile, the Indonesian military maintained a very brutal control there. In fact, estimates of the numbers killed over the years either directly or indirectly as a result of the occupation are, according to a recent independent report, from 84,000 to 183,000 people.

Sadly for the people of East Timor, there was almost no international awareness of their plight from the mid 1970s through the early 1990s when word of the horror going on there began to be better publicized. Most important in that growing international awareness of the crisis in East Timor was the massacre that took place in Dili in 1991. On that occasion, hundreds of East Timorese, perhaps emboldened by the presence of members of the world press, openly defied Indonesian authorities while attempting to commemorate the recent death of an East Timorese activist.

At the cemetery, ignoring the presence of western reporters, the Indonesian military opened fire killing an estimated 70 to 200 people. Despite the horror, it also marked the beginning of a greater global awareness of events in East Timor because of the coverage it received. Thus, after a generation of suffering the East Timorese finally found a growing body of international supporters after what became known as the Santa Cruz Massacre.

Later the East Timorese nationalists got a much needed boost in 1996 when two of their most prominent members were awarded the Nobel Peace Prize for their efforts. Bishop Carlos Filipe Ximenes Belo, who continued to live in East Timor, and Jose Ramos Horta, a militant leader of the

movement in exile, shared the award which gave the struggle of East Timor much more global attention.

Asian Economic Crisis and the fall of Suharto

East Timor's fate began to change dramatically only in the years after the Asian economic crisis that saw the authoritarian government of former General Suharto finally fall from power. His successor, B.J. Habibie, perhaps seeking a dramatic gesture to respond to the long running crisis of East Timor, announced in January 1999 that the unhappy province would be allowed to have a referendum on staying within Indonesia. The decision, while greeted enthusiastically by most East Timorese was seen as a disaster by many Indonesian immigrants to East Timor and the Indonesian army that had fought to retain the area. Indonesian attitudes were not surprising. Not only had many Indonesians in the military served in East Timor. Many were heavily invested in the region's economy. There was also a reasonable and understandable fear that East Timor's freedom might provoke the many other restless parts of Indonesia to secede.

The Referendum

The months leading up to the August 1999 referendum were both a time of crisis and excitement for the East Timorese. On one hand international observers arrived to supervise their long awaited opportunity to vote on ending their relationship with Indonesia. On the other hand, local militia, supported and supplied by the Indonesia military, violently attacked those supportive of independence and threatened a blood bath if the vote resulted in a choice to leave.

152

President Jose Ramos-Horta

The actual referendum went fairly calmly. However, as soon as it became clear that the East Timorese had voted against autonomy within Indonesia and more specifically for independence, an explosion of violence racked East Timor. Pro-Jakarta militias clearly backed by elements of the Indonesian military went on a rampage that saw perhaps 1,500 people slaughtered. Thousands more fled to West Timor, where they ended up in refugee camps often still harassed by the pro-Jakarta militias that opposed East Timor's independence.

Eventually, as the outrage grew and public awareness of the crisis expanded, the Australians agreed to lead an international force, which included troops from Thailand, Singapore, Malaysia, and the Philippines to East Timor to help restore order. Even China sent members of her security forces to work in East Timor. In the following months the United Nations established itself in East Timor and administered it with funds provided by nations ranging from Norway and Sweden to the Netherlands and Portugal.

After most of the violence ended, thousands of East Timorese returned home from refugee camps in West Timor even though reports of continued harassment and persecution of those still in West Timor are common. It is also clear that the militias have not only made it very difficult for the refugees to return to East Timor. They have also murdered foreign peacekeepers. Those refugees who have returned went home to a devastated land.

FROM UN CONTROL
TO A FREE EAST TIMOR

Meanwhile the East Timorese under their most popular leaders from Xanana Gusmao to Bishop Bello built the rudiments of a future government that would administer East Timor when the United Nations forces known as UNAMET pulled out. In the period after the departure of the Indonesian troops East Timor did not experience its long anticipated calm. There was considerable tension between the UNAMET administration of East Timor and local leaders who have vehemently complained of being ignored by the United Nations professionals. East Timorese leaders have also accused the aid agencies of underpaying their own workers and being more interested in earning money than delivering aid. Some East Timorese have also been upset with the number of outsiders the United Nations authorities hired to administer programs there.

By the time the United Nations officially turned power over to the incoming East Timor administration an enormous amount had been accomplished during its 32-month tenure. Large numbers of building had been rebuilt and many businesses reopened. Thousands of new civil servants were hired and trained to administer the new country. While a new central bank, a new public television station and customs service was established. Moreover, hundreds of schools were repaired and teachers hired. There was still much to do, but considering the state East Timor had been after the initial and devastating Indonesian departure, it was all quite impressive.

FORMING A GOVERNMENT

In late August of 2001 East Timorese went to the polls again in the on-going effort to build a new political future. At stake was the election of an 88-person assembly that was being chosen to write a constitution for the new government and to set a more specific timetable for the nation to emerge beyond the controls of the UN. Over 425,000 voters were involved and a wide range of parties offered themselves up for the voter's choice.

Not surprisingly, once the votes were counted *Fretilin*, now led by Mari Alkatiri, won 55 of the possible 88 seats. This win allowed Alkatiri to become the prime minister. *Fretilin*'s count might have been even higher if tensions had not developed between the national liberation party and its former leader Xanana Gusmao. He decided to campaign for the more minor parties based on the argument that it was important that no one party dominate East Timor's immediate future.

Xanana Gusmao's behavior was unusual in other ways as well. Unlike so many independence leaders who have anxiously awaited the opportunity to finally lead their nations, Gusmao appeared to be a very reluctant leader. In fact, he initially seemed quite reluctant to stand for election at all. Nevertheless, once committed Gusmao went on to win the April of 2002 presidential contest easily.

Most dramatically, East Timor's real day of reckoning occurred on May 20, 2002, when it celebrated its official independence. While its resources were limited, there was no shortage of hope. Certainly, that seemed apparent during the spring of 2002 when thousands of East Timorese refugees began returning home in anticipation of beginning life anew under their new government.

While East Timor had finally gained its independence, enormous problems still faced the society. Unemployment was very common, and there was considerable concern about the upsurge in criminal violence. More significant politically was

East Timor Coastline

Photo by Marc Cassidy

East Timor

the rising anger against the new government's inability to deal effectively with the nation's many problems. That frustration became abundantly obvious at the end of 2002 when angry crowds burned down not only Prime Minister Alkatiri's home, but those of his relatives and several Western businesses.

Perhaps most discouraging was that the local security situation forced the decision, during the late spring of 2004, to ask that the United Nations put off the departure of its security forces, originally scheduled for May 2004, for another year. That request was granted. By the spring of 2005 the last of the United Nations 450 peace keeping forces—of a contingent that had once numbered around 11,000 people—departed, leaving only a group of around 150 civilian administrators and security advisors. But that has hardly calmed matters completely. By the spring of 2006 East Timor's internal problems had once again made the international news as members of the security forces went on strike. Their eventual dismissal by the government then set off a series of riots that initially culminated in the prime minister's resignation.

Over the last few years a new alignment of political power had been forming in East Timor. The internationally famous Nobel Prize winner, Jose Ramos-Horta, replaced Alkatiri as prime minister and then subsequently won an election to replace outgoing President Xanana Gusmao. As for the former president and leader of East Timor's national struggle for freedom, by mid-summer 2007 he was campaigning to become prime minister, a position that in East Timor holds more executive power than that of the president.

Unfortunately, when the election took place, the results only created more tension. Fretilin, the former national resistance party that led the national resistance struggle and dominated politics in the years since nationhood, won the elections. But the final numbers did not give them enough of a parliamentary majority to create a government.

Over the next several months Fretilin was unable to reestablish a working coalition. Eventually Xanana Gusmao, with the support of his political ally Jose Ramos-Horta, formed a governing coalition with his own newly formed party and two other allied parties. From the perspective of Xianana Gusmao's previous allies in Fretlin, that was completely unacceptable. The formation of the new government, with Gusmao as prime minister, set off yet another round of riots.

But riots were the least of the new leadership team's problems. In February 2008 a rebel army commander attempted to assassinate both Prime Minister Gusmao and President Ramos-Horta. Luckily, for

Former President and current Prime Minister Jose Xanana Gusmao

the long-time resistance leader, Gusmao managed to avoid injury. But President Ramos-Horta was critically wounded and flown to Australia for treatment. After a very dramatic recovery effort, the nation's president was eventually able to return home having barely survived the ordeal.

DEFENSE AND FOREIGN RELATIONS

Aside from the United Nations and the international donor community the new nation's most significant foreign relations are with Indonesia and Australia. With Indonesia, the most important issue is that Indonesia's government will not make life more for complicated for East Timor by supporting those who retain desires to undermine the new nation. Happily, though progress has been on the relationship between the two countries as both civilian legislators and military officers from the two countries have met recently to improve cooperation.

Relations with Australia are equally important but for quite different reasons. From Australia is expected to come tourist dollars and lucrative investments that could help East Timor make some headway in building a new and stable community. And Australia has been committed to that relationship. Not only have the Australians supported the call for the United Nations to extend their stay in East Timor they are working with the government of Mozambique to help train East Timorese policemen. Perhaps more dramatically Australia's Prime Minister, Kevin Rudd, a former diplomat himself, has made it absolutely clear that his government will do everything it can to help maintain stability in East Timor.

Beyond relations with their more immediate neighbors, East Timor's leaders also successfully guided their nation into becoming the 25th and newest member of the regional organization, ASEAN. Setting their sights even further, then prime minister of East Timor, Mari Alkatiri, also traveled to Beijing to meet China's leaders with the hope of expanding relations with the People's Republic.

SOCIETY

Like their neighbors in Indonesia most of the peoples of East Timor are of Indonesian-Malay stock while within the mountainous regions live peoples of Melanesian ethnicity. In contrast with their neighbors though, Catholicism rather than Islam is particularly widespread and in fact grew significantly during the years of Indonesian control. Animism, Protestantism and Islam are present. Although Muslims constitute only about 5% of the population, East Timor's first prime minister was a Muslim.

The vast majority of East Timorese work in subsistence-level agriculture in the countryside. While agriculture has recovered from the devastation brought about during the Indonesian withdrawal, much of the rest of the society remains deeply impacted by those events. Most people speak either Indonesian or Tetum. The language of the former colonial power, Portuguese, is still spoken by the older generation. The effort to make it the official language has caused considerable tension among the many people who do not know it.

As we have seen, the struggle produced thousands of refugees and the separation of many families, including children separated from their parents into various camps in West Timor. Over the last several years many of those families have attempted to make their way back to East Timor again. Jose Xanana Gusmao has been especially involved in encouraging them to return. The fact that the country has one of the lowest per capita crime rates in the world probably helps.

The strong sense of family in East Timor has also had an impact on how it has sometimes been perceived on the broader world stage. Responding to both its strong Catholic heritage and to unpopular family planning efforts carried out by its former Indonesian occupiers, the people of East Timor have often been displeased with international calls discouraging them from criminalizing abortion. But those calls have been largely ignored as East Timor prepared its new legal code. Moreover practices from contraception to efforts to enhance the rights of women have often been frowned upon by the citizens of this society, which in many ways is still quite traditional.

Political rally for East Timor

ECONOMY

The most obvious reality is that East Timor's economy is in a disastrous way. Not only was it largely undeveloped before the violence of recent years, but it also has important work to do to set up a legal system that will attract outside investors. The most basic issues are on the table from laws on buying and selling goods to the question of whether foreign firms will be able to buy land. Making progress is incredibly important as the urban areas are said to have an unemployment rate of around 80%. Of course, refugees, who need employment, have returned home in large numbers.

News of the recent riots and the well known United Nation's concern about the new country's general level of security will not make it easier to attract outside money. But things are not all bad. Outside donors have promised some $360 million over the next few years. Such foreign aid is not always as impressive as it might sound when one only considers the raw figures. An outside monitoring agency reported in 2010 that relatively little of the approximately eight billion dollars that had been donated to East Timor in the years since independence had ended up in the local economy. Most of it was spent for the salaries of foreign administrators, imports and administration.

The new nation has also developed an important revenue stream through monies earned from natural gas and oil from the Timor Gap. Unfortunately, working out that oil and gas deal with Australia was quite difficult. The government refused to ratify a proposed treaty that would have given East Timor only 18% of the potential oil revenues while Australia was to have received 82%. The core problem was just where the proposed line between the two nations was to be officially demarcated. Dili insisted that the line lie at the midpoint between the two nations rather than where it had been designated in 1975. Given the extraordinary financial needs of the East Timor government, it was not surprising that Dili continued to insist that the final arrangements maximize their small nation's future oil income. Eventually a compromise was worked out for the two nations to share the potential financial gains while they put off further discussion of the territorial borders between the two nations for fifty years. The agreement could not have come at a better time. East Timor's population remains very poor. Life expectancy is in the mid-50s, twenty percent of the urban work force is unemployed, and a fifth of the nation still lives on less than a dollar a day.

The government also has ambitious plans to turn East Timor into a free-trade port and tax haven, which should help as well although there is some concern that East Timor might find itself involved in international money laundering that could cause significant problems.

THE FUTURE

It will not be easy for East Timor to establish itself as an economically viable nation. Still it does have some obvious advantages. The international community is concerned about its fate, and countries from Australia to Portugal are committed to helping out. For example, the United States recently offered $25 million to help strengthen the nation's democratic infrastructure. East Timor has also become involved with the larger Portuguese speaking community. Its prime minister, the former president, Xanana Gusmao, visited Angola, another former Portuguese colony, in an effort to expand cooperative efforts.

Significant money, reportedly around $5 billion, has already begun to flow in from East Timor's energy resources. Such revenues can be absolutely vital to a nation's future. But merely having the money is not enough. It is vitally important that the money be spent well, not only in building up the nation's current infrastructure, but in holding funds aside for the benefit of future generations.

Unfortunately, the political crisis and attempted assassinations that captured international headlines in 2008 will hardly attract the foreign investment that East Timor's growth requires. However, there are some signs of better days. It is in the process of becoming a formal member of the Association of Southeast Asian Nations. It also had the chance to highlight its recovery from the violence that attracted international attention in 2008 by sponsoring an international bicycle tour in 2009.

Considering that it has only been ten years since the nation emerged from Indonesian repression, the country seems reasonably on track despite the 2008 political crisis. As mentioned above, the fact that it could boast of an especially low per capita crime rate was something about which to be satisfied. The fact that it has maintained a relatively healthy growth rate in the seven to eight percentage range is also impressive considering how many other countries around the world moved into negative numbers after 2008's economic free fall.

Portuguese caravels enroute to Asia and East Timor

The Republic of Indonesia

At the Mall in Bandung, Indonesia

Photo by Steven Leibo

Area: 741,040 sq. mi. (1,906,240 sq. km., covering an expanse equal to the width of the U.S. coast-to-coast)

Population: 234,693,997 (July 2007 estimate)

Capital City: Jakarta (Pop. 8,792,000. 2004 estimate) Jakarta is actually administered as a province

Climate: Tropical, with a monsoon season from November to March

Neighboring Countries: Malaysia and the Philippine Republic (North); Australia (South); Papua New Guinea (East)

Official Language: Bahasa Indonesia (a formal version of the Malay language)

Other Principal Tongues: Malay, Common Malay (a dialect), and about 250 other Malayo-Polynesian languages and dialects, such as Sundanese and Madurese, Japanese, Dutch, Chinese

Ethnic Background: Javanese 45%, Sundanese 14%, Madurese 7.5%, coastal Malays 7.5%, other 26%

Principal Religion: Overwhelmingly Muslim, with small groups of Christians, Hindus and Buddhists

Main Exports (to Japan, Singapore, South Korea, China, Germany, Malaysia: Petroleum, liquefied natural gas, carpets, fruits, nuts and coffee, plywood, textiles, rubber, electrical appliances

Main Imports (From U.S., Singapore, Japan, China, Thailand, Saudi Arabia: Aircraft and equipment, cotton textile fibers, engines, civil engineering equipment, pulp, chemicals, foodstuffs, fuel

Currency: Rupiah

Former Colonial Status: Dutch Colony from about 1625 to 1949.

Independence Day: December 27, 1949 (August 17th, the anniversary of the 1945 date when revolutionaries proclaimed the Republic of Indonesia.)

Chief of State: Susilo Bambang Yudhoyono, President (since September, 2004)

National Flag: Two horizontal bands; the top is maroon and the bottom is white

Per Capita GDP Annual Income: $3,900 (2008 est. purchasing power parity)

Stretched along the Equator between Australia and the Asian mainland for a distance horizontally of about 3,000 miles, Indonesia consists of some 13,000 individual islands. The actual number seems to change frequently as improved visual technology reveals more islands even as rising waters submerges others. The largest are Sumatra and Java. Kalimantan occupies the southern portion of the Island of Borneo, and Irian Jaya is the western portion of the island of New Guinea. About one-fourth of the land is covered with inland waters.

If Indonesia did not have a great variation in elevation, its climate would be uniformly oppressive because of its equatorial location. The heat and humidity of the coastal areas give way to more moderate temperatures as the altitude rises to breathtaking heights. Although Irian Jaya is predominantly low and swampy, as is Kalimantan, there are mountains that are snow-covered throughout the year on New Guinea.

This is an area of volcanic peaks—some dormant and some active—that have enriched the soil greatly during their centuries of destructively explosive activity. Krakatoa, located on a tiny island between Java and Sumatra, exploded with such force in 1883 that it produced a tidal wave that was felt around the world and that inundated parts of nearby seacoasts. In other areas of the world, torrential rainfall such as occurs during the monsoon season is the enemy that washes valuable topsoil to the sea, exposing infertile land to the sun. In Java, the downpours are welcome. They wash away old soil and expose even richer volcanic ash and dirt which is fertile almost beyond belief.

The wildlife of Indonesia is more interesting and varied than in almost any other country of the world. The Komodo dragon, ten feet long and a remnant of prehistoric times, inhabits the island of Komodo east of Java. The Javanese rhinoceros makes increasingly rare appearances in the Udjung Kulon ("western tip") preserve on the end of Java, where successive governments have tried to maintain the natural setting of plants and animals. The gibbon, most agile among the primates, swings overhead in the tall trees that provide thick shade for the banteng, a native ox with white legs that resembles an ordinary dairy cow. Although crowded by a multitude of species adapted to its character, this area, as well as most of the interior of the Indonesian islands, is extremely inhospitable to modern man.

History

Fossils and other prehistoric remnants of human skeletons indicate that Indonesia was one of the earlier areas of the world to be inhabited by humans. The present population of the area acquired its somewhat uniform appearance about the second millennium B.C., a time when there was gradual intermarriage and mixture between native Polynesians and people from the Asian mainland. This combination, relatively stable since that time, is now referred to as Malayo-Polynesian.

Early Indonesian history is best seen as a regional history of diverse communities rather than as a unified early state directly tied through time to modern Indonesia. In fact many different communities existed though there were several commonalities among them, especially the presence of Hinduism and Buddhism, and their role in early international trade.

The arrival of Indian cultural, religious and commercial influences around the 1st century A.D. greatly influenced the people. Eventually Hinduism and Buddhism mingled with the ancient animist background of the Indonesians and produced an extremely complex, varied and unique culture, especially on Java and nearby Bali. The advances brought by the Indians

and the availability of good harbors in the Malacca and Sunda Straits were the basis for the rise of two powerful commercial and naval empires at the beginning of the 7th century, A.D. Srivijaya was based on the island of Sumatra; Sailendra arose on neighboring Java. The empires thrived on a lively trade centered on the production of spices treasured throughout the rest of the world, though available only here. Especially important was the islands' control of the trade routes between India and China and, in Srivijaya's case, its ties to imperial China. Taxes were imposed on passing ships based on the number of passengers and the cargo carried.

If Hinduism and Buddhism were prevalent in the early traditions of these island kingdoms, their modern heritage lies elsewhere. Indian merchants also brought Islam to the islands at the beginning of the 11th century, but it did not have much influence at first. The development of the Indonesian empires was briefly disrupted in the 13th century by a naval expedition sent by the powerful Mongol emperor of China, Khubilai Khan. Shortly afterward, a new empire, known as Majapahit, became dominant, and seized control of the valuable spice trade. Majapahit was the last major Indonesian kingdom headed by a Hindu.

After their departure from the scene, Islam became more and more common. It had long been spreading, and by the end of the 16th century the vast majority of the people had become Muslims. In a sense the early South Asian influence continued, but now in its Islamic, rather than Hindu

form. Today only Bali, the famous tourist destination within Indonesia, remains deeply committed to its traditional Hindu heritage.

The Colonial Period

Though Europeans had longed for the spices of the East for centuries (European spices were limited to salt, garlic and vinegar), the profits from those valuable commodities were largely in the hands of Muslim middlemen during the pre-modern era. What the Europeans wanted was to gain access to those profits. This explains the push in the 15th century to find new trade routes to the East. These images of fantastic wealth to be earned in the spice trade first brought Europeans to the East Indies, or Dutch East Indies as the islands were later called. The spices were, and even now are, grown principally in the Moluccas (Spice Islands) and on Java.

There was a keen interest in the area on the part of Portugal and Great Britain, but it was the Dutch who were ultimately successful in dominating Indonesia, controlling the area through a commercial organization, the Dutch East India Company. By then the Majapahit Empire was already in decline leaving the island of Java as a relatively easy conquest. It was quickly identified as the most strategic and fertile of the islands and one that could produce coffee, indigo and some spices. The local leaders were either militarily defeated or intimidated by the Dutch, who compelled them to deliver produce to the Company.

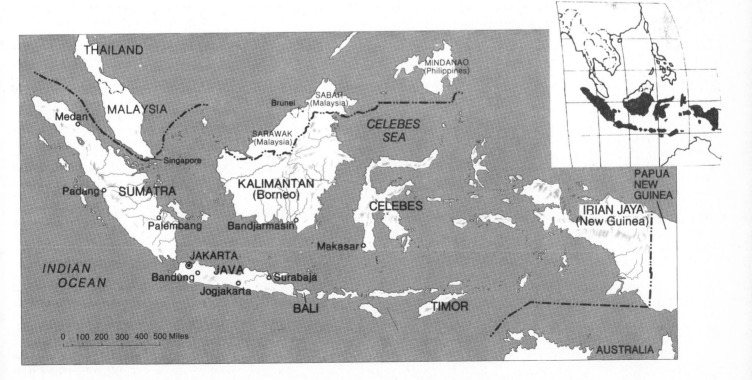

Indonesia

The colonial experience of the East Indies, as Indonesia was then known, was much the same as in other parts of the colonized world: centered on the process of extracting wealth from the colony. As was so common during colonialism, this was often carried out without any concern for the welfare of the indigenous peoples. Thus for example, in an effort to drive up prices, the Dutch destroyed some island communities' ability to produce spices, devastating their economies and people in the process.

With the wealth gained, Holland emerged as one of the most powerful European countries of the early modern period and one that supported an impressive navy. But as would be the case in the 20th century their control over the East Indies was temporarily interrupted in the nineteenth century due to developments back in Europe.

The Napoleonic Wars resulted in a brief period of British occupation of Java from 1811 to 1816. But once the Napoleonic war was over the Dutch were able to reestablish their control partly because the British, wanting to maintain a balance of power on the European continent, knew that Holland would need Indonesian wealth to contribute to European stability. It would not be the last time the states of Southeast Asia were sacrificed to the needs of internal European politics.

By then the East Indies had passed from administration by the Dutch East Indies Company to that of the Dutch crown. However, direct crown control proved difficult as it undertook administrative and judicial changes that challenged the power of the Javanese aristocratic class and provoked a war in the 1820s. The Dutch won but only after great loss of life. An especially exploitative economic system known as the *Cultivation System* was introduced. It was designed to gain maximum economic advantage for Holland from their control over the islands. This system added further to the hardships of the native Indonesians.

Eventually, in the last part of the 19th century there was a return to free economic development based on private investment. During this era there was considerable Western investment and the introduction of railroads. Large amounts of new land were put under cultivation. Indonesia emerged as the world's largest producer of tin and rubber. The islands became so associated with the production of products such as coffee that the term "java" became synonymous with the drink itself.

By the late nineteenth century, feelings against Dutch control were growing in both Indonesia and the Netherlands itself. Responding to these new sentiments, the colonial government adopted the "Ethical Policy," under which strenuous efforts

Farming in Indonesia

were made to promote the welfare of the Indonesians through public works and health measures. The government even announced that it would no longer take any surplus revenues generated by Indonesia and canceled the colony's debts.

Direct control over the East Indies grew during the early twentieth century even as new transportation methods allowed the Dutch themselves to become increasingly more remote from Indonesian society. They could, after all, send their children to schools in Europe and develop their own society more distant from that of the Indonesians they ruled. The phenomenon was a common one throughout much of the colonial world.

Local education was neglected and little serious effort toward preparation for self-government occurred despite the more general calls in the post World War I era for national self-determination. There was thus a rapid growth of both nationalism and communism in the interwar period in spite of increasingly harsh Dutch police measures.

World War II

When the Pacific War began in December 1941 Indonesia was, due to its great natural wealth, a prime target for the Japanese offensive in Southeast Asia. Weakly defended by a Dutch government-in-exile that had been driven from its own European homeland by the Germans, the islands rapidly came under Japanese control in early 1942.

As was the case elsewhere, many Indonesians warmly greeted the Japanese and sincerely believed their claims that they had come to free Asia from Western colonialism. Many Indonesians, either for convenience or commitment, made the decision to work with the Japanese. Sukarno,

the long term Indonesian nationalist, was among those who decided to use the occupation as a tool to help realize Indonesia's goal of national freedom. Eventually, he even managed to convince the Japanese authorities to help arm and train Indonesians in the struggle against the West.

The initial enthusiasm not withstanding, the Japanese administration soon convinced many Indonesians, as was to occur elsewhere in Asia, that they were hardly liberators, but merely new conquerors come to exploit the resources of Indonesia as the Dutch had before them. If the Japanese hoped to build a new colonial base in Indonesia, their real impact was rather in fundamentally destroying the old colonial mentality rather than building a new one.

Moreover, although they were foreign conquerors, the Japanese not only destroyed the prestige of the Dutch in the eyes of the Indonesians. They gave the latter valuable experience in political activity and public administration.

A New Nation

As soon as the war was over, Sukarno and fellow nationalist leader Mohammed Hatta immediately proclaimed the independent Republic of Indonesia. This move had widespread support of other leaders and among the population of the outlying islands. It paralleled similar anti-colonialist developments elsewhere such as those of Ho Chi Minh in Vietnam. But declaring independence and actually winning it were not the same thing.

British forces soon arrived and used their power to help the Dutch reestablish themselves, though not before a massive public outbreak of anti-Dutch feelings and considerable violence. For the moment, the Dutch would be able to reestablish themselves, but over the next four years a

Richard M. Nixon (right) meets with Indonesia's leader Sukarno
Courtesy of Special Collections, University of Virginia Library

major independence struggle took place, which eventually saw the Dutch withdraw. A settlement was reached at the end of 1949. It recognized the independence of Indonesia, which was supposed to be linked to the Netherlands through the Dutch Crown. West Irian, part of the island of New Guinea, was not included in the agreement. Dutch-owned industry and investment were to remain intact.

The new Republic of Indonesia, based on Java, promptly abolished the federal system created by the Dutch administration and established a unitary republic that later cut all ties with the Netherlands. Over the first several years, it would operate as a parliamentary democracy with the charismatic Sukarno at its head.

The Indonesians faced independence under almost insurmountable difficulties. There were geographic and cultural differences, poor communications between the islands, and the dominant power of the Javanese, resented in the other islands—referred to as "Outer Islands." The political turmoil left by the years of Japanese occupation followed by battle against the Dutch, and the primitive state of economic and political development, were adverse influences. In addition to these liabilities, there was the leadership role of Sukarno himself.

The Sukarno Years

Flamboyant, popular, unpredictable, self-indulgent, articulate, dictatorial and lovable are all adjectives that have been used to describe Sukarno. During the years of his control he moved Indonesia from a parliamentary system to a more authoritarian one called "Guided Democracy." Denouncing Western democratic traditions, he practiced a political leadership that stressed Indonesian nationalism

above regionalism and non-alignment in the Cold War between Washington and Moscow. Although not a communist, he frequently worked closely with the *PKI*, the *Indonesian Communist Party*. The U.S., alarmed by this, arranged a tryst for Sukarno with a beautiful woman at his hotel in New York while he was appearing at the UN. Cameras recorded the whole event in detail. When confronted with it, accompanied by threats of being disgraced, he was delighted. He asked for a copy to play publicly in Indonesia to visually demonstrate his sexual prowess.

Politics in those years became a complicated mixture of *PKI* communists led by the young and energetic Aidit, the army and Sukarno. The charismatic Sukarno was usually able to command the support of both the communists and the army. But his economic policies weakened the country. Promises had been given to leave foreign investment intact, but these were not kept. Dutch assets were seized in 1957. Some Chinese investment was nationalized in the following years. Most American assets were confiscated in 1963–1964.

Supported by Soviet diplomacy, Sukarno, in 1962, threatened West Irian, today known as Irian Jaya, with a substantial Soviet equipped military force. Under American pressure and mediation, the Dutch finally surrendered the western portion of New Guinea that they had until then continued to hold.

Sukarno then turned his attention toward Malaysia, which had been created by the British when they united Malaya, Singapore and North Borneo (Sabah and Sarawak) into a single, independent nation in 1963. In contrast to the Dutch in West Irian, the British were willing to fight to protect Malaysia.

The confrontation with Malaysia, launched in 1963 by Sukarno, led the *PKI*,

which already had achieved considerable power, to demand the arming of communist-led "workers and peasants." That demand was resisted by the army, but endorsed by China and given an increasingly enthusiastic reception by Sukarno in 1965.

The events that followed remain unclear to this day although their impact transformed the country. What we do know is that a group of dissident military officers plotted to overthrow their more senior commanders. The exact relationship between the *PKI*, Sukarno, and the plotters remains uncertain. However, the results are not.

As dramatized in the film, "A Year of Living Dangerously," events moved quickly during the fall of 1965. The coup attempt failed, and the army, now under the leadership of General Suharto, emerged in power. Suharto then crushed the rebellion. Resentment against the *PKI*, which had been smoldering in the islands for years, erupted into a massive slaughter of hundreds of thousands of people suspected of being communists or their sympathizers. While the army itself was directly involved, a large percentage of the deaths seem to have actually been carried out by civilians with the military's encouragement. The total number killed remains unclear. The *PKI* was almost annihilated and was outlawed as a political party. The army soon stripped Sukarno of all power. He died in 1970.

Former President Suharto

Indonesia

Suharto

If Sukarno had led an authoritarian government with leftist-leaning nationalist sentiments, Suharto would now offer his own version of authoritarianism but one that was more open to the West and based on the military. Ideologically it had been built around the idea of *Pancasila*. This state ideology incorporated the five principles of nationalism, democracy, internationalism, social justice, and belief in one God. All political parties were required to accept them, and the armed forces had been given a legitimate role in the political process through the official government party, *GOLKAR*.

After the 1965 coup, the appointed *Provisional People's Consultative Congress (MPRS)* was purged of pro-communist elements. Later in March 1967 it proclaimed Suharto president for five years.

Having achieved effective control of Indonesia, Suharto and the army ended the confrontation with Malaysia and began to tackle Indonesia's massive economic problems. Steps were taken to rejoin the UN, from which Sukarno's government had withdrawn in 1965. An interest was shown in resuming normal economic relations with the non-communist world, including the Netherlands and the United States.

Communist China, in contrast, denounced the new military regime as a gang of fascists, particularly after the extensive anti-Chinese violence following the military seizure of power. The Soviet Union had more mixed feelings; it did not wish for communists to be slaughtered, but since the *PKI* had adopted the Chinese side of the disputes in international communism, the Soviets undoubtedly were

gratified by the example of its failure—an example to other communist movements of the world which had sided with Beijing.

Unlike his rejection of Sukarno's anti-Malaysian foreign policy, Suharto's regime continued the latter's interest in West Irian. When the Dutch withdrew from West Irian in 1962, the UN promised that a popular vote would be taken to determine the will of the people. The alternatives were independence or union with Indonesia. However, Indonesian military officers present in West Irian in 1969 rigged a unanimous vote for union with Indonesia. Thus the region, known today as Irian Jaya, came to be part of Indonesia though even through the 1990s problems of anti-Jakarta regionalism have continued.

After the failure of the 1965 coup in Indonesia and the end of the confrontation with Malaysia, Indonesia joined with Malaysia, Singapore, Thailand and the Philippines to form the Association of Southeast Asian Nations (ASEAN). Brunei joined in 1984. The original purpose of this organization was to help stabilize regional power, develop the area economically and support the American struggle in Vietnam.

Its main visible functions were to maintain easy access for its members' raw materials to the markets of the developed countries, and to cooperate to a limited extent against communist insurgency. After the Vietnamese invasion of Cambodia at the end of 1978, ASEAN, with Thailand as the "frontline" state, began to play an important role in trying to negotiate an end to the struggle on terms that would include a Vietnamese military withdrawal.

It was announced in late 1969 that general elections would be held in mid 1971 in Indonesia. The result was an over-

whelming victory for the government party, the Sekber *GOLKAR*, a federation of about 260 trade, professional and regional groups which enjoyed an overwhelming advantage over the other legal parties.

Widespread discontent over the lack of political freedom and social justice erupted in serious riots in early 1974. Most of the anger was nurtured by inflation, commodity shortages and was mainly aimed against the government. Other elements included dissatisfaction with the growing economic influence of Japan, and the commercial influence of local Indonesian Chinese whose preeminent role in the economy has often led to outbursts of anti-Chinese sentiment.

In the wake of the riots, President Suharto made some changes, but government corruption, food shortages, a weak educational system, tensions between the Indonesian majority and the important Chinese minority continued to plague the country.

Nevertheless, in Indonesia's third general election in 1977, *GOLKAR* won 230 out of 360 seats in the House of Representatives. A few years later, in 1982, *GOLKAR* was again predictably victorious. Overall the system allowed for the appearance of a more democratic system while maintaining military domination.

Despite the authoritarian and military nature of the regime, Suharto's generation-long control over the country was economically successful for most of his tenure in power. In fact, the government specifically defended the lack of political progress made over the years precisely on the grounds of economic development. And those boasts were not without merit. Very real social and economic progress was made in Indonesia during the last quarter of the 20th century. The Suharto government, despite its many faults dramatically improved the educational level of the Indonesian people. Real wages went up as social conditions improved markedly. Per capita GDP had, for example, risen more than 4% annually for the first twenty years after 1965. After 1988 the figure for the last decade of Suharto's control was closer to 7%—impressive figures indeed.

These changes occurred in part because Suharto's regime was committed to integrating Indonesia into the world economy. During these important years Indonesia was able to successfully offer its services as an assembly area for products produced in the dynamic Asian economies of its neighbors from South Korea and Taiwan to Singapore and Hong Kong. Indonesia had long had the advantage of having considerable oil, gas and timber reserves. Now these additional efforts at diversifying the economy were quite effective and improved the lives of Indonesians a great deal.

Children at play in a poorer part of Jakarta ...

Still, Suharto's rather heavy-handed rule had naturally aroused opposition. There were two small legal opposition parties: the *Indonesian Democratic Party* and the *United Development Party* (the latter is Moslem-based). Interestingly those parties were not even officially allowed to call themselves "opposition" parties nor were they in a position to seriously challenge *GOLKAR* and the military due to the latter's overwhelming political and financial advantages.

Administratively, the general trend from the 1960s was toward a greater centralization of authority at the national level in Jakarta. But, perhaps under the impact of democratic developments in the Philippines and South Korea, there was, during Suharto's last decade in power some liberalization of the authoritarian political system. One form this trend took was a lessening of some central control—at least in the politically less sensitive areas of fiscal and technological authority. Another form was the revival of unofficial, as well as official, interest in the personality and career of the late President Sukarno, a development that has played a role in the recent prominence of his daughter.

One feature of the tensions that became more evident in recent years was anger at the ability of well-connected individuals and groups to dominate the economy. This was hardly new. Both the Dutch colonial system as well as that employed during the years of Japanese occupation and under Sukarno had seen the economy tightly controlled by those with special advantages. But in recent years expectations had changed, and these long-established economic controls were no longer acceptable.

The longtime domination of Suharto's family and friends in the Indonesian economy particularly aroused concerns that their activities were actually stifling the economy. These concerns were so significant that they, at times, even provoked challenges to Suharto from within the ranks of the usually supportive Indonesia military. Most of these tensions however remained fairly subtle till the crisis of 1998.

Suharto's government also kept the pressure on the media. In 1994 it arrested three members of the Alliance of Independent Journalists for slandering the government through their publication *Independent*. The government even set up an Association of Indonesian Journalists that all reporters were required to join. But things have not always gone as smoothly as the government wanted. In fact, Suharto's regime was already looking vulnerable even before the 1998 crash.

The Fall of Suharto

After the blood bath of 1965, Indonesian politics remained reasonably calm until

Morning exercises in Jakarta

Photo by Steven Leibo

the economic turmoil that developed in late 1997. The military and its partner, *GOLKAR*, allowed the impression of political harmony while maintaining a tight grip on political power. Nevertheless, even before the economic meltdown of the region during late 1997 and early 1998 Suharto's grip was being challenged.

The military's long term domination of the country, the growing disparity between rich and poor, the economic domination of Suharto's family and more general frustrations with pervasive levels of corruption all played a role in the developing tensions. But the more immediate cause was the entrance into Indonesian politics of the daughter of Indonesian nationalist hero Sukarno.

Until 1987, Megawati Sukarnoputri, the former president's daughter was not involved in politics. Only in the late 1980s was she elected to parliament. Somewhat later, in 1993, she emerged as the leader of the Indonesian Democratic Party, one of the two parties the government allowed to exist. But while many had dismissed the college-educated former housewife, President Suharto did not. He moved to weaken the political base of this cautious leader who carries with her the legacy of a powerful name in Indonesia's national memory.

Not content to harass her, Suharto's government engineered her ouster as leader of the *PDI* by pro-government supporters within the party. No doubt the hope had been to remove Megawati's official base but doing so appeared to backfire when, in the summer of 1996, government backed hoodlums attempted to force her supporters from the *PDI* headquarters. Rather than go quietly, her supporters quickly gathered and a confrontation

ensured which eventually saw several deaths and hundreds wounded.

The government's strong-arm tactics had done no more than solidify her leadership before her followers and raise the international prestige of her movement. By late fall she was being coupled in the public mind with other Southeast Asian women who have challenged dictatorial governments. These women ranged from Corazon Aquino of the Philippines to Aung San Suu Kyi of Burma. In late 1997, as the economic meltdown began to hit throughout the country, Megawati Sukarnoputri even announced she was ready to replace the president when his term ended in March 1998.

Her offer was not taken up. Rather, the government's political arm, *Golkar*, backed by the army, proceeded to reelect the 77-year-old president once again. Far more significant for the nation's future, Suharto chose Research and Technology Minister B.J. Habibie as his vice-president and presumably his successor.

Habibie, a 61 year-old engineer, had the confidence of the president and the technical background Suharto was said to have been looking for. Unfortunately, his reputation among the international financial community was not very positive. He was seen as a volatile leader and an economic nationalist too infatuated with unrealistic showcase style industrial goals. Nor did the ever-influential army have any affection for him. Suharto favored him and that was enough. By March 1998, newly elected President Suharto and his new vice-president were in place. But by then Indonesian politics were starting to move far beyond Suharto's control.

By mid-May 1998 the loss of confidence in Suharto's regime had become simply

Indonesia

too great. Initially aroused by the rising prices of basic commodities, as mandated by the IMF's recovery program, Jakarta and other cities saw demonstrations by at first students and then others against the regime. After more than a quarter of a century in power, Suharto had lost the confidence of more than just the younger and poorer members of society. By late May, even his most trusted loyalists and many of the country's leading political, intellectual and religious leaders had withdrawn their support. After one bloody clash between the students and the army, many even within the army leadership itself, were apparently ready to abandon Suharto and more importantly to help the country make the transition toward new leadership. With encouragement of General Wiranto, the Chief of the Indonesia Armed Forces, President Suharto finally resigned on the 21st of May and allowed his newly chosen vice-president Habibie to assume office.

We still have much to learn about the details of Suharto's fall, but it appears that members of the Indonesian military, most notably those led by Suharto's son-in-law, were probably working to bring about a situation which would have allowed the military to suppress the demonstrations and retain its influence. General Wiranto, the Minister of Defense and Security apparently had other ideas and threw his weight behind those hoping for a more peaceful resolution of the crisis, including the newly installed president.

Indonesia Enters a New Era

The 76-year-old Suharto had stepped down after 32 years in power. But the Indonesian establishment, military, political and financial was still largely in place. The new president, Habibie, had no popular mandate or even strong support among the military to help him lead. Unfortunately for the new president, nor was he able in the months following the fall of Suharto to develop such a following. In fact, his attitude, relatively cautious and incremental did little to build popular support and merely reminded many of his fundamental ties to the Suharto years.

Habibie did manage to move the country toward new elections. First parliamentary elections took place in June 1999, and then the presidential contest was followed later that year. The earlier elections proved to be a vindication for Megawati Sukarnoputri, whose Indonesian Democratic Party won 34% of the votes and 153 seats in the legislature. Despite those who thought *Golkar*'s strength had totally failed it, the former "government" party came in second with 120 seats. Altogether 21 parties managed to win seats in the 500 seat

Former President Abdurrahman Wahid

**Former President
Megawati Sukarnoputri**

Indonesian House of representatives—down from the 200 parties that were competing earlier in the year.

Though *Golkar*'s continuing strength was a surprise to some observers the really big winner in the contest was Megawati who seemed on a clear path to the presidency. But the presidential election that occurred the following October turned out quite differently from what many expected. Sukarno's daughter may have been very popular with the Indonesian public, but winning the presidency required far more than that. Megawati was hurt by a reputation for indecision. Most importantly she was far less effective than others in building the necessary support within the legislature. When the vote took place, the aging and partially blind Muslim leader, Abdurrahman Wahid, outmaneuvered not only Megawati but Suharto's chosen successor, Habibie, to emerge as Indonesia's new President.

That Indonesia had moved beyond Suharto and Habibie was certainly exciting for those who had hoped for a more open Indonesia. Wahid had long been known as an open-minded and tolerant leader. Nevertheless, Megawati's supporters were very disappointed. The newly elected president's decision to tap her as the nation's vice-president satisfied many, and the new team was duly sworn in.

Indonesia sorely needed a period of stability following the Asian economic collapse and the parallel fall of Suharto's long-lived dictatorship. Unfortunately Abdurrahman Wahid's presidency proved to be a disaster. Almost from the start, the new president failed to establish himself as an individual capable of guiding Indonesia. Many of his comments and acts were erratic, and corruption charges weakened his hold on power. Not only did he manage quickly to anger his own vice-president, Megawati, but his relations with the influential House of Representatives deteriorated rapidly over the months.

By the summer of 2001 Wahid, acting as if Indonesia remained the dictatorship it had once been, attempted to use his presidential authority to declare a state of martial law that would have allowed him to suspend the legislature. But support for the president had collapsed by then. In July the newly empowered national legislature voted to remove him and allow Megawati to take over as president.

Thus, in one stroke, the daughter of Indonesia's founding figure, the woman who had risen from the position of President Suharto's most vocal opponent to the biggest winner in Indonesia's first post Suharto's elections, had finally become president. In doing so she became the first female leader of the world's largest Muslim nation.

Once she assumed office, though, Megawati's presidency proved something of a mixed blessing. Some, for example, found her indifferent to the details of government. Moreover, a reputation for excessive caution surrounded her leadership. Still, Indonesia's political transformation has gone far beyond the question of what particular individual will lead the country next.

In the years following the election Indonesia worked vigorously to reorganize its political selection process. Most importantly, it adopted a more direct and democratic voting procedure to pick the country's leaders. Thus, unlike the preceding elections, Indonesia's next president was to be chosen after a two-part direct election.

As the time for the new parliamentary and presidential elections grew closer, hundreds of parties began to play a role in the campaign. Eventually two dozen parties qualified to contest the election of

April 2004. Not surprisingly the PRI-P of President Megawati and Golkar, the former ruling party, were at the forefront of the struggle.

Initially President Megawati retained considerable popularity, and many assumed she had a good chance of being re-elected. But that became less certain as her government found itself facing a wide variety of challenges. Among the most immediate problems she had was the challenge raised by the American campaigns in Afghanistan and Iraq. On the one hand, Megawati's government understood the importance of maintaining close ties with the influential Americans. Given the bombings in Bali and Jakarta over the last few years, it was understandable that she had committed her country to supporting the American war on terrorism.

On the other hand, many of Indonesia's hundreds of millions of Muslim voters were vehemently opposed to Washington's military campaigns in Afghanistan and Iraq, a sentiment that forced Indonesia's leaders into a complicated balancing act between Washington D.C. and their own people. The most obvious example of that tension was the original ambivalence that Jakarta showed to Washington's claims of an al-Qaeda's presence within Indonesia. Eventually, of course, the fall 2002 terrorist bombings in Bali did stir Indonesia's leadership toward a crackdown on some of the most extremist Islamic militants within the country.

Those difficulties and others played a role in the outcome of the parliamentary elections of April 2004. To the surprise of many pundits, Megawati's political party, the PDI-P, which had won 34% of the votes in the previous parliament, saw its share drop to a mere 19.67%. Golkar, the former ruling party, emerged triumphant with 20.99% of the vote. Given the outcome, it was now clear that the president's own re-election was likely to be a far more difficult challenge than many had previously assumed. Even worse was the news that according to polls more than 80% of the Indonesians claimed to want her to be replaced. Such a candidate was at hand to do that.

During the spring of 2004 Megawati's former security minister, retired General Susilo Bambang Yudhoyono, surged ahead in the polls as the candidate most likely to win the upcoming presidential elections. There were other candidates as well jockeying for position, including another military officer, General Wiranto, whom the newly triumphant Golkar chose to lead their effort to recapture the presidency.

By the time the presidential elections of 2004 finally arrived it was clear that the vast majority of Indonesian voters wanted a change in government. In the first round of voting that took place in July the 55 year old Susilo Bambang Yudhoyono received 34% of the vote while Megawati trailed by seven points, enough to retain her status as a candidate for that fall's run off but certainly a deep disappointment for her followers. That disappointment would continue though the fall when, despite the decision by the former ruling party Golkar's to support her re-election, Megawati was trounced by Susilo Bambang Yudhoyono in the late September run off.

Politically, the two finalists had a great deal in common. Both were secular nationalists committed to economic growth and resisting the forces of secession that have so often complicated Indonesia's political life. Nevertheless, Megawati had become quite unpopular and the reality that 40% of the working population remained underemployed, despite the very real economic improvements experienced by the country in recent years, deeply hurt her.

For his part, the new president, Mr. Yudhoyono, brought an impressive background to his new challenge. He had a newly minted doctorate in agricultural policy, (earned during the campaign itself) coupled with many years as a professional military officer. Plus, he had served in Megawati's cabinet where he was her minister of security, a position that allowed him many opportunities to serve as the government's principal spokesperson before his resignation. Indonesia's new leader also has another major advantage. He speaks fluent English an absolutely essential skill in today's globalized international community.

Significantly, Susilo Bambang Yudhoyono had taken office as the first directly elected president since Suharto fell. He leads a government that has undergone profound reforms in order to make the system more democratic. In fact, those changes were as dramatic as the election itself. Known collectively as *Reformasi*, the reforms have ranged from having the police and army formerly separated to fundamental alterations of the structure of parliament to make it more democratic. In the same vein, Indonesia had introduced a constitutional court and basic human rights protections. Of particular significance given their past role in national politics, Indonesia's parliaments no longer have special seats reserved for the military establishment.

But the new president hardly had time to get his administration formed before one of the worst natural disasters in modern history pummeled the island. In late December 2004 an enormous tsunami struck. Although the exact numbers will probably never be known, estimates were that around 132,000 people in Indonesia, particularly in the long troubled Aceh province, were killed while another 700,000 were left homeless. Moreover, almost 40,000 remained missing long after the disaster. Half of the capital city of Banda Aceh was leveled, and an enormous percentage of the community's infrastructure from homes and roads to universities was destroyed. It was a challenge with which any leader, let alone a newly inaugurated one, would be hard pressed to deal.

To make matters worse, the president had to deal with the challenge without full

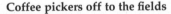

Coffee pickers off to the fields

Indonesia

control of the government of the nation's parliament. President Susilo Bambang Yudhoyono's party had won 7.5% in the elections, leaving him with control over only 120 seats in a parliament of 550. Still the president had important allies. His vice president, Jusuf Kalla, an accomplished businessman and politician in his own right, emerged as one of the principal organizers of the massive relief effort that saw outside agencies and numerous Indonesian organizations rushing in to offer help.

Despite such challenges, Indonesia's current president has proven to be a formidable leader. Particularly important in his initial popularity was the anti-corruption campaigns his government carried out and his accomplishments dealing with the troubled province of Aceh. More recently the government's popularity weakened when it was forced to lessen its domestic fuel subsidizes as world prices spiked over the last few years. Public frustration with the government's belt tightening apparently did not weaken the president significantly. Indeed, during the spring elections of 2009 his party did exceptionally well while those of the more religious parties went down dramatically.

Indonesian Regionalism and East Timor

When studying the modern history of communities like Indonesia it is important to remember that they were not single ethnic/linguistic/political communities before the colonial era. Rather, it was often the colonial experience itself that helped create the generation of nationalists like Sukarno or Hatta who led the struggle for independence. But like nations throughout the world, whose political borders were shaped by outside colonial powers, it has often been difficult to keep focused on their identities as Indonesians in the face of strong regional and ethnic ties. During the heady days of economic growth,

Jakarta street scene   Photo by Steven Leibo

Men on the way to work

pride in those accomplishments helped to strengthen Indonesia's national identity. Nevertheless, strong separatist sentiments and movements continued to be influential in regions from Aceh, near Malaysia, to Irian Jaya far to the east. And it was not just the power of separatism that challenged Indonesia's leadership in recent years. The larger geographic region also included militant Muslims who advocated the creation of an entirely new Islamic nation that would include countries from Indonesia and Malaysia to Singapore, Brunei and the Southern Philippines.

No Indonesian area experienced as much international attention for the level of its struggle and suffering as East Timor. Unlike much of the rest of Indonesia, which had been administered as the Dutch East Indies, East Timor had been a Portuguese colony for hundreds of years. Rather like Portuguese Goa in India or Macao near Hong Kong, it was a small reminder of the once energetic Portuguese role in colonization.

But just as India's government had moved into Goa in the early 1960s, and China took back Macao in December of 1999, Indonesia decided to absorb East Timor in 1975. The logic of Indonesian nationalism might have made the move seem appropriate, but culturally Indonesians and the East Timorese were quite different. Indonesia, although it includes many religions including millions of Christians, is largely Muslim, while East Timor, by grace of its centuries as a Portuguese colony, and more importantly the tensions which existed after Indonesia occupied it, is primarily Catholic and animist.

However significant the religious differences are, the real problems were probably the lack of a shared historical experience between the two peoples and especially

the brutality of the Indonesian occupation. The Indonesian move into East Timor was resisted by a leftist-nationalist movement called *Fretilin*, the Revolutionary Front for an Independent East Timor, and widely condemned internationally. In fact, only Indonesia's ASEAN partners and Australia actually recognized the legality of the occupation. Throughout the 1990s, reports of significant human rights abuses continued to be a problem for the Suharto government and aroused the sympathy of an increasingly large group of international sympathizers.

But it was not until the fall of Suharto in 1998 that the situation began to change. Once in power the new government of President Habibie indicated interest in trying to resolve the long-standing struggle. Clearly hoping to move toward some sort of autonomy, the regime made a series of dramatic admissions regarding its previous role in East Timor and claimed to be withdrawing some of its troops from the region. Not surprisingly leaders in East Timor were more interested in real independence than Jakarta's offer of greater autonomy.

Habibie blundered deeply by not ensuring that the Indonesian military was on board before offering the East Timorese an opportunity to vote on their future. In the months leading up to the August 1999 vote, it became clear that elements of the Indonesian military were supporting a terrorist campaign within East Timor to disrupt the referendum.

Eventually the violence, after the results of the vote for independence were announced, became so blatant that the United Nations supported by a force from Australia and other regional powers assumed control over East Timor from an extremely embarrassed and humiliated Indonesian military leadership. (For more information on East Timor, see the section dedicated to its recent development.)

Indonesia's former president, Megawati, came to power after East Timor had departed from Indonesia. While we have no way of knowing exactly what she might have done had she arrived in power earlier, once in office, she allied herself with those nationalists who wanted to insure that East Timor would remain the exception to the continuing unity of the nation her father did so much to build.

That understandable commitment to maintaining the territorial integrity of Indonesia, despite the loss of East Timor, was particularly obvious in her government's relations with the other rebellious province of Aceh. Thus, while formally apologizing to the people of Aceh for human rights abuses of the past, Megawati made it clear, she would oppose any independence efforts they might mount.

Nevertheless tensions continued. By the early spring of 2003 Jakarta began yet another military campaign to ensure that Aceh remained under its control. By the early summer hundreds of people from Aceh had been killed and thousands more made homeless as the central government made a dramatic effort to wipe out the region's nationalist movement.

Worse yet, the government moves against Aceh's separatists turned out to be the least of their problems when the horrific tsunami that hit the Indian Ocean in late December 2004 particularly devastated Aceh, destroying many of its population centers. But that horrific crisis did turn out to have a positive dimension as well.

In the aftermath of the tsunami, an agreement was worked out during the summer of 2005 to end the insurgency that had lasted over thirty years and killed more than 15,000 people. According to the agreement, the Achenese would disarm their forces while the government agreed to withdraw its troops, grant the province more autonomy and allow the formation of Achenese political parties. As of 2006 that agreement was apparently working, and plans were underway to integrate the former rebels into the provincial political system.

Society and Culture

Indonesia is a nation of islands that traditionally had mainly indirect contact with each other—a nation more recently ruled in effect by a cultural minority located on the island of Java. The vast majority of Indonesians are Muslims though other important groups of Christians and Chinese Buddhists are also present. Animism, a common tradition throughout Southeast Asia, is also found among some of the more isolated communities. Bali,

President Susilo Bambang Yudhoyono

the island fabled in story and song in the western world, is the one significant part of Indonesia that still practices Hinduism, the tradition that once dominated the entire region.

Thus, Indonesia is a country of great cultural differences. More than three hundred specific groups are recognized and over three hundred and fifty different languages are spoken. The dominant Javanese themselves constitute about 50% of the population. The largest non-indigenous community is the ethnic Chinese who, while constituting only around 3% of the population, are especially dominant in private economy.

The economic accomplishments of the era from the 1970s through the mid 1990s brought into being a new middle class that enjoyed many of the material comforts such groups enjoy elsewhere. Unlike the middle classes in other parts of East and Southeast, though, they did not appear to be particularly politicized or willing to challenge Suharto's regime until the drama of the late 1990s. Now the situation is quite different.

Modern Indonesia has developed as a community that draws sources from many different groups from Javanese and Malay traditions to those from the West and derived from Islamic society. Normally, non-violence and courteous agreement are a tradition in Javanese culture. Open disagreement is avoided—differences are buried in an atmosphere of agreement, no matter how unreal. Still, once it becomes apparent that differences cannot be hidden, violence has at times become painfully real.

In recent years a revival of an Islamic emphasis by some Javanese has tended at times to make the Christian and Chinese communities feel more insecure than in previous years. Of course, within the Indonesia, the tendency has long existed to blame the nation's economic crises on its influential Chinese minority a phenomenon that has sometimes resulted in violent attacks upon that community.

More positively Indonesia's large Chinese community has seen its circum-

stances evolve dramatically in recent years. It has now become not only legal but common for the local Chinese community to embrace their ethnicity and culture publicly. This is a far cry from the years when under the Suharto military dictatorship any show of Chinese culture could bring severe retribution.

But that does not mean ethnic relations are uniformly improving. Over the last few years, and especially as Indonesia's economic has weakened, there have been more and more outbreaks of communal violence. Especially violent outbreaks of fighting between Dayak tribesmen against Muslim Madurese settlers in Kalimantan have regularly created thousands of casu-

Statue of the young Barack Obama who grew up, in part, in Jakarta

Photo by Steven Leih

Indonesia

alties and refugees. Dramatic and bloody confrontations between Indonesia's Christian and Muslim communities have broken out as well. Clearly Indonesia is a country deeply affected by various communal tensions.

As is often the case within Muslim societies, the question of how closely secular law should parallel Islamic Shari'ah law became an issue again over the last year. The occasion was the introduction into the national legislature of a proposed law that would have expanded the role of Shari'ah law in society. The bill was opposed by a wide variety of interests groups, from predominantly secular ones to more traditional but non-Muslims groups. It was eventually modified enough to remove most of the controversial elements.

Indonesian Women

As is the case in many countries throughout the world, Indonesian women have many disadvantages when compared to men. Officially, they have the same rights but reality is often quite different. Those who work in industry usually get lower pay than men and often without the benefits men receive. Traditional Islamic family law prevails, making it legal for men to have more than one wife. Nevertheless, during President Suharto's period in power, the practice was

that senior level officials and officers were forbidden to do so. At the lower levels of the civil service it was tolerated, but men wishing to take another wife were required to get the permission of their supervisor as well as of their first wife.

Women's lower status is especially evident in the laws of citizenship. Women are not allowed to pass on their citizenship to their children. Thus a woman who becomes pregnant by a non-Indonesian citizen takes the risk of seeing her own children deported. In contrast to some other Asian societies there is much less social preference for boys over girls.

Some real improvements were being made in recent years. The number of young women graduating from high school went up enormously in the last generation, and the number graduating from college tripled in the years from 1980 to 1990. Additionally, a number of women's organizations have appeared to help improve the lives of Indonesian women.

Moreover, at the upper more educated levels, the gap between women's and men's salaries lessens. Many women now work at important mid-level positions in both government and the private sector. Unfortunately, the lives of both women and men were dramatically affected by the economic collapse of the late 1990s. Spousal abuse was reported to have risen as families experienced more tension, and

women were less able to afford the contraceptives they previously had used to help control their own fertility.

Although President Megawati was not able to win reelection in her own right after inheriting power from President Wahid, her tenure in power represented an enormously significant development. Under her leadership Indonesian Muslims had had the opportunity once again to show to the world that despite the common believe that women have no place in the politics of Islamic societies, that was hardly the case in Indonesia. A women there had risen to ultimate power within the largest Muslim country in the world, as they already had in other parts of the Islamic world.

Foreign Relations

Recent years have been a very complicated for Indonesia's relations with the outside world. Not only have Indonesian based forest fires often filled the entire region with choking smoke that hardly endeared her to her neighbors, but her ongoing battles during the late 1990s with the International Monetary Fund often complicated the regions efforts to recover from the Asian economic collapse of the late 1990s. And of course the struggle over East Timor not only soured relations with Australia and much of the international community but forced Jakarta to accept a humiliating presence of foreign troops on land she had until recently vehemently insisted was her sovereign territory.

That was ironic given that Indonesia has usually played an important and respected role in the region. As the fourth most populous country in the world, Indonesia has always considered itself to be number one among equals within the Association of Southeast Asian Nations (ASEAN). It is fair to say that the other ASEAN states have usually accepted the "big brother" role of Indonesia. The ASEAN headquarters is located in Jakarta. For its part, Indonesia has worked within the context of ASEAN although Jakarta has often been less enthusiastic about the rapid elimination of trade barriers since it is the least developed of the member states.

In the past Indonesia prided itself on being an arbiter of disputes and a conciliator. Indonesia played a role in the settlement of disputes in Cambodia and was helpful in having the Burmese activist Aung San Suu Kyi released from house arrest during the mid-1990s. Indonesia has also sponsored several seminars on the conflicting territorial claims in the South China Sea, and especially the Spratly Islands.

During the Cold War Indonesia was a key player in the Non-Aligned Movement that traced its beginnings back to the Ban-

Bandung side street

Photo by Steven Leibo

dung (Indonesia) conference of 1955. Nevertheless under former President Sukarno, the policy definitely leaned left. Sukarno tried to organize the New Emerging Forces that linked Indonesia to such countries as China, North Korea and Vietnam. After Sukarno's fall, President Suharto placed the country on a much more centrist path and one more tied to Western economic ideas. This generally non-aligned policy was evidenced for example in that the country did not develop defense treaties with any major outside power or group of powers. This set Indonesia apart from most of her ASEAN neighbors.

The country's territorial waters expanded greatly when the UN Law of the Sea Convention went into effect. Under the convention, all of the waters between the country's numerous islands, officially set at 17,500, now became Indonesian territorial waters.

But Indonesia's important and influential role regionally and economically began to unravel in late 1997 as her economy was struck by the same economic crises that had begun in Thailand and swept on toward South Korea. But unlike the situation both in Thailand and South Korea, there initially seemed no new or alternative leadership ready in the wings to take charge of getting the country back on track.

Unfortunately for Indonesia its long entrenched leadership, led by Suharto, seemed unwilling to find a way to work with the International Monetary Fund even as it requested funds from the agency. Thus by early 1998 the world was treated to an ongoing series of major world financial figures each making their way to Jakarta to meet its aging leadership hoping to encourage a more cooperative stance from the Indonesian government.

Certainly there were reasons for Jakarta to balk at some of the IMF's stringent financial demands for economic restructuring which would only add to the financial distress of the Indonesia people and hurt Suharto's own family's financial interests. Nevertheless, the open struggle with the IMF only added to those doubts about whether Indonesia's leadership would be able to make the hard choices necessary to recover and gain the confidence of the world financial markets.

Relations with the People's Republic of China, which were strained by the anti-Indonesian Chinese riots of 1998, have improved. In fact, former President Wahid even indicated an interest in improving relations with neighbors from China to India in order to offer a counter-balance to the enormous Western influence in the region.

Like much of the world Indonesia was deeply impacted by the September 2001 terrorist assault against the United States.

But for Indonesia the challenges were particularly daunting. Especially so as its secular and nationalist minded leader Megawati publicly supported the United States, while many others, in this largest of Muslim countries on the planet, including her own newly chosen vice-president were publicly critical both of her association with the United States and the latter's military activities in Afghanistan.

Those tensions only became more complicated when in the spring of 2003 the United States used its enormous power to overthrow the government of Saddam Hussein in Iraq. While most Americans seemed to support the campaign, within Indonesia Washington's efforts were enormously unpopular.

Although tensions over American policy in Iraq had an impact on Indonesia's international position, it played out as well on a regional level given the fact that Australia not only supported Washington's efforts, but it sent its own contingent of troops to the struggle. Clearly all this is yet another complication in Indonesian-Australian relations that were already complicated enough by Australia's role in the loss of East Timor only a few years earlier. On the more positive side, Indonesia's recent evolution toward a more democratic society and its increasing commitment and success in the war against Muslim Jihadist terrorism, despite the obvious setbacks, have helped enormously in improving Indonesian Western relations.

Economy

Until very recently the local economy was in shambles. Long proud of the steady economic progress they had made over the last generation, Jakarta suddenly found itself caught in the currency collapse begun in Thailand in the summer of 1997. Over the next months, as the rupiah lost an increasing percentage of its value, Indonesian businesses were unable to pay their U.S. dollar-based international debts. As the crisis grew worse, more and more Indonesian firms began failing and laying off their workers. For much of the country and so many of its citizens, all that they had worked so hard for over the previous generation was collapsing around them.

Initially working closely with the IMF, an enormous aid package of 43 billion dollars was arranged. Suharto's government started to act decisively by promising to close banks that were insolvent and to take "belt tightening" economic decisions. While the economic crisis grew, social and political cracks within the society, long present, added to the tensions. As the century drew to a close, riots broke out as people protested higher food and fuel prices. All this was in such contrast to the economic experience of Indonesia over earlier decades.

For much of the previous generation Indonesia had had a diversifying economy. Economic growth in Gross Domestic Product (GDP) had averaged about 7% annually since the 1970s. Foreign investment grew enormously. Indonesia's participation in the "growth triangle" with Singapore and Johore state in West Malaysia appeared to prove the merits of the private sector in the development process.

Despite the enormous economic growth and social improvements accomplished over those decades, 26 million of the country's 200 million people were said to be living in poverty, as defined by the World Bank even before the economic problems of 1997–1998. But with the onset of the Asian economic crisis, the situation grew

Indonesia

dire. Millions were pushed back into poverty as unemployment soared and more than two thirds of the population fell below even the more modest Indonesia poverty line. Unfortunately, as Indonesia moved more deeply into the new century, its recovery clearly lagged behind many other East and Southeast Asian nations that have already managed the recovery from the debacle of 1997.

Happily Megawati's arrival in power ended the uncertainty that surrounded her predecessor's chaotic administration and things began to improve. While growth rates have hardly returned to the heady figures of the 1980s, recent years have seen the GDP rise modestly. Other factors also indicate an improving economic reality for Indonesia. Domestic consumption has risen and the banking sector has seen significant improvement. Unfortunately while more stable leadership has brought about an improvement in confidence, the spill over within Indonesia surrounding the September 11 terrorists attacks in the United States, the subsequent campaigns in Afghanistan and Iraq and the more immediate horrors of the 2002 and 2005 Bali bombings have not encouraged investment.

More positively, Indonesian authorities have been particularly successful in their efforts to deal with local terrorist networks and have managed to arrest a significant number of them. But these efforts have also been very controversial as significant elements within Indonesian society have seen the American "War on Terrorism" as a campaign designed to weaken Islam itself,

a perception hardly helpful to Indonesia's leaders.

If the concerns about terrorism, and sectarian violence were not enough of a problem for both Indonesians and their economy, the horrendous earthquake and subsequent Tsunami that hit the country, especially the Aceh province of Northern Sumatra during late 2004, were particularly horrific. A hundred thousand were said to have been killed in Indonesia alone while perhaps up to 200,000 died throughout the region.

By the spring of 2008 the economy was still moving on the path of solid economic expansion. The growth figures around 6.3% were certainly positive, but unfortunately they are not high enough to create the new jobs its growing population requires. The fact that Indonesia, despite its significant oil reserves, has become a net importer of oil is also an issue of concern, given world oil prices. Nevertheless, the combination of reasonable growth rate and modest growth in foreign investment was obviously important and a positive development at least until the fall of 2008 when the most recent global economic slowdown began.

Environmental Issues

The late December 2005 Tsunami may have reminded Indonesians of how vulnerable we all are to natural phenomena like the earthquakes that sent those huge waves toward the nation's shores. But not all environmental threats emerge beyond humanity's influence. Within Indonesia

decisions are regularly made that have immediate and long-term implications for the nation.

Most important is the burning of Indonesia's forests, which regularly send huge plumes of smoke throughout the regional atmosphere hurting not only locals but their national neighbors. Of course, the smoke they create is only part of the problem. The cutting down of Indonesia's forest coverings, like similar activities in Brazil, is also contributing to the destabilization of global climate patterns by adding to the greenhouse gases that cause global warming. This happens in two ways. First, the burning of Indonesia's forests, particularly serious in the aftermath of the Asian economic crisis of the late 1990s, releases massive amounts of CO_2 that had been retained by the trees. Second, the cleared land no long absorbs CO_2, thus keeping more in the atmosphere.

The situation is so dramatic that Indonesia is among the top three emitters of green house gases in the world. This is true even though its output of the industrial-based green house gas emissions, while rising, remains relatively small.

In a dramatic gesture in the build up to the late-2007 meeting in Bali to expand the international efforts to confront global warming, the nation's president along with huge numbers of his fellow citizens worked to plant millions of new trees. It was a dramatic effort that President Bambang Yudhoyono proclaimed as Indonesia's gift to the international community. At the conference itself significant progress was made in creating an international formula that, it

The author meeting with Indonesian Climate Change activists

is hoped, will eventually offer financial incentives for nations like Indonesia to preserve their tropical forests. Developing such an international system is vitally important because forests play an important role in maintaining the world's current climate balance. Moreover, Indonesia is home to huge peat swamps that also contain enormous amounts of CO_2 that are now slowly being released as the swamps are drained and the resulting drying out process releases their long-stored gases.

Since the Bali Climate Conference, Indonesia's commitment to dealing with the related energy challenges has continued unabated. In the early spring of 2010 the World Bank announced efforts to help the nation develop its geothermal energy capacity. According to Bank officials, Indonesia is said to have the largest potential geothermal sources in the world. Meanwhile, officials have announced plans to reduce the growth of Indonesian-produced green house gases by 25% over the coming decade. Complementing that goal was the recent announcement of a new set of green energy building design guidelines.

Meanwhile the general population is also getting deeply involved. Recently dozens of climate activists who had been personally trained by Al Gore fanned out across Indonesia to offer a series of presentations on the impact of climate change globally and within the country itself. Of course, it is not surprising that the Indonesians have been especially sensitive to the world's most dramatic environmental challenge.

As a nation of relatively low-lying islands, Indonesia is thought to be particularly vulnerable to the rising waters brought about by climate instability. Most dramatically, its people experienced the power of the early 21st century's increasingly powerful rainstorms in February 2007 when around 400,000 residents of Jakarta were displaced by huge floods released by horrendous rainstorms. Unfortunately flooding has now become a regular feature of life for many of the residents of the Jakarta.

Future

Indonesia has experienced a great deal since the Asian economic crash and the fall of Suharto. For a time previous to those dramatic days, continued growth appeared about to put Indonesia firmly into the mid-level developing nations category. But the 1997–1998 economic crash and resulting political transformation ended those hopes. Once Suharto fell, the immediate challenge was to establish a stable transition toward a more open society. However, the first three presidents after Sukarno—Habibie, Wahid and Megawati Sukarnoputri—were all unable to generate enough lasting popular support and stability to allow that to happen.

The current president, Susilo Bambang Yudhoyono, has been able to create a much more politically stable environment. The president himself remains popular, and he easily won reelection in July 2009. Still, while Indonesia has obviously made enormous progress developing a mature democratic system, old habits die hard. The government still regularly bans books on topics it finds unacceptable. These include accounts of the still deeply controversial massacres of 1965 and guidebooks that cover regions the government does not want travelers exploring.

Indonesia's international standing was also raised when it hosted the 13th Conference of the United Nations Framework on Climate Change, which met in December 2007. Called to pave the way for a new international treaty on global warming to complement what was accomplished in 1997 at Kyoto, the conference attracted more than 10,000 people from more than 180 countries. Many saw it as a better organized effort than the Copenhagen conference that followed it.

One of the problems Indonesia faces is its relatively negative international reputation. We are often told that the nation's capital, Jakarta, is pollution-ridden and ensnarled by traffic and that its urban environment is so burdened by terrorism that most would want to avoid it. It is a very unfair reputation. Neither Jakarta's pollution nor its traffic is significantly worse than in many more popular Asian destinations, such as Bangkok, Ho Chih Min City and Hong Kong. Indeed Jakarta is an altogether charming and in many areas quite modern international city. As for it reputation for terrorism, the record in Jakarta is not significantly worse than in many world capitals. In short, Jakarta, like India's Calcutta and America's Pittsburgh, is a significantly more pleasant city than its international reputations suggests.

But the question of its reputational weaknesses is not the only way Indonesia has impacted the international consciousness. In fact, its international status seems likely to rise over the next years. The American President, Barack Obama, has deep ties to Indonesia. He lived there for a time as a child and is likely to use his ties with Indonesia as one part of his stated intention to improve America's relationship with the Muslim world. When he eventually decides to make a return visit, it will allow Indonesians to show the world how much more modern and sophisticated the nation is than its reputation. For the moment, though, the Indonesians have settled, not without some controversy, for the erection of a small statue of the president as a child in a park near his boyhood home.

Indonesia

. . . while the capital's business district plays the stock market.

The Laos People's Democratic Republic

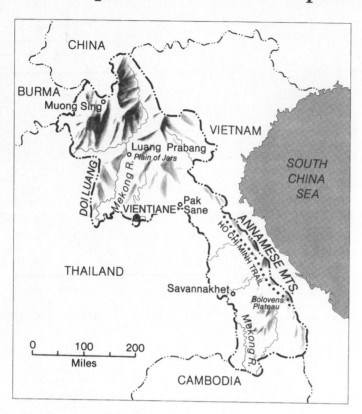

Area: 91,400 sq. mi. (234,804 sq. km., somewhat smaller than Oregon).

Population: 6,993,767 (July 2010 est.)

Capital City: Vientiane (Pop. 200,000, estimate 2005)

Climate: Tropical, with a rainy monsoon from May–October and a dry season from November–April

Neighboring Countries: China (North); Vietnam (East); Burma (Northwest); Thailand (West); Cambodia (South)

Official Language: Lao

Other Principal Tongue: French

Ethnic Background: Lao Loum (lowland) 68%, Lao Theung (upland) 22%, Lao Soung (highland) including the Hmong ("Meo") and the Yao (Mien) 9%, ethnic Vietnamese/Chinese 1%

Principal Religion: Buddhism; animism is predominant among the tribes

Major Exports: to Thailand, Vietnam, France, Germany U.K. Electric power (to Thailand): timber and textiles, garments, wood, coffee

Main Import from Thailand, Russia, Japan, France, China, Singapore, Vietnam: Rice, petroleum products, machinery and vehicles

Currency: Kip

Former Colonial Status: French protectorate (1893–1949); member of the French Union (1949–1954).

Loatian landscape

National Day: December 24, 1954
Chief of State: Lt. Gen. Choummali Saignason, President (since June 2006).
Head of Government: Prime Minister Bouasone Bouphavanh (since 8 June 2006).
National Flag: Two red stripes (top and bottom), a wide blue stripe between them upon which is centered a white circle.
Per Capita GDP Income: $2,100 (2010 estimate, purchasing power parity)

Laos is a landlocked country, largely covered with mountains and tropical forests, interrupted by patches of low scrub vegetation in the areas where the soil is poor. It is an extremely undeveloped country with few roads where the natural beauty has not been greatly altered by the presence of man.

Most of the fertile land lies along the valley of the Mekong River, where it is eroded and flows as silt to the rice paddies in the Mekong Delta in southern Vietnam. The land receives ample rainfall, but the sandstone soils have little capacity to retain the moisture. In the last part of the dry season from November to May, the air becomes oppressively hot and very dry. This is when tribesmen living in the mountain forests burn the trees to clear the land. The practice, coupled with natural forest fires, sadly robs the land of much of its fertility.

History

The Lao people moved into northern Laos from the southwestern Chinese province of Yunnan beginning in the 11th century A.D. During the succeeding centuries they slowly expanded toward the south, founding two communities in central and southern Laos. In their efforts to settle, the additional lands they came into frequent conflict with the Burmese and Thai who were also active in this part of Southeast Asia.

The French established their colonial authority over neighboring Vietnam by 1893. When there was a dispute between Thailand and Laos over demarcation of the border, the French proclaimed a protectorate over Laos in 1893, making it a dependency within the French Indochinese Empire. Because of its remoteness and lack of natural resources, the French did almost nothing to develop Laos; they did succeed in ending the payment of tribute to the kings of Thailand, however.

When the Japanese soldiers conquered Southeast Asia in 1942, Tokyo supported their Thai ally in taking some border territory from Laos. A nationalist movement, known as the Lao Issara and directed mainly against the Japanese occupation forces, arose during World War II. When the French reentered after the defeat of the Japanese, Thailand was forced by Britain and the U.S. to return the territory it had acquired while allied with Japan. The Lao Issara promptly started anti-French activity from bases in Thailand. Preoccupied with resistance movements in Vietnam, the French granted Laos internal self-government within the French Union in 1949, thus splitting the resistance movement while the non-communist majority took a leading role in the new government.

Meanwhile the pro-communist forces formed themselves into a new party known as the Pathet Lao which became increasingly associated with Ho Chi Minh's movement in North Vietnam. By the mid-1950s, The North Vietnamese help allowed the Pathet Lao to gain control over provinces along the border with Vietnam, even as Laos finally gained full independence from France in late 1954.

Within Laos a small-scale civil war broke out with both sides the United States and North Vietnam contributing respectively to their different allies. By the early 1960s Laos had become a hot bed of coups and countercoups as each side sought to gain advantage.

Evidently realizing that such chaos did not serve the aims of either side, U.S. President Kennedy and Soviet Premier Khrushchev agreed in 1961 that Laos should be neutralized. Following intense jockeying for position, the Pathet Lao withdrew from the coalition government that had just been set up. The result was continuation of a highly complex and somewhat obscure, undeclared civil war.

During the following years most military activity was directly tied to the Ho Chi Minh Trail, which was vital to the North Vietnamese war effort in South Vietnam. Hanoi sought to keep it open, while the U.S. tried periodically to close it. Later, as part of the accord supposedly settling the Vietnamese conflict, an agree-

President Choummali Saignason

ment was reached regarding Laos. It included many of the Pathet Lao demands and tended to lessen the influence of the right wing in the central government.

A coalition government was not installed until April 1974. It became a means whereby the Pathet Lao greatly strengthened its political influence. Prince Souvanna Phouma's age and ill health reduced his role, and Prince Souphanouvong, the leading Pathet Lao in the coalition government, assumed the chairmanship of the Political Council. He in effect made it, rather than the National Assembly, the real legislative body. Although the Pathet Lao military located themselves in the government areas, non-communists were not allowed to function politically in or even to enter areas held by them. North Vietnamese troops remained in the highlands after the coalition government was formed.

A heart attack suffered by Premier Souvanna Phouma in mid-1974 made things easier for the Pathet Lao. The early months of 1975 saw demonstrations by pro-communist elements (students, etc.) in some towns, as well as fighting in remote areas. But the fall of South Vietnam and Cambodia, in the spring of 1975, made a Pathet Lao takeover inevitable; the right-wing members of the government resigned in May. Soon there was a shift in favor of "hardline" communism. The monarchy was abolished and a new government was created with Souphanouvong as President. By 1977 the ex-king was under arrest.

By 1976, the political "re-education" of the Lao people had begun. Additionally a sizable Soviet aid program, including the building of an airfield on the Plain of Jars, was developed. Vietnamese influence was also very great, and their troops remained on Laotian soil. Using "yellow rain" (Soviet-made natural poisons) for a

**Prime Minister
Bouasone Bouphavanh**

Laos

Pha That Luang, The Major Stupa of Vientiane

time, they fought Lao insurgents, some of whom were supported by China. The new socialist government also attempted to put in place a communist command economy though the efforts were not sustained and the commitment to a centrally planned economy did not last.

By the 1980s the situation had begun to evolve again. At a congress of the ruling Lao People's Revolutionary Party held in November 1986, there were some leadership changes, with younger and better-trained men rising to the top. The change reflected new attitudes on economic development. The party, in line with developments elsewhere in the communist world, and concerned by the poor state of the Laotian economy, called for better relations with China, Thailand and the U.S. They also began to move away from a rigid communist economic system in favor of a more open system along the model of the People's Republic of China and the economic renovation then going on in neighboring Vietnam and other former hard line communist systems. To that end, the government has more recently added official protections for private property to the national constitution and become more interested in bringing Laos more deeply into the world economy.

Politics and Government

Under the 1991 Constitution, the Lao People's Democratic Republic (LPDR) continues to have a Marxist-Leninist style political system, though in reality its economy is more and more open to capitalist style practices as well. Political power rests with the Pasason, the central organ of the Lao People's Revolution Party (LPRP).

The unicameral Assembly operates under the principle of democratic centralism, which allows the leadership of the LPRP to control the legislative process. Khamtay Siphandon is the LPDR President and the most influential leader of the country.

The LPRP also controls the electoral process. Candidates for the National Assembly are approved by the LPRP and in some cases picked by government departments. Assembly members also receive political training before assuming their responsibilities. As has been the case in communist countries elsewhere the LPRP has moved the country closer to a market economy and away from socialism though the effort, like the earlier effort to introduce a more centrally planned economy has been a relatively casual affair.

Like their Vietnamese and Chinese neighbors, the Laotian leadership apparently wants economic reform while maintaining their hold on political power. Until recently the LPRP maintained firm control. There was no real political opposition in the country. The National Assembly had been trained to avoid politics and tend to other matters, including economic development. During the mid-1990s the political landscape began to change with the passing of 86-year-old Souphanouvong, known as the "Red Prince" and Phoumi Vongvichit, a leader of the Pathet Lao, who died in 1994. Virtually all of the founding members of the LPRP have now either died or retired and the general trend of

Laotian politics has since them moved rather dramatically away from its recent history. In the immediate aftermath of the Asian economic meltdown the most obvious political change in Laos was the lessening influence of more modern technically trained administrators. In the last year the government called for early elections that brought forward a newer and better-educated group of representatives although that hardly changed matters dramatically. Of those winning membership in the assembly only one non-communist was included.

In 1998 a military leader, Khamtay Siphandon, became president and, as we have seen, the dominant leader of the country. But his promotion was more than a personal gain. Equally important is the recent rise of various generals who have taken over many of the cabinet portfolios and other key positions. Relative to the party, the army itself appears increasingly powerful. In fact, some have suggested that Laos is moving toward the sort of military government common in Burma and during Suharto's term in Indonesia. That fact that during 2005 eight of the eleven-person Politburo were either active duty military or retired officers certainly seems to reinforce that impression.

But regardless of the military ties of many politburo members, the party itself still appears firmly in control. In early 2006 a large closed-door session of the Lao People's Revolutionary Party gathered to solidify future plans and appoint new leaders. To replace the 82-year-old departing President Khamtay Siphan-

172

done, the somewhat younger 79-year-old Choummali Saignason was chosen while Bouasone Bouphavanh, a relatively new member of the politburo, became the new prime minister.

Among the other important recent changes has been a general move toward decentralization of the Laotian governing system. If these efforts are successful, which includes the opportunity for the various local areas to retain a higher percentage of the tax revenues they collect, it could have a significant impact on how Laos is governed. Moreover, the individual provinces are now allowed as well to compete with each other to attract foreign investment.

As has often been the case elsewhere in East and Southeast Asia the Laotian military has been a major player in Laos' economic development. Dividing the country into three regions, the military has been deeply involved economically in everything from tourism to timber products.

The military may well be the only organization with the skills necessary to administer the process of economic modernization. Nevertheless, their control is hardly likely to allow the sort of vigorous economic growth that a more open system might offer. Still Laos clearly appears on the road to a more open economic system and this has included creating, as China started a generation ago, the opening up of its own Special Economic Zone to facilitate foreign investment.

While the general commitment toward market economics has continued, many influential Lao conservatives have also been concerned about their impact on Lao society. Increases in crime have been noted with fears that the reforms may have gone too far. Those concerns were acted upon during 1999 as the government made a conscious effort to emphasize what it called "traditional Lao values" as a counterweight to the growing obsession with making money. Considering the economic distress that hit he region in recent years, those that have remained more skeptical about market reforms probably feel vindicated. That effort to draw upon Laotian tradition to shore up the nation's leaders has continued.

In sharp contrast to the socialist government's previously antagonistic stance toward the nation's monarchial past, the nation's leaders have more recently been showing considerable respect for that very past. That is quite ironic given that relations with the surviving members of the Laotian royal family remain quite tense. Nevertheless today's Laotian leaders have been making significant efforts to enhance the population's awareness of Laos' imperial past, and to link the current government to that heritage.

Over the last few years, tensions have begun to surface. A bombing campaign began, even as some students started taking to the streets to question the government's authority. Within the rural area rebels from the minority, Hmong people have attacked Laotian targets. As of the spring of 2004 those attacks did not appear to be significant enough to genuinely threaten the nation's leaders but news of the occasional assaults that have killed civilians and foreigners alike have hardly helped the effort to attract outside investment or tourism. Reports more recently have suggested that agreements may have been made with some of the Hmong insurgents to lay down their arms but the details appear far from certain.

Foreign Relations

LPDR foreign policy had a decided "Look East" orientation for years. The country has had a long-standing relationship with Vietnam. In 1977 the two countries signed the Treaty of Friendship and Cooperation. The agreement gave the Vietnamese, among other things, the authority to enter Laos whenever it is deemed necessary. Though the Vietnamese troops were withdrawn from Laos in 1989, there are credible reports that the Vietnamese remain involved in helping Lao's authorities deal with the challenge Hmong insurgents have put up against the regime.

Laos is also especially involved with its neighbor to the West, Thailand, which has been a major investor in the Laotian economy. The recently opened Mitraphap Bridge spans the Mekong River and links Vientiane, the capital of Laos, to Nongkhai, Thailand. That connection was complemented in 2008 by the opening of the first rail line between the two countries. The ceremony was presided over by the Thai Princess, Maha Chakri Sirindhorn, and was opened with great enthusiasm. For Laos, it is the nation's first international train link. It is hoped that it will eventually become part of a long-planned international train line throughout much of eastern Asia. Given that Laos is landlocked, the railroad has the potential to play a very significant role in the nation's future. Because of Laos' interest in selling the energy from its hydroelectric industry to Thailand, these ties are likely to become even more important over the years.

As is the case elsewhere in the region, the influence of the People's Republic of China has grown in Laos although that relationship has not always worked out

Lane Xang Avenue in Vientiane

Laos

Buddha

tion and curbing the production of opium for export. Washington and Vientiane have also worked to resolve the status of Americans missing in action since the Vietnam War. Today, reasons for cooperation are obvious as Laos struggles with decisions about opening the country more and attracting outside investment. There was even talk recently of the U.S. granting Laos "most favored nation" status which would make it much easier for Laos to export its products to the United States. One element, though, that has made relations more complicated is that Laos has been accused by many in the United States of having a questionable human rights record. One the other hand, Laos' commitment and apparent success in dramatically lessening opium production are certainly an improving factor in their relations. The immediate example of that improvement was President Bush's recent granting of "normal trading relations" to the country.

Laos has also signed an agreement for foreign assistance with North Korea. However, in recent years it seems Laos, despite all its problems, is in a better position to give assistance than to receive it from that beleaguered state. The most obvious sign of Laos' emergence from its self-imposed isolation is the fact that it finally became an official member of ASEAN during the summer of 1997. Even more significantly, by 2005 Vientiane played host to a meeting of the Association of Southeast Asian Nations, a clear sign that the nation was successfully moving to enhance its integration into the larger Southeast Asian community.

Culture and Society

In physical appearance and culture, the Lao are regarded as "cousins" of the Thai. In fact the two groups are so similar that Laos has even asked Bangkok for special consideration for Laotians in matters related to visas and work permits. Overall the Lao are an extremely easygoing people and their country was relatively peaceful in modern times until the turmoil brought about by the Vietnamese revolutionary struggle nearby.

Although the government abandoned formal communist economic controls for a more open economic system after 1986, real changes in people's living standards are only just now beginning to be felt. Some wealthy urban dwellers now have the money for cars and TVs. The capital, Vientiane, has itself seen important changes. Foreign newspapers are now available along with the relatively new Vientiane Times. Laos is now available on the Internet and has its own e-mail service provider. Not surprisingly the growth of

well. China's Yunnan airline recently took a controlling interest in the Lao National Airline, but within a few years relations went bad, and Lao Aviation withdrew its cooperation. More recently there has been talk of building a road that would run from China through Laos and into Thailand. If completed, it would certainly have an important impact on the economy of the entire region. Lao officials and the authorities from the People's Republic have also pledged to significantly expand the

bilateral trade between the two countries. From the perspective of Laos' leaders, greater ties became especially important after the Asian economic crisis of the late 1990s made it obvious that their country would be better off if it was not so exclusively dependent on Thailand for their economic health.

Relations with the United States have been on good terms in recent years. The two countries have worked together successfully in the areas of refugee repatria-

recent years is uneven. Only 18% of the population is in the region around Vientiane while almost eighty percent of the population lives in the rural areas.

Around one third of the population remains below the World Bank's poverty line. Half the adult population is illiterate, and malnutrition is common among children. Life expectancy is significantly lower than in neighboring Thailand.

Since the majority of the population still lives as subsistence farmers, they have to deal on an almost daily basis with the perils of unexploded military ordinance. These explosions have killed around 12,000 people since the end of the Vietnam War era, and to this day they make tilling the soil in large parts of the country very dangerous.

Women

The new constitution provides equal rights for women though the traditional culture still favors men. Today women occupy positions of responsibility in business and government. In addition, they have improved their representation in the latter recently. The government, working through women's organizations, has also moved to educate young women about the dangers of labor recruiters who lure young girls to the sweatshops and brothels of Thailand. As is frequently the case, the more educated urban women have more opportunities than the majority of the women who live in the countryside where many remain illiterate.

Economy

From the standpoint of economic geography, Laos falls into two clearly divided areas. In the Mekong Valley, agriculture centered on rice prevails. In the hills, the remote tribesmen sporadically cultivate the poor soils in a migratory fashion. Development is retarded by the poorly developed infrastructure of roads and other means of communication and transportation around the country. Like the adjacent highlands of Burma, Thailand and China, the Laotian mountains are among the main opium producing regions of Asia. Most of this narcotic substance is smuggled out by air, though increasingly addiction is becoming a problem for the Laotian people as well.

In the years after the communists came to power, they enforced a socialist economic system but by the mid 1980s, that system began to change. The People's Democratic Republic (LPDR) launched the New Economic Mechanism (NEM) in an attempt to modernize the country's economy. Since 1990, reforms have included the introduction of a new accounting system for production and domestic trade, assigning a permanent staff to monitor budgetary revenue, creation of central banking laws, and the integration of official and parallel exchange rates. The number of state run enterprises has dropped dramatically as well. More recently serious efforts have begun to train civil servants in English so they can more easily work with their counterparts in ASEAN.

Foreign investment regulations were also liberalized in 1989 and again in 1994. In 1994–1995, the country attracted significant foreign investment for the development of hydroelectric power. The second-largest sector for investment is tourism, followed by mining and manufacturing, including clothing. One of the hydroelectric projects will be built by an Australian concern and is expected to be the world's second-highest concrete-faced, rock-filled dam. The government has planned to sell a significant percentage of the newly generated power to Thailand although progress on the dams was not initially very rapid. Hopes for the project were finally enhanced in 2005 when the World Bank gave its official "go ahead" for the effort.

By 2006 two major hydroelectric projects had begun construction. A year later the projects began to have a significant impact on Laos's economy. Not only were the two large hydroelectric dams finally being constructed but Australian firms had also become very involved in developing a mining industry.

For most of the last decade, the nation's GDP growth has hovered around 6% annually. Unfortunately, that growth has been quite uneven. Wealthier Laotians exist but more than 75% of the people earn less than two American dollars a day and while many of the people living in the lowlands of Laos are doing better, the poorest still live in the upland areas farther away from the Mekong River. Overall, Laos remains among the poorest countries in the world with a life expectancy of only fifty-three years for males and fifty-seven for women.

The country's first casino is now up and running hoping to attract gamblers with Thai Baht to spend. Over the last few years there has finally been some cause for optimism as the economy has started to

The Patouxai or "victory gate" Vientiane

Laos

improve. Real progress is being made on the hydroelectric projects. Tourism, another important revenue source in Southeast Asia, has begun to pick up. In 2007–08 Laos' exports reached a significant milestone when they finally hit the $1 billion mark. About half of those exports have come from mining commodities like copper and gold.

One of the more positive, if controversial, economic developments in recent years was the introduction in 2009 of a plan to develop the northern-most provinces using significant amounts of Chinese investments. The plan is to develop a zone of industries from mining and agriculture to tourism although the level of Chinese investment has raised concerns in some quarters.

Still there are other areas of concern as well. Over the last few years weakening public confidence in the local currency caused problems and the remaining state enterprises continued to lose money and to drag down the nation's banks which have many "bad loans" on their books caused by efforts to prop up those failing state businesses. Unfortunately, given the size of the country and the relatively small population the government has not felt much pressure to reform.

Perhaps one of the most important economic issues facing the Laos government is bringing the nation into the World Trade Organization. If that is not done, Laos will find itself at a clear exporting disadvantage relative to its neighbors who have joined. More immediately, of course, Laos faces the same problem most of the world faces: the economic slowdown that began to envelope the world by the fall of 2008.

The Future

Laos faces many challenges. The combination of divisions within the ruling elite and external challenges to their rule suggests that the relative calm of Laos during recent years may not last. People are apparently more willing to criticize the government's inability to improve the economy fundamentally. The recent willingness to re-embrace traditional Laotian values and to allow greater decentralization may very well reflect the regime's general concern about maintaining its authority. The fact that there has also been a significant effort to bring younger and more educated leaders into the power structure is certainly another sign of that concern.

Moreover relations with Thailand continue along their complicated "love-hate" route, but have been improving significantly. Still Laos is now a member of ASEAN and likely to benefit from those improved ties. It is also attempting to broaden its relations by strengthening links with other countries, especially the People's Republic of China and Vietnam.

The long-term efforts to revitalize the entire Mekong river area and to make it a more effective tool for trade throughout the region are eventually likely to be very beneficial to Laos. The regional development of the Mekong region, coupled with efforts to build new highways that would run through Laos and more directly and conveniently link the nation with its neighbors from China and Vietnam to Thailand, is likely to have a major impact on Laos' future.

The fact that Laos has managed to make significant progress in its efforts to eradicate the cultivation of opium-producing poppy plants has already improved its relations with the Western powers. This culminated in the granting of more favorable trading relations with the United States in 2004. The relationship remains complicated at times by memories and battles dating back more than three decades. In mid-2007, for example, a former general in the anti-communist Laotian army was indicted in an American court for conspiring to organize a coup against the Laotian government.

Overall, the government has increasingly committed itself to further integration both within South East Asia, best exemplified by its sponsoring of the 2009 games in Vientiane, and its continuing effort to join the World Trade Organization.

Young Laotian Monk   Courtesy of Rusty and Marilyn Staff, Asia Transpacific Journeys

Malaysia

The modern city of Kuala Lumpur

Courtesy: Embassy of Malaysia

Area: 128,775 square miles

Population: 26,160,256 (July 2010 est.)

Capital City: Kuala Lumpur (Pop. 1,479,388, estimate 2004)

Climate: Tropically hot and humid

Neighboring Countries: Thailand (north); Singapore (south); Indonesia (south and southwest)

Official Languages: Malay and English

Other Principal Tongues: Chinese, Tamil

Ethnic Background: Malay and other indigenous 58%, Chinese 24%, Indian 8%, others 10% (2000 estimate)

Principal Religions: Islam, Buddhism, Hinduism, and Christianity

Main Exports (to Japan, Singapore, U.S., China, Thailand) Natural rubber, palm oil, tin, timber, petroleum, and electronic goods

Main Imports (from Japan, Singapore, China, Thailand, Taiwan South Korea, Indonesia, Germany, U.S.) chemicals, machinery, electronics, transportation equipment, plastics, iron, steel

Currency: Ringgit

Former Colonial Status: British commercial interests acquired the islands of Penang in 1786 and port city of Melaka in 1824. The various states of Malaya entered into protectorate status from 1874 to 1914; they remained British colonies or protectorates until 1957 with the exception of the Japanese occupation from 1942 to 1945. Sabah was administered by the British North Borneo Company from 1881 to 1941, occupied by the Japanese from 1942 until 1945 and was a British Colony from 1946 to 1963. Sarawak was granted to Sir James Brooke by the Sultan of Brunei in 1841; it became a British protectorate in 1888; after the Japanese were expelled in 1945, Sir Charles Vyner Brooke, the ruling Raja, agreed to administration as a British Crown Colony, which lasted until 1963.

National Day: August 31st, 1957

Chief of State: His Majesty Sultan Mizan Zainal Abidin (since April 2007)

Head of Government: Prime Minister Mohamed Najib bin Abdul Razak (since 3 April 2009);

National Flag: Fourteen horizontal stripes of red and white with a dark blue rectangle in the upper left corner containing a yellow crescent and a 14-pointed star

Per Capita GDP Annual Income: $14,800 (2009 est. purchasing power parity)

Located at the southern end of the Malay Peninsula, the mainland portion of Malaysia consists of a broad central belt of forested mountains. In the areas of Malaysia where the mountains give way to low plains the vegetation turns into a thick green jungle situated on swampy plains, particularly in the coastal area. The climate is uniform during the year because of the closeness to the equator—hot and humid.

The Borneo states, also known as East Malaysia, contain wide coastal lowlands that have relatively poor soil and are interrupted by frequent rivers. The altitude rises in the south as the border with Indonesia is approached. The division between the two occupants of the island straddles a scenic range of rugged mountains the highest of which is Mt. Kinabalu, towering majestically to a height of 13,000 feet. Few people of the western world have penetrated Borneo to view this remote area, which is inhabited by an indigenous people who have advanced little beyond Stone Age life. The people of Malaysia are quite similar to their Indonesian neighbors—a mixture of Polynesian, Mongol, Indian and Caucasian origins.

Malaysia

There is also a large minority of Chinese who are descendants of laborers brought in by the colonial British.

History

The history of Malaysia, as a country, really begins during the colonial period, when the British started to establish their holdings in the area. Before that, the various regions that today are associated with Malaysia were part of several different political communities ranging from the mainland based Siamese kingdom to the north to the various commercial empires in what later became Indonesia.

The Malay language was prominent enough in the region's early life to serve as the principal language for commercial activities until the early modern era. Throughout the region, regardless of a person's ethnicity, knowing Malay was absolutely necessary to take part in the international trade of the region.

Malaya would probably have been colonized sooner than it was if the Dutch had not focused their attention on the fabled riches of Indonesia. The colonial history of both nations is very similar. The absence of Dutch control permitted the British to enter the area without opposition. In order to protect their trade routes the British compelled the rulers of the small individual states of Malaya to accept "protection." This included the presence of a British advisor at each Malay court to insure that British goals were achieved. Four outlying, impoverished states of Siam (Thailand) in the north were added to Malaya in 1909.

The rubber tree was brought from Brazil and planted in the rich soil to grow in an almost ideal climate. Drawn by the natural resources and the stability of the area, British capital poured in. There was also a mass influx of Chinese and Indian laborers to work the rubber plantations and the tin mines. In many cases the Chinese soon entered commerce and some became extremely wealthy and influential.

The arrival of immigrants from China and India created the ethnic mix which has been the most fundamental feature of modern Malaysian social and political life, the tripartite division of the population between native Malays who constitute around half the population and the Chinese and Indian communities who make up very significant minorities. In fact the Chinese, in contrast to their numbers that usually average around 10% throughout the region, make up closer to 40% of the population in Malaysia.

During the British rule the later "division of labor" also began to appear as Chinese moved into the economy with the Malays largely remaining less urbanized or in some cases becoming part of the British civil administration of the area. The British often favored the Malays, at the expense of the Chinese, a preference that more recent Malaysian governments have also followed. More importantly, British rule not only saw the evolution of the region from one that was relatively homo-

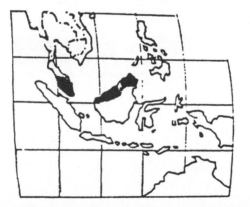

geneous to the more multi-ethnic society of modern Malaysia. As elsewhere British policy was to retain its authority by "divide and rule" processes that have certainly contributed to the problems that have affected Malaysia in later years.

World War II

When the Japanese arrived in 1942, they treated the Chinese with much greater brutality than they did the Malays. In reaction, the local Chinese, whose own politics were more tied to developments within China, formed an anti-Japanese guerrilla force of Chinese, most of them communists, who operated from bases deep within the thick jungles. Receiving weapons smuggled in by the British, the guerrillas fought their non-communist rivals as well as the Japanese. In contrast to the Chinese community, there was some sympathy among Malayans for the Japanese activities. Many people in Southeast Asia had been attracted to the Japanese calls to free the region from Western colonialism. The Chinese, well aware of the atrocities the Japanese had committed in China, did not view Japan's forces so positively.

After the war, the British moved to unify the various regions that would later come to form modern Malaysia. A major problem, though, was the indigenous Malay concerns about maintaining their own dominance in a future independent Malay state. The eventual compromise offered freedom within a constitutional structure which included support for the traditional Malay leaders, the recognition of Malay and Islam as the official language and religion respectively, and an overall structure that favored the Malay over non-Malay peoples.

The arrangement, as it was called, included an understanding that, while the

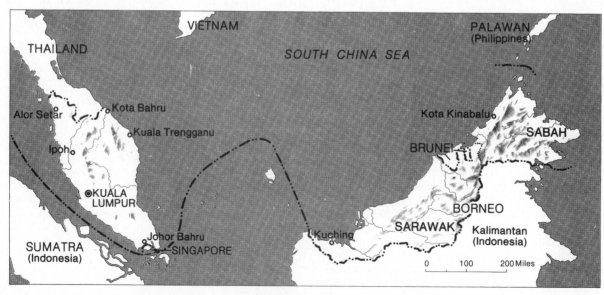

178

Malaysia

Malays would control politics, the economy would be dominated by the non-Malay citizens. Not all members of the Chinese community were happy with the agreement, and for the next decade a major insurrection developed led by local Chinese communists who had earlier been active in the resistance against the Japanese. While the entire period, known as "The Emergency," was very traumatic for the region, the rebellion was never able to draw much popular support and especially not from the Malay community. The British mounted a huge military effort that reduced the rebellion to almost nothing within a few years.

A New Nation Emerges: 1957

The British granted Malaya internal self-government in 1955 and full independence in 1957. Under the able leadership of Prime Minister Tunku Abdul Rahman, head of the dominant *Alliance Party*, (now known as *the National Front*), which included then and now, a dominant Malay party known as the *United Malay National Organization (UMNO)* as well as other parties representing the Chinese and Indian communities. UMNO, which has dominated Malaysian political life ever since, originally emerged as a reaction to British efforts to grant more rights to non-Malays. The party has not, in the years since, lessened its commitment to strengthening the position of Malay peoples within modern Malaysia. As we will see below, UMNO has dramatically improved the social and economic standing of the average Malay citizen but tensions over such favoritism continue to plague the country.

By the early 1960s Malaysia's chief problem, though, was not about indigenous ethnic tensions but with their immediate neighbors, especially with Sukarno, the fiery nationalist leader of Indonesia. Faced with Sukarno's increased interest in dominating the region, and a marked swing to the left in Singapore politics, Rahman and the British devised a plan to unite Malaya, Singapore, Sabah and Sarawak into the Federation of Malaysia. The tiny, oil-rich Sultanate of Brunei was also invited to join, but declined. After many complicated negotiations the federation came into existence in September 1963.

Sukarno, encouraged by his success in acquiring West Irian, (now Irian Jaya) from the Dutch without a fight, was furious about the federation's formation. A confrontation with Malaysia was started, which involved sporadic fighting in the remote parts of Borneo, and unsuccessful attempts to land Indonesian guerrillas in Malaya. The confrontation was quietly discontinued in the mid-1960s after General Suharto seized power from Sukarno.

The new Malaysian Federation faced significant domestic problems as well. There was continuing tension between the Chinese and Malays, especially over the role of Singapore, whose population is overwhelmingly Chinese, and which resented Malay domination of the central government. When Prime Minister Lee Kuan Yew of Singapore tried to increase his party's influence and power beyond Singapore and within the Malaysian Federation at large, a crisis erupted. It led to the expulsion of Singapore from Malaysia in August 1965.

**Former Prime Minister
Dato Seri Dr. Mahathir Mohamed**

A Challenge to the System

If Singapore's expulsion from the federation only two years after its formation had lessened tensions between Kuala Lumpur and Singapore, the core issues of Malay, non-Malay relations continued. As will be recalled, the compromise of the late 1940s has seen a political system which favored ethnic Malays while allowing the non-Malays to dominate the economy.

In the years leading up to 1969, the Malay leadership had been able to successfully dominate the country's political system. But the elections of 1969 challenged the political and economic compromise that had been at the root of the new nation's stability. Non-Malay parties won more votes than those of the Malay allies. While no dramatic change in government direction was immediately in the offing, it aroused the concerns of the Malay population, and hundreds died in the resulting communal violence.

This led the government to proclaim a state of emergency and to suspend the constitution; parliamentary government was, however, restored in early 1971. In the following years the government committed itself to improving the status of Malays, economically and socially. The hope was that if Malays were more integrated into the economic life of the community there would be less cause for the sort of social tensions that so commonly existed.

In the general elections of 1974 the *National Front* (the *Alliance Party* plus some smaller ones) won a sweeping victory. During the elections, strong precautions were taken to avoid the violence of 1969. In fact, to preserve social peace it became illegal to even discuss the issues that separated the different ethnic communities or the various programs designed to promote the economic life of the Malays.

Dr. Mahathir Emerges

In the mid 1970s a new political activist emerged who would eventually dominate Malaysian politics over the next generation. First chosen as prime minister in 1981 Dr. Mahathir Mohamad, a physician by training, was the first non-aristocrat to become first minister and a man whose political views have led him, along with Singapore's Lee Kuan Yew, to be seen as one of the most articulate, if at times deeply controversial, spokesmen for an "Asian Voice" in world affairs.

In the years after his arrival to power, Mahathir managed to grow increasingly influential. He consistently prevailed over

Mahathir originally gained public attention with a series of articles and then a book dealing with what he called the *Malay Dilemma*, which dealt with what he described as the second class status of Malays. A fervent nationalist, who wrote in English and even addressed such controversial subjects as the emancipation of women, his work was banned by the authorities when it came out in 1970. For a time he even had to go into hiding from the authorities for his outspoken comments against the leadership.

But given his support among younger Malays he was eventually invited back into *UMNO* and by the mid 1970s began his assent toward the premiership. In the years since, Dr. Mahathir has become one of the most outspoken leaders of his generation and a frequent and regular critic of the West even as he has successfully worked to integrate Malaysia itself into the modern industrialized world economy. Since his retirement he has emerged as a frequent critic of the government and his successors.

Malaysia

Petronas Towers, among the tallest buildings in the world

United States. During the economic crisis of mid 1997 it was Mahathir who was most ready to propose regional solutions to the area's problems from the use of local currencies for trading to a regional equivalent of the International Monetary Fund.

Dr. Mahathir's ideas were not always well received in either Australia or the United States or even among his Asian economic partners. Still, he was increasingly admired as an outspoken voice for the "non-Western" and specifically Asian communities. After the infamous terrorist attacks of September 11, 2001 many in the Western predictably gained a new appreciation for Dr. Mahathir, who was increasingly seen as a more moderate and "modern" Islamic leader in a world increasingly influenced by radical Islamic militants like Osama Bin Laden or those who had only recently dominated Afghanistan's Taliban-led government.

Contemporary Politics

Malaysia, a member of the British Commonwealth, is nominally a constitutional monarchy with a bi-cameral legislature composed of the Senate, Dewan Negara, and House of Representatives, Dewan Ra'ayat. The parliament in Malaysia is not an effective institution for the discussion of public policy. The opposition has limited time to speak and often receives bills for consideration the same day on which they are to be voted. The Standing Order of Parliament prohibits treasonable or seditious words, the interpretation of which is left up to the Speaker of the Dewan Ra'ayat who is appointed by the

opponents within his own party, UMNO, and over other centers of power within Malaysia. Over the years the Mahathir government also tried to curb the constitutional powers of the various Malay Sultans. In January 1984 it was successful in abolishing the Yang di-Pertuan Agong's power to veto legislation.

Several political problems of fairly serious proportions appeared in the last decade. One was leadership struggles within both the main components of the ruling coalition which governs the country: the dominant *United Malay National Organization (UMNO)*, and the less powerful *Malayan Chinese Association (MCA)*. Another was a rise in the activity of militant Islam, especially among the 20,000 Malaysian students in the United States and in Sabah (North Borneo), where there were violent Muslim demonstrations early in 1986 against the state government.

There were serious tensions within UMNO in 1987, reflecting a leadership struggle, a generational gap and a growing feeling that the party was strong enough to govern without the inconve-

nience of a coalition with other parties representing different races. Prime Minister Mahathir won a close vote for the party leadership in April and then purged some of his rivals. The relatively passive *Malayan Chinese Association* was troubled not only by a leadership problem, but also by a challenge from outside the National Front by the *Democratic Action Party (DAP)*, a younger and more vigorous party.

In a series of sudden arrests that were strongly criticized within and outside the country, the government cracked down on its opponents in 1987. Some of them were UMNO members, but more of them belonged to the DAP.

Prime Minister Mahathir long admired the economic dynamism of Japan and South Korea and often sought to use them as models for Malaysia. More broadly, he emphasized an "Asian" approach to economic issues. He spoke enthusiastically of an economic organization (the East Asian Economic Grouping) that would include the ASEAN states, China, South Korea, Taiwan, Hong Kong, and Japan, but would exclude other nations particularly the

PENINSULAR MALAYSIA
The nine states with hereditary rulers, and Penang and Malacca

government (prime minister). Questions about how representative the system really is were raised anew recently when a new law was passed that made it illegal to question voting roles. The opposition parties, which opposed the new legislation, had argued that checking the roles was important as many claimed they continued to list people who died.

Certain topics such as the special rights of Malays are not subject to discussion. Tough questioning by the opposition is rare and would not be widely reported in the media in any case, since it is either owned or licensed by the government. Overall, the prime ministership of Mahathir, who served from 1981 to 2003, evolved into a particularly powerful position.

The country has an unusual system for selecting the ceremonial leader the Yang di-pertuan Agong (King). The Yang di-pertuan Agong serves for five years and is selected on a rotational basis from among the hereditary rulers from nine of Malaysia's 13 states.

Elections in Malaysia have generally been clean, unlike those in many other developing countries. The single-member district formula benefits the government as does the fact that districts are often gerrymandered to favor the Malay voter.

Although important opposition parties are quite active Malaysian politics have long been dominated by the *United Malay National Organization (UMNO)* that has ruled in coalition with other small parties. In practical terms, really significant political issues and the fate of individual governmental leaders has largely been determined more within the *UMNO* and her coalition partners. Among the opposition parties *PAS*, the *Parti Islam Se Malaysia,* has been openly advocating the creation of an Islamic State in Malaysia.

The PAS's momentum, though, was somewhat weakened after the September 11, 2001 terrorist attacks in the United States and the commencement of the world wide campaign against terrorism that Malaysia's own government, under the strongly secular-minded Dr. Mahathir took part in. PAS has become a significant player in Malaysian politics. It may become even more so under its new more radically conservative leader Abdul Hadi Awang if the PAS's new, more outspoken leadership does not backfire by alienating the more moderate Malaysian voters.

Certainly among the most significant issues of the 1990s was the question of who would assume the mantle of Prime Minister Mahathir's authority after the long dominant leader left the scene. One early element of that issue was addressed in November 1993 when the *United Malay National Organization (UMNO)* was in-

Parliament House, Kuala Lumpur

volved in selecting a deputy president. This post, within Malaysia's dominant political party, was tantamount to a guarantee of gaining the post of deputy prime minister, and eventually the prime ministership. The contest involved the Minister of Finance, Anwar Ibrahim, and the then Deputy Prime Minister, Ghafar Baba. The Prime Minister, Dr. Mahathir seemed to prefer Ghafar Baba, but Anwar won a decisive victory and was appointed deputy prime minister.

Thus began a complicated relationship that has seen Anwar over the years become the most obvious heir to Mahathir's leadership and then later the powerful prime minister's most implacable opponent, an imprisoned felon, and a contemporary political opposition leader. More than personalities initially separated the two leaders. For example, relations with the more activist Islamic community have often been problematic. One significant challenge for the government in recent years came from the radical Islamic group, Al-Arqam. The sect was eventually banned. Al-Arqam had been operating hundreds of schools and many businesses throughout the country. As mentioned above, *PAS*, the party most openly advocating an Islamic state, has become more important in recent years.

As with other issues, the style of Dr. Mahathir and his former ally Anwar differed. The prime minister, at times, seemed to go

out of his way to challenge conservative Muslims by suggesting that a too rigid adherence to Islam might impede economic growth. Interestingly, the question of whether one wore a beard became an important issue in measuring the growth of Islamic influence in party politics. Anwar, a former Muslim activist, wore a very discrete goatee, while Mahathir went clean shaven, a subtle difference, but one that does carry considerable symbolism. The issue was reflected as well in the clothing choices of their wives. Mrs. Mahathir wore her hair uncovered while Anwar's wife covered her head in public.

For most of his period in power, Mahathir's leadership was largely unquestioned. Nevertheless, in October 1996, the party's convention saw very real competition between the prime minister's followers and those of Anwar Ibrahim. For a time it even looked like Anwar's supporters were pulling ahead. By the time the polling was completed a balance had been maintained between the two groups and Mahathir's power to sway his party's loyalists confirmed.

The following year, as the full brunt of the economic crises hit Malaysia, the long outspoken Mahathir lashed out at those he felt had brought on the crisis. His primary target was international currency traders. While many perhaps more objective economists have come to the same conclusion,

Malaysia

his comments, coupled with suggestions about controlling the financial markets with new laws, seemed to make the situation worse. Fear that such laws might hamper international currency movement caused Malaysia's currency to drop even further.

Meanwhile, provoked by the worsening situation, Anwar stepped forward to calm the markets by denying any such plans. Anwar was wrong. Mahathir not only introduced controls on some currency and stock exchanges but imposed price controls on a limited number of commodities as well. As for his long time deputy, while Anwar's monetary policies as the nation's long time finance minister had put him largely within the range of international opinion on economic decision-making, they contrasted deeply with those of his boss, Prime Minister Mahathir.

Over the summer of 1998, it was clear that behind the scenes the prime minister was moving against Anwar's supporters. By early September, the strong-minded leader had driven his most important financial advisers from power including his long time heir, Anwar Ibrahim. In fact, over the next week, Anwar found himself not only imprisoned, but beaten by his jailers and charged with an enormous range of sexual and corruption charges. The arrest and subsequent conviction of Anwar on charges of corruption sparked considerable international media, attention and inspired large pro-Anwar demonstrations throughout Malaysia. The former deputy prime minister himself was to remain imprisoned until he was released by the courts in the months after Dr. Mahathir left office.

In the elections that followed the crisis Mahathir's ruling National Front Coalition still did quite well, winning 148 seats of a possible 193. Nevertheless, it was clear that significant problems were brewing below the surface. For the first time most Malays voted against Mahathir's own UMNO organization. In fact, Mahathir's coalition had won due to the support of Indian and Chinese voters. Some of them were apparently nervous about the influence of Islamic groups among the opposition.

Dr. Mahathir had clearly survived the many challenges he faced not only from the internal politics of Malaysia but the impact of the Asian economic crisis. By the summer of 2002 he was ready to make his future plans publicly known. He did so in a particularly dramatic fashion, announcing tearfully in June that he was resigning from government a move that apparently shocked everyone in attendance. What happened next, though, was enough to make observers quite skeptical as within the hour he had taken back the resignation and announced that he would temporarily put off his departure. Moreover, he was

**Former Prime Minister
Datuk Seri Abdullah Badawi**

**Prime Minister
Mohamed NAJIB bin Abdul Razak**

supporting as his replacement his new deputy prime minister, Abdullah Badawi.

Malaysia Enters the Post Mahathir Era

Dr. Mahathir was Malaysia's 4th prime minister and in that capacity served the country for over twenty years. These were years that saw the nation transformed in countless ways. While he was at times extraordinarily controversial both within Malaysia and on the international scene his impact on Malaysia was largely a positive one. He promoted a multi-racial society while maintaining the centrality of the Malay community. Moreover he worked diligently to bring Malaysia into the world economy and encouraged an important role for a moderate and modern minded Islamic experience.

By October 2003 it was time for the sometimes larger than life Dr. Mahathir to

leave office, replaced by his chosen successor Datuk Seri Abdullah Ahmad Badawi. Early impressions can be deceiving, but it initially appeared that Prime Minister Badawi's differences with Dr. Mahathir's would be more those of style than substance. He remained committed to most of his predecessor's policies, including the controversial decision to introduce the teaching of science and math in English. The purpose was to prepare Malaysian students better for the globalized competition they would soon face, while being more closely linked than Dr. Mahathir to his nation's Islamic heritage.

However, Abdullah's approach to Islam was hardly that envisioned by Islamic hardliners. After coming into office, he worked to promote a vision of Islam that is as much cultural as religious. He strove to encourage better dialogue between the Islamic community and the West. At the same time, he was quick to shut down a Malaysian newspaper that printed copies of the infamous Danish cartoons that provoked such international outrage in 2006.

If the new prime minister's basic policies were a continuation of those of his predecessor's, his personal style was more conciliatory. This approach won him improved relations with countries from Australia to the United States. Coupled with Abdullah's early initiative—an anti-corruption campaign especially centered on the police—it was popular enough to give UMNO a major victory in the parliamentary elections of 2004.

His success though did not turn out to be long lived. During the late fall of 2007, the largest political rally in over a decade took place in Kuala Lumpur. Tens of thousands of people, led by the controversial former deputy prime minister, Anwar Ibrahim, called for electoral reforms. This is hardly a surprising demand given that Malaysia likes to think of itself as a democracy. Nevertheless, it has been governed by the same political party since 1957.

By the spring of 2008 the calls for reform had culminated in a humiliating showing by the government at the polls. The elections that took place in March resulted in a huge defeat for UMNO. It lost control of several state governments, from Penang and Selangor to Perak and Kedah, while the current coalition, which has led Malaysia since 1969, dropped a significant number of seats in the national parliament. The primary defectors were the government's ethnically Indian and Chinese supporters.

Opposition votes went to a coalition of different parties that had forged an alliance against the UMNO. Especially significant was the political re-emergence of Malaysia's former deputy prime minister, Anwar Ibrahim, who had earlier endured six years in jail after his falling out with

Dr. Mathathir. To make matters even more complicated, not only has Dr. Mathathir's disgraced former deputy begun a major comeback, but the nation's outspoken former leader has been feuding with his chosen successor, Prime Minister Badawi, whom he blamed for the weakening state of the UMNO.

By August 2008 Anwar Ibrahim's effort to stage a fuller political comeback were well underway. He won a seat in parliament while Badawai lost control of his party and eventually the prime ministership when his former deputy, Mohamed Najib bin Abdul Razak, assumed leadership of the party and government. In some ways, the new prime minister has offered a fresh perspective. He has spoken openly of the need to discuss publicly some of the more controversial elements of Malaysian society, such as the deep ethnic tensions that can bubble dangerously to the surface. His predecessors had been silent about this. More dramatically, he proceeded to remove some of the more discriminatory government policies that reserved special hiring privileges for ethnic Malays.

On the other hand, his government has continued the effort to undermine Mr. Ibrahim. In what appears to be yet another attempt to undermine Ibrahim's electoral popularity, the government has once again accused him of the sort of sexual misbehavior reminiscent of the very dubious charges that had caused him to languish in jail earlier in the decade.

Foreign Relations

Malaysia has been an effective actor in international politics for some time. In

Seeking public awareness of AIDS

fact, Malaysia has increasingly taken the liberty of speaking for the developing countries in the world community and particularly in international forums like APEC and the WTO. Malaysia, along with Singapore, have emerged as the most effective representatives of an Asian vision for the future and one that was strongly backed by the economic accomplishments of both regimes over the last generation. More recently the government has also moved to strengthen its ties to the People's Republic of China.

Relations with both Indonesia and the Philippines were significantly strained recently when Malaysia's government announced a draconian deadline for all illegal immigrants to leave. The decision not only created a massive human rights crisis as thousands of people found themselves suddenly housed in refugee centers, but it also weakened the domestic Malaysian construction industry, which relied on their labor. Eventually, after complaints from the construction industry, some elements of crackdown were modified. In addition, problems have developed with Thailand over charges that the Malaysians have harbored and perhaps trained members of the southern Thai Islamic resistance fighters.

Other issues have as well affected regional relations. Disputes continue over the many islands that dot the area. The disagreement with Indonesia over Sipadan and Ligitan islands off the coast of Sabah, East Malaysia, remained causes of concern during the 1990s. The dispute over Pulau Batu Putih ("White Rock Island") with Singapore was referred to The Hague by mutual agreement. The claims and counter claims continue throughout the region. For example, China, Malaysia and four other countries claim all or part of the South China Sea and the Spratly Islands.

Former Prime Minister Mahathir was particularly incensed by the United Nation's decision to have Australia lead the peacekeeping force sent to East Timor in the aftermath of the August 1999 referendum there. Mahathir had not opposed the necessity of intervention but made it clear that he felt it would have been better if the entire force came from Indonesia's Asian neighbors. More recently Australia's decision to take part in the American led invasion of Iraq hardly improved relations between Malaysia and their more "Western" neighbor to the south.

Malaysia maintains strong ties with the Islamic countries of the Middle East, but it has also officially attempted to improve relations with Israel. On a more practical level, that has not always been easy. A vis-

Rural life, Penang

Malaysia

Malaysia's "Come Back Kid"
Anwar Ibrahim

iting Israeli cricket team was greeted with protests during its spring 1997 visit to this heavily Muslim country. Nevertheless, as within practically all Islamic societies, sympathy with the Palestinians in their struggle with Israel as well as a criticism of recent American policies in Iraq and Afghanistan find many in agreement.

Relations with America have usually been quite complicated as well. The former prime minister seemed at times to go out of his way to arouse the concerns of many in the United States, the last superpower and an important Malaysian market. Not only did he charge in 1997 that Western financial speculators had caused the economic meltdown, but went on to claim that Jews were behind the "attack" against Muslim countries like Indonesia and Malaysia. If that were not enough to arouse the ire of many in Washington, he subsequently led a large entourage to Cuba to encourage trade with the Castro regime.

The Americans retaliated when the former U.S. Vice President Albert Gore chose the fall 1998 meeting of APEC, which took place in Kuala Lumpur, to denounce the Malaysian government's treatment of Anwar Ibrahim. Some might have wondered if the Americans were more upset about Mahathir's anti-democratic activities or his effort to impose currency controls. In either case, having Gore act as if Anwar were a hero not unexpectedly turned to the prime minister's advantage as many Malaysians resented the American interference.

More recently, though given that many in Malaysia have sided with the more anti-American Islamic activists and denounced the American bombing in Af-

ghanistan and the invasion of Iraq, the prime minister found himself in a complicated situation. On the one hand, he remained a vehement critic of the West. On the other hand, Mahathir also spoke out against the dangers of Islamic activism in politics and most recently against suicide bombers. Because of that stance the American administration, which has often shunned him, began working to improve relations with Malaysia's particularly influential moderate and secular Muslim national leader.

He was even received as a guest in Washington D.C. during the spring of 2002. That is not surprising because while Malaysia under the leadership of Dr. Mahathir often irritated the United States with his vehement criticism of both America and Israel. He has as well been a genuine voice of moderation within the Islamic world and has not hesitated to criticize his fellow Muslims for not advocating policies that would better integrate people into the modern technologically advanced world.

Overall, the last few years have been relatively successful for Malaysian foreign relations especially with respect to ASEAN. Singapore and Malaysia came to an agreement on their territorial waters boundary. They also reached agreement over Malaysian restrictions of the importation of Singaporean petro-chemicals. Still, as often in the past, issues such as water can make relations between Singapore and Kuala Lumpur complicated. Fairly recently, Singapore finally agreed to significantly raise the fees it pays for Malaysian water.

Society and Culture

Malaysia's population is very young. About 33% are under the age of 15. A high percentage of the people are literate; primary and secondary school education is provided for all, and there are a number of colleges and five universities. Although Islam is the state religion and Muslims enjoy certain special privileges by law, there is complete freedom of worship for other faiths. Nevertheless, Islamic departments within the government do have the power to arrest people for inappropriate behavior although after a recent incident they were formally told they would need official police permission to do so. The government has also made it clear that critics of Malaysian family law could be charged with sedition of they were seen as attacking Islam itself. But that hardly ended the tension.

Tensions that have long existed quietly within Malaysia have come to the surface more and more frequently. This was demonstrated in an especially dramatic fashion when Muslim activists destroyed a Hindu temple that was said to have been

built illegally in the nineteenth century. During 2009 Muslims in Selangor State provocatively protested the construction of a Hindu temple by marching through the streets carrying the head of a cow, the animal held sacred by Hindus. Not surprisingly, boar heads have been found on the grounds Muslim mosques, and a regular series of bombings has been directed toward churches. One of the most explosive recent issues has been Muslim displeasure with Christian use of the word "Allah" to refer to Christian God. While technically correct, given that Jews, Christians and Muslims, despite their different religious practices, are worshipping the same God, such scholarly explanations have little impact when emotions are aroused.

Malaysians are also great sports enthusiasts. Although more traditional ball game forms have dominated in the past, soccer is now the nation's most popular pastime. There is also tremendous interest in horseracing as seen by the country's five first-rate turf clubs.

The majority of the Malay community used to live in a fairly traditional manner, principally engaged in farming and fishing, but modern Malays are increasingly entering the trading, professional and other sectors of the modern economy. Today, Malaysia has a significant Malay middle- and upper-middle class. There are also a significant number of very wealthy Malays, some

Tri-shaw in Malaysia

of whom have made fortunes by having access to lucrative government contracts. With the exception of Singapore, Malaysia also has the highest percentage of Chinese in Southeast Asia. The community is divided into several linguistic groups that reflect the origins of their ancestors who migrated from China. Many educated Chinese, particularly among the younger generation, learn English and Malay. The more educated Malays usually speak English. That is likely to become an even more significant reality in upcoming years as the government, hoping to improve Malaysia's long-term economic prospects, has begun insisting that subjects such as science and math be taught in the English language.

Despite the recent crises, the impact of sustained economic growth over the last generation remains very visible. Longer life, improved health care, a significant increase in the number of people owning telephones, and an expanding national highway system were all indicators of the country's economic success over the last decade. Sadly, one effect of the recent economic problems is the reduction of the number of Malaysian families able to send their children abroad for higher education. While staying at home to save money might be a logical option, Malaysian universities have not been able to accommodate the larger numbers of potential students. Nevertheless, Prime Minister Mahathir did improve his standing among many non-Muslim Malaysian citizens by making it easier for outstanding non-Malay students to win places at the nation's universities.

Overall, in recent years there has been a growing sense that the official policy of Malay Rights, the preference for Malays over other Malaysian citizens has been something of a drain on the economy. As we have seen, Malaysia's most recent prime minister has moved to lessen some of those preferences.

Of more immediate concern in recent years has been the spate of violent and well publicized murders. They have aroused national concern and pushed the government into a more concerted effort to make the nation's security forces more effective.

Women

In Malaysia, Muslim women are subject to Islamic legal codes. In contrast, non-Muslim women are subject to the more secular civil code. For Muslim women that means that practices such as polygamy are allowed. On a practical basis of course the situation is more complicated. While at least one Malay state has made it somewhat easier for a man to meet the requirements to take more than one wife (not, for example, having to gain the first wife's permission), Former Prime Minister Mahathir made it clear that he disapproved of the practice as have other national leaders elsewhere in the region. Mrs. Mahathir would not even welcome second wives into her home.

Dr. Mahathir's daughter has also made her opinions known. Marina Mahathir has emerged as a well-known AIDS, human rights and democracy advocate. She has also spoken out against a too strong emphasis on Islam in Malaysian life and insisted that Malaysian Muslim women are still being treated as second-class citizens by Islamic family laws that do not even apply to non-Muslims. Most dramatically Ms. Mahatir set off a firestorm of controversy when she likened the situation of women in Malaysia to that of blacks under South Africa's former apartheid regime.

The fact is Islamic domestic law is widely used and it does favors males in matters of inheritance, but its application in Malaysia has varied from that practiced elsewhere. In 1989 the Islamic Family law was revised to give Muslim Malaysian women more rights in such personal matters as divorce. Nevertheless, in some regions, where Islamic parties have been influential, in Kelantan, for example, their rights have been lessening lately. Overall, one notes that the nation's Islamic heritage has been more reinforced in recent years. For example, in one state, Terengganu, the government established a phalanx of religious monitors to make sure that at least in public appropriate behavior between the sexes was enforced.

Malaysian women's rights and the nation's Islamic heritage have been particularly in the news lately because of the attempt by a young female Christian convert to have her former religious affiliation—Islam—removed from her identity card so that she can marry her Christian fiancé. Her long-time legal battle ended abruptly during the early summer of 2007 when Malaysia's high court dramatically ruled against her wishes. In doing so the high court specifically rejected the constitution's guarantee of religious freedom.

Looking at today's Malaysia, women are still under-represented in decision-making positions and their role in the professions is only recently growing. Happily, as has been the case so often elsewhere, the next generation of Malaysian women seems well situated to gain more control over their lives than women of earlier generations. Today's civil law grants them equal rights in work and education and today they are well represented among university student ranks. Women have served in cabinet level positions and they represent between 6% and 7% of those who serve in the various regional and national legislatures and a women, Malaysia's first astrophysicist even serves as the director-general of the nation's National Space Agency.

But more than Malaysian citizens find themselves within the country. For many foreign women the experience can be quite different. Malaysia has been accused of being part of an international network of human sex trafficking that often sees refugees from Myanmar being sent off to work in the brothels of Thailand.

Economy

Until the economic crash of 1997, Malaysia had one of the strongest and fastest growing economies in the Asia-Pacific region. Many expected Malaysia to become the "fifth tiger," joining Hong Kong, Singapore, South Korea, and Taiwan in the

National Planetarium

Malaysia

developed country ranks. Under Dr. Mahathir, the country had even developed enormously ambitious plans from the erection of the world's tallest building to hopes of turning Malaysia into a center for world telecommunications. The Malaysian national development plan had called for the country to achieve fully developed status by 2020. Under an earlier economic policy, the government was also able to substantially raise the level of Malay (rather than Chinese) participation in the non-agricultural sectors of the economy.

When the 1997 economic crises hit, Malaysia suffered the same fate as many of her neighbors. Its currency value dropped dramatically as did the local stock market. Initially, the government seemed confident it could manage the crises and unlike so many of her neighbors, Malaysia chose to confront the crises without borrowing funds from the International Monetary Fund. Given how strongly Malaysia's leadership has long felt about continuing Western influence within the world's financial institutions such as the IMF and the World Bank, this was a fairly predictable decision.

In response to the deteriorating situation, the government finally decided to cut its budget by a fifth and delayed some large infrastructure projects like the 550

million dollar monorail system that had been planned for Kuala Lumpur. By the fall of 1998 Mahathir, decided to go much further. Defying the international trend toward greater economic liberalization, he imposed controls against the trading of Malaysian currency or stocks outside the country. His goal, of course, was to shield the country from the sort of outside financial speculation he believed caused the crisis in the first place. The problem is that such a move can also end any hopes for outside investment. This is something most countries have felt necessary to help growth. The decision caused enormous and immediate political problems for the prime minister.

Despite the controversy, economic and political, Malaysia's economy in the following months did respond favorably. Although it was not clear if Malaysia's economy started to recover because of or despite the financial controls Dr. Mahathir imposed, they did improve. The year 2000 saw significant growth rates that by 2002 had become just over 4% annually. For a time though last year the nations' growth rate was expected to slow due to the financial setbacks associated with S.A.R.s outbreak that hit much of East and Southeast Asia during the winter and spring of 2003.

Recognizing the problem Dr. Mahathir's government responded with a combination of tax cuts and interest rate reductions in order to offer some relief to those hurt by the a potential economic downturn. Happily neither the dislocations caused by the U.S. war in Iraq nor the S.A.R.s virus significantly impacted on Malaysia's growth, which has continued its steady recovery from the crisis of 1997. The growth rate for 2004 came in at just over 7%, which is very healthy indeed.

One predicable problem has been higher international oil prices although Malaysia's government has been working hard to promote the production of palm oil as a fuel as well. Moreover, hoping to expand the economy further, government leaders have been working out stronger trade relationships with nations from Japan to Australia. Exports to both the United States and the People's Republic of China have also gone up significantly.

Abdullah Badawi, the former prime minister, also promoted agricultural improvements as a way to enable that industry to complement the contributions of the service and manufacturing sectors. In mid-2005, his government introduced a new "Malaysia Plan" that focused somewhat more on human "capital" improvements, laid greater stress on education,

and tried to improve economic conditions in the rural areas.

There has also been hope that Malaysia, given recent Western-Islamic tensions, would be able to attract more Muslim tourists over the next few years who might otherwise have done their leisure travel in the West.

Of course, the immediate recent challenge was coping with the world economic downturn that began in the fall of 2008. Like so many nations, from Japan and America to Britain and China, Malaysia developed its own $18 billion stimulus program to help the local economy weather the developing global recession. Some of their policies go further than those found elsewhere. For instance, the government ordered businesses to lay off foreign workers before local citizens. Nevertheless 2009's growth rate declined by a depressing 2.2%, a far cry from those healthier numbers that ranged somewhat over 6% in the year before the global recession set in.

Environmental Issues

Like the rest of the region, environmental problems are increasingly plaguing the country. The Science, Technology and Environment Ministry reported in late 1995 that two out of three rivers in Malaysia were polluted and that those left unpolluted were deteriorating rapidly as a consequence of industrial waste. It was estimated that seven million fish died off the coast of Perak state from exposure to potassium cyanide.

Another problem, which one finds throughout the region, is deforestation. It has even been estimated that the rain forest in the East Malaysia state of Sabah will soon have no more marketable timber left. Sadly native peoples are losing their lands to greedy state politicians and Japanese plywood manufacturers. On the more positive side, the governments of Malaysia, Indonesia and Brunei recently pledged jointly to protect 200,000 sq. kilometers of rainforest. This is a significant decision given how important rainforests are to the health of our planet.

In addition, had the new round of international climate talks that were held in Copenhagen at the end of 2009 been successful, the nation would have been in a good position to reap the benefits of the proposed plans to offer financial incentives to preserve their tropical rain forests. Unfortunately, no binding agreements came out of Copenhagen.

The Future

In the more than five years after he succeeded Dr. Mahathir, Abdullah Badawi clearly put his own stamp on the Malaysian administration. He worked to encourage a moderate cultural Islamic emphasis instead of the more controversial secularism often promoted by his successor. In practice, the effort had as its goal to limit the influence of the more radical Islamic activists. But as time went on, his leadership and that of the United Malay National Organization faltered while the formerly deposed and humiliated ex-deputy prime minister, Anwar Ibrahim, has made a remarkable comeback.

For the moment, though, the most obvious issue is the question of whether the nation's long-time leading party, the United Malay National Organization, will be able to maintain its hold over the nation's political life. It will be quite some time before we have a definitive answer. The next elections are not scheduled until 2013. Equally important is the question of whether long-simmering ethnic tensions of the sort that have so often disrupted societies elsewhere will become more problematic for Malaysia itself.

Meanwhile the Malaysian government has also committed itself to playing a major role in the emerging global Green Energy economy. Just last year they signed a $550 million deal with a Dutch firm to have the national car company, Proton, develop a line of fully electric cars for the Western market. The hope is to begin production of 40,000 automobiles annually in the very near future.

One of many beautiful mosques for the large Muslim population.

The Union of Myanmar
(*Burma*)

The ancient city of Bagan is located in Mandalay region

Area: 261,700 sq. mi. (676,600 sq. km., almost as large as Texas)

Population: 53,414,374 (2010 estimate)

Capital City: Yangon (also Rangoon, Pop. 4,082,000). The capital is currently being moved to Naypyidaw, located several hundred kilometers north of Yangon.

Climate: Tropical, with torrential rains during the summer monsoon (June–November) in the coastal areas.

Neighboring Countries: China (north and east); India, Bangladesh (west); Laos (east); Thailand (east and south)

Official Language: Burmese

Other Principal Tongues: English, Chinese, Karen, Shan

Ethnic Background: Burman 68%, Shan 9%, Karen 7%, Rakhine 4%, Chinese 3%, Indian 2%, Mon 2%, other 5%

Principal Religion: Buddhism 89% & other traditions, include Christianity, Islam and animist

Main Exports (to Japan, Singapore, China, Thailand, India and Hong Kong): Beans, teak, rice, hardwood, natural gas, fish

Main Imports (from Japan, China, Thailand, Singapore, South Korea, Malaysia): Machinery, transportation equipment, chemicals, food products, plastics and construction supplies

Currency: Kyat

Former Colonial Status: British dependency (1886–1947)

Independence Day: January 4, 1948

Chief of State: General Than Shwe, Chairman, State Peace and Development Council (since April 1992)

Prime Minister: Lt. General Thein Sein (since 24 October 2007)

National Flag: A red field with a blue union in the upper left-hand corner containing a large white gear (representing workers) superimposed with a sheaf of rice (representing peasants) surrounded by 14 small white stars symbolizing the states and divisions of the country.

Myanmar

Annual Per GDP Capita Income: $1,100
(2009 est. purchasing power parity)

(Note, the government of Burma has changed the name of the country to Myanmar. Where appropriate that term will be used in this text.)

The long western coastline of Myanmar faces the tropical waters of the Bay of Bengal in the north and the Andaman Sea in the peninsular southern regions. The northern part of the country is actually a moist and hot basin. It is separated from India and Bangladesh by high, forested ridges and lower valleys, and from China, Laos and Thailand by the mountains and by the Shan Plateau, which combine to form a crescent nearly enclosing Myanmar.

The mountains of the plateau region are not particularly high when compared to those in other countries of southern Asia; they reach a maximum height of about 9,000 feet. The Irrawaddy River originates in the mountainous region of the north, turbulently descending to the lowlands where it is transformed into a sluggish, muddy stream of water. It is along this river and the Sittang River that the largest cities of Myanmar are located, including Yangon and Mandalay.

The northern mountains are thinly inhabited by people who are mostly non-Burman. They live principally in the thick forests where teak and other valuable trees grow.

The great majority of the people live in the crowded central valley where great quantities of rice are raised each year, much of which is exported. The comparatively cool and dry season, which starts in November, ends in about mid-February when the wind changes from the north and begins to blow from the Bay of Bengal. The air becomes hotter during April and May, and periodic storms appear on the horizon.

In June, the full force of monsoon rains inundates the coastline. An average of 200 inches of rainfall each year, but the further inland regions receive less rain as their distance from the coast increases. The rains abate in late October; the wind again comes from the North, providing a cooler and drier relief from the oppressive moisture of the preceding months.

History

In the early centuries of the Common Era, the fertile coastal region of Myanmar was inhabited by the Mons, who had cultural characteristics quite similar to those of India. In about 1000 A.D., they converted to Theraveda Buddhism which had come from India by way of Ceylon (Sri

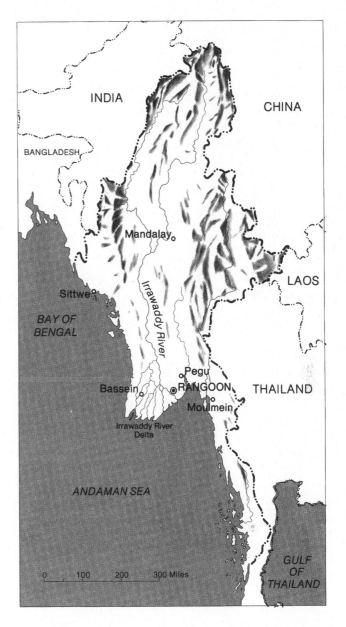

Lanka). The Mons in turn transmitted this tradition to the other people living in the region, including the Burmans.

The term "Burmese" is often used by outsiders to describe all of the people living within the country of present day Myanmar. "Burman" is correctly used to designate the largest ethnic group. Burmans are closely related in terms of language and appearance to the Tibetans, and seem to have moved southwest into Myanmar from the remote regions of eastern Tibet beginning about 800 A.D. Although they have oriental features, they usually do not have the eyelid fold of their Chinese neighbors; the color of their skin varies from deep brown to extremely light in color.

The Burmans emerged as the most powerful force in the country by the mid-11th century under King Anawrata, who established a national capital in the central city of Pagan, from which most of the country was subdued. The Shan (Thai) people, who lived in the northeastern part of Burma, disliked Burman rule, and in the late 13th century requested the protection of the Mongol empire which ruled China. The emperor Kublai Khan sent a large force of cavalrymen who invaded Burma, totally destroying the Burmese kingdom.

From about 1300 to the mid-18th century, Myanmar history is one of repeated destructive civil wars among the various ethnic groups that made up the population. No one emerged victorious; the wars served only to limit the development of what was to become Myanmar.

European merchants and explorers first appeared along the coast after 1500. Al-

Myanmar

Lord Louis Mountbatten, supreme allied commander in Southeast Asia (1943–46), later *Earl Mountbatten of Burna*, talks with British troops near Mandalay in April 1945

though the Dutch had trading bases there for a brief period, there was no early colonization of Myanmar. In 1753 a new Burmese kingdom emerged, rapidly reuniting the several small states into which Myanmar had been split by civil war. This warlike kingdom raided Thailand, fended off two invasions by the Manchu dynasty of China, and in the early 19th century, invaded Assam to the west.

The British East India Company, which controlled Assam, sent troops to push the Burmans out of the area in the First Burmese War (1824). The British then took over the Arakan and Tenasserim coasts and advanced up the Irrawaddy River. Faced with defeat, the Burmese surrendered those coasts and permitted the British to maintain a minister at the Burman capital of Ava. Relations with the British remained tense and eventually resulted in the Second Burmese War of 1852. A decade later, 1862, a commercial treaty gave the British the right to trade throughout Myanmar.

Thibaw became king in 1878, and rapidly alienated the British by again interfering with their trade and establishing

relations with the French. This resulted in the Third Burmese War (1885–1886), which ultimately ended Burman rule. The country was then governed as a province of British India until 1937 when it became a Crown Colony.

Myanmar as a British Colony

The emphasis during the British colonial period was on profitable trade rather than the welfare of the various ethnic groups in Myanmar. In depriving the Burmans of control, the British aroused the hatred of this the largest group. The minority Karen, Shan, Chin and Kachin peoples however looked to the British for protection from the Burmans, and thus were less antagonistic towards their colonial rulers. The British also undermined the influence of the Buddhist monasteries and imported large numbers of Indians to perform skilled and semi-skilled tasks rather than training the Burmans for these jobs. Thousands of Chinese also entered to engage in trade. The presence of these foreign minorities provoked anti-Indian and anti-Chinese riots in 1931. The anti-

foreign Burmese resisted adoption of European skills and cultural patterns more successfully than the people in almost all of the other British colonies.

Nevertheless there was considerable economic growth during the colonial period. Myanmar became the chief rice exporter of Southeast Asia; the lower Irrawaddy Valley was cleared of its dense forests and brought under cultivation. Burmese labor was used for the cultivation of the huge crops.

The British granted a degree of self-government to Myanmar in 1937 that included an elected legislature and a cabinet. Unfortunately the lack of experience in government on the part of the Burmans created a basic instability. Predictably there was little support among the people for the elected members and officials.

Thus, when the Japanese invaded Myanmar in 1942, they were welcomed by the people and Chief Minister Ba Maw of the colonial government accepted leadership in a puppet government later established by the Japanese in 1943. Even though the people had welcomed their conquerors, the Japanese quickly set up a very oppressive administration designed to exploit Myanmar's capacity to produce rice. Active resistance soon formed around the Anti-Fascist People's Freedom League (AFPFL), a political movement composed of left-wing nationalists and some communists, leading a guerrilla army under the Burman popular hero Aung San. The Allied forces, in an effort to establish a supply route to southwest China, slowly fought their way through Myanmar. The country was eventually liberated by mid-1945. The British then tried to establish a government along prewar colonial lines, but friction erupted immediately with the AFPFL led by Aung San. The British were then living under the anti-colonial *Labor Party* government of Prime Minister Attlee, which was in the process of giving up its control over India and Pakistan. It agreed in 1947 to give Myanmar its independence; the AFPFL chose then to leave the British Commonwealth entirely.

After Aung San was assassinated in 1947, U Nu, an attractive and fervently Buddhist member of the AFPFL, took control of the government. Burmese communists threatened the government of Myanmar in the years after 1948. In fact the government controlled little of the nation outside Rangoon. The lack of cooperation among the insurgents, though, enabled the Burmese army under Ne Win to reduce the rebellion to a much lower level by 1951.

China, Myanmar's largest neighbor, was not involved in the civil strife. The Burmese, although independent, were not experienced in operating an effective government; the AFPFL split and became a coalition of parties with a high degree of inefficiency, corruption and factionalism. The leftist-socialist group was led by U Nu while the more conservative wing was led by Ba Swe. The split between the two factions resulted in the forced resignation of U Nu in the fall of 1958; Myanmar was then ruled by the military, led by Ne Win. Little progress was made toward solving the political problems of the country, or toward getting the sluggish economy moving during this period of military rule.

Elections were permitted in 1960 that resulted in U Nu's faction being returned to office, but in 1962 adverse political and economic conditions again caused the military to intervene. This time, Ne Win abolished the existing political parties, imprisoned a number of political leaders, including the highly popular U Nu, and established a military dictatorship under the *Union Revolutionary Council*. He then announced that he would make Myanmar a completely socialist—although not a communist—state. Meanwhile the internal revolts had continued, particularly in rural areas during the post-independence years. Ne Win was unsuccessful in negotiating an end to these revolts despite new military operations.

Ne Win invited some of the former political leaders in early 1969 to advise him on Myanmar's political future. They urged a return to elected government instead of military rule. When Ne Win refused, U Nu went into exile and announced that he would try to lead a political movement for the overthrow of Ne Win; however, he eventually gave up the plan and returned to Myanmar. Meanwhile Ne Win launched an effort to make Myanmar a one-party state, controlled by the *Burma Socialist Program Party*, a leftist movement with some communist elements.

A new constitution was adopted by referendum at the beginning of 1974. Myanmar was renamed the *Socialist Republic of the Union of Burma*. Real power though was exercised by a 29-man Council of State, chaired by President Ne Win. The government remained repressive, unpopular and inept.

Inflation, shortages of rice, and floods contributed to political unrest in the mid 1970s. In December 1974, the funeral of U Thant, former Secretary General of the United Nations, provided the occasion for Buddhist and student organized riots that were quickly suppressed by the military. In 1983, Myanmar found itself dragged into the violent politics of the Korean peninsula when North Korean agents planted a bomb in a public monument that killed 17 visiting South Korean officials and journalists on October 9th. High Burmese officials were narrowly spared from this terrorist attempt. Infuriated, Ne Win

General Than Shwe

shook up the security services and broke diplomatic relations with North Korea.

Domestically the army improved its position against insurgency during the mid 1980s as China reduced its support for the communists in the Wa and Shan states and as a number of Karen insurgents were driven across the border into Thailand. On the other hand, the so-called Shan United Army, which in addition to defending the interests of the Shan tribes in Myanmar and Thailand, was involved in the opium trade, transferred its operation from Thailand to Myanmar.

Meanwhile the National Democratic Front, a coalition of ethnic insurgent groups, attempted to engage the government in talks on the key issues of ending military rule and restoring parliamentary government and autonomy for ethnic minorities. In August 1987, Ne Win made an unprecedented public admission that he and his government had made some mistakes. These included authoritarian policies that led to demonstrations, which had in turn caused the closing of all educational institutions at the secondary and higher levels.

An Epic Struggle for Democracy

In March 1988, a long series of massive demonstrations against the ruling regime by students, monks, and urban residents seemed to promise a democratic or liberal revolution like those in the Philippines and South Korea. The army, however, proved too strong and determined to tolerate such an outcome. Unlike similar struggles elsewhere, it did not have the world's press to worry about. Rangoon was neither Manila nor Seoul and it was far easier to use brute force with impunity. The long time dictator, Ne Win, officially resigned in July as chairman of the ruling *Myanmar Socialist Program Party*, but nevertheless stayed in the Rangoon area and continued to give orders to the army from behind the scenes.

At the end of July, Ne Win was succeeded by a close associate and tough former general, Sein Lwin, who became president of the Union of Myanmar. He proclaimed martial law in Rangoon and

tried to control the pro-democracy demonstrations by military force but failed.

The leadership then turned to a relatively moderate civilian, Maung Maung, who pledged multiparty elections in which none of the current leaders would run for office. There was great popular joy at this, but also a widespread demand for an immediate interim government. In September of 1988 former Prime Minister U Nu proclaimed such a government, composed largely of opposition leaders. The nation's military leaders had other ideas. Defense Minister Saw Maung seized power on September 18 and assumed both the chairmanship of the ruling party (the *State* Law and Order Restoration Council (SLORC) and the presidency of the state.

Protest demonstrations were then violently and brutally suppressed by the army. Thousands of people died as the army drove the pro-democracy crowds from the streets. The military assault that followed was even more brutal than the more publicly viewed repression that occurred in the People's Republic of China the following year. Thousands of refugees eventually headed for Thailand and various border areas beyond the control of the government.

For the moment, efforts to end the generation long military dictatorship had failed but Myanmar's democratic activists soon had another opportunity to expand the nation's democratic base. The opposition, calling itself the National League for Democracy, discarded U Nu as its head and selected as its new leader the increasingly popular, Aung San Suu Kyi, the daughter of national hero Aung San (assassinated in 1947). She benefited not only from her name and memory but also from the atmosphere surrounding the funeral of her mother in January of 1989, which amounted to a peaceful demonstration against military rule. In preparation for the supposedly free election scheduled for 1990, the military leadership disqualified the most prominent opposition figure, Aung San Suu Kyi, from running. It placed her under house arrest in July of that year, together with other leading members of the opposition.

The opposition parties won over 80% of the vote for the National Assembly in the May 1990 elections. But the army refused to surrender power and intensified its campaign of repression. Attempting to assert themselves, Aung San Suu Kyi's party and the Karen guerrillas then symbolically proclaimed a coalition government in opposition to the army-dominated one.

In spite of the brutal repression by the military, unrest continued to grow, both in the cities and in the rural areas. The government responded by closing the universities in 1991. The army, strengthened by

Myanmar

purchases of more than $1 billion in arms from China, launched a series of offensives in ethnic minority areas. One result was a stream of refugees out of the country, including Muslims fleeing to Bangladesh.

In 1994 and early 1995, the State Law and Order Restoration Council (SLORC) neutralized much of the opposition by signing individual ceasefire agreements with rebel groups. Their support was thus denied to anti-government democratic forces in urban areas. Overall supporters of democracy have had very little opportunity to advance their goals in recent decades. Tensions with the various ethnic insurgent groups have grown in the run up to the government's efforts to institute a new constitution. (See below)

Government and Politics

After independence from the British at the end of 1947, the Burmese political system that emerged was nominally a parliamentary democracy under the leadership of Prime Minister U Nu. Unfortunately, the multiethnic nature of the state, the lack of experience with the Western-style government and the inability to confront important political, social and economic problems, eventually led to the military domination of the country.

The early assassination of the country's popular independence leader also complicated the situation. The independence struggle had been led by Aung San, viewed by many as the founder of modern Myanmar. He had been an effective leader of the nationalist movement and was expected to lead the first post-colonial government, but his death ended that possibility. Later, of course, his memory would help galvanize Burmese behind the pro-democracy movement of his daughter Aung San Suu Kyi, the 1991 winner of the Nobel Peace Prize.

Today the country is best characterized as a military dictatorship. The dominant political figure for many years was General Ne Win, who died in late 2002 at the age of 91 years old. He had ruled from 1962 through 1987 through the country's only political party, the Burmese Socialist Program Party (BSPP). This was, however, only a front for military rule.

The period from 1988 (after Ne Win resigned) to the present, as described in the previous section, was one of crisis in which the military sought a way to maintain control and regain legitimacy. It even went as far as ignoring the results of the 1990 election, which had been overwhelmingly won by the country's democratic party, the National League for Democracy.

The political culture of the country is both hierarchical and paternalistic. There is almost no real experience with demo-

Aung San Suu Kyi (1991 Nobel Prize Winner)

Photo by Leslie Kean, The Burma Project USA

cratic institutions despite the strong public support for Aung San Suu Kyi's efforts to create a democratic Myanmar. Effective control of the government rests with the military junta that was officially known as the State Law and Order Restoration Council (SLORC), until it renamed itself the more benign sounding *"State Peace and Development Council"* in late 1997. However, a military junta by any other name is still a military junta, and no real political openings have followed the change of names. In fact, the transformation appears to have indicated more of a generational change among the country's military leaders than any movement toward a greater political opening.

There is some evidence that there may also be some tension among the military elites. For example, in early 2002 the junta claimed it had suppressed a coup attempt by relatives of the former leader, Ne Win. They were subsequently condemned to death although the executions were not immediately carried out. More recently, General Khin Nyunt, the prime minister, was abruptly forced to retire.

Among the most important political issues in recent years has been the status of

Aung San Suu Kyi, the most famous opposition figure in the country. In the aftermath of the government's refusal to recognize her party's political victory she ended up under house arrest. In 1995 was released to great fan fare. But that turned out to be of little significance. Despite Aung San Suu Kyi's release from formal house arrest, it soon became clear that the government had no interest in allowing her to carry out her political activities. In fact, for all practical purposes she still remained under house arrest until the spring of 2002 when once again, to more fanfare she was temporarily released from confinement. Nevertheless, that did not last either. She was soon officially under house arrest again.

Overall, though, despite the occasional efforts at reconciliation Myanmar's leadership remains unwilling to allow her to play any role in the political life of the country. Throughout the late 1990s, her efforts to address her supporters were constantly interfered with and confrontations between students, monks and the government forces were a regular feature of life in the capital. During the fall of 1996 the NLD had even attempted to hold an official meeting within Myanmar that resulted in hundreds of arrests. Attempts in 1997 and 1998 fared no better and the NLD supporters found themselves under major pressure from the government. Many were jailed and SLORC even refused to allow the former president of the Philippines, Corazon Aquino, to visit Aung San Suu Kyi.

As mentioned above, for a time things did seem to have improved somewhat between Aung San Suu Kyi and the government. For example some of the offices of the NLD were allowed to reopen and a limited number of her followers were released from jail. Still, when the Malaysian Prime Minister Dr. Mahathir Mohammad tried to visit with her during his state visit to Myanmar the junta refused to allow the meeting as well. More significantly the long hoped-for direct discussion between the leader of Myanmar's democratic movement and the junta never materialized.

By the spring of 2003, most of the pressures against Aung San Suu Kyi and her party were put back into place. Most dramatically the backers of the junta attacked her convoy which had been traveling in the country side and arrested the famous democratic activist in a bloody assault that saw an unknown number of her supporters killed.

Over the following months Aung San Suu Kyi remained in "protective custody" while governments and people from around the world, most importantly from within the region, called for her release. While all this was going on, the junta went through a transition that saw long-time strong man, General Khin Nyunt, emerge temporarily as the prime minister.

Once in power the new prime minister announced a "road map" toward a more open society into order to placate some of the junta's critics. Eventually, by the fall of 2003 Myanmar's national heroine Aung San Suu Kyi was allowed to return home. Given these government actions there were some who speculated that the new Prime Minister might even be considered a relative "reformer" within the context of the very hard liners who dominated the junta. Whether that was true or not, what was clear was that no real change was going to be allowed. By the fall of 2004 Khin Nyunt had been removed from power by his opponents within the nation's leaders who accused him of "violating discipline." Eventually the fallen leader was given a forty-four year suspended sentence for corruption in a move that sent a clear signal even to those in the military that the top leadership would accept no deviation from their control.

Khin Nyunt was initially replaced as prime minister by Lt. Gen. Soe Win, who is said to have been involved in the deadly attack on Aung San Suu Kyi's convoy. Meanwhile, his close ally, General Than Shwe, the chairman of the state Peace and Development Council, remains deeply entrenched in power.

In the spring of 2004, before Khin Nyunt was removed from power the government, perhaps at his urging had convened what was presented as an historic meeting of the nation's national convention, which was charged with creating a new constitution. Aung San Suu Kyi's NLD refused to take part unless their leaders were released from jail. The government though has continued with the initiative claiming that the groups they had brought into the process were more representative than the NLD. What actually seems to be occurring is an effort by the junta to create a political system that will eventually allow the appearance of democratic governance even as it remains in absolute control.

2007's Dramatic Challenge to the Military Junta

But the government's efforts to present the impression of a more open society was clearly not convincing to those who actually lived under its dictatorial control. In August 2007 the largest demonstration in decades began. Initially stirred by a dramatic rise in the price of fuels and public transportation, thousands and eventually tens of thousands of Burmese, led by Buddhist monks, took to the streets to protest peacefully against the military junta that controlled their lives.

Former Prime Minister Soe Win of Myanmar

Quite dramatically, they even marched in front of the home of the long-time democratic leader, Aung San Suu Kyi who, of course, remained under house arrest. As expected the junta struck back. Beginning in late September, the troops were sent against the crowds, and late night arrests began against the demonstrators, Buddhist monks and civilians. Eventually thousands were detained and many killed. Just how many died in the crackdown is not known. Clearly, it was less than the larger numbers who died in the crackdown of 1988, but by the time it was over, the junta was just as much in control. However, it had been forced by both regional and international condemnation to open talks again with Aung San Suu Kyi.

The suffering of the people of Myanmar had hardly begun. By the spring of 2008, the nation was hit by a devastating cyclone that killed an estimated 140,000 people It also left sections of the nation devastated, especially the Irrawaddy River that historically has supplied much of the nation's food.

While weather had initiated the crisis, the junta's own incompetence almost immediately made it worse. Extraordinarily hesitant to allow outside foreigners to help bring in critically needed supplies, significantly more people ended up suffering far greater losses. In fact, it took weeks before the country's leaders made the concessions necessary to allow relatively large relief efforts to begin.

Meanwhile Myanmar's military leaders continue their effort to create the façade of a more open government. They are restructuring the nation's constitution to create a system that, while formally allowing elections will ensure permanent military domination. As of 2009, the junta had officially scheduled those elections for 2010. However, to ensure that Aung San Suu Kyi would not be in a position to impede their efforts, the military put the Nobel Peace Prize Lauriat on trial once again after an American fan was successful in secretly visiting her compound.

Eventually the American was released to the custody of a visiting American senator while Aung San Suu Kyi found herself back under house arrest. Meanwhile real politics within Myanmar played out as they have for decades between members of the nation's elite military rather than between the generals and the dispirited democratic movement.

Defense

Until recently much of Myanmar's defense policy was internally directed against the various ethnic groups that sought either total independence or some degree of autonomy. Progress, though, has

Myanmar

Mother and Daughter in front of Pagodas

been made in recent years. On January 14, 1996, SLORC improved its hold on the country when Khun Sa, the number one opium and heroin producer in the Golden Triangle, surrendered his 10,000 man Mong Tai army to Burmese officials. The "triangle" refers to the area where the borders of Myanmar, Thailand and Laos meet. In return for the surrender, Khun Sa was apparently assured that he would not be extradited to the United States. Amnesty from Rangoon and the right to maintain control over part of the Shan state with a downsized army may also have been part of the deal.

The Burmese government has also signed agreements with the New Mon State Party (NMSP). The military agreement gave Mon rebels control over 20 designated areas in their home state in return for a cease-fire. Rangoon has also been militarily successful against the *Karen National Union*. Overall these agreements are a clear indication of Rangoon's determination to put an end to rebel activities in the country. It also seems clear that unlike the situation in earlier years, Myanmar's

neighbors have not been involved in helping the insurgent forces. Overall considerable progress has been made and only remnants of the once strong ethnic armies still resist Yangon.

The military situation along the Thai-Burmese border still, at times, remains. Yangon has in the past accused Thailand of providing sanctuary and help for both the Karen and Shan rebels. Burmese military forces also have conducted raids against refugee camps across the Thai border. Most recently, issues ranging from the flow of Burmese drugs into Thailand to Bangkok's forced return of thousands of illegal workers to Myanmar as well as incidents associated with anti-Burmese junta activists in Thailand have strained relations. Sometimes the issues that separate the two peoples are less geopolitical and more tied to popular culture. Just recently, for example, significant tensions arouse over the depiction of Myanmar in a popular Thai feature film. Matters did not improve when reports arrived in Bangkok recently of alleged Burmese insults directed against the revered Thai

monarch. During both 2001 and 2002 the two nations' shared border was closed for a time, a move that especially hurt those Thai merchants who depend on trade with Myanmar.

In contrast, relations with the People's Republic of China are quite positive. Since the early 1990s, Myanmar has reportedly received huge amounts of military equipment from China. Trade between the two countries has become a very important factor in Myanmar's economy. Along with India and Russia, China has also used its international influence skillfully to help shield the junta from some of its international critics. It also seems likely that China, concerned that its support of the junta might mar its international reputation on the eve of the Olympic Games, counseled Myanmar's generals against using the sort of force they had employed in 1988. Whether that is true or not, when the inevitable crackdown did happen, it was significantly less violent than the previous clash between Myanmar's long suffering population and their military rulers.

Not surprisingly the growing ties between Myanmar and China have aroused concern among regional neighbors. India and Indonesia as well as the other ASEAN states appear concerned about Chinese access to various three strategic islands off the Burmese coast.

Foreign Policy

As Myanmar emerges from its self-imposed isolation, it faces a complicated international environment. Moreover, that effort is especially complicated by a split between many Western states and Myanmar's more immediate Southeast Asian nations on the question of relations with Myanmar and its controversial military government.

External to the region, its international support has practically vanished. The fame of Aung San Suu Kyi is spreading throughout the Western world, no doubt helped by the success of the film "Beyond Rangoon." In early 1997 she appeared on the cover of the influential *Parade Magazine*, a newspaper magazine that reaches millions of Americans every Sunday.

In the eyes of many Westerners, Myanmar may be emerging as the 'South Africa' of contemporary human rights concerns. Within the United States, individual states like Massachusetts have moved to bar their governments from working with any corporation active in Myanmar and efforts to boycott the developing tourist trade have begun as well. Furthermore, in April 1997 the United States government officially banned all new American investment in the country. The United States, along with other Western nations has become even more critical of Myanmar's military government.

Former Secretary of State Madeleine Albright, when she was still U.S. ambassador to the United Nations, visited Yangon and delivered the message that there would be no significant change in U.S. policy toward Myanmar until the government changed the way it treats the Burmese people. More recently former Secretary of State Condoleeza Rice called the country an "outpost of tyranny." Somewhat later, in the aftermath of the newest condemnation of Aung San Suu Kyi to house arrest, the Bush Administration extended the economic sanctions against Myanmar for another three years. Since the crackdown of autumn 2007, Washington's sanctions against the junta have continued to increase.

The combination of consumer boycotts of Burmese textiles and official sanctions have as well made it very hard for Myanmar to sell its products within the enormous American market. The regime is clearly concerned about this and even hired a western public relations firm to try to improve its image.

Myanmar's relations with its neighbors are even more complicated. Overall the closer nations, especially those in ASEAN, are interested in a policy of "constructive engagement" which finally allowed Myanmar to enter ASEAN as a full member during 1997.

The decision to allow Myanmar to enter ASEAN not unexpectedly aroused considerable concern in the Western world and created tension between the European Economic Community and ASEAN. ASEAN itself is keen on bringing Myanmar into the organization as a means of providing Yangon with other alternatives to China. While Myanmar's rulers wanted to enter it, they have probably not appreciated the widespread criticism they have received from many regional colleagues who have been quite out-spoken in their negative comments about Myanmar's human rights practices.

That criticism got very specific when Malaysia's outspoken prime minister, Mahathir Mohammad, arrived in Myanmar and took the opportunity to tell his hosts quite openly that their membership in ASEAN was causing significant problems between ASEAN and groupings like the European Union. Eventually Myanmar chose not to serve as the head of ASEAN's influential standing committee, as it was scheduled to. This was no doubt done to placate some of its critics.

Chinese influence in Myanmar is significant through the military assistance described above and because of significant immigration and trade, particular in lumber, from the provinces north of Myanmar.

This influence has created its own problems. India, for example, is said to be concerned about the growing Chinese presence in Myanmar.

India has also worked to warm relations with the junta perhaps to balance Chinese influence and to gain help dealing with her own insurgency movement along its northeastern frontier. Eventually, by the fall of 2004, that interest had grown enough that General Than Shwe, the chairman of Myanmar's ruling junta made the first visit by a Burmese leader to India in almost a quarter of a century. Interestingly, Pakistan, India's arch rival, has explored the possibility of building an air base in Myanmar—a development that is likely to complicate even further foreign relations in the area.

It is more than Myanmar's ties with China or Pakistan that have attracted New Delhi's concern. India's leaders are very interested in Myanmar's natural gas reserves. But dealing with the unsavory Myanmar regime comes at a price. The Shwe natural gas project in which both South Korea and India have invested has attracted the attention of political activists concerned that such investments only strengthen the ruling junta's power. Nevertheless, such projects continue to proliferate. Most recently, the Chinese government announced two new pipeline projects to pump crude oil and natural gas northward into China's Yunnan province.

Society and Culture

While Burmans constitute the largest ethnic group in the country, others such as the Karens, Shans, and Kachins are important. Much of modern Burmese history has been dominated by the efforts of these groups to gain greater autonomy from the Burmese Government.

Theravada Buddhism pervades almost every aspect of Burmese culture. In fact, the military junta has made efforts to link itself to Buddhism as a way to reinforce its legitimacy. Monks are numerous and influential; most Burmese males spend at

Young monks eating

Myanmar

least part of their lives in monasteries. The countless temples and shrines have been constructed with great care and with precious materials that combine to create structures of exquisite beauty; the best known of these is the huge and ornate Shwe Dagon in Yangon. There is also a widespread belief in animism, especially with respect to the existence and activities of "nats" which are spirits within objects. Christian and Muslim groups also exist although they operate under heavy controls imposed by the government.

While these religious traditions reinforce Myanmar's links to its cultural tradition, today's political policies are hurting the country's ties to the future. The regime is so concerned about the thousands of students who have so often protested against its rule that most of the nation's colleges have been closed to keep the opposition under control. The result, of course, has been a generation of Burmese who have either failed to gain the higher education they and their country need to move into the 21st century, or the departure of the very people Myanmar needs for the challenges of the new century. The regime thus has been sacrificing the nation's entire future, for that future will require trained Burmese professionals to ensure its own survival.

Of even more immediate concern, outside experts have estimated that more than 3,000 villages have been burned to the ground in recent years as a result of the junta's efforts to impose its power over various minority groups. The suffering has a real potential for growing even worse in the near future as Myanmar's military leaders push even harder to expand their control in the rebel held areas in the run up to the formal establishment of their new constitution. Though there are many examples of the regime's new effort to consolidate power in the various ethnic enclaves, the August 2009 assault on the Kokang people was particularly brutal. It forced 30,000 civilians to flee into Chinese territory.

Women

In contrast to the customs of both traditional India and China, Burmese women have enjoyed a high degree of freedom and social equality; they can inherit property, keep their maiden names after marriage and have equal rights in contracting marriage and suing for divorce. Reports of spousal abuse are infrequent. Nevertheless, for many young Burmese women, especially among minorities that live near the borders, life can bring great trials. There are frequent reports of young women having been lured across the border to Thailand to accept jobs which turn

out to be forced prostitution in Bangkok's brothels despite the original job offers. This is also true for members of the nation's various ethnic minorities, who have often ended up being sent by human traffickers to serve in those same Thai brothels after trying to flee the nation by sea.

Moreover, the government's policy of demanding forced labor from its citizens often leads to abuses. There are no independent women's rights organizations nor are there government ministries responsible for women's issues. With the exception of Aung San Suu Kyi, women play almost no role in the political life of the nation.

As elsewhere in the world and within the region, the women of Myanmar are increasingly faced with the risk of contracting the AIDS. Women are especially vulnerable to the disease since they tend to have less power than their male counterparts and frequently less access to the education necessary to prevent infection and later to the medications needed to deal the disease.

Economy

The government's initial success in trying to transform the economy from its earlier centrally planned socialist style econ-

Young nun and her mother

196

omy into a market orientated one lost enormous momentum. By 1997 the economy, having done somewhat better during the early 1990s, was again a disaster. Currently the more open economic policies of the early 1990s seem to have lessened and a new tone of corruption and patronage reestablished. All this was made worse by shortsighted government currency manipulation that only served to weaken further public faith in their country's money system. Just recently, for example, the economy was disrupted when the government limited how much people could withdraw from banks and forcing people who owed money to immediately pay back half of their loans. Moreover inflation has become rampant.

Most significantly, the World Bank has ended its relationship with the regime and thus sent a clear message that investment should be considered especially risky. Overall, despite the fact that the nation is quite rich in natural resources, the combination of poor governmental economic leadership and the international sanctions its policies have provoked combine to create very weak economic circumstances.

Tourism, an important industry for the region, has not played its usual role either. The government had dubbed 1996 as "visit Myanmar year." The junta's marketing campaign was weakened by the efforts of Aung San Suu Kyi to discourage tourism so as to avoid inadvertently helping the junta in its domination of the country.

The temporary reconciliation between Myanmar's Nobel Prize winning activist and the government did not significantly affect the number of tourist arrivals. They still remain far short of Myanmar's tourist potential. Still visits did climb in the early years of the new millennium as people who had originally planned Southeast Asian vacations to Indonesia redirected their sights toward Myanmar after the terrorist bombings in Bali.

The bottom line is that Myanmar remains a very poor country with an economy that seems to be getting worse by the day. Most notably, the nation will be deeply challenged for some time to come by the enormous damage caused by the devastating cyclone in 2008.

The problems include flood damage, significant foreign debt, unemployment, high inflation, an unrealistic exchange rate, a very poor infrastructure, (which is finally improving) a failed educational system, and the prospect of little immediate assistance from the international community as a result of the junta's anti-democratic behavior. Many foreign companies, including Eddie Bauer, Pepsi, Carlsberg, Heineken Beer, Liz Claiborne, Apple Computer, Levi Strauss. More recently Toyota and All Nippon Airways have discontinued or reduced

their operations because of the country's international reputation.

Given that the infamously poor treatment of Burma's Nobel Prize winner Aung San Suu Chi regularly attracts considerable international attention, we can probably assume that Westerners are not likely to become deeply involved in investment there any time soon. Another burden on the economy was the military junta's decision to build an entirely new capital at Naypyidaw. Given the regime's public incompetence in dealing with the recent cyclone damage, it is likely to add yet another level of reluctance to those considering investing there.

While it is true that a new Burmese middle class seems to be emerging, the average income is between two and three hundred dollars a year and few get any advanced education. Forty percent of the children never attend school and three-fourths never get past the fifth year of schooling. As mentioned above, especially significant is the country's failure to produce enough college-educated professionals to meet the new economic challenges of the globalized world economy.

Really significant economic gains have been made in the illegal but lucrative narcotics trade. Since SLORC came to power, Myanmar has become the world's main producer of opium and heroin and more recently has added the production of methamphetamines to its infamous production schedules. The government itself claims it has been actively working to reduce the production of opium and even forcibly relocating peasants to areas where they can cultivate crops other than opium.

The one area of Myanmar's economy that has seen impressive growth is that of pearl production. As of the spring of 2004 it looked like production figures will be the higher than they have been in 30 years. In contrast to other of Myanmar businesses, the pearl industry has been able to attract foreign investment. The oil and gas industry has attracted outside investment as well. Currently a South Korean company is involved in exploring for oil off Myanmar's western coast.

Moreover, commitments have been made by Myanmar's neighbors, particularly China, Thailand, India and the more distant Russians, to invest directly in Myanmar's energy sector. China alone has seen a very significant growth in its trade with Myanmar while transportation links with India were growing during 2008.

Burmese Monks Protest Junta

Myanmar

Perhaps one of the most important developments that may ultimately affect the economy is the growth of economic cooperation among Myanmar's neighbors, the recent trade fair held among the Greater Mekong Sub-region nations being only the most obvious example. Even more dramatically, the ongoing effort to dredge the Mekong to make it easier to navigate within the region occupied by China, Myanmar, Laos and Thailand is eventually likely to offer considerable economic benefits.

Nevertheless, growth figures remain difficult to gauge. The figures occasionally issued by the Burmese government differ dramatically from those offered by outside agencies like the Asian Development Bank. Following the 2003–2004 financial year, Yangon did not even publish growth figures, a decision that hardly suggests robust growth. More recently the situation has changed somewhat. The junta claimed very impressive double-digit growth rates while outsider agencies estimated the rates at somewhat over 2%. More recently the figure again set by outsiders has been a somewhat healthier 2.9 % for 2006. But those plunged again in the aftermath of the recent series of disasters. The year 2008 came in at a weak .9%, and that was before the full impact of the world economic downtown was felt late that year.

It is also true though that while the West may have spent years trying to use economic pressure to force the junta to improve its governing record, the country has weathered those pressures relatively well. Despite being largely isolated by the Western countries, Myanmar's neighbors, from China to India and Thailand, have been more supportive. China, for example, is particularly interested in using Myanmar as an oil transport resource that might allow it to depend less on the potentially unreliable waters around the Straits of Malacca.

Additionally at least in the runup to the planned elections, the nation's competing military elites have allowed a greater measure of economic freedoms. The leader-

Lt. General Thein Sein

ship has also shown more interest in seeking advice from leading international economic experts and has been making limited efforts to liberalize elements of the economy over the last year.

Environmental Issues

As is so common among its neighbors, protecting its natural environment and especially the nation's forest growth is an important challenge. In Myanmar's case timber smuggling remains a problem, and negotiations are currently under way to form a cooperative arrangement between the Myanmar and the Chinese government to deal with forestry issues along their shared border. Myanmar is also attracting unwanted attention from its Thai neighbors for the burning of rubbish and weeds that so often dramatically influences the air quality of its richer neighbor. These are, of course, practices that have gone on for ages. But in today's increasingly more environmental conscious world, it is more of an issue. Like many other countries whose tropical forests are being dramatically reduced by deforestation, Myanmar could potentially gain significantly if the world were finally to develop a system to make it financially advantageous to let forests remain healthy and capable of successfully absorbing the CO_2 green house gasses that are adding to the current challenge of climate change.

The Future

Myanmar's integration into ASEAN may help the regime emerge from its isolation, but nothing is certain. Southeast Asia does need an independent and economically stable Myanmar. However, it is as an even more repressive and economically weak nation that Myanmar enters the larger international community. For the moment, the government has strengthened itself through its ties to the People's Republic of China. Some economic indicators, from the rising numbers of tourists to foreign interest in the offshore oil possibilities in the Bay of Bengal, offer a somewhat more optimistic impression. Reconstruction efforts to repair the damage caused by the cyclone are likely be a drain for some time to come.

Myanmar's evolution toward a more democratic society is now less promising than at any point in the recent past. For a time it seemed that Myanmar, which had long remained on the "back burner" of Western human rights campaigns, was likely to become a more pressing international issue. But even that role is now less likely. Western activists have turned their attention to the more headline-grabbing issues that have dominated world news since the terrorist assaults of September 11, 2001.

Within Myanmar, the democratic movement is largely defunct. For the immediate future Myanmar can be expected to remain the most controlled society in Southeast Asia, led by a regime in many ways not very different from that found in North Korea. If there is any difference, it is probably that there appears to be significantly more jockeying for power among Myanmar's military elite than is apparently the case in North Korea. Nevertheless, neither is making any progress toward a more open society.

Papua New Guinea

Shipping at Port Moresby

Photo by Ray Witlin

Area: 178,260 sq. mi. (475,369 sq. km., somewhat larger than California)

Population: 6,064,515 (July 2010 est.)

Capital City: Port Moresby (Pop. 255,000, estimate 2000)

Climate: Tropical

Neighboring Countries: Australia (South); Indonesia (West).

Official Language: English

Other Principal Tongues: There are over 800 indigenous languages and a Pidgin English is spoken in much of the country.

Ethnic Background: Melanesian, Papuan, Negrito, Micronesian, Polynesian

Principal Religion: Traditional tribal beliefs, 34%, Roman Catholic 22%, Lutheran 16%, other 28%

Main Exports (to Japan, China, Germany, Australia): oil, natural gas, copper, gold, timber, coffee, rubber, palm oil, cocoa, crayfish

Main Imports (from Australia, Japan, Singapore): Machinery, consumer goods, food, fuel, transportation equipment, fuels, chemicals

Currency: Kina

Former Colonial Status: Until 1975, a United Nations trusteeship administered by Australia

National Day: September 16, 1975

Chief of State: Her Majesty Queen Elizabeth II, represented by Governor-General Sir Paulius MATANE (since 29 June 2004)

Head of Government: Michael Somare (since August 2002)

National Flag: Divided diagonally from top left to bottom right, the top a red field upon which is centered a yellow bird of paradise, the bottom a black field showing five white stars in the Southern Cross.

GNP Per Capita GDP: $2,400 (2009 est., purchasing power parity)

Occupying the eastern half of the large island of New Guinea, the western portion, Irian Jaya, being part of Indonesia, the nation was formed from Papua, the southeastern quarter of the island and the Territory of New Guinea, the northeastern quarter plus the nearby Admiralty, northern Solomon and Bismarck island groups.

The terrain is covered largely with very high mountains, swamps and jungles. The climate is uniformly tropical except in the more temperate altitudes of the mountains. There is an extremely small European minority; the indigenous inhabitants belong either to the Papuan group (on New Guinea) or to the Melanesian people (on the islands).

History

Until two centuries ago the people of Papua New Guinea were still living a lifestyle thousands of years older than what the population experienced in 18th century Europe. Still their societies—and there are a great many different communities among them—were quite sophisticated and ancient. In fact, it has been estimated that people have lived in New Guinea for at least 50,000 years. The evidence indicates that intensive agriculture has been carried out—probably using sugarcane—as the primary crop for several millennia. It is also possible that the cultivation of Taro root was an early part of the farmer's repertoire.

Archeological evidence suggests that such food production developed as early as 7000 B.C. and was accomplished indigenously rather than being imported from elsewhere. But that production accomplishment was not the work of a single group. In terms of human habitation, Papua New Guinea has long been one of the most diverse communities in the world. Even today, of the 6000 known languages in the world, 1000 of them are confined to New Guinea.

Despite that long historical presence in the region, the peoples of New Guinea lived in small villages without larger political organization or more sophisticated tools than those made out of stone. They did have the advantage of the Taro root as something that humans could domesticate, but the island lacked any of the larger animals that other societies have

199

Papua New Guinea

been able to domesticate. The only relatively large animals were flightless birds and small kangaroos. Neither is suitable for human use as are horses or camels found elsewhere.

The European Arrival

Prior to the late 19th century, apart from missionaries, New Guinea attracted two main types of Europeans: explorers and investors, lured by its supposedly substantial mineral resources. Dutch influence based on Indonesia became dominant in western New Guinea. The northeastern part of the big island and the smaller islands to the east were annexed by Germany in 1884. The southeastern part of the island known as Papua was placed under British protection in the same year, during the scramble for colonial possessions, which was then underway worldwide. Britain soon changed its policy toward Papua to a less possessive one, and later transferred the area to Australia.

The German holdings in northeastern New Guinea and the nearby islands were seized by Australia during World War I. They were then awarded to Australia under a League of Nations mandate that after World War II became a United Nations trusteeship. In reality, Australia administered the entire dependency until 1974 from Port Moresby without regard to the legal distinction between the status of Papua, a direct Australian dependency, and New Guinea, the trusteeship.

In 1942, the Japanese conquered the islands east of New Guinea and invaded parts of the large island, including both of the eastern regions. Some of the bitterest fighting of the Pacific war occurred during the next two years as Australian and American forces drove the Japanese out of all but a few strongholds. Following the end of the war, Australian civil administration was restored. In response to UN criticism and a growing demand for self-government, an elected assembly was established in 1968.

In elections in 1972 to the House of Assembly (the parliament), the National Coalition, led by Michael Somare was victorious. His program, which called for full self-government, was accepted by Australia soon afterward, even though it was opposed by many of the European inhabitants who were understandably concerned about the changing political environment.

Politics and Government

The political system of Papua New Guinea is a federally based parliamentary system which offers universal suffrage for its citizens. The judiciary is independent from the executive branch of the government. Although democracy has been successfully maintained, little has been accomplished in terms of the daily living standards of PNG citizens in the decades since full independence. The government is currently made up of representatives from thirteen different parties as well as twenty independents, a political diversity that makes it difficult to accomplish much politically. There have of course been efforts to reform the system. More recently, for example it has been made illegal for politicians to change their party affiliation after elections, a move that may offer more political stability.

Another governmental reform was undertaken, which resulted in the elimination of the country's nineteen provincial parliaments. Unpaid local government officials, along with the national parliamentary representatives, formed local assemblies. They took the place of some 600 paid politicians who composed the provincial parliaments. The MPs in the new assemblies with the largest representation became governors. They are to be the primary link between the local assemblies and the capital. The move may also have some impact on the unstable political party system, where new parties appear frequently, and where members regularly shift from one party to another.

Especially damaging over the years was the long running struggle with separatists from the island of Bougainville which not only caused tremendous suffering but dramatically impacted on the politics of the central government. For example, former Prime Minister Chan, who came into power in 1994, initially appeared to be in firm control, but he lost significant support due to questionable decisions regarding the insurrection in Bougainville.

Hoping to end the revolt once and for all, Prime Minister Chan, in early 1997, arranged for the hiring of a foreign mercenary contingent to deal with the rebels. But his own military refused to go along. Led by Brigadier General Jerry Singirok, the military demanded the termination of the mercenaries' contract. In the ensuing brouhaha, Prime Minister Chan was forced temporarily from office only to lose his own political seat in the July 1997 elections, the first sitting prime minister to do so.

Chan was followed in office by the flamboyant Bill Skate, who successfully held off a challenge by the nation's first prime minister, Sir Michael Somare, to return to office. Skate, the former Port Moresby governor, took office in July of 1997. His primary accomplishment, during what turned out to be a very short-lived administration, was ending the fighting in Bougainville by signing a peace treaty in early 1998. Unfortunately for Skate, within a year his tenure in office had become very rocky. The following July Skate was ousted from his position by a whopping 99 to 5 parliamentary vote.

His successor was the well-known economist and businessman, Sir Mekere Morauta, who promised a more stable financial and international administration. Unfortunately, the prime minister's hopes to use his extensive experience to improve the economy did not work out. In August 2002, for the third time, Papua New Guinea's founding prime minister, Michael Somare, returned to office. By 2007 he had been reelected to yet another term as prime minister. Unfortunately, none of

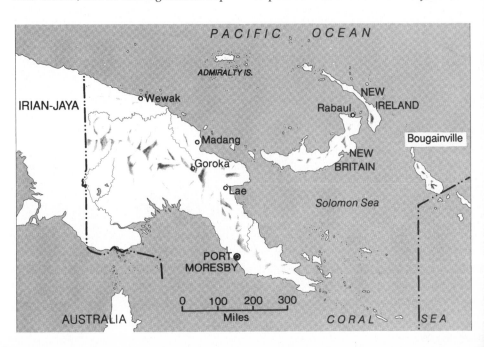

these changes seems to have improved the lives of the average citizen much.

Society and Culture

The vast majority of the population (around 85%) still lives at a subsistence level in isolated villages. Little headway has been made in developing the more industrial sectors of the economy or helping the villagers compete in the world agricultural market.

A small portion of the indigenous inhabitants still live at an Old Stone Age level-hunting and gathering for a living. The common impression that all of its citizens live under such traditional circumstances has—at times—made it difficult to attract foreign investment.

Most of people practice some sort of Protestant Christianity with the majority Lutherans. About one-third of them are Roman Catholic. Traditional religious practices are also an important part of the religious environment. Western missionaries, many of them American, are quite active in the area.

In recent years, the combination of the growth in the urban population and significant levels of unemployment has produced a major growth in crime which has made it even more difficult for the country to attract tourists to its shores. In fact, the crime rate has grown so significantly that the American Peace Corps even decided recently to pull its volunteers from PNG. These problems have aroused calls to break up the squatters camps around the main urban areas and to encourage people to return to their villages.

Women

Although government legislation gives women extensive rights, they are in practice still discriminated against, and some of the traditional cultural values that once offered women some protections have broken down in recent years. Polygamous marriages are allowed and often are at the root of domestic violence. It is, for example, not uncommon for a woman to be imprisoned for attacking another of their spouses' wives. The government has banned new polygamous marriages although the legislation does not affect previously established unions. Interestingly the new government has also introduced legislation designed to encourage the political parties to support female candidates. That is a worthwhile goal as only one member of the current parliament, Lady Carol Kidu, is a woman, though female activists do hope to eventually expand that number.

Only 57.7% of PNG women are literate (male literacy is around 71.1%), and a third do not attend primary school. Still, some women have established themselves in many upper level positions in business and government. Nevertheless, traditional practices still tend to treat women as property that adds to the perception of them as second-class citizens or even less.

Traditional expectations of women were very publicly challenged recently. The drama began when a young rural woman refused to cooperate when her family agreed to turn her over to another clan in compensation (along with $15,000 and 25 pigs) for the killing of a clan leader. The young woman fled to Port Moresby, where she gained legal support for her refusal to cooperate.

Perhaps even more significant, in the run-up to the upcoming elections, scheduled for 2007, a number of women from the more rural upland areas have declared their candidacy for political office. Problems associated with the treatment of women have become acute enough that a conference was recently organized, attended by representatives from a wide range of groups including police officials and health services personnel, to highlight the growing problem of violence against women.

Foreign Policy

The most controversial aspect of PNG's foreign policy in recent years was former Prime Minister Chan's decision to resolve the Bougainville crisis by employing a mercenary contingent. The incident temporarily soured relations with Australia that had been especially angry about the employment of the South African mercenaries. Matters were not helped when a confidential Australian government document, which negatively evaluated PNG's leadership, was leaked to the press during the summer of 1997.

PNG's southwestern neighbor New Zealand also played an important role in trying to reconcile the opposing sides in the on-going Bougainville crisis. Later, PNG's neighbors contributed to the resolution of the problem by agreeing to supply troops from New Zealand, Australia, Tonga, Fiji and Vanuatu. One of the most significant accomplishments of the former Prime Minister Sir Mekere Morauta was the completion of a final peace treaty on this issue which has so disrupted life in Papua New Guinea. The agreement that finally resolved the long-running crisis was to allow Bougainville to become a special autonomous region able to take more control over its own fate. And by the late spring of 2005 its people were doing precisely that. Over 130,000 of them registered to vote in the region's first ever autonomous election, a polling that was carried out smoothly under the watchful eye of a dozen international observers.

Among the most complicated of Papua New Guinea's international relationships is with its neighbor Australia. On the one hand, the Australian government contributes hundreds of millions of dollars in aid the frequently hard pressed nation needs. On the other hand, former Australian Prime Minister Howard made it clear that he wanted more accountability on how that aid was spent. He dispatched 200 Australians to help improve the nation's public administration, a move that

Mountain children

Papua New Guinea

was not well received by Papua New Guinea's Prime Minister Michael Somare.

Eventually a more formal "Enhanced Cooperation Program" was put into place. It allowed 300 Australian experts to serve in a variety of governmental posts from the local police and courts to immigration and customs offices. However, that agreement collapsed in May 2005 amidst more tensions between Prime Minister Somare and the Australians. Once Australia's next Prime Minister Kevin Rudd assumed office in 2007, there was significantly more effort on Australia's part to help PNG deal with the challenge of climate change and the all-important effort to reduce carbon emissions globally. In the most recent example, Rudd (whose party replaced him as prime minister in June 2010) offered help in reducing carbon emissions associated with deforestation in PNG.

Economy

The economies of the two areas, Papua (in the south) and New Guinea (in the north), are similar except that most of the mineral deposits (copper, gold and silver) so far discovered are located in New Guinea. The external trade of Papua New Guinea is largely with Australia, the United States and Germany. More than 50% of PNG's economy is owned by large Australian firms.

Almost 70% of PNG's exports come from mining. There are also substantial oil and gas deposits. Regrettably, production has often been disrupted by bandits and local armed gangs.

In spite of the country's political difficulties, economic growth was impressive in the early 1990s, but it weakened in the following years. In 1995, the country narrowly avoided financial collapse. During the Asian economic crisis of the late 1990s, PNG was hurt as the economies of its neighbors went into decline. Its logging industry, which had thrived on the needs of the growing Asian economies, largely collapsed. The year 1997 saw the nation's growth rate drop by over 5% with 1998 dropping by another 3 percent. As the new century opened, PNG's economic situation significantly improved, especially because its natural resources, like natural gas, began to be more available for the international market. The big news for 2010 was the decision to award Exxon-Mobil a large contract to exploit the nation's natural gas resources for eventual shipment to energy customers from Taiwan to China and Japan.

Over the years, the World Bank and other international observers have expressed concern over how the country's budget is handled. One of the major priorities of Prime Minister Somare's government in recent years has been to improve transparency of the nation's economic circumstances. Additionally an Investment Promotion Authority was initiated with the power to allow increased foreign equity in designated national industries. Giving foreign investors a greater share of ownership is a common mechanism to induce increased foreign investment.

The country has faced extraordinary challenges. Though its economy was less directly affected by the Asian economic crisis of the 1990s than some of its neighbors, the El Niño weather system devastated the country's farming community. Hundreds of thousands of people died from a famine caused by a drought. Almost as soon as that crisis eased, the country was hit by devastating tidal waves.

There have been some positive economic developments. For example, Australia's problems with the arrival of Central Asians seeking asylum turned out to PNG's advantage as the government agreed to house some of the refugees for a price. The Japanese have been building a methanol plant while PNG has been working with its regional neighbors to attract more Japanese tourists to the country. There is good news as well from the

Mekeo Tribesmen in ceremonial dress   Courtesy: Colin Freeman

oil industry. Not surprisingly, the recent rise in world oil prices has helped the nation's income.

The Environmental Challenge

Because Papua New Guinea remains one of the least explored areas in the contemporary world, it has drawn a lot of attention from those concerned about its fate if the world's climate changes as much as some have predicted. The glaciers on the island's highest mountain have retreated significantly in the last thirty years. It is also feared that further warming will eliminate many of the indigenous and poorly known species that live in the country's high elevations. As for the inhabitants themselves, responding to concerns about global warming and the more immediate rise in the price of expensive imported fuels, they are now producing automobile fuel from coconut oil. But such efforts have not held off some of the most dramatic changes brought about by climate change.

The people of the Carteret Islands, located in the eastern-most part of Papua New Guinea, are already living through what may soon become a common plight for the hundreds of millions of people around the world who live close to sea level. Today the island's population of some 2,600 people is facing an environmental disaster. The ocean is progressively rising and slowly devastating their once beautiful island chain. Even when the waters recede, as they still frequently do, salt water is destroying the islands' vegetation making it increasingly difficult for this long isolated community to survive. Perhaps more ominously are reports that efforts by some of Carteret Island's threatened inhabitants to relocate to other nearby islands were rebuffed by locals. This is perhaps a hint of the challenges much of the world may face as rising waters limit livable land along the coasts.

Opinions differ about the exact cause of PNG's local challenge. It could be a more general ocean rise caused by the increase in green house gasses in the upper atmosphere. Or it could be a more immediate and local problem. Some believe the problem is the sinking of an ancient volcano. Regardless of the specific circumstances, the challenge of rising waters is one that more and more communities in the 21st century face.

Given that concern, it is not surprising that during the late spring of 2009 PNG's leadership participated alongside its regional neighbors in an effort to get the United Nations' General Assembly to encourage the UN Security Council to take more direct responsibility in confronting climate change. Although the vote was largely symbolic, it passed the assembly in early June. It was the first resolution specifically to link climate change to security issues. It was also recognition of how the "security" issues of the 20th century are evolving as we proceed in the 21st century.

The Future

PNG's biggest problems are both natural and political. Resolving the conflict on Bougainville was very important for bringing a measure of stability to the country. Now the goal will be to make sure the fighting does not begin again.

The best news for PNG is that significant progress is being made in developing the nation's natural gas industries. Given the growing need to decarbonize the world's energy resources, the fact that natural gas is so much less carbon intensive than other fossil fuels like coal makes it likely to become an even more valuable financial resource for PNG over the coming decades. The current plan PNG worked out with Exxon Mobil to supply its neighbors with natural gas is reported to be a deal worth around 15 billion dollars.

Courtesy Laura Tamakoshi

The Republic of the Philippines

Majestic Mayon volcano, the most symmetrical mountain on earth, looms mistily over Legaspi City at the southern tip of Luzon. Still active, a curlicue of smoke issues from its summit.

Area: 115,700 sq. mi. (300,440 sq. km., somewhat smaller than New Mexico)

Population: 99,900,177 (July 2010 est.)

Capital City: Manila Pop. 10, 444, 527 (estimates vary widely)

Climate: Tropically warm with rainy monsoons in the summer

Neighboring Countries: The Philippines' closest neighbors are Republic of China on the island of Taiwan (North) and Malaysia (Southwest)

Official Languages: Filipino (a formal version of Tagalog) and English

Other Principal Tongues: Tagalog and tribal dialects of principally Malay origin, including Visayan, Ilocano and Bicol

Ethnic Background: Christian Malay 91.5%, Muslim Malay 4%, Chinese 1.5%, other 3%

Principal Religion: Christianity, predominantly Roman Catholic (about 83%), Protestant 9%, Islam (about 5%), Buddhist & others (3%)

Main Exports (to U.S., Netherlands, China, Singapore, Malaysia, Taiwan, and Japan): coconut products—copra, oil and fibers, abaca—Manila hemp, timber, Philippine mahogany, sugar, iron ore, electronic equipment, optical equipment, garments

Main Imports (Saudi Arabia, U.S., Japan, Taiwan, South Korea, China, Malaysia): Industrial equipment, wheat, petroleum, vehicles, plastics, chemicals

Currency: Philippine Peso

Former Colonial Status: Spanish colony (about 1570–1898); U.S. colony (1898–1946); occupied by the Japanese (1941–1945).

National Day: July 4, 1946. (June 12 the anniversary of the proclamation of independence from Spain in 1898, is a national holiday)

Chief of State: Benigno "Noynoy" Aquino III President. Since June 30, 2010

National Flag: The left edge is the base of a white equilateral triangle containing a yellow sun and three yellow stars; the rest of the flag is divided into two horizontal stripes with blue on the top, red on the bottom.

Per Capita GDP Income: $3,300 (2009 est., purchasing power parity)

The land which makes up the territory occupied by the Republic of the Philippines consists of a portion of a mountain chain running from northern Siberia in Russia through the China Sea to Borneo and New Guinea and the small islands of eastern Indonesia, and then southward through eastern Australia. Countless ages ago the sea invaded the lower part of these mountains—the Philippines are a small portion of the top of this mountain range that has sufficient height to rise above the surface of the tropical waters of the Southwest Pacific.

The nation includes eleven larger islands with more than 1,200 square miles of land on each island: Luzon, Mindanao, Samar, Negros, Palawan, Panay, Mindoro, Leyte, Cebu, Bohol and Masbate. More than 95% of the nation's land and people are located on these islands.

The remaining islands, around 7000 are desolate, jungle-covered and mostly uninhabited. Few have an area of more than one square mile, and about 4,500 of them exist as land masses in the 21st century only because it is impossible to sail across them. They are dots on navigation charts not even possessing the dignity of a name.

The temperature is consistently warm. Much of the terrain lies above an altitude of 1,600 feet. Almost all of the islands are mountainous, containing a multitude of dead and active volcanoes. The eastern slopes receive ample rainfall during all months of the year. The westward-facing

The Arrival of the Spanish

Ferdinand Magellan, the famed Portuguese explorer who, sailing under the Spanish flag, directed the first successful voyage around the world, was killed in the islands in 1521. There was no serious attempt by the Spanish to establish a colony until fifty years later when the Spanish forces, based in their colony of Mexico, dispatched an expedition to the Philippines. The initial settlement was small and had as its only contact with the European world the annual visit of the "Manila Galleon" sent to Mexico once a year. This is not very surprising because, unlike many of the other island communities to their south and east, the Philippines did not produce many of the spices that had attracted the Europeans to Asia in the first place.

As they had done in Central and South America, the Spanish gave large tracts of fertile land to prominent Spaniards who had almost complete authority over their domains, and exploited the native inhabi-

parts are drenched by the southwest monsoon from May to October. All areas of the islands have periodic, often devastating typhoons which bring torrential rains.

The land is covered with vast expanses of thick jungle that grows with incredible rapidity and contains among its taller trees the timber from which Philippine mahogany is marketed to the world. The part that has been tamed by the population varies from a thick growth of poor grass that supports grazing to plantation producing coconut, rubber, pineapple and other tropical crops.

History

Unlike some of the communities discussed in *East, and Southeast Asia*, the Philippines did not have a unified history before the arrival of the colonial powers. Rather, like Indonesia, it is made up of widely diverse groups of communities that had largely gone their separate ways before the conquerors, first the Spanish and later the Americans, forced them into a single administrative unity. What we know of the years before colonization is relatively limited.

Research has shown that about two centuries before the Common Era a fairly advanced people from what is now northern Vietnam and southern mainland China migrated to the large islands of the Philippines. They practiced a system of communal agriculture based on irrigation. Many of their descendants live in the islands today as small non-Christian communities. The larger number of Filipinos, who are of Malayo-Polynesian origin, arrived in the islands from the 8th to the 15th centuries from Java and the Malay Peninsula. Their migrations occurred principally during the period of the strong Srivijaya kingdom in the Indonesia-Malaya area and during the Majapahit kingdom on Java, which dominated a large area up to the beginning of the 13th century Muslim traders and pirates later arrived during the 14th century. There has also long been a small Chinese community.

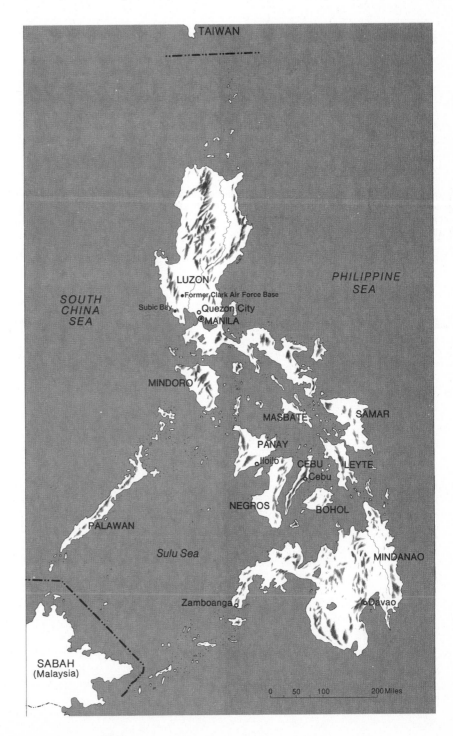

Philippines

tants without interference. Many of the native Filipinos, driven from their farms by the Spanish, went to the more hilly and mountainous areas of the islands to continue farming. Faced with the steep slopes of these regions they developed new agricultural plots based on intricate stone terracing of the steep sides to allow their crops to grow on artificially leveled land.

Given the especially harsh treatment the Filipinos received from their Spanish military occupiers, the best friends that the Filipinos initially had among the early Spanish were the Catholic monks who protested their treatment by the secular authorities. Eventually the harsh treatment of the natives reached the ears of King Philip who, by the mid 16th century, granted primary responsibility for the islands to the Catholic monastic orders. Over the next centuries, the various Catholic orders acquired huge estates and became increasingly resistant to efforts at reform.

Compared to the Spanish civilian officials the friars had far more power and influence, the most obvious example, their successful conversion of the islands over the centuries to their current status as the most Catholic country in Asia. In sharp contrast to the Americans who later made the teaching of English a major priority during their own colonial years or even their own brethren in Latin America, the Spanish religious authorities discouraged the teaching of Spanish which it was felt would make the Filipinos more difficult to control. Moreover, even as they converted many Filipinos to Catholicism, they resisted the ordination of native priests.

The Catholic religious establishment was involved in all aspects of the colony's civilian administration from collecting taxes and doing budgets through control over the recruiting for the army and the police. Predictably, the tight control of the ecclesiastic authorities eventually aroused tension with the indigenous Filipinos. Over time various leaders arose to challenge the Spanish Friar's authority, frequently over the latter's unwillingness to ordain Filipino priests. A trio of reformists, accused of questioning Spain's authority, were publicly executed by the authorities in 1872 in front of a huge crowd that watched the unhappy prisoners being slowly strangled to death.

Spain's attitude toward the islands had evolved during the century. After it lost its colonies in Central and South America during the first part of the 19th century, the Philippines assumed an even more important position. Nevertheless, efforts to develop the colony's economy were largely unsuccessful. So were the attempts to subdue the Muslims communities of the southern islands. Predictably, the slow but steady growth of education and the spread

of European ideas like nationalism and unrest, which were caused by oppressive Spanish economic policies, gave rise to a small group of educated Filipinos who demanded independence from Spain.

Among the best known of these Filipino nationalists was Jose Rizal, a passionate intellectual whose fictional portrayal of life in the Philippines, in a novel published in 1887 and smuggled into the islands, aroused considerable public sentiment and the anger of the Church authorities. Eventually, associated by the government with another revolt that had broken out, Rizal was executed in 1896, yet another martyr to the Philippine nationalist cause. But his death did not end the cries against Spanish control. A late 19th-century insurrection would emerge even as international events beyond the Philippines were soon to transform the circumstances of the islands almost completely.

Jose Rizal y Mercado

The Arrival of the Americans

Taking advantage of Spain's preoccupation with Cuba during the Spanish-American War of 1898, local Philippine nationalists proclaimed an independent Republic of the Philippines and quickly adopted a European-type constitution. Given the well-known American feelings against colonialism, the Filipino leaders, assuming the United States supported them in their fight for independence, joined the Americans in a combined assault against the remaining Spanish forces in the islands. Their assumptions about America's intentions were wrong.

To the frustration of the Philippine nationalists, the U.S. government decided to keep the islands for itself. This was partly out of fear that some other power, such as Germany, would seize the Philippines, and this policy was influenced by the young American assistant secretary of the navy, Teddy Roosevelt. Understandably

feeling betrayed by the Americans with whom they had fought against the Spanish for the previous six months, the rebel forces led by General Emilio Aguinaldo's immediately went into armed revolt against the United States.

During the Spanish American War itself, the Philippine struggles had merely been a sideshow to the American war with Spain over Cuba. Few Americans, save the young Teddy Roosevelt and his colleagues, were even interested in following the European powers in the exercise of empire building. In fact, when the clash over the Philippines actually came, even the president of the United States had to use a map to find where the islands were.

Once the decision was made to conquer the islands, the United States committed itself to put down the forces of the Philippine nationalists. The resulting struggle was carried out in a fashion very similar to the Vietnam struggle of several generations later.

As the tensions began, Aquinaldo, the leader of the Philippine nationalists, declared his nation free and independent and moved to occupy as much territory as possible before the Americans established themselves. The goals of the movement were quite impressive for their age. They envisioned a democratic Philippines, which would even include votes for women. This was something that was not yet a reality in the United States. But Philippine aspirations were of little interest to the Americans, who by then had their own plans for the islands' future.

The inevitable clash finally occurred in February 1899 as fighting broke out between the American and Philippine forces. Over the next few years the United States was forced to commit three-quarters of its entire military, about 75,000 soldiers, to the struggle.

Before it was declared over by President Teddy Roosevelt in 1902, approximately 200,000 people had died. Most of them were Filipino civilians, but the figure also included more than four thousand American soldiers as well. It was a bloody affair that included atrocities on both sides that would sound ominously familiar to later generations who came of age hearing horror stories about the Vietnam struggle. In the end, though, American power and divisions among the Filipinos weakened Aguinaldo's effectiveness. His capture, after a daring American raid, determined the fate of the islands. Among the most prominent of the Americans who commanded there during the struggle was Arthur MacArthur, father of Douglas MacArthur, whose boyhood experiences in the islands would affect the rest of his career.

General Emilio Aguinaldo

Though the Americans had fought hard to establish their control over the islands, there was enough ambivalence about the blatantly imperialist effort for Washington also to commit itself to preparing the islands for eventual independence. Unlike some of the other colonial powers, the United States did make a clear effort to share administration with the Filipinos from the colony's earliest years. In fact, the American-sponsored assembly that was soon formed had the distinction of being the first elective legislative body in the entire region. But while the United States increasingly turned over internal decision making to the Filipinos, control over defense and foreign policy remained tightly in American hands.

Education was a major goal of the islands' new administration, and large numbers of young Americans were recruited to serve as teachers, especially English teachers. The program was in many ways rather like the Peace Corps efforts later in the century. The major emphasis on education and English soon had a considerable impact. Literacy rates improved markedly and English became in more common use among the island's inhabitants.

By 1916, the United States had committed itself to the goal of establishing eventual independence for the islands. It had also begun the creation of internally self-governing institutions. The colonial administration also made efforts in the fields of communication, public works and education.

Nevertheless, the emphasis was on creating areas for profitable American investment. There was little done to develop the economy as a whole for the benefit of the Filipinos, especially the poorer classes. A foreign trade emerged that was almost totally linked to and dependent on the U.S. market. Sadly, while the Americans were quite influential in

Grounds of the Pacific War Memorial, Corregidor

Philippines

moving Filipinos into governing positions and improving literacy rates, their economic policies did little to address the economic domination the land-owning elite held over the population.

Feudal systems of sharecropping in the rural areas, which had arisen under the Spanish as a result of land grants, continued and became an even worse problem. The local elected governments permitted by the colonial administration drifted toward control by Filipino political machines and bosses who bore a remarkable resemblance to some of their contemporaries in Latin America.

In the 1930s, Manuel Quezon, who formed and led the Nationalist Party, emerged as the leading politician and eventually president. Political idealism was one factor that prompted the United States to adopt legislation providing for an almost fully self-governing Commonwealth to be established in 1935. The other was pressure from U.S. sugar interests for protective tariffs against Philippine sugar, which were impossible unless it was independent.

Toward World War II

The growing threat of the Japanese in Asia, in the late 1930s, lessened the desire for total independence on the part of the more radical Filipinos, who saw the need for U.S. protection. Partly as an assurance of further American support, Quezon hired Douglas MacArthur, son of the island's late military governor and former American army's Chief of Staff to serve as the Philippine's "Field Marshal." But despite MacArthur's reputation as an outstanding military strategist, the Philippines were not at all prepared for the assault they were to experience as the forces of imperial Japan attacked in December of 1941.

The islands were quickly overrun by a force of well-trained Japanese soldiers who inaugurated, in 1942, the same harsh military rule that was their policy in the other areas of Southeast Asia they conquered. As was the case elsewhere, many Filipinos, including the father of the later martyred hero, Benigno Aquino, took the Japanese at their word about freeing Asia from the Western colonialists and collaborated with them. This was often true of the Philippine elite that had earlier worked with the Spanish, then the Americans, and now the Japanese occupiers. Many other Filipinos eventually took up arms against Japan's forces.

This resulted in a limited guerrilla movement operating clandestinely in the rural areas to sabotage the military installations of the Japanese. Quezon and his government went into exile in the United States, where he died in 1944. His successor, Sergio Osmena, was eventually able to return to the Philippines as a result of the progress of General Douglas MacArthur's forces in liberating the islands.

MacArthur, in sharp contrast to his later role as a social revolutionary in Japan, chose to reestablish the Philippine land-owning elite in power even overlooking their role as frequent wartime collaborators with the Japanese. Not surprisingly, that enraged many of the leftist guerrillas who had fought Japan and had long harbored hopes for a more equitable land distribution after the war. Given American concerns about socialism and fear of communism, the likelihood that the U.S. would have supported their wartime peasant allies in efforts at significant land reform was small indeed. Most groups, like the leftist Huks, were simply demobilized and sent home only to emerge in later years as a new threat to the government. On a political level though, the United States did officially grant the islands their independence on July 4, 1946.

The economy had been devastated by the war, and it was necessary for the United States to pour in huge sums for relief and rehabilitation and to grant duty-free status to Philippine exports in the American market until 1954. Much of the aid did not reach those who needed it. Osmena died in 1946. For the next twenty years the Philippines were ruled, with one exception, by a succession of colorless, corrupt and inefficient leaders, and behind the scenes the United States remained especially influential.

Ramon Magsaysay, who served as president during the mid-1950s was, for example, especially close to the American intelligence community that had sponsored his rise in Philippine politics. Once in power he maintained a consistently pro-U.S. policy and took the Philippines into SEATO, the Southeast Asia Treaty organization in 1954. In spite of his strenuous efforts the power of the small group of families who dominated agriculture, industry and trade—the descendants of the Spanish aristocratic class, continued. Unfortunately for the Americans who valued their ties to him, Magsaysay was killed in an airplane crash in 1957.

The next few years saw little change in the Philippines. There was a limited growth of anti-Americanism as some of its leaders dabbled in an active, anti-U.S. foreign policy intended to make the Philippines more popular, powerful and acceptable in the Asian community.

The Marcos Years

Ferdinand Marcos of the Nationalist Party was elected president in 1965 amid a general sense of an urgent need for change among the people. His election was helped by his claim, later disproved, to have been an influential leader in the anti-Japanese guerrilla movement. Marcos embarked upon a reform platform similar to that of Magsaysay, but met the same intractable obstacles as his predecessor. Corruption remained a virtual custom among minor government officials and employees for the next twenty years. The Communist Party (PKP) abetted by discontent among the poverty-stricken rural people, also resumed its guerrilla activity against the state. Traditional rivalry between the Nationalist Party and the Liberal Party continued.

President Marcos was reelected in 1969 over a Liberal Party opponent by a large majority and became the first Philippine president to win a second term. Nationalist majorities in both houses of the Assembly were sizable. But student and labor demonstrations in Manila were symptoms of the country's malaise. Some of the dissent had an openly anti-U.S. tone.

Among Marcos' most outspoken opponents was the young Benigno Aquino, a former journalist and popular politician. Aquino and his later internationally famous wife, Corazon Aquino, came from elite Filipino families. Having been unable to run against Marcos in the 1969 election, it was expected that Benigno Aquino would run for president in the next elections but those elections never came about. Ferdinand Marcos, already the first Philippine president to serve two full terms, had other plans.

Marcos had no intention of running for office again. Rather, after staging a series of violent incidents that added to the sense of crisis in the country, he declared martial law and canceled the upcoming elections. Large numbers of his political enemies were imprisoned. Aquino was to spend the next seven years in jail where much to Marcos' displeasure he came to be seen as the principal martyr of the developing dictatorship. Marcos justified his actions by claiming the islands were threatened by communism and needed authoritarian government for the moment.

Despite these actions, the influential Americans and the local business community as well as much of the population initially approved of the move. In the ensuing years Marcos had some success in improving the state of law and order except in Mindanao, where an ongoing Muslim revolt had been in progress for years. Of greatest importance, however, he received additional support by rigging a referendum on a new constitution under which he awarded himself virtual dictatorial powers for an unlimited period.

Principal opposition to the Marcos regime came from the Catholic Church and insurgent Muslims in the southern islands. The latter received support from other Muslim countries. Little progress though was made dealing with those problems until years later. Under Marcos, martial law delegated great political power to the armed forces, which became repressive and corrupt, even while providing a semblance of order.

insurgent Muslims in the southern islands. The latter received support from other Muslim countries. Little progress though was made dealing with those problems until years later. Under Marcos, martial law delegated great political power to the armed forces, which became repressive and corrupt, even while providing a semblance of order.

Imelda Marcos, the flamboyant wife of the president, became Governor of Manila and announced ambitious plans for its redevelopment. Even as she set up her own power base, she remained loyal to her husband. Still, her plans to succeed him were widely known. For a time the powerful couple seemed to be a Philippine equivalent of the glamorous Kennedys of American political life.

In the 1980s, the militant wings of the opposition groups began to resort to terrorist bombings. Insurgency, particularly Muslim and communist, became a continuing problem as well.

Despite the end of martial law in 1981, there was little improvement in the political situation. The country continued to be run by an alliance led by the aging Marcos, his wife Imelda, the armed forces, the ruling New Society Party and rich and powerful men close to the president who operated an economic system known informally as "crony capitalism." By the early 1980s more and more of the Philippine elite had lost faith in Marcos's government and its ability to deal with the economic crisis brought on by the rise in oil prices in the mid 1970s.

Marcos often talked of forcing the U.S. out of its huge air and naval bases in the Philippines, but that was almost certainly to divert popular attention from his domestic policies as well as to get greater concessions from the United States, including higher rents. In addition, he was determined to appear at home and abroad as entirely independent of the United States and as the leader of a truly Asian nation. Partly for this purpose, he visited and granted diplomatic recognition to the People's Republic of China in June 1975; another consideration was that he wanted, and apparently thought that he got, a pledge from Beijing not to support the small Philippine communist insurgent movement, the New People's Army. Marcos also established diplomatic relations with the Soviet Union in 1976.

Despite the occasionally nationalistic rhetoric, relations with the United States were reasonably good; President Ford visited in late 1975. During the late 1970s the United States' primary concern in the Philippines, especially after its loss in Vietnam, was to maintain its access to the bases. Marcos knew that and often offered himself to the Americans as their only

Ferdinand and Imelda Marcos at their zenith in 1972

guarantee that the bases would be maintained—assuming the Americans were willing to pay enough. An agreement concerning the base leases was finally concluded with the United States in 1978, and a second in late 1983.

The Aquino Challenge

The forces of opposition to Marcos' rule continued to grow. Had he been able to of-

fer a record of continuously strong economic growth, as had other Southeast Asian rulers of the era, his authoritarianism might have been tolerated. But that was not the case. As in the early 1980s, other regional economies started to take off, and the Philippines lagged behind, mired in economic problems.

In 1983, longtime opposition leader Benigno Aquino, probably encouraged by false reports that Marcos was about to undergo surgery, decided to return to Manila from the United States, where he had been serving as a fellow at Harvard University. Sadly, he had misjudged just how dangerous his decision was. As he was getting off the plane Aquino was summarily gunned down.

The opposition blamed the government, and more specifically, the armed forces, for the assassination. Huge demonstrations occurred in the cities against Marcos and in protest at the sham official investigation of the murder.

After an unnecessarily lengthy inquiry, armed forces Chief of Staff General Fabian Ver and 25 others were indicted in January 1985 for complicity in the assassination of Benigno Aquino. The trial began in February and continued for months. But when all the evidence was in and after the jury had retired to deliberate, the Philippine Supreme Court took the unheard of step of dismissing the charges on the grounds that there was insufficient evidence.

Despite their success in dealing with the events surrounding the assassination, the Marcos regime seemed to be unraveling. Marcos still had some major advantages,

Inside the Pacific War Memorial Museum on Corregidor

Philippines

the influential Americans were, as always, more interested in the security of the American bases than the welfare of the Philippines themselves. They still believed that his remaining in power was their best defense against losing the bases.

In fact, even as many officials among the Americans had lost faith, Marcos's long-term relationship with Ronald Reagan kept the United States from openly siding with his enemies until his regime was almost completely spent. Eventually, under American pressure, Marcos called a presidential election for early 1986.

By then, though, the opposition had managed to unite behind Corazon Aquino, the widow of Benigno Aquino. Her candidacy, which had the support of the Philippine Catholic hierarchy and its influential Archbishop of Manila, Jaime Sin, soon attracted widespread support, especially in the cities. She also had, at least for the moment, the support of her vice-presidential candidate, Salvador Laurel's powerful political organization. Although Marcos was officially declared to have won the election, which had been monitored by large numbers of mainly American official and unofficial observers, it soon became obvious that his supporters were guilty of massive fraud and that Mrs. Aquino had actually won.

The United States government was by now finally convinced that Marcos' time had passed and switched its support to Mrs. Aquino. A group of army officers belonging to a military reform movement usually known by its acronym RAM then began to plan a coup against Marcos.

Hearing of the plans for a coup, Marcos concluded that it was the work of Defense Minister Enrile and Vice Chief of Staff Fidel Ramos and began to move against them. They and their supporters, now including many Americans, promptly came out in support of Mrs. Aquino. Privately, the Americans supplied important intelligence to the insurgents. Cardinal Sin, meanwhile, urged the Catholic faithful to block the streets of Manila to prevent the movement of troops loyal to Marcos. This tactic was effective and later came to be known to the world as an example of "people power." Marcos had lost. After gaining an offer of asylum from the United States, provided he did not use force against his own people, Marcos went into exile in Hawaii and Mrs. Aquino was inaugurated President.

As president, Aquino repealed Marcos' repressive regulations and released his political prisoners. She also initiated steps to recover the enormous wealth—put at ten billion dollars by the CIA—that he had stashed abroad, mainly in the United States and Switzerland. President Aquino and her middle-class cabinet, faced with a pro-

Marcos majority in the Assembly and the Supreme Court, then declared a "revolutionary" government in order to be better able to eliminate the legacy of Marcos' rule.

About six months after her election, President Aquino began to move on her major challenges. She visited the U.S. in September, and the American Congress voted an extra $200 million in aid for the Philippines. She began then to work on an ambitious and difficult land reform program, which was badly needed. In late November she broke with her former supporter Defense Minister Juan Ponce Enrile, who had apparently been threatening a military coup against her. At that time, General Ramos ensured that the armed forces remained loyal to President Aquino. Aquino's most important military supporter, Fidel Ramos, later president Ramos, also pressed her to take a stronger

Former President Corazon Aquino

line against the communists and their New People's Army (NPA).

After long negotiations, the communists agreed to a 60-day truce, beginning in December 1986. The PKP used its interlude of legality to make energetic propaganda in the cities, but it ended by apparently alienating more people than it impressed. Accordingly, it refused to renew the cease-fire. President Aquino countered with an offer of amnesty to any insurgent who surrendered. In January 1987 another dissident movement, the (Muslim) Moro National Liberation Front (based in Mindanao), signed a peace agreement with the government. Unfortunately, it hardly solved the ongoing problems in the largely Muslim island.

There were also some serious disorders just before a referendum was to be held on a new constitution, but they were suppressed. Despite these problems Aquino's constitution got an unexpectedly high vote (about 75% of those casting ballots). It limited the president to one six-year term, created a bicameral legislature, granted the courts the power of judicial review of laws and provided that the U.S. bases be non-nuclear and could be continued after 1991 only on the basis of a treaty approved by at least two-thirds of the Philippine Senate.

President Aquino's supporters won a sweeping victory in elections for the Senate and House of Representatives held in May 1987. But in August of the same year, in the most serious of several attempts to overthrow President Aquino, a colorful paratrooper, Colonel Gregorio (Rambo) Honasan, led an attempted coup against her. It failed due to energetic action by loyal forces under Chief of Staff Ramos (made Defense Secretary in January 1988). For a time it appeared that President Aquino's position might be untenable. Increasingly, her former political allies were moving against her.

Despite the great hopes that had accompanied her arrival to power, the new president had difficulty living up to those expectations. The army disliked her efforts to reconcile with the long running communist insurgents. Those that hoped she would move against the entrenched landowners and institute true land reform were equally unhappy.

Given the unequal land distribution of the Philippines, it is hardly surprising that the communist insurgency continued to grow to the point where President Aquino apparently considered proclaiming a state of emergency. Frequently brutal anticommunist vigilantes also emerged in many areas.

Despite the victory of the democratic forces, Philippine political life remained riddled with corruption and factionalism on the part of elected and appointed officials. From Aquino's perspective, actually accomplishing something was quite difficult. The lower house of Congress was subservient to the popular Aquino, whereas the Senate, whose members were elected by the national electorate, rather than from local constituencies, was highly independent.

According to analysts, the core problem is that politics in the Philippines may appear democratic, but they are still largely tied to families and personalities rather than parties. Thus, the vast majority of the nation's politicians are not linked to particular parties or, more importantly, to specific policies whose success or failure can be used to judge their performance in

Workmen cut the bananas from the stalk and place them in a washing vat.

office. For that reason it has been very difficult for any national leader to build a stable and strong coalition around specific reform policies. For example, in June 1988, the Philippine Congress finally voted a moderate land reform program that managed to please neither the landlords nor the land hungry tenants. Social unrest and communist insurgency continued.

During these years, the presence of the U.S. bases, holdovers from the years when the Philippines were an American colony, became especially controversial in the eyes of the Philippine political elite and intellectuals. After difficult negotiations, an agreement was reached in October 1988, under which the U.S. was to give $481 million in economic aid (one-third of what the Philippine side had been demanding) in 1990 and again in 1991, when the current base agreement was set to expire.

Under the new constitution, any new agreement would have to be ratified by the Philippine Senate, and perhaps by a popular referendum. In May 1988, the Senate voted a ban on storage of nuclear weapons on the bases, but it appeared that in practice they could still be taken through in transit.

A series of developments, in late 1989 and early 1990, heightened the general impression that, under Aquino's indecisive leadership, the country was drifting or even regressing. In early December the sixth and most serious attempted military coup against her was quelled, but mainly because U.S. combat aircraft flew over the rebel positions. The fact that the United States had effectively used its Philippine-based military resources to intervene in local politics added a new and complicated dimension to the base issue.

The American side wanted continued access even after the bases passed to Philippine control. Manila wanted to get as much money as possible out of the entire transaction. Philippine nationalists found the presence of the bases to be a source of national shame. Filipinos employed at the bases were, of course, concerned about their continued employment.

Political unrest and attempted military coups continued to be a serious problem. As the end of President Aquino's term approached, various political figures began to jockey for succession. One of them was Imelda Marcos, the widow of Ferdinand Marcos. She returned from exile in November 1991 and gained government permission to bury her husband in his native province, Ilocos Norte. Although facing criminal proceedings on charges of corruption, she soon began to campaign as the champion of the poor, notwithstanding her vast fortune. But while the return of Imelda Marcos was something of a distraction, much more important issues demanded the government's attention.

In 1991 the Philippines suffered a series of natural disasters, including a storm that struck the central islands in November and caused unusually heavy damage (runoff and mud slides) because of heavy illegal logging and more dramatic, a volcanic eruption. Mt. Pinatubo, a volcano about 55 miles north of Manila, and only 10 miles from U.S.-controlled Clark Air Force Base, erupted in June of 1991 and fatefully determined the outcome of the long and complex negotiations between Manila and Washington on the future of the U.S. bases in the Philippines.

Before the eruption, Manila had been demanding $825 million per year for seven years in aid, in exchange for continuation of the base agreement. The American Congress was unwilling to appropriate that much, and Washington had been offering $520 million per year over 10–12 years. Certainly there were lots of reasons the Americans wanted to keep their bases in the Philippines. They were very valuable for repair and refueling of ships and aircraft and for training of personnel. Moreover, Filipino labor was plentiful, cheap, and skilled.

But as someone said at the time, the volcano had its own agenda, and it was clearly not the same as that of the negotiators. The eruption, apparently the most powerful anywhere in the twentieth century, heavily damaged the town of Angeles, near Clark, and covered the base with about a foot of ash, rendering it virtually useless. Subic Naval Base and its environs also suffered damage.

After the eruption, some haggling continued between the two sides, but the ne-

Philippines

gotiations were basically over. The bases had also become much less important to U.S. strategic interests since the collapse of the Soviet Union, the main regional threat.

In September of 1991, the Philippine Senate, in a nationalistic mood, voted not to ratify an agreement incorporating the U.S.'s final offer (Clark to be turned over, Subic to be kept for ten more years for $203 million per year). American forces then began to withdraw. The most graphic reminders of the American occupation of the Philippines were now to fade into history.

Politics and Government

The Philippine political system resembles that of the United States. Prior to 1987, the Philippines were governed under the U.S.-modeled 1935 constitution. That constitution provided a bill of rights, a bicameral legislature, an independent judiciary and a president with a four-year term. A new constitution was approved in 1987. It limits presidents to single six-year term. Close relatives of the president cannot be appointed to public office. Both the legislature and the judiciary may review the legal reasons for the imposition of martial law. The constitution also provides for civil liberties and is democratic in form. The legislative branch has a House of Representatives and a Senate. Under the constitution congress has the power to declare war, restrict presidential emergency powers and control the appropriation of revenue. The Senate has twenty-four members with six-year terms that are limited to two consecutive terms. The house can have up to 250 members elected from legislative districts apportioned by population. Twenty percent of the seats are filled through a party-list system. But whether that largely American-style system will continue is less than certain. As of summer 2008 controversial efforts were in progress drastically to revise the 1987 constitution into something more akin to a European-style parliamentary system.

The Philippines have historically been a two-party system. The *Nacional* and Liberal parties traded control of the government between 1946 and 1972. Both parties tended to serve the interests of the political elites in the country. During much of the Marcos era there was no effective political party opposition. Strong opposition began to emerge around 1980 with the formation of UNIDO which had the backing of anti-Marcos elites. Benigno Aquino Jr. established LABAN ("Fight") as a vehicle for his political ideas. The political party landscape fragmented somewhat during the Aquino years. Today politics continues to be highly personalized. Support is given to individuals, not platforms, programs or ideologies though that can be more com-

Philippines Street Scene

plicated lately given the fact that presidents are not eligible to run again.

As in many other communities in Asia and elsewhere, Philippine politics are much influenced by the presence of "patron-client relationships." Essentially, this means that political life centers on relationships that are personal and hierarchical. Political relationships are also built on the concept of *"utang na loob,"* obligations of indebtedness. Politics is therefore frequently dominated by personal loyalty to a hierarchical group. Patrons must provide resources to their clients to keep their loyalty. This has been a motivation for the corruption that has often weakened the Philippines. On a more practical level it also means that only the nation's president is particularly associated with specific policies against which they are eventually judged.

In this type of environment, institutions like interest groups, political parties and other organizations that could unite large segments of society are less effective than they might be. Thus, such institutions which have at times been so effective in countries from South Korea to the United States are of less value in the personalized political culture of the Philippines.

A New Beginning for the Philippines

Fidel V. Ramos was elected president of the Philippines in May 1992. However, as one of seven candidates, Ramos, in winning, received only 23.4% of the vote. To make matters more complicated, his closest challenger, Miriam Defensor Santiago, claimed fraud and managed to have the Supreme Court consider the charge. Ramos, in short, did not start off with a lot

of support, though Mrs. Aquino backed him strongly. Still, for most of his term, he was quite effective.

During the first years after his election, President Ramos and his government faced several significant challenges: the need to establish law and order, opposition to the current political process by groups including the National Democratic Front (representing the communists), the Muslim National Liberation Front, the Muslim Islamic Liberation Front, the military officers' group *RAM-YOU* and the continuing entrenched position of the old political elite. By his last year he also had to face the challenges of the Asian economic crisis of 1997, but that was much later. Initially, he was quite successful in dealing with the issues that faced him.

In fact, by early 1996, there were still plenty of problems but also signs of improvement. President Ramos and the MNLF leader, Nur Misuari, finally concluded an agreement that many hoped would contribute to ending the generation-long struggle that had taken more than 120,000 lives. Overcoming the opposition of minority Christian communities in the south, Ramos and Misuari agreed to form a special presidential council headed by Misuari which would have responsibility over development issues in fourteen of the southern provinces. The deal, part of a larger plan that included the formation of a more autonomous Muslim-dominated region after three years, marked a major breakthrough for efforts to reinforce Philippine stability. It was later to prove less successful in bringing in Misuari's more militant Muslim co-religionists.

Ramos even managed to gain an agreement with the Communist National Democratic Front in April 1998 which projected a series of negotiations intended to end the generation long communist rebellion. Economically, the Ramos administration had moved to reform the Philippine economy and further integrate it into world.

But, despite a very impressive record for most of his administration, President Ramos's last year in office was hurt both by forces he controlled and those he did not. Although Ramos never publicly said he wanted a second term—a clear violation of the new constitution—He let his followers try to modify the constitution in order to allow him to do so. The decision was inadvisable and he soon found even his former allies, President Aquino, Cardinal Sin, and much of the population aroused against the idea. In the end he backed down and disavowed the idea, but not before he had damaged his reputation. Then President Ramos, understanding his time at the helm was really up, chose House Speaker Jose de Venecia as his successor.

But while having Ramos' support was important, de Venecia still had to win the election. And that turned out to be a very daunting task, especially when facing the vice president Joseph Estrada. Estrada was a former actor, who wanted the job himself, and campaigned hard to get it. In contrast to the organizational skills of de Venecia, Estrada, despite his personal origins among the Philippine elite, cam-

Former President Fidel Ramos

paigned as a populist and was much more flamboyant as a public campaigner, a skill especially important in the May 1998 election which included not only Estrada and de Venecia but nine other candidates.

In the end, as the polls had long predicted, the people chose Joseph Estrada.

Estrada may not have had the support of many Philippine elites. In fact much of the leadership, from the military to the church, was skeptical; nevertheless, he won the presidency with an impressive 40% of the vote and drew his support from a wide range of voters. It was. In fact, a far better performance than Ramos had done in his own earlier effort. The victory was coupled with both President Ramos's willingness to accept the end of his term and with Estrada's decision to continue Ramos's economic policies. This seemed to put the Philippines on the verge of a much brighter future than many had expected.

President Estrada's popularity did not last as long as he probably hoped. As the months went on, his poll ratings dropped steadily. His administration was plagued by rumors of economic corruption, inattention to detail, favoritism and unpopular policies. The president soon found himself almost abandoned save for some members of the poorest classes. He was impeached by the Senate. The influential Philippine Catholic Church got involved as well as it denounced the besieged president for setting a bad moral example for the nation.

Eventually the backlash against Estrada grew so great that the President's support collapsed and his vice president, the American trained economist, Gloria Macapagal-Arroyo became president. Despite her as-

A panoramic view of the Sierra Madre slopes.

Philippines

sumption to power, the former president still had supporters. For years after his departure she faced a series of pro-Estrada demonstrations and various legal challenges to her authority which made it difficult for the new president to fully establish her authority.

While the Philippines' new president and Asia's newest contribution to the ever growing number of female national leaders may not be nearly as flamboyant as her disgraced predecessor, she has presided over a reasonably successful period in the life of the Philippines. Since she came to power, Arroyo, an economist, who had once been a Georgetown University classmate of Bill Clinton's, has helped keep the nations' inflation under control while making important progress in the areas of agricultural funding and an expansion of insurance coverage for the population. Her administration has also worked toward lowering the cost of power. Somewhat more controversial has been her direction of Philippine-American relations.

Former President Joseph Estrada

In contrast to many Asian leaders President Arroyo has been particularly supportive of the American War on Terrorism. In fact, her administration received considerable public criticism for inviting the American military to become active in the struggle against the Abu Sayyaf, the militant Muslim nationalists that have been so active in terrorism in the Southern Philippines. That cooperation has continued to the present and was an element in American Secretary of Defense Robert Gates' visit to the Philippines in 2009.

Overall, it would be hard to argue that President Arroyo has not performed the functions of her job with an enormously

greater commitment and professionalism than her "playboy" predecessor. But international and domestic challenges have made her tenure in office very challenging. Within the Philippines, the levels of crime, drug use and urban violence have become particularly significant with almost a score of gangs in Manila specializing in kidnapping the rich for ransom. The problem has become so great that the President has declared that crime problems have gone beyond being simply law and order issues and become fundamental threats to the National Security a move which has prompted not only an effort to reorganize the Philippine army to deal with these new threats but moves to have the United States offer assistance as well.

Other problems also made life difficult for the new president. Like her predecessor Corazon Aquino, President Macapagal-Arroyo has had to deal with the threat of military coups. In fact, during the summer of 2003, a group of some 300 soldiers took over a shopping mall in downtown Manila and demanded that the president resign. The group's mutiny, (they had apparently hoped to establish a military junta) was dealt with in only a few days, but it was only one example of the problems the President has faced since coming into power in the aftermath of President Estrada's departure in disgrace. The problem of violent challenges to her rule has not gone away. More recently, in 2008, the president reportedly was the target of another foiled assassination plot devised by the notorious Abu Sayyaf.

As the time grew closer for the presidential elections of 2004 the Philippines' "accidental" president initially announced that she did not intend to run for office again. Her public explanation was that she has wanted to save the country from a "prolonged period of political infighting." That explanation of course sounds good but it was hard to see how her not running would avoid that problem. And upon further reflection she apparently agreed because, by the fall of 2003, she reversed herself and declared her candidacy.

By the time those elections rolled around the President found herself facing a very wide range of opponents, from her own former education secretary Raul Roco to the controversial senator and former Chief of Police who ran for office even as the Supreme Court re-opened a case against him which dealt with the alleged official murder of a number of criminals who had been in his custody. One candidate even had to drop out for a time when he learned he had developed a case of prostate cancer.

In the end her chief competitor declared his candidacy. Fernando Poe was a man whose background closely resembled that

of her predecessor, President Estrada. He was a popular film star, who had dropped out of high school. As the time approached for election, the two of them were neck and neck in the polls.

Once the voters went to the polls, though, it soon became clear that Gloria Macapagal Arroyo had managed to win the presidency herself. At least that seemed to be the case. Unfortunately for the newly elected president, charges soon surfaced that she may have tampered with the counting process. For a time, as demonstrations grew in the streets and influential figures called for her resignation, it even looked like her situation was increasingly precarious. In the end, though, the president survived a call for her impeachment and remained in power.

But there was a clear price to pay. Both her son and husband ended up leaving the country to alleviate some of the charges of corruption that had surfaced although the antagonism against President Arroyo continued unabated. By early 2006 yet another military coup was apparently attempted against her. The effort was headed off by prompt government action. But it was obvious that the president's unpopularity went far beyond the military plotters. In the aftermath of the failed coup attempt, thousands of people, including Former President Corazon Aquino, went into the streets to call for her resignation.

Despite the complications of her initial election, the president's support did not wholly fail her. In the elections of May 2007, her supporters won 200 of the possible 219 seats that were up for reelection.

The late Cardinal Jaime Sin

This put them in a commanding position to control the new House of Representatives. However, her success in the lower house did not stop her many opponents from winning the majority of seats in the upper house. Unfortunately while the results of the elections were relatively positive for the government, more than a hundred people died in associated violence. The unrest reopened the angers associated with the controversies of 2004 election battle.

Another area of conflict between the former president and her political opponents were her efforts to modify the nation's constitution. Not surprisingly given that the country's current governmental structure emerged out of its experience as an American colony, the Philippines have operated as a presidential democracy. In the opinion of many, that system has not worked well. Thus Arroyo began an effort to replace the nation's bicameral presidential system with a unicameral parliamentary system. The new legislature would be led by a prime minister who presumably would be better able to facilitate the passing of needed legislation. In theory, it might be a good idea. But the nation's upper legislative chamber, the senate, is filled with people who, with good reason, fear that such a change would eliminate their power base.

By the early summer of 2008 the president's long-term goal of rewriting the 1987 constitution was gaining steam. The lower house of congress voted to transform itself into a constituent assembly in order to revise the constitution. But it has not just been members of the senate who have opposed the idea. Large popular demonstrations against the effort have regularly occurred. Part of the problem is that many of the president's critics claim the plan is merely a gimmick designed to maintain Arroyo's power. Others claimed there was a secret plan to delay the 2010 elections with the hope of using a revised parliamentary system to allow Arroyo to

return to power as a prime minister chosen by the lower house of congress.

Despite the fears of some, the presidential elections were held on schedule in the spring of 2010 with a campaign that featured very familiar names. Joseph Estrada, the former president whose failed administration had led to Arroyo's initial rise to the presidency, ended up running unsuccessfully against Senator Benigno S. Aquino III, son of the couple who had battled so dramatically to terminate the presidency of former Philippine Ferdinand Marcos in the mid-1980s.

It will be recalled that the new president's late father, Benigno Aquino, himself a very influential politician, had been murdered by Marcos' cronies previous to the famous "People Power" election that had brought his widow, Corazon Aquino, to power. The new president, who won an impressive electoral victory, campaigned on a platform that highlighted his family and anti-corruption policies. While his election over Mr Estrada may certainly have reflected such hopes, it was also true that his rise to power was yet another example of the influence of the small number of elite families who have dominated Philippine politics over the decades.

Culture and Society

Like so much of the developing world the contrasts in society are striking. Manila, a busy, modern city, has a sophisticated cultural atmosphere that can compare with most western cities. In recent years, a building boom has made it look even more like some of its more economically vibrant East and Southeast Asian neighbors. Still, many peasants live at poverty levels that are as extreme as anywhere in the world. The Philippines remain one of the most stratified countries in the world. It is a society where a significant percentage of the population cannot meet their basic nutritional and other needs while the richest ten percent possess thirty-six percent of all personal income. Despite the recent economic growth, the number who live in poverty has actually grown over the last few years. For example, in 2003 the official number living in poverty was reported to be around 30 percent. By 2008 it had risen to almost 33 percent.

The Filipino language, a refinement of the Tagalog spoken by many Philippine people, serves as the official language. Spanish is spoken by a dwindling number of descendants of the Spanish aristocracy. English is well known, and many educated Filipinos, unable to find work in their homeland, have left the country. For example, many Filipino medical doctors and nurses have settled in the United States. Large numbers of them work in the

various countries of the Middle East, a fact that makes the Philippines especially sensitive to what happens in that frequently volatile part of the world.

The influence of the Catholic Church is very important. The church controls enormous holdings, and, the late Archbishop Jaime Cardinal Sin, who was instrumental in helping to end the Marcos dictatorship and making sure President Ramos honored the constitution by not running again, was very influential. President Estrada weakened his political base by antagonizing the church officials due to his support of population control programs and the death penalty and to his leading a personal life style the church leaders found morally unacceptable.

The church has also played an important role in condemning corrupt political practices and campaigning for greater support for the poor. The church's strong stand against birth control has also made it very difficult for the Philippines to limit the country's soaring population. The nation's birth rate currently runs at 2.3% annually, a figure that adds an enormous burden on the national economy and is unsustainable given the country's relatively modest economic growth rates.

In recent years the administration has frequently come under fire for human rights violations. It has been reported that more than 1,000 people have disappeared, been killed or gone missing as a result of actions taken by the Filipino security forces. The nation's Supreme Court has accused the government of tolerating their behavior. The assaults have had their targets not only relatively young children but activists perceived to be threats to government. Most recently, in 2009, a union organizer for farm workers was shot dead only an hour after giving a speech criticizing the president.

The biggest challenge to people's lives in the last year was the enormous number, reports suggested over 500,000, who were forced to flee their homes in the wake of yet another failed effort to resolve the tensions between Manila and the Islamic southern providences. Initially it looked like real progress was being made. President Arroyo's government reached an agreement with the Moro Islamic Liberation Front that would have allowed local Muslims greater autonomy in an expanded area on the southern island of Mindanao. But that agreement was opposed by the Roman Catholic community of Mindanao, which eventually managed to get the nation's Supreme Court to block the settlement. Predictably the frustrated MILF began a new series of assaults on government troops and others. Eventually another cease fire of the sort that had been implemented in 2003 was reinstated, but

Philippines

Benigno Aquino III
The Philippines New President

not before almost one hundred people had died. And that has not really stopped the fighting.

It is not just tensions between the largely Catholic North and the Islamic community of the South that made Mindanao so dangerous at times. Rivalries between different Muslim clans have also provoked vicious fighting and most horrifically a major massacre of scores of people during the heat of the electoral process in the South. On that occasion a convoy of journalists, women and children were killed by members of a rival clan that opposed their political activities.

Women

Philippine women have not been influential in their country's politics. The careers of women such as Imelda Marcos, Corazon Aquino and President Arroyo, are more representative of the power of family connections than women's influence. In the same vein the current president is the daughter of a previous president. This is a circumstance that would hardly surprise most Americans.

In the workplace their salaries are usually one-third that of men. Philippine women often travel abroad to find work. They go to places like Singapore and the Persian Gulf States to serve as domestic servants. In the United States, they often serve as nurses. In fact, the Philippines supply more female overseas workers than any other country.

In the late 1980s a new family code was introduced in the Philippines to replace the older more traditional code that had earlier reinforced inequality between the sexes. Women gained the right to practice professions without having their husbands' permission. Women also gained more rights over their children and remarriage. As is the common case in East and Southeast Asia Muslim women are covered by separate legal codes that allow polygamy. Catholic practice is also very influential in the Philippines. Thus divorce is not legally available (though annulment is), and abortion is available only to save the life of a mother.

Former President Ramos made a significant contribution to the rights of women when he signed a new anti-rape law that offered more sensitivity to the rights of the victims. Still domestic violence against women, as elsewhere, is common. In contrast to most Asian countries, Philippine women go to college more often than men do. Around 10% of all women are college graduates. The figure is only about 7% for men. By 1992 women began to be admitted to the Philippine military academies.

About one-third of the workforce is female although women predominate at the lower levels earning the lowest wages. Women have made considerable gains in the field of law. They make up 26% of the trial court judges. They are also very involved in teaching at both the primary and secondary levels and outnumber men in civil service jobs though not at the highest levels.

Women have served both in the country's parliament and as cabinet level ministers though in relatively small numbers as yet. And of course during the most recent presidential election, Gloria Macapagal-Arroyo, daughter of a former leader was elected vice-president and later succeeded to the presidency with the collapse of President Estrada's administration. Somewhat later she won the presidency in her own right. Thus the Philippines have in recent years been led by two different women, Corazon Aquino and President Macapagal-Arroyo.

Foreign Policy

Philippine foreign policy has often wavered between developing closer ties to its regional neighbors and focusing on its relationship with the United States. During his term in office former President Ramos made it a personal priority to strengthen ties with his regional neighbors and traveled extensively to do so. Ramos felt it was particularly important for the Philippines to improve relations with other members of ASEAN, the Association of Southeast Asian Nations. President Ramos, for example, visited Indonesia to discuss the possibility of links between Mindanao, in the southern Philippines, and Indonesia. Eventually, the Indonesian government offered important help in his efforts to bring the confrontation with the *MNLF* Muslim leadership to resolution.

Once in office President Arroyo continued the focus on Asia by visiting many neighboring states with a special emphasis on improving relations with Malaysia. Unfortunately, relations with Malaysia were nevertheless strained for a time over Kuala Lumpur's abrupt decision to expel large numbers of illegal aliens, a move that caused considerable hardship to thousands of people, many of them from the Philippines.

Under President Gloria Macapagal-Arroyo, relations with the United States have remained especially important as well. The president was educated in the United States and was among the first Asian leaders to lend her support to the Americans in the immediate aftermath of the September 2001 terrorist attacks on the U.S. Later, as the American campaign in Afghanistan wound down, Arroyo made the controversial decision to invite American advisors to assist Philippine soldiers in the struggle against the Muslim Abu Sayyaf group that has long been known for its terrorist activities and kidnappings of foreign tourists.

Her decision offered benefits and problems. On the one hand, the American administration offered her government millions of dollars in aid to help deal with the Abu Sayyaf which Manila considers simple criminals. On the other hand, her approval of the return of American troops aroused considerable controversy and provoked massive demonstrations in the southern parts of the country. That commitment has turned out to be a longer one than many anticipated. Washington, after sending the first troops during the winter of 2002, pulled most of them out again by the following summer. But by the spring

Former President Macapagal Arroyo

of 2003, after President Arroyo made an official state visit to the White House, Washington announced that more American troops were being sent. The president has also paid a political price for her controversial decision to send Filipino soldiers to serve in Iraq in support of the American occupation there. Thus she not surprisingly decided in the weeks before the presidential election to suspend plans to send any additional troops to Iraq.

More recently the Philippine role in Iraq took a more dramatic turn as a Philippine truck driver was taken hostage and threatened with beheading. President Arroyo then made the controversial decision to expedite the departure of her troops in order to win the release of the hostage. In doing so, she pleased many people in the Philippines, but she came in for considerable criticism not only from the United States but from her Australian neighbors as well.

During the 1990s, relations with the People's Republic of China also proved complicated at times. By far, China's occupation of Mischief Reef in the South China Sea constituted the most serious problem. In early 1995, Manila discovered that one of the small islands in the Spratley chain about 150 miles off the Philippine coast had been occupied by members of the Chinese navy.

In May 1995 Philippine military officials tried to take a boatload of journalists to see the reef but a Chinese patrol boat blocked their path. The Philippine navy then detained a number of Chinese fishermen who were illegally in the country's territorial waters.

Later, at the ASEAN Regional Forum, ARF, the ASEAN states spoke with one voice in raising concern about the Chinese occupation. Beijing subsequently agreed to deal with the conflicting claims in the South China Sea multilaterally. Thus, Manila would have its fellow ASEAN member states as partners in negotiations over the Spratley Islands. This was far more preferable than going one-on-one with the PRC.

The struggle has at times turned out to be rather embarrassing for the Philippines. During the spring of 1997 the Philippine navy dramatically arrested some Chinese fishermen and drove some Chinese ships from Scarborough Shoal to the west of Luzon Island. Unfortunately, for Philippine authorities, upon closer inspection it became clear that particular shoal was beyond Philippine territorial waters. But that did not terminate the nation's claim to the disputed islands.

Economy

The Philippine Republic is fairly rich in natural resources and, with the exception of the Manila plain, not overpopulated. The post-World War II economy was quite weak until the mid-1990s when it started showing signs of the sort of economic vitality that many of its neighbors had demonstrated during the 1980s.

Still, much of the wealth winds up in the hands of a small group of rich individuals and families. Corruption and inflation have been a continuing problem. Under former President Marcos's "New Society," a limited land reform program was in progress. Landlords, as part of the establishment, were well compensated by the government for what land they had lost, and this further inflated the economy. President Marcos sold highly profitable monopolies of such commodities as coconuts and sugar to his friends, a system known to the opposition as "crony capitalism."

Under President Aquino, a less stifling, but still harmful version of the "crony capitalism" that had flourished under Marcos emerged. Her successor, President Fidel Ramos, was much more successful with economic reforms and carried out a significant amount of land reform and other economic efforts. Called "Philippines 2000," the government strove to change its traditional agrarian-based, paternalistic economy to an industrial and market-driven one. They have moved, for example, to liberalize rules for investment, trade and banking among other economic activities.

During the mid-1990s the economy was finally showing signs of strength. The 5.1% growth figure of 1994 paled when compared to double-digit numbers of some of its neighbors. But economic indicators were finally showing substantive growth that would continue at about the same average rates over the next decade or so. This was true despite the occasional dramatic dip as larger regional and global events washed over the islands.

Despite earlier fears, the economy has also weathered well the departure of the Americans. The former American Clark Air Force Base, now recovered from the volcano eruption, is operating as a civilian charter airport (which the American military has again begun using) and the former naval base at Subic Bay is serving as a successful tax-free port and industrial base. The American-based FEDEX Company even made it its regional hub.

By the time President Ramos hosted the Asia-Pacific Economic Cooperation (APEC) forum in November 1996, he had plenty of reasons to be pleased. The facilities at the Subic Bay were ready to convince the arriving dignitaries that the Philippines, so long the laggard in the regime's economic spurt was ready to make its own effort to become a new "Asian Tiger!"

When the Asian economic crisis hit in mid-1997, the Philippines were as vulnerable as many of her neighbors and saw her own currency take a plunge. But unlike them the Philippines initially weathered well the international economic stresses and began not only to recover but pull ahead. The Philippine economy was helped by former President Ramos' reforms and especially by the political stability that seemed in place.

More recently the economy has shown a modest growth rate and inflation some-

Philippine street traffic

Courtesy of Raeann Rebanal

Philippines

what lessened, two factors which contributed to the generally improving situation. Unfortunately, news of scandals, financial and otherwise, became very common during President Estrada's term in office and hurt the country economically. With the arrival of the professionally trained economist Gloria Macapagal-Arroyo to the presidency, the Philippine economy has done relatively well. Growth rates have average around 5%. The GDP rate for 2005 was a very healthy 6%, up from the previous year, while 2007 was over 7%. The year 2008 came in at 5.4% although that was before the greatest impact of the most recent global economic downturn was felt. But even as the full impact of the global slowdown hit economic growth rates for the Philippines, growth continued at least in the very modest positive area of just under one percent for 2009.

Like that of many of its neighbors, the economy in the Philippines is particularly tied to the international economic situation. From Malaysia to Israel and throughout large parts of the Middle East, many Filipinos work abroad and the money they send home plays a significant part in the health of the local economy. When various crises affect the lives of those overseas workers the nation itself suffers as well. As the world economy has improved those remittances have gone up and played a significant role in pushing consumer spending higher. On the other hand, the weakening of the global economy lessens those remittances and prompts the return of those same laborers from abroad thereby adding to the number of people looking for work locally.

The Philippines do at times have trouble competing for outside investment with many of its neighbors because the local minimum daily pay rate, at around U.S.$5.23, while much lower than in countries like the United States or Japan, is not an advantage when competing with countries like China, where the going rate can be as low as 31 cents a day or even Vietnam which comes in at around 92 cents. That higher figure is unfortunately not complemented by utility rates for power that also exceed their rivals as well.

Still that reality has not always been an impassible barrier. Mitsubishi recently decided to make the Philippines the hub of its Southeast Asian production facilities for sports utility vehicles headed for markets from Southeast Asia to Latin America, a decision that certainly helped improve the local economy and complemented other positive trends.

But other problems persist. On the more immediate local level, the increasing ugly urban crime in Manila and especially the ongoing regularity of kidnappings of the elite for ransom are clearly having an impact on the ability of the Philippines to attract outside business investment and are driving some business people out of the country. But there is as well some positive news. President Arroyo has made significant progress dealing with some economic issues such as inflation, and the recent opening of a new natural gas field has promised to be a very helpful boon to the economy. Despite the new natural gas field, the Philippines remain an importer of oil and, like so many other nations around the world, have been deeply hurt by the rising cost of oil.

While the Philippines generally have reason to be satisfied with recent economic developments, it is also true that its relative position has fallen over the last half century. In the years before World War II, the Philippines had the highest per capita income in Southeast Asia. In the early 1950s its per capita income was far ahead of Thailand while today the average Thai has twice the income of the average Filipino. The real problem for the Philippines is not growth per se, but the fact that the society is especially divided along economic lines. The vast majority is quite poor and burdened by a birth rate that makes economic progress very difficult.

Environmental Issues

As is usually the case elsewhere, the environment of the Philippines has been deeply impacted by the economic demands of its growing population. Deforestation has become a significant problem, and the air quality has been deeply affected. On a national level the government has shown an interest in confronting these problems, but progress has been very limited. Efforts at reforestation have not been very successful. Those will likely be improved if the various international efforts to retain tropical forests are successfully implemented as part of the international climate change negotiations scheduled for Copenhagen in December of 2009.

Like the rest of its neighbors, the Philippines are experiencing the slowly rising temperatures associated with the thickening of green house gasses. While the temperature rise is not as dramatic as recently seen in the higher areas of the northern hemisphere, changes are beginning to occur. The islands are becoming dryer, and tropical diseases like Dengue fever are becoming more and more common. At base, of course, the primary impact of manmade climate change is about water. In some places there is too little, in others too much. Thus even as parts of the Islands are becoming dryer, Manila itself has been hit particularly hard by ever more powerful hurricanes. This happened most dramatically in the fall of 2009 when Typhoon Ketsana (Ondoy) flooded large sections of Manila and subjected the city to levels of rainfall not seen in generations.

On the positive side, Philippine citizens are becoming increasingly aware of the challenge of climate change. In the spring of 2008, around 10,000 people took part in a huge conference in Zamboanga City. It was addressed by an impressive array of scientists, NGO representatives and political leaders. Perhaps even more exciting and certainly more tangible has been cooperation with Icelandic companies to introduce geo-thermal energy production on Biliran Island in the Leyete region of the country.

The Future

During the upcoming year a number of different issues are likely to challenge the people of the Philippines. Most immediately, of course, is making a smooth transition from the administration of President Gloria Macapagal-Arroyo to that of Benigno S. Aquino III. President Arroyo may have had many political problems. The ambiguities of her last election only exacerbated them. But unlike her predecessor, the flamboyant Joseph Estrada, she was a serious-minded professional economist. Under her leadership the islands maintained a relatively healthy growth rate. Her own successor, Benigno S. Aquino III, comes to power with a famous name and a great deal of good will. But he has a relatively limited record of real accomplishments behind him.

Second, but no less alarming, is the continuing inability to reconcile the needs of the local Christian communities with southern Muslim demands for their own separate autonomous state, as represented by the Moro Islamic Liberation Front. The future does not seem likely to offer a realistic resolution to this long-term struggle, which has divided Philippine society for generations.

The Republic of Singapore

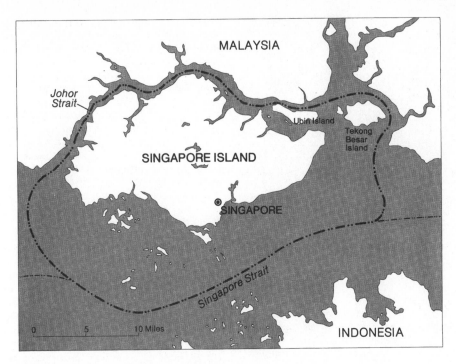

Area: 239 sq. mi. (692.7 sq. km., somewhat smaller than New York City)

Population: 4,701,069 (July 2010 est.)

Capital City: Singapore 4,163,700 (estimate)

Climate: Tropically hot and humid

Neighboring Countries: Malaysia (North); Indonesia (South)

Official Languages: Chinese (Mandarin dialect), Malay, Tamil, English

Ethnic Background: Chinese (about 77%); Malay 14% Indian (about 7%)

Principal Religions: Buddhism, Hinduism, Islam, and Christianity, Daoism

Main Exports: Rubber, petroleum, tin and manufactured goods mainly to Malaysia, U.S., Japan, China, Taiwan, Thailand, S. Korea

Main Imports: Manufactured goods, petroleum, fuels, chemicals and foodstuffs, chiefly from Japan, U.S., Malaysia, Taiwan, S. Korea, Thailand

Currency: Singapore Dollar

Former Colonial Status: Possession of the British East India Company (1819–1867), British Crown Colony (1867–1958), occupied by the Japanese (1941–1945), internally self-governing (1958–1963).

National Day: August 9, 1965 (Independence Day)

Chief of State: President S.R. Nathan since Sept. 1999

Head of Government: Prime Minister Lee Hsien Loong since August 2004

Dominant Political Figure: Lee Kuan Yew, Mentor Minister.

National Flag: Divided horizontally, with a white crescent moon and five white stars on a red field at the top and a white bottom.

Annual Per Capita GDP Income: $50,300 (2009 est. purchasing power parity)

The small island of Singapore is separated from Johor State at the southern tip of West Malaysia by a narrow strait of water; road and railway bridges provide access to the mainland. Although tropical, the island is highly urbanized. The city occupies the more agreeable part of the island on the southeast coast. Its harbor is naturally a good one, and it lies at the crossroads of Southeast Asia at one end of the Straits of Malacca. This is the best and shortest passage between the Indian Ocean and the South China Sea, and Singapore has been an important naval base and commercial port for almost two centuries.

History

Prior to the arrival of Europeans, Singapore was a small insignificant part of the Malay world, inhabited by a few fishermen but not much more. Sir Thomas Stamford Raffles of the British East India Company occupied the island in 1819 after realizing the commercial possibilities of the harbor given its very strategic location. The decision to make it a free port was quite important to the city's later growth. By 1867 it had been made a British Crown Colony. In spite of Dutch competition based on neighboring Java and Sumatra, the colony began to achieve the size of a major commercial port. The opening of the Suez Canal in 1869 attracted even heavier traffic from Europe to the Straits of Malacca.

This commercial development also resulted in the migration of many Chinese to the island. They quickly became the majority ethnic group as they labored to process rubber and tin. Over time, Singapore became the principal British stronghold in the region.

A large British naval base was constructed in the 1920s, equipped with coastal defenses designed to protect it from attack by sea. Unfortunately, the new defenses were not finished by the start of World War II and the Japanese assault. When World War II began British plans came to naught. Three days after the attack on Pearl Harbor in 1941, Japanese torpedo planes sank the Prince of Wales and the Repulse, two mammoth British warships, which had been dispatched to Singapore to help in the defense of the port. In addition, an invasion of Malaya was carried out by a large, highly trained Japanese army. It fell to the invaders within four weeks, and the siege of Singapore began. The British held out for two weeks before the Japanese finally captured Singapore and 60,000 prisoners on February 15, 1942. It was one of the worst military defeats ever suffered by Great Britain.

Prime Minister Lee Hsien Loong

Hon. Lee Kuan Yew

Singapore

Contrasts in urban Singapore

As elsewhere in Southeast Asia, the Japanese often mistreated the people they had conquered, particularly those of Chinese origin. Ultimately, as the war neared its conclusion, the Japanese were isolated from Singapore by American sea and air action. The British peacefully returned to the island when Japan collapsed in 1945.

After the war Britain used Singapore as its headquarters in the region. Over time, Britain began slowly to withdraw. It did retain its bases, but decreased their size as it embarked on a pullout. During the process the U.K. maintained control over Singapore's external relations, but permitted increasing degrees of internal self-government. The government nurtured by the British was faced with serious civil strife in the mid-1950s which was promoted by labor unions and student organizations, both communist controlled.

After a new constitution was adopted, the leftist People's Action Party, the PAP, came to power in an electoral landslide in 1959. Although he had ties to the communists, the new Prime Minister, Lee Kuan Yew, quickly moved to lessen their potential influence. Sensing British and Malayan concerns over his election, he made strenuous efforts to improve relations.

A widespread and ambitious program of centralized economic development and social welfare programs was instituted which caused the communists to redouble their efforts to seize control of the government; they feared a possible increase in popularity of the People's Action Party. During those early years of the new state, the principal tensions were within the People's Action Party, between the moderate socialists who favored more ties with Malaysia, and their more extremist communist allies. Eventually the PAPs principal leftists quit to form the Barisan Socialist Party.

The apparent strength of the left in Singapore was a major source of concern to Britain and Malaya. Thus, Prime Minister Tunku Abdul Rahman of Malaya immediately proposed that Malaya, Singapore and the Borneo territories of Sabah and Sarawak be joined into the Federation of Malaysia. His purpose was twofold: to protect the stability and progress of the entire region, and to control the leftist trend in Singapore. Prime Minister Tunku Abdul Rahman had reason to be concerned. Had Singapore become a communist state, Malaya would have suffered a serious economic blow, since the island processed and shipped the bulk of the rubber and tin which produced most of Malaya's foreign exchange. It would have posed a political threat as well.

In spite of opposition by the Barisan Socialist Party, the Malayan Communist Party, and the vehement opposition of Indonesia's President Sukarno, the Federation of Malaysia came into existence in 1963. Sukarno immediately declared that Indonesia was in a state of "confrontation" (a sort of undeclared, irregular war) with Malaysia, severing all trade relations. Singapore suffered somewhat from this step, since Indonesia had been one of its most important trading partners, but Indonesia suffered as well. Actually, the economic needs of both gave rise to a widespread smuggling operation which helped to offset the effect of the official boycott.

The short-lived union of Singapore with the Federation of Malaysia came to an end in 1965. The Federation may have solved the immediate problems of a potential communist takeover. But it did not resolve the more basic antagonism between the Malays and Chinese that has long been the greatest internal problem within Malaysia. The Malay-dominated government of the Federation preferred to deal at arms-length with the Chinese-controlled regime on the island rather than to add more Chinese to the Federation's population. Lee Kuan Yew's vision of a more multi-cultural Malaysian Federation was clearly threatening to the Malay leaders of Kuala Lumpur. When he energetically tried to extend the activities of the People's Action Party to mainland Malaya and to exert greater influence throughout the Federation, matters came to a head. Singapore was forced out of the Federation, left to survive on its own.

Birth of a New City

Although the separation of Singapore from the Federation of Malaysia was described as a matter of mutual consent, in reality Singapore was confronted with a demand to withdraw. It had no choice but to do so. Within Singapore, leaders like Lee Kuan Yew had serious doubts that the newly independent country could survive on its own. There was, though, little choice but to try.

The immediate problem for Singapore was survival. But happily the new city-state had the advantages of excellent leadership under Lee Kuan Yew and a population committed to accomplishing that goal. In fact, under the paternalistic leadership of Prime Minister Lee and PAP, Singapore did more than survive. It prospered and became one of the most successful economies of Southeast Asia while maintaining a major commitment to improving the living standards of its people. By late century, its population enjoyed the highest standard of living in the region and was generally one of the safest societies. Some though have come to believe that Singapore's citizens have paid a high price in political freedoms for PAP's economic successes.

Former Prime Minister Goh Chok Tong

Singapore

Political developments during the early 1960s complemented PAP's ability to dominate the new nation's political life. In elections held in 1963, the People's Action Party elected 39 representatives to 23 from the Barisan Socialist Party. But even then Prime Minister Lee Kuan Yew so dominated the political scene in Singapore that members of the opposition party angrily stalked out of the Parliament in 1966.

Since then the People's Action Party has been in almost complete charge although a new, leftist opposition party formed in April 1971, was successful in electing one member in 1981. In 1984 it doubled its holding to two, but that barely made a dent on the PAP's monopoly of political power.

In 1986, the debates in parliament began to be televised. This gave wide publicity to the speeches of one of the only two opposition members, an articulate ethnic Indian, J.B. Jeyaretnam, who in September of that year was expelled from the body for having allegedly defamed the impartiality of Singapore's judiciary.

From time to time, the government, which maintains a limited amount of censorship, has tried to penalize foreign publications that contain articles it does not like. Punishments have ranged from financial pressures to outright lawsuits.

As concerns about Singapore's immediate survival have given way to economic success, Prime Minister Lee, who ran the country directly till 1990, began to concern himself with slowing the spread of what he believed were negative Western values. Distressed by the materialistic outlook of Singapore's "yuppies," he has tried to revive a modern version of Confucianism. He and other government officials have enthusiastically embraced Confucianism's more communal values and hierarchal perspective as more suitable for Singapore's predominantly Chinese population than Western individualism.

While this emphasis on a Chinese approach to values has also encouraged the study of Mandarin Chinese in the schools of Singapore, the government has treated with considerable disdain and hostility those it perceives as pushing multi-cultural Singapore too far in the direction of being an exclusively Chinese nation. Important as well has been Lee Kuan Yew's concern that Singapore's people continue their commitment to learning English, an increasingly important language throughout the world.

Over the years Singapore's leaders have viewed their nation as particularly fragile because of its ethnic diversity and vulnerable because of its small size when compared to its neighbors. Accordingly, they have done whatever they considered necessary for domestic and external security. The armed forces are large for the size of the country and are impressively modern. The Internal Security Act—inherited from the British—is used by the Internal Security Department, to make dissent difficult.

Government and Politics

Lee Kuan Yew, in office from 1959, retired as prime minister in November 1990 in favor of his handpicked successor, Deputy Prime Minister Goh Chok Tong. The change, though, made little difference in the political realities of Singapore. Lee Kuan Yew remained in the government with the title of "Senior Minister" and has continued to be influential. The Goh Chok Tong government largely followed the path of the previous government.

Singapore Skyscrapers

221

Singapore

The January 1997 elections saw Prime Minister Goh more genuinely come out from under Lee Kuan Yew's shadow. This time PAP even won a greater electoral victory than previously. The election though was more than a triumph of Prime Minister's Goh's new authority. PAP and the government used all their power to ensure a victory. They even announced that the government planned improvements in the city's housing infrastructure within which most of the city's citizens live and often own apartments. Interestingly, the government warned that those districts that voted against PAP would be last on the waiting list for improvements.

The most intriguing development has been the emergence of the son of Lee Kuan Yew, Lee Hsien Loong, into the political limelight. Until recently the younger Lee served as the nation's deputy prime minister under Prime Minister Goh but all that changed in August 2004 when Lee Hsien Loong became prime minister in his own right. While the son of Singapore's founder leader Lee Kuan Yew might be said to have had an advantage in his political aspirations, his rise was hardly a quick one. Born in 1952, the younger Lee studied at both Cambridge and Harvard where at the latter he eventually earned a masters degree in public administration. Named deputy prime minister in 1990, Lee has long been expected to become prime minister though how much of the nations' ultimate decision making now lies within his hands remains uncertain. His eighty year old and still very vigorous father has been elevated to a newly created position of "minister mentor" while his former boss Prime Minister Goh retains official influence as the nations' senior minister.

It does appear that the new prime minister is determined to make his own mark on the nation's leadership. He has spoken frequently of the need to build a more open and politically responsive system within Singapore, and laws that previously required police permission to hold indoor meetings have been rescinded. Such changes will most likely allow a somewhat more open environment for political activity over the next few years though how significant such efforts might become is less clear.

For the moment, though, the People's Action Party and its candidates remain firmly in control. During the August 2005 presidential election, the official election committee rejected all candidates for office save those of the incumbent S.R. Nathan. More recently, in the spring of 2006, the long-awaited general elections offered very few surprises. The ruling People's Action Party won 82 of the 84 seats in parliament although their winning percentage (66.6%) was significantly lower than their 2001 win, which had come in at 75.5%.

The one thing probably most certain is that Lee Kuan Yew, the nation's long-time preeminent leader, will remain influential as long as he is able. But, not surprisingly, having the former prime minister's son serve as Singapore's leader raises questions about how politically open Singapore's is capable of becoming. The Lee family is not just influential within the nation's political system. The new prime minister's wife serves as the executive director of the national investment firm Temasek Holdings.

The government's heavy hand is not the only thing that impedes the growth of a more inclusive political system. PAP has been in power so long and has been so successful in improving living standards that few Singapore citizens actually trust the opposition. Well aware of that sentiment, the opposition parties have been careful not to field a full list of candidates during elections. The logic has been that if the voters know that PAP would win regardless of how they voted, the electorate would be more willing to allow an opposition to emerge within the parliament. In practice, it has not mattered much. The opposition currently holds only two of the 84 seats in the nation's parliament.

What is most obvious is that PAP is going to remain in control for quite some time to come. Indeed, the government has made it quite difficult for its opponents to even build support for their causes. One opposition politician, Chee Soon Juan, was jailed for publishing and giving speeches the government did not support. Somewhat later Chee spent twelve days in jail for giving a political speech without a permit and long-time opposition leader J.B Jeyaretnam has been no luckier in his opposition to government policies.

Responding to criticism, the government recently decided to follow the model made famous in London by authorizing the creation of a "Speaker's Corner" in Singapore, where people could voice their opinions in public. But it was hardly a genuine move toward a more open political debate. Aspiring speakers were told they had to register with the police in advance and could still be sued for libel for their comments. How much those controls will remain in place given the new prime minister's talk of a more open society is less sure. Singaporeans were allowed to see somewhat greater openness than in the past during the recent controversy over allowing casinos to open within the normally staid city state. While the eventual decision, influenced by the hope of attracting more tourists, favored the idea, open public forums were allowed. Even senior government ministers were free to express their convictions.

That hardly created a revolution in Singapore's attitude toward free speech. In the early summer of 2008 a naturalized American citizen from Singapore was arrested for writing insulting comments about a local judge in his Internet blog. Insulting a public servant remains a criminal offense punishable by a fine and possible imprisonment.

For the moment the government is facing a series of genuine challenges, which if not handled well could eventually begin to undermine PAP's leadership in the future. Those challenges range from the increasing crime rate and economic setbacks to a growing terrorist presence. Still the government has reason to be satisfied. At least within the city-state itself the regional Islamic militant organization, Jemaah Islamiyah, appears to have been neutralized.

Foreign Policy

Singapore, as an independent mini-state, cannot hope to survive without friends. The strategy has been to make the country so valuable to the region that no one would wish its booming economy destroyed because of the repercussions that would be

Singapore

Courtesy of Frank Conlon

Singapore entrepreneur and family

felt throughout the area. This approach has succeeded. Singapore is one of the world's busiest ports and is the center of economic activity in Southeast Asia. It intends to keep its value high by always being the best.

Relations with Malaysia, though, can at times be complicated. Singapore has though come to an agreement with Malaysia on its international sea boundary. A flap over a Malaysian tariff on Singapore petrochemicals was recently put to rest also. Unfortunately, more problems surfaced early in the late 1990s when Senior Minister Lee Kuan Yew made disparaging remarks about crime problems in one of the Malaysian cities closest to Singapore. The comments were resented and Lee later apologized. Nor were relations improved when Lee later published the first volume of his memoirs about the early years of the city. Many in Malaysia were unhappy with his comments about some of their previous leaders.

The reality is Malaysian-Singapore relations are often tense. Considering that Singapore gets most of its food and water from Malaysia, having a good relationship is especially important. In fact, the price of Malaysian-supplied water was taken to the International Court of Justice for arbitration. Given the recent leadership changes within both Malaysia and Singapore some analysts claim there is reason to expect the all too often tense relationship between the two neighboring countries is likely to lessen.

The most important challenge of recent years has been to help Indonesia through the economic and political challenges it faces. Singapore had good relations with Suharto but with the dictator's departure a new and stable relationship needs to be developed. Here again, the outspoken Lee Kuan Yew has at times complicated matters by making disparaging remarks about Suharto's designated vice-president and

then successor, B.J. Habibie. Of course Singapore's citizens could hardly remain indifferent to the fate of so many Indonesian ethnic Chinese who found themselves threatened by the violence unleashed during Suharto's fall from power. While Singapore did not send troops to East Timor during the later crisis and intervention of 1999 it did send a medical team and provide aid.

In the months after Abdurrahman Wahid came to power in Indonesia Singapore attempted to improve relations with him. Wahid's government reciprocated, by asking Lee Kuan Yew to serve on a panel of outside advisors for Indonesia. More recently Prime Minister Goh Chok Tong visited Indonesia to help coordinate a major new Singapore investment program there and to establish an agreement under which Indonesia will supply natural gas to the Chinese city-state.

Until recently perhaps the most profound aspect of Singapore's foreign relations was the influence it has had on the region as a model of economic and social growth under a non-communist but authoritarian regime. Despite Western preferences and claims that a free and vibrant economy cannot exist without a politically open system, Lee Kuan Yew and the PAP long seemed to have demonstrated that they apparently can. It is an example that countries as close as Malaysia and as far as the People's Republic have watched closely.

As has been the experience of other nations in the region, the on-going "War on Terrorism," carried out by the Bush administration, has impacted on Singapore as well. In the island nation's case, it contributed personnel to the group of countries that supported the American activities in Iraq, and was rewarded for its troubles by being designated a major American ally which carries with it political and economic advantages. But working too closely with the increasingly unpopular Americans can be potentially dangerous as well given that Singapore is surrounded by Muslim countries that have at times often been very critical of the United States. As mentioned above within Singapore, the nation's security forces do appear to have been successful in their efforts against Jemaah Islamiyah, the most dangerous regional Islamic militant group.

Despite the complicated issues arising out of the world wide "war on terrorism" it was regional issues that dominated Singapore's international affairs over the last year, especially so when the soon to be named Prime Minister made what was said to be on an official visit to Taiwan to consult with that nations' leaders. Predictably, Beijing was very unhappy with the visit though perhaps somewhat mollified later on when Taiwan became angry

over warnings from Singapore that its independence drive was "dangerous."

As a nation whose economic prosperity is particularly tied to the free navigation of the world's oceans, it will not be a surprise that Singapore has chosen to take part in the international coalition of naval forces that are working to protect shipping off the coast of Somalia. The plan put into effect in early 2009 called for the country to supply a tanker ship, two helicopters and around 200 personnel in order to police the regional waters and confront the threats emanating from the Somali pirates who captured headlines early in the year.

Culture

Singapore is a more multi-cultural city than many people realize. The vast majority of the population is Chinese, but they emigrated from several parts of southern China and thus tended to speak mutually unintelligible dialects until the government began its emphasis on learning "Mandarin" Chinese. That is also one of the reasons English has long been used as the official language of instruction, business and in government. Moreover, the community includes a significant minority of Malays and South Asians. Over the last year, given the increased concern about the presence of terrorist cells in Singapore some have feared that this might result in an increased prejudice against local Muslims, a development that would hurt the social cohesiveness of Singapore and certainly add to the tensions which arise with Malaysia from time to time.

The main feature of society in Singapore today is that it is centered around the industry of a bustling port and its very urban citizens who enjoy the highest standard of living of the region. Rather than living in the countryside, they live in apartments that the government built and that they have been encouraged to purchase.

A Very Well Organized Society?

Singapore's leadership has made extraordinary improvements in the life of its citizens. It has done so at a price that some might find excessive. The government has over the years intervened in many aspects of the lives of its citizens, thus creating an astoundingly regulated society. Still, as a result of the government's almost puritanical attitude, Singapore has been viewed as one of the safest and cleanest places in the world. Though, that reputation was tarnished somewhat when during the aftermath of the World Trade attack of September 2001 it became clear that a terrorist cell had been operating in Singapore. The crime rate (hardly significant when compared to

Singapore

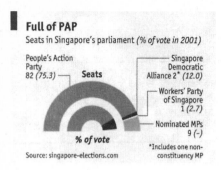
many of its neighbors) has also tarnished that "squeaky clean" image somewhat.

However, the social success of Singapore has not always been sufficient to keep the country's best and brightest at home. Significant numbers of highly educated young citizens have left the country in search of greater political freedom. While some have returned, the fact that the usually prosperous environment alone has not been sufficient to keep younger people from leaving should give the government cause to ponder how much authoritarianism is appropriate for a modern, well-educated society.

Education is highly admired in Singapore, and the society is moving smoothly into the computer age. Increasing numbers of households have personal computers and more and more of them are connected to the Internet. Predictably, that has opened up yet another vehicle of potential disruption the government would rather avoid. There have been moves to liberalize the social policies that are so influential in Singapore as well. In recent years the government has become somewhat more tolerant of activities and behaviors from bungee jumping to homosexuality.

Overall, the island has acquired a genuinely cosmopolitan atmosphere with people from all over the world present. The city-state serves as a major international port that lies at the crossroads of Asia. For a modern urban society Singapore is still a very safe city whose crime rates remain quite low—certainly lower than in many urban centers in America or many other places in Asia. In fact, until recently it could boast that the crime rate had gone down every year for almost a decade.

There are other concerns as well. The birthrate is declining, and the government has begun a concerted effort from making it easier for foreigners to become citizens to encouraging parenthood to address the problem. There has also been a growth in the gap between rich and poor. The nation's leadership has addressed this by introducing a compulsory annuity program that should help poorer citizens to retire with more of the funds they need to live.

While Singapore may be an unusually stable society, very public controversies of the sort common elsewhere certainly do break out from time to time. Most recently the question of homosexuality became a public topic when a dramatic struggle broke out among conservative women. They had became involved in a struggle over the question of whether an organization founded to support gender equality had become too involved in what some saw as promoting homosexuality.

In other incident, a Christian preacher had to apologize publically for derogatory comments he made on YouTube about Taoist religious practices. Clearly, Singapore may pride itself on the sophistication of its multicultural society, but it is as vulnerable to outbursts of intolerance as many of its neighbors.

Women

Women in Singapore have the same civil rights as men. In contrast to some other parts of Asia, Muslim women are covered by most of the provisions of the Women's Charter although in matters of polygamy and divorce Islamic law prevails. The government has also mandated that women should get equal pay for equal work and no longer allows separate pay scales.

Inequalities do exist. For example, women do not have the same rights males have in passing on their citizenship automatically to their children. Moreover, medical benefits available to the families of male civil servants are denied to families of female employees. And quotas that limit the number of women in the nation's medical schools were only just being addressed recently. On the more positive side two women currently serve as ministers in the nation's government.

Economy

In a fashion similar to that pioneered in Japan, Singapore's economy has been developed along the lines some refer to as "Asian Capitalism," though without the corruption often associated with the term. In contrast to "Anglo-American capitalism's" ever present suspicions about government, Singapore's government has played an important role in guiding the nation's economy. Employing institutions like the Economic Development Board and the Trade Development Board, the leadership has helped guide and set priorities for the economic evolution of Singapore. Such institutions have been especially helpful as Singapore has moved through various economic stages from the processing of primary products to the new information technologies.

As one of the first nations to embrace what is now known as "globalization," Singapore is heavily dependent on foreign trade and investment, all of which it is doing its best to promote. Since the mid-1980s the economy had been growing at a rate of about 8% a year. Because of its high level of development and its "contribution" to the U.S.'s trade imbalance, Singapore lost its preferential tariff status under the United States' Generalized System of Preferences (GSP) in 1988. Nevertheless, in the mid 1990s the growth rates averaged around nine percent.

Even before the onset of the economic crisis of 1997, the island suffered a glut of empty retail spaces and very high rents. Wages were high and rising because labor was chronically short. It was in the context of these problems that Singapore, along with its neighbors, experienced the many economic problems 1997 brought.

Singapore waterfront

Courtesy of Frank Conlon

Singapore

Not only did its currency plunge, but tourist arrivals—no doubt frightened by the stories of the choking atmosphere of a few years before—dropped significantly.

Responding proactively, the government continued to develop new industries, such as those in information technologies, electronic commerce and most recently biotechnology. In fact, the government has made it clear that it hopes to see Singapore become especially involved in new biomedical breakthroughs associated with stem cell research. As the island nation entered the new century, the economy initially appeared on track again with a growth rate of 9.9% for 2000. Unfortunately, 2001 turned out be a disaster, literally the worse GDP—it fell by 2%—in the nation's history. That downturn was clearly tied not only to the worldwide glut of electronic products, but to the more general international economic slowdown, especially within the United States and its important domestic market.

Responding to the problem, the government worked not only on long-term solutions like the diversification of the economy and moving away from the dependence on electronics, but also on immediate changes to the corporate tax system to make Singapore more attractive to business leaders. It was especially important to lower the local wage bills. To deal with the problem, new policies were put into place, including lowering taxes to encouraging new bilateral trade agreements with nations like Canada and Sri Lanka. Especially important in that regard was the signing of the long-negotiated Singapore-U.S. free-trade agreement.

The economy has also been helped by the growth of Southern India, with which Singapore has deep cultural and economic ties. As a sign of how Singapore might evolve in the future, the controversial decision was taken to allow two casinos to be built. This was a clear recognition of the success nearby Macau has had with its own efforts to expand its gambling revenues and of the importance for Singapore to continue to diversify its revenues. One casino, run by the Las Vegas Sands Hotel group, was built in downtown Singapore.

Regardless of what combination of factors has been most influential in Singapore's recovery, the economy in recent years was rebounding nicely. Economic growth for 2006 was around 7.4 %, and 2007 was about the same. In fact, the most immediate concerns were an overheating economy and inflation. There was also a real estate boom as the value of condominiums rose dramatically. In yet another sign of what some have called the emerging Asian century, Merrill Lynch, the powerful American investment house, sold billions of dollars in stock to a Singapore investor as the U.S. firm struggled to get its financial house in order in the wake of the American home loan debacle.

But Singapore's status as one of the world's most globalized nations has a price. The global recession that set in so dramatically in the late fall of 2008 deeply affected the local economy. By early 2009, the economy had dropped precipitously although the eventual year-end figures were not as bad as some had initially feared.

Like so many of the other governments in the world, Singapore's government moved quickly to put in place its own $13.7 billion economic package to revise the economy. Moreover, in the early spring the government moved to devalue its currency somewhat in hopes of making its exports relatively more attractive to international buyers.

The Energy and Environmental Challenge

Given how often hot ash from the regular burning of Indonesian forests arrives to hang over the city, environmental issues are rarely far from people's minds in Singapore. As for the larger issues of energy use and the challenges of global warming, Singapore's obligations under the Kyoto Protocol on climate change came into effect during 2006. Unlike China, Singapore already generates the bulk of its electrical energy needs from natural gas, a cleaner technology than coal. Moreover a campaign to enhance energy efficiency is underway. Greater tax breaks for purchasers of hybrid cars have been implemented along with experiments with hydrogen cars. But while the small island nation's ability fundamentally to influence global climate change is relatively small, its vulnerability is great. A good chunk of the nation's entire business district, airport and important naval facilities is somewhat less than two meters above sea level. Given that reality, the country's authorities have begun discussions with the Dutch government on what the Netherland's has learned in its long fight against the sea.

The Future

The success of Singapore may have less to do with the distinct values its leaders talk about than with the country's manageable size and optimum location. Some educated youth already find the tradeoff between the general economic prosperity and restricted political and social freedom difficult. The arrival to adulthood of a generation—which takes the material advantages of life in Singapore for granted and is thus not so afraid of losing them—may one day demand greater political participation than the government will be willing to grant.

Singapore's new leader, himself part of the younger generation, is aware of this problem. He has been moving to address some of those concerns, at least in his rhetoric if not, thus far, in many actual decisions.

In the same vein, if the PAP is not able to deliver the economic prosperity of the past, future voters may not see its leadership as quite so vital. That challenge is a real one. The SARs crisis of 2003 may have proven to have been a short-time problem. But the island nation's economic prosperity remains deeply tied to what is going on in the rest of the world. Of course, fears of a deadly outbreak of Avian flu are quite real. Like so many other highly developed nations, the biggest challenge for Singapore will be to build upon its accomplishments as one of the world's first globalized nations. This would ensure that its success continues as so many of its regional neighbors, from India to China, begin to compete in that same economic arena.

Of course, the immediate challenge has been to weather the global recession that began in late 2008 and hit Singapore especially hard because of its close integration with the world economy. As the downturn struck, the government used the tools at its disposal, including an economic stimulus program of something just under 14 billion dollars, to improve Singapore's economic prospects. As we have seen elsewhere, the downturn did not turn out to be quite as dramatic in Asia has some had feared. However, Singapore still entered 2010 with negative growth rates.

Not surprisingly given Singapore's reputation as one of the most high tech and globalized countries in the world, the nation's leaders utilized the occasion to use government resources to stimulate another expansion in the nation's internet infrastructure. They put into place even more fiber optic networks that can carry data at speeds most Americans could not even imagine.

Famous Singapore Flyer

225

The Kingdom of Thailand (before 1935 known as Siam)

River Traffic in Bangkok

Area: 198,455 sq. mi. (514,080 sq. miles)

Population: 66,404,688 (2010 estimate)

Capital City: Bangkok Pop. 6,355,144 (2000 estimate)

Climate: Tropically hot with a wet monsoon season (May–October) dry and increasingly hot (November–April)

Neighboring Countries: Malaysia (South); Burma (Northwest); Laos (Northeast); Cambodia (Southeast)

Official Language: Thai (about 75%)

Other Principal Tongues: Chinese (about 14%); other (about 11%)

Ethnic Background: Thai (about 75%); Chinese (about 14%); Malay (about 4%); inland tribal groups (about 2%); Cambodian refugees (about 2%); other (about 3%)

Principal Religions: Theravada Buddhism, Islam

Main Exports (to Japan, U.S., China, Malaysia, Hong Kong, Singapore): textiles, footwear, cars, computers, rice, sugar, corn, rubber, tin, timber, fishery products

Main Imports (from Malaysia, Singapore, Japan, U.S., Saudi Arabia): Machinery and transport equipment, petroleum, chemicals, fertilizer, consumer goods

Currency: Baht

Former Political Status: Siam avoided becoming a European colony; it was a nominal ally of Japan during World War II.

National Day: December 10th (Constitution Day)

Chief of State: King Bhumibol Adulyadej (b. 1927).

Head of Government: Prime Minister Abhisit Vejjajiva (Since December 17, 2008)

National Flag: Five horizontal stripes from top to bottom; red, white, blue (wider than the others), white and red.

Per Capita Income: $8,100 (2009 est., purchasing power parity).

The broad central plain of Thailand, through which flows the Chao Phraya River, is the most fertile and productive area of the country and contains the principal cities, including Bangkok. Viewed from the foothills, which are found on the western edge of the plain, the land resembles an almost endless window with countless "panes of glass" when the precisely divided rice paddies are flooded with water.

The northern areas are more mountainous, and are covered with jungles containing timber and mineral resources. Valuable teakwood is still brought from the jungle on the tusks of the Asian elephant. The northeast region is dominated by the arid Korat Plateau. Ample rainfall occurs in the plateau, but it is not absorbed by the sandstone soil—it quickly collects into streams and rivers and runs to the sea instead of enriching the land. More people live here than can be supported by the limited agriculture that is possible. The southern region consists of the narrow Kra Isthmus and the coastal belt.

History

People of Thai origin today not only inhabit Thailand but also live in the adjacent regions of all of Thailand's neighbors with the exception of Malaysia. The original home of these people was in southwest China where they were ruled by a highly organized kingdom in the 7th century A.D. The pressure of the Chinese and later the Mongols caused a migration of the Thais southward where they eventually founded a new state in what is now northern Thailand.

In sharp contrast to governmental traditions in China, the Thai kings ruled as autocratic divine beings. Although they had not ruled directly for much of the 20th century, elements of this earlier tradition continue in the deep reverence the Thai people still hold for their monarchy.

During centuries of slow expansion they were eventually able to crush the Khmer Empire in neighboring Cambodia. In the 16th century, Siam, as it was then called, was conquered by the Burmese. Apart from sporadic contact by French merchants, the Europeans did not enter the area during the early centuries of exploration and colonization.

There was another Burmese invasion in 1767, but shortly thereafter Burma was invaded by the Manchu empire of China. That development eventually allowed the Siamese to win their freedom again. The present reigning dynasty came to power in 1782, and moved the capital city to the more secure location of Bangkok. Siam again emerged as a strong state. But though Siam's relations were already complicated, they were about to get much more so.

The Arrival of the West

Early in the 19th century, Siam began to have more extensive contacts, commercial and otherwise, with Westerners. Moreover, the British gradually established control over Burma, and the French asserted their power over Vietnam. Laos and Cambodia had formerly been tributary states of Siam, but the French were ultimately able to combine them with Vietnam in their colony of Indochina. Thus, Siam was surrounded with the British on the west, the French on the east and the Manchu empire of China to the north.

Siam managed to avoid becoming a European colony by a lucky combination of factors. First were the advantages of having not one but two European colonial powers on their borders (who could then be played off against each other). Second was enlightened leadership, which moved to strengthen the country through an in-

Prime Minister Abhisit Wetchachiwa

creasing degree of modernization. It was a combination too few other non-Western states enjoyed.

In Siam's case, two important monarchs, during the critical late nineteenth and early twentieth centuries, helped shield them from the worst of imperialism. The first was Mongkut, who reigned in the critical the mid-nineteenth century, and his son Chulalongkorn who followed him in power. Mongkut who was the monarch described in the book Anna and the King of Siam which eventually inspired a musical and two feature length films.

Phra Maha Chulalongkorn, his son, was king from 1868 to 1910. He gained fame not only by abolishing Siam's feudal system, but also by modernizing the government and the army and by introducing such conveniences as the telegraph and railroad. He also paid an extended visit to the European capitals.

Both monarchs, father and son, recognizing the seriousness of the Western threat, took significant steps to educate themselves in Western issues and to find ways to lessen the growth of Western power in Siam. Overall their policies were a combination of tactical acceptance of various legal and territorial demands made by the Europeans while working to maintain the ultimate sovereignty of the Siamese state.

As part of some early 20th century treaties the borders with Laos and Cambodia were adjusted. Under these treaties, regions were traded back and forth between France and Siam. In order to keep other colonial powers out of Siam, France and Britain established "spheres of influence"—the French east of the Chao Phraya River and the British west of the river. As a result of its somewhat limited, but significant, modernization program, and the fact

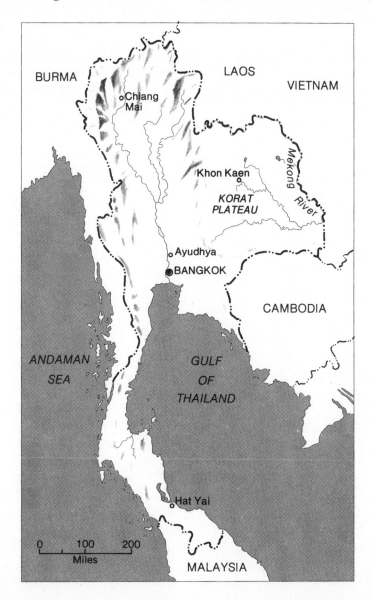

Thailand

Wat Po

that it escaped being a colony of a European power, Thailand today lacks the sense of resentment toward the industrialized nations that many people still feel in the countries of the former colonial world.

A New Political System

After World War I there was a period of extravagant spending by the royal government, which was followed by a worldwide economic depression. This created discontent within Thailand and gave rise to intense political activity. The result was a bloodless overthrow of the autocratic monarchy in 1932 by a combination of civilian politicians and military leaders.

The two groups cooperated in the adoption of a constitution that limited the power of the king and established a parliamentary form of government. The first prime minister was a brilliant lawyer named Pridi Phanomyong. The king, dissatisfied with this system, abdicated in 1935, and was succeeded by his ten-year-old nephew and a regency council. This and other unsettling conditions, including the increased power of Japan in Asia, led to the overthrow of Pridi by Marshal Pibul Songgram. As World War II approached Marshal Pibul would prove to be especially nationalistic and pro-Japanese.

In theory the country continued to be governed by a coalition consisting of the prime minister, the military and Luang Pradit, the foreign minister. As the military acquired increasing political power, they displayed their nationalism by such means as legislation aimed at curbing the role of the Chinese commercial community, and changing the nation's name from Siam to Thailand, meaning "Land of the Free." In the years following the 1932 coup the Thai military, like the later Burmese and Indonesian military, would insist on an important place for itself in national decision-making.

The Pacific War

Three weeks after the bombing of Pearl Harbor by the Japanese, Thailand signed a treaty of alliance with Japan. War was declared on the United States and Great Britain on January 25, 1942. With the support of Japanese troops, Thailand compelled the French to cede some border territories in Laos and Cambodia. The four southern states of Thailand, which had earlier been given to the British in Malaya were now returned to Thailand by the Japanese after they seized the British colony of Burma. Thailand probably had little choice in cooperating with the armies of imperial Japan. The Japanese certainly had the means to impose their will and had demonstrated their strength in early clashes with the Thai forces.

As the war began to turn against Japan, the Thai government, which has a long history of protecting itself through power politics, began to change sides. An anti-Japanese guerrilla movement arose, and American military intelligence officers were able to operate almost openly in Bangkok during the last months of the war.

Pibul, himself, the pro-Japanese premier, resigned in 1944. At the end of the war, Britain took the position that Thailand was an enemy country and compelled payment of reparations in the form of rice, which was sent to Malaya. The U.S. however viewed Thailand as a more reluctant Japanese ally, and was able to persuade the British to adopt a similar policy.

Thailand's most immediate problem in the postwar years was to reintegrate itself into the world community after having been allied with imperialist Japan, and to establish a stable government. The former proved easier than the latter. The lands taken from France and Britain during the war were returned. Thailand was admitted to the UN in 1946.

Political stability, however, proved more difficult. The king, who had only recently been enthroned, was found dead of a gunshot wound in 1946. Premier Pridi, who was accused, apparently falsely, of having played some part in the slaying, was deposed. The army, still led by Pibul, again seized power. It was a pattern that was to continue through the 1990s.

The Cold War

Initially it appeared uncertain as to what position Thailand would take in the Korean War. Once it decided to support the American-backed UN troops, it began to receive U.S. military aid. This further strengthened the political position of the army in domestic affairs, making it more and more powerful within Thailand and, given the economic support of the wealthy Americans, helping to build the country's economic infrastructure.

The early 1950s saw many leaders like Nehru of India and Sukarno of Indonesia attempting to build a nonaligned movement during the height of the Cold War. Some governments accepted this position, but Thailand chose to align itself more directly with the Americans. Thailand became a founding member of SEATO, the Southeast Asian Treaty Organization (designed to be an Asian equivalent of NATO), and supported the American war in Vietnam.

Premier Pibul did permit freer discussion of political issues and began to encourage a growth of neutralism. Concerned about potential Communist Chinese influence he also took steps against the local Chinese community that traditionally had been involved in the economy but refrained from taking part in politics. Nevertheless, Communist gains in Laos created more uneasiness in Thailand, which was dispelled when the U.S. pledged direct assistance in the event SEATO failed to fully support Thailand.

Pibul was overthrown in 1958 by Marshal Sarit, who kept Thailand firmly in an anti-communist posture. The country had an orderly, stable and not overly intrusive

228

government. As was true in so many nations, the military leaders were able to accumulate vast private fortunes through corruption.

Less effective military leadership continued after 1963 under subsequent leaders. Reliance was placed upon the ability of the popular royal family to maintain the unity of the Thai people, as well as on an increased degree of official respect shown for Buddhism and its various organizations. However, communist-inspired unrest in the poverty-stricken northeast region became more serious. The government treated this as a genuine threat, though perhaps partly to obtain additional American aid.

Once the United States fully committed to the struggle in Vietnam, Thailand permitted the Americans to use its air bases for attacks on North Vietnam and the Viet Cong. Thailand sent about 11,000 troops to fight in Vietnam and Laos. Having sided with the Americans, Thailand was able to gain enormous economic aid.

The reaction from the communist side was predictable—as Thailand increased its assistance to the U.S. and South Vietnam, the communists stepped up their guerrilla activities within the country. The increased U.S. military buildup in Thailand was thus paralleled by a greater flow of U.S. aid to the Thai armed forces. But if Thailand's association with the anticommunist side was clear in these years its own domestic politics were less so.

The National Assembly was dissolved in 1968, leaving no representative body in Thailand. Eventually, a constitution was drafted by a Constituent Assembly and promulgated by the king in mid-1968. Elections in 1969 gave the United Thai People's Party, the government party, the victory. The Senate was appointed by the government.

But, the powerful military, unhappy with developments, suspended the parliament and reshuffled the cabinet. In 1972 a new constitution was proclaimed under which 299 members of a National Assembly were all appointed by the government, in other words by the army.

Democratic Momentum?

The next year, the army-dominated government was toppled by student demonstrations that had the support of the King and at least part of the army. A civilian government was then ushered in, committed to greater freedom and reform. It was yet another step, such as in 1932, when the autocratic monarchy had ended, that gave Thailand the possibility of moving toward a more democratic form of government. In this case, it was partially as a result of the intervention of the monarchy itself that

had not played a political role since 1932. As the new government was formed in 1973, Thailand seemed on the verge of taking yet another step toward more inclusive political decision-making.

But true parliamentary government was not to develop in Thailand, at least not during those years. A combination of insecurity caused by the growing strength of Communism in the region—Vietnam had been unified under Hanoi and Cambodia taken over the Khmer Rouge—as well as unhappiness about the open political battles within the new democratic government moved the military to once again reassert itself in 1976. In October of that year, with the backing of the King, the government was overthrown and the democratic constitution suspended.

Over the next years Thailand's politics were moved by several factors—the emerging democratic movement, which had its first real chance to govern in the mid 1970s, the ever influential Thai military and the King, who has continued to be revered and has demonstrated a willingness to intervene in the governing system when he deems it appropriate.

An informal power-sharing arrangement between the army, civilian politicians and officials has been common over the last few generations. Army leadership itself has been divided between those willing to work with civilians and those who are not. Rule has shifted between civilian and military-dominated governments, with and without ex-generals in the premiership, and outright military rule. Corruption has been commonplace. However, there were signs during the early 1990s that the military's domination of Thai politics was being increasingly challenged by the growth of a more politically conscious middle class.

In 1991 another civilian government was overthrown. Rule then shifted to the military dominated National Peacekeeping Council. In March 1992, a three-party coalition favored by the Council won control of the government with 53% of the seats in the lower house of parliament. The NPC then appointed all 270 members of the upper house with most having military backgrounds or connections.

When agreement could not be achieved on a new prime minister, the leader of the "junta," General Suchinda Krapayoon, a key figure in the coup, and an individual especially unpopular with those who supported democracy, stepped into the post. Public demonstrations against Suchinda then led to severe repression by the Thai military. The level of violence against the civilian population was unparalleled in the recent Thai history.

The king stepped in to calm the crisis. On May 20, Suchinda appeared on na-

tional television kneeling before King Bhumibol. He was ordered to settle the crisis peacefully. After a short period of "caretaker" government, new elections were held on September 13, 1992. Chuan Leekpai was chosen as prime minister. The constitution now required that the prime minister be chosen from the lower house of parliament. The new government was ruled by a five-party coalition. This made it difficult to proceed with the legislative agenda that centered on constitutional reform. The army had been warned. It could no longer assume the civilian population would simply go along with anything it attempted.

In May 1995, Prime Minister Chuan Leekpai was forced to dissolve parliament when the Palang Dharma party pulled out of the ruling five-party coalition. Elections took place the following July which saw the prime minister's coalition lose. Thai voters then elected the Chart Thai party's Banharn Silpa-Archa as prime minister. The Banharn government was built around a seven party coalition led by his party, Chart Thai, and the Palang Dharma which defected from Chuan's coalition prior to the election. But the new government came under fire almost immediately for a kickback scheme involving the prime minister's party and a Swedish submarine manufacturer, and for protecting a minister involved in vote-buying.

The military's recent reticence to intervene seemed less sure when a military radio broadcast criticizing the government

Traditional Thai dancer

Thailand

The Royal Family of Thailand

for its management of the economy raised concerns in Bangkok and abroad. A disagreement over military promotions between the Minister of Defense and the Army Commanding General, Wimol Wongwanich, also worsened civil-military relations. To make matters worse, the King criticized the government for the traffic chaos in Bangkok. By mid-1996 prospects were not looking bright for the Banharn government, and by November new elections brought Chavalit Yongchaiyudh, the Defense Minister, from the previous government, to power.

As a former Armed Forces Chief, Chavalit had close ties not only to the Thai military but to Burma's military junta as well. The new leader was 65 and claimed he was committed to cleaning up corruption. That was probably a good idea since his own party, the New Aspiration Party, was said to have been the most involved in buying votes during the elections.

Chavalit had his work cut out for him. Even before the economic crisis of 1997 his government had to face calls for a new constitution in order to reduce corruption. As has been the case in so many other countries, Thai electoral politics has been driven by money. In fact, enormous sums are usually spent to influence elections including even the direct purchase of votes in rural areas.

To address the problem a group of former parliamentary members and legal experts were chosen to write a new constitution. The results were presented to the nation's legislature during the fall of 1997. At that point Chavalit, despite his earlier promises, seemed more in support of those who feared the new constitution would hurt their personal interests. Foremost among the changes were the direct election of senators, rather than appointment by the prime minister, more regulations to promote public accountability and further guarantees of individual rights.

The rules for election to the senate were particularly creative. To make the election as incorruptible as possible, those running were not allowed to make any public announcements about proposed goals once in office. Later after the early 2000 senate elections occurred, it became especially clear that the commitment to ensuring a more honest electoral process was still firmly in place. To the surprise and irritation of many senatorial candidates, the electoral commission, citing concerns about corruption, revoked the victories of more than a third of the winners and called for new supplemental elections.

Happily, for those who supported the new constitution, the new charter has had the support of both the population and the military.

It was a difficult fight and, in the end, one of the few significant accomplishments of Prime Minister Chavalit's term in office, even accepting his somewhat ambivalent support. As the battle over the constitution was going on during the fall, the more immediate crisis over the economy was raging. In that battle the prime minister, in office for less than a year, would not prevail.

The turmoil now known as the "Asian Economic Crisis" began in 1997 with a drop in the value of Thailand's national currency, the Baht. Unfortunately, the Prime Minister seemed bewildered by the crisis and many in the country quickly concluded he lacked the skills to take on the challenge. Thus Prime Minister Chavalit became the region's first political casualty of the economic crisis.

His replacement was former Prime Minister Chuan Leekpai, who returned to power in November. When Chuan Leekpai, 59, assumed office again, many in Thailand voiced a collective sense of relief that he would be better able to deal with the crisis than his predecessor. Certainly no one could single handedly pull the country back from the brink, but Chuan did move quickly to build a strong support team around himself and then set off for an important meeting in Washington where he was successful in improving relations with the United States. Most importantly, he resolved a problem over new defense aircraft Bangkok had ordered and which it could no longer afford. The trip turned out so well that even his opponents seemed satisfied.

Despite the early confidence he had received from the public, Chuan Leekpai's popularity did not last as long. By mid-1999, much of his authority was weakened by revelations of corruption among some of his political coalition partners. The prime minister, working to retain his authority responded by inviting new partners into the ruling coalition.

Although Prime Minister Chuan offered sophisticated leadership during Thailand's struggle to recover from the impact of the Asian economic crisis, his efforts were not enough to keep in him office. In January 2001, Thais went to the polls for the first time since 1997 to elect a new government. This time they voted under the new electoral rules.

New electoral changes had been designed to reduce the influence of money in Thailand's electoral process. Nevertheless, money remained especially important to the final outcome of the election as the Thai telecommunications tycoon billionaire Thaksin Shinawatra used his abundant cash not only to form a new party, the Thai Loves Thai party, but to win a major victory at the polls. In fact, his electoral domination was the largest in Thailand's parliamentary history and ushered Thaksin into power with an extraordinary 70% popularity in the polls.

Thai Politics at a Crossroads?

The last few years have proven quite significant for Thailand both politically and socially. In the years after Thaksin Shinawatra came to office, he significantly increased his power. He initially did so by relying more on the nation's traditional elites and the military while, according to some critics, backing away from plans for more significant political reforms. The government was also accused of using its power to pressure both the international and domestic media. Leading journalists reportedly had their bank accounts scru-

Former Prime Minister Chuan Leekpai

tinized, possibly a tool of intimidation while prominent writers and editors were forced from their positions.

Some observers even suggested that the prime minister's long-term political goal was to move his nation's political system closer to the one-party dominated systems of Singapore and Malaysia, rather than to a more genuinely open political system. The prime minister himself was quite open about his negative attitude toward democracy, which he clearly saw as "overrated."

There were certainly plenty of examples of the government's authoritarianism. The prime minister developed an almost dictatorial control over the parliament. Moreover he put his cousin in charge of the Thai army. His family's financial holdings also grew enormously after coming to power.

Nevertheless, much of the population remained quite supportive of the prime minister. Understandably, people were initially pleased by Thailand's recovery from the devastating economic downturn of the late 1990s. His very severe and violent crackdown against the Thai illegal drug industry was also largely appreciated by the masses. Many have also reacted positively to his promises of significantly reducing poverty and terrorism. Ironically, the tsunami of late 2004 further strengthened the prime minister as he was frequently shown in the media dynamically confronting the challenges brought by the waging waters. That publicity paid significant dividends only a few weeks later in early 2005 when the results of the general elections handed him and his party another big electoral boost.

With that second win, some feared that, given the prime minister's authoritarian predilections, Thailand would remain democratic in name only. However, that impression did not last long. Over the following months, as the economy lost its earlier momentum and the insurgency in

Floating market in Ratchaburi Province south of Bangkok   Photo by Karla Allan

Thailand

the south failed to be resolved, much of Prime Minister Thaksin Shinawatra's momentum seemed to fade.

Making matters worse was the emergence of a huge political scandal concerning the questionable sale of the prime minister's family's media holdings to a Singapore company. Huge demonstrations became common in the streets of Bangkok while he found his political legitimacy collapsing. Hoping to renew his political mandate amidst the crisis, Thaksin called for a snap election in early April 2006.

However, the opposition candidates boycotted them. Not unexpectedly this created a situation where at least on paper Thaksin's political party, Thai Loves Thai, was in a position to dominate the parliament. Over the next few months, Thai politics continued to get more complicated, while in Southern Thailand the Muslim insurgency, another matter for which Thaksin's detractors blamed the prime minister, continued to worsen.

Saving or Destroying Thai Democracy?

Suddenly in September 2006 the situation changed dramatically as the Thai military, so often a major player in the nation's political history, staged a coup as the now acting Prime Minister Thaksin was in New York attending the United Nations. While the role of the nation's deeply revered monarch, King Bhumipol Adulyadej, remains somewhat murky, it was immediately obvious once the military coup occurred that it clearly had the king's support.

Ironically, although much of the world initially condemned the actions of Thailand's military, the move was received relatively positively within the country and even among many of the nation's most ardent supporters of democracy. That was not surprising as many had come to believe that Prime Minister Thaksin himself had been fundamentally opposed to Thailand's democratic tradition.

Once the military fully established itself, a new prime minister, Surayud Chulanont, a retired general with close ties to the king and a known supporter of Thai democracy was named p.m. At the same time plans were announced for a temporary suspension of democracy. The world was told that the delay was necessity given the importance of modifying the constitution in light of recent developments.

Meanwhile, during the summer of 2007 the Thai courts officially banned Thaksin, along with many senior members of his party, from taking part in the nation's politics for five years. The other political parties whose activities had also been banned were now allowed to resume them. As for the nation's political constitution, sus-

pended since the coup, the new military-dominated government issued its own revised version, which won a 57% approval during the subsequent referendum.

Nevertheless, the divisions within Thai society clearly remained. The more than 40% of the population that voted against the new constitution usually lived in the rural areas that remained strongly supportive of Thaksin. Bangkok's population, on the other hand, was strongly critical of Thaksin's years in office.

By late 2007, the question became even more complicated whether Thailand would continue on the road toward the vibrant democracy it had become in the years before the pro-democratic military coup.

Ousted Thai Prime Minister Thaksin Shinawatra

New elections were allowed to proceed again. In a stunning reversal of fortune, the newly formed People's Power Party, the successor to the exiled former Premier Thaksin's Thai Rak Thai party, easily defeated its rivals and came very close to gaining a governing majority in the nation's parliament. While their actual win, only a few votes short of an absolute majority, was significantly lower than those they had won during the last few convoluted elections before the coup, it was nevertheless significant.

Clearly, the majority of Thailand's voting population, and especially those in the rural areas that had long supported Thaksin, had fundamentally rejected the military's intervention and had thrown their support to the former minister's hand-picked successor, Samak Sundaravej. By February 2008, the new prime minister was able to form a cabinet, which the king then swore in.

A close look at the newly formed government revealed a few clues about Thai-

land's future. On the one hand, it was largely made up of the ousted Prime Minister Thaksin's supporters. On the other hand, many of his closest former colleagues were unable to take part because of laws that had officially banned them from politics for five years. Most interestingly, Samak Sundaravej himself took the post of defense minister, an unusual role for a civilian leader. However, it was an understandable decision given the tensions with the nation's military leaders.

Despite the fact that Samak himself, like his sponsor, had a checkered past, Thai voters clearly preferred the People's Power Party and its promises of a renewal of Thaksin's economic policies, which had included specific populist policies for the rural poor. Nevertheless, the election results, which could so obviously be interpreted as a vindication of ousted Prime Minister Thaksin, hardly ended the issue. In fact, the struggle merely entered another stage.

The simple fact was that while Thailand's rural poor may have continued to support Thaksin's political movement, it had developed over the years an impressive array of enemies. They came from diverse sectors of Thai society: from the military to the financial community and, more subtly but equally obviously, from the monarchy itself. Given that reality, it is not surprising that by August 2008 a new seemingly populist and certainly militant movement, known as the People's Alliance for Democracy (PAD), emerged to challenge the authority of the government and Thaksin's supporters.

Over the next month, the movement's middle-class supporters successfully occupied major government buildings and ultimately Thailand's ultra-modern international airport. The movement seemed at first glance to be quite rowdy. However, it was obvious upon closer inspection that it was linked to a very well organized and funded movement with relatively visible ties to those segments of the population that had risen to oppose everything Thaksin represented: the monarch, the police and the financial elite.

Most significantly, Thailand's demonstration of what might be seen as pseudo-people power had real clout. After pushing one prime minister from power, the movement ultimately saw yet another pro-Thaksin prime minister, Somchai Wongsawat, his brother-in-law, forced from power by the Thai Supreme Court, which accused him of corruption. It dissolved his political party.

Eventually a new prime minister, Abhisit Vejjajiva, who hailed from the ranks of those who have been so critical of Thaksin, took office in December of 2008. Almost three full years of political uncer-

Lumphini Park, Bangkok

tainty—from Thaksin's bid to solidify his party's absolute control to the military coup that overthrew him to the new elections that brought his supporters back to power and more recently to the political activism of the PAD—all combined to ensure that Thailand's political future remained up in the air. A dramatic year it was.

The turmoil continued throughout 2009 and well into 2010 as the opposing forces, dubbed red shirts for Thaksin's rural supporters, vehemently opposed the unelected new Prime Minister Abhisit Vejiajiva. They faced off with the "yellow shirts," the more urban-based royalist anti-Thaksin activists. By March a new populist movement, known as the United Front for Democracy Against Dictatorship, emerged from the ranks of the Red Shirt movement that carried out a series of mass demonstrations in the capital. Eventually the violence that included the assassination of a former Thai general who had become a leader in the Red Shirt movement was quelled. In May the Thai military intervened to end the disturbances.

For many on the outside, the struggle had been seen simplistically as a struggle between the masses supporting a democratic movement and an authoritarian military influenced by the monarchy. On the ground, the situation was much more complicated. It is perhaps best discussed in the context of populist rural forces supporting an anti-democratic former prime minister against more urban and democratically minded military, and royalist figures. This proves that in Thailand, as in so many other societies, it is difficult to simplify political battles into cartoon-like descriptions.

The Restive Muslim South

Going beyond the question of how Thailand will be governed, the last years have revealed an even greater challenge to the nation's fundamental stability. Outsiders tend to forget that although a large Buddhist majority lives in the north near the major cultural and industrialized parts of the country Thailand has a significant population of Muslims of Malay ethnicity who live in the southern part of the country. It is not just outsiders who have at times apparently forgotten about those who live in the south. For years many southern Muslims have complained about being ignored by the nation's leaders.

The long simmering tension erupted dramatically during the spring of 2004 when hundreds of young Muslim men assaulted several government facilities in an apparent attempt to find the military equipment necessary to support a separatist movement. It was the first significant outbreak of sectarian violence since 1993. Of even more concern was that the attacks demonstrated a growing military and organizational sophistication that suggested to some observers that local Muslim insurgents were benefiting from outside training.

The Buddhist-dominated government based in Bangkok responded by declaring martial law in the three southern provinces. Unfortunately, the crisis that began anew in 2004 has turned into an on-going crisis, the roots of which have been growing for years.

One of the more immediate causes was former Prime Minister Thaksin's decision, after some initial hesitation, to enroll Thailand as a major supporter of the American President George W. Bush's Iraq campaign.

Thailand

The decision to support the overthrow of Saddam Hussein was, of course, controversial around the world. But among Muslims it has been especially so, and it added to tensions within Southern Thailand. But recent political decisions have only been one element of the growing tensions.

For years the southern Muslim provinces have felt that Bangkok was not supportive enough of their cultural heritage that so obviously differed from the Buddhist dominated north. It was more than local issues that had changed the situation. As was the situation elsewhere within the Muslim world, local Thai Muslims had been drawn more and more deeply into the world Islamic community. Today, significant numbers of Thais have studied in the Islamic universities of the Persian Gulf and Pakistan.

Prime Minister Thaksin's approach was strongly to support the Thai military's efforts to suppress the insurgents while working to improve the southern economic infrastructure. Whether such economic growth can lessen the growing tensions in the south is something only time will tell. Certainly it has been obvious to the government that merely using strong arm tactics has not worked.

In fact, General Sonthi Boonyaratkalin, himself a Muslim and the general who initially led the September 2006 coup against the prime minister, was reported to have been partly motivated by his dissatisfaction with the prime minister's failures in dealing with the southern provinces. But once in power the military did not accomplish much more than the former prime minister had. The insurgency has continued and has managed significantly to weaken the economy of the region.

Governmental System

The Thai political system is nominally a constitutional monarchy usually governed with a democratic-style parliamentary system. The military remains very influential, but in recent years until the events of September 2006 it had chosen to remain largely out of domestic affairs. As we have seen, though, Thailand has struggled since 1932 to evolve a modern workable political system. The first four decades of the constitutional period were dominated largely by the military.

Civilian-led governments, though, became more common in the 1970s. But they have not always been very stable. In order for true democratic civilian government truly to establish itself, several things must take place. First, corruption must be curtailed. As Thailand's educated middle class grows, this segment of society, like elements of the military, will no longer accept the old ways of doing

things. It has been revealed recently that the nation's extraordinarily revered king is especially concerned that the level of corruption is undermining the nation's future.

The aggressive effort of former Prime Minister Thaksin Shinawatra to expand the authority of his office and political party seemed for a time dangerously close to tipping the balance of power away from the more open system that had been evolving. However, the military coup of 2006 temporarily ended that threat with an equally undesirable and unfortunate return military rule.

But then the first elections after the coup brought Mr. Thaksin's authoritarian-minded supporters back to power leaving the prospect of Thailand's authentic democratic future still in doubt. That sudden reversal turned out to be only one more step in the emerging drama that would see over the past year a dramatic rise in street demonstrations in support of various governments that have rotated back and forth in power. While Thaksin's supporters no longer control the prime minister's office, that development is more a product of court decisions than electoral politics. From a distance it can easily look like a struggle between the military and those favoring a more democratic Thailand. Up close, though, the struggle appears far less simplistic.

For the moment, the only thing that can be said for certain about the Thai governing system is that the momentum of stable democratic growth has fallen away as the society struggles to develop a new legitimacy that the majority of Thais can accept. That effort is especially difficult these days as the nation's core symbol of legitimacy, King Bhumibol Adulyadej, who has reigned since the mid 1940s, increasingly leaves the scene weakened by illness and age.

**Former Prime Minister
Surayud Chulanont**

Foreign Policy

Thailand's foreign relations are driven by its geographic location and pragmatism. It has a fascinating history of keeping enemies at bay through diplomatic and other means that generally have not involved the direct use of force. Of particular importance has been the relationship with its enormous northern neighbor, the People's Republic of China.

Thai officials profess not to be worried about China's growing military might. However, there is concern over the potential for large scale Chinese migration into the country and the possible impact from a flood of inexpensive products from the north that could undercut sectors of the Thai economy. These concerns are long term and unpublicized but they are real. Nevertheless, rather than shut China out, Thailand wants to see relations between the two countries expanded. President Jiang Zemin of the People's Republic recently visited, and Thai Queen Sirikit made a state visit of her own to China. More recently overland transportation routes between the two nations were improved as well.

Because of its well integrated overseas Chinese community, which dominates the business sector, Thai officials and businessmen feel they have an advantage over other Southeast Asian states in opening up new economic links with China. Some even believe they can provide a link for the other ASEAN states to the People's Republic. In contrast to many other Southeast nations, the local Chinese community takes an active part in politics.

During the 1990s, the huge explosion in the study of Mandarin was welcomed in Bangkok. Beijing was also particularly helpful during the early stage of the Asian economic crisis when it agreed to buy large amounts of Thai rice to help the struggling economy. Beijing contributed a billion dollars to the IMF bail-out funds that were arranged to help Thailand. It also avoided devaluing its own currency which would have made recovery much more difficult.

Thailand has moved to become more involved in broader international activities. During the crisis over East Timor, Bangkok decided to dispatch around 1,500 soldiers to reestablish stability in that troubled community. A Thai officer became second in command over the entire military operation.

Relations with Myanmar remain complex. The 1995 defeat of the Karen rebels in Myanmar sent thousands of refugees across the Thai border and which altered relations between the two countries. The Burmese believed the Thais were aiding the Karens. Bangkok was upset because of Burmese military raids on refugee camps

Princess Maha Chakri Sirindhorn visited the Sage Colleges in May 2009.

Photo Credit: Harvey Vlahos

a strong backer of the American military campaigns in Afghanistan and Iraq. Predictably, the decision to send military personnel to Iraq aroused considerable ire among many Thais Muslims and Buddhists alike. In fact, by the spring of 2004 the prime minister, aware of how controversial his decision to send military personnel to Iraq had been, was talking of removing them if the situation became any more unstable there.

Of course, the campaign against terrorism has hardly been something Thailand has watched as a disinterested observer. In the late spring of 2003 the prime minister officially admitted that there were members of the infamous, Indonesian-based Jemmah Islamiyah present in Thailand. Moreover, it has become increasingly obvious in recent years that the insurgency in the south has developed ties with other Muslim activists beyond the region.

Society and Culture

Shortly after their arrival in Southeast Asia, the Thai were converted to the Theravada school of Buddhism, which came from the island of Sri Lanka. The numerous colorful festivals and the participating monks almost completely dominate the traditions of the people. Thai architecture is unique, colorful and particularly elaborate.

The customs and traditions of Bangkok and the larger cities have been modified greatly by increased contacts with the West, particularly with Americans. In fact, Thailand is among those developed countries with the greatest divergence between the very urbanized middle classes of Bangkok and the peasant farmers in much of the rest of the country.

For years visitors to the city have had to put up with some of the worst traffic in the world. Today the situation is improving. Parts of the Bangkok expressway are now open, and it is now possible to get from one part of the city to another far easier than it was only a few years ago.

Significant among social issues has been the government's aggressive campaign to ban smoking anywhere near the nation's schools. It is clear that Bangkok is quite serious in this effort to make smoking less common. By the fall of 2003 the plan was to extend the ban throughout many public areas from internet cafes to beauty parlors.

On an even more serious matter—the use of illegal drugs—the government has been even more committed. During the spring of 2003 a major and quite aggressive campaign against drug dealers was carried out. It resulted in tens of thousands being arrested and hundreds dying in the crackdown. Prime Minister Thaksin

inside Thai territory. Later that spring, Burmese officials closed a major border crossing at Mae Sod that resulted in a significant economic loss for businesses on the Thai side of the line.

Burmese authorities were also incensed over what they perceived to be the "gentle handling" of Burmese dissidents who, in the fall of 1999, took over Rangoon's Bangkok embassy. This resulted in yet another border closing which, unfortunately, has become a common occurrence. More recently, tensions associated with the production of drugs in Burma that eventually find their way across the border has added to the problems.

Other concerns, including competing off-shore territorial claims, have also impacted in the region. In May 1995, Thai and Vietnamese navy patrols exchanged gunfire off the Thai coast. Thai fishing boats and crews have also been seized by the Vietnamese. In recent years though relations with Vietnam have improved considerably, and Bangkok and Hanoi have been working well together, especially in terms of a mutual understanding regarding their respective strategic and military circumstances.

To the south border tensions have risen recently between Thailand and Cambodia. Ironically, today's popular culture has also had an impact on Thailand's foreign affairs as locally produced historically based feature length films have managed to antagonize both their Lao and Burmese neighbors. Recently the supposed remarks by a Thai actress that the extraordi-

nary Cambodian historic site, Angkor Wat, should rightfully belong to Thailand set off weeks of angry and expensive tensions and violence with Phnom Penh. Especially controversial has been the competing claims over the ancient temple of Preah Vihear that provoked a dramatic military confrontation in the summer of 2008 and caused several deaths. This was not just an international matter for Thailand. The controversy that swirled around the temple even added to the animosity of internal Thai politics. Prime Minister Samak's tenure in office was weakened as well when he appeared to support Cambodia's claims to the revered temple site. The fact that Cambodia's long time ruler, Hun Sen, recently chose to hire Thailand's most controversial recent prime minister, Thaksin, as an advisor has certainly not improved relations either.

Relations with the United States are also important and at times difficult. During the early development of the Asian economic crisis many felt that the U.S. had been slow in reacting to the gravity of the economic problems that beset the region. Fortunately, as the crisis developed and the Americans became more actively involved in trying to resolve the situation, these concerns became less significant.

After the September 2001 assault and the "War on Terrorism" rose to the top of the international agenda, Thailand was initially unwilling to even admit the there was a terrorist presence within Thailand. As time past, Bangkok's attitude changed. Thaksin's government eventually became

Thailand

Shinawatra said at the time that his goal was to eliminate the use of such drugs.

Women

As elsewhere, Thai women have grown up in a region that generally values boys more than girls. Today, the situation of women in Thailand is especially complex and combines examples of considerable progress and proof of their continuing lack of control over their own lives.

The military has allowed a few women into their upper ranks, but women are still not allowed to attend the nation's military academies. Women have fewer rights than men in obtaining documents like passports, and domestic law favors husbands. Men, for example, also have more rights under the divorce laws. Women are less than 10% of those appointed to the Thai senate. On the other hand, young women have far more access to education today and half of the college graduates are female. The problem is especially acute among the thousands of young women from Thailand's poorer neighbors, especially like Vietnam and Myanmar, who are lured to Bangkok with offers of jobs and then find themselves in virtual debt slavery in the brothels of that huge city.

In the mid 1990s an ominous cloud appeared on the horizon. A report by an international organization revealed that Thailand had developed the fastest growing AIDS population in all of Asia. In spite of a very successful birth control program, there has been little public education about AIDS until recently. Figures for young women especially in northern Thailand are very high. In Bangkok, a significant portion of the prostitute community is infected. To make matters worse, a new more powerful strain of AIDS was discovered in Thailand in 1995. The Thai government has attempted to move against the traffickers, and various international organizations have attempted to improve the situation of these young women. Nevertheless, rthe situation remains a very tragic one today.

Economy

For years the Thai economy was one of the fastest growing in Asia. Many had expected it to become one of the "Asian Tigers" like Taiwan, Hong Kong, Singapore, and South Korea which had so impressed the world during the last decades of the century. In fact, according to the World Bank Thailand's growth between 1985 and 1994 was a robust 8.2%, even better than South Korea in those years. Even in early 1997, things still looked good. The huge American company, General Motors, signed a deal for a new car plant said to be worth over $750 million dollars and which promised 1,500 new jobs. Though the situation seemed to change suddenly during the summer of 1997, in truth the problems had been building for quite some time.

In the first half of the 1990s, it appeared for a time that the infrastructure of the country was simply unable to keep pace with the rapidly growing economy. Efforts were then made to construct a mass transit system in the congested Bangkok area. Progress in building up the country's infrastructure in a logical way was also made. New factories are being located outside the Bangkok area in industrial parks. Each is required to have its own wastewater treatment plant. The water coming out of these plants today is far cleaner than the water industries take in for their use.

Bangkok had been making progress in helping the country deal with its growing involvement in the world economy, and though the economy had slowed down, few anticipated the developments of July 1997. That summer, international currency speculators aroused by Thailand's huge private foreign debt began to speculate against the value of the baht. Though the government defended the price of the local currency through the summer, it was forced by July to devalue the baht. Thailand's economic bubble began to burst. Especially hurt were the many business people who seeking better loan rates abroad had gone heavily in debt over loans pegged in currencies like the American dollar. Whether the loans had been economically viable when they were originally made or not, they became impossible burdens when Thai locals had to buy much more expensive American dollars to repay them.

The economic crisis had begun. Thailand would not be the only nation caught in the collapse. Soon, Thailand had to turn to the International Monetary Fund to gain the financial resources needed to deal with the crisis though as always those funds came with demands for economic reforms and budget cutting that few countries take easily. By the spring of 1999, Thailand seemed to be gaining the reputation as one of the nations of the region that had most responsibly taken on the challenges of the economic crisis.

Thailand's leaders had reason to be pleased as the nation entered the new century. Once again, the economy was going strongly. If the growth rates were not what they had been at points during the previous generation, growth rates of 3–4% were being projected. Clearly, it looked as if the worst of the 1997 crisis was finally over. But as the new century dawned, the economy remained very fragile, and the slow

Class outing in Bangkok

down in the United States affected Thailand as well. Things became even more complicated during 2001 as Prime Minister Thaksin Shinawatra spoke openly of employing more economic nationalism. This tended to make outside investors nervous.

Even as Bangkok seems determined to crawl back from the brink, the country faced serious problems with its natural resources and a limited technological base. Because so much of the country's timber has been cut, erosion is rampant. The quality of the soil is being negatively affected, and flooding is common. While the environment remains a critical problem and will be for decades to come, there is now visible evidence of government efforts. One can now see miles of newly planted trees along major highways and the ban on cutting teakwood is apparently strongly enforced.

The most immediate challenge of course, is maintaining a stable economy. Over the last few years considerable progress has been made, and the most recent gains as the new century developed have been in the area of growing domestic consumption that insulates the economy from too great a dependence on exports. Unlike the disastrous era of the Asian Economic Crisis the Thai bhat has been considerably healthier. Large infrastructure projects that had been put on hold during the late 1990s seem again back on track as well.

The economy had been recovering well from the economic setbacks of the late 1990s. Tourism, deeply hurt by the tsunami of late 2004, had begun to recover. Meanwhile the growth rate for 2005 came in at a healthy 4.4%, while the next year until 2008 averaged around 5%. Then came 2008, and by year's end the emergence of the current international recession had hit Thailand especially hard. In fact, growth figures for 2009 came in at more than two percentage points in the negative. Of course, the economic shock in late 2008 only "complemented" the domestic political instability that had already undermined Thailand's earlier reputation as one of the most stable in Southeast Asia.

The Future

The last several years have been very complicated for Thailand. While the economy had been doing relatively well until recently, the tsunami in late 2004 was an enormous challenge to overcome. The ongoing struggle in the nation's southern provinces has also disrupted lives and drained resources.

On the political side, the situation had by the fall of 2006 become practically intolerable. It was obvious that something dramatic was likely to occur. In September it did so when the military, with the rather obvious support of the popular king, overthrew the popularly elected government of Thaksin Shinawatra. This set off a horrendously complicated set of revolving door governments and massive demonstrations for and against the various prime ministers who have come in and out of power over the last couple of years.

Now, three years later, the real question remains how well Thai democracy will be able to reestablish itself once things begin to calm again. It is hoped that it will do so along healthier less authoritarian lines than was the case during the rule of the controversial prime minister Thaksin and the perhaps equally unpopular military intervention that followed. However, that future remains uncertain. For the moment, the core question is who really represents a more successful future for the people of Thailand: former Prime Minister Thaksin's supporters or his detractors? For the outside world, the question is whether Thailand is going to become stable again soon enough to consider it a safe place for outside investment or vacation travel. Another critically uncertain factor within Thailand is the fact that the nation's greatest living symbol of legitimacy and stability, King Bhumibol himself, is likely to leave the scene soon.

Demonstrations in Thailand, 2008

The Socialist Republic of Vietnam

Communist Party of Vietnam headquarters in Ho Chi Minh City

Area: 329,560 sq. miles
Population: 89,571,130 (July 2010 est.)
Capital City: Hanoi (Pop. 3,083,800. Estimated 2004)
Climate: Subtropical, with cooler weather in the higher elevations. The Mekong Delta area is hot and humid.
Neighboring Countries: China (North); Laos and Cambodia (West)
Official Language: Vietnamese
Other Principal Tongues: some French and Chinese, mountain area languages (MonKhmer and Malayo-Polynesian)
Ethnic Background: Vietnamese (about 85%); Thai, Cambodian, Lao, Chinese, tribesmen (about 15%)
Principal Religions: Buddhism, Taoism, Confucianism subdivided into many sects, Christianity, animism, Islam and syncretistic traditions like Caodaism, a blend of eastern and western traditions
Main Exports: (to U.S., Japan, China, Australia, Germany, Singapore, U.K.): agricultural products, especially rice, coffee, coal, minerals oil, clothing, shoes, rubber
Main Imports: (from China, Taiwan, South Korea, Japan, Singapore, Thailand): steel products, railroad equipment, chemicals, medicines, petroleum, fertilizer, cotton, grain, cement, motorcycles

Currency: Dong
Former Colonial Status: French colony (1883–1954); occupied by the Japanese (1942–1945); anti-French struggle (1945–1954); civil war (1954–1975)
National Day: September 2, 1945, when independence from the French was declared and the Democratic Republic of Vietnam was proclaimed
Chief of State: Nguyen Minh Triet, President (since June 2006)
Head of Government: Nguyen Tan Dung, Prime Minister (since June 2006)
Chairman, Communist Party: This post has been vacant since the death of Ho Chi Minh in 1969
General Secretary, Communist Party: Nong Duc Manh (since April 2001)
National Flag: A red field with a five-pointed yellow star in the center.
Per Capita GDP Income: $2,900 (2009 est. purchasing power parity)

Very narrow in the middle, the map of Vietnam is shaped somewhat like a dumbbell. The northern "bell" is an area formerly known as Tonkin. It is quite mountainous, with peaks as high as 10,315 feet, close to the southern Chinese border. The mountains gradually diminish in height as they approach the plains and river deltas closest to the Gulf of Tonkin.

The Red River originates in the lofty plateaus of the Chinese province of Yunnan, some 8,000 feet above sea level, and forms the border with China for a distance of about 30 miles. When it enters northern Vietnam, it is 260 feet above sea level, descending through a narrow gorge until it widens; after being joined with the River Claire it meanders 93 miles to the sea, flowing in a shifting, irregular course that is 140 miles of curving and twisting water.

The two principal cities of northern Vietnam, Hanoi and Haiphong, are situated on the river and flooded by its waters during the wet season each year. They are colored red by the silt washing to the sea from the highlands. It is in this river delta region that much of the food of northern Vietnam is produced by peasants laboring in the fields with the same basic tools used by their forebears.

The narrow middle part of the country is a thin, coastal plain, closely confined on the west by the Annam Cordillera, a north-south range of mountains forming a natural barrier between Vietnam and Laos to the west. This coastal belt is narrow and somewhat inhospitable. Its lands

Vietnam

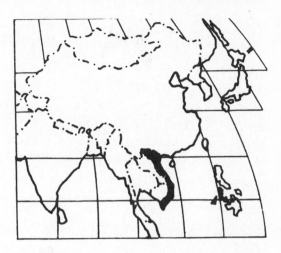

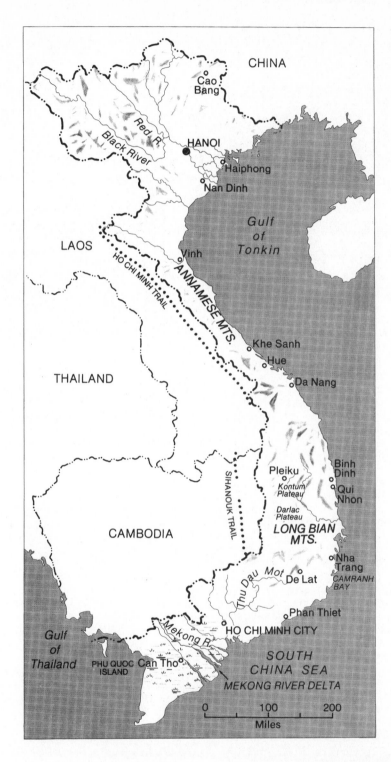

Intensive agriculture, dominated by rice production, has enabled the people living in the Mekong River Delta to produce large surpluses of food in the past and present. Traditionally, two harvests of wet paddy rice are possible each year, a feat possible in very few places of the world. In contrast, only dry field rice can be grown in parts of northern Vietnam.

History: Before the Chinese Arrival

Linguistically the Vietnamese speak a MonKhmer language that includes a lot of Chinese and French words. In appearance the Vietnamese most resemble other Asian peoples of mongoloid origin although their ethnicity seems more correctly tied to both the Mongolian peoples of their north and the Austroasiatic-Indonesian peoples to their south.

Among the non-Han peoples of Southeast Asia the Vietnamese were the people most influenced by Chinese culture. Nevertheless, Vietnamese culture had developed a sophisticated sea-oriented civilization long before the era of significant Chinese influence. Known as the Dongson Culture or Lac-Viet era, early Vietnamese civilization in those years was especially influenced by the more southern communities of the coasts and islands of Southeast Asia.

By the third century B.C., pressured by both Chinese armies and arriving immigrants, Vietnam fell deeply under the influence of Chinese civilization. Eventually conquered by the powerful Han dynasty of China, Vietnam remained part of the Chinese empire for most of the next millennium. For the Chinese, in those years before the region around Guangzhou (Canton) was developed, controlling Vietnam was especially important as its occupation facilitated Chinese trade with the island communities of Southeast Asia.

It was natural that during those centuries the Vietnamese adopted many as-

are not enriched by the silt of any large river, and the typhoons of the South China Sea frequently do considerable damage.

The lower portion starts with an area of central highland plateaus that are heavily forested and inhabited by more traditional peoples who till the limited available land after clearing it by burning. These highlands gradually give way to the Mekong Delta, near where Ho Chi Minh City (formerly Saigon) is located.

The Mekong River starts in remote Tibet where snows gradually melt in the thin, icy air, gathering into small streams. Before reaching Vietnam, the waters travel almost 3,000 miles through some of the most rugged country in the world. The river is yellow and sluggish by the time it enters the country. The tides of the sea are felt as far back as Phnom Penh in Cambodia during the dry season and even further upriver during the wet months each year.

Vietnam

Town on the Mekong River

pects of the Chinese political system and cultural patterns. The Chinese language and writing system became well known among the elite as did the Confucian social system. Eventually the Vietnamese developed their own version of the famous Confucian civil service exam system and used it as a tool to choose many of their elites. Despite China's enormous political and cultural influence, many core elements of Vietnamese civilization, from a greater role for women to the language itself, have survived to help define Vietnamese identity.

Not surprisingly, the Vietnamese often feel a combination of respect, dislike and fear toward the Chinese. In fact, throughout history the Vietnamese have at times tried simultaneously to be "more Confucian than the Chinese" while vehemently working to avoid becoming too "Chinese like." Alternatively, as one well-known scholar has put it, "the Vietnamese could easily become Chinese but have no interest in doing so."

That attitude played a significant role over the centuries as various Vietnamese leaders, among them the famous Trung Sisters of the early 1st century A.D., led a series of unsuccessful revolts against Chinese control. The rebellion led by the two sisters is particularly notable not only because of its role in inspiring future generations to resist the Chinese. It also serves as an important reminder of how important women have been in Vietnam's long history of fighting for its independence from the era of the Trung Sisters (39–43 A.D.) to the struggles against the French and later the United States.

After the collapse of the Tang dynasty in China in the early 10th century, the Viet-

namese finally broke away from direct Chinese control. Still, over the centuries China has attempted more than once to reassert its authority over its southern neighbor.

Independent Vietnam

Somewhat after Vietnam's leaders established their independence in the late 10th century, the first more recognizably modern Vietnamese kingdom, known historically as the Da Viet, emerged under the leadership of the Ly dynasty, which located its capital at what would later be known as Hanoi. However, establishing a stable and unified Vietnam soon proved beyond the capacity of the Ly family. Over the next several centuries, Vietnam found itself regularly facing new threats from the north, such as when the Mongols sought to occupy the country in the 13th century and when the Chinese Ming dynasty effectively did so for a short time in the 15th century. Divisions existed as well among the Vietnamese themselves as many southerners resisted efforts to unify the country under northern control. In fact, it was not until the late 18th and early 19th centuries that Vietnam emerged under the unified control of the Emperor Gia Long. His dynasty would lead Vietnam from Hue, modern Vietnam's best-known imperial city.

Vietnam's relationship with its enormous neighbor to the north was not the only challenge faced by the Vietnamese. To their south lay the lands of Champa, a South Asian-influenced community of Malayo-Polynesian stock which had established a kingdom that lasted from the 2nd to the 17th century. Unfortunately, for the Cham peoples their kingdom slowly collapsed during a series of struggles with

both the Khmer peoples of Cambodia and the Vietnamese. Finally, in the years from the 15th through 17th centuries the originally northern-based Vietnamese conquered the last of the lands once held by Champa. Today, the Cham people survive as a small Muslim minority community in both Vietnam and Cambodia.

French Colonialism

French interest in Indochina, the name given to the eastern portion of mainland Southeast Asia, began in the 18th century. Initially taking the form of commercial and missionary contacts, the French effort did not become serious until the mid-19th century. Forces of Napoleon III conquered Vietnam in a series of military campaigns, beginning in the South and working slowly northward. Initially, the French navy was far more interested in the region than the French government, but over time the national commitment grew. The proclamation of a protectorate over the Annamese (Vietnamese) state in 1883 was followed by a short war with the Chinese to force the Manchu emperors to recognize the end of the tributary status of Annam.

The French divided their newly won possession into three segments: Tonkin in the North, Annam in the narrow middle belt and highland plateaus of the South, and the colony of Cochin China in the Mekong Delta. Those three areas were ruled by a governor-general who also presided over Cambodia and Laos after 1887.

Actual administration of the colonies was by the French during the colonial period although an imperial court was permitted to exist in Annam. The French introduced a narrow-gauge railroad from

Hanoi to Kunming in China that allowed them to extract mineral wealth from the North. In addition, intensive cultivation methods were introduced to produce large quantities of rubber.

During the early colonial period the French encouraged the migration of people from Tonkin in the north to the delta of Cochin China. Immigrant Chinese were also permitted in the southern colony although at times the European businessmen there resented their competition.

Considerable effort was put into the promotion of French culture among the Vietnamese. As a result, an upper class of Vietnamese eventually emerged that was fluent in French, at home in French culture, and often Roman Catholic. But over time they were often bitterly resentful of French political domination. It was a pattern that was followed frequently throughout the colonized world.

The World Wars and Nationalist Struggles

Shortly after World War I, a nationalist group, composed of people supported by the French-speaking upper class emerged, competing with a communist movement led by a dedicated patriot known as Ho Chi Minh. Both of these movements attempted unsuccessful armed uprisings against the French. In 1930, Ho brought together the various communist groups into a single new movement known as the Indochinese Communist Party.

Once the Second World War had begun, the Japanese took Indochina by default after Germany installed the puppet French Vichy government. Japan demanded the right to land forces in the area, which was granted by the French. Within three months the Japanese controlled all of northern Viet-

nam. In July 1941 they occupied the south as well.

In contrast to other leaders of anti-colonial Asian movements, like Sukarno of Indonesia, Ho Chi Minh did not collaborate with the Japanese. Rather, being a fluent speaker of English, he aligned himself with the allied forces and spent the war years often working closely with the Americans.

In 1945, the Japanese ousted the local French authorities whom they correctly suspected of being in contact with General de Gaulle and the Allies. Direct Japanese authority, though, was short-lived. Surrender came within six months. At the Potsdam conference in 1945, the Allied powers decided to divide Vietnam at the 16th parallel for the purpose of disarming and evacuating the Japanese. The southern region was to be occupied by the British and the north by the Nationalist Chinese. For Ho and other nationalists this was a serious development given the long Chinese interest in Vietnamese territory. For the immediate period one of Ho's most important goals would be to make sure the Chinese did not come to stay.

For him the moment he had long waited had finally come. He hastily proclaimed the Democratic Republic of Vietnam in Hanoi at a big public rally on September 2, 1945. Given later events, it is ironic that Ho, an admirer of the United States, began his speech with lines chosen from the American Declaration of Independence.

Shortly thereafter, the forces of the Chinese Nationalists moved into the northern region. Meanwhile, Ho expanded his power in the rural areas of the north, eliminating his Vietnamese Nationalist rivals and managing to co-exist uneasily with the Chinese occupation forces that gave

every indication of wishing to remain in Vietnam. Ho's movement, known as the Viet Minh was certainly not the only nationalist movement in Vietnam. Indeed, there were others who were nationalist but not communist. But Ho Chi Minh was widely admired and helped by his reputation for having close ties to the increasingly powerful Americans.

Meanwhile in the south, the British suppressed activity by the Viet Minh and quickly returned the area to the French. Seeking a withdrawal of the Chinese in the north, Ho and the French put pressure on them. Fortuitously, the outbreak of civil war in China helped instigate a Chinese withdrawal in early 1946.

Ho permitted the French to reenter northern Vietnam, promising to keep the Democratic Republic of Vietnam within the French Union, as so long as its autonomy was respected and providing it was allowed to control all of Vietnam. He certainly wanted French economic aid, but the chief reason for this attitude was probably Stalin's attitude at the time. The Russians wanted a French communist victory at the polls in France, and did not wish to alienate French voters by supporting a communist revolt in Vietnam.

An Anti-Colonial Struggle

The French colonial regime, however, refused to allow Viet Minh control of Cochin China. France was committed to reestablishing its control over Vietnam, an effort Ho and his movement opposed. By the end of 1946, fighting erupted between the French and the Viet Minh, who retreated to the mountains above Hanoi to conduct a guerrilla war. In an effort to find a political cover for their desire to reestablish

Ho Chi Minh leaves the French Foreign Ministry, July 1946

Vietnam

Ho Chi Minh

their former colony, the French selected Bao Dai, the hereditary Emperor of Annam and a descendant of the royal family that had once ruled from a massive palace at Hue, as the new official leader of the country. Bao Dai officially accepted the French offer in 1946. He then became provisional president and later permanent chief of state of a government obviously organized by the French to maintain their power in Indochina. The arrangement hardly pleased real nationalists like Ho, and the struggle continued.

The American attitude toward Vietnam in the immediate aftermath of World War II was ambivalent. America had a long-term commitment to anti-colonialism, and President Franklin D. Roosevelt had long made it clear that he did not favor the simple resumption of European colonies in Asia after the war. These American attitudes were well known. In fact, as early as 1919, the young Ho Chi Minh had attempted unsuccessfully to meet President Woodrow Wilson at the Paris Versailles Conference to discuss Vietnam with the influential American president who was so associated with the idea of "national self-determination." A generation later, Ho, having just finished working with the Americans during the war, still hoped to gain U.S. support for his fledgling nation.

However, in the years after World War II there was also an interest among the Americans in strengthening their erstwhile allies, the French. Paris wanted its former colony back. Thus, those U.S. officials who were concerned about ensuring that France remained strong as an ally in Europe prevailed over those who were more concerned about America opposing the anti-colonial Vietnamese communist movement.

As the tensions between East and West grew, American attitudes hardened. When the Cold War set in during the late 1940s, Ho's nationalist credentials loomed far less large in the minds of American decision-makers than his equally strong commitment to communism. Now many American decision makers would develop a strong antipathy for Ho and his movement. In their minds they were merely an extension of world communism directed from Moscow. However, it would be another generation before they would act directly on those attitudes.

In early 1950, the Viet Minh received diplomatic recognition from newly communist China. With Chinese military aid, they cleared French troops from the border areas of northern Vietnam later in that year. What had been an anti-colonial struggle was evolving into a major theater of the Cold War in Asia, a fact that led to increased involvement of the United States and of the People's Republic of China.

France initially had trouble convincing the Americans to support its efforts. Nevertheless, they had little trouble convincing America that France was now fighting on the front lines against communist expansion, as was the U.S. in Korea. Ho Chi Minh, a nationalist and communist, had not changed, but the "context" in which he was viewed by the powerful Americans had.

By the spring of 1953, the French prospects in Vietnam were bleak; the approaching end of the Korean War was expected to enable greater Chinese effort in Vietnam. In desperation, the French granted further political, economic, and military concessions to the non-communist Vietnamese state and substantially increased their own military activities. Their purpose was not to defeat the Viet Minh, since such a goal was unrealistic, but rather to obtain a "face saving" political settlement. The U.S., the Soviet Union, Britain and France decided that a conference should be held in the spring of 1954 in Geneva, Switzerland, to deal with the questions of Indochina and Korea. But developments in the battlefield were moving faster than diplomacy.

Dienbienphu

The French had fortified a position at Dienbienphu in northwest Vietnam in response to a Viet Minh thrust into neighboring Laos. The Viet Minh then surrounded the French with artillery and mortars supplied by the Chinese and laid siege to the French camp. Although the decision to make Dienbienphu the central symbol of the struggle over Vietnam only came slowly, the battle eventually grew into one that symbolized the entire Franco-Vietnamese war. Overly confident, the French assumed their position within a

valley surrounded by soldiers who held higher ground, would not be a problem. They were wrong. The Viet Minh quickly destroyed the airstrip to prevent reinforcements and supplies from being sent in, and the siege began in earnest.

Even as the battle raged, many within the American administration argued that as the symbolism of Dienbienphu grew, the United States should intervene. Though there was considerable opposition to doing so unilaterally, Washington did go so far as to approach London about a joint effort to save the French. But Winston Churchill, again the British Prime Minister, declined. The French were left to fight alone. The tiny base fell on May 7, 1954, the day before the matter of Indochina was to come before the Geneva conference.

There were few times in recent history when the fate of a small country so depended on world politics. The French wanted to get out of Indochina on any reasonable basis. The Soviet Union did not want to press France to the extent that it would join the European Defense Community, a multi-country army then being proposed. Russia desired even less a direct clash with the U.S., which had only recently completed a massive series of hydrogen bomb tests in the Pacific. The People's Republic of China also wished to avoid conflict with the U.S. and apparently did not want Ho Chi Minh to achieve too much power.

The Geneva Settlement

Ho Chi Minh's delegation to the conference arrived with a demand that the three nations of Indochina be treated in such a manner that would have produced a communist victory not only in Vietnam, but also in Cambodia and Laos. But the Chinese delegation conceded that a final settlement would treat the three countries separately. Ultimately, the final settlement contained some minor concessions to the communist movement in Laos, but none in Cambodia.

Vietnam was divided at the 17th parallel, considerably farther to the north than had been demanded by Ho Chi Minh. National Elections were scheduled for mid-1956. Military details of withdrawal, etc., were left to the French and Vietnamese. This was a defeat for Ho, who desired immediate elections before a non-communist government could solidify itself in the south. He was sure of victory in the north, since he was credited with expelling the French colonial government. In fact, it was generally agreed by most observers, including the Americans, that Ho Chi Minh, the long-time leader of the Vietnamese struggle for independence, would easily win the scheduled elections. Ho appeared poised to win at the ballot box what he had largely won on the battlefield already.

In order to exclude American military forces from Indochina, the settlement prohibited any foreign power from maintaining forces in Vietnam. A general political agreement was included in the final version in which many things were left subject to interpretation. The U.S., not surprisingly, was very unhappy with the settlement which appeared likely to bring into existence a unified Vietnam under communist control. It declined to sign the agreement. Angered by this refusal, the Chinese agreed to accept an informal American promise not to "disturb" the agreement. The settlement was then "adopted" in July 1954 without actually being signed by the representative of any nation.

Ho Chi Minh's regime promptly took over North Vietnam from the French. It began to build a strong and effective regime with large amounts of economic and military aid from the Soviet Union and China. Exhibiting revolutionary zeal, the new government embarked on an extremely brutal program of collectivization that soon cost the party considerable popularity. In fact, the program provoked a peasant revolt in Nghe An, the southernmost province, which had to be suppressed by government troops in 1956. Ho was forced to moderate his programs in order to regain his popular support.

Ngo Dinh Diem and the Americans

Nearly everyone at the Geneva conference had expected South Vietnam to collapse, or to go communist via the ballot box. Bao Dai had no real authority and was under the influence of corrupt military leaders. In mid-1954, however, he appointed Ngo Dinh Diem premier. Diem, an energetic Catholic and committed nationalist, had strong ties to the Americans. In fact he had only just recently returned from an extended stay in the United States. Having appointed the anticommunist Diem, Bao Dai then resumed his luxurious life in France. Diem later deposed him.

In October 1956, Diem proclaimed South Vietnam a republic and assumed the office of president. From the time of his appointment, Diem had enjoyed the support of prominent U.S. officials. They hoped to strengthen his position enough to allow him to serve as a non-communist alternative to Ho Chi Minh.

Diem also received the support of the several hundred thousand of his Catholic co-religionists who, partially inspired by C.I.A propaganda, fled into the South in 1954. Diem also gained the allegiance of the traditionally corrupt army and managed to impose his authority over South Vietnamese religious sects that were hostile to his government.

The United States backed Diem's 1956 decision against holding the national elections called for in the Geneva Convention and his efforts to establish South Vietnam as a separate country. For the Americans Diem's regime seemed a way to stop the unification of the country under Ho Chi Minh, which Vietnam-wide elections would probably have brought about. The U.S. now offered massive amounts of military and economic aid just as it had earlier supported the French effort against Ho.

North Vietnam was furious and called for international action against Diem, but it received no support from the Soviets or the Chinese. Initially hoping that Diem's regime would collapse from its own weight of dishonesty and corruption, Ho discouraged the communist guerrillas, who had remained within South Vietnam after the Geneva division of the country, from taking action. However, in 1957 the rebels, called Viet Cong, undertook a terrorist campaign to force village support of their communist movement.

Diem and his supporters responded by setting up a virtual police state which smothered all opposition, non-communist and communist. He was able to withstand a military revolt in 1960 and tried to promote the regime's power in rural areas by use of anti-Viet Cong measures. Diem's crackdown against the Viet Cong was successful enough to push them to adopt new, more militant tactics. However, initial southern success turned into a virtual loss of control over much of the countryside as Viet Cong strength swelled and its military activities increased.

In contrast to the conservative American assumption of an unrelenting global conspiracy to spread communism throughout the world, there was no major direct support of the Viet Cong by North Vietnam until 1959 because of the reluctance of the Soviets and Chinese to provoke another crisis in the region. Moreover, because of serious economic difficulties in 1960, China sharply reduced its aid to North Vietnam. Despite the international situation, Hanoi did begin to give substantial and active support to the Viet Cong in the south.

In response, the United States, during the first months of the Kennedy administration, increased its aid to the Diem government and raised the number of American military advisers to the South Vietnamese army. The Chinese, in return for Vietnamese support in their ideological disputes with the Soviet Union, also increased their support of Ho's effort to bolster the Viet Cong.

The dictatorial Diem government further alienated public opinion in South Vietnam, which resulted in growing support for the Viet Cong. Moreover, Diem, whose own background was among the minority Catholics, infuriated the Buddhist community by publicly allowing discrimination against their practices while supporting Catholic activities. By the spring of 1963, he had alienated the most influential segment of the public by his harsh measures.

Aroused by government attempts to ban Buddhist public religious displays, Buddhist demonstrators were fired upon by government troops. Soon the international news was filled with images of Buddhist monks burning themselves to death to protest the actions of the American-backed Diem regime.

Predictably, the U.S. government was becoming increasingly embarrassed and

Eisenhower and Ngo Dinh Diem

Vietnam

Black smoke covers areas of Saigon during the Tet offensive

disgusted with Diem. An army group, with American support, deposed him in late 1963, resulting in his violent death. Over the next year or so, the government of South Vietnam was in uncertain hands. For a time, leadership was held by General Duong Van Minh, but he proved too independent for the Americans and was quickly deposed. Power was supposedly centered in Saigon, but local military leaders in the provinces were all but independent of the central government. Entering an election campaign in 1964, the U.S. did not want to disturb the shaky status quo.

That uncertain period after Diem's death was interrupted in August when news reports indicated that North Vietnamese torpedo boats had attacked a U.S. destroyer in the Tonkin Gulf. Public reports at the time suggested that on two different occasions North Vietnamese boats had threatened the American ships. More recent evidence suggests that, though no one was hurt, the American ships operating off the coast of North Vietnam may have provoked one attack and that the second reported assault probably never occurred.

Nevertheless, at the time, given the fact that the United States government had been actively looking for an excuse to step up its efforts, the reports were not questioned. President Johnson manufactured a crisis out of the event and secured a vague resolution from Congress authorizing him to take military action in response. Eventually, the Tonkin Gulf vote would be viewed as the single most important ele-

ment in U.S. congressional support of the war. In fact, it became a de facto declaration of a war although such a declaration never formally occurred.

Because of their opposition to Diem's harsh rule, a great many non-communists also supported the Viet Cong and its political arm, the National Liberation Front. When he was deposed, this ended. Feeling the need of greater support and believing it more probable that military action would succeed after the downfall of Diem, the Viet Cong embarked on wider military efforts. In 1964, they were, for the first time, joined by regular units of the North Vietnamese army. There was a rapid increase in the area under communist control, particularly in the central highlands of South Vietnam. The Russians, sensing an imminent victory, sent their premier to Hanoi in early 1965 to give assurances of Russian support. The Americans feared South Vietnam would soon be lost. For the United States, which had been traumatized internally during the previous decade over the issue of "who had lost China?", such a development had to be stopped at all costs. More direct action was taken.

The American War

By 1965, the United States was bombing North Vietnam and deploying U.S. Marine and Army combat units. The days of the "advisors" were over. Now American troops under U.S. officers would fight the

North Vietnamese and their supporters directly. South Vietnam finally had the formal direct support of its major superpower ally, the United States. Given the changing circumstances, Hanoi would need similar help, but developments within the communist world were getting more complicated.

Ideological differences had led to a breakdown in Soviet-Chinese relations. The differences between the two communist giants now included disputes about what role each nation should play in aiding Ho Chi Minh's forces. After 1965, China's leadership resented the superior economic ability of the Russians to buy influence in Hanoi and limited its own assistance to the maintenance of the Chinese-North Vietnamese rail line and the shipment of infantry weapons. Although there was an agreement to ship Soviet equipment through China to North Vietnam, the trains were often delayed and harassed by "Red Guards" active in Mao's Great Cultural Revolution, then in progress in China.

Meanwhile, in Saigon a dashing young Air Force general, Nguyen Cao Ky, emerged as a leading figure in the military establishment of South Vietnam. In mid-1965, he became premier and retained that position for two years. This provided a welcome respite from the seemingly continuous change of rulers in the country. It became clear, though, that during his rule the armed forces exercised almost all-political power. This continued to arouse Buddhist opposition.

The cost to the U.S. rose to more than $30 billion a year, placing a serious strain on the American economy and on its political system. Within the U.S., opposition to the war began to grow more and more significant, especially among college-age students who did not share their leadership's obsession with anti-communism and who were more likely to view the struggle in South Vietnam as a civil war rather than as a part of a world-wide struggle between communism and capitalism. Moreover, the clearly undemocratic nature of the South Vietnamese regime made it hardly seem worthy of the sacrifices Americans were increasingly being asked to make. Recognizing that last issue, President Lyndon Johnson set out to improve Saigon's image.

Due to pressure from Washington to offer at least the appearance of a democratic regime, some political progress took place in South Vietnam. A constitution was enacted, and elections for a new National Assembly were held in 1967. Military intrigue reduced General Ky to the candidacy for vice president. General Nguyen Van Thieu, a Catholic, was elected president though in a relatively poor showing that saw a considerable number of votes going to an anti-military "peace" candidate.

The new government had a broader base, but the habit of jailing political opponents persisted. The military situation, bolstered by a half million U.S. troops, improved. The South Vietnamese army alone simply could not hold its own against North Vietnam and Viet Cong units. The government did gain control of half the land area by the end of 1967, but in many cases, its hold was shaky.

TET: A Battle Won and Lost

As 1968 began, both sides found themselves involved in a terribly costly and bloody conflict. Yet little was being accomplished to resolve the struggle. The U.S. was distracted by the 1968 elections, in which President Lyndon Johnson had declined to run, and the Soviets dared not appear to be less revolutionary than the Chinese. On Tet, the Lunar New Year holiday traditional to the Vietnamese, the communist forces started an unexpected all-out offensive. They invaded most of the provincial capitals and parts of Saigon, and they held a portion of the ancient imperial capital, Hue, for several days. U.S. encampments and installations were attacked, causing tremendous losses of material and manpower. Moreover monsoon rains prevented effective American defensive air strikes.

In the end, the spectacular offensive was dramatically defeated although it had certainly revealed the weaknesses of the South Vietnamese and U.S. forces and driven them back temporarily. The communist goal of generating a popular uprising was a dismal failure. Nevertheless, official American claims to the contrary, the North had proven that Americans were not winning the war and that it was likely to go on for many years. For Hanoi, committed as it had been for generations to the unification of the country under its rule, that price was acceptable. For the United States, by now more interested in simply finding a way out of the costly but ultimately peripheral struggle, it was not.

Seeking "Peace with Honor"

A desperate U.S. President Lyndon Johnson suspended the bombing of North Vietnam (except the southern provinces) in 1968 and proposed talks between the combatants. Knowing he could probably not be re-elected, Johnson, as stated, declined to run again. At last, negotiations were begun, but organizational issues, such as the status of the Viet Cong and seating arrangements at the conference table, resulted in endless haggling and little progress. But events within the United States were moving faster than the negotiations.

After a divisive campaign that saw the Democratic Party almost destroy itself over the war, Richard M. Nixon, the former Republican vice president, who had once advocated American intervention at Dienbienphu, was elected president of the U.S. During the campaign, Nixon had spoken somewhat vaguely about a "secret plan" to end the war. Once in power his plans became clearer.

The newly elected president was no longer primarily interested in South Vietnam, but in ending the war in a fashion that would retain American influence in the postwar era. This would not have been accomplished by simply pulling out, as many Americans had advocated. Rather, Nixon feared, it would send shock waves through the entire American alliance system. Thus, he wanted a way to withdraw that would allow U.S. prestige to continue undiminished.

His method to accomplish these goals came to be known as "Vietnamization." What Nixon and his soon famous advisor Henry Kissinger had in mind was to transfer the bulk of the ground war to the Army of the Republic of South Vietnam. In their plan, the United States would withdraw to the relatively safer position of offering air support. The goal was to reduce the number of American casualties while building up South Vietnam's ability to defend itself. Certainly, a good idea in theory, the plan dangerously reduced American military force in Vietnam even as its prestige remained closely tied to events there.

U.S. troop withdrawals thus started in 1969. From Hanoi's perspective their chances of victory probably seemed closer than ever. In mid-1969 they proclaimed a "provisional government" for the South. 1969 also saw the death of their long time leader Ho Chi Minh.

The Saigon government of President Thieu then turned to what it considered the most reliable elements for support: the armed forces and Catholics. Spurred by land reform in the south, the economy improved. Thieu was reelected (unopposed) in late 1971 in a contest his opponents charged was rigged. Although he made an attempt to build an effective government party, disruption came when the northern provinces of South Vietnam were struck by a massive North Vietnam invasion in March 1972.

President Nixon, who was facing a reelection contest responded by ordering the mining of Haiphong Harbor. This precipitated yet another international "crisis." The military stalemate was acutely embarrassing to Nixon as the fall elections approached. Yet, for a time it seemed "that peace was at hand," as Kissinger was publicly quoted. But no formal agreement was reached before Nixon's landslide reelection victory of 1972. Once reelected, Nixon ordered a resumption of the heavy bombing of North Vietnam in an attempt to persuade Hanoi to accept terms acceptable to the Saigon government.

The End

After the intense December 1972 bombing, the North Vietnamese verbally agreed to end the conflict. The formal agreement was signed on March 2, 1973. The U.S. had already given up its insistence on a North Vietnamese withdrawal from South Vietnam and continued its own withdrawal. In exchange, it got American prisoners back although some insist to this day that many were held against their will in violation of the promise.

Hanoi accepted a political arrangement that did not guarantee the overthrow of

South Vietnamese President Nguyen Van Thieu decorates soldiers

Vietnam

The Mausoleum of Ho Chi Minh in Hanoi

the Thieu government as had been previously demanded. Realistically neither North nor South Vietnam had any genuine interest in abiding by the political provisions of the January 1973 agreement, which called for a vaguely defined coalition government and general elections.

To strengthen its hand, Hanoi, with the help of military aid from the Soviet Union and China, then began to create a "third Vietnam" under the nominal control of the Viet Cong in the highlands of South Vietnam. This activity, much of which was in flagrant violation of the agreement, included road building, troop buildups, the stockpiling of weapons and other measures.

Meanwhile, Saigon's principal supporter, the United States, was sinking deeply into the Watergate scandal that eventually destroyed the Nixon administration. Deprived of American air support by Congressional prohibitions and unwilling to commit its own air force against communist-held areas in the highlands, South Vietnam made no genuine military effort to contain their long-time foe.

In the Saigon-controlled areas, the Thieu government continued its own repressive policies. Although Thieu fired a number of corrupt military and civilian officials, there was no basic change in the style of the regime. Anti-Thieu protest movements arose in 1974 among both the Buddhists, who stressed liberalization and peace, and the Roman Catholics, who emphasized opposition to corruption. Concessions were promised to both in late 1974, but little happened. By early 1975, five major opposition newspapers were closed down.

Meanwhile, North Vietnam was developing its economy through aid from the Soviet Union and China. The military strength of Hanoi was built up as was that of the Viet Cong in the highlands of South Vietnam. A strategy of "accelerated erosion" began against Saigon's military positions in both the highlands and in the Mekong Delta. This approach was obvi-

ously inadequate to achieve Hanoi's two principal objectives: imposition of the political provisions of the January 1973 agreement and/or the downfall of Thieu. One reason for this cautious approach was probably the attitude of the Soviet Union and China, which did not want their rapprochement with the United States to be endangered by a major resurgence of fighting in Vietnam.

The North Vietnamese capture of two provincial capitals in early 1975, and another closer to Saigon, was the beginning of the end. Shocked by the loss of these towns and unquestionably worried by the refusal of the U.S. Congress to vote further large-scale military aid, Thieu simply abandoned the three provinces in March. What was perhaps meant as a retreat quickly turned into a rout as Hanoi's forces, taking advantage of the dry season and the government withdrawals, moved forward. By the end of March, the two important coastal cities of Hue and Danang had fallen to the communists. Saigon fell at the end of April in a morass of confusion as people with close contacts with the Thieu administration or the Americans desperately tried to flee in overcrowded boats and planes.

The behavior of the leadership during 1975 in South Vietnam demonstrated that their concern was mainly for their personal safety rather than for the future of South Vietnam. Thieu issued military orders that were disastrous, changed daily, and led nowhere. Many field officers deserted to seek safety for themselves and their families. Several hundred thousand refugees fled, most ultimately to the U.S. Thieu went to Taiwan. Almost the entire leadership was able to depart with substantial wealth, in contrast to most of the refugees who had little more than the clothes they wore. Most dramatically, thousands of South Vietnamese suddenly abandoned their G.I. issued boots to avoid being recognized as former South Vietnamese soldiers.

The reasons for the loss of the war were many, but especially important was the weakness of the southern regime. Despite its access to American support, it never developed deep roots among the Vietnamese population, certainly nothing similar to what Hanoi was able to call upon from the populations under its control. When South Vietnam started to lose the support of even the Americans, its ability to maintain itself became even more problematic.

A Unified Vietnam

If Hanoi's tenacity had allowed it finally to unify the country under its own control, actually ruling a united Vietnam would require very different skills. Unified Vietnam's new leaders had an enormous challenge ahead of them, for the country had been devastated by the years of war. Over eight million tons of bombs had been dropped. The Vietnamese had experienced some two million casualties—tremendous numbers of whom would have to be taken care of for years. The people hurt and killed by the war were not the only victims. Vietnam's land had suffered horribly.

More than eleven million gallons of Agent Orange had been sprayed over the country by the United States in order to destroy the vegetation cover used by the communist forces. According to the United Nations, U.S. chemical warfare created "black zones" within the countryside whose ability to produce crops was radically reduced. In addition, like many American Vietnam veterans, many Vietnamese and their families would suffer from the affects of Agent Orange years after the fighting ended. Unfortunately for the nation that had already experienced so many hardships, Hanoi's post-victory policies often created even more problems, as it attempted both to centralize authority and to build a communist "command economy."

After its "liberation" from the Thieu regime, South Vietnam was run by men sent from Hanoi. Chief among them was Pham Hung who, although a southerner, was a member of the top leadership of the Vietnam Workers Party, the communist party. Imposition of communist controls on the South proceeded fairly slowly.

Nevertheless, tens of thousands were executed while millions were forced into political "re-indoctrination" camps. Former employees of the Thieu regime found it difficult for years to find jobs and even food. Sadly, the ostracizing of family members often continued down into the next generation as many of their children experienced continuing prejudice.

The new regime worked to reduce the population of Saigon, now renamed Ho Chi Minh City, through forced resettlement in the countryside. Their reasoning is understandable given how much the city's population had swollen with refugees from the countryside and how little work there was once the free spending Americans left. The policies, though, caused suffering for thousands as they were forced to abandon their lives in the city for the backbreaking labor of the countryside.

The party held its Fourth Congress in late 1976, at which it renamed itself the Vietnam Communist (rather than "Workers") Party. The north's domination over the south was clear. Soviet aid to and influence on the new regime was also substantial. The Soviets also took over the huge naval base at Camranh Bay built by the U.S. In contrast, Chinese influence was considerably less than that of the Soviets. Clearly Vietnam was tilting toward Moscow as the Sino-Soviet disputes continued.

Meanwhile, Hanoi naively continued to hope for the $3.25 billion in reconstruction aid Nixon was said to have promised. But no aid was forthcoming as little progress was made on the Missing-in-Action (MIA) matter, and Hanoi was widely disliked within the United States.

Having finally won its long independence and unification struggle, Hanoi then moved to impose a socialist economy on the south. That effort was not well received by the southerners who passively resisted efforts to collectivize agriculture and redistribute land. When efforts to socialize the urban area brought an end to the free market system of the south, large numbers of indigenous Chinese, the backbone of the urban economy, fled the country. This created yet another wave of "boat people," who had already filled refugee camps throughout Southeast Asia.

These policies hardly helped strengthen the country, and in the late 1970s Vietnam's leadership already started looking for new solutions to the nation's problems. Hanoi then moved to integrate itself into the world economic community by joining organizations like the World Bank and the Asia Development Bank. It sought outside development funds for the exploration of natural resources such as oil. In 1977, it announced it would honor the former South Vietnamese government's debts to both France and Japan (necessary to build future economic relations). The decision was even made in 1979 to slow down the process of collectivization of agriculture.

Unfortunately, these early examples of practical economic decision-making did not bear the fruit for which one might have hoped. Other problematic relationships continued to complicate Hanoi's efforts. The Americans continued to maintain their economic embargo, and newly developing tensions with China over Vietnam's role in Cambodia were soon to complicate matters even more.

My Lai Memorial Peace Park   Photo by Steven Leibo

Vietnam's Cambodia Involvement

In the late 1970s, Vietnam developed a border conflict with Cambodia, which was then controlled by the murderous and vehemently nationalist Pol Pot regime. In 1978, Vietnam launched a full-scale invasion of the country. In doing so, Hanoi claimed they were responding to frequent border provocations and to the Khmer Rouge's genocidal killing within Cambodia. Under the circumstances, many Cambodians initially viewed the invading Vietnamese and their supporters as liberators. Nevertheless, despite the general hatred of the Pol Pot regime, Vietnam's own invasion was also widely condemned. The Chinese, who had been especially supportive of the Khmer Rouge, were outraged. They saw Hanoi's actions as an extension of their enemy's, the Soviet Union's, influence in Southeast Asia. From Beijing's perspective that was unacceptable.

In retaliation for this strike against its ally, China began to pour troops over the Vietnamese border in early 1979, occupying, despite heavy fighting, a portion of its northern territory. Beijing's efforts, though, were less successful than expected. The Chinese troops, who had not fought in a generation, were hard pressed to deal with the Vietnamese military fresh from its generation-long struggle with the United States. China's efforts to teach

Hanoi a "lesson" had failed, and Chinese troops were withdrawn within a few weeks. After that Beijing directed itself more toward supporting the fallen Khmer Rouge and making life "difficult" for the Vietnamese in Cambodia.

Over the next decade, Vietnam's commitment to Cambodia and its allied government would become a major burden on the regime. Predictably, as time went on, the Vietnamese, who had initially been welcomed as liberators, were themselves seen as aggressive occupiers. Finally, in the late 1980s Hanoi began its withdrawal from Cambodia after a decade that had seen the commitment there contribute to the weakening economic conditions in Vietnam itself and its international isolation.

A New Economic Path

Economically the first decade of independence was a disaster. The most productive citizens had been driven from the country, and the socialist economic planning had alienated many others. The war in Cambodia had so alienated countries, including China and the United States, that it was particularly difficult for Vietnam's economy to move meaningfully toward recovery.

The aging, largely North Vietnamese leadership and its economic policies had not helped the economy grow. The contin-

Vietnam

Rice paddy work in Northern Vietnam   Photo by Sara Zaidspiner-Leibo

uing isolation of the regime due to the American-led boycott had hurt. Meanwhile, the efforts of many communist states from Eastern Europe to improve ties with Beijing meant less enthusiasm for Vietnam. Hanoi's economic crisis was growing.

For example, inflation was running at around 700%. By the mid 1980s, it was clear that a new direction was required. Not surprisingly this new thinking emerged as China, under Deng Xiaoping, was several years into a major economic reform program itself. More importantly given the Soviet Union's considerable influence in Vietnam, the actions and advice of its reforming leader, Mikhail Gorbachev, was

particularly important in the decision to fashion a new economic policy.

The new direction also became more possible with the death in July 1986 of Le Duan, the longtime General Secretary of the Communist Party of Vietnam, the most powerful political office. He was succeeded by Truong Chinh, also elderly but more flexible and with a reputation for being pro-Chinese. Accordingly, at a Party Congress held in December 1986, Truong Chinh, Le Duc Tho and Pham Van Dong "resigned" from the Politburo although all continued to be "advisors." Chinh retained the presidency of the state and Dong the premiership. A new General Secretary of the party, Nguyen Van Linh,

a Southerner and an economic reformer, was elected. In 1987 there were major personnel changes in the government although Chinh and Dong remained in place; the newcomers were mostly southerners with some economic expertise. The new leadership group was clearly interested in moving more decisively away from central control of the economy.

Over the next several years, agriculture was de-collectivized and many financial reforms were put into place. State factory managers were given more authority, and a partial revival of private enterprise was permitted. By 1989, Vietnam had re-emerged as a major rice exporter and is now the world's second-largest. Private businesses, such as restaurants and shops, were opened and flourished as well.

The changes were inspired both by internal developments in Vietnam as well as by the new Gorbachev leadership in the Soviet Union. These changes came to be known as Doi Moi, or "renovation." If they are less well known than the famous Glasnost and Perestroika of Gorbachev, they were born of the same problems in the socialist world. Eventually, while the initial decision to open the economy was inspired by developments within the socialist block, by the early 1990s the Soviet Union had collapsed, and Vietnam was forced to integrate itself more deeply into the world's newly globalized economies.

A similar relaxation of controls occurred in Vietnam in the late 1980s, which also paralleled developments in both the Soviet Union and the People's Republic of China. Greater press and religious freedom became possible, as well as the introduction of Western music videos. Some 6,000 political prisoners were released in 1987.

Another milestone was reached in 2007 when Vietnam achieved its goal of joining the World Trade Organization. At the beginning of the year the nation became the 150th country to join. Overall, the idea of a "new Vietnam," one that was eager for foreign contacts, was energetically promoted by the government.

Vietnamese Domestic Politics

The dramatic developments of 1989–1991 in the Soviet Union and Eastern Europe had a serious impact on the Vietnamese leadership. The basic reaction was one of alarm and a determination that the erosion of the ruling party's power would not be repeated in Vietnam. Particularly shocking for Vietnam's leadership was the bloody fall of the Nicolae Ceaucescu regime in Romania in December 1989.

Political opposition in Vietnam had been almost non-existent. Accordingly, the regime had felt free to proceed along the

Ford Plant East of Hanoi   Courtesy: Ed Tick

same lines as in China: minimal political reform combined with some reasonably effective economic reform. However, the events of the 1989–1991 era had clearly shown how easily reform efforts in the communist world could swirl out of control. The Party had no desire to lose its mandate on power. The key appeared at least to make reasonable progress on economically improving people's lives without loosening up on political controls.

One requirement was the establishment of normal commercial relations with the industrial countries. The 1989 withdrawal from Cambodia was fundamental to that process and made improved relations with the rest of Vietnam's neighbors far more possible. Relations with the U.S. remained difficult, especially as controversies continued around the political sensitive issue of American Missing-in-Action (MIA). Thus, constrained by anti-Hanoi sentiments in the U.S., Washington continued to withhold diplomatic recognition and trade from Hanoi.

Finally, as time passed Hanoi became increasingly more cooperative on the MIA issue, and by the end of 1991 the State Department even began to authorize tour groups of Americans to visit Vietnam. The U.S. presidential election prevented rapid action, but in late 1992 President George H.W. Bush finally permitted U.S. companies to open offices in Vietnam and begin negotiations for future trade relations.

Throughout the early 1990s, many signs pointed to the continued opening of Vietnam to the outside world. Vietnamese officials were being trained in contemporary diplomatic practice, a Fulbright program was begun, and American professors were in the country at several institutions teaching business and economic courses. Americans also visited Vietnamese military bases and government offices in search of additional information on American MIAs. Vietnamese were also being trained to aid them in the process of determining the fate of their own MIAs that far outnumber the

Americans lost. Unfortunately, Vietnam has lacked the financial resources to seek out the ultimate burial places of most of their own war dead. This is an issue that is often very painful to the many Vietnamese who see so much money being spent to locate the remains of lost Americans.

A new leader also emerged over the last decade. In the spring of 2001 a new general secretary, Nong Duc Manh, was chosen to head the communist party. Manh had come to power as a replacement to the more conservative Le Kha Phieu. His selection was greeted enthusiastically by many. He joined in leadership Prime Minister Phan Van Khai and President Tran Duc Luong. To the disappointment of some, though, in the time since he came to power, Manh has taken a relatively cautious approach to reform. Nevertheless, there have been some provocative new changes.

One particularly interesting development was the government's decision to allow communist party members to be officially involved in private business activities. There has even been talk of allowing people from the private sector to join the party, a practice already allowed in the People's Republic of China.

While Vietnamese politics remains largely beyond the view of outsiders, it has become more and more obvious that the upper leadership has been torn by infighting. Information about some of this has leaked to the general public. The best known example are the accusations that members of the nation's military intelligence services fabricated information to make it appear that top Vietnamese Communist Party officials had secretly collaborated with the American Central Intelligence Agency. Examples of intra-party struggles have become more and more publicly known. In fact, some very well-known officials have circulated documents critical of recent decision making.

Problems within the ruling elite have also been manifested in more public concerns about the party. Once the respected

leader of the nation's struggle to free and then unify the nation, today's Vietnamese Communist Party has been experiencing considerable public dissatisfaction over the government's record of corruption. The most dramatic recent example of such corruption was the case of a high official of the Ministry of Transport and Communications. He was accused in 2006 of having lost seven million dollars in public funds betting on European soccer matches.

So serious has this loss of faith become that the party has officially committed itself not only to root out corruption, but to restore public confidence. There are plenty of reasons for them to be concerned about that loss of public confidence.

More and more commonly, the government has had to face peasant unrest aroused by excessive taxation and corrupt local officials. Especially significant has been tension between the government and the ethnic minorities of Vietnam's central highlands. According to reports from the region, the problems have been caused by the new arrivals' confiscation of lands owned by the ethnic minorities and pressure against their local, often protestant churches. The problem has, at times, grown so explosive that many of the tribal people from the central highlands have fled into Cambodia, a development that also added to the tensions between the two nations.

In April 2004, thousands of Vietnamese ethnic minorities staged a huge demonstration that apparently clashed with security forces resulting in hundreds of injuries and perhaps a dozen deaths. Given Hanoi's control of the media, the details of the reported clashes are often sketchy, but the impression is that these disturbances have been quite serious. More recently, in early 2008, similar tensions resulted in mass demonstrations carried out by the Degar peoples in the provinces of Dak Lak and Gia Lai.

Vietnam's leaders do appear to have taken some of the tensions seriously. There have been efforts to confront corruption

President Nguyen Minh Triet

Prime Minister Nguyen Tan Dung

General Secretary Nong Duc Manh

Vietnam

Photo by Steven A. Leibo

and to expand decision making, for example making sure that the full central committee is not overshadowed by the smaller politburo and working to ensure a younger and more professionally trained bureaucracy. Nevertheless, the changes have obviously not been enough to calm the tensions that regularly develop in the Central Highlands.

Society and Culture

The Vietnamese have been influenced by the culture of the Chinese to a greater extent than all other nations of Southeast Asia, except Singapore, where there is a Chinese majority. Chinese characters were used to write the Vietnamese language until the French replaced them with quoc-ngu, a system based on the French alphabet. The Red River in North Vietnam is controlled with dikes of Chinese design.

Religiously Vietnam includes a large number of followers of Mahayana Buddhism, whose practices vary widely, and many Roman Catholics. Vietnamese Buddhism includes traditions ranging from animism and Taoism to Confucianism and Buddhism and is often simply called the Triple Religion or "Vietnamese Buddhism." Along with Korea and the Philippines, Vietnam has one of the highest percentages of Christians in Asia. There is also a considerable number who follow minority traditions like the Cao Dai and Hoa Hao sects. Compared to the situation in earlier years, Vietnam has become much more religiously tolerant.

More dramatic over the last few years, however, has been the ongoing confrontation between the authorities and local Catholics over property rights. More specifically it concerns the control of church lands in Hanoi and along the central coast at Dong Hoi that have seen a series of demonstrations, arrests and a rising tone of conflict. Moreover, religious organizations that are not officially sanctioned, such as Mennonites or dissident Buddhists, regularly feel the weight of government displeasure.

Most citizens are ethnically Vietnamese with a small percentage of Chinese and a block of some 54 different smaller groups that are sometimes collectively known as Montagnards. The Vietnamese tribal communities have often experienced prejudice directed against them by the majority Vietnamese people. From time to time a significant number of demonstrations and clashes has occurred in regions of the central highlands.

Unlike China, which has committed itself to reducing population growth, Vietnamese efforts have not been nearly as dedicated. Few restrictions exist to limit the number of children a family might want. Abortion is very common, and about twenty percent of those who do have them are young people. There is also a significant rise in HIV/AIDS. As in other Asian countries, more male births are reported than female. This suggests that female fetuses are more likely to be aborted than male.

The government, like that in neighboring Thailand and China, has become par-

ticularly involved in trying to limit the number of Vietnamese who smoke. Currently about half of all Vietnamese men do so. To reduce that number, the government has now banned smoking scenes in all Vietnamese films.

Most of the population remains poor and largely rural. The real economic changes made in recent years have been significant, but they have also added to the gap between the rich and poor. This is particularly true when one looks both regionally and ethnically. Some regions, like those around Ho Chi Minh City, have grown far faster than the area around the Mekong Delta and the central highlands. Ethnic Vietnamese from the lowlands have moved into the central highlands weakening the economic circumstances of the ethnic minorities who previously predominated in those areas.

Nevertheless, considerable progress has been made. According to the World Bank, 58% of the Vietnamese population lived in poverty during 1992–1993. By 1997–1998 only 37% were officially living in poverty, and by the first years of the new century the number living under the official poverty rate continued to decline significantly.

However, the burdens on people have also changed as the nation's emphasis on a less state-dominated economic system has grown. Health care, for example, can be very expensive, and peasants who have members of their families needing major medical treatment can often only obtain the treatment by selling off family land.

The government has acted to remove street children from the cities by pressuring them to return to their villages or to live in charity centers. The goal is to have them living in regular charity centers, where they can be trained to do more than sell souvenirs or lottery tickets.

If the situation in Vietnam is more open today than in the past, the government is still quite willing to come down hard on those it perceives as undermining its authority. In early 2009, one of Vietnam's most prominent lawyers was arrested for challenging state power. The government claimed he had been drafting a revised constitution. Later in the year, six dissidents were arrested for hanging banners in the port city of Haiphong that demanded greater political freedoms. At least one of them was sentenced to a five-year term for subversion.

For those who avoid arousing the leadership anger, today's Vietnamese government controls people's lives far less than it once did. It still decides how much free speech and press freedoms are allowed. Outside sources of information, ranging from telephones to e-mail and faxes, are controlled. Nevertheless, one of the most obvious things one notices when traveling regularly in Vietnam is that change is coming fast. The Internet is increasingly available, and many have access to e-mail through the popular internet cafes and international accounts such as Hotmail.

Moreover, there have been enough improvements in recent years that many Vietnamese who fled earlier are returning home. Some are even buying and building homes often in more western styles. The most dramatic example was the 2004 return by the former South Vietnamese leader Nguyen Cao Ky, who made his first visit in almost thirty years. Those who have returned either for visits or to stay are not allowed to take part in public activities.

Another obvious change that even the most casual visitors will notice is the growing gap between the generations in Vietnam. The older generation, those who grew up during Vietnam's nationalist struggle against the French and the later "American" war, has far different memories and life experiences than the new generation that has come of age in a largely peaceful Vietnam ever more deeply involved in global economic activities. Given the facts that 60% of the population is under thirty and that only 15% is over 40, it is a community with very different memories of Vietnam's modern experience than earlier generations.

Perhaps most interestingly, the Pew Organization, which is known for its international polling, reported recently that Vietnamese are among the most content and optimistic of the peoples around the world. This is an incredible rating for a people who suffered so much deprivation during the last century. Statistics back up that level of optimism. Life expectancy has recently gone up by two years for the average Vietnamese. Today the average is 71.58 years, a figure more similar to those of the developed world than the developing world in which Vietnam is more appropriately listed.

Vietnamese Women

As mentioned in the background section of East and Southeast Asia, Southeast Asian women have historically enjoyed more rights than their sisters in other parts of Asia. In ancient Vietnam women were especially important, and many played significant roles in Vietnam's long struggle against Chinese domination. In modern Vietnam, women often played very important roles in the nationalist struggle against both the French and later the Americans. Still, the first female did not take her place in the party's all-important politburo until the summer of 1996. Women still represent only 21% of the managerial positions in business, and within the central committee of the Communist Party males hold 89% of

. . . even as the Internet has arrived.

Photo by Steven A. Leibo

the seats. Within the society at large people still prefer male babies to females although that attitude is more common among the more conservative northerners than among their southern cousins.

That said, women are nevertheless an important part of the Vietnamese work force. In Hanoi, for example, they make up more than half of the local work force. Still, according to international reports, Vietnamese women only make around 89% as much money as men do. One especially interesting development within Vietnam that particularly affects women has been the government's campaign to reduce the number of Vietnamese couples who live together instead of marrying. Divorce is also common, and women more often than men initiate the efforts usually for reasons that range from spousal abuse to adultery and economic conflicts.

The challenges that continue to face Vietnamese women are perhaps best revealed by the reality that thousands of them have opted to offer themselves to Taiwanese men as "male order brides." Doing so allows them to live in Taiwan earning significantly more money than is possible in Vietnam. That money can then be sent home to their families.

For visitors to Hanoi interested in women's history, one especially important visit should be to the wonderfully organized and very modern museum of Vietnamese women. Along with the Ho Chi Minh museum, it is far and away one of the best in the country.

Foreign Relations

Looking at Vietnam's foreign relations from the broadest view, two obvious periods emerge in the years since the war ended. First, the initial decade after the war saw Vietnam increasingly dependent on the Soviet Union. Later, after its invasion of Cambodia, Vietnam found itself alienated from much of the rest of the world. Her foreign policy was particularly ideological in those years as Vietnam attempted to orient its diplomatic decision-making within the framework of the Cold War era. But that approach did not prove effective and eventually moved Vietnam's leaders to reevaluate their approach.

By the mid-1980s, as Vietnam's economic problems and diplomatic isolation proved more and more problematic, its leaders began not only their effort to renovate the economy but to open Vietnam up more to the world community. Fundamental to that effort was, of course, the withdrawal from Cambodia, a move that opened up a new era in Vietnamese foreign relations.

Having removed the foremost impediment to deepening its involvement in the world community, Vietnam during the 1990s set out in a new direction. In July 1993, President Bill Clinton ended U.S. opposition to International Monetary Fund (IMF) loans to Vietnam. Somewhat later Clinton announced that American companies could bid on infrastructure projects funded by the international lending agencies.

The next year the 19-year U.S. trade embargo was finally ended. Full diplomatic relations were announced in July 1995. More recently it has become easier for American businessmen to invest and trade with Vietnam. Vietnam has even gone as far as paying back monies the former government of South Vietnam owed to the United States. Cooperation on a range of issues between the two wartime enemies

Vietnam

became even more possible after former U.S. Secretary of Defense William Cohen's highly successful trip to Hanoi in early 2000 and even more dramatically after President Clinton's own extremely well received visit during the last weeks of 2000.

It was after all only a few years ago that Vietnam was finally granted "most favored nation" (more correctly, normal trading status) by the Americans. That was important because it allowed Vietnamese goods to enter the U.S. as cheaply as those from America's other trading partners. In July 2000, the United States and Vietnam finalized an official trade treaty that was expanded by yet another agreement reached in early 2006.

Clearly, normalization of relations with the United States has been a major element in Hanoi's efforts to strengthen the economy. By 2004 the United States had become the Vietnam's 11th largest investor, and trade relations were growing rapidly. Vietnam's total exports to the United States went up over 127%, earning the country almost two billion dollars in revenues while the Americans sold almost 600 million dollars worth of goods to Vietnam. By 2005, Vietnamese sales to the United States had reached $8.5 billion, while in early 2006 the American company, Lockheed Martin, won the contract to launch Vietnam's first telecommunications satellite.

Overall, American firms have become deeply involved in the Vietnamese economy though some, like Nike, have come under considerable public criticism for the

work conditions they established there. True, things have not always worked out as hoped. The Procter and Gamble Company's soap- and shampoo-making facility was plagued by legal and supply problems, and in March 1998, it was temporarily shut down. More recently American charges that Vietnam has been "dumping" catfish and shrimp on the American market have contributed to the tensions. The same applies to the recent American State Department's designation of Vietnam as a country that does not respect religious freedom. This is a charge to which Hanoi may object, but there is significant evidence behind it to validate it.

Nevertheless, the relationship appears quite healthy, in fact so healthy that Vietnamese Prime Minister Phan Van Khai made a historic visit to the United States during the summer of 2005. The visit was the first by a Vietnamese leader since the end of the Vietnam War. While in the U.S., Phan Van Khai was received at the White House by President George W. Bush. Eventually, agreements were even reached on Vietnam's participation in some American military training programs. Phan's 2005 visit was followed up by Prime Minister Dung in June 2008. Of course, recent American presidents, Bill Clinton and George W. Bush, visited Vietnam during their terms in office.

Most interesting to those who lived through the era of the Vietnam War is that their respective military leaders have visited and consulted with their counter-

parts. For the first time in a generation, an American naval vessel docked in Vietnam, and its sailors were allowed to wander like tourists within the country.

But improving relations with America has not stopped Vietnam's leadership from developing stronger ties with the United States' long-time arch enemy, Cuba, formerly led by Fidel Castro. Some have speculated that the visit of Vietnam's leader, Nong Duc Manh, to the ailing Castro in mid 2007 might be a precursor to a Cuban effort to emulate some of the more open economic policies Hanoi has developed in Vietnam itself since the 1980s.

Especially important as well has been Vietnam's integration with its Southeast Asian neighbors. Vietnam is now a member of ASEAN (Association of Southeast Asian Nations). Membership provides important economic and strategic benefits. For example, being a member of ASEAN can provide Vietnam with support in its relations with China. An important example of this occurred when the ASEAN states recently spoke out with one voice at the second ASEAN Regional (security) Forum in Brunei on the issue of conflicting claims in the South China Sea (which Vietnamese call "East Sea"). China had insisted that these claims be addressed on a bilateral basis. Countries like Vietnam and the Philippines, who have had run-ins with the Chinese military in the sea, preferred the multilateral approach.

As is often the case, Sino-Vietnamese relations remain problematic. After almost two decades of closure, the border between them was recently opened for rail service. Both Presidents Jiang Zemin and Hu Jintao of the People's Republic have visited. In addition, in 2006 Party Secretary-General Nong Duc Manh made his first official trip to China and negotiated an agreement designed to facilitate a more exact determination of the border between the two countries.

Nevertheless, problems remain, most notably over the annual midsummer Chinese moratorium against fishing in the South China Sea. This ban comes at the very height of the Vietnamese fishing season. It regularly involves Chinese ships aggressively driving Vietnamese ships from the region. The ban, which has been in place over the last decade, was ostensibly proclaimed by Beijing as a way to preserve the vital fishing resources of the area. But it has been seen more widely as an example of China's growing assertion of their claims to the region's offshore resources. However, if today's relationship between Vietnam and China is a somewhat mixed one, it is certainly an improvement over their earlier one.

The two fought one conflict in 1979 and have come to blows over conflicting claims

Tourists explore Vietnam's Citadel

Courtesy of Sara Zaidspiner-Leibo

in the South China Sea several times. As recently as 1994, a Vietnamese patrol boat seized three Chinese fishing vessels off Bach Long Vi, an island claimed by Hanoi and located half way between Vietnam and Hainan Island (Chinese territory). The next day a Chinese boat opened fire on another patrol, wounding two Vietnamese. More recently, though, progress has been made in resolving this important issue. As we have seen, the fishing moratorium remains a continuing source of tension.

In large measure, after Vietnam's withdrawal from Cambodia and the end of its relationship with the Soviet Union, after the latter's collapse in 1991, only the issue of competing claims over the various disputed islands kept the two nations somewhat apart. During 2008, those improving relations were solidified by visits to Beijing by most of Vietnam's top leadership and the signing of an agreement on the border between the two nations.

Vietnam also continued to talk with Cambodian officials about the treatment of ethnic Vietnamese living along the border just inside Cambodian territory. Relations, though, are not the best and they could deteriorate easily. In fact, there was considerable tension recently between the two as Cambodia claimed that Vietnam had actually moved the border markers between the two countries. Nor did the Cambodian government appreciate it when Hanoi, after some hesitation, followed their ASEAN colleagues' lead and temporarily halted Cambodia's entrance into ASEAN in the weeks after Hun Sen's coup. As mentioned above, relations were complicated as well when many Vietnamese ethnic-minority people fled to Cambodia after tensions over land use exploded in the Central Highlands.

Of particular interest has been Vietnam's effort to reach out to the other non-Asian developing nations. During the spring of 2003 Hanoi played host to representatives from nineteen African nations who arrived to discuss issues of mutual concern. Nor has Hanoi forgotten its important relationship with France, the nation that so dominated its recent modern history. This time, though, relations are on a much more equal basis. In recent years a renewed official relationship was established between the French and Vietnamese national assemblies.

Meanwhile, Hanoi restored diplomatic relations with Chile. The two countries had broken relations after Chile's democratically elected Marxist president, Salvador Allende, was overthrown in 1973. The move was yet another sign that the tensions that had dominated the world during the Cold War have largely passed into history. More recently, Hanoi successfully hosted the fifth Asia-Europe summit.

The meeting was almost disrupted by the European nations' reticence to deal with Myanmar's presence at the conference because of its human rights record.

Even official anger at the Vatican's canonization in mid-1988 of 117 Vietnamese martyrs of the 17th and 18th centuries was not allowed to derail a policy of increased toleration of religion, including Catholicism. Still, Hanoi remained suspicious of the Vatican, given the deeply anti-communist reputation of the former Polish Pope John Paul II and the Church's strong ties to the hated Diem regime. The usual tensions between Vietnam and the Catholic Church became particularly heated during 2008 because of government confiscations of lands the Church claimed in Hanoi. Public demonstrations broke out, and it was reported that government supporters attacked a peaceful march organized by Church members. A similar series of confrontations took place the following year in the city of Dong Hoi along the coast in central Vietnam.

One of the most obvious examples of Vietnam's increasing integration with the wider world community was its election as a non-permanent member of the United Nation's Security Council in late 2007.

Vietnam's leadership has traveled very extensively around the world promoting the nation's economic and political interests.

Economy

Vietnam has for years appeared as if it were on the verge of becoming another "Asian Tiger." The term, especially common before the 1997 "Asian Economic Crash," referred to the rapidly growing economies of Asia: Singapore, Taiwan, South Korea and Hong Kong. The term is no longer used as often. However, the reality of Vietnam's transition from a centrally controlled communist economy to a much more dynamic economy remains true. Today Vietnam is more and more influenced by capitalism, and it is moving into the global market.

Beginning in the late 1980s the country experienced a real economic boom with the economic growth rate during the 1990s averaging around 7.5%. That average includes even the slowdown that took place during the Asian economic crisis of 1997–1998. The momentum has continued. In recent years, Vietnam's growth has been hovering around 8%. That is a respectable rate that is higher than many of its neighbors. It even managed a respectable 5.2% for 2009 despite the global slowdown.

These changes were initially a result of the Communist Party's policy of doi moi, or restructuring, which ushered in a series of market reforms. A great many restrictions on the private sector were removed and the decision to move Vietnam more deeply into the world economic system largely embraced. Nevertheless, none of those domestic changes would have mattered much if economic globalization in the late 1990s had not created a more integrated planetary economic system of which Vietnam could take advantage. One result, for example, is that Vietnam is currently among the world's largest exporters of rice (second in world) and coffee (third in world). The results have been impressive.

If 1995, per capita income was still only about $270, or using figures adjusted for living standards, around $1,310. By the first

Fishing in central Vietnam

Courtesy of Barbara Leibo

Vietnam

years of the new century, Vietnam had changed even more. The per capita income had risen to $400 or $1,950 when so adjusted. More recently, the figure based on the more realistic purchasing power parity had the Vietnamese per capita income at just under $3,000 while the poverty rate has been reduced to around 12%.

Still there have been plenty of impediments to further integration in the world economy. One is the government's on-going commitment to the state firms. Hanoi may be siphoning off resources needed by the private sector to help state enterprises. For example, textiles made in state concerns are given preference for export. These companies also benefit from better access to foreign currency loans. Foreign companies are even being forced to form joint ventures with local state-owned businesses.

State-run companies still produce a significant percentage of the national GDP. In contrast to China, which apparently wants the importance of such state companies to diminish over time, Hanoi's leaders hope they will remain significant. Still not all have remained economically viable. It has also been necessary for the economy to absorb excess labor from closed state enterprises. This has been partly accomplished by creating millions of new jobs in the private sector.

For urban laborers, 2008 was a particularly tense year. Due to rising inflation, more and more workers found themselves losing purchasing power. This was a situation that eventually resulted in hundreds of strikes. For the most part it was the foreign-owned companies near Ho Chi Minh City that bore the brunt of the labor unrest. The workers did manage to win a few concessions and somewhat higher wages.

Especially interesting is that Vietnam has finally developed a stock market as China its giant neighbor did some years ago. Experts were hired from Taiwan to help set one up, and in July of 2000 it opened in Ho Chi Minh City to great fanfare. Another major government goal was to join the World Trade Organization (WTO). The new economic agreement worked out in 2006 between the United States and Vietnam went a long way toward accomplishing that goal. In the fall of 2006 the WTO officially recommended that Vietnam be admitted as its 150th member.

In the early years of the new millennium a number of problems arose to challenge the Vietnamese. The September 11, 2001, terrorist attack against the United States slowed the all-important American economy. Subsequently Vietnam found itself affected as well. Moreover, tourism was deeply impacted. Later, in 2003, fears of the SARS influenza-like disease weakened many Asian economies, including Vietnam's. Fear of SARS hurt Vietnam's economic growth despite the fact that Hanoi received a great deal of positive international publicity for its quick and professional response.

Just as Vietnam and much of the rest of Asia appeared to be moving past the problem, a new medical crisis appeared on the horizon. This time it was bird flu that began to kill people in various parts of Southeast Asia, including Vietnam. Local authorities destroyed millions of chickens and other poultry to stop the outbreak. Predictably, Vietnam found countries around the world banning the import of Vietnamese chickens just as many of those same countries had earlier banned American beef after reports of a cow carrying mad cow disease were published. In the end, all the effort seemed to have been worth it. Over time the number of cases dropped dramatically.

There were plenty of other bright spots in Vietnam's economic situations. The tourist industry has generally been growing well and becoming more and more important to the country's economy. Vietnam is even attracting significant numbers of Americans interested in learning more about the country that so transformed their own, now more than a third of a century ago.

Vietnam is looking forward to the future when agriculture production will not be such a fundamental part of the average Vietnamese's life. Not only has the government announced plans to build over 30 new power production plants, but ambitious plans have been announced to develop an aerospace industry that will help develop technologies associated with satellite constructions and launching facilities. Those who a generation ago saw Vietnam as only a terribly poor country of peasants would find this quite amazing. More immediately Vietnam has been working with its neighbors who also live along the great Mekong River to transform it into a true vehicle to facilitate trade along its entire route. This is an effort that will require expensive engineering projects to accomplish. But it might one day bring enormous benefits to the entire community of perhaps 250 million people who live along the river's route. It is also an effort that has aroused significant opposition from environmentalists, who fear that the development of so many new dams along the river, needed for electricity production, will negatively impact fishing, an industry the nation also requires.

As is the case elsewhere in Southeast Asia, the level of Chinese investment is becoming increasingly controversial. Over the last year, an enormous controversy developed over the government's decision to award a Chinese company the right to mine bauxite in the Central Highlands. The opposition included a coalition of environ-

mental, academic and religious leaders. They were against the project on both environmental and national security grounds. Even the nation's most prominent activist war hero, General Vo Nguyen Giap, who was nearing his ninety-ninth birthday, was among the opponents. In the end, the impressive coalition managed to get the government to revise its plans somewhat.

Of course, Vietnam, like the rest of the world, has had to struggle with the burden of the slowing global economy in the aftermath of the 2008 American housing meltdown. In Vietnam's case, initial hopes for growth of over 6.5% had been scaled back to something in the range of 5%. Eventually the growth rate for 2009 came in close to expected figures, specifically 5.3%, but not without the government having to devalue the currency by more than 5% to compensate for the weak economy.

Vietnam's Environmental Challenge

The most recent "impacts" section of the International Governmental Panel on Climate Change listed Asia and Africa as being among the regions likely to be most impacted by growing climate instability. Vietnam is no exception to that general trend, and the nation's scientists are increasingly studying the problem. Of particular importance is the fact that much of Vietnam's 3,000 kilometer coastline is a meter or less above sea level. This makes the nation especially vulnerable not only to rising sea levels, but to the more powerful storms that rising air temperatures

are thought to bring. Two regions are particularly vulnerable—southern Vietnam's Mekong Delta and the Red River valley in the north. Both are areas where agricultural activities are at risk.

Along with most nations of the world, Vietnam signed the Kyoto protocol. Within its borders it is planning to confront the growing challenge of finding alternative fuels. But it is also realistically working to prepare for an era when its vulnerability to the loss of coastal land, increased salinization of agricultural land and greater tropical storms will largely be beyond its control. The nation is looking to move to less fossil-based fuels. It is currently in negotiations with various international energy companies to begin the development of nuclear plants to help generate the energy it needs.

One of the more immediate environmental challenges is the condition of the Mekong River, which feeds a good part of the nation. Human activity along the river, from dam building to polluting, is deeply impacting the Mekong. At least one species whose habitat lies upstream from Vietnam itself, the Mekong dolphin, is said be moving toward extinction.

The Future

The end of the U.S. embargo, the entrance into the World Trade Organization, and the arrival of significant foreign investment and personnel into the country are hastening the pace of change. Not all of this will be good. The environment has already suffered significantly, and many individu-

als have not benefited from the initial stages of economic growth and development. Nevertheless, a new middle class is emerging, and people's lives have improved enormously over the last decade despite the more recent economic slowdown. Vietnam is gaining a reputation as an attractive place for investment that can even compare satisfactorily with the long-dominant People's Republic of China.

Of course, the issue of China is never far from the Vietnamese concerns. China's increasing presence, both as an investor within Vietnam and an impediment to its offshore goals, remains a constant issue. Increasingly within the country, tensions are emerging regarding a wide range of Chinese-related matters. These include the potential dangers of extensive Chinese economic power and the Chinese laborers who have entered the country. They are said to have taken advantage of job opportunities many felt should go to the locals. When the government has sponsored such immigration, it itself has become a common focus of popular anger.

For now, the Communist Party still runs the country although Vietnam also has a new constitution and a National Assembly that has been given a greater voice in public affairs. It has even shown a willingness to use it. More significantly, tensions within the ruling elite have begun to highlight the question of how long the party will be able to maintain its domination. For the moment, though, the party has made it continuingly clear that any effort to challenge it will bring a swift response from the leadership. The arrest in early 2009 of one of the nation's leading civil rights lawyers made that abundantly clear.

Despite all the recent challenges, Vietnam's leadership has plenty of reasons to be pleased. Not least among them are recent Pew international polls indicating that the Vietnamese were among the happiest and most optimistic of all the national communities surveyed. The fact that Vietnam appears to have successfully confronted the challenge of avian flu is another reason for optimism. On the other hand, challenges like climate instability caused by global warming are largely beyond the nation's ability to confront significantly. Given that reality, the nation's scientists are trying to develop plans to adapt to such changes if and when they arrive.

For the moment, though, the more immediate need to control more of its own fossil fuels has trumped the larger international goal of lessening global reliance on them. Vietnam has partnered with Saudi Arabia to develop the nation's oil and gas industry. The effort includes not only the development of a Vietnamese-based refinery industry, but efforts to develop its own oil resources.

Fishing boats along the coast

Australia

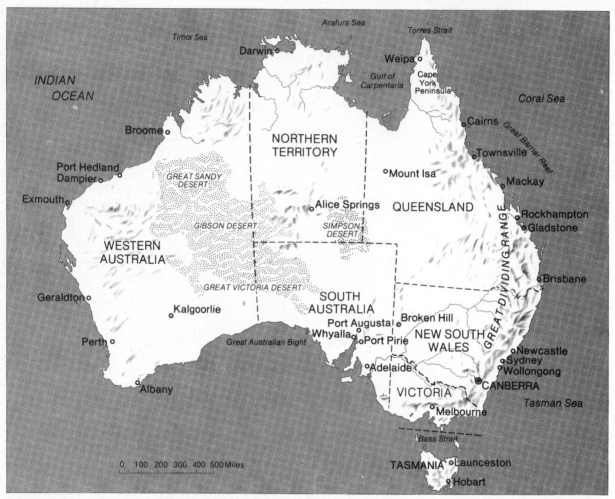

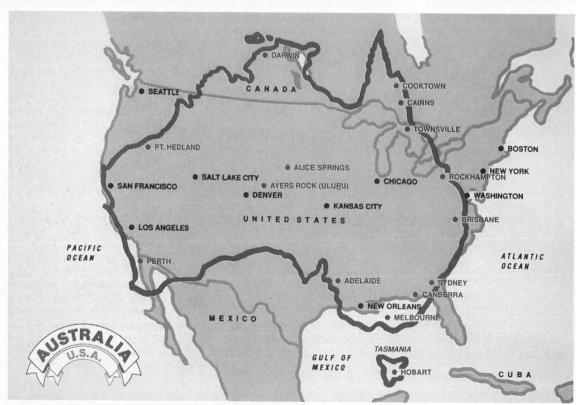

Area: 7,686,850 sq. km.

Population: 21,515,754 (July 2010 est.)

Capital City: Canberra Pop. 334,000 (estimates vary)

Climate: Tropical to subtropical in the north, temperate in the south; the interior is highly arid

Neighboring Countries: Indonesia, Papua New Guinea lie to the north; New Zealand to the southeast

Official Language: English

Ethnic Background: Caucasian 92%, Asian 7%, aboriginal and other 1%

Principal Religion: Christianity, small communities Buddhists and Muslims

Main Exports: (to U.S., China, S. Korea, India, U.K., New Zealand): Coal, gold, wool, meat, iron ore, aluminum ore, transportation equipment

Main Imports: (from U.S. China, Japan, Germany, Singapore, U.K) Automobiles, computers, petroleum and telecommunication and transportation equipment

Currency: Australian Dollar

Former Colonial Status: British dependency (1788–1900).

National Day: January 26 (anniversary of the first British settlement at Sydney in 1788)

Head of State: Her Majesty Queen Elizabeth II, represented by governor general Quentin Bryce (since 5 September 2008)

Head of Government: Prime Minister Julia Eileen Gillard (since 24 June 2010)

National Flag: A blue field with the Union Jack in the upper left quarter, a seven-pointed star in the lower left corner, and five stars at the right side

Per Capita Annual: $38,800 (2009 est. purchasing power parity)

The enormous island called Australia is so immense that it is classified as a continent; at 2.97 million square miles it is almost the size of the continental United

Julia Gillard
Australia's First Female Prime Minister

States. Its 12,000 miles of coastline is relatively smooth with few harbors, but in the northeast the sandy coast is in the lee of the Great Barrier Reef, a 1,200 mile chain of coral reefs and islands extending north almost to Papua New Guinea. With its vivid coral and a profusion of other marine life, the reef is one of the world's natural wonders and a magnet for scientists and tourists.

Australia is one of the oldest of the continents and one of the flattest and driest. Its few mountains have been worn with the passage of time and the highest peak today is Mt. Kosciusko at only 7,300 feet. The largest chain of mountains is found in the east and is called the Great Dividing Range; in the southeast, they are known as the Australian Alps. They divide the narrow crescent of land along the coastline from the vast interior. It is in the fertile eastern coastal area that the great majority of Australians live and their largest cities are located.

To the west are large lowlands and plateaus that begin the vast interior region known to Australians as the Outback. This is the region containing the two-thirds of Australia classified as desert (fewer than 10 inches of rain annually) or semi-desert (fewer than 15 inches). The region's "rivers" often are chains of waterholes and flow only following infrequent rains. Most never reach the sea, but instead widen into areas called lakes which most of the time are actually mud flats encrusted with salt. By drilling to great depths, it is possible in some parts of this region to locate limited amounts of ground water, making possible the raising of livestock. However, large areas are needed to support even small numbers of animals. Some outback cattle ranches in Australia are larger than the smaller European countries. Apart from mining settlements, population is scattered and averages fewer than two persons per square mile.

Australians many years ago introduced the Royal Flying Doctor Service, utilizing two-way radio and light aircraft to bring medical services to those living in this isolated environment. Outback children also use the radio system as students of the School of the Air, working through their daily lessons with a teacher in a studio-classroom in the nearest township hundreds of miles away. Large parts of the region are not inhabited at all. An occasional thunderstorm moistens the thirsty land, and grasses and wildflowers rapidly spring up, flower, wither and die, dropping their seeds to the ground to wait many months before the next rainfall.

Apart from its dry center, Australia has a widely varied climate. It covers more than 30 parallels of latitude and more than a third of the country is in the tropics.

Normally snow falls only on the southeastern ranges during the winter as Australia's position surrounded by sea and the absence of marked physical features give a more temperate climate than other land in corresponding latitudes. Because of the low humidity in many places, the high summer temperatures are not as enervating. The north is subject to tropical cyclones (hurricanes), and the city of Darwin was almost completely destroyed by Cyclone Tracy in 1974.

Isolation from other countries by wide expanses of water has affected Australia in many ways from its plant and animal life to its contemporary culture. Australia has many wildflowers found nowhere else. The main native trees are 500 varieties of eucalyptus and 600 species of acacia (known to Australians as wattle and akin to the mimosa of North America). About half of Australia's native mammals are marsupials—animals that produce their young in embryo form which is a tiny fraction of the adult weight of the parent. The newborn offspring finds its way miraculously to the adult's pouch where it continues its development; the mammary glands on which it suckles are located within the pouch. Only when it is the equivalent of a three-to five-year-old human does it leave the pouch, returning for nourishment as needed until even more mature. Marsupials include members of the kangaroo family, the koala, the wombat and possums. Australia is also the home of another of nature's oddities— the duck-billed platypus, a cross between bird and mammal. It lays eggs, but then nurses its young after they have hatched, yet its body is covered with fur and it lives in a water habitat. Australia's 800 bird species include the ostrich-like emu and many brightly colored parrots.

Australia

This painting by Algernon Talmage shows the unfurling of the British flag at Sydney Cove. Captain Arthur Phillip and his men drink to the health of King George III.

Australian Information Service

History

During the many centuries of development of the Western world, Australia was thinly populated by an estimated 300,000 aborigines, a nomadic, tribal hunting and gathering society. About 160,000 aborigines remain today, but many have embraced a largely Western life style; some later racially intermixed with the European settlers. They now are a disadvantaged and increasingly assertive minority and Australian politics often revolves around questions relating to their treatment both today and in the past.

Ships of the Dutch East India Company touched on the Australian coastline in the early 17th century; the Dutch explorer Tasman circumnavigated the continent in 1642–43. The first real penetration was by the British, led by Captain James Cook, who claimed the eastern portion of the island in 1770 in the name of the British Crown.

The principal interest of Britain in Australia was initially as a penal colony where its criminals could be exiled or held in prison. The first settlers, numbering 270 soldiers and sailors and 760 convicts, landed on the present site of the city of Sydney in 1788 to establish the colony of New South Wales under the royally appointed Governor, Captain Arthur Phillip.

The Crown later permitted non-convict settlers to emigrate from the British Isles to Australia. Most of them became interested in raising sheep for which the island was ideally suited. A close social organization quickly emerged among these free settlers; they dominated the New South Wales Corps, which was a special military police force. They became very influential and struggled with a succession of royal governors, sometimes gaining the right to use the services of convict labor at a low wage, and to expand their sheep-raising activities. They also sought control over internal and external trade.

The notorious Captain Bligh, the former commander of HMS Bounty, struggled with the New South Wales Corps when he was governor in 1805 and lost. The next governor, Macquarie, was much more respected and successful. He curbed the power of the police force, set limits on land grants and organized and permitted rapid economic development. No more convicts were sent to Australia after 1868.

The discovery of gold in 1851 gave a great boost to the Australian economy and was accompanied by disorders in the mining camps, similar to those in the American West during the same period. In the succeeding decades, additional immigration of free settlers, exploration of the eastern and later the western parts of the continent, and general economic development took place at a steadily accelerating rate.

Six British crown colonies were successfully established in Australia from 1788 through the first half of the 19th century. All had been granted self-governing independence by the end of that century. In 1901, the colonies became the six States of an Australian Federation under the title Commonwealth of Australia. This status continues today.

Although an independent, self-governing nation, Australia, along with other countries of the British Commonwealth, recognizes the British sovereign as the head of state, symbolizing historical links with Britain. The Queen is represented in Australia by a governor-general. Australia's chief executive is a prime minister elected by members of the majority party in the federal parliament. The parliament consists of a Senate and a House of Representatives functioning under a written constitution that borrows from both British and

American experience. There is no elected president. Cabinet officers must also be members of parliament.

Australia sent volunteer units that fought bravely on the Allied side in the Middle East and on the Western Front during World War I. The demands of the British war effort benefited the Australian economy. During the period between the two World Wars, it continued to experience growth, as well as the emergence of a powerful labor movement pressing for benefits for workers. It was gripped by the worldwide depression, with a sharp drop in trade in 1931 and the following years.

Prior to World War II, the foreign policy of Australia was one of comparative isolation from the community of nations. In spite of this, Australia responded to the outbreak of World War II by coming to the aid of the British in the European War in 1939, and after 1941 joined the Allied war effort in the Pacific. For Australia, the war was made much more complicated and dangerous because of the closeness of Japan.

Japanese troops quickly conquered most of Southeast Asia by mid-1942. Australia became the base for the headquarters of General Douglas MacArthur after the fall of the Philippines. The main concern of the Australians was that they also might be invaded next. Darwin, the northern seaport, suffered heavy Japanese bombing raids. However, Allied victories in the Pacific and fighting by Australian troops in New Guinea prevented a Japanese invasion.

The Labour Party, led by Prime Minister John Curtin, came to power in late 1941 and was responsible for major changes in Australian international thinking during World War II. After such close cooperation with the United States in achieving ultimate victory, Australian strategic thinking turned towards the United States after the war.

The end of World War II brought another period of growth and prosperity. Substantial immigration, encouraged by the government, resulted in a larger population, primarily Caucasian. Until 1966 Australian immigration policies discriminated against non-Europeans, and in earlier years this had been known as the "white Australia" policy. Since 1966, successive governments have removed discriminatory restrictions. However, the overall rate of immigration was reduced during the 1970s though it has picked up dramatically in recent decades. Today, the influx of newcomers has brought marked changes in Australian society, lifestyle and culture.

The country was governed by a coalition of the Liberal Party and the Country Party between 1949 and 1972, for 17 years under its leader, the colorful Sir Robert Menzies, then Harold Holt, John Gorton and William McMahan. All maintained steady support for U.S. policies and efforts in Southeast Asia. Australian troops took part in the war in Korea, the campaign against communist terrorists in Malaya (1948–1960) and the Vietnam War.

Elections in 1972 returned the Labour Party to power. The new Prime Minister, E. Gough Whitlam, a man of strong personality and intellect, recognized the People's Republic of China and established diplomatic relations with North Vietnam, North Korea and East Germany. He also withdrew the remaining Australian troops from South Vietnam and moved to establish closer economic relations with Japan. He then abolished the draft, lowered the defense budget, began fairer treatment of the Aborigines and introduced ambitious domestic social programs.

The world oil crisis of the early seventies affected Australia as it did other communities. Both inflation and unemployment went up. Faced with these problems, Whitlam called an election in April 1974 that reduced his majority in the House of Representatives but did enable him to continue in office.

By late 1975, the continuously poor state of the economy and controversy over various Labour Party programs prompted the Liberal and National Country parties (the latter previously known as the Country Party) opposition to press for new elections. When Whitlam refused, the opposition took the unprecedented action of using its Senate majority to block the government's budget appropriation bills, leaving it without authority to pay its creditors, including federal employees and recipients of social security and other benefits. As the government's reserves of money ran out, the constitutional crisis intensified. It is at this point that one of the more peculiar features of Australia's government became apparent.

The Governor-General, the representative of the British Crown, stepped in, dismissed the sitting Prime Minister and asked J. Malcolm Fraser to form a new Liberal government. The party, in a coalition with the National Party, won the next election. Thus, a representative of a foreign nation was able substantially to interfere in Australia's domestic political process and no doubt added to the number of Australians who were increasingly dissatisfied with their ongoing relationship with the British Crown.

Eventually the question of Australia's relationship with Britain was put before the public in a referendum that raised the question of replacing the Governor-General, the representative of Great Britain's monarch, with a president chosen by the Australian parliament. It was a struggle that revolved both around questions of Australia's continuing ties to Great Britain and whether a president chosen by the parliament rather than at large by the population was a good idea. In the end, the referendum went down to defeat when only 45% of the population voted to support it while 55% opposed the idea.

A very different sort of controversy arose in 2003 when a series of sexual misconduct charges, personal and some associated with his earlier responsibilities as an Anglican Archbishop, began swirling around Peter Hollingworth, the then governor-general. With his public support collapsing, he became only the second governor-general in Australian history to resign.

Government

Australia is a parliamentary democracy whose political institutions and practices follow the Western democratic model, reflecting both the British and American experience. The Australian federation has a three-tier system of government: the na-

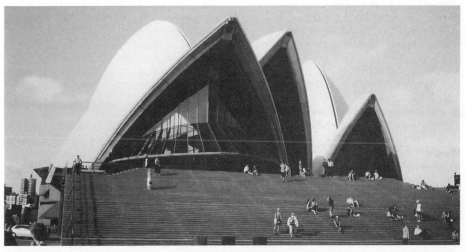

Sydney Opera House

Australia

Team march at lifeguard competition, Manley Beach, Sydney

tional government consists of Parliament (House of Representatives with 150 seats and the Senate with 76 seats) and the Government. The party or parties with a majority in the lower house constitute the government, controlling all ministries; six state governments, the Capital Territory and Northern Territory (similar to states); and some 900 local governmental bodies at the city, town, municipal and shire level. Senators in the Federal Parliament serve six-year terms (senators for the two territories serve three-year terms), and representatives serve for three years.

Australia has a written constitution that came into force on January 1, 1901, when the colonies federated to form the Commonwealth of Australia. The constitution can be amended if a majority of voters in a majority of states plus an overall majority approve the change. Proposed changes must also be passed by an absolute majority in both houses of parliament. If an amendment is passed twice by one house but fails in the other, the governor general may submit the amendment to the electorate.

Australia pioneered the secret ballot in parliamentary elections and has used the system since 1879. Voting is compulsory at the national level. The franchise extends to everyone over 18 years of age except criminals and the mentally incompetent. The Australian system of law resembles the British system from which it was taken. Australian law places great importance on the rights of the individual. The law provides for habeas corpus (which prevents arbitrary arrest or imprisonment without a court hearing), bail, trial by judge and jury, the presumption of innocence until proven guilty, and prevention from double jeopardy.

The High Court resembles the American Supreme Court and deals with federal and state matters. It has original jurisdiction in important areas, including inter-

pretation of the Constitution, determination of legal disputes between the federal government and state governments, suits between state governments, and suits between citizens of different states. The Court has a chief justice and six other justices. The Federal Court is a specialized court dealing with matters such as copyrights, industrial law, trade practices, bankruptcy, and administrative law, appeals from territory supreme courts and tribunals administering federal laws. The other specialized court is the Family Court which deals with divorce, custody of children, and associated matrimonial property disputes.

All states and territories have supreme courts and magistrates' courts, and several have intermediate district or county courts that deal mainly with state laws, federal criminal offenses and federal income tax. The supreme courts have the same role at the state level as the High Court does federally. Magistrates' courts deal summarily with most ordinary offenses and preliminary hearings to determine whether sufficient grounds exist in more serious offenses to be tried before a judge and jury. The capital territory and external territories of Norfolk Island, Christmas Island and the Cocos islands have court systems similar in general to the states. Australia has independent federal, state and territory police.

Contemporary Political Issues

Today the major political parties are the Australian Labour Party (ALP), the Australian Democrats (AD) and the conservative Liberal Party. The ALP controlled the government from the early 1980s through the mid-1990s. A new party, the One Nation Party, appeared on the scene in 1997 and at times gathered significant support based on its strong anti-immigration policy. Especially dramatic in recent years

was the first successful election of a representative of the Australian Green Party to the federal parliament.

For most of the last decade or so, the government was directed by John Howard of the conservatives who won a fourth term in November 2004. This resurgence of the conservative Liberal Party began in the middle of the last decade. After John Howard was selected as the new party leader in 1996, the conservative Liberal-National coalition won a landslide victory in national elections which gave the new government a 40-seat margin in the lower house of Parliament. Two years later Howard called for elections again with a platform advocating tax code changes and was reelected.

The new coalition government, which was formed after the October 1998 election, included both Howard's Liberal Party and the National Party. Together, the two parties won 49% of the vote. In 2001 Howard's party won an unprecedented third term in office. Nevertheless, the conservative trend of those years had gone beyond the policies advocated by Howard himself.

In 1996, a newly elected political independent, a former operator of a fish and chips shop named Pauline Hansen, rose to give her maiden speech in parliament. Once standing, she proceeded to attack the Australian Asian and Aboriginal community with considerable vehemence. Hansen claimed that Asian immigration was swamping Australia. Her attacks on Australia's non-white community were nothing new. Indeed, for much of Australian history a largely "whites only" policy had been the norm. However, this was in late 1996, and after years of official attempts by the government and business community to improve their relationship with Asia. The storm of controversy she began has not yet let up. Indeed, early political polls showed that 10% of the population supported her racist comments and many showed support for her new political movement, the One Nation party, which she launched during the spring of 1997.

Although he was pushed to do so for months, not until March 1997 did the conservative prime minister, John Howard, launch an official effort to discredit the racism of Hansen's rhetoric. Still, over time, the momentum of her movement seemed to slow down. By late 1999, Hansen had lost her parliamentary seat, and considerable internal dissension had broken out within her One Nation Party. For a time she even found herself in jail due to violations associated with the original registration of her party.

Nevertheless, the antipathy toward foreigners, especially non-whites that Hansen had tapped into had attracted 8% of the vote in the national elections of October 1998 and played an important role, not so much in the Hansen's fortunes but those of the conservative Liberal party. That reality was particularly apparent during the summer and fall of 2001 when a weakening Liberal Government found itself faced with the imminent arrival of a ship carrying over four hundred refugees from Iran, Iraq and Afghanistan.

Taking a strong stand against allowing the refugees to land in Australia Howard's popularity rose considerably and allowed him to win an election in November for a third term as prime minister. Eventually the Liberal government funded neighboring governments to establish temporary reception centers. Eventually some Iraqis were able to gain refugees status in Australia but those from Afghanistan were less successful. Over all, the anti-asylum policy has continued to be a mainstay of Liberal politics, and former Prime Minister Howard made it clear that refugee seekers should have no hope to establish themselves on the Australian mainland. Rather, he made sure that any who tried were arrested and sent to detention centers, such as that on Christmas Island.

As Australia neared the fall of the 2004 electoral season, the Liberal Party, under John Howard's leadership, remained relatively popular. The opposition Labour Party also seemed to be growing stronger under the direction of their new leader Mark Latham, who had taken a strong stand against Prime Minister Howard's decision to send troops to serve in the American occupation of Iraq. Nevertheless, relatively few Australians had actually taken part in the unpopular campaigns in Iraq, and the numbers who had done so had already been significantly re-

duced, making the issue not something that would in the end fundamentally alter the election.

When the votes were actually cast, domestic economic issues were clearly uppermost in the voter's minds. Prime Minister Howard's Liberal Party managed to win an unprecedented fourth term in office and significantly strengthen his party's ability to pass favored legislation. By the time the new seats were allocated, Howard's party controlled both of the legislative chambers. This was a position of influence no prime minister had had in more than twenty-five years.

By 2007, though, the political mood in Australia had changed dramatically. Despite the fact that the economy had continued to do well under the Liberal's, the Labor party, under the leadership of the former diplomat Kevin Rudd, not only won a significant victory in the parliamentary elections, but Mr. Howard lost his own seat.

Many issues featured in Howard's defeat, not least simply fatigue over Howard's long tenure in office; he had become the second-longest serving leader in Australian history. Certainly, the opposition to the government's long-standing commitment to the American policy in Iraq had played a part. However, that had been an issue in 2004 as well. Nevertheless, it had apparently not had a significant impact.

This time, though, there was an additional issue. Rudd proclaimed on the eve of the historic vote that dealing with the challenge of climate change was his number-one priority and that if elected he would lead Australia's delegation to the upcoming international climate change conference in Bali. Certainly, his attitude was in clear contrast to the Liberal Party's John Howard, who had long followed a policy of dismissing the issue of global warming. He had positioned Australia as the only developed country that followed the American lead in rejecting the Kyoto Treaty on climate change. The news in Australia had in recent years been particularly dominated by problems associated with draught. Even Howard had publicly asked people to pray for rain. Thus, the question of climate change denial had become an increasingly untenable political position.

However, Rudd's tenure in office turned out to be dramatically less successful than that of his conservative rival John Howard. Originally coming into power with very strong polling numbers, Rudd soon found himself unable to carry out some of his most important legislative priorities, such as climate-change legislation, while his popularity plunged. By the spring of 2010, after two failed efforts to pass climate legislation, he had given up. He had alienated many in his own party for what were described as poor leadership skills.

Eventually in late June 2010 in a surprisingly quick process, Rudd's premiership seemed to collapse almost overnight. His party replaced him with Julia Gillard, who became Australia's first female prime minister. Gillard herself had been a close ally of Rudd and is strongly associated with his policies. Nevertheless, her supporters hope she will prove more successful in implementing the party's legislative agenda and better represent the party in the upcoming elections.

Society and Culture

In the years after Europeans first began settling in Australia, it quickly became a society largely dominated by Westerners whose culture resembled that of North America and England. The original aboriginal peoples, like Native Americans, increasingly lost their land to the aggressive Westerners and immigration laws strongly discriminated against Asians. This "whites only" attitude was a feature of Australian society until fairly recently. Within those parameters, Australians built a society similar to many other Western societies.

Education is free and compulsory through the secondary school level. There are no tuition fees at the 18 government-funded universities and at many colleges offering diplomas, degrees and postgraduate studies.

Because of the climate, outdoor sports such as swimming, surfing, football and tennis are very popular. Horseracing is widely enjoyed, and betting on the horses is a consuming topic of interest among many.

Though it has vast spaces and relatively few people, Australia is highly urbanized,

The Rt. Hon. John Howard
Former Prime Minister

Aboriginal Art, "Going for Honey Ants"

Australia

perhaps because most population growth and development has taken place only over the past 75 years. More than 80% of the population lives in urban centers and more than 60% are concentrated in five major state capitals.

Two cities dominate urban life. Sydney faces the southeast coast and has a population of more than 4.5 million; Melbourne (4 million) faces the southern Bass Strait. All of the cultural entertainment and events common to Europe and America are abundant in both. Perth, with a population of around a million and a half and lying on the southwestern coast, is caressed by a gentle climate similar to that found in the Mediterranean and Caribbean resorts of the Western world.

Australia's Federal Capital is Canberra, the basic plan for which was conceived by Chicago architect Walter Burley Griffin shortly before World War I. Today, it is a garden city with over 8 million trees planted in the last half century—and it occupies the site of a former sheep station (ranch) in the foothills of the Australian Alps.

As mentioned above the world of white Australia has usually not been shared equally with that of the aboriginal community whose lot is decidedly less attractive. Aboriginal Australians can expect to live twenty years less than whites and a quarter of them are unemployed.

Of late, new controversies have entered the public arena and aroused even more tensions between the two communities. On one hand there is growing sentiment against the social welfare programs the government supplies for the aboriginal community but on the other, great anxiety about a number of recent court decisions that have authorized greater aboriginal rights to millions of acres of land now being used by Australian ranchers.

To some aboriginal leaders, these new rights should allow their people to wean themselves from government welfare programs, something whites should theoretically welcome. But since aboriginal economic empowerment is, in the case of the land, tied to competing white claims, the problems are not likely to be resolved soon.

More recently as well, Australia has been facing up to other realities of their historical treatment of Aborigines. Over the last few years, a greater sensitivity has developed about aboriginal history. This growing consciousness had taken the form of rewriting Australian history to include aboriginal perspectives and heroes as well as recognizing culturally "genocidal" policies like those that had seen generations of lighter-skinned Aborigines taken from their families to be raised in the white world.

During the run-up to the successful Olympics of 2000, there was speculation that the Aborigines might demonstrate during the games. But nothing very dramatic actually happened. More recently, there has been considerable discussion within Australia over issuing a formal apology for white Australia's historic treatment of them. But, the movement toward greater sensitivity has hardly made the tensions between the majority white community and Australia's Aboriginal community a thing of the past.

In February 2004, Sydney experienced the worst outbreak of civil unrest in over a decade after the death of a young aboriginal cyclist was blamed on the police. The subsequent rioting, which lasted over nine hours, left scores of police and civilians injured and was an obvious sign of the importance of making progress on one of the most long-standing issues within Australian society.

Once in power Kevin Rudd moved quickly to address the long simmering tensions with the Aboriginal community. In February 2008, the new prime minister officially apologized to Australian's indigenous community for their treatment at the hands of Australia's European settlers. On a more practical level, Rudd committed his government to lessening the 17-year gap in life expectancy between Aboriginal and non-Aboriginal Australians and bringing more early childhood education to their communities.

Relations between the larger majority community and the aboriginal peoples are not the only source of ethnic tensions that have complicated Australian life in recent years. During late 2005, an outbreak of attacks by white gangs against Middle Eastern-looking men shocked locals and gained Australia a considerable amount of unwanted international attention. Eventually Prime Minister Howard undertook a series of efforts to try to lessen the tensions. His primary goal was to bring Australia's Muslim community more into the mainstream of national life while rooting out extremists.

Foreign Relations

As is often the case, Australian foreign relations have revolved around its relationships with its geographic neighbors, the Asian states of the region and the Western countries whose cultures are similar to those of Australia. Historically, Australia tended to orient itself toward the Western communities of North America and Europe but in recent years the emphasis has been more on its regional relationships. That movement was begun by the former Australian Labour Party governments.

Race riots in Australia

In early 1996, however, there were indications that the new more conservative government intended to orient the country's foreign affairs position once again to emphasize Australia's relationships with the West. There were even some tensions with China during Howard's early months in office especially when he seemed to associate himself with those Americans who were talking of "containing" China.

Indeed for a time the new government seemed to be backing away from integrating Australia more closely into Asia but that change never developed into anything significant. By 1997, Howard had led an influential group to Beijing and then later received the soon to be Chinese Prime Minister Zhu Rongji as his guest. More recently, China's then President Jiang himself visited Australia.

Under the then new prime minister, Australia continued its growing involvement in East Asia. Kevin Rudd is a professionally trained diplomat with long experience in China and speaks Mandarin Chinese well. However, that did not mean a completely smooth relationship. Last year, as Tibet's capital Lhasa erupted in riots against the Chinese, Australia and the United States no doubt irritated Beijing by encouraging it to open a dialogue with the Dalai Lama.

However, encouraging a dialogue with the Dalai Lama was hardly Australia's only sin in Beijing's eyes. Especially irritating was the government's unwillingness, despite the Chinese government's request, to refuse entry to Rebiya Kadeer, an ethnic Uighur whom the Chinese accuse of instigating the recent unrest. Once praised by Chinese authorities as a very successful example of Uighur business success, Kadeer eventually earned Beijing's ire by campaigning for the rights of her Uighur compatriots, a campaign that earned her first imprisonment and eventual exile. The fact that Rudd's government had been willing to grant her a visa eventually provoked cancelation of the visit by none other than the Chinese Vice Minister He Yafei.

Australia has also become more involved with the nations of Southeast Asia and especially their regional organization, ASEAN which for the first time invited representatives from Canberra to their meeting in Laos last year. Australia has also been working with its Asian neighbors and the U.S. to create an Asia-Pacific Climate-control regime. But Australia's efforts to integrate itself more deeply within ASEAN have not always been appreciated, a sentiment Malaysia's Prime Minister Abdullah Badawi recently vocalized.

It was not merely the early conservative government's policies that caused occasional strains with Asia. The overt racism of the One Nation party obviously also

Kevin Rudd
Former Prime Minister of Australia

caused problems. Certainly, such developments have reinforced those in the Asian community who have not welcomed Australia's recent attempts to associate itself more closely with Asia. Nevertheless, concerns about possibly anti-Asian sentiments have certainly not deterred many Asians from visiting. Most recently the number of tourists from mainland China has risen significantly. Australia's economic ties to the People's Republic have grown considerably in recent years.

But it was relations with Indonesia that especially complicated Australia's international position recently. Reversing themselves after a generation of supporting Indonesia's control over East Timor, the Australians began supporting East Timorese independence aspirations. Eventually, they ended up leading the United Nations international intervention force, which included 5,000 Australians, into East Timor in the late summer of 1999. Realistically the government had little choice.

Although a generation of Australia's leaders had understandably believed that Canberra's relationship with the entire country of Indonesia was more important than the East Timorese plight, the wave of violence that occurred after Jakarta agreed to the referendum in East Timor aroused the ire and sympathy of the Australian population. Within Indonesia, there was an outpouring of popular Indonesian anger over the loss of East Timor that was often directed against the Australians.

The level of tensions subsided over time and in recent years the relationship has been improving. In June of 2001 Indo-

nesia's president, Abdurrahman Wahid visited Australia, the first such visit by leader from Jakarta in a generation. Later, when Wahid's problems within his own country forced him from office Australia's Howard was among the first foreign leaders to visit the new President, Megawati Sukarnoputri. But that did not stop an outpouring of anger against Indonesian officials during the spring of 2005 when a young Australian women was imprisoned in Indonesia on drug charges that most Australians thought were false.

Understandably, developments within in Indonesia are likely to remain especially important to Australia. Instability within a neighbor as large and as close to Australia as Indonesia is, is something Canberra has been concerned about for a long time. During the fall of 2002, Australians found out just how deadly Indonesia frustration and anger against the West and in particular, Australia could be. For that was the year that, at a popular Bali nightclub, a horrific bombing set off by Islamic terrorists with ties to the infamous Al Qaeda killed almost two hundred people, around a hundred of them from Australia. It was the first time that the potentials of terrorism had been so dramatically brought home to most Australians. Australia had, of course, long supported the American "war on terrorism" initiated after the September 11, 2001, assaults on New York and Washington. However, its government under John Howard also made the decision to align his nation closely with the more controversial American policy of overthrowing the government of Saddam Hussein in Iraq.

In fact, Australia went considerably beyond mere support and sent around 2,000 troops to take part in the fighting. This was a move that not only aroused unprecedented criticism within Australia but a highly publicized resignation by a senior intelligence analyst and a very public rebuke against the prime minister by the Australian Senate.

Nevertheless, the prime minister has remained adamant in his support of American President George W. Bush's Iraq policy. Although the number of Australian troops dropped from the initial 2,000 employed during the initial occupation campaign to only 850, the Australian government, despite growing public opposition to the deployment, continued to insist that their troops would remain in Iraq until the country was deemed sufficiently stabilized for the Australian contingent to be withdrawn. Despite Australia's long-term ties to the United States, its government has also been committed to balance that relationship with its growing relationship with the People's Republic of China.

As has been the case around the world, Australia's role in Iraq has become a cen-

Australia

tral feature within the nation's internal political environment. Howard's opponent in the national elections of late 2004, then Labour Party Leader Mark Latham, came out very publicly not only against Australia's role in the Iraq occupation, but against the entire American effort there as well. Latham was, of course, unsuccessful. But Labour won the next election, and Kevin Rudd, the new prime minister who had campaigned on a promise to withdraw the country's forces in Iraq, acted. By June of 2008, the last of the Australian troops were home.

Perhaps one of the most obvious changes in Australia's foreign policy since the Labour Party's arrival to power has been Australia's relationship with many of its South Pacific Islands neighbors. Given the new government's recognition of the challenges climate change is creating for these very low lying island communities, it has been more supportive of their efforts to press the United Nations to take the matter more seriously.

Economy

Australia's economy has changed much in the last fifty years from one that relied heavily on primary production to a mature, diverse one with nearly two-thirds of production in the service sector. World War II and post-war immigration spurred rapid expansion of secondary industry, diversifi- cation and overall economic growth. Large investments were made in mining and energy projects. Although the agricultural and mining sectors account for a small part of the country's production, they make a large percentage of total exports. Australia leads the world in wool production and is a major supplier of wheat, meat and sugar. Australia is also a leading exporter of coal and a major supplier of coal, iron ore, gold, bauxite, and alumina.

The export base was diversified in the 1980s, with the fastest growth in manufactured products and in services. Tourism has also been strong. Overall Australia entered the new century with a relatively strong economy. And unlike some of its neighbors, it was not merely recovering from the regional economic downturn of previous years. Australia was not significantly affected by the Asian economic crisis that enveloped so many of its neighbors. Even at the height of the crisis in 1998 Australia kept its economy in the black with its GNP registering a respectable 3% growth rate.

Like much of the world, Australia's economy experienced the same global slowdown that much of the world encountered. Several major firms went under, most notably Ansett, Australia's second largest airline. There have been more recent concerns about a slowing of the oil production from some of the nation's older fields that have spurred recent ef-

Koala munching on his favorite food, eucalyptus leaves.

forts to develop new supply areas. Doing so is important because Australia is currently producing about 80% of its own petroleum needs and has developed a growing natural gas export industry. Still, those figures were not enough to insulate Australia against rising costs as elevated prices for oil worked its way through the Australian economy.

The government has also strengthened its formal economic ties with other nations. Free-trade agreements have been signed with Thailand, and the prime minister and ex-President George W. Bush signed their own free trade pact. Overall growth rates have been relatively healthy. The year 2007 came in with a rate around 4% while 2008 was only a bit over 2.3%.

Of course, that was before the full impact of the most recent global economic slump had hit. By the time 2009 expired, the nation's growth rate, while not in the negative numbers, had plummeted to around 1% annual growth rate. The fact that the numbers had remained out of the red was apparently only because of the nation's trade with China, which had managed to pull itself back from the brink much faster than many of the world's industrial nations had. Still there was plenty to feel good about. Almost alone among the developed world, Australia had kept up its economic growth, and 2010 looked likely to be a relatively strong year as well.

Tom Roberts, *The Golden Fleece*, 1894

Australia's Environmental Challenge

Like the United States, Australia signed but did not initially ratify the Kyoto Climate Change Treaty of 1997. In some ways, that was rather curious as its negotiators had worked out a particularly advantageous position for Australia within the treaty. Nevertheless, along with the United States, Australia eventually became a prominent hold-out against the protocol. Over the last few year or so, though, Australia's position on climate change has begun to change. Former American Vice President Al Gore has been running training sessions in Australia to create a cadre of local climate change educators.

Meanwhile the population has become more sensitized to environmental concerns. The core issue is that Australia has been experiencing a long-term drought in the very areas where most of the population lives. Moreover, reports have gained a lot of attention that the Great Barrier Reef, one of Australia's most famous natural coral sites, is starting to die because of coral bleaching. This is a phenomenon associated with warming waters.

Overall, the concern about global warming was particularly obvious in March 2007 when many of the lights in Sidney were switched off to help raise consciousness about the challenge of global warming. Nevertheless, unlike the Conservative party politicians in Britain, the former Australian conservative Prime minister, John Howard, was unwilling to commit the nation to taking on the transition to a less carbon-emitting society.

Still the government began to encourage the replacement of the older incandescent bulbs for more modern, energy-efficient ones. But those tentative steps were clearly not enough for the Australian population. In what may have been the first election to turn primarily on the issue of climate change, Howard's Liberal government went down in a flaming defeat in November 2007 to a resurgent Labor Party leader, Kevin Rudd, who vowed to make climate change his highest priority. He promised to take Australia into the emerging international consensus symbolized by the conferences at Kyoto and Bali.

However, As the American President Obama has himself learned, promising to make progress on moving toward a more green economy and actually passing the legislature necessary to encourage that evolution are quite different things. Rudd's efforts were, as we have seen, stalled by significant opposition from the nation's conservatives, who during their own governing years had largely refused even to recognize the problem. Rather in August and then again in December Rudd failed to win a majority on legislation to introduce carbon permits that were expected to help spur movement toward a more green energy infrastructure.

But even as Australia was making progress in recognizing the importance of confronting climate change, and fighting over the legislative tools required actually to do so, its own particularly great vulnerability became especially obvious. It had long been warned by organizations like the Intergovernmental Panel on Climate Change that it was especially vulnerable to fires caused by its decade-long drought. Those predictions became painfully true in early February 2009 when horrendous fires—the worst in Australian history—broke out in areas near South Australia, Victoria and New South Wales. The fires claimed over 180 lives and destroyed more than a thousand square miles of territory.

Because of global warming, Australia may soon find itself in a particularly unusual situation. Not only is the nation itself especially vulnerable to the sort of drought contemporary climate change makes more likely. But it has the added problem of dealing with its island neighbors, who face not a lack of water but literally too much of it. The reason, of course, is because so many of Australia's Pacific island neighbors inhabit low-lying atoll islands that are deeply at risk from rising sea waters.

The Future

Australia faces no immediate external threats. Its growing involvement with the countries of Asia, particularly the ASEAN states of Southeast Asia, can only help to improve its regional position. But it will require a sophisticated handling of the recent resurgence of some white Australian racist sentiments. Of course, as the influence and power of China grow, that relationship will continue to be complicated given Australia and China's often divergent world views even as their economic relations grow tighter.

Economically the situation seems bright as well. Unlike the United States and so many of its European allies, Australia's economy has been doing well and is making up for the lost momentum of 2009 quite well.

The long-term situation is significantly more complicated. The nation is among the most vulnerable of the developed world to the ravages of climate change. The horrific fires that engulfed the nation in 2009 were a product of years of increasing drought that parched the land. Beyond Australia's shores, its regional neighbors, especially those of the South Pacific islands from Tuvalu to Kirabati, are seeing their own homes even more threatened by rising waters. Under the circumstances, Australia's people will be faced even more often than in the past with the challenge posed by increasing numbers of potential refugees. However, in the future such refugees are as likely to be consequence of climate change as the geopolitical struggles that had previously brought them to the Australia's shores.

New Zealand

Aukland

Area: 103,000 sq. mi. (268,276 sq. km., the land surface somewhat smaller than Colorado)

Population: 4,252,277 (July 2010 est.)

Capital City: Wellington (larger region) 445,406 (2002 estimate)

Climate: Temperate, with ample rainfall; subtropical conditions at the northern tip of the North Island, with colder temperatures in the South Island.

Neighboring Countries: Australia, about 1,200 miles to the northwest.

Official Language: English and Maori

Ethnic Background: European 69.8%, Maori 7.9%, Asian 5.7%, Pacific islander 4.4%, other 0.5%, mixed 7.8%, unspecified 3.8% (2001 census)

Principal Religion: Protestant Christianity (82%)

Main Exports (to Australia, China, U.K., Japan, U.S.): Meat and dairy products, fish, wool, wood products, machinery

Main Imports (Australia, China, Germany, Japan, U.K. U.S.): Petroleum, cars, trucks, iron, steel, plastics, textiles, vehicles, aircraft

Currency: New Zealand Dollar

Former Colonial Status: British Colony (1839–1907)

National Day: February 6 is Waitangi Day, anniversary of the signing of the Treaty of Waitangi in 1840 between the British and the Maoris.

Chief of State: Her Majesty Queen Elizabeth II, represented by Governor General, Anand Satyanand (since 2006)

Head of Government: John Key, Prime Minister (since 19 November 2008)

National Flag: A purple field with the Union Jack in the upper left corner and four 5-pointed stars in the right half of the field

Per Capita GDP Income: $27,300 (2009 est. purchasing power parity)

The remote islands of New Zealand are about 1,200 miles from their nearest neighbor, Australia. Prior to the advent of air transportation New Zealand was one of the world's most isolated nations. The North Island is the more habitable of the two, and, though smaller than the South Island, it has more than half the country's population.

In the North Island there are volcanic and thermal areas dominated by three volcanic peaks, Ruapehu, Ngauruhoe and Tongariro. All of them are active and given to occasional eruptions of steam and ash. In the central plateau area there is activity caused by the thermal pressure from deep within the earth in the form of geysers, hot springs, steam vents and foul-smelling deposits of sulfur. The average annual rainfall for the whole country is about 60 inches, which allows for quick growth of rich vegetation to feed the millions of sheep that abound in New Zealand.

The South Island is much more rugged and contains the Southern Alps that equal their European namesake in beauty and wildness. In this mountainous region, the climate can sometimes be sub-Arctic. In contrast to the abundant growth of the North Island, the grasses of the South Island are more suited to rearing Merino sheep, which have a fine coat to protect them from the chilly air. Most of the sheep of the North Island are crossbreeds, designed to produce both meat and wool. It is interesting for those who live in the Northern hemisphere that the reversal of warm and cold zones and of summer and winter in the Southern Hemisphere make northern New Zealand the warmer, more subtropical area while the southern region is considerably colder.

History

Though it is known that the Maori, the original peoples of New Zealand, initially came from Eastern Polynesia, the dating of this event varies widely. Their arrival has been dated from as early as the 3rd century of the common era to as late as the 13th. An extraordinary people, they were the heirs of one of the most impressive seagoing communities the world has ever seen. Even today the descendants of those great sea voyagers live throughout much of the Pacific.

Establishing themselves in their new home must have been especially demanding given that their society had originated in the warmer climates to the north. Upon arrival the most important food was the flightless birds, the moa, which they initially found in large numbers. Over time these animals were apparently hunted to extinction. Other foodstuffs, from marine life to small-scale farming, also contributed to the diet of these early peoples.

The Maori were not a united community. Rather, they were divided along both tribal lines and the different locations of their settlements. Once the Europeans arrived in the 17th century, access to advanced Western weapons became available thus making intra-tribal warfare even more deadly. Other factors also lowered the local population. As was common throughout the colonized world, the Maori lacked the antibodies necessary to resist Western diseases which depleted their numbers.

The first well documented European visit is that of Abel Janszoon Tasman, a Dutch sailor who apparently visited the islands around 1642. An account still remains of the first encounter that saw several Maori row out to the Dutch ship attempting to communicate. Unfortunately, that effort turned ugly, and only a short time later, Tasman lost three of his sailors

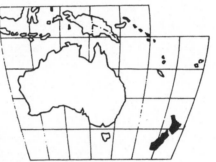

in a clash with Maori from the southern Island. Discouraged by that first encounter, the Dutch sailed away leaving only their naming of the place, initially Nieuw Zeeland, as a contribution.

More than a century after Tasman left, the famous Captain James Cook arrived for an extended visit. Cook's stay included charting of the islands and a much more sophisticated contact with the Maori, whom Cook described as quite intelligent in his well known work, *A Voyage Towards the South Pole and Round the World* (1777). Unfortunately for the Maori, Cook also wrote of the suitability of the islands for colonization. Over the next decades visits by various Europeans became common.

The growth of the whaling industry in the early 19th century also affected the islands. It attracted increasing European interest as whalers, especially those from Australia, created bases in New Zealand. The Maori were also drawn into the whaling economy as they supplied the Europeans with provisions and received rum and weapons from the outsiders. One Maori leader not only traveled to Australia and England, but bought weapons abroad which he later used to attack rival Maori tribes. Predictably, these bloody struggles disturbed local life enough to make settlement easier for the arriving Europeans.

Along with whalers and escaped convicts, religion also came to New Zealand via Australia. Missionaries settled in 1814 and quickly began the task of converting the Maoris to Christianity. Despite the Maori reputation for aggressiveness and cannibalism, some early missionaries were convinced that the Maori would be good candidates for conversion. Several branches of Western Christianity were active among Maori with denominations ranging from Anglicans to Catholics and Methodists. Eventually most Maori came to embrace some form of Christianity.

Over time, the islands became increasingly integrated with other British holdings in the South Pacific. Initially considered part of their Australian holdings they soon became a separate crown colony. In 1840, with the signing of the Treaty of Waitangi, Britain assumed direct control and according to the terms of the treaty was obligated not only to protect the Maori but ensure their land holdings. Not surprisingly, those promises were not upheld and by mid-century, the English found themselves often in open warfare with the Maori community. As was the case elsewhere, the indigenous community was not able to successfully resist the powerful Europeans and over time the Maori not only lost lands but saw their own numbers dwindle significantly. As time passed the Maori population also underwent a gradual transformation. Many of them adopted

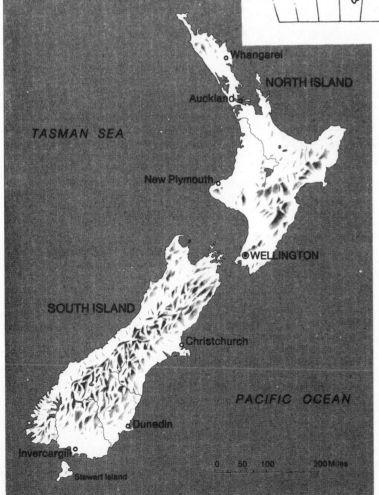

New Zealand

Late afternoon at Lake Hayes, South Island

Courtesy: New Zealand Information Service

western dress, and began to practice agriculture and animal husbandry in the manner of the English. Even for the European settlers, the economy of the islands allowed only a very difficult existence until the turn of the 20th century, when faster ships and refrigeration boosted the export of New Zealand's agricultural products.

Among the settlers the main political issue during the 19th century was the demand for greater representative government for the colony. By the mid 1850s, with the establishment of the New Zealand Constitution Act, the settler community gained more authority over domestic matters. Nevertheless, the British governors remained powerful and their clashes with elected local assemblies over their respective authority not infrequent.

New Zealand was granted dominion status within the British Commonwealth in 1907 as a result of a new vigor imparted

to the country's politics and administration by energetic Liberal leader Richard John Seddon, prime minister from 1893 to 1906. For all practical purposes, New Zealand was independent from that time on. Nevertheless, it would not become officially independent until 1947.

As it entered World War I, New Zealand was governed by the Reform Party, and later by a coalition government. New Zealand fought on the allied side especially in battles such as Gallipoli. Though their soldiers won admiration for their fighting skills the losses were enormous. Later, New Zealand took part as an independent state in the peace settlement at Versailles. It also joined the League of Nations and was awarded a mandate over the islands of Western Samoa that had been captured from the Germans.

Adverse economic conditions from 1920–1940 created an increase in labor organi-

zation and unrest. However, by the late 1930s, prosperity began to return, aided by an ambitious program of public works and social security under a succession of Labour Party governments.

New Zealand took an active part in World War II. After the Pacific War began in 1941 its troops were engaged in battle not only in Europe but against imperial Japan. During the war years, both Labour and National worked together in a coalition. Once the war was over, Labour's political domination continued through the late 1940s when the more conservative National Party returned to power.

Despite New Zealand's ties to Great Britain, it was understood that its wartime defense depended more on the Americans than on the British. Thus, after the war, recognizing the declining influence of Great Britain and the rise of U.S. as an Asian power, New Zealand joined the

ANZUS treaty (Australia, New Zealand and the U.S.) to provide security. It also joined the American led Southeast Asian Treaty Organization (SEATO) to meet the threat posed by the growth of communism in the region. During the 1960s New Zealand supplied troops for the American war in South Vietnam.

In 1972, The Labour Party came to power once again on a platform of more welfare benefits. The move to the left was reversed by late 1975 when Labour was defeated by a reinvigorated National Party that returned to power. Over the next few years, as so often in previous decades, the two parties rotated in power as New Zealand, buffeted by the loss of its British markets due to the growth of the European Common Market suffered financially.

During the mid 1980s ties to the United States were strained when the Labour Party run government announced that no nuclear-armed U.S. naval vessels would be allowed to call at New Zealand's ports. Since the U.S. refused on principle to say whether any particular vessel was nuclear-armed, this meant that no U.S. naval vessel could dock in New Zealand. As the U.S. began to apply counter-pressures, including the withholding of some intelligence information and threats to cut back on imports from New Zealand, the ANZUS alliance came under serious strain.

Finally, in June 1986, at a meeting in Manila between Prime Minister David Lange and U.S. Secretary of State George Shultz, the chain broke, at least temporarily. Good naturedly, Shultz admitted to the press that, "we part company on security matters as friends, but we part." Lange was equally gracious, but he stood by his government's policy. Eventually the U.S. suspended its security arrangements with New Zealand until "adequate corrective measures" were taken. This ended New Zealand's military alliance with the United States.

New Zealand does maintain defense ties with Australia. The Lange government also proposed in 1987 a buildup of New Zealand's defensive forces. His stand was quite popular and contributed to Labour's reelection.

In 1987 the Labour Party won reelection with a 15-seat majority in the 120 seat parliament. In sharp contrast to previous Labour government policies Lange's administration now worked for economic liberalization and privatization that eventually weakened its support.

In 1990 the National Party, under the leadership of Jim Bolger, again returned to power. However, the votes for him appeared to be more tied to domestic concerns over the state of the economy than to the continuing controversy with the United States over its nuclear weapons.

Politics and Government

New Zealand is a member of the British Commonwealth with a parliamentary form of government. Differences with the British model include a unicameral House of Representatives, which until the last election held 120 seats. Today, as a result of a new proportional representation system, it includes 121 members. The prime minister's term is three years. The political system is multiparty in nature with the major parties being the National Party, Labour Party, The Maori Party, The Progressive Party, ACT New Zealand, and New Zealand First. The Queen of England is represented by a governor general, a post currently held by Dame Silvia Cartwright, whose presence complements the particularly important role women play in New Zealand's government and society.

As has long been the case in neighboring Australia, there are those in New Zealand who have questioned the continuing influence of the British crown in the local affairs. That sentiment was particularly obvious recently when a new local supreme court, a court of last appeal, was created the replace the one long based in London. New Zealand's leaders also moved to deemphasize the revered tradition of knighthoods that have for so long been associated with British traditions. The changes were dramatic enough that the Labour Party, which then led the country, was accused by its opponents of the National Party of trying to turn New Zealand into a republic.

Other recent changes have included modification of the electoral laws to create a mixed-member proportional representation system. Proportional representation, which awards seats in a district based on the percentage of votes won by a party, tends to help smaller parties and encourage a multi-party system. Six seats in parliament are specifically reserved for Maoris.

Until fairly recently the National Party led the country. Their last elective victory though was in 1996. Nevertheless, the 1990s were years of realignment among the country's political parties. The National Party under the leadership of then Prime Minister Jim Bolger maintained control, but its majority eroded and a coalition with minor parties was required to remain in office.

Particularly significant in recent years was the growing strength of the New Zealand First Party. Long led by Winston Peters, a Maori lawyer, it has lashed out against Asian immigration that its supporters claimed had swamped the country with people who lacked a commitment to New Zealand. As we have seen in Australia, the anti-immigration campaign has attracted not only considerable attention and controversy but political support as well.

Thus, it is not surprising that Winston Peters ended up in a coalition government again headed by the National Party's Jim Bolger. Peters took the post of deputy, and treasurer. But that relationship, controversial in itself, did not work well. Over time tensions between Peters and his political colleagues fell to such an all time low that they caused Bolger to lose his position as both head of the Nationalists and Prime Minister.

In November of 1997 Jenny Shipley, the transport minister, successfully challenged Bolger, taking over the party leadership and becoming the prime minister. If she had acted to strengthen the conservatives, it was too late, for polls had been

Opening day at a Christchurch prep school

New Zealand

showing that the National Party was losing support to New Zealand's Labour Party, led by Helen Clark.

By 1999 Labour had returned to power alongside the smaller Alliance party. For Clark, a university lecturer in political science, it must have been a gratifying moment indeed. Clark had led the party since the early 1990s and had, twice before, almost become prime minister. Unfortunately for Clark, her support of various left-wing causes from Maori activism to her environmental policies alienated many moderate voters and made her first years in office quite difficult.

More recently, though, Clark's leadership has gained far more support, and she has managed to win back many voters who were initially quite unhappy with some of her policies. Most notable are those associated with her effort to re-impose a level of economic regulation rejected by her predecessors. In fact, by the elections of July 2002 Clark solidified her leadership by leading her party to a significant victory 41.3% of the votes over the rival National Party's 20.9%, or 52 seats to the Nationals 27.

That victory, along with Clark's ability to win allies among the 120-seat parliament, strengthened her hold on power. During the September 2005 election, she was able to retain her hold on power by forming a collation with four of the smaller parties. Of particular significance was that Winston Peters, the long time leader of the New Zealand First Party, emerged as the nation's first Maori Foreign Minister.

As so often happens in politics, the population's support for Helen Clark's Labour party ran its course by late 2008. In the November elections Clark's nine-year tenure in power came to an end. The resurgent National Power roared back to life with 58 seats to Labour's 43 elected to the House of Representatives.

Australia's Maori Community

While the evolving political landscape often attracts the most attention, other issues have played out dramatically as well. Race relations between the indigenous Maoris and the British-descended New Zealanders have been especially complicated in recent years. The problems date back to the 1840 Treaty of Waitangi which first saw the British officially establish themselves in New Zealand and, of course, the loss of so much Maori land to the new Anglo immigrants.

Today, the Maori constitute somewhere between 9% and 15% of the population (estimates vary), but they have shared little in the development of modern New Zealand. After public demonstrations in early 1995, both sides agreed to a multi-million dollar settlement involving both money and the return of some Maori lands. The May 1995 deal also included an official apology for land that was confiscated as a result of conflict in the 1860s. By 1997 the government had agreed to the return of an equivalent of $450 million and some expected the eventual total to reach $750 million.

More symbolic but nevertheless important, the country's highest peak has now been renamed from Mount Cook (named after the explorer) to Aoraki which means Cloud-Piercer in Maori. All these changes, like those going on in Australia, or for that matter, the United States, have been part and parcel of an attempt to make peace with the injustices of the past while not totally transforming the present.

Most New Zealanders hoped these settlements would mark the beginning of improved relations. But realistically, they are no more than partial payments on past debts. Much more will have to occur before a society emerges where the Maori share equally with the more recent New Zealanders the fruits of their society. For the moment that seems less likely. Just recently, the government ruled against Maori demands that the national sea beds be considered Maori holding and designated the areas part of the "public domain." While then Prime Minister's Clark's party continued to support the separate Maori seats in parliament her opponents in the National Party have tried to eliminate them. The National Party's former leader, Don Brash, even went so far as to accuse the then prime minister of running a government with a "pro-Maori bias."

Society and Culture

Apart from the Maori community, life in New Zealand has for generations been predominantly British, more so than in any other nation of the British Commonwealth except for the British Isles. Isolated and relatively small, it has a reputation for being somewhat provincial and conservative, whereas British cultural values have rapidly changed since World War II. Thus, the old saying that New Zealanders are more British than the British has some validity today.

But the New Zealand of old has been changing rapidly. More than 200,000 Asian immigrants have established themselves in New Zealand and it is now estimated that by 2021 more than 13% of the country will be of Asian origin, a fact that has in recent years created an environment of racial ten-

Former Prime Minister Helen Clark
Leader, *Labour Party*

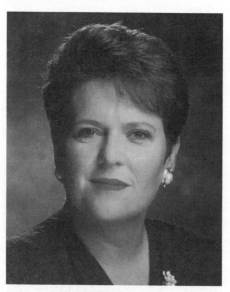

Rt. Hon. Jenny Shipley
Former Prime Minister

Prime Minister
John Key

sion that is unfamiliar to many there. A recent human rights study reported that the vast majority of New Zealanders feel that the new arrivals experience a significant amount of discrimination.

The indigenous Maori community though increasingly politically active, nevertheless lags behind its non-Maori neighbors in the basic social indicators such as longevity and unemployment. Most of the Maori live in urban areas having lost the bulk of their lands to the whites during the nineteenth century. Today there is considerable intermarriage between the Maori and the non-Maori New Zealanders. Nevertheless, as a group they are less represented in the professional classes. Unfortunately, they are over represented among prison populations, and experience a far higher unemployment record than their neighbors.

Compared to their non-Maori neighbors they are also more likely to depend on the government for employment. There has though been one bright spot lately for the Maori. Long a people that few outsiders had ever heard of, the brilliant feature length film "The Whale Rider" captured the attention of a worldwide audience. The film certainly put the Maori people on the "map of world consciousness" in a way they never have been before.

The special Maori representatives in the nation's House of Representatives have become controversial. The then leader of the opposition, John Key of the National Party, announced the goal of abolishing them. As we have seen, John Key became New Zealand's new prime minister as a result of the 2008 elections.

One particularly interesting element of New Zealand's modern development has been the growing influence of women in the political life of the nation. Not only was the former prime minister a female, but her immediate predecessor was also a women. A woman also emerged as the nation's first speaker of the House of Representatives. Overall, women are especially well represented within the government and professional organizations. Clearly the women of New Zealand have taken their place within the highest levels of decision making—political, legal and academic—in a way that few other countries could possibly boast.

Foreign Policy

Over the last few years, there has been more contact between New Zealand's leaders and those of the United States. In 1995, a significant step was taken to put New Zealand-U.S. relations back on track when Prime Minister Bolger headed for Washington for a meeting with President Bill Clinton. Leaders of the two countries had not met since former Prime Minister David Lange banned a U.S. ship suspected of carrying nuclear weapons from entering a New Zealand port. More recently Secretary Albright made the first visit by a U.S. Secretary of State since the Tripartite ANZUS pact ended. Relations have improved somewhat in recent years though Prime Minister Clark's decision to favor New Zealand's army over its air force has upset both the United States and the Australians who were concerned about having to fill the gap in their surveillance of the region.

Once the American-led "War against Terrorism" began, New Zealand became involved, sending her troops to serve alongside those from Australia in Afghanistan. But that improved relationship, after so many years of tension with the United States did not last long. Unlike its neighbor

Maori performer in Auckland

Australia, whose leadership committed itself deeply to the American occupation of Iraq, New Zealand's government refused to support the effort unless the United Nations sanctioned it.

When that did not occur, New Zealand refused to take part. This decision hardly improved relations with Washington. On the other hand, during 2009 New Zealand's new conservative government committed even more resources to the less controversial NATO effort in Afghanistan. Around seventy special elite military personal were sent to join the 150 non-combatants that were already serving there.

Since the establishment of a free trade area with Australia, the economies of the two nations have been closely intertwined though that has not always guaranteed that the two former British colonies would get along well. The two have differed, for example, on the details of the Bougainville settlement in Papua New Guinea's civil war. New Zealand, like Australia, has also attempted, over the last generation, to turn more toward Asia with its tremendous potential as an export market.

Like Australia, New Zealand too has been working to improve its relations with the People's Republic of China. It has finally concluded the first bilateral trade agreement with Beijing, and it is working to establish a free-trade relationship with Hong Kong and South Korea as well.

Again, like Australia, New Zealand became embroiled in regional politics as it

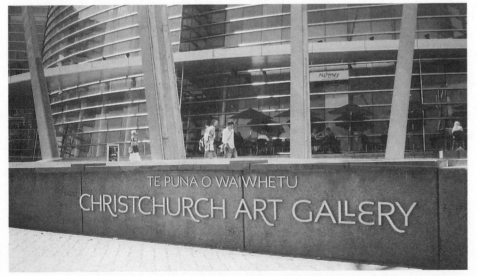

Maori-English bilingualism

New Zealand

also contributed to the international intervention in East Timor although its ability actually to support such an effort turned out to highlight significant deficits in the country's military equipment. In the aftermath the government made plans to spend several additional billions of dollars to modernize their military forces.

During her tenure in office Prime Minister Clark worked to transform New Zealand into a world leader in national sustainability. She officially declared the goal of making government services carbon neutral by 2012. This is a transformation that many other countries are likely to find themselves contemplating soon as consciousness grows about the threat of climate change.

Once New Zealand's Conservatives returned to power, though, there was initial concern about how the new government would deal with the challenge of Climate Change, given new Prime Minister John Key's well known skepticism about the entire issue. Nevertheless, once in office, his government has continued down the path of building a legislative economic environment that complements the move toward a more green-energy economy. This is despite the opposition the effort has raised among some members of the population and industry.

Economy

Agriculture, raising livestock and dairying predominate in the New Zealand economy. Mining and other industries have been added in the post World War II

Milford Sound in Fjordland National Park

era which will continue gradual expansion. Over the last two decades, the economy has become much more involved in industrial production as well. The economy is also very dependent on foreign trade and this has caused some difficulty for unskilled workers. The government has taken the position, however, that this is the best course for the country in the long term. Recent governments have undertaken significant privatization efforts. The past years have seen a restructuring of the economy that makes it one of the least regulated in the world though in recent years there has been something of a reversal in that regard. Still though, according a 2003 World Trade Organization report, New Zealand remains one of the most open economies in the world.

During the mid-1990s, the economy grew at a healthy rate of around 6%. But the economy has slowed considerably over the last few years and was stagnating even before the global recession of 2008–9 set in. Tourism, which dropped during the Asian economic crisis of the late 1990s, has begun to show considerable improvement.

The spectacular success of the Lord of the Rings movies has also played an important part in that industry's growth. The three films, all of which were filmed in New Zealand, highlighted far more than the storytelling genius of J. R. R. Tolkein, the original books' author, how extraordinarily beautiful parts of New Zealand are—a publicity bonanza New Zealand's tourist industry is busily taking advantage of.

Efforts to enhance New Zealand's trading relationships have picked up steam as well with progress made on establishing such ties with Singapore, South Korea and possibly even Chile. Over the last few years efforts were also begun to create a free-trade agreement with the People's Republic of China. During 2008, that effort was accomplished with the signing of a comprehensive agreement that would evolve over time and included both labor and environmental clauses.

Meanwhile the nation has worked to develop closer economic relations with India and the membership of the Association of Southeast Asian Nations (ASEAN). There has even been discussion of an Asia-Pacific free-trade zone.

There is hope that such an arrangement can also be established with the United States, as Australia has already done. For the moment, though, there is little reason

Christchurch Cathedral

for significant optimism about the economy. Real growth in 2007 was only around 3%, and 2008 was much lower at negative 1%. More significantly, that was before the full impact of the most recent global economic slowdown had begun. When 2008's global recession hit, it was quite significant and worse than that experienced by its near neighbor, Australia. 2009's growth rate was in the low negative rate of over 1.4% while the government carried out a host of measures. They included subsidizing employers who lowered the work week to encourage more hiring and funding various public works and infrastructure projects, such as a plan to build a bike network across the nation.

The Environment

In Australia, as we have seen, one of the issues that divided the two major parties was their respective acceptance or rejection of the growing scientific consensus on the dangers of global warming. Under the circumstances, the defeat of the Australian conservatives made a very significant difference in that nation's goals relating to climate change. That is apparently not the case in New Zealand. John Key, the new National Party prime minister, has stated publically that he understands the threat of climate change. More importantly there were news reports in the early summer of 2009 that the government was working with the leaders of the defeated Labour Party to develop a coordinated policy on that important issue. Doing so is especially important given that New Zealand, like Australia, faces the challenge of potentially large numbers of climate refugees from the nearby Pacific islands. On a positive note, New Zealand's relatively small population and less intense industrialization compared to some other nations makes it less environmentally damaged.

But the nation does make its own special contribution to the growing density of global green house gasses. In this case the culprit is the nation's large sheep and cattle herds, which emit into the atmosphere significant amounts of methane—a much more powerful green house gas than CO_2. This problem is recognized, and experiments are being carried out to introduce modified bacterium into the intestines of the animals that would help lessen the problem. However, according to at least one recent survey, the population is somewhat ambivalent about whether that is a good idea. The larger legislative efforts to move toward a greener energy infrastructure have also aroused opposition.

The Future

Compared to so many of its neighbors, New Zealand has plenty to be grateful for. The economy has remained reasonably stable and does seem to be slowly pulling out of the most recent recession relatively well. Some progress has been made in dealing with the injustices of the past through efforts at reconciliation with the Maori people. Plans are currently under way to attempt a settlement with the Maori over historical claims arising out of Treaty of Waitangi. The goal is finally to reconcile such claims by 2020. By June 2009 progress was already being made as a treaty was signed with the Ngati Whare people of New Zealand's North Island. The "agreement in principal," as it was termed, offered a series of cultural and historic redress measures that are part of the larger effort to settle long-standing inequities stemming from the colonial era.

With all the publicity her beautiful landscape earned from the three Lord of the Rings films, the New Zealand tourist industry is well positioned to grow significantly. For a relatively small country like New Zealand, those tourist dollars can be especially significant.

New Zealand also continues to be a social trend setter internationally. The growing strength of women throughout its political infrastructure continues unabated. As it once pioneered the role of women as voters, it more recently passed a law allowing civil union between homosexuals. On the other hand, there are limits to the toleration of New Zealand's political decision makers. An effort by the Green Party to legalize marijuana for medicinal purposes was voted down quite handily.

Rural scene North Central Island   Courtesy Tom Waters

Island Communities of the Western and Southern Pacific

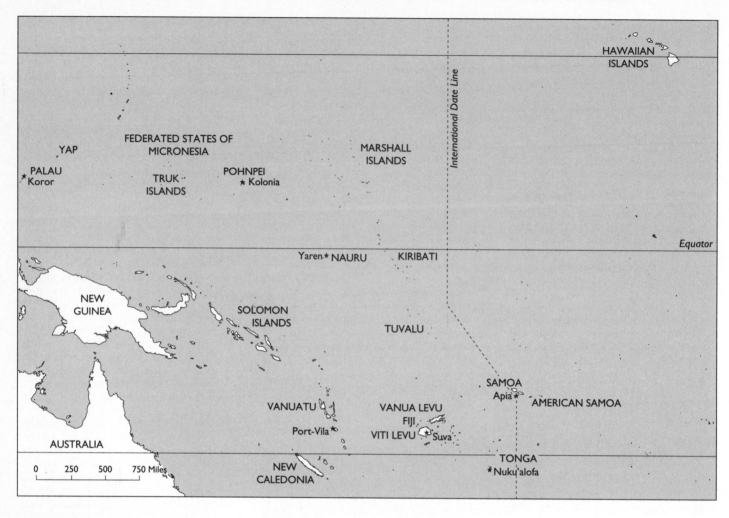

"... the seas bring us together, they do not separate us ..."

(From the preamble to the Constitution of the Federated States of Micronesia)

Scattered like brilliant pieces of jade across an area covering more than 3 million square miles of the Pacific Ocean lies a number of island nations. Most of them have achieved independence. They range in population from Fiji's 944,000 to Nauru's 14,000 inhabitants. Most islanders are ethnically Polynesian, Melanesian or Micronesian, although some Asian groups, such as Indians, Chinese and Vietnamese, have settled in the islands. Over the years these island communities have lived under the control of a range of outside countries including Britain, Germany, France, the United States, Japan, Australia and New Zealand.

Many of the islands also bear the scars and rusted armaments left to them by the savage engagements waged throughout the region during World War II. Gentle wavelets brush the bows of hulking battleships sunk during those years, while palm trees sway in the cooling breezes that moderate the tropical climate.

Long before the Common Era, Asian peoples migrated into the area. Much later Spanish explorers combed the region for gold and spread Christianity, a belief that was often blended with the traditional religious practices. In the latter 1800s, German control was imposed over much of the region. After World War I, Japan, a wartime partner of the victorious allies, was rewarded with possession of the former German-held islands north of New Guinea.

During World War II, an island-by-island struggle by Allied troops wrested the area from the Japanese. Eventually the islands came under control of the United States, Great Britain, France, Australia and New Zealand. Over the following decades, most of the islands achieved independence although some, like French Polynesia, remain colonial possessions.

Following World War II, the United Nations established a trusteeship over three of the primary archipelagos north of the equator: the Carolinas, the Marshalls and the Marianas. The U.S. became the trustee, and the Department of the Interior took jurisdiction over the islands from the Navy in 1951. In 1975, the Northern Mari-

anas were given separate status as a commonwealth. The rest of the territory was divided into the Marshall Islands (in the East), the Federated States of Micronesia (FSM, in the South), and the Republic of Palau (in the Southwest).

In January 1986, the United States approved a Compact of Free Association for the islands. It consists of two agreements included in the same act of Congress—one between the U.S. and the Federated States of Micronesia, and the other between the U.S. and the Marshall Islands. The Compact provides for extensive cooperation in numerous areas, such as law enforcement, narcotics control, economic and technical assistance, resolution of nuclear-cleanup programs, health care, fishing rights, etc. With the enactment of the Compact, the Trust Territory of the Pacific Islands ceased to exist. The FSM and the Marshall Islands are now independent republics and members of the United Nations. American Samoa, in contrast, is considered a territory of the United States.

The Solomon Islands, Tonga, and Vanuatu are members of the (British) Commonwealth of Nations. Nauru and Tuvalu are special members. In other words, they may participate in all functional Commonwealth meetings and activities, but do not have the right to attend meetings of the Commonwealth Heads of Government. The states of this region, including Australia and New Zealand, have also formed an organization called the South Pacific Forum. In 1985 they signed a South Pacific Nuclear-Free Zone Treaty barring such weapons from the region's territories, but not banning transit of its waters by nuclear-armed or nuclear-powered ships. More recently, an organization emerged called the Forum Economic Minister's Meeting (FEMM), which held its first meeting at Cairns, Australia. The new group, which has largely been sponsored by Australia, was partly a result of the latter's concern about the increasing economic weakness of its South Pacific island neighbors.

Contemporary issues in the Region

Economically the different communities are relatively varied. Some islands are very specialized, such as Nauru with its dependence on phosphate deposits. Others produce in varying quantities basic products of a tropical climate: coconut and palm oil, fish, copra, fruits and—in the case of Fiji—sugar and some gold. Timber is also an important export for both Fiji and the Solomon Islands. Another prime source of income is tourism. The strength of their economies varies as well. Fiji has been doing quite well, with a 2004 growth rate of almost 4%, while Nauru is undergoing a period of significant economic crisis.

While people might consider these small communities far from the mainstream of modern international life, they have often been deeply impacted by current developments. In fact, some islands, Nauru for example, have become refugee centers for Iraqis and Afghans who had initially tried to enter Australia. Palau made international news as well in early 2009 when it agreed to take some of the prisoners the new American administration needed to relocate after its decision to close the American detention camp at Guantanamo Bay.

Meanwhile Russian policy goals have also enriched the region's coffers. Nauru recently earned a $50,000 aid package merely for recognizing the controversial territories of Abkhasia and South Ossetia over which Russia has been feuding with Georgia.

A number of these island communities have cashed in on the globalized economy by selling their Internet country codes to those looking for easy and readable worldwide web addresses. Within the globalized economy, these new roles have

also brought new problems. This is especially the case as some have been under considerable international pressure lately to pass laws against money laundering.

In recent years, there has been talk of expanding cooperation between the nations of the region on global political and economic issues. Those talks came to fruition when the new South Pacific Free-trade Area was created. Such a move had been felt necessary in order to have a unified voice speak for these communities in negotiations with emerging trade blocks like the Northern American Free-Trade Association (NAFTA) and the European Union (EU).

With such ideas in mind, several of these island nations recently joined the United Nations in order to give more voice to their concerns within the forums of the international community. The perils of not having such a voice were especially obvious during the era of nuclear testing.

In the 1950s during the Cold War, the Eniwetok and Bikini atolls in the Marshalls were the site of H-bomb tests. Such testing deeply disrupted the lives of many of the region's people. Not surprisingly there was considerable local discontent over the use of the area as a nuclear testing zone. The most recent incident arose when, in 1995, the French announced plans to resume nuclear testing. The decision resulted in an unsuccessful effort by New Zealand to use the International Court of Justice to pressure Paris not to start testing again. There was also a world-wide protest that included both government religious and anti-nuclear groups.

Finally, in January 1996, then French President Jacques Chirac announced that, having carried out six of the originally planned eight nuclear tests, the program would be discontinued. But while nuclear testing has been ended, the demands for compensation continue. In May 2005, the Marshall Islands once again unsuccessfully made their case to Congress and the Bush Administration for increased compensation.

Of particular importance has been the end of the long-running civil war in Papua

New Guinea. The situation was resolved after agreement was reached between many of the states in the region to provide military units for peace-keeping on Bougainville. Happily the situation has improved in recent years. Still, many of these communities have continued to experience instability. Among the best known are, for example, an uprising of armed militias in the Solomons and significant political instability in Tonga, Fiji, Nauru and Kiribati over the last decade.

One of the most interesting challenges for the region will be the introduction of new technologies that will allow for mining the sea during the 21st century. At that point, some have speculated that the ocean floors surrounding these islands may be worth billions of dollars. Working out the legal and financial details now will facilitate harvesting the advantages in the future. On that front Fiji requested that the United Nations recognize its claim to an extended continental shelf. If accepted, that would facilitate the nation's ability to exploit those undersea resources.

Once idyllic and isolated communities, these nations are increasingly part of the globalized world community. Their new status can have an impact on a very personal level. The people of Palau, for example, were recently cited by the World Health Organization as the seventh-fattest people on the planet for the all-too-common habit of living without proper exercise "complemented" by a poor diet full of Western fast foods. Meanwhile HIV/AIDS has become increasingly common. But in many ways these island nations were not just experiencing some of the worst habits of the larger industrialized nations. They are, in fact, likely to be among the first victims of the West's development choices. On the other hand, there are certainly advantages in becoming more integrated with the world community. Nauru implemented its first national cellular and internet service in 2009. The event was so celebrated that the nation's president declared a national holiday.

The Fate of Nations: Rising Waters and Low Lying Atolls

Dwarfing all other issues is the reality that the terrain of the majority of these island communities is quite low, sometimes only a few feet above sea level. Given growing fears about global warming producing a rise in sea levels, many of the region's inhabitants are deeply concerned about their nations' long-term future.

Over the years their officials have at times spoken out forcibly, as Tuvalu's former leader did at a recent World Summit on Sustainable Development. He denounced both the United States' and Aus-

The Islands

tralia's "contribution" to the growing problem. Tuvalu's leaders have plenty of reason for concern. Ocean levels around the Islands have been rising almost an inch a year. Some believe the Islands themselves might be submerged by 2040.

Unfortunately, these island communities often find themselves in a difficult position politically. New Zealand's government has long been more and more conscious of the growing threat of climate change. However, Australia, their other large and influential neighbor, remained until quite recently one of the last nations on earth not to sign the Kyoto Climate Protocols. With the election of the new Labour government in Australia, which campaigned on a platform committed to confronting climate change, at least that complication has been removed. In fact, Australia's former prime minister, Kevin Rudd, committed his government to helping the islands deal with the many challenges associated with climate change. Rudd's successor from his own Labour Party, Julia Gillard, promised to continue his climate related policies

Politics aside, the realities of the threat continue. In 1999 two of Kiribati's unin-habited islands disappeared under the ocean. The remaining 33 islands remain at risk. The residents of Tegua, Vanuatu, were forced to abandon their island in December 2005.

It is not clear how long it will be before the permanent rising of the oceans threatens the homes of even larger numbers of people. Nevertheless, increasing numbers are already at risk during water surges brought on by stronger tropical storms, which are themselves made more powerful by the warming waters.

Rising water is not the only concern. As it happens, the coral reefs that surround these atoll nations may be among the earliest victims of global warming. These reefs are very sensitive to rising temperatures. They have long served as something akin to Holland's dykes in holding back the strongest of the ocean's surges during storms. Given that the region contains the largest collection of coral communities in the world, this issue is particularly important. The local communities depend on the coral for everything from defense against the sea, fishing, and the all-important ability to attract the money of visiting tourists.

Some Pacific Island leaders have done what they could to protect their people. The government of Tuvalu has already negotiated emigration rights for its entire citizenry to depart for New Zealand if the situation becomes critical. The emerging climate crisis, though, is not merely the fault of outsiders far from these chains of island communities. The Solomon Islands have themselves been chastised for unsustainably logging their forests, which has a direct negative impact on global warming.

On an international level these island communities have also been quite active. In the early summer of 2009 a coalition of the islands successfully urged the United Nations General Assembly to pass a resolution encouraging the Security Council to recognize the threat climate change poses to their peoples. Meanwhile Tuvalu was particularly active at the Copenhagen Climate meeting in encouraging the international community to adopt a more serious attitude about carbon reductions. It announced its own plans to spend twenty million dollars to employ enough renewable technologies to supply the entire country with green energy by 2020.

Fiji's Daydream Island—At Risk From Rising Waters

Selected Bibliography of Key English Language Sources

WEB SITES
Useful General Sites:

The author, Steven A. Leibo's World Watch blog is available at: http://sagethoughts.wordpress.com/

www.un.org (Web site for United Nations. Many links.)

www.unsystem.or (Official UN website)

http://en.cop15.dk/ United Nations Climate Change Conference official site

www.oecd.org/daf/cmis/fdi/statist.htm (OECD site)

www.osce.org (Site of OSCE)

www.wto.org (World Trade Organization site)

www.worldbank.org/html/Welcome.html (World Bank news, publications with links to other financial institutions)

http://www.ncuscr.org/ National Committee on United States-China Relations

www.ceip.org (Carnegie Endowment for International Peace, using a fully integrated Web-database system)

www.cia.gov/index.html (Central Intelligence Agency)

http://climateprogress.org/ (Best website to follow the science & politics of climate change

www.odci.gov/cia (Includes useful CIA publications, such as *The World Factbook* and maps)

www.state.gov/www/ind.html (U.S. Department of State, including country reports)

http://usinfo.state.gov (U.S. Department of State)

lcweb2.loc.gov/frd/cs/cshome.html (Library of Congress with coverage of over 100 countries)

www.embassy.org/embassies (A site with links to all embassy web sites in Washington D.C.)

www.psr.keele.ac.uk\official.htm (Collective site for governments and international organizations)

http://www.ruf.rice.edu/tnchina/ (Excellent site on various aspects of China)

http://www.crisisgroup.org/home/index.cfm? International Crisis Group-excellent for dealing with specific contemporary issues.

Newspapers, Journals, Television, Radio with good coverage on international affairs:

www.chicagotribune.com (Named best overall US newspaper online service for newspapers with circulation over 100,000.)

http://foreignpolicy.com/ *Foreign Policy* excellent journal of Global Politics

www.currenthistory.com *Current History*, features monthly issues on specific areas

www.csmonitor.com (Respected U.S. newspaper, *Christian Science Monitor*.

Named best overall US newspaper online service for newspapers with circulation under 100,000.)

www.economist.com (British weekly news magazine)

www.nytimes.com (Respected U.S. newspaper, *The New York Times*)

www.washingtonpost.com (Good international coverage)

www.foreignaffairs.org (One of best-known international affairs journal)

www.cnn.com (Latest news with external links)

www.news.BBC.co.uk (British Broadcasting Corporation site)

www.c-span.org (Includes C-SPAN International)

www.xe.com/ucc/ current exchange rate of currencies

iTunes Apple's website designed to support its various iPods allows one to subscribe to an enormous range of free international news services that are being delivered as podcasts.

General Books and Reports

Arifin, Evi Nurvidya editor, *Older Persons in Southeast Asia*: An Emerging Asset Singapore, Institute of Southeast Asian Studies, 2009.

Bracken, Paul. *Fire in the East: the Rise of Asian Military Power and the Second Nuclear Age.* New York: HarperCollins Publishers, 1999.

Britannica, Encyclopedia *2010 Book of the Year*, Encyclopedia Britanica, Inc. Chicago, 2010

Clifford, Mark L. and Peter Engardio. *Meltdown: Asia's Boom, Bust, and Beyond.* Upper Saddle River, NJ: Prentice-Hall Press, 1999.

Das, Dilip K., ed. *Emerging Growth Pole: the Asia-Pacific Economy.* Upper Saddle River, NJ: Prentice Hall, 1997.

Dutta, Manoranjan. *Economic Regionalization in the Asia-Pacific: Challenges to Economic Cooperation.* Northampton, MA: Edward Elgar Publishing, 1999.

Eccleston, Bernard and Michael Dawson, eds. *Asia Pacific Profile.* New York: Routledge, 1998.

Flannery, Tim, *The Weather Makers: How Man is Changing the Climate and What it Means for Life on Earth*, New York, NY: Grove Press, 2005.

Flynn, Norman. *Miracle to Meltdown in Asia: Business, Government and Society.* New York: Oxford University Press, 2000.

Ikenberry, G. John and Inoguchi, Takashi. *Reinventing the Alliance. US-Japan Security Partnership in an Era of Change.* NY: Palgrave, 2003.

Institute of Southeast Asian Studies, *Energy Perspectives on Singapore and the Region*, Singapore, Institute of Southeast Asian Studies, 2007.

Institute of Southeast Asian Studies, *Regional Outlook Southeast Asia 2005–2006*. Singapore, Institute of Southeast Asian Studies, 2006.

Institute of Southeast Asian Studies, *Southeast Asian Affairs 2004*. Singapore, Institute of Southeast Asian Studies, 2004.

Kristoff, Nicholas D. and Sheryl WuDunn. *Thunder from the East: Portrait of a Rising Asia.* New York: Alfred A. Knopf, 2000.

Lal, Rollie, *Understanding China & India: Security Implications for the United States & the World*, Westport Connecticut, Praeger Security International, 2006.

Liu, Ts-ui-jung, ed. *Asian Population History.* New York: Oxford University Press, 1999.

Mahbubani, Kishore, *The New Asian Hemisphere: The Irresistible Shift of Global Power to the East.* Public Affairs, New York 2008.

Muhlhausler, Peter. *Linguistic Ecology: Language Change and Linguistic Imperialism in the Pacific Rim.* New York: Routledge, 1996.

Olds, Kris. *Globalisation and the Asia-Pacific: Contested Territories.* New York: Routledge, 1999.

Preston, Benjamin et al. *Climate Change in the Asia/Pacific Region: A consultancy Report Prepared for the Climate Change and Development Roundtable.* October 2006 available at www.csro.au

Rohwer, Jim. *Re-Made in America: How Asia Is Rebuilding Its Economies American-Style.* New York: Crown Publishing, 2001.

Rubinstein, Murray A. *Taiwan: A New History, Expanded Edition.* M.E. Sharpe, Armonk, N.Y. 2007.

Simone, Vera and Anne T. Ferara. *The Asian Pacific: Political and Economic Development in a Global Context.* White Plains, NY: Longman Publishing Group, 1999.

Marcelo M. Suarez-Orozco and Desiree Baolian Qin-Hilliard, *Globalization Culture and Education in the New Millennium.* Berkeley and Los Angeles: University of California Press, 2004.

Tan, Gerald. *The Newly Industrializing Countries of Asia.* Portland, OR: Times Academic Press, 2000.

Terry, Edith B. *How Asia Got Rich: the Rise and Fall of Asia's Miracle Economies, What Went Wrong, and How to Fix It.* Armonk, NY: M.E. Sharpe, 2000.

Thompson, Roger C. *The Pacific Basin since 1945: a History of the Foreign Relations of the Asian, Australasian, and American Rim States and the Pacific Islands.* White Plains, NY: Longman Publishing, 1994.

The Wilson Chronology of Asia and the Pacific. Bronx, NY: H.W. Wilson, 1999.

The World Watch Institute. *The State of the World 2006 Special Focus China and India,*

New York, NY: WW Norton & Company 2006.

Yomamato, Yoshinobu, ed. *Globalism, Regionalism, and Nationalism: Asia in Search of Its Role in the 21st Century*. Malden, MA: Blackwell Publishers, 1999.

East and Southeast Asia

Abuza, Zachary. *Militant Islam in Southeast Asia: Crucible of Terror*. Boulder, CO: Lynne Reinner, 2003.

Adams, F. Gerard and Shinichi Ichimura, eds. *East Asian Development: Will the East Asian Growth Miracle Survive?* Westport, CT: Greenwood Publishing Group, 1998.

Athukorala, Prema-Chandra and Chris Manning. *Structural Change and International Labour Migration in East Asia*. New York: Oxford University Press, 2000.

Barlow, Colin, ed. *Institutions and Economic Change in Southeast Asia: the Context of Development from the 1960's to the 1990's*. Northampton, MA: Edward Elgar Publishing, 2000.

Bessho, Koro. *Identities and Security in East Asia*. New York: Oxford University Press, 1999.

Christie, Clive J. *A Modern History of Southeast Asia: Decolonization, Nationalism, and Separatism*. New York: Tauris Academic Studies, 1996.

Cohen, Warren I. *East Asia as the Center: Four Thousand Years of Engagement with the World*. New York: Columbia University Press, 2003.

Collins, Alan. *Security and Southeast Asia: Domestic, Regional, and Global Issues*. Boulder, CO: Lynne Reinner, 2003.

Compton, Robert W., Jr. *East Asian Democratization: Impact of Globalization, Culture and Economy*. Westport, CT: Greenwood Publishing Group, 2000.

Devasahayam, Theresa W. editor, *Gender Trends in Southeast Asia*, Singapore, Institute of Southeast Asian Studies, 2009.

Dickinson, David and Andrew W. Mullineux, eds. *Finance, Governance and Economic Performance in Pacific and South East Asia*. Northampton, MA: Edward Elgar Publishing, 2001.

Dittmer, Lowell, et al., eds. *Informal Politics in East Asia*. New York: Cambridge University Press, 2000.

Fogel, Joshua A. *A History of East Asia*. Upper Saddle River, NJ: Prentice Hall, 2001.

Harland, Bryce. *Collision Course: America and East Asia in the Past and in the Future*. New York: St. Martin's Press, 1996.

Heidhues, Mary Somers. *Southeast Asia: a Concise History*. New York: Thames & Hudson, 2000.

Ho Khai Leong, editor, *Connecting And Distancing: Southeast Asia and China*, Singapore, Institute of Southeast Asian Studies, 2009.

Huxley, Tim and Susan Willett. *Arming East Asia*. New York: Oxford University Press, 1999.

Ikeo, Aiko, ed. *Economic Development in Twentieth Century East Asia: the International Context*. New York: Routledge, 1997.

Keay, John. *Empire's End: a History of the Far East from High Colonialism to Hong Kong*. New York: Scribner, 1997.

Kelly, David and Anthony Reid, eds. *Asian Freedoms: the Idea of Freedom in East and Southeast Asia*. New York: Cambridge University Press, 1998.

Kim, Samuel S. *East Asia and Globalization*. Lanham, MD: Rowman & Littlefield Publishers, 2000.

Leifer, Michael, ed. *Dictionary of the Modern Politics of South-East Asia*. New York: Routledge, 1995.

Levine, Alan J. *The United States and the Struggle for Southeast Asia, 1945–1975*. New York: Praeger, 1995.

McCloud, Donald G. *Southeast Asia: Tradition and Modernity in the Contemporary World*. Boulder, CO: Westview Press, 1995.

Morley, James W. *Driven by Growth: Political Change in the Asia-Pacific Region*. Armonk, NY: M.E. Sharpe, rev. ed. 1998.

Mulder, Niels. *Inside Southeast Asia: Religion, Everyday Life, Cultural Change*. Boston, MA: Charles E. Tuttle Company, 1997.

Murphey, Rhoads. *East Asia: a New History*. Reading, MA: Addison-Wesley Educational Publishers, 1997.

Montesano, Michael, J. editor *Regional Outlook: Southeast Asia 2010–2011*, Singapore, Institute of Southeast Asian Studies, 2010.

Neher, Clark D. *Southeast Asia in the New International Era*. 4th ed. Boulder, CO: Westview Press, 2002.

Ramesh, M. and Mukul G. Asher. *Welfare Capitalism in Southeast Asia: Social Security, Health and Education Policies*. New York: Saint Martin's Press, 2000.

Ravich, Samantha F. *Marketization and Democracy: East Asian Experiences*. New York: Cambridge University Press, 2000.

Reid, Anthony. *Southeast Asia in the Age of Commerce, 1450–1680, Volume 1: the Lands below the Winds*. New Haven, CT: Yale University Press, 1990.

Reid, Anthony. *Southeast Asia in the Age of Commerce, 1450–1680, Volume 2: Expansion and Crisis*. New Haven, CT: Yale University Press, 1993.

Rodrigo, G. Chris. *Technology, Economic Growth and Crises in East Asia*. Northampton, MA: Edward Elgar Publishing, 2000.

Rowen, Henry S. *Behind East Asian Growth: the Political and Social Foundations of Prosperity*. New York: Routledge, 1998.

SarDesai, D.R. *Southeast Asia. Past and Present*. 5th ed. Boulder, CO: Westview, 2003.

Shaffer, Lynda N. *Maritime Southeast Asia to 1500*. Armonk, NY: M.E. Sharpe, 1996.

Dingh, Daljit & Tin Maung Maung Than, Editors, *Southeast Asian Affairs 2008*. Singapore, 2008, Institute of Southeast Asian Studies. 2008.

Sajise, Percy E. editor, *Moving Forward: Southeast Asian Perspectives on Climate Change and Biodiversity*, Singapore, Institute of Southeast Asian Studies, 2009.

Sponsel, Leslie E., ed. *Endangered Peoples of Southeast and East Asia*. Westport, CT: Greenwood Publishing Group, 1999.

Tarling, Nicholas, ed. *The Cambridge History of Southeast Asia, Volume 1: from Early Times to c. 1800*. New York: Cambridge University Press, 1992.

Tartling, Nicholas, ed. *The Cambridge History of Southeast Asia, Volume 2: the Nineteenth and Twentieth Centuries*. New York: Cambridge University Press, 1992.

Tongzon, José L. *The Economies of Southeast Asia: the Growth and Development of ASEAN Economies*. Northampton, MA: Edward Elgar Publishing, 1998.

Trocki, Carl. *Gangsters, Democracy, and the State in Southeast Asia*. Ithaca, NY: Cornell University Press, 1998.

Viviano, Frank. *Dispatches from the Pacific Century*. Reading, MA: Addison-Wesley, 1993.

Wolters, Oliver W. *History, Culture, and Region in Southeast Asian Perspectives*. Ithaca, NY: Cornell University, Southeast Asia Program Publications, 1999.

Woo-Cumings, Meredith. *Development States in East Asia*. Ithaca, NY: Cornell University Press, 1999.

World Bank Staff. *East Asia: the Road to Economic Recovery*. Washington, DC: The World Bank, 1999.

Yamamoto, Tadashi, ed. *Emerging Civil Society in the Asia Pacific Community: Nongovernmental Underpinnings of the Emerging Asia Regional Community*. Seattle, WA: University of Washington Press, 1995.

Zhao, Suisheng. *The Dynamics of Power Competition in East Asia: from the Old Chinese World Order to the Post-Cold War Regional Multipolarity*. New York: Saint Martin's Press, 1997.

Australia

Adelman, Howard, et al., eds. *Immigration and Refugee Policy: Australia and Canada Compared*. Toronto: University of Toronto Press, 1994.

Andrews, E.M. *The Anzac Illusion: Anglo-Australian Relations during World War I*. New York: Cambridge University Press, 1993.

Argy, Fred. *Australia at the Crossroads: Radical Free Market or a Progressive Liberalism?* Concord, MA: Paul & Company Publishers Consortium, 1998.

The Australian Reference Dictionary. New York: Oxford University Press, 1992.

Baker, Richard W., ed. *The ANZUS States and Their Region: Regional Policies of Australia, New Zealand, and the United States*. New York: Praeger, 1994.

Bassett, Jan. *The Oxford Illustrated Dictionary of Australian History*. New York: Oxford University Press, 1996.

Beilharz, Peter. *Transforming Labor: Labour Tradition and the Labor Decade in Australia.* New York: Cambridge University Press, 1994.

Bell, Stephen, ed. *The Unemployment Crisis in Australia: Which Way Out?* New York: Cambridge University Press, 2000.

Bennett, Tony, et al. *Accounting for Tastes: Australian Everyday Cultures.* New York: Cambridge University Press, 1999.

Brawley, Sean. *The White Peril: Foreign Relations and Asian Immigration to Australasia and North America, 1919–1978.* Sydney: University of New South Wales Press, 1995.

Broeze, Frank. *Mr. Brooks and the Australian Trade: Imperial Business in the Nineteenth Century.* Melbourne: Carlton University Press, 1993.

Butlin, N.G. *Forming a Colonial Economy, Australia 1810–1850.* New York: Cambridge University Press, 1994.

Castles, Stephen, et al. *Immigration and Australia.* Concord, MA: Paul & Company Publishers Consortium, 1998.

Davidson, Alastair. *From Subject to Citizen: Australian Citizenship in the Twentieth Century.* New York: Cambridge University Press, 1997.

Davidson, Alastair. *The Invisible State: the Formation of the Australian State, 1788–1901.* New York: Cambridge University Press, 1991.

Davidson, Graeme, et al., eds. *The Oxford Companion to Australian History.* New York: Oxford University Press, 1998.

Dean, Mitchell, ed. *Governing Australia: Studies in Contemporary Rationalities of Government.* New York: Cambridge University Press, 1998.

Docherty, James C. *Historical Dictionary of Australia.* Lanham, MD: Scarecrow Press, 2nd ed. 1999.

Emy, Hugh V., ed. *Australia and New Zealand.* Brookfield, VT: Ashgate Publishing Company, 1999.

Fischer, Gerhard and John Docker, eds. *Race, Colour and Identity in Australia and New Zealand.* Randwick, NSW: New South Wales University Press, 2000.

Grey, Jeffrey. *A Military History of Australia.* New York: Cambridge University Press, rev. ed 2000.

Hassam, Andrew. *Sailing to Australia: Shipboard Diaries by Nineteenth-Century British Emigrants.* New York: Manchester University Press, 1994.

Heathcote, R.L. *Australia.* London: Longman Scientific & Technical, 2nd ed. 1994.

Inglis, K.S. *Australian Colonists: an Exploration of Social History 1788–1870.* Carlton, Victoria: Melbourne University Press, 1993.

Inglis, K.S. and Craig S. Wilcox, eds. *Observing Australia, 1959–1999.* Carlton, Victoria: Melbourne University Press, 2000.

Irving, Helen, ed. *The Centenary Companion to Australian Federation.* New York: Cambridge University Press, 2000.

Jamrozik, Adam, et al. *Social Change and Cultural Transformation in Australia.* New York: Cambridge University Press, 1995.

Jayasuriya, Laksiri, et al, eds. *Legacies of White Australia. Race, Culture and Nation.* University of Western Australia Press, 2003.

Kenny, John. *Before the First Fleet: Europeans in Australia, 1606–1777.* Kenthurst, NSW: Kangaroo Press, 1995.

Lines, William J. *False Economy: Australia in the 20th Century.* Portland, OR: International Specialized Book Services, 1998.

Macintyre, Stuart. *A Concise History of Australia.* New York: Cambridge University Press, 2000.

McGarvie, Richard E. *Democracy: Choosing Australia's Republic.* Carlton, Victoria: Melbourne University Press, 2000.

McIntyre, W. David. *Background into the ANZUS Pact: Strategy and Diplomacy, 1945–55.* New York: Saint Martin's Press, 1995.

Mediansky, Fedor A., ed. *Australian Foreign Policy: into the Next Millennium.* Concord, MA: Paul & Company Publishers Consortium, 1998.

Meredith, David and Barrie Dyster. *Australia in the Global Economy: Continuity and Change.* New York: Cambridge University Press, 2000.

Monfries, John, Editor, *Different Cultures: Shared Futures: Australia, Indonesia and the Region.* Singapore: Institute of Southeast Asian Studies. 2006

Murphy, Brian. *The Other Australia: Experiences of Migration.* New York: Cambridge University Press, 1993.

Okamoto Jiro, *Australia's Foreign Economic Policy And ASEAN,* Singapore, Institute of Southeast Asian Studies, 2010.

Painter, Martin. *Collaborative Federalism: Economic Reform in Australia in the 1990s.* New York: Cambridge University Press, 1998.

Paul, Erik. *Australia in Southeast Asia: Regionalism and Democracy.* Concord, MA: Paul & Company Consortium Publishers, 1998.

Reynolds, Henry. *Aboriginal Sovereignty: Reflections on Race, State and Nation.* New York: Paul & Company Publishers Consortium, 1997.

Robinson, Guy. *Australia and New Zealand: Economy, Society and Environment.* New York: Edward Arnold, 2000.

Scates, Bruce. *A New Australia: Citizenship, Radicalism and the First Republic.* New York: Cambridge University Press, 1997.

Simon, Julian L. *The Economic Consequences of Immigration.* Ann Arbor, MI: University of Michigan Press, rev. ed. 1999.

Singh, Anoop. *Australia: Benefiting from Economic Reform.* Washington, DC: International Monetary Fund, 1998.

Smith, Gary. *Australia in the World: an Introduction to Australian Foreign Policy.* New York: Oxford University Press, 1998.

Smyth, Paul and Bettina Cass, eds. *Contesting the Australian Way: States, Markets and Civil Society.* New York: Cambridge University Press, 1999.

Trainor, Luke. *British Imperialism and Australian Nationalism: Manipulation, Conflict and Compromise in the Late Nineteenth Century.* New York: Cambridge University Press, 1994.

Uhr, John. *Deliberative Democracy in Australia: the Changing Place of Parliament.* New York: Cambridge University Press, 1998.

Wiseman, John. *Global Nation? Australia and the Politics of Globalisation.* New York: Cambridge University Press, 1998.

Brunei *Darussalam*

Ranjit Singh, D.S. *Historical Dictionary of Brunei Darussalam.* Lanham, MD: Scarecrow Press, 1997.

Burma (Myanmar)

Becka, Jan. *Historical Dictionary of Myanmar.* Lanham, MD: Scarecrow Press, 1995.

Carey, Peter, ed. *Burma: the Challenge of Change in a Divided Society.* New York: Saint Martin's Press, 1997.

Chao Tzang Yawnghwe, *The Shan of Burma: Memors of a Shan Exile,* Singapore, Institute of Southeast Asian Studies, 2010.

Falco, Mathea. *Burma. Time for Change.* Washington D.C.: Brookings, 2004.

Fink, Christina. *Living Silence. Burma under Military Rule.* New York: Palgrave, 2003.

Ganesan N. & Kyaw Yin Hlang, *Myanmar: State, Society and Ethnicity.* Singapore: Institute of Southeast Asian Studies, 2007.

Herbert, Patricia M. *Burma.* Santa Barbara, CA: ABC-CLIO, 1991.

Lintner, Bertil. *Burma in Revolt: Opium and Insurgency since 1948.* Boulder, CO: Westview Press, 1994.

Rotberg, Robert I., ed. *Burma: Prospects for a Democratic Future.* Washington, DC: Brookings Institution Press, 1998.

Seekins, Donald M. *Historical Dictionary of Burma (Myanmar).* Lanham, Maryland: Scarecrow Press, 2006.

_____. *Burma and Japan since 1940: From 'Co-Prosperity' to 'Quiet Dialogue,'* Nordic Institute of Asian Studies monograph 106. Copenhagen: NIAS Press.

Suu Kyi, Aung S., edited by Michael Aris, foreward by Vaclav Havel. *Freedom from Fear and Other Writings.* New York: Penguin, 1991.

Suu Kyi, Aung S. *Letters from Burma.* New York: Viking Penguin, 1998.

Cambodia

Ayers, David M. *Anatomy of a Crisis: Education, Development and the State in Cambodia, 1953–1998.* Honolulu, HI: University of Hawaii Press, 2000.

Chandler, David P. *A History of Cambodia.* Boulder, CO: Westview Press, 3rd ed. 2000.

Chandler, David P. *Brother Number One: A Political Biography of Pol Pot.* Rev. ed. Thailand: Silkworm Books, 2000, originally published by Westview Press, 1999.

Chandler, David P. *Facing the Cambodian Past: Selected Essays, 1971–1994*. Seattle, WA: University of Washington Press, 1998.

Curtis, Grant. *Cambodia Reborn? The Transition to Democracy and Development*. Washington, DC: Brookings Institution Press, 1998.

Dith, Pran and Kim DePaul, eds. *Children of Cambodia's Killing Fields: Memoirs of Survivors*. New Haven, CT: Yale University Press, 1997.

Ebihara, May M., et al., eds. *Cambodian Culture since 1975: Homeland and Exile*. Ithaca, NY: Cornell University Press, 1994.

Kamm, Henry. *Cambodia: Report from a Stricken Land*. New York: Arcade Publishing, 1998.

Kiernan, Ben, ed. *Genocide and Democracy in Cambodia: the Khmer Rouge, the United Nations and the International Community*. New Haven, CT: Yale University Southeast Asia Studies, 1993.

Kiernan, Ben. *The Pol Pot Regime: Race, Power, and Genocide in Cambodia under the Khmer Rouge, 1975–79*. New Haven, CT: Yale University Press, 1996.

Lizée, Pierre. *Peace, Power and Resistance in Cambodia: Global Governance and the Failure of International Conflict Resolution*. New York: Saint Martin's Press, 2000.

Mabbett, Ian and David Chandler. *The Khmers*. Malden, MA: Blackwell Publishers, 1995.

Marin, Marie Alexandrine. *Cambodia: a Shattered Society*. Berkeley, CA: University of California Press, 1994.

Morris, Stephen J. *Why Vietnam Invaded Cambodia: Political Culture and the Causes of War*. Stanford, CA: Stanford University Press, 1998.

Osborne, Milton. *The Mekong: Turbulent Past, Uncertain Future*. New York: Grove/Atlantic, 2000.

Peou, Sorpong. *Cambodia: Change and Continuity in Contemporary Politics*. Brookfield, VT: Ashgate Publishing, 2000.

Ung, Loung. *First They Killed My Father: a Daughter of Cambodia Remembers*. New York: HarperCollins Publishers, 2000.

Ung, Loung. *Lucky Child: A Daughter of Cambodia Reunites with the Sister She Left Behind*. New York, Harper Collins, 2005.

Welaratna, Usha. *Beyond the Killing Fields: Voices of the Cambodian Survivors in America*. Stanford, CA: Stanford University Press, 1993.

China

Adshead, Samuel Adrian Miles. *China in World History*. New York: Saint Martin's Press, 2000.

Barme, Geremie R. *In the Red: Contemporary Chinese Culture*. New York: Columbia University Press, 1999.

Becker, Jasper. *The Chinese*. New York: The Free Press, 2000.

Bolt, Paul J. and Albert S. Willner, eds. *China's Nuclear Future*. Boulder, CO: Lynne Rienner, 2005.

Blunden, Caroline and Mark Elvin. *Cultural Atlas of China*. Rev. ed. New York: Facts on File, 1998.

Brook, Timothy. *Quelling the People: the Military Suppression of the Beijing Democracy Movement*. New York: Oxford University Press, 1992.

Brown, Harold et al. *Chinese Military Power*. Washington D.C.: Brookings, 2004.

Burstein, Daniel and Arne J. De Keijzer. *Big Dragon: China's Future: What It Means for Business, the Economy, and the Global Order*. New York: Simon & Schuster, 1998.

Buruma, Ian, *Bad Elements: Chinese Rebels from Los Angeles to Beijing*, New York, NY: Vantage Books, 2006.

Chan, Anita. *Transforming Asian Socialism: China and Vietnam Compared*. Lanham, MD: Rowman & Littlefield Publishers, 1999.

Chang, Jung and Jon Halliday. *Mao: The Unknown Story*. New York, Knopf, 2005.

Chang, Tony H. *China during the Cultural Revolution, 1966–1976: a Selected Bibliography of English Language Works*. Westport, CT: Greenwood Publishing Group, 1999.

Cheng, Chu-Yuan. *Behind the Tiananmen Massacre*. Boulder, CO: Westview Press, 1990.

Clough, Ralph N. *Cooperation or Conflict in the Taiwan Strait?* Lanham, MD: Rowman & Littlefield Publishers, 1999.

Day, Kristen A. *China's Environment and the Challenge of Sustainable Development*. Armonk, NY: M.E. Sharpe, 2005.

Dreyer, June T. *China's Political System*. Reading, MA: Addison-Wesley Educational Publishers, 2000.

Dryer, Edward L. *China at War, 1901–1949*. White Plains, NY: Longman Publishing, 1995.

Finkelstein, David Michael. *Washington's Taiwan Dilemma, 1949–1950: from Abandonment to Salvation*. Fairfax, VA: George Mason University Press, 1993.

Fishman C. Ted. *China Inc. How the Rise of the Next Superpower Challenges America & the World*. New York: Scribner, 2005.

Fitzgerald, John. *Awakening China: Politics, Culture, and Class in the Nationalist Revolution*. Stanford, CA: Stanford University Press, 1996.

Foot, Rosemary. *The Practice of Power: US Relations with China since 1949*. New York: Oxford University Press, 1995.

Gamer, Robert E., ed. *Understanding Contemporary China*. Boulder, CO: Lynne Reinner, 2003.

Garrison, Jean A. *Making China Policy: From Nixon to G.W. Bush*. Boulder, CO: Lynne Rienner, 2005.

Giquel, Prosper. Edited and translated by Steven A. Leibo. *A Journal of the Chinese Civil War, 1864*. Honolulu, HI: University of Hawaii Press, 1985.

Gittings, John. *The Changing Face of China: From Mao to Market*. NY: Oxford, 2005.

Grunfeld, Thomas, ed. *The Making of Modern Tibet*. Rev. ed. Armonk, NY: M.E. Sharpe, 1996.

Goldstein, Melvyn C. *The Snow Lion and the Dragon*. Berkeley, University of California Press, 1997.

Guldin, Gregory E., ed. *Farewell to Peasant China: Rural Urbanization and Social Change in the Late Twentieth Century*. Armonk, NY: M.E. Sharpe, 1997.

Gurtov, Mel and Byong-Moo Hwang. *China's Security: the New Role of the Military*. Boulder, CO: Lynne Rienner Publishers, 1998.

Harris, Richard B. *Wildlife Conservation in China*. Armonk, NY: M.E. Sharp, 2008.

He, Henry Yuhuai. *Dictionary of the Political Thought of the People's Republic of China*. Armonk, NY: M.E. Sharpe, 2000.

Henderson, Callum. *China on the Brink: the Myths and Realities of the World's Largest Market*. New York: McGraw-Hill, 1999.

Holz, Carsten, *The Role of Central Banking in China's Economic Reforms*. Ithica, NY: Cornell University Press, 1993.

Hook, Brian and Dennis Twitchett. *The Cambridge Encyclopedia of China*. New York: Cambridge University Press, 2nd ed. 1991.

Hsieh, Chiao-Min, ed. *Changing China*. Boulder, CO: Westview Press, 2000.

Huang, Ray. *Broadening the Horizons of Chinese History: Discourses, Syntheses, and Comparisons*. Armonk, NY: M.E. Sharpe, 1999.

Hui, Wang. *China's New Order. Society, Politics, and Economy in Transition*. Cambridge, MA: Harvard University, 2003.

Hung-Mao, Tien and Yun-Han Chu, eds. *China under Jiang Zemin*. Boulder, CO: Lynne Rienner Publishers, 2000.

Huot, Claire. *China's New Cultural Scene: a Handbook of Changes*. Durham, NC: Duke University Press, 1999.

Ji, You. *Armed Forces in China*. New York: I.B. Tauris & Company, 2000.

Jiaqi, Yan and Gao Gao. Translated by D.W.K. Kwok. *Turbulent Decade: a History of the Cultural Revolution*. Honolulu, HI: University of Hawaii Press, 1996.

Joseph, William A., ed. *China Briefing: the Contradictions of Change*. Armonk, NY: M.E. Sharpe, 1997.

Kennedy, Thomas L. *The Arms of Kiangnan: Modernization in the Chinese Ordnance Industry, 1860–1895*. Boulder, CO: Westview Press, 1978.

Ke-wen, Wang, ed. *Modern China: an Encyclopedia of History, Culture, and Nationalism*. New York: Garland Publishing, 1999.

Kornberg, Judith F. and John R. Faust. *China in World Politics: Policies, Processes, Prospects*. 2d ed. Boulder, CO: Lynne Rienner, 2005.

Leibo, Steven A. *Transferring Technology to China: Prosper Giquel and the Self-Strengthening Movement*. Berkeley, CA: University of California Press, Institute of East Asian Studies, 1985.

Leung, Edwin Pak-Wah, ed. *Historical Dictionary of Revolutionary China, 1839–1976*. Westport, CT: Greenwood Press, 1992.

Levine, Marilyn Avra. *The Found Generation: Chinese Communists in Europe during the Twenties.* Seattle, WA: University of Washington Press, 1993.

Lin, Bih-Jaw and James T. Myers. *Contemporary China and the Changing International Community.* Columbia, SC: University of South Carolina Press, 1994.

Lo, Dic. *Market and Institutional Regulation in Chinese Industrialization, 1978–94.* St. Martin's Press, 1997.

MacFarquhar, Roderick, ed. *The Politics of China: the Eras of Mao and Deng.* New York: Cambridge University Press, 1997.

MacKerras, Colin and Donald H. McMillen, eds. *Dictionary of the Politics of the People's Republic of China.* New York: Routledge, 1998.

McGiffert, Carola, *China in the American Political Imagination.* Washington, Center for Strategic and International Studies, 2003.

Malik, Hafeez, ed. *Roles of the United States, Russia and China in the New World.* New York: Saint Martin's Press, 1997.

Mann, James, *The China Fantasy: How Our Leaders Explain Away Chinese Repression,* New York, NY: Penguin Group Inc. 2007.

Marti, Michael E. *China and the Legacy of Deng Xiaoping: From Communist Revolution to Capitalist Evolution.* Washington, D.C.: Brassey's Inc. 2002.

Mathias, Jim, ed. *Computers, Language Reform, and Lexicography in China: a Report.* Pullman, WA: Washington State University Press, 1980.

Meisner, Maurice. *The Deng Xiaoping Era: an Inquiry into the Fate of Chinese Socialism, 1978–1994.* New York: Hill & Wang, 1996.

Miles, James A. *The Legacy of Tiananmen: China in Disarray.* Ann Arbor, MI: University of Michigan, 1995.

Mok, Ka-Ho. *Intellectuals and the State in Post-Mao China.* New York: Saint Martin's Press, 1998.

Murowchick, Robert E., ed. *China: Ancient Culture, Modern Land.* Norman, OK: University of Oklahoma Press, 1994.

Nathan, Andrew J. *The Great Wall and the Empty Fortress: China's Search for Security.* New York: W.W. Norton & Company, 1997.

Nie Zeng Jifen. Translated and annotated by Thomas L. Kennedy; edited by Thomas L. Kennedy and Micki Kennedy. *Testimony of a Confucian Woman: the Autobiography of Mrs. Nie Zeng Jifen, 1852–1942.* Athens, GA: University of Georgia Press, 1993.

Pearson, Margaret M. *China's New Business Elite: the Political Consequences of Economic Reform.* Berkeley, CA: University of California Press, 1997.

Perkins, Dorothy. *The Encyclopedia of China: the Essential Reference to China, Its History and Culture.* New York: Facts on File, 1998.

Richter, Frank-Jurgen, ed. *The Dragon Millennium: Chinese Business in the Coming World Economy.* Westport, CT: Greenwood Publishing Group, 2000

Saw Swee-Hock, editor, *Regional Economic Development in China,* Singapore, Institute of Southeast Asian Studies, 2009.

Sautman, Barry Ed. *Contemporary Tibet: Politics, Development, and Society in a Disputed Region.* Armonk, NY: M.E. Sharpe, 2006.

Schell, Orville. *Mandate of Heaven: a New Generation of Entrepreneurs, Dissidents, Bohemians, and Technocrats Lays Claim to China's Future.* New York: Simon & Schuster, 1994.

Segal, Gerald and Richard H. Yang, eds. *Chinese Economic Reform: the Impact on Security.* New York: Routledge, 1996.

Shakya, Tsering. *The Dragon in the Land of the Snows: a History of Modern Tibet since 1947.* New York: Columbia University Press, 1999.

Shambaugh, David. *Beautiful Imperialist: China Perceives America, 1972–1990.* Princeton, NJ: Princeton University Press, 1991.

Shambaugh, David, ed. *China's Military in Transition.* New York: Oxford University Press, 1998.

Shambaugh, David, ed. *Is China Unstable? Assessing the Factors.* Armonk, NY: M.E. Sharpe, 2000.

Shaoguang, Wang and Hu Angang. *The Political Economy of Uneven Development: the Case of China.* Armonk, NY: M.E. Sharpe, 2000.

Shirk, Susan L. *China: Fragile Superpower.* New York: Oxford University Press, 2007.

Shaughnessy, Edward L., ed. *China: Empire and Civilization.* NY: Oxford University Press, nd.

Shenkar, Oded, *The Chinese Century.* Upper Saddle River, NJ: Wharton School of Publishing, 2006.

Sidhu, Waheguru and Jing-dong Yuan. *China and India: Cooperation or Conflict?* Boulder, CO: Lynne Reinner, 2003.

Smith, Christopher J. *China in the Post-Utopian Age.* Boulder, CO: Westview Press, 2000.

Sun, Yan. *The Chinese Reassessment of Socialism, 1976–1992.* Princeton, NJ: Princeton University Press, 1995.

Tanner, Murray Scott. *The Politics of Lawmaking in Post-Mao China: Institutions, Processes, and Democratic Prospects.* New York: Oxford University Press, 1999.

Teiwes, Frederick C. and Warren Sun. *China's Road to Disaster: Mao, Central Politicians and Provincial Leaders in the Unfolding of the Great Leap Forward, 1955–1959.* Armonk, NY: M.E. Sharpe, 1998.

Terrill, Ross. *The New Chinese Empire. Beijing's Political Dilemma and What it Means for the United States.* Boulder, CO: Westview, 2003.

Tien, Hung-mao and Yun-han Chu, eds. *China Under Jiang Zemin.* Boulder, CO: Lynne Reinner, 2000.

Tyler, Patrick, *A Great Wall: Six Presidents And China,* New York, A Century Foundation Book, 1999, 2000.

Vogel, Ezra F., ed. *Living with China: U.S.—China Relations in the Twenty-First Century.* New York: W.W. Norton & Company, 1997.

Wang, Gabe T. *China's Population: Problems, Thoughts, and Policies.* Brookfield, VT: Ashgate, 1999.

Wang Lixiong and Tsering Shakya, The Struggle for Tibet; Tibet's Last Stand? The Tibetan Uprising of 2008 and China's Response, *London,* Verso, 2009

Wang, Shaoguang and Angang Hu. *The Political Economy of Uneven Development: the Case of China.* Armonk, NY: M.E. Sharpe, 1999.

Wasserstrom, Jeffrey N. and Elizabeth J. Perry, eds. *Popular Protest and Political Culture in Modern China.* Boulder, CO: Westview Press, 1994.

Waters, Harry J. *China's Economic Development Strategies for the 21st Century.* Westport, CT: Greenwood Publishing Group, 1997.

Weston, Timothy B. and Lionel M. Jensen, eds. *China beyond the Headlines.* Lanham, MD: Rowman & Littlefield Publishers, 2000.

Winckler, Edwin A., ed. *Transition from Communism in China: Institutional and Comparative Analysis.* Boulder, CO: Lynne Rienner Publishers, 1999.

Wortzel, Larry M. *Dictionary of Contemporary Chinese Military History.* Westport, CT: Greenwood Publishing Group, 1999.

Wu, Yanrui. *China's Consumer Revolution: the Emerging Patterns of Wealth and Expenditure.* Edward Elgar Publishing, 1999.

Zhai, Qiang. *The Dragon, the Lion, and the Eagle: Chinese-British-American Relations, 1949–1958.* Kent, OH: Kent State University Press, 1994.

Zhang, Wei W. *Transforming China.* New York: St. Martin's Press, 2000.

Zhang, Xiaoguang. *China's Trade and International Comparative Advantage: Studies in the Modern Chinese Economy.* New York: Saint Martin's Press, 2000.

Hong Kong

Butenhoff, Linda. *Social Movements and Political Reform in Hong Kong.* Westport, CT: Greenwood Publishing Group, 1999.

Callick, Rowan. *Comrades and Capitalists: Hong Kong since the Takeover.* Portland, OR: International Specialized Book Services, 1998.

Chan, Ming K., ed. *Precarious Balance: Hong Kong between China and Britain.* Armonk, NY: M.E. Sharpe, 1994.

Cohen, Warren I., ed. *Hong Kong under Chinese Rule: the Economic and Political Implications of Reversion.* New York: Cambridge University Press, 1997.

Hsiung, James C. *Hong Kong and the Super Paradox: Life after Return to China.* New York: St. Martin's Press, 2000.

Keay, John. *Empire's End: a History of the Far East from High Colonialism to Hong Kong.* New York: Scribner, 1997.

Ku, Agnes S. *Narratives, Politics, and the Public Sphere: Struggles over Political Reform in the Final Transitional Years in Hong Kong (1992–1994).* Brookfield, VT: Ashgate, 1999.

Lam, Wai-man. *Understanding the Political Culture of Hong Kong.* Amonk, NY: M.E. Sharp, 2004.

Meyer, David R. *Hong Kong as a Global Metropolis.* New York: Cambridge University Press, 2000.

Pang-Kwong, Li. *Hong Kong from Britain to China: Political Cleavages, Electoral Dynamics and Institutional Changes.* Brookfield, VT: Ashgate Publishing, 2000.

Patten, Christopher. *East and West: the Last Governor of Hong Kong on Power, Freedom and the Future.* New York: Times Books, 1998.

Postiglione, Gerald A. and James T. H. Tang, eds. *Hong Kong's Reunion with China: the Global Dimensions.* Armonk, NY: M.E. Sharpe, 1997.

Roberti, Mark. *The Fall of Hong Kong: Britain's Betrayal and China's Triumph.* New York: John Wiley & Sons, 1994.

Roberts, Elfed Vaughan, et al. *Historical Dictionary of Hong Kong and Macau.* Lanham, MD: Scarecrow Press, 1992.

Shipp, Steve. *Hong Kong, China: a Political History of the British Crown Colony's Transfer to Chinese Rule.* Jefferson, NC: McFarland & Company, 1995.

Thomas, Nicholas. *Democracy Denied: Identity, Civil, Society and Illiberal Democracy in Hong Kong.* Brookfield, VT: Ashgate Publishing Company, 1999.

Tsang, Steve. *Modern History of Hong Kong, 1841–1998.* London: I.B. Tauris & Company, 1998.

Van Kemendade, William. *China, Hong Kong, Taiwan, Incorporated.* New York: Alfred A. Knopf, 1997.

Indonesia

Baker, Richard W. *Indonesia: the Challenge of Change.* New York: St. Martin's Press, 1999.

Bresnan, John. *Managing Indonesia: the Modern Political Economy.* New York: Columbia University Press, 1993.

Cribb, Robert. *Historical Atlas of Indonesia.* Honolulu, HI: University of Hawaii Press, 1998.

Cribb, Robert. *Historical Dictionary of Indonesia.* Lanham, MD: Scarecrow Press, 1992.

Cribb, Robert, ed. *The Late Colonial State in Indonesia: Political and Economic Foundations of the Netherlands Indies, 1880–1942.* Leiden: KITLV Press, 1994.

Cribb, Robert and Colin Brown. *Modern Indonesia: a History since 1945.* New York: Longman, 1995.

Crouch, Harold, *Political Reform in Indonesia after Soeharto,* Singapore, Institute of Southeast Asian Studies, 2010.

Emmerson, Donald K., ed. *Indonesia beyond Suharto.* Armonk, NY: M.E. Sharpe, 1998.

Frederick, William H. and Robert L. Worden, eds. *Indonesia: a Country Study.* Washington, DC: U.S. GPO, 5th ed. 1993.

Friend, Theodore. *Indonesian Destinies.* Cambridge, MA: Harvard University, 2003.

Gardner, Paul F. *Shared Hopes, Separate Fears: Fifty Years of U.S.—Indonesian Relations.* Westport, CT: Westview Press, 1997.

Hill, Hal. *The Indonesian Economy since 1966.* New York: Cambridge University Press, 2000.

Hilmy, Masdar: *Islamism and Democracy in Indonesia: Piety & Pragmatism,* Singapore, Institute of Southeast Asian Studies, 2010.

Kipp, Rita Smith. *Dissociated Identities: Ethnicity, Religion, and Class in an Indonesian Society.* Ann Arbor, MI: University of Michigan Press, 1993.

Martin, Ian. *Self-Determination in East Timor: The United Nations, the Ballot, and International Intervention.* Boulder, CO: Lynne Reinner, 2001.

Platzdasch, Bernhard, *Islamism In Indonesia: Politics in the Emerging Democracy,* Singapore, Institute of Southeast Asian Studies, 2009.

Ramage, Douglas E. *Politics in Indonesia: Democracy, Islam, and the Ideology of Tolerance.* New York: Routledge, 1995.

Ricklefs, Merle Calvin. *A History of Modern Indonesia: c. 1300 to the Present.* Stanford, CA: Stanford University Press, 1993.

Schiller, Jim and Barbara Martin-Schiller, eds. *Imagining Indonesia: Cultural Politics and Political Culture.* Athens, OH: Ohio University Press, 1997.

Schwartz, Adam. *A Nation in Waiting: Indonesia in the 1990s.* Boulder, CO: Westview Press, 1994.

Simons, G.L. *Indonesia: the Long Oppression.* New York: Saint Martin's Press, 2000.

Smith, Michael G. and Moreen Dee. *Peacekeeping in East Timor: The Path to Independence.* Boulder, CO: Lynne Reinner, 2003.

Uhlin, Anders. *Indonesia and the "Third Wave of Democratization": the Indonesian Pro-Democracy Movement in a Changing World.* New York: St. Martin's Press, 1997.

Vatikiotis, Michael R.J. *Indonesian Politics under Suharto: the Rise and Fall of the New Order.* New York: Routledge, 1999.

Japan

Abe, Etsuo and Robert Fitzgerald, eds. *The Origins of Japanese Industrial Power: Strategy, Institutions and the Development of Organisational Capability.* Portland, OR: Frank Cass & Company, 1995.

Alinson, Gary D. and Yasunori Sone, eds. *Political Dynamics in Contemporary Japan.* Ithaca, NY: Cornell University Press, 1993.

Aoki, Masahito and Gary R. Saxonhouse, eds. *Finance, Governance and Competitiveness in Japan.* New York: Oxford University Press, 2000.

Banno, Junji. *The Establishment of the Japanese Constitutional System.* New York: Routledge, 1995.

Beasley, W.G. *The Japanese Experience: a Short History of Japan.* Berkeley, CA: University of California Press, 1999.

Bix, Herbert P. *Hirohito and the Making of Modern Japan.* New York: HarperCollins Publishers, 2000.

Browring, Richard and Peter Kornicki, eds. *The Cambridge Encyclopedia of Japan.* New York: Cambridge University Press, 1993.

Buckley, Roger. *Japan Today.* New York: Cambridge University Press, 1999.

Carlile, Lonny E. and Mark Tilton, eds. *Is Japan Really Changing Its Ways? Regulatory Reform and the Japanese Economy.* Washington, DC: Brookings Institution Press, 1998.

Christensen, Ray. *Ending the LDP Hegemony: Party Cooperation in Japan.* Honolulu, HI: University of Hawaii Press, 2000.

Cohen, Stephen D. *An Ocean Apart: Explaining Three Decades of U.S.-Japanese Trade Frictions.* Westport, CT: Greenwood Publishing Group, 1998.

Curtis, Gerald L., ed. *Japan's Foreign Policy after the Cold War: Coping with Change.* Armonk, NY: M.E. Sharpe, 1993.

Curtis, Gerald L., ed. *Politicians and Policymaking in Japan.* Washington D.C.: Brookings, 2002.

Dower, John. *Embracing Defeat: Japan in the Wake of World War II.* New York: W.W. Norton & Company, 1999.

Drysdale, Peter and Luke Gower. *The Japanese Economy.* New York: Routledge, 2000.

Edstrom, Bert. *Japan's Evolving Foreign Policy Doctrine: from Yoshida to Miyazawa.* New York: St. Martin's Press, 1999.

Eisenstadt, Samuel N. *Japanese Civilization.* Chicago: University of Chicago Press, 1998.

Fessler, Susanna, *Wandering Heart: The Work and Method of Hayashi Fumiko.* Albany: SUNY Press, 1998.

Fessler, Susanna, *Musashi in Tuscany: Japanese Overseas Travel Literature 1860–1912.* Ann Arbor, Michigan: Center for Japanese Studies, 2004.

Flath, David. *The Japanese Economy.* New York: Oxford University Press, 2000.

Fukushima, Akiko. *Japanese Foreign Policy: the Emerging Logic of Multilateralism.* New York: St. Martin's Press, 1999.

Garon, Sheldon. *Molding Japanese Minds: the State in Everyday Life.* Princeton, NJ: Princeton University Press, 1997.

Giffard, Sydney. *Japan among the Powers, 1880–1990.* New Haven, CT: Yale University Press, 1994.

Gordon, Andrew, ed. *Postwar Japan as History.* Berkeley, CA: University of California Press, 1993.

Green, Michael J. *Arming Japan: Defense Production, Alliance Politics, and the Postwar Search for Autonomy*. New York: Columbia University Press, 1995.

Green, Michael JU. *Japan's Reluctant Realism. Foreign Policy Challenges in an Era of Uncertain Power*. New York: Palgrave, 2003.

Hall, Ivan P. *Cartels of the Mind: Japan's Intellectual Closed Shop*. New York: W.W. Norton & Company, 1997.

Hall, Maximilian J. *Financial Reform in Japan: Causes and Consequences*. Northampton, MA: Edward Elgar Publishing, 1999.

Heneshall, Kenneth G. *A History of Japan: from Stone Age to Superpower*. New York: Saint Martin's Press, 1998.

Herbig, Paul A. *Innovation Japanese Style: a Cultural and Historical Perspective*. Westport, CT: Quorum Books, 1995.

Herzog, Peter J. *Japan's Pseudo-Democracy*. New York: New York University Press, 1993.

Holgerson, Karen M. *The Japan-U.S. Trade Friction Dilemma: the Role of Perception*. Brookfield, VT: Ashgate Publishing Company, 1998.

Hrebenar, Ronald J. *Political Parties and Elections in Japan: the Post–1993 System*. Boulder, CO: Westview Press, 2000.

Hsu, Robert C. *The MIT Encyclopedia of the Japanese Economy*. Cambridge, MA: MIT Press, 1994.

Huber, Thomas M. *Strategic Economy in Japan*. Boulder, CO: Westview Press, 1994.

Huffman, James L. *Modern Japan: an Encyclopedia of History, Culture, and Nationalism*. New York: Garland Publishing, 1999.

Inoguchi, Takashi. *Japan's Foreign Policy Today*. New York: Saint Martin's Press, 2000.

Iriye, Akira. *Japan and the Wider World: from the Mid-Nineteenth Century to Present*. New York: Longman, 1997.

Irokawa, Daikichi. Translated by John K. Urda. *The Age of Hirohito: in Search of Modern Japan*. New York: Free Press, 1995.

Itoh, Mayumi. *Globalization of Japan: U.S. Efforts to Open Japan from Commodore Matthew Perry to Defense Secretary William Perry*. New York: St. Martin's Press, 1998.

Jansen, Marius B. *The Making of Modern Japan*. Cambridge, MA: Harvard University Press, 2000.

Japan: an Illustrated Encyclopedia. 2 vols. New York: Kodansha America, 1994.

Johnson, Chalmers. *Japan: Who Governs?* New York: W.W. Norton, 1995.

Johnson-Freese, Joan. *Over the Pacific: Japanese Space Policy into the Twenty-First Century*. Dubuque, IA: Kendall/Hunt Publishing, 1993.

Koppel, Bruce M., ed. *Japan's Foreign Aid: Power and Policy in a New Era*. Boulder, CO: Westview Press, 1993.

Lincoln, Edward J. *Japan's New Global Role*. Washington, DC: Brookings Institution Press, 1993.

Luney, Percy R., Jr. and Kazuyuki Takahashi, eds. *Japanese Constitutional Law*. Tokyo: University of Tokyo Press, 1993.

Maher, John C. and Gaynor Macdonald, eds. *Diversity in Japanese Culture and Language*. New York: Kegan Paul International, 1995.

Mann, Thomas E. and Sasaki Takeshi, eds. *Governance for a New Century. Japanese Challenges, American Experience*. Washington D.C.: Brookings, 2002.

McCargo, Duncan. *Contemporary Japan*. New York: St. Martin's Press, 2000.

McNeil, Frank. *Democracy in Japan: the Emerging Global Concern*. New York: Crown Publishing, 1994.

Mochizuki, Mike M. *Japan Reorients: the Quest for Wealth and Security in East Asia*. Washington, DC: Brookings Institution Press, 2001.

Nathan, John. *Japan Unbound: A Volatile Nation's Quest for Pride and Purpose*. NY: Houghton Mifflin, 2004.

Nester, William R. *American Power, the New World Order and the Japanese Challenge*. New York: Saint Martin's Press, 1993.

Porter, Michael, et al. *Can Japan Compete?* New York: Basic Books, 2000.

Reischauer, Edwin O. and Marius Jansen. *The Japanese Today*. Cambridge, MA: Harvard University Press, rev. ed. 1995.

Richardson, Bradley M. *Japanese Democracy: Power, Coordination, and Performance*. New Haven, CT: Yale University Press, 1997.

Sakakibara, Eisuke. *Structural Reform in Japan. Breaking the Iron Triangle*. Washington D.C.: Brookings, 2003.

Sato, Kazuo, ed. *The Transformation of the Japanese Economy*. Armonk, NY: M.E. Sharpe, 1999.

Sato, Ryuzo. *The Chrysanthemum and the Eagle: the Future of U.S.-Japan Relations*. New York: New York University Press, 1994.

Schaller, Michael. *Altered States: the United States and Japan since Occupation*. New York: Oxford University Press, 1997.

Schoppa, Leonard J. *Bargaining with Japan: What American Pressure Can and Cannot Do*. New York: Columbia University Press, 1997.

Smith, Patrick. *Japan: a Reinterpretation*. New York: Pantheon, 1997.

Stockwin, J.A. *Governing Japan: Divided Politics in a Major Economy*. Malden, MA: Blackwell Publishers, 1998.

Sugimoto, Yoshio. *An Introduction to Japanese Society*. New York: Cambridge University Press, 1997.

Uriu, Robert M. *Troubled Industries: Confronting Economic Change in Japan*. Ithaca, NY: Cornell University Press, 1996.

Weiner, Michael, ed. *Japan's Minorities: Illusion of Homogeneity*. New York: Routledge, 1997.

Woronoff, Jon. *The Japanese Social Crisis*. New York: Saint Martin's Press, 1997.

Wicaksono, Agung, *Energy Efficiency in Japan*, Singapore, Institute of Southeast Asian Studies, 2098.

Yasutomo, Dennis T. *The New Multilateralism in Japan's Foreign Policy*. New York: Saint Martin's Press, 1995.

Zhang, Wei-Bin and Ake E. Andersson. *Japan Versus China in the Industrial Race*. New York: Saint Martin's Press, 1998.

Korea

Alford, C. Fred. *Think No Evil: Korean Values in the Age of Globalization*. Ithaca, NY: Cornell University Press, 1999.

Becker, Jasper *Rouge Regime: Kim Jong Il and the Looming Threat of North Korea*, New York, Oxford University Press 2005.

Bedeski, Robert E. *The Transformation of South Korea: Reform and Reconstitution in the Sixth Republic under Roh Tae Woo, 1987–1992*. New York: Routledge, 1994.

Buzo, Adrian. *The Making of Modern Korea. A History*. NY: Routledge, 2002.

Chinoy, Mike, *Meltdown The Inside Story of the North Korean Nuclear Crisis*. New York, St. Martin's Press, 2008.

Cumings, Bruce. *Korea's Place in the Sun: a Modern History*. New York: W.W. Norton, 1997.

Eberstadt, Nicholas. *Korea Approaches Reunification*. Armonk, NY: M.E. Sharpe, 1995.

Hamm, Taik-Young. *Arming the Two Koreas: State, Capital, and Military Power*. New York: Routledge, 1999.

Helgensen, Geir. *Democracy and Authority in Korea*. New York: Saint Martin's Press, 1998.

Hulbert, Homer B. *History of Korea*. Honolulu, HI: University of Hawaii Press, 1998.

Hunter, Helen-Louise. *Kim Il-Sung's North Korea*. Westport, CT: Greenwood Publishing Group, 1999.

Jung, Walter and Xiao-Bing Li, eds. *Korea and Regional Geopolitics*. Lanham, MD: University Press of America, 1998.

Kihl, Young Whan. *Korea and the World: beyond the Cold War*. Boulder, CO: Westview Press, 1994.

Kim, Dae Jung. *Mass Participatory Economy: Korea's Road to World Economic Power*. Lanham, MD: University Press of America, 1996.

Kim, Eun M. *Big Business, Strong State: Collusion and Conflict in South Korean Development, 1960–1990*. Albany, NY: State University of New York Press, 1997.

Kim, Gye-Dong. *Foreign Intervention in Korea*. Brookfield, VT: Dartmouth Publishing Company, 1993.

Kim, Hakjoon. *Korea's Relations with Her Neighbors in a Changing World*. Elizabeth, NJ: Hollym International, 1993.

Kim, Samuel S., ed. *Korea's Globalization*. New York: Cambridge University Press, 2000.

Kim, Samuel S., ed. *The North Korean System in the Post-Cold War Era*. New York: Palgrave, 2003.

Lancaster, Lewis R., et al. *Religion and Society in Contemporary Korea*. Berkeley, CA: Institute of East Asian Studies, 1998.

Lee, Chae-Jin. *China and Korea: Dynamic Relations*. Stanford, CA: Hoover Institution Press, 1996.

Lee, Hyung-Koo. *The Korean Economy: Perspectives for the Twenty-First Century.* Albany, NY: State University of New York Press, 1996.

Lee, Kenneth B. *Korea and East Asia: the Story of a Phoenix.* Westport, CT: Greenwood Publishing Group, 1997.

Lee, Peter H., ed. *Sourcebook of Korean Civilization, vol. 1: from Early Times to the Sixteenth Century.* New York: Columbia University Press, 1993.

Lee, Peter H., ed. *Sourcebook of Korean Civilization, vol. 2: from the Seventeenth Century to the Modern Period.* New York: Columbia University Press, 1996.

Lee, Yur-Bok and Wayne Patterson, eds. *Korean-American Relations, 1866–1997.* Albany, NY: State University of New York Press, 1998.

Lie, John. *The Political Economy of South Korea.* Stanford, CA: Stanford University Press, 1998.

Macdonald, Donald Stone. *The Koreans: Contemporary Politics and Society.* Bouder, CO: Westview Press, 3rd ed. 1996.

Martin, Bradley, *Under the Loving Care of the Fatherly Leader, North Korea and the Kim Dynasty,* New York, St. Martins Press, 2004.

Mazarr, Michael J. *North Korea and the Bomb: a Case Study in Nonproliferation.* New York: St. Martin's Press, 1995.

McNamara, Dennis L. *Trade and Transformation in Korea, 1876–1945.* Boulder, CO: Westview Press, 1996.

Nahm, Andrew C. *Historical Dictionary of the Republic of Korea.* Lanham, MD: Scarecrow Press, 1993.

Natsios, Andrew S. *The Great North Korean Famine.* Herndon, VA: U.S. Institute of Peace Press, 2002.

Noland, Marcus. *Avoiding the Apocalypse: the Future of the Two Koreas.* Washington, DC: Institute for International Economics, 2000.

Oberdorfer, Don. *The Two Koreas: a Contemporary History.* Rev. ed. Boulder, CO: Westview, 2001.

Oh, John K. *Korean Politics: the Quest for Democratization and Economic Development.* Ithaca, NY: Cornell University Press, 1999.

Oh, Kongdan, ed. *Korea Briefing, 1997–1999: Challenges and Change at the Turn of the Century.* Armonk, NY: M.E. Sharpe, 2000.

Oh, Kongdan and Ralph C. Hassig. *North Korea through the Looking Glass.* Washington D.C.: Brookings, 2000.

O'Hanlon, Michael and Mochizuki, Mike. *Crisis on the Korean Peninsula. How to Deal with a Nuclear North Korea.* Washington D.C.: Brookings, 2003.

Oliver, Robert T. *A History of the Korean People in Modern Times: 1800 to the Present.* Cranbury, NJ: University of Delaware Press, 1993.

SaKong, Il. *Korea in the World Economy.* Washington, DC: Institute for International Economics, 1993.

Savada, Andrea Matles, ed. *North Korea: a Country Study.* Washington, DC: U.S. GPO, 4th ed. 1994.

Savada, Andrea Matles and William R. Shaw, eds. *South Korea: a Country Study.* Washington, DC: U.S. GPO, 4th ed. 1992.

Sigel, Leon V. *Disarming Strangers: Nuclear Diplomacy with North Korea.* Princeton, NJ: Princeton University Press, 1998.

Simons, Geoff. *Korea: the Search for Sovereignty.* New York: Saint Martin's Press, 1995.

Sun, De-Soon, ed. *North Korea after Kim Il Sung.* Boulder, CO: Lynne Rainier Publishers, 1998.

Swartout, Robert R. *Mandarins, Gunboats, and Power Politics: Owen Nicker son and the International Rivalries in Korea.* Honolulu, HI: Asian Studies Program, University of Hawaii, 1980.

The Two Korea and the United States: Issues of Peace, Security and Economic Cooperation. Armonk, NY: M.E. Sharpe, 2000.

Laos

Bourdet, Yves. *The Economics of Transition in Laos: from Socialism to ASEAN Integration.* Northampton, MA: Edward Elgar Publishing, 2000.

Castle, Timothy N. *At War in the Shadow of Vietnam: U.S. Military Aid to the Royal Lao Government, 1955–1975.* New York: Columbia University Press, 1993.

Cordell, Helen. *Laos.* Santa Barbara, CA: ABC-CLIO, 1991.

Pholsena, Vatthana. *Post-War Laos: The Politics of Culture, History and Identity.* Singapore. Institute of Southeast Asian Studies, 2006.

Savada, Andrea Matles. *Laos: a Country Study.* Washington, DC: U.S. GPO, 3rd ed. 1995.

Stuart-Fox, Martin. *A History of Laos.* New York: Cambridge University Press, 1997.

Stuart-Fox, Martin. *Historical Dictionary of Laos.* Lanham, MD: Scarecrow Press, 1992.

Than, Mya and Joseph L.H. Tan, eds. *Laos' Dilemmas and Options: the Challenge of Economic Transition in the 1990s.* New York: St. Martin's Press, 1997.

Macau

Cheng, Christina M. *Macau: a Cultural Janus.* Hong Kong: Hong Kong University Press, 1999.

Porter, Jonathan. *Macau, the Imaginary City: Culture and Society, 1557 to the Present.* Boulder, CO: Westview Press, 1996.

Roberts, Elfed Vaughn, et al. *Historical Dictionary of Hong Kong and Macau.* Lanham, MD: Scarecrow Press, 1992.

Shipp, Steve. *Macau, China: a Political History of the Portuguese Colony's Transition to Chinese Rule.* Jefferson, NC: McFarland & Company, 1997.

Malaysia

Beng, Oui Kee, *Era of Transition: Malaysia after Mahathir.* Singapore: Institute of Southeast Asian Studies, 2006.

Bruton, Henry J. *Sri Lanka and Malaysia.* New York: Oxford University Press, 1992.

Drabble, John H. *An Economic History of Malaysia, C. 1800–1990: the Transition to Modern Economic Growth.* New York: St. Martin's Press, 2000.

Gomez, Edmund T. *Malaysia's Political Economy: Politics, Patronage and Profits.* New York: Cambridge University Press, 1997.

Kaur, Amarjit. *Historical Dictionary of Malaysia.* Lanham, MD: Scarecrow Press, 1993.

Kaur, Amarjit. *The Shaping of Malaysia.* New York: St. Martin's Press, 1999.

Lucas, Robert E. *Restructuring the Malaysian Economy: Development and Human Resources.* New York: St. Martin's Press, 1999.

Milne, R.S. *Politics under Mahathir.* New York: Routledge, 1999.

Munro-Kua, Anne. *Authoritarian Populism in Malaysia.* New York: St. Martin's Press, 1997.

Mongolia

Kotkin, Stephen, ed. *Mongolia in the Twentieth Century.* Armonk, NY: M.E. Sharpe, 2000.

Nordby, Judith. *Mongolia.* Santa Barbara, CA: ABC-CLIO, 1993.

Rossabi, Morris. *Modern Mongolia: Descendants of Khubilai Khan in Transition.* Berkeley, CA: University of California Press, 2005.

Sanders, Alan J.K. *Historical Dictionary of Mongolia.* Lanham, MD: Scarecrow Press, 1996.

Worden, Robert L. and Andrea Matles Savada, eds. *Mongolia: a Country Study.* Washington, DC: U.S. GPO, 2nd ed. 1991.

New Zealand

Alves, Dora, ed. *The Maori and the Crown: an Indigenous People's Struggle for Self-Determination.* Westport, CT: Greenwood Publishing Group, 1999.

Barretta-Herman, Angela. *Welfare State to Welfare Society: Restructuring New Zealand Social Services.* New York: Garland Publishing, 1994.

Boston, Jonathan, et al., eds. *Redesigning the Welfare State in New Zealand: Problems, Policies, Prospects.* New York: Oxford University Press, 1999.

Clements, Kevin P. *Breaking Nuclear Ties: New Zealand's Nuclear-Free Course.* Boulder, CO: Westview Press, 2000.

Emy, Hugh V., ed. *Australia and New Zealand.* Brookfield, VT: Ashgate Publishing Company, 1999.

Fischer, Gerhard and John Docker, eds. *Race, Colour and Identity in Australia and New Zealand.* Randwick, NSW: New South Wales University Press, 2000.

Jackson, William K. and Alan McRobie. *Historical Dictionary of New Zealand.* Lanham, MD: Scarecrow Press, 1996.

McKinnon, Malcolm. *Independence and Foreign Policy: New Zealand in the World since 1935*. Auckland: Auckland University Press, 1993.

Miller, Raymond, *New Zealand Government and Politics*. New York: Oxford University Press, 2006.

McLeay, Elizabeth. *The Cabinet and Political Power in New Zealand*. New York: Oxford University Press, 1995.

Rice, Geoffrey W., ed. *The Oxford History of New Zealand*. New York: Oxford University Press, 2nd ed. 1992.

Robinson, Guy. *Australia and New Zealand: Economy, Society and Environment*. New York: Edward Arnold, 2000.

Rudd, Chris, ed. *The Political Economy of New Zealand*. New York: Oxford University Press, 1997.

Sharp, Andrew, ed. *Leap into the Dark: the Changing Role of the State in New Zealand since 1984*. Auckland: Auckland University Press, 1994.

Sinclair, Keith, ed. *The Oxford Illustrated History of New Zealand*. New York: Oxford University Press, 2nd ed. 1996.

Wood, G. A. and Rudd, Christ. *Politics and Government of New Zealand*. University of Otago Press, 2003.

Papua New Guinea

Dinnen, Sinclair. *Law and Order in a Weak State: Crime and Politics in Papua New Guinea*. Honolulu, HI: University of Hawaii Press, 2000.

Gewertz, Deborah B. and Frederick K. Errington. *Emerging Class in Papua New Guinea: the Telling of Difference*. New York: Cambridge University Press, 1999.

Rannells, Jackson. *PNG: a Fact Book on Modern Papua New Guinea*. New York: Oxford University Press, 2nd ed. 1995.

Turner, Ann. *Historical Dictionary of Papua New Guinea*. Lanham, MD: Scarecrow Press, 1994.

The Philippines

Broad, Robin. *Plundering Paradise: the Struggle for the Environment in the Philippines*. Berkeley, CA: University of California Press, 1993.

Corpuz, O.D. *An Economic History of the Philippines*. Honolulu, HI: University of Hawaii Press, 1999.

Cullather, Nick. *Illusions of Influence: the Political Economy of United States-Philippines Relations, 1942–1960*. Stanford, CA: Stanford University Press, 1994.

Guillermo, Artemio R. *Historical Dictionary of the Philippines*. Lanham, MD: Scarecrow Press, 1997.

Karnow, Stanley. *In Our Image: America's Empire in the Philippines*. New York: Ballantine Publishing Group, 1989.

Kwiatkowski, Lynn M. *Struggling with Development: the Politics of Hunger and Gender in the Philippines*. Westport, CT: Westview Press, 1998.

Reid, Robert H. and Eileen Guerrero. *Corazon Aquino and the Brushfire Revolution*. Baton Rouge, LA: Louisiana State University Press, 1995.

Steinberg, David. The *Philippines*. 4th ed. Boulder, Co: Westview, 2000.

Singapore

Clammer, John. *Race and State in Independent Singapore: the Cultural Politics of Pluralism in a Multiethnic Society*. Brookfield, VT: Ashgate Publishing Company, 1998.

Gopinathan, S., et al., eds. *Language, Society and Education in Singapore: Issues and Trends*. Portland, OR: International Specialized Book Services, 1998.

Haas, Michael, ed. *The Singapore Puzzle*. Westport, CT: Greenwood Publishing Group, 1999.

Hill, Michael and Lian Kwen Fee. *The Politics of Nation Building and Citizenship in Singapore*. New York: Routledge, 1995.

Huff, W.G. *The Economic Growth of Singapore: Trade and Development in the Twentieth Century*. New York: Cambridge University Press, 1994.

Kong, Lily. *Singapore: a Developmental City State*. New York: John Wiley & Sons, 1997.

Lee, Kuan Yew. *From Third World to First: the Singapore Story, 1965–2000*. New York: HarperCollins Publishers, 2000.

Leifer, Michael. *Singapore's Foreign Policy: Coping with Vulnerability*. New York: Routledge, 2000.

Leong, Ho Khai. *Shared Responsibilities, Unshared Power. The Politics of Policymaking in Singapore*. Eastern Universities Press, 2003.

Ling, Qui G. *The City and the State: Singapore's Built Environment Revisited*. New York: Oxford University Press, 1997.

Mauzy, Diane K. and R.S. Milne. *Singapore Politics. Under the People's Action Party*. NY: Routledge, 2002.

Mulliner, K. and Lian The-Mulliner. *Historical Dictionary of Singapore*. Lanham, MD: Scarecrow Press, 1991.

Rodan, Garry, ed. *Singapore Changes Guard: Social, Political and Economic Directions in the 1990s*. New York: St. Martin's Press, 1993.

Von Alten, Florian. *The Role of Government in the Singapore Economy*. New York: Peter Lang Publishing, 1995.

Taiwan

Bullard, Monte. *The Soldier and the Citizen: the Role of the Military in Taiwan's Development*. Armonk, NY: M.E. Sharpe, 1997.

Chao, Linda. *The First Chinese Democracy: Political Life in the Republic of China on Taiwan*. Baltimore, MD: Johns Hopkins University Press, 1997.

Clough, Ralph. *Cooperation or Conflict in the Taiwan Strait?* Lanham, MD: Rowman & Littlefield Publishers, 1999.

Copper, John F. *Taiwan. Nation-state or Province?* Boulder, CO: Westview, 2003.

Copper, John F. *Historical Dictionary of Taiwan*. Lanham, MD: Scarecrow Press, 2nd ed. 2000.

Finkelstein, David Michael. *Washington's Dilemma, 1949–1950: from Abandonment to Salvation*. Fairfax, VA: George Mason University Press, 1993.

Garver, John W. *The Sino-American Alliance: Nationalist China and American Cold War Strategy in Asia*. Armonk, NY: M.E. Sharpe, 1997.

Hickey, Dennis Van Vranken. *United States Taiwan Security Ties: from Cold War to Beyond Containment*. New York: Praeger, 1994.

Hood, Steven J. *The Kuomintang and the Democratization of Taiwan*. Boulder, CO: Westview Press, 1997.

Hughes, Christopher. *Taiwan and Chinese Nationalism: National Identity and Status in International Society*. New York: Routledge, 1997.

Lasater, Martin L. *U.S. Interests in the New Taiwan*. Boulder, CO: Westview Press, 1993.

Lee, Bernice. *The Security Implications of the New Taiwan*. New York: Oxford University Press, 2000.

Maguire, Keith. *The Rise of Modern Taiwan*. Brookfield, VT: Ashgate Publishing Company, 1998.

McBeath, Gerald A. *Wealth and Freedom: Taiwan's New Political Economy*. Brookfield, VT: Ashgate Publishing Company, 1998.

Rawnsley, Gary D. *Taiwan's Informal Diplomacy and Propaganda*. New York: St. Martin's Press, 2000.

Rubinstein, Murray A., ed. *Taiwan: a New History*. Expanded Edition, Armonk, NY: M.E. Sharpe, 2007.

Schive, Chi. *Taiwan's Economic Role in East Asia*. Washington, DC: Center for Strategic and International Studies, 1995.

Shambaugh, David, ed. *Contemporary Taiwan*. New York: Oxford University Press, 1998.

Skoggard, Ian A. *The Indigenous Dynamic in Taiwan's Postwar Development: the Religious and Historical Roots of Entrepreneurship*. Armonk, NY: M.E. Sharpe, 1996.

Sutter, Robert G. and William R. Johnson, eds. *Taiwan in World Affairs*. Boulder, CO: Westview Press, 1994.

Tsang, Steve and Hung-mao Tien. *Democratization in Taiwan: Implications for China*. New York: St. Martin's Press, 1999.

Tsang, Steve, ed. *In the Shadow of China: Political Developments in Taiwan since 1949*. Honolulu, HI: University of Hawaii Press, 1993.

Wachman, Alan M. *Taiwan: National Identity and Democratization*. Armonk, NY: M.E. Sharpe, 1994.

Wu, Jaushieh Joseph. *Taiwan's Democratization: Forces behind the New Momentum*. New York: Oxford University Press, 1995.

Zhao, Suisheng. *Power by Design: Constitution-Making in Nationalist China*. Honolulu, HI: University of Hawaii Press, 1996.

Thailand

Campbell, Burnham O., et al., eds. *The Economic Impact of Demographic Change in Thailand, 1980–2015.* Honolulu, HI: University of Hawaii Press, 1993.

Chachavalpongpun, Pavin, *Reinventing Thailand: Thaksin and His Foreign Policy,* editor, Singapore, Institute of Southeast Asian Studies, 2010.

Dixon, Chris. *The Thai Economy: Uneven Development and Internationalism.* New York: Routledge, 1999.

Funston, John, *Southern Thailand: The Dynamics of Conflict,* Singapore, Institute of Southeast Asian Studies, 2008.

Hall, Denise. *Business Prospects in Thailand.* Upper Saddle River, NJ: Prentice Hall, 1997.

Jansen, Karel. *External Finance in Thailand's Development: an Interpretation of Thailand's Growth Boom.* New York: St. Martin's Press, 1997.

Krongkaew, Medhi, ed. *Thailand's Industrialization and Its Consequences.* New York: Saint Martin's Press, 1995.

Mulder, Niels. *Inside Thai Society: an Interpretation of Everyday Life.* Boston, MA: Charles E. Tuttle, 1997.

Muscat, Robert J. *The Fifth Tiger: a Study of Thai Development Policy.* Armonk, NY: M.E. Sharpe, 1994.

Phongpaichit, Pasuk and Sungsidh Piriyarangsan. *Corruption and Democracy in Thailand.* Seattle, WA: University of Washington Press, 1998.

Phongpaichit, Pasuk. and Chris Baker, *Thaksin.* Chiang Mai: Silkworm Books, 2009.

Skagner, Kerbo. *Modern Thailand.* New York: McGraw-Hill, 1999.

Vietnam

Anderson, David L. *Facing My Lai: Moving Beyond the Massacre.* Lawrence, KS: University Press of Kansas, 2000.

Arkadie, Brian and Mallon, Raymond. *Viet Nam: A Transition Tiger?* Asia Pacific Press, 2003.

Ashwill, Mark A. *Vietnam Today: A Guide to a Nation at a Crossroads* Yarmouth, ME, Intercultural Press, 2005.

Chan, Anita. *Transforming Asian Socialism: China and Vietnam Compared.* Lanham, MD: Rowman & Littlefield Publishers, 1999.

Chapuis, Oscar M. *A History of Vietnam: from Hong Bang to Tu Duc.* Westport, CT: Greenwood Press, 1995.

Cima, Ronald J., ed. *Vietnam: a Country Study.* Washington, DC: U.S. GPO, 1989.

Clodfelter, Michael. *Vietnam in Military Statistics: a History of the Indochina Wars, 1772–1991.* Jefferson, NC: McFarland & Company, 1995.

Davidson, Phillip B. *Vietnam at War: the History, 1946–1975.* New York: Oxford University Press, 1991.

Duiker, William J. *Historical Dictionary of Vietnam.* Lanham, MD: Scarecrow Press, 1997.

Duiker, William J. *Ho Chi Minh: a Life.* New York: Hyperion, 2000.

Elliott, David. *The Vietnamese War: Revolution and Social Change in the Mekong Delta.* Armonk, NY: M.E. Sharpe, 2001.

Harvie, Charles and Tran Van Hoa. *Vietnam's Reforms and Economic Growth.* New York: St. Martin's Press, 1997.

Hunt, Michael H. *Lyndon Johnson's War: America's Cold War Crusade in Vietnam, 1945–1968.* New York: Hill & Wang, 1996.

Jamieson, Neil L. *Understanding Vietnam.* Berkeley, CA: University of California Press, 1993.

Kamm, Henry. *Dragon Ascending: Vietnam and the Vietnamese.* New York: Arcade Publishing, 1996.

Kerkvliet, Benedict J. Tria and Doug J. Porter, eds. *Vietnam's Rural Transformation.* Boulder, CO: Westview Press, 1995.

Lamb, David. *Vietnam Now.* Boulder, CO: Westview, 2002.

Langguth, A.J. *Our Vietnam: a History of the War, 1954–1975.* New York: Simon & Schuster, 2000.

Lomperis, Timothy J. *From People's War to People's Rule: Insurgency, Intervention, and the Lessons of Vietnam.* Chapel Hill, NC: University of North Carolina Press, 1996.

Luong, Hy V. *Post War Vietnam: Dynamics of a Transforming Society.* Singapore: Institute of Southeast Asian Studies and Rowman & Littlefield Publishers, 2003.

McNamara, Robert T. *Argument without End: in Search of Answers to the Vietnam Tragedy.* New York: Public Affairs, 1999.

Morley, James W. and Masashi Nishihara, eds. *Vietnam Joins the World.* Armonk, NY: M.E. Sharpe, 1997.

Moses, George D. *Vietnam, an American Ordeal.* Upper Saddle River, NJ: Prentice-Hall, 1994.

Murray, Geoffrey. *Vietnam: Dawn of a New Market.* New York: St. Martin's Press, 1997.

Osborne, Milton. *The Mekong: Turbulent Past, Uncertain Future.* New York: Grove/Atlantic, 2000.

Rotter, Andrew J., ed. *Light at the End of the Tunnel: a Vietnam War Anthology.* Wilmington, DE: Scholarly Resources, 1999.

SarDesai, D.R. *Vietnam: Past and Present.* Boulder, CO: Westview Press, 1998.

Schulzinger, Robert D. *A Time for War: the United States and Vietnam, 1941–1975.* New York: Oxford University Press, 1997.

Stern, Lewis M. *Imprisoned or Missing in Vietnam: Policies of the Vietnames Government Concerning Captured and Unaccounted for United States Soldiers, 1969–1994.* Jefferson, NC: McFarland & Company, 1995.

Tucker, Spencer C. *Vietnam.* Lexington, KY: University Press of Kentucky, 1999.

Vandemark, Brian. *Into the Quagmire: Lyndon Johnson and the Escalation of the Vietnam War.* New York: Oxford University Press, 1991.

Wolff, Peter. *Vietnam: the Complete Transformation.* Portland, OR: Frank Cass Publishers, 1999.

Pacific Islands

Craig, Robert D., ed. *Historical Dictionary of Oceania.* Westport, CT: Greenwood Press, 1981.

Gorman, G.E. and J.J. Mills. *Fiji.* Santa Barbara, CA: ABC-CLIO, 1994.

Hanlon, David L. *Remaking Micronesia: Discourses over Development in a Pacific Territory.* Honolulu, HI: University of Hawaii Press, 1998.

Hill, Hal and Saldanha, João M., eds. *East Timor. Development Challenges for the World's Newest Nation.* NY: Palgrave, 2003.

Lal, Brij V. *Broken Waves: a History of the Fiji Islands in the Twentieth Century.* Honolulu, HI: University of Hawaii Press, 1992.

Leibowitz, Arnold H. *Embattled Island: Palau's Struggle for Independence.* New York: Praeger, 1996.

Levy, Neil M. *Micronesia Handbook.* Chico, CA: Moon Publications, 4th ed. 1997.

Sahlins, Marshall D. *Islands of History.* Chicago: University of Chicago Press, 1987.

Stanley, David. *South Pacific Handbook.* Chico, CA: Moon Publications, 6th ed. 1996.

Wuerch, William L. and Dirk Anthony Ballendorf. *Historical Dictionary of Guam and Micronesia.* Lanham, MD: Scarecrow Press, 1994.